Follett Vest-Pocket 50,000 Words

Follett
Vest-Pocket

50,000
Words

compiled and edited by
HARRY SHARP

(*formerly entitled*
VEST-POCKET
WORD DIVIDER)

50,000 Words and
3400 Variants Spelled,
Pronounced, and Divided

FOLLETT PUBLISHING COMPANY

Chicago

Library of Congress Catalog Card Number 64-10914

Manufactured in
The United States of America

11121314/8079787776

ISBN 0-695-89110-3

Contents

Preface

Proper word division is one of the many problems generated by man's need to write. Closely related is the problem of spelling. Both issues, since writing is essentially an artificial development, depend upon adopted conventions and are not inherent in the spoken language itself.

Until the invention of printing, there were no standardized rules for word division. Then the need for rapidly produced lines of type with set margins made a uniform system for dividing words imperative. Gutenberg, Caxton and their followers had no ready guides. They had to work out their own rules; conventional usages were established long before the first dictionaries were printed.

In organizing these conventions into a set of written rules, English presents innumerable puzzles. In most other languages the procedures are so simple that no one feels the need for a handbook or a dictionary. This is due largely to a fairly simple and regular word stress pattern. But in English the pattern is far from simple. The word *rebel* is stressed one way as a noun, another way as a verb. In fact, it would be more accurate to say that there are two words spelled *rebel*.

Early dictionaries made no attempt to show word division points, just as they failed to indicate pronunciation. The inclusion of word division is a relatively recent development, and is largely American. The English have tended to a less prescriptive approach and frequently use divisions Americans frown upon. Unfortunately, however, although every modern American dictionary of consequence indicates word division, no two publishers seem to agree. Indeed, the desk dictionary is frequently in conflict with the unabridged dictionary issued by the same publisher. The *Follett Vest-Pocket 50,000 Words* was initiated as an attempt to provide a handy reference to the most common division points currently in use.

This compiler has noted two main streams of practice in word division: the *etymological* and the *pronouncing* schools. The etymological school prefers divisions that preserve the "roots" of the word. The pronouncing school says: "Divide the way you pronounce." In general, the English follow the etymological and the Americans the pronouncing system. Thus the Oxford University Press insists on *bio-graphy,* while American sources indicate *bi-og-ra-phy.* The English argue that since the word comes from the Greek *bios,* life, and *graphein,* to write, the units *bio-* and *-graphy* should be preserved. The Americans argue that since the stress is on the second syllable, *-og-,* this is the unit to be kept intact.

The present compiler, like most American typesetters and proofreaders, has strong roots in the pronouncing school, to which he owes his training. He believes that *Wed-nesday* is bad and that *Wednes-day* is good, that *Wor-cestershire* is impermissible and that *Worcester-shire* is permissible, and that *knowl-edge* is far more knowledgeable than *know-ledge.*

Unfortunately, this American rule of thumb—divide the way you pronounce—does not solve all problems. To begin with, we don't all pronounce the same word the same way. Some say "apparatus" with the sound of the word *rate;* others say it with the sound of the word *rat.* Either one is acceptable. However, according to the pronunciation school the word is divided *ap-pa-ra-tus* if the first pronunciation is used, and *ap-pa-rat-us* if the second pronunciation is used. Thousands of English words present this alternative division and pronunciation problem.

Moreover, many English words are homographs —spelled and pronounced alike, but radically different in meaning. The word *founder* may be a verb, meaning *to collapse* or *to sink;* but it may also be either of two nouns, one meaning *originator,* the other *foundry-worker.* We pronounce all these words the same way, but convention long ago fixed different division points: the verb is *foun-der,* the nouns are *found-er.*

Printers and secretaries used to have an easy solution for these word division problems: look it up in Webster. This was easy to say—and simple to put into effect—provided everyone meant the same thing by "Webster." Although there were, and still are, other works including this name in their titles, for a long time the usual reference was to the unabridged dictionary published by the G. & C. Merriam Company. Then in the fall of 1961, the Merriam Company published *Webster's Third New International Dictionary,* and a new war of words broke out.

Many of the word division forms presented in the new edition are at variance with the forms indicated in previous editions. *Organize* is divided *or-ga-nize,* while earlier editions show *or-gan-ize.*

PREFACE

Multiply this instance by thousands, and the number of different and conflicting ways of division now in practice becomes apparent.

On the plus side, though, the new "Webster" put an end to such poor practices as cutting a word after a one-letter syllable and clearly showed the difference between the "orthographic hyphen," which is essential to the meaning of a word and is retained always, and the dividing hyphen, which is used only for division. In the *Follett 50,000 Words* the "orthographic hyphen" is illustrated with the entries spelled *refuse*. There are three of these. The verb *refuse*, as in *We refuse to go*, is pronounced quite differently from the noun *refuse*, as in *We burned the refuse*. In addition, there is another verb *re=fuse*, with two meanings: *We re=fuse the silver to purify it*, or *We re=fuse the circuit, and the lights go on*. The symbol = tells the user that the word involved has an orthographic hyphen, which must be retained regardless of word division. It should be noted also that if a word with an orthographic hyphen must be divided, a strong attempt should be made to use the orthographic hyphen as the point of division.

The *Follett Vest-Pocket 50,000 Words* has been compiled to solve such problems and puzzles as are suggested above. It is designed to help the professional typesetter and proofreader as well as the secretary and office typist. The author gratefully acknowledges as his primary source *Webster's Third New International Dictionary*, published by G. & C. Merriam Co., Springfield, Mass. Their kind permission has made this work possible. Other word division books and booklets were also helpful guides. Special mention should be made of the *Word-Division* booklet published by the Government Printing Office (the newest edition appeared while this book was being prepared) and *How Divide the Word,* by Southern Publishers, Kingsport, Tenn.

Although this divider has largely followed the "new Webster," in some instances it has followed widespread convention rather than authority. For example, not many advertisers would care to proclaim:

> Only the best in ser-
> vice is offered our clients.

The objection, of course, is that some readers will look at the second line independently of the first. Hence, following the usual American typesetting and publishing practice, this word divider favors *serv-ice,* rather than *ser-vice.*

The *Follett 50,000 Words* differs from previous books on the subject in two respects. First, this book indicates the major instances in which authorities disagree on the division of a particular word. The main listing normally shows the division recommended in *Webster's Third New International Dictionary;* an asterisk (*) following an entry shows that the word is divided differently in *Webster's New International Dictionary, Second Edition;* a dagger (†) following the entry shows that there is a different division in Funk & Wagnalls *New Standard Dictionary of the English Language.* All these variant divisions are clearly indicated in the Appendix of Variants beginning on page 435.

A second difference involves the treatment of

such words as *ameba* and *insomnia*. Though the initial *a* in *ameba* and the final *a* in *insomnia* are separate syllables, the conventions of good usage clearly forbid any division that leaves a single letter from a word isolated either at the beginning or at the end of a line. Consequently, in this word divider no hyphen has been inserted where no division is permissible. To indicate syllabication in such instances, a colon has been used: *in-som'-ni:a, a:me'-ba.* If the one-letter syllable is stressed, an accent mark is used instead of a colon: *i'o-dine.* The same treatment has been extended to compounds of such words: *end-a:me'-ba, tri-i'o-dide.*

In short, one simple rule will guide the reader through this entire book: *divide only where a hyphen has actually been marked down.*

This book contains over 50,000 entries with indications of proper word division and stress.

The compiler assumes full responsibility for any errors of omission or commission. All users of this word divider are urged to submit suggestions for the improvement of future editions.

Harry Sharp

Acknowledgment

By permission, the following system of syllabication is based on Webster's Third New International Dictionary, *copyright 1961 by G. & C. Merriam Co., Publishers of the Merriam-Webster Dictionaries.*

In a few instances the compiler has preferred word divisions based on convention, especially American typesetting and publishing practice. In the Appendix of Variants are syllabications derived from Webster's New International Dictionary, Second Edition, *and* Funk & Wagnalls New Standard Dictionary of the English Language.

KEY TO SYMBOLS

- This is the dividing hyphen. It shows where words should be divided.

= This is the orthographic hyphen. It must always be used, since it shows the compounding of the word. Use it whether dividing or using the word entirely undivided. If you are dividing, the orthographic hyphen is the best place for the division.

: This is an unaccented syllable. Do *not* divide here.

' This is an accented syllable. Do not divide here *unless* a hyphen follows, as '-

* Asterisk indicates that *Webster's New International Dictionary, Second Edition* gives a variant division, which has been listed in the Appendix of Variants beginning on page 435.

† Dagger indicates that Funk & Wagnalls *New Standard Dictionary of the English Language* gives a variant division, which has been listed in the Appendix of Variants beginning on page 435.

aard'-vark
Aa'-ron*†
Aa-ron'-ic
ab'a (altazimuth)
a:ba'† (cloth)
ab-a-ca'*
a:back'
a'-baft'
ab-a-lo'-ne
a:ban'-don
a:ban'-doned
a:ban'-don-er
a:ban'-don-ment
a:base'
a:based'
a:bas'-ed-ly
a:base'-ment
a:bash'
a:bash'-ment
a:ba'-si:a
a:bas'-ing
a:bat'-a:ble
a:bate'
a:bate'-ment
a:bat'-ing
ab'-a-tis
a:ba'-tor
ab'-at-toir†
ab'-ba-cy
ab-ba'-tial
ab-bé'
ab'-bess
ab'-bey
ab'-bot
ab'-bot-cy
ab-bre'-vi-ate
ab-bre'-vi-at-ed
ab-bre'-vi-at-ing
ab-bre-vi-a'-tion
ab'-di-ca-ble
ab'-di-cate
ab'-di-cat-ing
ab-di-ca'-tion
ab'-di-ca-tor
ab'-do-men
ab-dom'-i-nal
ab-du'-cent
ab-duct'
ab-duc'-tion
ab-duc'-tor
a:beam'
a:be-ce-dar'-i-an
a:bed'
A:bed'-ne-go
A'bel
Ab'-e-lard
ab-en-ter'-ic

Ab'-er-deen
Ab'-er-deen An'-gus
Ab-er-do'-ni-an
ab-er'-rance
ab-er'-ran-cy
ab-er'-rant
ab-er-ra'-tion
ab'-er-rom'e-ter
a:bet'
a:bet'-ted
a:bet'-ting
a:bet'-tor
a:bey'-ance
a:bey'-ant
ab-hor'
ab-horred'
ab-hor'-rence
ab-hor'-rent
ab-hor'-ring
a:bid'-ance†
a:bide'
a:bid'-ing
ab'-i-e-tate
Ab'-i-gail
Ab'-i-lene
a:bil'-i-ties
a:bil'-i-ty
a:bi-o-gen'-e-sis*†
a:bi-o-ge-net'-ic*†
a:bi-og'-e-nist*†
ab-ject' (ab'-ject)
ab-jec'-tion
ab-ject'-ly
ab-ju-ra'-tion
ab-jur'-a-to-ry†
ab-jure'
ab-jur'-ing
ab-late'
ab-la'-tion
ab'-la-tive
a:blaze'
a'ble
a'ble=bod'-ied
a'bler
a:bloom'
ab-lu'-tion
ab-lu'-tion-ar:y†
a'bly
ab'-ne-gate
ab-ne-ga'-tion
ab'-ne-ga-tive
ab-nor'-mal
ab-nor-mal'-i-ties
ab-nor-mal'-i-ty
ab-nor'-mal-ly
ab-nor'-mi-ty
a:board'
a:bode'

1

a:bol′-ish
ab-o-li′-tion
ab-o-li′-tion-ism
ab-o-li′-tion-ist
a-o-ma′-sum
A′=bomb
a:bom′-i-na-ble
a:bom′-i-na-bly
a:bom′-i-nate
a:bom′-i-nat-ed
a:bom-i-na′-tion
ab-o-rig′-i-nal
ab-o-rig′-i-ne
a:bort′
a:bor′-ti-cide
a:bor′-ti-fa′-cient
a:bor′-tion
a:bor′-tion-ist
a:bort′-ive*†
a:bound′
a:bound′-ing
a:bout′
a:bout=face′
a:bove′
a:bove′-board
ab-ra-ca-dab′-ra
a:brad′-ant*†
a:brade′*†
a:brad′-ed*†
a:brad′-ing*†
A′bra-ham
a:bran′-chi-an
a:bran′-chi-ate
a:bra-si-om′-e-ter*
a:bra′-sion*†
a:bra′-sive*†
ab-re-ac′-tion
a:breast′
a:bridge′
a:bridge′-a-ble
a:bridg′-ing
a:bridg′-ment
a:broad′
ab′-ro-ga-ble
ab′-ro-gate
ab′-ro-gat-ed
ab′-ro-gat-ing
ab-ro-ga′-tion
ab′-ro-ga-tive
ab′-ro-ga-tor
ab-rupt′
ab-rup′-tion
ab-rupt′-ly
ab-rupt′-ness
A:bruz′-zi
Ab′-sa-lom
ab′-scess
ab′-scessed

ab-scis′-sa
ab-scis′-sion
ab-scond′
ab-scond′-ed
ab-scond′-er
ab′-sence
ab′-sent (adj.)
ab-sent′ (v.)
ab-sen-ta′-tion
ab-sen-tee′
ab-sen-tee′-ism
ab′-sent-ly
ab′-sent-mind-ed
ab′-sinthe
ab-sin′-thi-an
ab′-so-lute
ab′-so-lute′-ly
ab-so-lu′-tion
ab′-so-lut-ism
ab′-so-lut-ist
ab-so-lu-tis′-tic
ab′-so-lu-tive
ab-sol′-u-to-ry
ab-solv′-a-ble
ab-solve′
ab-solved′
ab-sol′-vent
ab-solv′-er
ab-solv′-ing
ab-sorb′
ab-sorb-a-bil′-i-ty
ab-sorbed′
ab-sorb′-ed-ly
ab-sor-be-fa′-cient
ab-sorb′-ent†
ab-sorb′-ing
ab-sorp′-tion
ab-sorp′-tive
ab-stain′
ab-stained′
ab-stain′-er
ab-ste′-mi-ous
ab-ste′-mi-ous-ly
ab-sten′-tion
ab-sten′-tious
ab-ster′-gent
ab-ster′-sion
ab′-sti-nence
ab′-sti-nent
ab′-stract (n., adj.)
ab-stract′ (v.)
ab-stract′-ed
ab-stract′-ed-ly
ab-strac′-tion
ab-strac′-tive
ab′-stract-ly
ab-stric′-tion
ab-struse′

ab-struse'-ly
ab-surd'
ab-surd'-i-ty
ab-surd'-ly
a:bu'-li:a
a:bu'-lic
a:bun'-dance
a:bun'-dant
a:bun'-dant-ly
a:buse'
a:bused'
a:bus'-er
a:bus'-ing
a:bu'-sive
a:bu'-sive-ly
a:bu'-sive-ness
a:but'
a:bu'-ti-lon
a:but'-ment
a:but'-tal
a:but'-ted
a:but'-ter
a:but'-ting
A:by'-dos
a:bysm'
a:bys'-mal
a:bys'-mal-ly
a:byss'
a:byss'-al†
Ab-ys-sin'-i:a
Ab-ys-sin'-i-an
a:ca'-cia
ac'-a-deme
ac-a-dem'-ic
ac-a-dem'-i-cal
ac-a-dem'-i-cal-ly
ac-a-de-mi'-cian*†
ac-a-dem'-i-cism
a:cad'-e-my
A:ca'-di:a
A:ca'-di-an
ac'-a-leph
ac-a-na'-ceous
ac-an-tha'-ceous
a:can-tho-ceph'-a-lan
a:can'-thoid
a:can'-thous
a cap-pel'-la
a cap'-su-lar
A:ca-pul'-co
a-ca-ri'-a-sis
ac'-a-roid
a:car'-pel-ous
a:car'-pous
a:cat-a-lec'-tic
a:cau'-dal
a:cau'-date

a:cau-les'-cent*†
a:cau'-line
ac-cede'
ac-ced'-ence†
ac-ce-le-ran'-do*
ac-cel'-er-ate
ac-cel-er-a'-tion
ac-cel'-er-a-tive
ac-cel'-er-a-tor
ac-cel'-er-a-to-ry
ac'-cent (n., v.)
ac-cent' (v.)
ac-cen-tu-al'-i-ty
ac-cen'-tu-ate
ac-cen-tu-a'-tion
ac-cept'
ac-cept-a-bil'-i-ty
ac-cept'-a-ble
ac-cept'-ance†
ac-cep-ta'-tion
ac-cept'-ed
ac-cept'-er
ac-cep'-tor
ac'-cess
ac-ces'-sa-ri-ly
ac-ces'-sa-ry
ac-ces-si-bil'-i-ty
ac-ces'-si-ble
ac-ces'-sion
ac-ces-so'-ri-al
ac-ces'-so-ri-ly
ac-ces'-so-ry
ac-ciac-ca-tu'-ra
ac'-ci-dence
ac'-ci-dent
ac-ci-den'-tal
ac-ci-den'-tal-ly
ac-cip'-i-tral
ac-cip'-i-trine
ac-claim'
ac-claim'-ing
ac-cla-ma'-tion
ac-clam'-a-to-ry
ac-cli'-mat-a-ble†
ac-cli'-mate
ac-cli'-mat-ed
ac-cli-ma'-tion
ac-cli-ma-ti-za'-tion
ac-cli'-ma-tize
ac-cliv'-i-ty
ac-cli'-vous
ac-co-lade'
ac'-co-lade
ac-com'-mo-date
ac-com'-mo-dat-ing
ac-com'-mo-da'-tion
ac-com'-mo-da-tive
ac-com'-pa-nied

ac-com′-pa-nies
ac-com′-pa-ni-ment
ac-com′-pa-nist
ac-com′-pa-ny
ac-com′-plice
ac-com′-plish
ac-com′-plished
ac-com′-plish-ment
ac-compt′
ac-cord′
ac-cord′-a-ble
ac-cord′-ance
ac-cord′-ant
ac-cord′-ed
ac-cord′-ing
ac-cord′-ing-ly
ac-cor′-di-on
ac-cor′-di-on-ist
ac-cost′
ac-couche-ment′
ac-cou-cheur′
ac-count′
ac-count-a-bil′-i-ty
ac-count′-a-ble
ac-count′-an-cy
ac-count′-ant
ac-count′-ing
ac-cou′-ter
ac-cou′-ter-ment
ac-cred′-it
ac-cres′-cence
ac-cre′-tion
ac-cre′-tive
ac-cru′-al
ac-crue′
ac-crue′-ment
ac-cru′-ing
ac-cum′-ben-cy
ac-cum′-bent
ac-cu′-mu-late
ac-cu′-mu-lat-ing
ac-cu′-mu-la′-tion
ac-cu′-mu-la-tive
ac-cu′-mu-la-tor
ac′-cu-ra-cy
ac′-cu-rate
ac′-cu-rate-ly
ac′-cu-rate-ness
ac-curs′-ed
ac-cus′-al
ac-cu-sa′-tion
ac-cu′-sa-tive
ac-cus′-a-to-ry*
ac-cuse′
ac-cused′
ac-cus′-er
ac-cus′-ing
ac-cus′-ing-ly

ac-cus′-tom
ac-cus′-tomed
ac-e-naph′-thy-lene
a:ceph′-a-lous
ac′-er-ate†
a:cer′-bi-ty
ac′-er-ose†
a:ce′-rous† (hornless)
ac′-er-ous† (needlelike)
a:cer′-vate†
a:ces′-cent
ac-e-tab′-u-lum
ac-et-al′-de-hyde
a:cet′-a-mide*†
ac-et-an′-i-lid
ac′-e-tate
a:ce′-tic
a:ce′-ti-fy*†
ac-e-tom′-e-ter
ac′-e-tone
ac′-e-ton-ic
ac-e-to-phe-none′
a:ce′-tous*†
a:ce′-tyl*†
a:ce′-tyl-ac′-e-tone*†
a:cet-y-la′-tion†
a:cet′-y-lene
ac-e-tyl′-ic
a:ce′-tyl-sal-i-cyl′-ic
A:chae′-an
A:chai′a†
A:chai′-an
A:cha′-tes
ached
a:che′-ni-al
Ach′-er-on†
a:chiev′-a:ble
a:chieve′
a:chieved′
a:chieve′-ment
a:chiev′-ing
Ach-il-le′-an
A:chil′-les
ach′-ing-ly
a:chla-myd′-e-ous*†
ach-ro-mat′-ic
ach-ro-mat′-i-cal-ly
a:chro′-ma-tism
a:chro′-ma-tize
a:chro′-ma-tous
a:cic′-u-lar
a:cic′-u-lar-ly
ac′-id
a:cid′-ic
a:cid-i-fi-ca′-tion
a:cid′-i-fied
a:cid′-i-fy

4

ac-i-dim′-e-ter
a:cid-i-met′-ric*†
a-ci-dim′-e-try
a:cid′-i-ty
ac-i-doph′-i-lus
ac-i-do′-sis
ac′-id-proof
a:cid′-u-late
a:cid-u-la′-tion
a:cid′-u-lous
ac′-i-er-ate
a:cin′-i-form
ac′-i-nous
ac′-i-nus
ac-knowl′-edge
ac-knowl′-edge-a-ble
ac-knowl′-edg-ing
ac-knowl′-edg-ment
a:clin′-ic
ac′-me
ac′-ne
ac-no′-dal
ac′-o-lyte
a:con′-dy-lous
ac′-o-nite
ac-o-nit′-ic
a:con′-i-tine
ac-o-ni′-tum
a:con′-ti-um
a′corn
a:cot-y-le′-don
a:cous′-tic
a:cous′-ti-cal
a:cous′-ti-cal-ly
ac-ous-ti′-cian
A:cous′-ti-con
a:cous′-tics
ac-quaint′
ac-quaint′-ance†
ac-quaint′-ance-ship†
ac-quaint′-ed
ac-qui-esce′
ac-qui-es′-cence
ac-qui-es′-cent
ac-qui-esc′-ing
ac-quire′
ac-quire′-ment
ac-quir′-er
ac-quir′-ing
ac-qui-si′-tion
ac-quis′-i-tive
ac-quit′
ac-quit′-tal
ac-quit′-tance
ac-quit′-ted
ac-quit′-ting
a′cre
a′cre-age

ac′-rid
ac′-ri-dine
a:crid′-i-ty
ac′-rid-ly
ac-ri-mo′-ni-ous
ac′-ri-mo-ny
ac′-ro-bat
ac-ro-bat′-ic
ac-ro-bat′-ics
ac′-ro-gen
a:crog′-e-nous
a:cro′-le-in
ac′-ro-lith
ac-ro-me-gal′-ic
ac-ro-meg′-a-ly
a:cro′-mi-on
a:cron′-i-cal
ac′-ro-nym
a:croph′-o-ny
a:crop′-o-lis
a:cross′
a:cros′-tic
a:crot′-ic
ac′-ro-tism
a:cryl′-ic
ac-ry-lo-ni′-trile
ac′-ry-lyl*
act′-a-ble
Ac-tae′-on
ac′-ti-nal
act′-ing
ac-tin′-i:a
ac-tin′-ic
ac′-ti-nism*†
ac-tin′-i-um
ac′-ti-noid
ac-ti-nol′-o-gy
ac-ti-no-my′-cin
ac-ti-no-my-co′-sis
ac′-tion
ac′-tion-a:ble
Ac′-ti-um
ac′-ti-vate
ac-ti-va′-tion
ac′-ti-va-tor
ac′-tive
ac′-tive-ly
ac′-tiv-ist
ac-tiv′-i-ties
ac-tiv′-i-ty
ac′-tor
ac′-tress
ac-tu-al
ac-tu-al′-i-ty
ac′-tu-al-ly
ac-tu-ar′-i-al†
ac′-tu-ar-ies†

ac'-tu-ar:y†
ac'-tu-ate
ac'-tu-at-ing
ac-tu-a'-tion
ac'-tu-a-tor
ac'-u-ate
a:cu'-i-ty
a:cu'-le-ate
a:cu'-men
a:cu'-mi-nate
a:cu-mi-na'-tion
ac'-u-punc-ture
a:cute'
a:cute'-ly
a:cute'-ness
a:cy'-clic†
ac'-yl-ate†
ad'-age
a:da'-gio
Ad'-am
ad'-a-mant
ad-a-man'-tine
A:dam'-ic
Ad'-ams
A:dam'-si:a
Ad'-am-son
a:dapt'
a:dapt-a-bil'-i-ty
a:dapt'-a:ble
ad-ap-ta'-tion
a:dapt'-er
a:dapt'-ive*†
a:dap'-tor
ad-ax'-i-al
add'-a-ble
add'-ed
ad-den'-da
ad-den'-dum
ad'-der (snake)
add'-er (one who adds)
add'-i-ble
ad'-dict (n.)
ad-dict' (v.)
ad-dict'-ed
ad-dic'-tion
Ad'-dis Ab'-a-ba†
Ad'-di-son
ad-dit'-a-ment
ad-di'-tion
ad-di'-tion-al
ad-di'-tion-al-ly
ad'-di-tive
ad'-dle
ad'-dled
ad-dress'
ad-dress-ee'
ad-dress'-er
ad-dress'-ing

Ad-dres'-so-graph
ad-dres'-sor
ad-duce'
ad-du'-cent
ad-duc'-i-ble†
ad-duc'-ing
ad-duct' (v.)
ad'-duct (n.)
ad-duc'-tion
ad-duc'-tor
Ad'-e-la
Ad'-e-laide
A'den
a:de'-nia
a:den'-i-form
ad-e-ni'-tis
ad-e-no-fi-bro'-ma
ad'-e-noid
ad'-e-noi'-dal
ad-e-no'-ma
a:dept' (adj.)
ad'-ept (n.)
a:dept'-ly
a:dept'-ness
ad'-e-qua-cy
ad'-e-quate
ad'-e-quate-ly
ad-here'
ad-her'-ence
ad-her'-ent
ad-he-res'-cent
ad-her'-ing
ad-he'-sion
ad-he'-sive
ad-he'-sive-ly
ad-hib'-it
ad-hi-bi'-tion
ad-i-a-bat'-ic
ad-i-an'-tum
ad-i-aph'-o-rous
a:di-a-ther'-man-cy*†
a:dieu'
ad in-fi-ni'-tum
ad in'-ter-im*†
a:dios'†
a:dip'-ic
ad-i-poc'-er-ous
ad'-i-pose
ad-i-pos'-i-ty
Ad-i-ron'-dack
ad-ja'-cen-cy
ad-ja'-cent
ad-ja'-cent-ly
ad-jec-ti'-val
ad'-jec-tive
ad-join'
ad-joined'

6

ad-join′-ing	a:do′
ad-journ′	a:do′-be
ad-journed′	ad-o-les′-cence
ad-journ′-ment	ad-o-les′-cent
ad-judge′	Ad′-olph
ad-judg′-ing	A:don′-ic
ad-ju′-di-cate	A:don′-is*†
ad-ju′-di-cat-ing	a:dopt′
ad-ju-di-ca′-tion	a:dopt′-a-ble
ad-ju′-di-ca-tive	a:dopt′-er
ad-ju′-di-ca-tor	a:dop′-tion
ad′-junct	a:dop′-tive
ad-junc′-tive	a:dor′-a-ble
ad-ju-ra′-tion	a:dor′-a-bly
ad-jur′-a-to-ry†	ad-o-ra′-tion
ad-jure′	a:dored′
ad-ju′-ror†	a:dor′-er
ad-just′	a:dor′-ing
ad-just′-a-ble	a:dorn′
ad-just′-er	a:dorned′
ad-just′-ment	a:dorn′-ing
ad-jus′-tor	a:dorn′-ment
ad′-ju-tant	a:down′
ad′-ju-tant gen′-er-al	ad-re′-nal
ad′-ju-vant (v., adj.)	Ad-ren′-a-lin*†
ad=lib′ (v., adj.)	A′dri-an
ad lib′-i-tum	A:dri-a-no′-ple*†
ad-mi-nic′-u-lar	A:dri-at′-ic
ad-min′-is-ter	a:drift′
ad-min′-is-trate	a:droit′
ad-min′-is-tra′-tion	a:droit′-ly
ad-min′-is-tra-tive	a:droit′-ness
ad-min′-is-tra-tor	ad-sci-ti′-tious
ad-min′-is-tra-trix	ad-sorb′
ad′-mi-ra-ble	ad-sorb′-ent
ad′-mi-ra-bly	ad-sorp′-tion
ad′-mi-ral	ad-sorp′-tive
ad′-mi-ral-ty	ad-u-lar′-i:a†
ad-mi-ra′-tion	ad′-u-late
ad-mire′	ad-u-la′-tion
ad-mired′	ad′-u-la-to-ry
ad-mir′-er	a:dult′
ad-mir′-ing	a:dul′-ter-ant
ad-mir′-ing-ly	a:dul′-ter-ate
ad-mis-si-bil′-i-ty	a:dul-ter-a′-tion
ad-mis′-si-ble	a:dul-ter-a′-tor
ad-mis′-sion	a:dul′-ter-er
ad-mis′-sive	a:dul′-ter-ess
ad-mit′	a:dul′-ter-ous
ad-mit′-tance	a:dul′-ter:y
ad-mit′-ted	a:dult′-hood
ad-mit′-ted-ly	a:dult′-i-cide
ad-mit′-ting	ad-um′-bral
ad-mix′-ture	ad-um′-brant
ad-mon′-ish	ad′-um-brate
ad-mon′-ish-ment	ad va-lo′-rem
ad-mo-ni′-tion	ad-vance′
ad-mon′-i-to-ry	ad-vanced′

ad-vance'-ment
ad-vanc'-ing
ad-van'-tage
ad-van-ta'-geous
ad-van-ta'-geous-ly
ad-ve'-nience*
ad'-vent
Ad'-vent-ism
Ad'-vent-ist
ad-ven-ti'-tious
ad-ven-ti'-tious-ly
ad-ven'-tive
ad-ven'-ture
ad-ven'-tur-er
ad-ven'-ture-some
ad-ven'-tur-ess
ad-ven'-tur-ous
ad'-verb
ad-verb'-i-al*†
ad'-ver-sar-ies†
ad'-ver-sar:y†
ad-ver'-sa-tive
ad'-verse
ad'-verse-ly
ad-ver'-si-ty
ad-vert'
ad-vert'-ence†
ad-vert'-ent†
ad-vert'-ent-ly†
ad'-ver-tise
ad-ver-tise'-ment
ad'-ver-tis-er
ad'-ver-tis-ing
ad-vice'
ad-vis-a-bil'-i-ty
ad-vis'-a-ble
ad-vise'
ad-vised'
ad-vis'-ed-ly
ad-vise'-ment
ad-vis'-er
ad-vis'-ing
ad-vi'-sor
ad-vis'-o-ry*†
ad'-vo-ca-cy
ad'-vo-cate
ad'-vo-ca-tor
ad-voc'-a-to-ry†
a:dy-nam'-i:a*†
a:dy-nam'-ic*†
ad'-y-tum
ae'-ci-um
a:e'-des
ae'-dile
Ae-ge'-an
Ae-gi'-na
ae'-gis
Ae-gis'-thus

Ae-ne'-as
Ae-ne'-id
a:e'-ne-ous
Ae-o'-li-an
ae-o-lot'-ro-py
Ae'-o-lus
ae'-on
aer'-ate
aer-a'-tion
aer'-a-tor
aer'-i-al*†
aer'-i-al-ist*†
ae'-rie*†
aer-if'-er-ous
aer-i-fi-ca'-tion
aer-o'-bic
aer:o-do-net'-ics
aer:o-dy-nam'-ic
aer:o-dy-nam'-ics
aer-og'-ra-phy
aer-ol'-o-gy
aer-om'-e-ter
aer'o-mo-tor
aer'o-naut
aer:o-nau'-ti-cal
aer:o-nau'-ti-cal-ly
aer:o-nau'-tics
aer'o-plane
aer'o-scope
aer:o-scop'-ic
aer-os'-co-py
ae'-rose
aer'-o-sol
aer:o-ther-a-peu'-tics
ae-ru'-gi-nous
a'er:y
Aes-chy-le'-an
Aes'-chy-lus
Aes-cu-la'-pi-an
Aes-cu-la'-pi-us
Ae'-sir
Ae'-sop
aes'-thete
aes-thet'-ic
aes-thet'-i-cal-ly
aes-the-ti'-cian
aes-thet'-i-cism
aes-thet'-ics
ae'-ther
Aet'-na
a:far'
a:feb'-rile*
af-fa-bil'-i-ty
af'-fa-ble
af'-fa-bly
af-fair'
af-fect'
af-fec-ta'-tion

8

af-fect'-ed
af-fect'-i-ble
af-fec'-tion
af-fec'-tion-ate
af-fec'-tion-ate-ly
af-fec'-tive
af'-fer-ent
af-fi'-ance
af-fi'-anced
af-fi'-ant
af-fi-da'-vit
af-fil'-i-ate
af-fil-i-a'-tion
af-fin'-i-ties
af-fin'-i-ty
af-firm'
af-firm'-a-bly
af-firm'-ance
af-fir-ma'-tion
af-firm'-a-tive
af-firm'-a-tive-ly
af-firm'-a-to-ry
af-fix' (v.)
af'-fix (n.)
af-fla'-tus
af-flict'
af-flic'-tion
af-flict'-ive*†
af'-flu-ence
af'-flu-ent
af'-flu-ent-ly
af-ford'
af-for-es-ta'-tion*
af-fray'
af-fric'-a-tive
af-fright'
af-front'
af-front'-ive*†
af-fu'-sion
Af'-ghan
Af-ghan'-i-stan
a:field'
a:fire'
a:flame'
a:float'
a:flut'-ter
a:foot'
a:fore'-men-tioned
a:fore'-said
a:fore'-thought
a-fore'-time
a-for-ti-o'-ri
a:foul'
a:fraid'
a:fresh'
Af'-ric
Af'-ri-ca

Af'-ri-can
Af-ri-kan'-der
af'-ter*
af'-ter-birth*
af'-ter-burn-er*
af'-ter-care*
af'-ter-deck*
af'-ter-ef-fect*
af'-ter-glow*
af'-ter-life*
af'-ter-math*
af-ter-noon'*
af'-ter-taste*
af'-ter-thought*
af'-ter-ward*
af'-ter-wards*
a:gain'
a:gainst'
a:ga'-ma†
Ag-a-mem'-non
a:gam'-ic
a:gam-o-gen'-e-sis*†
ag'-a-mous
ag-a-pan'-thus
a:gape' (ajar)
a:ga'-pe*† (love feast)
a'gar
a'gar=a'gar
ag'-a-ric*†
a:gar-i-ca'-ceous
Ag'-as-siz
ag'-ate
ag'-ate-ware
Ag'-a-tha
ag'-at-ize†
a:ga'-ve
aged (ag'-ed)
age'-less
a'gen-cies
a'gen-cy
a:gen'-da
a:gen'-dum
a'gent
a:gen'-tial
a:gen-ti'-val
ag-er-a'-tum*†
ag-glom'-er-ate
ag-glom-er-a'-tion
ag-glu'-ti-nant
ag-glu'-ti-nate
ag-glu-ti-na'-tion
ag-glu-ti-na-tive
ag-gra-da'-tion
ag-gran'-dize
ag-gran'-dize-ment
ag'-gra-vate
ag'-gra-vat-ed
ag'-gra-vat-ing

9

ag-gra-va'-tion
ag'-gra-va-tor
ag'-gre-gate
ag'-gre-gate-ly
ag'-gre-gat-ing
ag-gre-ga'-tion
ag'-gre-ga-tive
ag'-gre-ga-to-ry
ag-gres'-sion
ag-gres'-sive
ag-gres'-sive-ness
ag-gres'-sor
ag-griev'-ance
ag-grieve'
ag-grieved'
a:ghast'
ag'-ile
ag'-ile-ly
ag'-ile-ness
a:gil'-i-ty
Ag'-in-court†
ag'-ing
a:gio-tage'*†
ag'-i-tate
ag'-i-tat-ed
ag'-i-tat-ed-ly
ag'-i-tat-ing
ag-i-ta'-tion
ag'-i-ta-tive
ag'-i-ta-tor
a:gleam'
ag'-let
a:glow'
ag'-mi-nat-ed
ag-na'-tion
Ag'-nes
ag-no'-men
ag-nom'-i-nal
ag-no'-si:a
ag-nos'-tic
ag-nos'-ti-cal
ag-nos'-ti-cal-ly
ag-nos'-ti-cism
a:go'
a:gog'
a:gon'-ic
ag-o-nis'-tic
ag'-o-nize
ag'-o-niz-ing
ag'-o-ny
ag'-o-ra
ag-o-ra-pho'-bi:a
A'gra
a:graph'-i:a
a:grar'-i-an†
a:gree'
a:gree-a-bil'-i-ty
a:gree'-a-ble

a:gree'-a-bly
a:greed'
a:gree'-ing
a:gree'-ment
a:gres'-tic
A:gric'-o-la
ag-ri-cul'-tur-al
ag-ri-cul'-tur-al-ist
ag'-ri-cul-ture
ag-ri-cul'-tur-ist
ag'-ri-mo-ny
A:grip'-pa
a:grol'-o-gy
ag-ro-nom'-ic
ag-ro-nom'-ics
a:gron'-o-mist†
a:gron'-o-my†
ag-ros-tol'-o-gy
a:ground'
ag-ryp-not'-ic
A'guas-ca-lien-tes
a'gue
a'gue-weed
a'gu-ish
A'hab
a:head'
a:hoy'
A:i'-da
aide'=de=camp
ai-grette'
ai-guille'
ai-lan'-thus
ai'-le-ron*
ail'-ment
aim'-less
Ai'-nu
air base
air'-borne
air brake
air'-brush
air coach
air'=con-di'-tion
air'=con-di'-tioned
air'=cool
air'-craft
air'-drome
air'-drop (n.)
air'=drop (v.)
Aire'-dale
air ex-press'
air'-field
air'-foil
air force
air'-freight
air hole
air'-i-ly
air'-i-ness
air'-ing

air'-less
air lift (pump)
air'-lift (aviation supply line)
air line (line suppling air)
air'-line (aviation company)
air'-mail
air'-man
air'=mind'-ed
air-om'-e-ter
air'-plane
air pock'-et
air'-port
air pres'-sure
air'-proof
air pump
air raid
air ri'-fle
air'-ship
air'-sick-ness
air space (enclosure for air)
air'-space (air under a nation's control)
air'-speed
air'-strip
air'-tight
air'-way
air well
air'-wor-thy
air'y
aisle
Aisne
Aix=la=Cha-pelle'
A:jac'-cio
a:jar'
A'jax
a:kim'-bo
a:kin'
Ak'-ron
Al-a-bam'a†
Al-a-bam'-i-an
al-a-bam'-ine
al'-a-bas-ter
a la carte
a:lack'
a:lac'-ri-ty
A:lad'-din
a la king
Al-a-me'-da
Al'-a-mo†
a la mode
Al'-an
al'-a-nine
al'-a-nyl
a'lar
al'-a-ric

a:larm'
a:larm'-ing
a:larm'-ing-ly
a:larm'-ist
a:lar'-um
a'la-ry
a:las'
A:las'-ka
A:las'-kan
Al'-ban
Al-ba'-ni:a
Al-ba'-ni-an
Al'-ba-ny
al'-ba-tross
al-be'-it
Al'-be-marle
Al'-bert
Al-ber'-ta
Al'-ber-tine
al-bes'-cent
Al-bi-gen'-ses
al'-bi-nism
al-bi'-no
al-bi'-nos
Al'-bi-on
al-bo-lite
al-bu-gin'-e-ous
al'-bum
al-bu'-men (egg white)
al-bu'-me-nize*
al-bu'-min (class of proteins)
al-bu'-mi-nize*†
al-bu-mi-noi'-dal
al-bu-mi-no'-sis
al-bu'-mi-nous
al-bu-min-u'ri:a*†
al-bu-min-u'ric*†
Al'-bu-quer-que
al-bur'-num
Al-cae'-us
al-cal'-de
al'-ca-mine
Al'-ca-traz
al-ca-zar*
Al-ces'-tis
al-chem'-ic
al-chem'-i-cal-ly
al'-che-mist
al'-che-my
Al-ci-bi'-a-des
Al'-ci-des
al'-co-hol
al-co-hol'-ic
al-co-hol-ic'-i-ty
al'-co-hol-ism
Al'-cott
al'-cove

11

ALCOVINOMETER

al-co-vi-nom'-e-ter
Al-cy'-o-ne
Al-deb'-a-ran
al'-de-hyd-ase†
al'-de-hyde
Al'-den
al'-der
al'-der-man
al-der-man'-ic
Al'-der-ney
Al'-dine
al'-drich
a'le-a-to-ry
a'lef
a'lef=null'
ale'-house
a:lem'-bic
A:len'-çon (A:len-çon')
a'leph
a'leph=null'
a'leph=ze'-ro
A:lep'-po
a:lert'
a:lert'-ly
a:lert'-ness
A:les-san'-dri:a
al'-eu-rone*†
A:leut'*†
A:leu'-tian†
Al-ex-an'-der
Al-ex-an-dret'-ta
Al-ex-an-dri:a
Al-ex-an'-dri-an
Al-ex-an'-drine
a:lex'-i:a
A:lex'-is
a-fal'-fa
Al-fon'-so
Al'-fred
al-fres'-co
al'-ga
al'-gae
al-gar-ro'-ba
al'-ge-bra
al-ge-bra'-ic
al-ge-bra'-i-cal
al-ge-bra'-i-cal-ly
Al-ge-ci'-ras
al-ge-fa'-cient
Al-ge'-ri:a
Al-ge'-ri-an
al-gid'-i-ty
Al-giers'
al-go-lag'-ni:a
al-gol'-o-gy
al-gom'-e-ter
al-go-met'-ri-cal
Al-gon'-qui-an
Al-gon'-quin

al-go-pho'-bi:a
Al-go-rab'
al'-go-rism
al'-go-rithm
Al-ham'-bra
Al-ham-bresque'
A'li
a'li-as
A'li Ba'-ba
al'-i-bi
al'-i-bi-ing
al-i-bil'-i-ty
Al'-ice
al'-i-dade
al'-ien
al-ien-a-ble
al'-ien-ate
al'-ien-at-ing
al-ien-a'-tion
al'-ien-ist
a:lif'-er-ous
a:light'
a:lign
a:lign'-ment
a:like'
al'-i-ment
al-i-men'-tal-ly
al-i-men'-ta-ry
al-i-men-ta'-tion
al'-i-mo-ny
a:line'
a:line'-ment
al'-i-ped
al-i-phat'-ic
al'-i-quant
Al-i-quip'-pa
al'-i-quot
Al'-i-son
al-i-un'-de*†
a:live'
a:li-vin'-cu-lar*†
a:liz'-a-rin
al'-ka-li
al-ka-lim'-e-ter
al-ka-lim'-e-try
al'-ka-line
al-ka-lin'-i-ty
al-ka-li-za'-tion
al'-ka-lize
al'-ka-loid
al-ka-loid-al*†
al'-ka-net
al'-ke-nyl
al'-kyl
al'-kyl-ate
al'-kyl-ene†
al'-kyl-ize†
Al'-lah
all=A:mer'-i-can

12

Al'-lan
al-lan-to'-ic
al-lan-toi'-dal
all'=a:round'
al-lay'
al-lay'-ing
al-le-ga'-tion
al-lege'
al-lege'-a-ble
al-leged'
al-leg'-ed-ly
Al-le-gha'-nies
Al-le-ghe'-ni-an†
Al-le-ghe'-nies†
Al-le-ghe'-ny†
al-le'-giance
al-leg'-ing
al-le-gor'-ic
al-le-gor'-i-cal
al'-le-go-ries
al'-le-go-rist
al'-le-go-rize
al'-le-go-ry
al-le'-gro
al-le-lu'-ia
Al'-len
Al'-len-by
Al'-len-town
al'-ler-gen
al-ler'-gic
al'-ler-gy
al-le'-vi-ate
al-le'-vi-at-ing
al-le-vi-a'-tion
al-le'-vi-a-tive
al'-ley
al'-leys
al'-ley-way
al-li-a'-ceous
al-li'-ance
al-lied'
al-lies'
al'-li-ga-tor
all'=im-por'-tant
Al'-li-son
al-lit'-er-ate
al-lit-er-a'-tion
al-lit'-er-a-tive
al'-lo-ca-ble
al'-lo-cate
al'-lo-cat-ing
al-lo-ca'-tion
al-log'-a-mous
al-log'-a-my
al-lom'-er-ism
al-lom'-e-try
al'-lo-path
al-lo-path'-ic

al-lo-path'-i-cal-ly
al-lop'-a-thy
al-lo-phyl'-li-an
al-lot'
al-lot'-ment
al-lo-troph'-ic
al-lo-trop'-ic
al-lot'-ro-py
al-lot'-ted
al-lot'-ting
all=o'ver
al-low'
al-low'-a-ble
al-low'-ance
al-lowed'
al-low'-ed-ly
al'-loy
all right
all'=round
all'-spice
al-lude'
al-lure'
al-lured'
al-lure'-ment
al-lur'-ing
al-lu'-sion
al-lu'-sive
al-lu'-sive-ly
al-lu'-sive-ness
al-lu'-vi-al
al-lu'-vi-on
al-lu'-vi-um
al'-ly' (n.)
al-ly' (v.)
al-ly'-ing
al'-lyl
al'-lyl-a:mine'†
al-lyl'-ic
Al'-ma
al'-ma-gest
al'-ma ma'-ter
al'-ma-nac
al-might'y
al'-mond
al'-mo-ner*†
al'-most
alms'-house
al'-ni-co
a:lo'-di-um
al'-oe
al'-oes
al'-oes-ol
al-o-et'-ic
a:loft'
al'-o-gism
a:lo'-ha
al'-o-in
a:lone'

13

a:long'
a:long-side'
A:lon'-so (A:lon'-zo)
a:loof'
a:loof'-ness
al-o-pe'-ci:a
a:loud'
Al-o-ys'-i-us
al-pac'a
al'-pha
al-pha-bet'-ic
al-pha-bet'-i-cal
al'-pha-bet-ize
al'-pha-nu-mer'-ic
Al'-phe-us
Al-phon'-so
Al'-pine
Al'-pin-ism
al-read'y
al-right'
Al'-sace
Al'-sace=Lor-raine'
Al-sa'-tian
al'-sike
al'-tar
al'-ter
al-ter-a-bil'-i-ty
al'-ter-a-ble
al-ter-a'-tion
al'-ter-cate
al-ter-ca'-tion
al'-ter e'go
al-ter'-nant
al'-ter-nate
al'-ter-nat-ed
al'-ter-nate-ly
al'-ter-nat-ing
al-ter-na'-tion
al-ter'-na-tive
al-ter'-na-tor
al-the'a
al-though'
al-tim'-e-ter
al-tis'-o-nant
al'-ti-tude
al-ti-tu'-di-nal
al-ti-tu-di-nar'-i-an†
al'-to
al'-to-geth-er
Al'-ton
Al-too'-na
al'-tru-ism
al'-tru-ist
al-tru-is'-ti-cal-ly
al'-u-del
al'-um
a:lu'-mi-na

a:lu-mi-nif'-er-ous
al-u-min'-i-um
a:lu'-mi-nize
a:lu'-mi-nous
a:lu'-mi-num
a:lum'-na
a:lum'-nae
a:lum'-ni
a:lum'-nus
A:lun'-dum
al'-u-nite
Al'-va
al-ve'-o-lar
al-ve-o-la'-tion
al-ve'-o-lus
al'-ways
a:lys'-sum
a'mah
a:mal'-gam
a:mal'-ga-mate*
a:mal'-ga-ma'-tion*
a:mal'-ga-ma-tor*
A:man'-da
a:man-u-en'-sis
am'-a-ranth
am-a-ran'-thine
Am-a-ril'-lo
am-a-ryl'-lis
a:mass'
a:mass'-a-ble
a:mass'-ment
am'-a-teur
am'-a-teur-ish
am'-a-teur-ism
A:ma'-ti
am'-a-tol
am'-a-to-ry
am-au-ro'-sis
a:maze'
a:mazed'
a:maz'-ed-ly
a:maze'-ment
a:maz'-ing
a:maz'-ing-ly
Am'-a-zon
Am-a-zo'-ni-an
am'-a-zon-ite
am-ba'-gious-ly
am-bas'-sa-dor
am-bas-sa-do'-ri-al
am-bas'-sa-dress
am'-ber
am'-ber-gris
am'-bi-dex-ter
am-bi-dex-ter'-i-ty
am-bi-dex'-trous
am'-bi-ent
am-bi-gu'-i-ty

14

am-big'-u-ous
am-bip'-a-rous
am-bi'-tion
am-bi'-tious
am-biv'-a-lence
am-biv'-a-lent
am'-ble
am'-bled
am'-bling
am'-bling-ly
am-blys'-to-ma
Am'-brose
am-bro'-si:a
am-bro'-si-al†
am-bro'-si-an†
am'-bry
ambs'-ace
am-bu-lac'-rum*†
am'-bu-lance
am'-bu-lant
am'-bu-late
am-bu-la'-tion
am'-bu-la-to-ry
am'-bus-cade
am-bus-cad'-er
am'-bush
am'-bushed
am'-bush-er
am'-bush-ment
am'-bush
am'-bush
me'-ba
me'-bic
me'-boid
me'-lia*
me-lio-ra-ble*
me-lio-rate*
me-lio-ra'-tion*
me-lio-ra-tive*
me-lio-ra-tor*
men'
me-na-bil'-i-ty
me'-na-ble
mend'
mend'-a-ble
mend'-a-to-ry
mend'-ed
mend'-ment
mends'
men'-i-ties
men'-i-ty
men-or-rhe'a
a'-ent
a-en-ta'-ceous
men'-ti:a
a-en-tif'-er-ous
men'-tu-lum
merce'
mer-i-ca
mer'-i-ca

A:mer'-i-can
A:mer-i-can'a*†
A:mer'-i-can-ism
A:mer-i-can-i-za'-tion
A:mer'-i-can-ize
am'-e-thyst
am-e-trom'-e-ter
am-e-tro'-pi:a
Am'-herst
a:mi-a-bil'-i-ty
a'mi-a-ble
a'mi-a-bly
am-i-ca-bil'-i-ty
am'-i-ca-ble
am'-i-ca-bly
am'-ice
a:mi'-cus cu'-ri-ae
a:mid'
am'-ide
a:mid'-ic
a:mi'-do
a:mid'-ships
a:midst'
Am'-i-ens
a:mi'-go
a:mine'†
a:mi'-no†
a:mi'-no ac'-id†
a:mi-no-ben-zo'-ic†
Am'-ish (A'mish)
a:miss'
a:mi-to'-sis*†
a:mi-tot'-ic*†
am'-i-ty
am'-me-line
am'-me-ter
am-mi-a'-ceous
Am'-mon
am-mo'-ni:a
am-mo'-ni-ac
am-mo'-ni-ate
am-mon'-ic
am'-mo-nite†
Am'-mon-ite
am-mo'-ni-um
am-mu-ni'-tion
am-ne'-sia*†
am'-nes-ty
am-ni-ot'-ic
a:moe'-ba
am-oe-bae'-an
a:moe'-boid
a:mo'-le
a:mong'
a:mongst'
A:mon-til-la'-do
a:mor'-al

15

a:mo-ral'-i-ty
a:mor'-al-ly
am'-o-rous
a:mor'-phism
a:mor'-phous
am-or-ti-za'-tion*†
am'-or-tize*†
am'-or-tiz-ing*†
A'mos
a:mount'
a:mour'
A'moy
A'moy-ese*
am'-per-age
am'-pere
am'-per-sand
am-phi-ar-thro'-sis
Am-phib'-i:a
am-phib'-i-an
am-phib-i-ol'-o-gy
am-phi-bi-ot'-ic
am-phib'-i-ous
am-phib'-i-ous-ly
am-phib-ol'-ic
am-phib'-o-lite
am-phib-o-log'-i-cal
am-phib'-o-lous
am-phi-coe'-lous
am-phic'-ty-on
am-phi-dip'-loi-dy
am'-phi-gen
am-phig'-e-nous
am-phi-gor'-ic
am'-phi-go-ry
am-phip'-o-da
am'-phi-the-a-ter
am-phi-the'-ci-um
Am'-phi-tri-te
am'-pho-ra
am'-ple
am'-ple-ness
am-plex'-i-caul
am-pli-a'-tion
am-pli-fi-ca'-tion
am-plif'-i-ca-to-ry†
am'-pli-fied
am'-pli-fi-er
am'-pli-fy
am'-pli-fy-ing
am'-pli-tude
am'-ply
am'-poule
am-pul'-la
am-pul-la'-ceous
am'-pu-tate
am'-pu-tat-ed
am'-pu-tat-ing
am-pu-ta'-tion

am'-pu-tee'
am-ri'-ta
Am-rit'-sar
Am'-ster-dam
a:muck'
am'-u-let
A'mund-sen
a:mus'-a-ble
a:muse'
a:mused'
a:mus'-ed-ly
a:muse'-ment
a:mu'-si:a
a:mus'-ing
a:mus'-ive*†
Am'-vets
A'my
a:myg'-da-la
a:myg'-da-lase
a:myg'-da-lin
a:myg-da-loi'-dal
am'-yl
am-y-la'-ceous
am'-yl-ene†
am-y-loi'-dal
am-y-lol'-y-sis
am-y-lo-lyt'-ic
am-y-lop'-sin
am'-y-lose*
am'-y-lum
an'a
an-a-bae'-na
An'-a-bap'-tist
an'-a-bas
a:nab'-a-sis
an-a-bat'-ic
an:a-bi-o'-sis
an-a-bol'-ic
a:nab'-o-lism
a:nach'-ro-nism
a:nach'-ro-nis'-tic
a:nach'-ro-nous-ly
an-a-clas'-tic
an-a-cli'-nal
an-a-clit'-ic
an-a-co-lu'-thon
an-a-con'-da
A:nac'-re-on
an-a-cru'-sis
an-a-di-plo'-sis
a:nad'-ro-mous
a:nae'-mi:a
an-aer-o'-bi:a
an-aer-o'-bic†
an-aes-the'-si:a
an-a-glyph'-ic
a:nag'-ly-phy
an-a-glyp'-tics

an-a-gog'-i-cal
an'-a-gram
an-a-gram-mat'-ic
a'nal
a:nal'-cite
an'-a-lects
an-a-lep'-tic
an-al-ge'-si:a
an-al-ge'-sic
an-a-log
an-a-log'-ic
an-a-log'-i-cal
an-a-log'-i-cal-ly
a:nal'-o-gies
a:nal'-o-gist
a:nal'-o-gize
a:nal'-o-gous
a:nal'-o-gous-ly
an'-a-logue
a:nal'-o-gy
a:nal'-y-ses
a:nal'-y-sis
an'-a-lyst
an-a-lyt'-ic
an-a-lyt'-i-cal
an-a-lyt'-i-cal-ly
an'-a-lyze
an'-a-lyz-ing
an-am-ne'-sis
an-an'-drous
An-a-ni'-as
an-a-paes'-tic
a:naph'-o-ra
an-aph-ro-dis'-i-ac
an'-a-plas-ty
an-ap-tot'-ic
an'-arch
an-ar'-chic
an-ar'-chi-cal
an'-ar-chism*†
an'-ar-chist*†
an-ar-chis'-tic†
an'-ar-chy*
an'-ar-throus
an-as'-tig-mat†
an-a-stig-mat'-ic*†
a:nas-to-mo'-sis
a:nath'-e-ma
a:nath'-e-ma-tize
An-a-to'-li:a
An-a-to'-li-an
an-a-tom'-i-cal
a:nat'-o-mist
a:nat'-o-mize
a:nat'-o-my
a:nat'-ro-pous

an'-ces-tor
an-ces'-tral
an'-ces-tress
an'-ces-try
An-chi'-ses
an'-chor
an'-chor-age
an'-cho-ret
an'-cho-rite (hermit)
an'-chor-ite (mineral)
an-cho-rit'-ic
an'-cho-vies
  (an-cho'-vies)
an'-cho-vy (an-cho'-vy)
an'-cient
an'-cient-ly
an'-cil-lar:y†
an'-con
An-co'-na
an-co'-ne-al
an-cy-lo-sto-mi'-a-sis*†
An-da-lu'-si:a
An-da-lu'-sian
An'-da-man
an-dan'-te
An-de'-an
An'-der-sen
An'-der-son
An'-des
an'-de-site*
and'-i-ron
An-dor'-ra
An'-do-ver
An-dre'
An'-drew
An'-drews
An'-dro-clus
an-droe'-ci-um
an'-dro-gen
an-drog'-y-nous
An-drom'-a-che
An-drom'-e-da
An'-dros
an'-dro-sin
an-dros'-te-rone*
an'-ec-dot-al*†
an'-ec-dote
an-ec-dot'-ic
an-ec-dot'-i-cal
an'-ec-dot-ist
a:ne'-mi:a
a:ne'-mic
an-e-mo-log'-i-cal
an-e-mom'-e-ter
a:nem'-o-ne
an-e-moph'-i-lous
an-e-mo'-sis
a:nent'

an'-er-oid†
an-es-the'-sia
an-es-the-si-ol'-o-gist
an-es-thet'-ic
a:nes'-the-tist*†
a:nes'-the-tize*†
a:neu'-ri:a
an'-eu-rysm
a:new'
an-frac-tu-os'-i-ty
an'-ga-ry
an'-gel
An'-ge-la
an-gel'-ic
an-gel'-i-ca
an-gel'-i-cal
an-gel'-i-cal-ly
An'-gell
An'-ge-lo
An'-ge-lus
an'-ger
An'-ge-vin
an-gi'-na
an-gi'-na pec'-to-ris
an'-gi-o-cyst
an-gi-o'-ma
an-gi-om'-a-tous
an-gi-op'-a-thy
an'-gi-o-sperm
an-gi-o-sperm'-mous
an-gi-os'-to-my
Ang'-kor
an'-gle
an'-gler
an'-gle-worm
An'-gli-can
an'-gli-cism
an-gli-ci-za'-tion
an'-gli-cize
an'-gling
An'-glo=A:mer'-i-can
An'-glo-phile
An'-glo=Sax'-on
An-go'-la
An-go'-ra
an'-gri-ly
an'-gri-ness
an'-gry
ang'-strom
an'-guish
an'-guished
an'-gu-lar
an-gu-lar'-i-ty
An'-gus
an-he'-dron
an-hi-dro'-sis
An'-hwei
an-hy'-dride

an-hy'-drous
an'-ile
an'-i-lide
an'-i-line
a:nil'-i-ty
an-i-mad-ver'-sion
an-i-mad-vert'
an'-i-mal
an-i-mal'-cu-lar
an-i-mal'-cule
an'-i-mal-ism
an-i-mal'-i-ty
an'-i-mate
an'-i-mat-ed
an'-i-mat-ed-ly
an'-i-mat-ing
an-i-ma'-tion
an'-i-mism
an-i-mos'-i-ty
an'-i-mus
an'-i:on
an'-ise
an'-i-seed
a:nis'-i-dine
an-i:som'-er-ous
an-i:so-me-tro'-pi:a
an-i:so-trop'-ic
an-i:sot'-ro-py
An-jou'
an'-kle
an'-klet
an-ky-lo'-sis
an-ky-los'-to-ma
an'-nal
an'-nal-ist
an-nal-is'-tic
an'-nals
An'-nam
An'-nam-ese*†
An-nap'-o-lis
Ann Ar'-bor
an-neal'
an-nealed'
an'-ne-lid
An-nette'
an-nex' (v.)
an'-nex (n.)
an-nex'-a-ble
an-nex-a'-tion
an-ni'-hi-la-ble
an-ni'-hi-late
an-ni-hi-la'-tion
an-ni'-hi-la-tor
An'-nis-ton
an-ni-ver'-sa-ries
an-ni-ver'-sa-ry
an'-no Dom'-i-ni
an'-no-tate

18

an-no-ta'-tion
an'-no-ta-tor
an-nounce'
an-nounce'-ment
an-nounc'-er
an-nounc'-ing
an-noy'
an-noy'-ance
an-noyed'
an-noy'-ing
an'-nu-al
an'-nu-al-ly
an-nu'-i-tant
an-nu'-i-ty
an-nul'
an'-nu-lar
an-nu-lar'-i-ty
an'-nu-let
an-nulled'
an-nul'-ling
an-nul'-ment
an'-num
an-nun'-ci-ate
an-nun-ci-a'-tion
an-nun'-ci-a-tor
an-nun'-ci-a-to-ry
An-nun'-zi:o
an'-ode
an'-o-dyne
a:noint'
a:noint'-ed
a:noint'-er
a:noint'-ment
an'-o-lyte
a:nom'-a-lism
a:nom-a-lis'-tic
a:nom'-a-lous
a:nom'-a-lous-ly
an'-o-nym
an-o-nym'-i-ty
a:non'-y-mous
a:non'-y-mous-ly
A:noph'-e-les
an-op'-si:a
an'-o-rak*
an-or'-thite
an-or'-tho-site
an-os'-mi:a
an-oth'-er
An'-schluss
An'-selm
an'-ser-ine
an'-swer
an'-swer-a-ble
an'-swered
an'-swer-ing
an'-ta

ant-ac'-id
An-tae'-us
an-tag'-o-nism
an-tag'-o-nist
an-tag-o-nis'-tic
an-tag'-o-nize
ant-al'-ka-line
Ant-arc'-tic
Ant-arc'-ti-ca
An-tar'-es†
an'-te
ant'-eat-er
an'-te-bel'-lum
an-te-ced'-ence†
an-te-ced'-en-cy†
an-te-ced'-ent†
an'-te-cham-ber
an'-te-date
an-te-di-lu'-vi-an
an'-te-lope
an'-te me-rid'-i-em
an-ten'-na
an-te-pen'-di-um
an'-te-pe'-nult
an-te-pe-nul'-ti-mate
an-te'-ri-or
an'-te-room
ant-he'-li-on
ant-hel-min'-tic*
an'-them
an-the'-mi-on
an'-ther
an'-ther-al
an-ther-id'-i-um
an-the'-sis
an-tho-cy'-a-nin
an-tho'-di-um
an-thog'-e-nous
an-tho-log'-i-cal
an-thol'-o-gist
an-thol'-o-gize
an-thol'-o-gy
An'-tho-ny
an'-tho-tax:y
an'-thra-cene
an'-thra-ces
an'-thra-cite
an-thra-qui-none'
an-thra-qui-no'-nyl
an'-thrax
an-thro-po-gen'-e-sis
an-thro-pog'-e-ny
an-thro-pog'-ra-phy
an'-thro-poid
an-thro-po-log'-i-cal
an-thro-pol'-o-gist
an-thro-pol'-o-gy
an-thro-pom'-e-ter

19

an-thro-po-met'-ric
an-thro-pom'-e-try
an-thro-po-morph'-ic*†
an-thro-pon'-y-my
an-thro-pop'-a-thy
an-thro-poph'-a-gi
an-thro-poph'-a-gous
an-thro-poph'-a-gy
an'-ti
an'-ti-air'-craft
an'-ti-ar
an-ti-bi-ot'-ic
an'-ti-bod-ies
an'-ti-bod:y
an'-tic
an-ti-cat'-a-lyst
an-ti-cath'-ode
an'-ti-chlor
an-ti-chlo-ris'-tic
An'-ti-christ
an-tic'-i-pant
an-tic'-i-pate
an-tic'-i-pat-ed
an-tic'-i-pat-ing
an-tic-i-pa'-tion
an-tic'-i-pa-tive
an-tic'-i-pa-to-ry
an-ti-cler'-i-cal
an-ti-cli'-max
an-ti-cli'-nal
an-ti-cli-no'-ri-um
an-ti-cy'-clone
an-ti-cy-clon'-ic
an'-ti-dot-al†
an'-ti-dote
an-ti-drom'-ic
An-tie'-tam
An-ti-fed'-er-al-ist
an'-ti-freeze
an'-ti-gen
An-tig'-o-ne
An-tig'-o-nus
An-ti'-gua
an-ti-he'-lix
an-ti-his'-ta-mine
an-ti-ke-to-gen'-e-sis
An-til'-les
an-ti-log'-a-rithm
an-til'-o-gism
an-til'-o-gy
an-ti-ma-cas'-sar
an-tim'-er-ism†
an-ti-mis'-sile
an'-ti-mon-ic*
an'-ti-mo-ny
an-tin'-o-my
An'-ti-och
An-ti'-o-chus

an-ti-pas'-to
an-ti-pa-thet'-ic
an-ti-pa-thet'-i-cal
an-tip'-a-thy
an'-ti-phon
an-tiph'-o-nal
an-tiph'-o-nar:y†
an-tiph'-ra-sis
an'-ti-pode
an-tip-o-de'-an
an-tip'-o-des
an-ti-quar'-i-an†
an'-ti-quar:y†
an'-ti-quate
an'-ti-quat-ed
an'-ti-quat-ing
an-tique'
an-tiq'-ui-ty
an-ti-re-mon'-strant
an-tir-rhi'-num
an-ti=Sem'-i-tism
an-ti-sep'-sis
an-ti-sep'-tic
an-ti-sep'-ti-cize
an-ti-se'-rum
an-ti-slav'-er:y
an-ti-so'-cial
an-tis'-tro-phe
an-ti-stroph'-ic
an-tith'-e-sis
an-ti-thet'-ic
an-ti-thet'-i-cal-ly
an-ti-tox'-ic
an-ti-tox'-in
an-ti-tra'-gus*†
an'-ti-trust'
an-ti-typ'-ic
an-ti-typ'-i-cal
ant'-ler
ant'-lered
An-toi-nette'
An-to'-ni:a
An-to-ni'-nus
An-to'-ni:o
An-to'-ni-us
An'-to-ny
an'-to-nym
an-ton-y-my
ant'-proof
An'-trim
an'-trorse
an'-trum
Ant'-werp
an-u'-rous†
a'nus
an'-vil

anx-i'-e-ty
anx'-ious
anx'-ious-ly
an'y
an'y-bod:y
an'y-how
an'y-one
an'y-place
an'y-thing
an'y-way
an'y-where
a'o-rist
a:o-ris'-tic
a:or'-ta
a:or'-tic
a:pace'
a:pache' (Parisian gangster)
A:pach'e (Indian tribe)
Ap-a-lach-i-co'-la
ap'-a-nage
a:pa-re'-jo
a:part'
a:part'-heid
a:part'-ment
ap-as'-tron
ap-a-tet'-ic
ap-a-thet'-ic
ap-a-thet'-i-cal-ly
ap'-a-thy
ap'-a-tite
ape'-like
Ap'-en-nines
a:pe'-ri-ent
a:pe-ri-od'-ic
a:per-i-tif*‡
ap'-er-ture
a:pet'-al-ous†
a'pex
a:phaer'-e-sis
aph'-a-nite
aph-a-nit'-ic
a:pha'-si:a
a:pha'-si-ac
a:pha'-sic
aph-e'-lion*†
aph-e-li-ot'-ro-pism*†
aph'-e-sis
a'phid†
A'phis
a:phlo-gis'-tic†
a:pho'-ni:a
a:phon'-ic
aph'-o-rism
aph-o-ris'-tic
a:pho'-tic
a:phra'-si:a
aph-ro-dis'-i-ac
Aph-ro-di'-te

a:phyl'-lous
a:pi-an
a:pi-ar'-i-an†
a:pi-a-rist
a:pi-ar:y†
ap'-i-cal
ap'-i-ces
a:pi-cul'-tur-al
a:pi-cul-ture
a:piece'
a:pi-ose
ap'-ish
ap'-ish-ly
a:piv'-o-rous
ap-la-nat'-ic
a:plen'-ty
a:plomb'
ap'-ne:a
a:poc'-a-lypse
a:poc-a-lyp'-tic
ap-o-car'-pous
ap-o-chro-mat'-ic
a:poc'-o-pe
A:poc'-ry-pha
a:poc'-ry-phal
a:poc'-y-na'-ceous
ap'-o-dal
Ap'-o-des
ap-o-dic'-tic
a:pod'-o-sis
ap-o-gam'-ic
a:pog'-a-my
ap-o-ge'-al
ap-o-ge'-an
ap'-o-gee
A:pol-li-nar'-is†
A:pol'-lo
a:pol-o-get'-ic
a:pol-o-get'-i-cal
a:pol-o-get'-i-cal-ly
a:pol-o-get'-ics
ap-o-lo'-gi:a
a:pol'-o-gies
a:pol'-o-gist
a:pol'-o-gize
a:pol'-o-gized
a:pol'-o-giz-ing
ap'-o-logue
a:pol'-o-gy
ap-o-neu-ro'-sis
ap-o-pemp'-tic
a:poph'-y-ge
ap-o-phyl'-lite*†
ap-o-plec'-tic
ap-o-plec'-ti-cal
ap'-o-plex:y
ap-o-si-o-pe'-sis
a:pos'-ta-sy

21

a:pos'-tate
a:pos'-ta-tize
a pos-te-ri-o'-ri
a:pos'-tle
a:pos'-tle-ship
a:pos'-to-late
ap-os-tol'-ic
ap-os-tol'-i-cal
ap-os-tol'-i-cism
a:pos-to-lic'-i-ty
a:pos'-tro-phe
ap-os-troph'-ic
a:pos'-tro-phize
a:poth'-e-car-ies†
a:poth'-e-car:y†
ap-o-the'-ci-um
ap'-o-thegm
ap-o-theg-mat'-ic
a:poth-e-o'-sis†
ap-o-the'-o-size*
Ap-pa-la'-chi-an*†
ap-pall'
ap-palled'
ap-pall'-ing
ap-pall'-ing-ly
ap'-pa-nage
ap-pa-rat'-us*†
ap-par'-el
ap-par'-eled
ap-par'-ent
ap-par'-ent-ly
ap-pa-ri'-tion
ap-par'-i-tor
ap-peal'
ap-peal'-a-ble
ap-pealed'
ap-peal'-er
ap-peal'-ing
ap-peal'-ing-ly
ap-pear'
ap-pear'-ance
ap-peared'
ap-pear'-ing
ap-peas'-a-ble
ap-pease'
ap-pease'-ment
ap-peas'-er
ap-peas'-ing
ap-peas'-ing-ly
ap-pel'-lant
ap-pel'-late
ap-pel-la'-tion
ap-pel'-la-tive
ap-pel-lee'
ap-pel'-lor
ap-pend'
ap-pend'-age†
ap-pend'-aged†

ap-pend'-an-cy
ap-pend'-ant†
ap-pen-dec'-to-my
ap-pend'-ed
ap-pen'-di-cal
ap-pen-di-ci'-tis
ap-pen-dic'-u-lar
ap-pen'-dix
ap-per-ceive'
ap-per-cep'-tion
ap-per-cep'-tive
ap-per-tain'
ap'-pe-ten-cy
ap'-pe-tite
ap-pet'-i-tive*†
ap'-pe-tiz-er
ap'-pe-tiz-ing
Ap'-pi-an
ap-plaud'
ap-plaud'-er
ap-plaud'-ing
ap-plause'
ap-plaus'-ive*
ap'-ple
ap'-ple-jack
ap'-ple-sauce
Ap'-ple-ton
ap-pli'-ance
ap-pli-ca-bil'-i-ty
ap'-pli-ca-ble
ap'-pli-ca-bly
ap'-pli-cant
ap-pli-ca'-tion
ap'-pli-ca-tive
ap'-pli-ca-to-ry
ap-plied'
ap-pli'-er
ap-pli-qué'
ap-ply'
ap-ply'-ing
ap-pog-gia-tu'-ra
ap-point'
ap-point'-a-ble
ap-point'-ed
ap-poin-tee'*†
ap-point'-er
ap-point'-ing
ap-point'-ive*†
ap-point'-ment
ap-poin'-tor
Ap-po-mat'-tox
ap-por'-tion
ap-por'-tioned
ap-por'-tion-er
ap-por'-tion-ing
ap-por'-tion-ment
ap-pos'-a-ble
ap-pose'

ap'-po-site
ap-po-si'-tion
ap-pos'-i-tive
ap-prais'-a-ble
ap-prais'-al
ap-praise'
ap-praised'
ap-praise'-ment
ap-prais'-er
ap-prais'-ing
ap-prais'-ing-ly
ap-pre'-cia-ble*†
ap-pre'-ci-ate
ap-pre'-ci-at-ed
ap-pre'-ci-at-ing
ap-pre-ci-a'-tion
ap-pre'-cia-tive*†
ap-pre'-cia-tive-ly*†
ap-pre'-cia-to-ry*†
ap-pre-hend'
ap-pre-hend'-ed
ap-pre-hend'-ing
ap-pre-hen-si-bil'-i-ty
ap-pre-hen'-si-ble
ap-pre-hen'-sion
ap-pre-hen'-sive
ap-pre-hen'-sive-ly
ap-pren'-tice
ap-pren'-ticed
ap-pren'-tice-ship
ap-prise'
ap-prised'
ap-pris'-ing
ap-proach'
ap-proach-a-bil'-i-ty
ap-proach'-a-ble
ap-proached'
ap-proach'-ing
ap-pro-ba'-tion
ap'-pro-ba-tive
ap'-pro-ba-tive-ness
ap'-pro-ba-to-ry
ap-pro'-pri-a-ble
ap-pro'-pri-ate
ap-pro'-pri-at-ed
ap-pro'-pri-ate-ly
ap-pro'-pri-ate-ness
ap-pro'-pri-at-ing
ap-pro-pri-a'-tion
ap-pro'-pri-a-tive
ap-prov'-a-ble
ap-prov'-al
ap-prove'
ap-proved'
ap-prov'-ing
ap-prov'-ing-ly
ap-prox'-i-mate
ap-prox'-i-mat-ed

ap-prox'-i-mate-ly
ap-prox'-i-mat'-ing
ap-prox-i-ma'-tion
ap-pui'
ap-pur'-te-nance
ap-pur'-te-nant
a'-pri-cot
A'-pril
a pri-o'-ri
a:pri-or'-i-ty
a'-pron
a'-pron-ful
ap'-ro-pos
apse
ap'-si-dal
ap'-sis
Ap'-ter:a
ap'-ter-al
ap-te'-ri-um
ap'-ter-ous
ap'-ti-tude
apt'-ly
apt'-ness
A:pu'-li:a
a:py-ret'-ic†
aq'-ua†
aq'-ua-lung
aq-ua-ma-rine'†
aq'-ua-plane†
aq'-ua-relle
a:quar'-i-um†
A:quar'-i-us†
a:quat'-ic
a:quat'-i-cal-ly
aq'-ua-tint†
a:quat'-ive-ness
aq'-ue-duct
a'-que-ous
Aq'-ui-la
aq'-ui-line
A:qui'-nas
Aq'-ui-taine
Aq-ui-ta'-ni:a
Ar-ab
Ar-a-bel'-la
ar-a-besque'
A:ra'-bi:a
A:ra'-bi-an
Ar'-a-bic
Ar'-ab-ist†
ar'-a-ble
Ar'-a-by
a:ra'-ceous
A:rach'-ne
a:rach'-nid
A:rach'-ni-da
a:rach'-noid
Ar'-a-gon

ARAGONESE

Ar-a-go-nese'
Ar'-al
Ar-a-mae'-an
Ar-a-ma'-ic
Ar-a-min'-ta
A:rap'-a-ho
Ar'-a-rat
Ar'-as
A:rau-ca'-ni-an
ar'-ba-lest
ar'-bi-ter
ar'-bi-tra-ble
ar'-bi-trage
ar'-bi-trag-er
ar'-bi-tral
ar-bit'-ra-ment
ar'-bi-trar-i-ly†
ar'-bi-trar:y†
ar'-bi-trate
ar'-bi-trat-ed
ar'-bi-trat-ing
ar-bi-tra'-tion
ar'-bi-tra-tive
ar'-bi-tra-tor
ar'-bi-tress
ar'-bor
ar-bo'-re-al
ar-bo-res'-cent
ar-bo-re'-tum
ar'-bo-rize*†
ar'-bor-ous
ar'-bor-vi'-tae
ar-cade'
Ar-ca'-di:a
Ar-ca'-di-an
ar-ca'-num
ar'-ca-ture
ar-chae-ol'-o-gist
ar-chae-ol'-o-gy
ar-cha'-ic
ar-cha'-i-cal-ly
ar'-cha-ist
ar-cha-is'-tic
ar'-cha-ism
arch'-an'-gel
arch'-bish'-op
arch-bish'-op-ric
arch'-dea'-con
arch'-dea'-con-ry
arch'-di'-o-cese
arch'-du'-cal
arch'-duch'-ess
arch'-duch'y
arch'-duke'
arche- (see archae-)
Ar-che'-an
arched

arch'-en'-e-my
ar-che-o-log'-ic
ar-che-o-log'-i-cal
ar-che-ol'-o-gist
ar-che-ol'-o-gy
arch'-er'
arch'-er:y
ar'-che-spore
ar'-che-typ-al†
ar'-che-type
ar-che'-us
arch'-fiend'
Ar'-chi-bald
ar-chi-e-pis'-co-pa-cy
ar-chi-e-pis'-co-pal
ar'-chi-mage
Ar-chi-me'-de-an
Ar'-chi-me-des
ar-chi-pe-lag'-ic
ar-chi-pel'-a-go
ar-chi-pel'-a-goes
ar'-chi-tect
ar-chi-tec-ton'-ic
ar-chi-tec'-tur-al
ar'-chi-tec-ture
ar'-chi-trave
ar-chi'-val
ar'-chive
ar'-chi-vist
arch'-ness
ar'-chon
arch'-priest'
arch'-way
arc'-ing
Arc'-tic
Arc'-tic Cir'-cle
Arc-tu'-rus
ar'-cu-ate
Ar'-den
ar'-den-cy
Ar-dennes'
ar'-dent
ar'-dent-ly
ar'-dor
ar'-du-ous
ar'-du-ous-ly
ar'-e:a*†
ar'-e-al*†
ar'-e:a-way*
a:re'-ca*†
a:re'-na
ar-e-na'-ceous
ar-e-nic'-o-lous
a:re'-o-la
ar-e-ol'-o-gy
ar-e-o-log'-i-cal
Ar-e-op'-a-gus†
A'res

Ar-e-thu'-sa
ar'-gent
ar-gen'-tal
ar-gen'-te-ous
Ar-gen-ti'-na
Ar'-gen-tine
ar-gen'-tous
ar-gen'-tum
ar'-gil
ar-gil-la'-ceous
ar-gil-lif'-er-ous
ar'-gil-lite
Ar'-give
ar'-gol
Ar'-go-lis
ar'-gon
Ar'-go-naut
Ar-gonne'
Ar'-gos
ar'-go-sy
ar'-gu-a-ble
ar'-gue
ar'-gued
ar'-gu-ing
ar'-gu-ment
ar-gu-men-ta'-tion
ar-gu-men'-ta-tive
Ar'-gus
Ar'-gyle
Ar'-gyll
ar'-gy-rol
a'ri:a
Ar-i-ad'-ne†
Ar'-i-an†
ar'-id
a:rid'-i-ty
ar'-id-ness
Ar'-i-el†
A'ri-es
a:right'
A:ri'-on
a'ri-ose*†
a:ri-o'-so
A:ri-os'-to
a:rise'
a:ris'-en
a:ris'-ing
Ar-is-ti'-des
ar-is-toc'-ra-cy
a:ris'-to-crat
a:ris-to-crat'-ic†
a:ris-to-crat'-i-cal-ly†
Ar-is-toph'-a-nes
Ar-is-to-te'-li-an
Ar'-is-tot-le
a:ris'-to-type
a:rith'-me'-tic (n.)
ar-ith-met'-ic (adj.)

ar-ith-met'-i-cal
a:rith-me-ti'-cian
ar-ith-mom'-e-ter
Ar-i-zo'-na
Ar-i-zo'-nan
Ar-i-zo'-ni-an
Ar-kan'-san
Ar'-kan-sas
Ark'-wright
Ar'-ling-ton
ar-ma'-da
ar-ma-dil'-lo
Ar-ma-ged'-don
ar'-ma-ment
ar'-ma-ture
arm'-chair
Ar-me'-ni:a
Ar-me'-ni-an
Ar-men-tieres'
arm'-ful
arm'-hole
ar'-mies
ar'-mi-ger
ar'-mil-lar:y†
Ar-min'-i-an
ar-mip'-o-tent
ar'-mi-stice
arm'-let
ar'-mor
ar'-mor=bear-er
ar'-mored
ar'-mor-er
ar-mo'-ri-al
ar'-mor=plat'-ed
ar'-mo-ry*
arm'-pit
Arm'-strong
ar'-mure
ar'-my
ar'-ni-ca
Ar'-no
Ar'-nold
ar'-oid
a:roi'-de-ous
a:ro'-ma
ar-o-mat'-ic
ar-o-mat'-i-cal-ly
a:ro'-ma-tize
a:rose'
a:round'
a:rous'-al
a:rouse'
a:rous'-ing
ar-peg-gio
ar'-que-bus
ar-raign'
ar-raign'-er
ar-raign'-ment

25

Ar'-ran
ar-range'
ar-range'-a-ble
ar-range'-ment
ar-rang'-er
ar-rang'-ing
ar'-rant
ar'-ras
ar-ray'
ar-ray'-al
ar-rayed'
ar-ray'-ing
ar-rear'
ar-rear'-age
ar-rest'
ar-rest'-ed
ar-rest'-er
ar-rest'-ing
ar-res'-tive
ar-res'-tor
ar-rhyth'-mi:a
ar'-ris
ar-riv'-al†
ar-rive'
ar-riv'-ing
ar-ro'-ba
ar'-ro-gance
ar'-ro-gan-cy
ar'-ro-gant
ar'-ro-gate
ar'-ro-gat-ing
ar-ro-ga'-tion
ar-ron-disse'-ment
ar'-row
ar'-row-head
ar'-row-root
ar'-row:y
ar-roy'o†
ar'-se-nal
ar'-se-nic (n.)
ar-sen'-ic (adj.)
ar-sen'-i-cal
ar'-se-nide
ar-se'-ni-ous
ar-sine'
ar'-sis
ar'-son
ar'-son-ist
ar-so'-ni-um
ars-phen'-a-mine†
ar'-tal
Ar-ta-xer'-xes
Ar'-te-mis
ar-te'-ri-al
ar'-ter-ies
ar-te-ri-o-scle-ro'-sis
ar-ter:y

ar-te'-sian
art'-ful
art'-ful-ly
ar-thrit'-ic
ar-thri'-tis
ar-throg'-e-nous
ar'-thro-pod
Ar-throp'-o-da
ar-throp'-o-dal
Ar'-thur
Ar-thu'-ri-an
ar'-ti-choke
ar'-ti-cle
ar'-ti-cled
ar-tic'-u-lar
ar-tic'-u-late
ar-tic'-u-lat-ed
ar-tic-u-la'-tion
ar-tic'-u-la-tive
ar-tic'-u-la-tor
art'-i-er
ar'-ti-fact
ar'-ti-fice
ar-tif'-i-cer
ar-ti-fi'-cial
ar-ti-fi-ci-al'-i-ty
ar-ti-fi'-cial-ly
ar-til'-ler-ist
ar-til'-ler:y
ar-til'-ler:y-man
ar-ti-o-dac'-tyl
ar'-ti-san
art'-ist
ar-tiste'
ar-tis'-tic
ar-tis'-ti-cal
ar-tis'-ti-cal-ly
ar'-tist-ry*†
art'-less
art'y
Ar'-un-del (family)
A:run'-del (Maryland
    town)
a:run-di-na'-ceous
Ar'-yan
ar-y-te-noi'-dal
A'sa
as-a-fet'-i-da
as-bes'-tos
As'-bu-ry†
As-ca'-ni-us
as-car'-i-dole
as-cend'
as-cend'-a-ble
as-cend'-an-cy†
as-cend'-ant†
as-cend'-ing
as-cen'-sion

as-cent'
as-cer-tain'
as-cer-tain'-a-ble
as-cer-tain'-ment
as-cet'-ic
as-cet'-i-cal-ly
as-cet'-i-cism
As'-cham
as-cid'-i-an
as-ci'-tes
As-cle'-pi-us
as-co-go'-ni-um
as-co-my-ce'-tous
a:scor'-bic
as-co-spor'-ic
as-co-spor'-ous*†
As'-cot
as-crib'-a-ble
as-cribe'†
as-crib'-ing†
as-crip'-tion†
a:sep'-sis
a:sep'-tic
a:sep'-ti-cal-ly
a:sex'-u-al
a:sex-u-al'-i-ty
As'-gard
a:shamed'
a:sham'-ed-ly
ash bin
ash cart
ash'-en
Ashe'-ville
ash=free
ash'-man'
a:shore'
A'shur†
ash'y
A'sia
A'sia Mi'-nor
A'sian
A:si-at'-ic
a:side'
as'-i-nine
as-i-nin'-i-ty
a:skance'
a:skew'
a:slant'
a:sleep'
as-par'-a-gus
As-pa'-sia
as'-pect
as'-pen†
as'-per-ate
as-perge'
as-per-gil'-lum
as-per-gil'-lus
as-per'-i-ty

as-perse'
as-pers'-er
as-per'-sion
as-per-so'-ri-um
as'-phalt
as-phal'-tic
as-phal'-tum
as'-pho-del
as-phyx'-i:a
as-phyx'-i-ate
as-phyx'-i-at-ing
as-phyx-i-a'-tion
as-phyx'-i-a-tor
as'-pic
as-pi-dis'-tra
as'-pi-rant*†
as'-pi-rate
as'-pi-ra'-tion
as'-pi-ra-tor
as'-pi-ra-to-ry
as-pire'
as'-pi-rin
as-pir'-ing
as-pir'-ing-ly
As-ple'-ni-um
As'-quith
as'-sa-gai
as-sail'
as-sail'-a-ble
as-sail'-ant
as-sail'-ment
As-sam'
as-sas'-sin
as-sas'-si-nate
as-sas-si-na'-tion
as-sas'-si-na-tor
as-sault'
as-sault'-a-ble
as-sault'-er
as'-say (n.)
as-say' (v.)
as-say'-a-ble
as-sayed'
as-say'-er
as-say'-ing
as'-se-gai
as-sem'-bla-ble
as-sem'-blage
as-sem'-ble
as-sem'-bling
as-sem'-bly
as-sem'-bly-man
as-sent'
as-sen-ta'-tion
as-sent'-er
as-sent'-ing-ly
as-sen'-tor
as-sert'

27

as-sert'-er
as-ser'-tion
as-ser'-tive
as-ser'-tor†
as-ser'-to-ry
as-sess'
as-sess'-a-ble
as-sess'-ee
as-sess'-ment
as-ses'-sor
as-ses-so'-ri-al
as'-set
as-sev'-er-ate
as-sev-er-a'-tion
as-si-du'-i-ty
as-sid'-u-ous
as-sid'-u-ous-ly
as-si-ette'
as-sign'
as-sign-a-bil'-i-ty
as-sign'-a-ble
as'-sig-nat
as-sig-na'-tion
as-sign-ee'
as-sign'-er
as-sign'-ment
as-sign'-or
as-sim-i-la-bil'-i-ty
as-sim'-i-la-ble
as-sim'-i-late
as-sim'-i-lat-ing
as-sim-i-la'-tion
as-sim'-i-la-tive
as-sim'-i-la-tor
as-sim'-i-la-to-ry
as-sist'
as-sist'-ance†
as-sist'-ant†
as-sist'-ed
as-sist'-er
as-sist'-ing
as-sis'-tor
as-size'
as-so'-cia-ble
as-so'-ci-ate
as-so'-ci-at-ing
as-so-ci-a'-tion
as-so'-cia-tive
as'-so-nance
as'-so-nant
as-sort'
as-sort'-ed
as-sort'-ment'
as-suage'
as-suage'-ment
as-suag'-ing
as-sua'-sive
as-sum'-a-ble

as-sum'-a-bly
as-sume'
as-sum'-ed-ly
as-sum'-er
as-sum'-ing
as-sump'-sit
as-sump'-tion
as-sur'-a-ble
as-sur'-ance
as-sure'
as-sured'
as-sur'-ed-ly
as-sur'-ed-ness
as-sur'-ing
as-sur'-gent
As-syr'-i:a
As-syr'-i-an
As-tar'-te
a:stat'-ic
as'-ter
as-te'-ri:a
as'-ter-isk
as'-ter-ism
a:stern'
a:ster'-nal
as'-ter-oid
as'-ter-oi'-dal
as-ter-oi'-de-an
as-the'-ni:a
asth'-ma
asth-mat'-ic
asth-mat'-i-cal
asth-mat'-i-cal-ly
a:stig'-ma-tism
a:stir'
as-ton'-ish†
as-ton'-ished†
as-ton'-ish-ing†
as-ton'-ish-ing-ly†
as-ton'-ish-ment†
As'-tor
As-to'-ri:a
as-tound'†
as-tound'-ed†
as-tound'-ing†
as-tound'-ing-ly†
a:strad'-dle
as'-tra-gal
as-trag'-a-lus
as'-tra-khan
as'-tral
a:stray'
as-tric'-tion
a:stride'
as-trin'-gen-cy
as-trin'-gent
as'-tro-labe
as-trol'-o-ger

as-tro-log'-i-cal
as-tro-log'-i-cal-ly
as-trol'-o-gy
as-trom'-e-try
as'-tro-naut
as-tron'-o-mer
as-tro-nom'-ic
as-tro-nom'-i-cal
as-tro-nom'-i-cal-ly
as-tron'-o-my
as-tro-phys'-i-cal
as-tro-phys'-i-cist
as-tro-phys'-ics
as-tu'-cious
as-tute'
as-tute'-ly
as-tute'-ness
a:sty'-lar
a:sun'-der
a:sym-met'-ric
a:sym-met'-ri-cal
a:sym-met'-ri-cal-ly
a:sym'-me-try
as'-ymp-tote†
a:syn-ap'-sis
a:syn'-chro-nism
as-yn-det'-i-cal-ly
a:syn'-de-ton
a:sys'-to-le
at'-a-bal
At-a-lan'-ta
at'-a-vic*‡
at'-a-vism
at'-a-vist
at-a-vis'-ti-cal-ly
a:tax'-i:a
a:tax'-ic
Atch'-i-son
a:te-lier'*
ath-a-na'-sia
Ath-a-na'-si-an
Ath-a-na'-si-us
a'the-ism
a'the-ist
a:the-is'-tic
a:the-is'-ti-cal
a:the-is'-ti-cal-ly
ath'-e-ling*
Ath'-el-stan
A:the'-na
ath-e-nae'-um
A:the'-ne
ath-e-ne'-um
A:the'-ni-an
Ath'-ens
a:thirst'
ath'-lete

ath-let'-ic
ath-let'-i-cal-ly
ath-let'-i-cism
ath-let'-ics
Ath'-os
a:threp'-si:a
a:thwart'
a:tilt'
a:tin'-gle
At-lan-te'-an
At-lan'-tic
At'-las
at'-mo-sphere*†
at-mo-spher'-ic*†
at-mo-spher'-i-cal*†
at-mo-spher'-i-cal-ly*†
at'-oll†
at'-om
a:tom'-ic
a:tom'-i-cal
at-o-mic'-i-ty†
at'-om-ism
at-om-is'-tic
at-om-i-za'-tion
at'-om-ize
at'-om-iz-er
at-om-ol'-o-gy
at'-o-my†
a:ton'-al
a:ton'-al-ism
a:ton-al-is'-tic
a:to-nal'-i-ty
a:tone'
a:tone'-ment
a:ton'-ic
a:ton'-ing
at'-o-ny
a:top'
A'treus
a'tri-um
a:tro'-cious
a:tro'-cious-ly
a:troc'-i-ty
a:troph'-ic
at'-ro-phied
at'-ro-phy
a:trop'-ic
at'-ro-pine
At'-ro-pos
at-tach'
at-tach'-a-ble
at-ta-ché'
at-tached'
at-tach'-ment
at-tack'
at-tacked'
at-tack'-er
at-tack'-ing

at-tain'
at-tain-a-bil'-i-ty
at-tain'-a-ble
at-tain'-a-ble-ness
at-tain'-der
at-tain'-er
at-tain'-ment
at-taint'
at-tain'-ture
at'-tar
at-tem'-per
at-tempt'
at-tempt'-a-ble
at-tempt'-er
at-tend'
at-tend'-ance†
at-tend'-ant†
at-ten'-tion
at-ten'-tive
at-ten'-tive-ly
at-ten-u-a'-ate
at-ten-u-a'-tion
at-test'
at-test'-ant†
at-tes-ta'-tion
at-test'-er
at'-tic
At'-ti-ca
At'-ti-la
at-tire'
at-tire'-ment
at-tir'-ing
at'-ti-tude
at-ti-tu'-di-nize
at-tor'-ney
at-tor'-ney = at=law
at-tor'-ney gen'-er-al
at-tract'
at-tract-a-bil'-i-ty
at-tract'-a-ble
at-tract'-a-ble-ness
at-tract'-ant†
at-trac'-tion
at-tract'-ive*†
at-tract'-ive-ly*†
at-tract'-ive-ness*†
at-trac'-tor
at-trib'-ut-a-ble†
at'-tri-bute (n.)
at-trib'-ute (v.)
at-tri-bu'-tion
at-trib'-u-tive
at-tri'-tion
at-tri'-tus
at-tune'
at-tune'-ment
at-tun'-ing
a:typ'-i-cal

au'-burn
auc'-tion
auc-tion-eer'
au-da'-cious
au-dac'-i-ty
au-di-bil'-i-ty
au'-di-ble
au'-di-bly
au'-di-ence
au'-dile
au'-di:o
au-di-o-gen'-ic
au'-di-o-phile
au'-dit
au-di'-tion
au'-di-tor
au-di-to'-ri-um
au'-di-to-ry
Au'-du-bon
au'-ger
aught
au'-gite
au'-gi-tite
aug-ment' (v.)
aug'-ment (n.)
aug-ment'-a-ble
aug-men-ta'-tion
aug-men'-ta-tive*
au gra'-tin
Augs'-burg
au'-gur
au'-gu-ry
Au'-gust
au-gust'
Au-gus'-ta
Au-gus'-tan
Au'-gus-tine
   (Au-gus'-tine)
Au-gus-tin'-i-an
Au-gus'-tus
auk
auld lang syne
au'-lic
au'-ra
au'-ral
au-re-ate
Au-re-li:a
Au-re'-li-an
Au-re'-li-us
au'-re-ole
Au-re-o-my'-cin
au re-voir'
au'-ric
au'-ri-cle
au'-ri-cled
au-ric'-u-lar
au-rif'-er-ous
au-ris'-co-py

30

au'-rist
au-ro'-ra
au-ro'-ra bo-re-al'-is*
au-ro'-ral
au-ro-re'-an
au'-rous
au'-rum
aus'-cul-tate
aus-cul-ta'-tion
aus'-pi-cate
aus'-pice
aus-pi'-cial
aus-pi'-cious
aus-pi'-cious-ly
aus-tere'
aus-tere'-ly
aus-ter'-i-ty
Aus'-ter-litz
Aus'-tin
Aus-tra-la'-sia*†
Aus-tra-la'-sian*†
Aus-tra'-lia*
Aus-tra'-lian*
Aus-tra'-sian
Aus'-tri:a
Aus'-tri:a=Hun'-ga-ry
Aus'-tri-an
Aus'-tro=Ma-lay'-an
au-tar'-chic
au'-tar-chy*
au-then'-tic
au-then'-ti-cal-ly
au-then'-ti-cate
au-then-ti-ca'-tion
au-then-tic'-i-ty
au'-thor
au'-thor-ess
au-thor-i-tar'-i-an†
au-thor'-i-ta-tive
au-thor'-i-ty
au-tho-ri-za'-tion*†
au'-tho-rize*†
au'-tho-rized*†
au'-tho-riz-ing*†
au'-thor-ship
au'-tism
au'-to
au-to-bi-og'-ra-pher
au-to-bi-o-graph'-ic
au-to-bi-o-graph'-i-cal
au-to-bi-og'-ra-phy
au-toch'-thon
au-toch'-tho-nous
au-to-co-her'-er
au-toc'-ra-cy
au'-to-crat
au-to-crat'-ic
au-to-crat'-i-cal-ly

au'-to=da=fé'
au-to-e-rot'-ic
au-to-er'-o-tism
au-tog'-a-my
au-to-gen'-e-sis
au-to-ge-net'-ic
au-to-gen'-ic
au-tog'-e-nous
au'-to-gi-ro
au'-to-graph
au-tog'-ra-pher
au-to-graph'-ic
au-tog'-ra-phy
au-to-gy'-ro
au-to-in-fec'-tion
au-to-in-oc-u-la'-tion
au-to-in-tox-i-ca'-tion
au-to-ki-net'-ic
au-tol'-y-sis
au'-to-mat
au-to-mat'-ic
au-to-mat'-i-cal
au-to-mat'-i-cal-ly
au-to-ma'-tion
au-tom'-a-tism
au-tom'-a-ton
au-to-mo-bile'
au-to-mo-bil'-ist
au-to-mo'-tive
au-to-nom'-ic
au-ton'-o-mist
au-ton'-o-mous
au-ton'-o-my
au-toph'-a-gi
au-toph'-o-ny
au'-top-sy
au-tos'-co-py
au-to-sug-ges'-tion
au-to-tox-e'-mi:a
au'-to-typ:y†
au'-tumn
au-tum'-nal
au-tum'-nal-ly
Au-vergne'
aux-il'-ia-ry
a:vail'
a:vail-a-bil'-i-ty
a:vail'-a-ble
a:vailed'
av'-a-lanche
Av'-a-lon
a:vant'=garde'
av'-a-rice
av-a-ri'-cious
av-a-ri'-cious-ly
av'-a-tar
a:vaunt'
a've

A've Ma-ri'a
av-e-na'-ceous
a:venge'
a:venged'
a:veng'-er
a:veng'-ing
av'-ens
Av'-en-tine
av'-e-nue
a:ver'
av'-er-age
a:ver'-ment
A:ver'-nus
a:verred'
a:ver'-ring
a:verse'
a:ver'-sion
a:vert'
a:vert'-ed
a:vert'-i-ble
a'vi-a-rist*
a'vi-ate
a'vi-a'-tion
a'vi-a-tor
a'vi-a'-trix
Av-i-cen'-na
a'vi-cul-ture
av'-id
a:vid'-i-ty
av'-id-ly
A:vi-gnon'
A'vis
av-o-ca'-do
av-o-ca'-dos
av-o-ca'-tion
a:voc'-a-to-ry
A:vo-ga'-dro
a:void'
a:void'-a-ble
a:void'-a-bly
a:void'-ance
a:void'-ed
av-oir-du-pois'
A'von
a:vouch'
a:vow'
a:vow'-al
a:vowed'
a:vow'-ed-ly
a:vun'-cu-lar
a:wait'
a:wake'
a:waked'
a:wak'-en
a:wak'-en-ing
a:wak'-ing
a:ward'

a:ward'-ed
a:ware'
a:ware'-ness
a:wash'
a:way'
awe
a:wea'-ry
a:weigh'
awe'-some
awe'-strick-en
awe'-struck
aw'-ful
aw'-ful-ly
a:while'
awk'-ward
awk'-ward-ly
awk'-ward-ness
awl
aw'-ning*†
a:woke'
a:wry'
ax
ax'-es
ax'-i-al
ax'-i-al-ly
ax'-il
ax-il'-la
ax'-il-lar:y†
ax'-i-om
ax-i-o-mat'-ic
ax-i-o-mat'-i-cal
ax-i-o-mat'-i-cal-ly
ax'-is
ax'-le
Ax'-min-ster
ax'-o-lotl
ax-om'-e-ter
ay
a'yah
aye
Ayr'-shire
a:za'-le:a
az-i-mi'-no
az'-i-muth
az'-i-muth-al
A:zores'
A:zo-to-bac'-ter†
Az'-tec
Az'-tec-an
az'-ure
az'-ur-ite*†
az'-y-gous

B

Ba'-al
ba'-bas-su'
bab'-bitt
bab'-bitt-ry

bab'-ble
bab'-bler
bab'-bling
Bab'-cock
Ba'-bel
ba'-bied
ba'-bies
ba-boon'†
ba'-by
ba'-by-hood
ba'-by-ing
ba'-by-ish
Bab'-y-lon
Bab-y-lo'-ni-a
Bab-y-lo'-ni-an
ba'-by=sit-ter
bac-ca-lau'-re-ate
bac'-ca-rat
bac'-cha-nal
bac-cha-na'-lia
bac-cha-na'-lian
bac-chant'
bac-chant'e
Bac'-chus
bac-cif'-er-ous
bac-civ'-o-rous
bach'-e-lor
bach'-e-lor-hood
bac'-il-lar:y†
ba-cil'-li
ba-cil'-lus
bac-i-tra'-cin
back'-ache
back'-bite
back'-bit-ing
back'-bone
back'-break-ing
back door
back'-drop
back'-er
back'-field
back'-fire
back'-gam-mon
back'-ground
back'-hand
back'-hand-ed
back'-ing
back'-lash
back'-log
back'-saw
back'-side
back'-slide
back'-slid-ing
back'-stage'
back'-stairs
back'-stitch
back'-stop
back'-stroke

back'-talk
back'-track
back'-ward
back'-ward-ly
back'-ward-ness
back'-wash
back'-wat-er
back-woods'
back-woods'-man
back-yard'
ba'-con
Ba-co'-ni-an
bac-te'-ri:a
bac-te'-ri-al
bac-te'-ri-cid-al
bac'-ter-id
bac-te-ri-o-log'-i-cal
bac-te-ri-ol'-o-gist
bac-te-ri-ol'-o-gy
bac-te-ri:o-lyt'-ic
bac-te-ri:o-phage
bac-te-ri-os'-co-py
bac-te'-ri-um
bac'-te-roid*
bac'-te-roi-dal
Bac'-tri:a
Bac'-tri-an
bac-u-li-form*†
Ba'-den
badge
badg'-er
bad-i-nage'†
bad'-ly
bad'-min-ton
bad'-ness
bad'=tem-pered
Bae'-de-ker
Baf'-fin
baf'-fle
baf'-fle-ment
baf'-fler
baf'-fling
baf'-fling-ly
baff'y†
ba-gasse'
bag'-a-telle'
Bag'-dad
bag'-gage
bag'-gage-man
bag'-gage-mas-ter
bag'-gage room
bagged
bag'-gi-ly
bag'-ging
bag'-gy
Bagh'-dad
ba-gnio*†

bag'-pipe
bag'-pip-er
ba-guette'
Ba-ha'i
Ba-ha'-ma
Ba-hi'a†
bailed
bail-ee'
Bai'-ley
bai'-lift*
bai'-li-wick*
bail'-ment
bail'-or
bails'-man
bairn
bait
baize
Ba'-ke-lite†
bak'-er
bak'-er:y
bak'-ing
bak'-ing pow-der
bak'-sheesh
Ba'-laam
bal-a-cla'-va
bal-a-lai'-ka
bal'-ance
bal'-anc-er
bal'-anc-ing
ba-la'-ta†
ba-laus'-tine
Bal-bo'a
bal-brig'-gan
bal'-co-nies
bal'-co-ny
bal'-der-dash
bald'-ness
bald'-pate
bal'-dric
Bald'-win
Bald'y
Bal-e-ar'-ic
baled
ba-leen'
bale'-ful
Bal'-four
Ba'-li
Ba-li-nese'
bal'-ing
Ba'-li-ol
bal-is-trar'-i:a*†
balk
Bal'-kan
Bal'-kan-ize
balk'-i-er
balk'-ing
balk'y
bal'-lad

bal-lade'
bal'-lad-ry
bal'-last
ball bear'-ing
bal-le-ri'-na
bal'-let
Bal'-li-ol
bal-lis'-ta
bal-lis'-tic
bal-lis-ti'-cian
bal-lis'-tics
bal'-lo-net'
bal-loon'
bal-loon'-ist
bal'-lot
bal'-lot box
ball'-play-er
ball'-room
bal'-ly-hoo
balm
bal-ma-caan'
balm'-i-ly
balm'-i-ness
Bal-mor'-al
balm'y
bal'-ne-al
bal-ne-a'-tion
bal-ne-ol'-o-gy
ba-lo'-ney
bal'-sa
bal'-sam
bal-sam'-i-cal-ly
Bal'-tic
Bal'-ti-more
Ba-lu'-chi-stan'
bal'-us-ter
bal-us-trade'
Bal-zac'
bam-bi'-no
bam-boo'
bam-boo'-zle
bam-boo'-zler
ban
ba'-nal (trite)
ban'-al† (of a banate)
ba-nal'-i-ty
ba-nan'a
ban'-at
ban'-ate
Ban'-bur:y
Ban'-croft
ban'-dage*†
ban'-dag-ing*†
ban-dan'-na
ban'-dar
band'-box
ban'-deau
ban'-de-role

ban'-di-coot
ban'-died
ban'-dit
ban'-dit-ry
ban-dit'-ti
band'-mas-ter
ban'-do-leer'
ban'-do-line
bands'-man
band'-stand
band'-wag-on
ban'-dy
ban'-dy-ing
ban'-dy=leg-ged
bane'-ful
Banff
ban'-ga-lore
Bang'-kok
Ban'-gor
ban'-ish
ban'-ish-ment
ban'-is-ter
ban'-jo
ban'-jos
bank' ac-count
bank'-book
bank' draft
bank'-er
bank'-ing
bank'-note
bank'-rupt
bank'-rupt-cy
bann
banned
ban'-ner
ban'-ner-et
ban'-ning
ban'-nock
banns
ban'-quet
ban'-quet-er
Ban'-quo
ban'-shee
ban'-tam
ban'-tam-weight
ban'-ter
ban'-ter-ing-ly
bant'-ling
Ban'-ting
Ban'-tu
ban'-yan
ban-zai'
ba'-o-bab
Baph'-i:a
bap'-tism
bap'-tis'-mal
Bap'-tist

bap'-tis-ter:y
bap-tize'
bap-tized'
bap-tiz'-ing
Bar-ab'-bas
Ba-rac'a
bar-a-the'a
Bar-ba'-dos
Bar'-ba-ra
bar-bar'-i-an†
bar-bar'-i-an-ism†
bar-bar'-ic
bar-bar'-i-cal-ly
bar'-ba-rism
bar'-ba-rize
Bar-ba-ros'-sa
bar'-ba-rous
bar'-ba-rous-ly
Bar'-ba-ry
bar'-be-cue
barbed
barbed wire
bar'-ber
bar'-ber-ry
bar'-ber-shop
bar-bette'
bar'-bi-can
bar'-bi-tal
bar-bi'-tu-rate†
bar-bi-tu'-ric
Bar'-bi-zon
barb'-less
bar'-ca-role
Bar-ce-lo'-na
bard
bard'-ic
bare
bare'-back
bared
bare'-faced
bare'-foot
bare'-foot-ed
bare'=hand-ed
bare'-head-ed
bare'-leg-ged
bare'-ly
bare'-ness
bar'-er
bar'-gain
bar'-gain-er
barge
barge ca-nal'
barge load
barge'-man
barge'-mas-ter
bar'-ic
bar'-ing

bar'-ite†
bar'-i-tone
bar'-i-um†
bar'-keep-er
bar'-ken-tine*
bark'-er
bark'-ing
Bar'-kis
bark-om'-e-ter
bar'-ley
bar'-ley-corn
bar'-maid
bar'-man
Bar'-me-cide
barm'y
Bar'-na-bas
bar'-na-cle
barn' dance
barn'-storm-er
barn'-storm-ing
Bar'-num
barn'-yard
bar'-o-graph
ba-rom'-e-ter
bar-o-met'-ric
bar-o-met'-ro-graph
bar'-on
bar'-on-age
bar'-on-ess
bar-on-et'
bar-on-et'-age
bar'-on-et-cy
ba-ro'-ni-al
bar'-on:y*†
ba-roque'
bar'-o-scope
bar-o-scop'-ic
ba-rouche'
bar'-racks
bar-ra-cu'-da
bar-rage'
bar'-ra-tor
bar'-ra-trous
bar'-ra-try
barred
bar'-rel
bar'-rel or'-gan
bar'-ren
bar'-ren-ness
bar-rette'
bar'-ri-cade
bar-ri-cad'-ing
bar-ri-ca'-do
Bar'-rie
bar'-ri-er
bar'-ring
bar'-ris-ter
bar'-room

bar'-row
bar'-tend-er
bar'-ter
Bar-thol'-di
Bar-thol'-o-mew
Bart'-lett
Bar'-ton
Ba-ruch' (Amer.
  statesman)
Bar'-uch (Biblical name)
bar'-y-lite
ba-ry'-ta
ba-ryt'-ic
bar'-y-tone
ba'-sal*
ba'-sal-ly*
ba'-sal me-tab'-o-lism*
ba-salt'
ba-sal'-tic†
ba-sal'-ti-form†
bas'-cule
base
base'-ball
base'-board
base'-born
base'-heart-ed
base' hit
Ba'-sel
base'-less
base' line
base'-ly
base'-man
base'-ment
base'=mind-ed
base'-ness
bas'-es
Ba'-shan
ba-shaw'
bash'-ful
bash'-ful-ness
ba'-sic*
ba'-si-cal-ly*
ba-sic'-i-ty
ba-sid'-i-um
bas'-il
bas'-i-lar
ba-sil'-i-ca
ba-sil'-i-cal
ba-sil'-i-can
bas'-i-lisk
ba'-sin
bas'-i-net'
bas'-ing
ba'-sis
bask
bas'-ket
bas'-ket-ball
bas'-ket-ful

36

bas'-ket-ry
bas'-ket-work
Ba'-sle
ba'-son
Basque
Bas'-ra
bas'=re-lief'
bass
bas'-set
bas-si-net'
bas'-so
bas-soon'
bas-soon'-ist
bas'-so=re-lie'-vo
bass vi'-ol
bass'-wood
bas'-tard
bas'-tard:y*
baste
bast'-er
bas-tille'
bas-ti-na'-do
bast'-ing
bas'-tion
Ba-su'-to-land
Ba-ta'-vi:a
Ba-ta'-vi-an
bate
ba-teau'
ba-teaux'
bat'-fish
bath (n.)
bathe (v.)
bath'-er
ba-thet'-ic
bath'-house
bath'-ic
bath'-ing
bath-o-lith'-ic
ba-thom'-e-ter
ba'-thos
bath'-robe
bath'-room
Bath-she'-ba
bath'-tub
Bath'-urst
ba-thys'-mal
bath'y-sphere
ba-tik'
ba-tiste'
ba-ton' (n.)
bat'-on (v.)
Bat'-on Rouge
ba-tra'-chi-an
bats'-man
bat-ta'-lia
bat-tal'-ion
bat'-ten

bat'-ter
bat'-ter-ies
bat'-ter-ing
bat'-ter-ing ram
bat'-ter:y
bat'-ting
bat'-tle
bat'-tle=ax
bat'-tle cruis'-er
bat'-tle cry
bat'-tle-dore
bat'-tle fa-tigue'
bat'-tle-field
bat'-tle-flag
bat'-tle-front
bat'-tle-ground
bat'-tle-ment
bat'-tle=scarred
bat'-tle-ship
bat'-ty
Ba-tum'
bau'-ble
bauch'-le†
Bau'-cis
Bau'-er
baulk
Bau-mé'
baux'-ite
Ba-var'-i:a†
Ba-var'-i-an†
baw-bee
bawd'-i-ly
bawd'-ry
bawd'y
bawl
Bay'-ard
bay'-ber-ry
Ba-yeux'
bay'-o-net
Ba-yonne'
bay'-ou
Bay'-reuth
ba-zaar'
ba-zoo'-ka
bdel'-li-um
beach
beach'-comb-er
beach'-head
bea'-con
Bea'-cons-field
bead'-ed
bead'-ing
bea'-dle
bead'-work
bead'y
bea'-gle
beaked
beak'-er

beak'-less
beamed
beam'-ing
beam'-ing-ly
beam'-less
beam'y
bear
bear'-a-ble
beard'-ed
beard'-less
bear'-er
bear'-ing
bear'-ish
bé-ar-naise'
bear'-skin
beast'-li-ness
beast'-ly
beat'-en
beat'-er
be-a-tif'-ic
be-at-i-fi-ca'-tion
be-at'-i-fied
be-at'-i-fy
beat'-ing
be-at'-i-tude
Be'-a-trice
beau
Beau'-fort
beau geste
Beau-mar-chais'
Beau'-mont
Beau're-gard
beau-sé-ant'
beau-te-ous
beau'-ties
beau-ti-fi-ca'-tion
beau'-ti-fied
beau'-ti-fi-er
beau'-ti-ful
beau'-ti-ful-ly
beau'-ti-fy
beau'-ti-fy-ing
beau'-ty
beaux
beaux arts
bea'-ver
be-calm'
be-came'
be-cause'
bec-ca-fi'-co
bé-cha-mel'†
Bech-u-an'-a-land†
Beck'-et
beck'-on
beck'-on-ing
be-cloud'
be-come'
be-com'-ing

Bec-que-rel'
be-daub'
be-daze'
be-daz'-zle
be-daz'-zling
bed'-bug
bed'-cham-ber
bed'-clothes
bed'-ded
be-deck'
be-dev'-il
be-dev'-il-ment
be-dew'
bed'-fast
bed'-fel-low
Bed'-ford
Bed'-ford-shire
be-dight'
be-dim'
Bed'-i-vere
be-di'-zen*†
bed'-jack-et
bed'-lam
Bed'-ou-in
bed'-pan
bed'-post
be-drag'-gle
bed'-rid-den
bed'-rock
bed'-room
bed'-sheet
bed'-side
bed'-sore
bed'-spread
bed'-spring
bed'-staff
bed'-stead
bed'-time
bed'-warm-er
Bee'-be
beech
beech'-en
beech'-nut
beef
beef'-eat-er
beef'-i-ness
beef'-steak
beef'y
bee'-hive
bee'-keep-er
bee'-line
Be:el'-ze-bub
beer
Be:er-she'-ba
beer'y
bees'-wax
beet
Bee'-tho-ven

38

bee'-tle
bee'-tle-browed
bee'-tling
beeves
be-fall'
be-fall'-en
be-fell'
be-fit'
be-fit'-ting
be-fit'-ting-ly
be-fog'
be-fogged'
be-fog'-ging
be-fool'
be-fore'
be-fore'-hand
be-fore'-time
be-foul'
be-friend'
be-fud'-dle
be-gan'
be-gat'
be-get'
beg'-gar
beg'-gar-li-ness
beg'-gar-ly
beg'-gar-weed
beg'-gar:y
beg'-ging
be-gin'
be-gin'-ner
be-gin'-ning
be-girt'
beg'-ohm
be-gone'
be-go'-nia
be-got'
be-got'-ten
be-grime'
be-grudge'
be-grudg'-ing
be-grudg'-ing-ly
be-guile'
be-guil'-er
be-guil'-ing-ly
be'-gum
be-gun'
be-half'
be-have'
be-haved'
be-hav'-ing
be-hav'-ior†
be-hav'-ior-ism†
be-hav'-ior-is'-tic†
be-head'
be-head'-ed
be-held'
be-he'-moth

be-hest'
be-hind'
be-hind'-hand
be-hold'
be-hold'-en
be-hold'-er
be-hold'-ing
be-hoof'
be-hoove'
be-hove'
beige
be'-ing
Bei'-rut
be-jew'-el
be-jew'-eled
Bel'a
be-la'-bor
be-lat'-ed
be-lay'
bel'-dam
be-lea'-guer
be-lea'-guered
be-lea'-guer-ment
Bel'-fast
Bel'-fort
bel'-fried
bel'-fry
Bel'-gian
Bel'-gium
Bel'-grade
Bel-gra'-vi:a
Be'-li-al
be-lie'
be-lief'
be-li'-er
be-liev'-a-ble
be-liev'-er
be-lieved'
be-liev'-er
be-liev'-ing
be-liev'-ing-ly
be-like'
be-lit'-tle
be-lit'-tling
bel-la-don'-na
bell'-boy
belle
Bel-leau'
Bel-ler-o-phon
belles let'-tres
bell'-flow-er
bell'-hop
bel'-li-cose
bel-li-cos'-i-ty
bel-lig'-er-ence
bel-lig'-er-en-cy
bel-lig'-er-ent
bel'-low

bel'-lows
bell'=shaped
bell'-tow-er
bell'-weth-er
bel'-ly
bel'-ly-band
Bel'-mont
Be-loit'
be-long'
be-longed'
be-long'-ing
be-long'-ings
be-loved' (be-lov'-ed)
be-low'
Bel-shaz'-zar
belt'-ed
belt'-ing
bel'-ve-dere
be-ly'-ing
be'-ma
be-mazed'
be-mire'
be-mir'-ing
be-moan'
be-moaned'
be-moan'-ing
be-mock'
be-muse'
be-mused'
be-mus'-ing
Be-na'-res
bench'-er
bend'-ed
bend'-er
bend'-ing
be-neath'
be-ne-di'-ci-te*†
ben'-e-dict
Ben-e-dic'-tine
ben-e-dic'-tion
ben-e-dic'-to-ry
ben'-e-fac-tion
ben'-e-fac-tor
ben'-e-fac-tress
be-nef'-ic
ben'-e-fice
ben'-e-ficed
be-nef'-i-cence
be-nef'-i-cent
be-nef'-i-cent-ly
ben-e-fi'-cial
ben-e-fi'-cial-ly
ben-e-fi'-cia-ries*
ben-e-fi'-cia-ry*
ben'-e-fit
ben'-e-fit-ed
ben'-e-fit-ing
Be'-nes

be-nev'-o-lence
be-nev'-o-lent
Ben'-gal
Ben-gal-ese'*†
Ben-gal'i
be-night'-ed
be-nign'
be-nig'-nan-cy
be-nig'-nant
be-nig'-nant-ly
be-nig'-ni-ty
be-nign'-ly
ben'-i-son
be-ni-to-ite
Ben'-ja-min
Ben'-nett
ben'-thos
Bent'-ley
be-numb'
benz-al'-de-hyde†
benz-am'-ide†
Ben'-ze-drine*
ben'-zene
ben'-ze-noid
ben'-zi-dine
ben-zil'-ic
benz-im-id-a'-zole*
ben'-zine
ben'-zo-ate
ben-zo'-ic
ben'-zol
benz-ox'-y-a:ce'-tic†
ben'-zo-yl
ben'-zo-yl-ate
ben'-zyl
ben'-zyl-ate
Be'-o-wulf
be-praise'
be-queath'
be-queath'-al
be-quest'
Bé-ran-ger'
be-rate'
be-rat'-ed
be-rat'-ing
Ber'-ber
ber-ceuse'
be-reave'
be-reaved'
be-reave'-ment
be-reav'-ing
be-reft'
Ber'-e-nice*†
Ber'-es-ford
be-ret'†
ber'-ga-mot
Ber'-gen
Ber'-ge-rac'

ber:i-ber'i
Ber'-ing*†
Berke'-ley
Berk'-ley
Berk'-shires
Ber-lin'
Ber'-li-oz
Ber-mu'-da
Ber-mu'-di-an
Ber'-nard-ine†
Bern-ese'*†
Bern'-hardt
ber'-ries
ber'-ry
ber-serk'
ber-serk'-er
berth
Ber'-tha
berth'-ing
Ber'-tram
Ber'-trand
ber'-yl
ber'-yl-line
be-ryl'-li-um
bes'-ant
be-seech'
be-seeched'
be-seech'-ing
be-seem'
be-set'
be-set'-ting
be-shrew'
be-side'
be-sides'
be-siege'
be-sieg'-er
be-sieg'-ing-ly
be-smear'
be-smirch'
be-smirch'-er
be'-som
be-sot'
be-sot'-ted
be-sought'
be-spake'
be-span'-gle
be-spat'-ter
be-speak'
be-spec'-ta-cled
be-spoke'
Bes-sa-ra'-bi:a
Bes-sa-ra'-bi-an
Bes'-se-mer
bes'-tial
bes-ti-al'-i-ty
bes'-tial-ize
bes'-tial-ly
bes-ti-ar:y†

be-stir'
best'=known'
best'=liked'
be-stow'
be-stow'-a-ble
be-stow'-al
best'=paid'
be-strew'
be-stride'
be-strode'
best' sell'-er
best'=sell'-ing
be'-ta
be'-ta-ine
be-take'
be'-ta-tron
be'-tel
Be'-tel-geuse†
Beth'-a-ny
Beth'-el
Be-thes'-da
be-think'
Beth'-le-hem
be-thought'
Beth-sa'-i-da
Be-thune'
be-tide'
be-times'
be-to'-ken
be-took'
be-tray'
be-tray'-al
be-tray'-er
be-troth'
be-troth'-al
be-throthed'
be-troth'-ment
bet'-ter
bet'-ter-ment
bet'-ting
Bet'-ty
bet-u-la'-ceous
be-tween'
be-twixt'
Beu'-lah
bev'-a-tron
bev'-el
bev'-eled
bev'-el-ing
bev'-er-age
bev'-ies
bev'y
be-wail'
be-wail'-ing
be-ware'
be-wil'-der
be-wil'-dered
be-wil'-dered-ly

41

be-wil'-der-ing
be-wil'-der-ing-ly
be-wil'-der-ment
be-witch'
be-witch'-ing
be-witch'-ment
be-wray'
bey
be-yond'
bez'-ant
bez'-el
be-zique'
be-zo''-ni-an
bi-a:nis'-i-dine
bi-an'-nu-al
bi-an'-nu-al-ly
Biar-ritz'†
bi'-as
bi'-ased
bi'-as-ing
bi-au-ric''u-lar
bi-ax'-i-al
bi'-be-lot†
Bi'-ble
Bib'-li-cal
Bib'-li-cal-ly
bib'-li-o-graph
bib-li-og'-ra-pher
bib-li-o-graph'-ic
bib-li-o-graph'-i-cal
bib-li-og'-ra-phy
bib-li-ol'-a-ter
bib-li-o-ma'-ni:a
bib-li-op''-e-gy
bib'-li-o-phile
bib-li-oph-i-lis'-tic
bib'-li-o-pol'-ic
bib'-u-lous
bi-cam'-er-al
bi-car'-bon-ate†
bi-cen-ten'-a-ry*†
bi-cen-ten'-ni-al
bi-ceph'-a-lous
bi'-ceps
bi-chlo'-ride
bi-chro'-mate
bi-cip'-i-tal
bick'-er
bick'-er-ing
bi-con'-vex
bi'-corn
bi-cor'-po-ral
bi'-cron
bi-cus'-pid
bi-cus'-pi-date
bi'-cy-cle
bi'-cy-cler
bi-cy'-clic†

bi'-cy-clist
bi-dar'-ka
bid'-da-ble
Bid'-de-ford
bid'-den
bid'-der
bid'-ding
bid'-dy
bide
Bid'-e-ford
bi-den'-tate
bid'-ing
bi-en'-ni-al
bi-en'-ni-al-ly
bier
bi-fa'-cial
bi-far'-i-ous-ly†
bi'-fid
bi-flag'-el-late
bi'-fo-cal
bi'-fur-cate
bi'-fur-cat-ed
bi-fur-ca'-tion
big'-a-mist
big'-a-mous
big'-a-mous-ly
big'-a-my
big'-ger
big'-head-ed
big'-heart-ed
big'-horn
bight
big'-ness
big-no-ni-a'-ceous
big'-ot
big'-ot-ed
big'-ot-ry
big'-wig
bi-hour'-ly
bi-ki'-ni
bi-la'-bi-al
bil'-an-der
bi-lat'-er-al
bi-lat'-er-al-ly
Bil-ba'o
bil'-ber-ry
bilge
bilg'y
bil-har-zi''-a-sis
bil'-i-ar:y†
bi-lin'-e-ar
bi-lin'-gual
bi-lin'-gual-ism
bi-lin'-gual-ly
bil'-ious
bil'-ious-ly
bil'-ious-ness
bill'-a-ble

bill'-board
bill'-er
bil'-let
bil'-let=doux
bill'-fish
bill'-fold
bill'-head
bil'-liard-ist
bil'-liards
Bil'-lings
Bil'-lings-gate
bil'-lion
bil'-lion-aire
bil'-lionth
bil'-low
bill'-low:y
bill'-post-er
bill'-stick-er
bil'-ly
bi-lobed'
bi-loc'-u-lar
bi-loc'-u-late
bim'-a-nous
bi-man'-u-al-ly
bi-mes'-tri-al
bi-me-tal'-lic
bi-met'-al-lism
bi-met'-al-list
bi-month'-ly
bi-mo'-tored
bi'-na-ry
bi'-nate
bin-au'-ral
bind'-er
bind'-er:y
bind'-ing
bind'-weed
bi-net'
bing'-ham-ton
bin'-go
bin'-na-cle
bin-oc'-u-lar
bi-no'-mi-al
bi-no'-mi-al-ly
bi:o-cat'-a-lyst
bi-o:cel'-late*
bi:o-chem'-i-cal
bi:o-chem'-ist
bi:o-chem'-is-try
bi:o-gen'-e-sis
bi'-o-graph
bi:o-graph'-ic
bi:o-graph'-i-cal
bi-og'-ra-phy

bi:o-log'-ic
bi:o-log'-i-cal
bi-ol'-o-gist
bi-ol'-o-gy
bi:o-lu-mi-nes'-cence
bi-ol'-y-sis
bi-om'-e-ter
bi:o-met'-ric
bi-om'-e-try
bi-on'-ics
bi:o-nom'-ics
bi'-op-sy
bi'o-scope
bi-os'-co-py
bi-os'-o-phy
bi:o-stat'-ics
bi-os'-ter-ol
bi'-o-tite
bi'-o-tit-ic
bi-pa-ri'-e-tal
bip'-a-rous
bi-par-ti-san
bi-par'-tite
bi-par-ti'-tion
bi'-ped
bi'-plane
bi-po'-lar
bi-quar'-ter-ly
bi-ra'-di-al
birch'-bark
birch'-en
bird'-call
bird'-lime
bird'-man
bird's=eye
bi-ret'-ta
Bir'-ming-ham
birth
birth'-day
birth'-mark
birth'-place
birth'-rate
birth'-right
birth'-stone
Bis'-cay
bis'-cuit
bi'-sect'
bi-sec'-tion
bi-sec'-tion-al-ly
bi'-sec'-tor
bish'-op
bish'-op-ric
Bis'-marck
bis'-muth
bi'-son
bisque
bis-sex'-tile
bis'-ter

bis'-tou-ry
bi-sul'-fate
bi-sul'-fide
bitch
bite
bit'-er
bit'-ing
bit'-stock
bit'-ten
bit'-ter
bit'-ter-ly
bit'-tern
bit'-ter-ness
bit'-ter-root
bit'-ters
bit'-ter-sweet
bit'-ter-weed
bi-tu'-men
bi-tu'-mi-nize
bi-tu'-mi-noid
bi-tu'-mi-nous
bi-va'-lence
bi-va'-len-cy
bi-va'-lent
bi'-valve
bi-val'-vu-lar
biv'-ouac†
biv'-ouacked†
biv'-ouack-ing†
bi-week'-ly
bi-zarre'
bi-zarre'-ness
Bi-zet'
blab
blab'-ber
black'-a-moor
black'-ball
black'-ber-ry
black'-bird
black'-board
black'-cap
black'-en
black'-ened
black'-en-er
black'-er
black'=eyed
black'-face
Black'-feet
Black'-foot
black fri'-ar
black'-guard
black'-head
Black Hills
black'-ing
black'-ish
black'-jack
black'-lead
black'-leg

black let'-ter
black'-list
black'-ly
black'-mail
black'-ness
black'-out
black'-poll
black sheep
black'-smith
black'-tail
black'-thorn
blad'-der
blade
blad'-ed
blade'-less
blame'-wor-thy
blam'-ing
blanch
blanch'-er
blanch'-ing
blanc-mange'
bland
blan'-dish
blan'-dish-ment
bland'-ly
bland'-ness
blank'-book
blan'-ket
blank'-ly
blank'-ness
blare
blar'-ney
bla-sé'
blas'-pheme
blas'-phem-er
blas'-phem-ing
blas'-phe-mous
blas'-phe-my
blast'-ed
blas-te'-ma
blast'-er
blas'-tic
blas'-to-coel
blas-to-gen'-e-sis
blas'-tu-la
bla-'tan-cy
bla'-tant
bla'-tant-ly
blath'-er-ing
blath'-er-skite
blaze
blazed
blaz'-er
blaz'-ing
bla'-zon
bla'-zon-ry
bleach'-er
bleak

bleak'-ly
blear'=eyed
blear'-i-ness
blear'y
bleat'-ing
bleb'-by
bleed'-ing
blem'-ish
blem'-ish-er
blend'-er
blend'-ing
Blen'-heim
bleph-a-ri'-tis
Blé'-riot†
bless
blessed (bless'-ed)
bless'-ed-ly
bless'-ed-ness
bless'-ing
blew
blight
blind'-er
blind'-fish
blind'-fold
blind'-ing
blind'-ly
blind'-ness
blink'-er
blink'-ing
bliss'-ful
bliss'-ful-ly
blis'-ter
blis'-ter:y
blithe
blithe'-ly
blithe'-some
blitz'-krieg
bliz'-zard
bloat
bloat'-er
bloc
block
block-ade'
block-ad'-ed
block-ad'-er
block-ad'-ing
block'-bust-er
block'-head
block'-house
block'y
block'-i-er
blon'-dine
blond'-ness
blood bank
blood'-cur-dling
blood'-ed
blood'-guilt
blood'-guilt:y

blood'-hound
blood'-i-est
blood'-i-ly
blood'-i-ness
blood'-less
blood'-let-ting
blood' mon-ey
blood poi'-son-ing
blood pres'-sure
blood'-root
blood'-shed
blood'-shed-ding
blood'-shot
blood'-stain
blood'-stained
blood'-stone
blood'-suck-er
blood'-thirst-i-ly
blood'-thirst:y
blood' ves-sel
blood'-wort
blood'y
bloom'-ers
bloom'-ing
bloom'-ing-ly
blos'-som
blos'-som:y
blotch
blotch'y
blot'-less
blot'-ted
blot'-ter
blot'-ting
blouse
blow'-er
blow'-fish
blow'-fly
blow'-gun
blow'-hole
blow'-i-ness
blown
blow'-out
blow'-pipe
blows'y
blow'-torch
blow'-tube
blow'-up
blow'y
blub'-ber
blub'-ber-er
blub'-ber:y
blu'-cher
bludg'-eon
blue
Blue'-beard
blue'-bell
blue'-ber-ry
blue'-bird

blue=black
blue'=blood-ed
blue'-bon-net
blue book
blue'-bot-tle
blue'-coat
blue'=eyed
blue'-fish
blue'-grass
blue'-jack-et
blue' jay
blue laws
blue moon
blue'=pen'-cil (v.)
blue'-print
blue'-stock-ing
blue'-stone
blu'-et
bluff'-er
bluff'-ing
blu'-ing
blu'-ish
blun'-der
blun'-der-buss
blun'-der-er
blun'-der-ing
blung'-er
blunt'-ly
blunt'-ness
blur
blurred
blur'-ring
blur'-ry
blurt'-ed
blushed
blush'-ing
blus'-ter
blus'-ter-ing
blus'-ter-ous
blus'-ter:y
bo'a
bo'a con-stric'-tor
boar
board'-er
board'-ing
board'-ing-house
board'-ing school
board'-walk
boast'-er
boast'-ful
boast'-ing-ly
boat'-bill
boat'-build-er
boat club
boat hire
boat'-hook
boat'-house
boat'-ing

boat'-load
boat'-man
boat'-swain
bobbed
bob'-bin
bob'-bi-net
bob'-bing
Bob'-by
bob'-by=sox-er
bob'-cat
bob'-o-link
bob'-sled
bob'-stay
bob'-tail
bob'-white'
bo-cac'-cio
Boc-cac'-cio
bo-dhi-satt'-va
bod'-ice
bod'-i-less
bod'-i-ly
bod'-kin
Bod-lei'-an*
bod'y
bod'y-guard
Boe-o'-tia
Boer
Bo-e'-thi-us
bo'-gey
bog'-gi-ness
bog'-gish
bog'-gle
bog'-gy
bo'-gie
bo'-gle
Bo-go-ta'
bo'-gus
bo'-gy
Bo-he'-mi:a
Bo-he'-mi-an
Boi-leau'
boil'-er
boil'-ing
Boi'-se
bois'-ter-ous
bois'-ter-ous-ly
Bo'-jer
Bo-kha'-ra
bold'-face
bold'=faced
bold'-ly
bold'-ness
bole
bo-le'-ro
bo-le'-tus
Bol'-eyn
Bol'-ing-broke
Bo-li'-var

Bo-liv'-i:a
Bo-liv'-i-an
boll
bol'-lard
boll' wee'-vil
boll'-worm
bo'-lo
Bo-lo'-gna
bo-lom'-e-ter
bo-lo-met'-ric
Bol'-she-vik
Bol'-she-vik:i
Bol'-she-vism
Bol'-she-vist
bol'-ster
bolt'-er
bolt' head
bolt'-less
Bol'-ton
bolt'-rope
bol'-us*†
bomb
bom-ba-ca'-ceous
bom-bard'
bom'-bar-dier'*
bom-bard'-ment
bom'-bar-don
bom'-bast
bom-bas'-tic
bom-bas'-ti-cal
bom-bas'-ti-cal-ly
Bom-bay'
bom-ba-zine'
bomb bay
bomb'-er
bomb'-proof
bomb'-shell
bomb'-sight
bo-na-ci'
bo'-na fide
bo-nan'-za
Bo'-na-parte
Bo'-na-part-ist
Bo-na-ven-tu'-ra
bon'-bon
bon-bon-nière'
bond'-age
bond'-ed
bond'-hold-er
bond'-maid
bond'-man
bond'-ser-vant*
bonds'-man
bond'-wom-an†
bone'-dry
bone'-less
bon'-er

bone'-set
bon'-fire
bon'-i-er
Bon'-i-face
bon'-i-ness
bon'-ing
bo-ni'-to
bon jour
bon mot
bon'-net
bon'-ni-ly
bon'-ny
bo'-nus
bon vi-vant'
bon vo-yage'
bon'y
bonze
boo'-bies
boo'-by
boo'-dle
boo'-dler
boog'-ie=woog'-ie
book
book a'gent
book'-bind-er
book'-bind-er:y
book'-case
book club
book col-lec'-tor
book'-deal-er
book'-end
book'-ie
book'-ish
book'-keep-er
book'-keep-ing
book'-let
book'-lore
book'-mak-er
book'-mark
book'-plate
book'-rack
book re-view'
book'-sell-er
book'-shelf
book'-shop
book'-store
book'-worm
Bool'-e-an
boo'-mer-ang*†
boon'-dog-gle
boor'-ish
boost'-er
boot'-black
boot'-ed
boo'-tee*
Bo-o'-tes
booth
boot'-jack

boot'-leg
boot'-leg-ger
boot'-leg-ging
boot'-less
boot tree
boo'-ty
booze
booz'-er
booz'-y
bo-peep'
bo-rac'-ic
bo-ra-cite
bor'-age
bor'-ak†
bo'-rate
bo'-rax
Bor-deaux'
bor'-der
bor'-dered
bor'-der-er
bor'-der-land
bor'-der-line
bor'-dure
bore
bo'-re-al
bo'-re-as
bore'-dom
bor'-er
Bor-ghe'-se
Bor'-gia
Bo'-ri
bo'-ric
bor'-ing
Bor'-is
born
borne
Bor'-ne-an
Bor'-ne:o
born'-ite
bo'-ron
bor'-ough
bor'-row
bor'-row-er
borsch
Bose
bosk'y
Bos'-ni:a
Bos'-ni-an
bos'-om†
Bos'-po-rus
boss'-ism
boss'y
Bos'-ton
Bos-to'-ni-an
bo'-sun
Bos'-well
bo-tan'-i-cal
bot'-a-nist

bot'-a-nize
bot'-a-ny
botch
botch'y
bot'-fly
both'-er
both-er-a'-tion
both'-er-some
Both'-well
bot'-ry-oi'-dal
Bot-ti-cel'-li
bot'-tle
bot'-tled
bot'-tle=fed
bot'-tle green
bot'-tle-neck
bot'-tle=nosed
bot'-tler
bot'-tle wash'-er
bot'-tling
bot'-tom
bot'-tom-land
bot'-tom-less
bot'-tom-ry
bot'-u-lism
bou-clé'
bou-doir'
bou-gain-vil'-le:a
bough
bough'-pot
bought
bou'-gie
bouil'-la-baisse'
bouil'-lon
boul'-der
bou'-le-vard
Bou-logne'
bounce
bounc'-er
bounc'-ing
bound
bound'-a-ries
bound'-a-ry
bound'-ed
bound'-en
bound'-er
bound'-less
boun'-te-ous
boun'-ti-ful
boun'-ty
bou-quet'
bour'-bon
bour'-geois
bour'-geoise
bour'-geoi-sie'
bourne
bourse
bou'-ton-niere'

bo'-vine
bowd'-ler-ize
bow'-el
bow'-er
bow'-er:y
bow'-fin
bow'-ie
bow'-knot
bowl
bow'-leg
bow'-leg-ged
bow'-line
bowl'-er
bowl'-ing
bowl'-ing green
bow'-man
bow'-shot
bow'-sprit
bow'-string
bow'-yer
box'-ber-ry
box'-car
box coat
box'-er
box'-ing
box kite
box'-thorn
box'-wood
boy
bo-yar'
boy'-cott
boy'-cott-er
boy'-hood
boy'-ish
boy'-ish-ness
Boyle
boy'-sen-ber-ry
brace'-let
brac'-er
brach'-i-al*
brach'-i-ate*
brach'-i-o-pod*
brach'y-ce-phal'-ic
brach'y-ceph'-a-ly
bra-chyl'-o-gy
brach'y-mor-phic
bra-chyp'-ter-ous
brach'-ysm
brach'y-u'ral
bra-chyt'-ic
rac'-ing
rack'-en
rack'-et
rack'-et-ing
rack'-ish
rac'-te-al
rac-te'-o-late

brad'-awl
Brad'-dock
Brad'-ford
Brad'-ley
brag-ga-do'-ci:o
brag'-gart
brag'-gart-ism
bragged
brag'-ger
brag'-ging
Brah'-ma
Brah'-man-ism
Brah'-ma-pu-tra
Brah'-min
Brahms
Braille
brain cell
brain'-i-er
brain'-less
brain'-pan
brain'-sick
brain'-wash-ing
brain'-work
brain'y
braise
braised
brais'-ing
brake
brake'-man
bram'-ble
bram'-bly
bran'-chi-al
bran-chif'-er-ous
Bran'-deis
Bran'-den-burg
bran'-died
bran'-dish
brand'=new
bran'-dy
Bran'-dy-wine
bran'-ni-gan
bras'-sage*
bras-sard'
bras-si-ca'-ceous
bras-sid'-ic
brass'-ie
bras-siere'
brass'-i-ly
brass'-i-ness
brass'-ware
brass'-work
brass'y
brat'-tice
bra-va'-do
brave'-heart-ed
brave'-ly
brav'-er:y
brav'-est

bra'-vo
bra-vu'-ra
brawl
brawl'-er
brawn
brawn'-i-er
brawn'-i-est
brawn'-i-ness
brawn'y
brax'y
braze
bra'-zen
bra'-zen-faced
bra'-zen-ly
bra'-zier
Bra-zil'
Bra-zil'-ian
braz'-i-lin
bra-zil'-wood
braz'-ing
breach
bread
bread'-fruit
bread'-pan
bread'-root
bread'-stuff
breadth
bread'-win-ner
break
break'-a:ble
break'-age
break'-down
break'-er
break'-fast
break'-neck
break'-through
break'-up
break'-wa-ter
breast
breast'-bone
Breas'-ted
breast'-ed
breast'-pin
breast'-plate
breast'-work
breath
breath'-a:ble
breathe
breath'-er
breath'-ing
breath'-less
breath'-less-ly
breath'-tak-ing
breath'y
brec'-cia
bred
breech
breech'-cloth

breech'-es
breech'-load-er
breech'=load-ing
breed
breed'-er
breed'-ing
breeze
breeze'-way
breez'-i-ly
breez'-i-ness
breez'y
breg'-ma
Bre'-men†
Brem'-er-ton
Bren'-ner
Bre-scia*†
Bres'-lau
Brest
Bre-tagne'
breth'-ren
Bret'-on
bre-vet'
bre-vet'-ted
bre'-via-ry*
bre-vier'
brev'-i-ty
brew'-er
brew'-er:y
brew'-ing
Bri-and'
bri'-ar
brib'-a:ble
bribed
brib'-er
brib'-er:y
brib'-ing
bric'=a=brac
brick'-bat
brick'-kiln
brick'-lay-er
brick'-lay-ing
brick'-work
brick'-yard
brid'-al†
bride'-groom
brides'-maid
bride'-well
bridge'-a:ble
bridge'-head
Bridge'-port
Bridg'-es
Brid'-get*
Bridge'-wa-ter
bridge'-work
bridg'-ing
bri'-dle
bri'-dling
brief'-ing

brief'-less
brief'-ly
bri'-er
bri'-er-root
bri'-er-wood
bri'-er:y
brig'-a-dier
brig'-and
brig'-and-age
brig'-an-dine
brig'-an-tine
bright'-en
bright'=eyed
bright'-ly
bright'-ness
Brigh'-ton
bright'-work
bril'-liance
bril'-lian-cy
bril'-liant
bril'-lian-tine
bril'-liant-ly
brim'-ful
brim'-less
brimmed
brim'-ming
brim'-stone
brin'-dle
brin'-dled
brine
Bri-nell'
bring
bring'-er
bring'-ing
brin'-i-ness
brink
brin'y
bri'-o-lette
bri-quet'
bri-quette'
bris'-ket
brisk'-ly
brisk'-ness
bris'-ling
bris'-tle
bris'-tle-tail
bris'-tli-ness
bris'-tling
bris'-tly
Bris'-tol
Bris'-tol-board
Brit'-ain
Bri-tan'-ni:a
Bri-tan'-nic
Brit'-i-cism
Brit'-ish
Brit'-ish-er

Brit'-on
Brit'-ta-ny
brit'-tle
broach
broad
broad'-ax
broad'-brim
broad'-cast
broad'-cloth
broad'-en
broad'-loom
broad'-ly
broad'=mind-ed
broad'=mind-ed-ness
broad'-side
broad'-sword
broad'-tail
Broad'-way
bro-cade'
bro-cad'-ed
broc'-a-telle'
broc'-co-li
bro-chette'
bro-chure'
Brock'-ton
bro'-gan
brogue
broi'-der
broi'-der:y
broil
broil'-er
bro'-kage
broke
bro'-ken
bro'-ken-heart-ed
bro'-ker
bro'-ker-age
bro'-mate
bro-me'-lia
bro-mell'-ite*
bro'-mic
bro'-mide
bro-mid'-ic
bro'-mine
bro'-mo-form
bro-mom'-e-try
bron'-chi-al
bron-chi'-tis
bron-chog'-ra-phy
bron'-cho-scope
bron-chos'-co-py
bron-chot'-o-my
bron'-chus
bron'-co
Bron'-te
bron'-to-saur
bronze
bronz'-ing

51

bronz'y
brooch
brood'-er
brood'-ing
brood'-ing-ly
brood'y
brook'-let
Brook'-line
Brook'-lyn
broom'-stick
broth
broth'-el
broth'-er
broth'-er-hood
broth'-er=in=law
broth'-er-li-ness
broth'-er-ly
brougham
brought
brow'-beat
brow'-beat-ing
Brown'-i-an
brown'-ie
Brown'-ing
brown'-ish
brown'-ness
brown'-out
brown'-stone
Browns'-ville
browse
brows'-ing
bru-cel-lo'-sis
bruc'-ine†
Bruges†
Brug'-ge
bru'-in
bruise
bruised
bruis'-er
bruis'-ing
bruit
bru'-mal
Brun-dis'-i-um
bru-net'
Brun'-hild
Bruns'-wick
brunt
brush'-wood
brush'-work
brush'y
brusque
brusque'-ly
brusque'-ness
Brus'-sels
bru'-tal
bru-tal'-i-ty
bru'-tal-ize
bru'-tal-ly

brute
brut'-ish
brut'-ish-ly
Bru'-tus
Bry'-an
Bry'-ant
Bryce
bry-o-log'-i-cal
bry-ol'-o-gy
bry'-o-ny
Bryth'-on
Bry-thon'-ic
bu'-ba-line
bub'-ble
bub'-bling
bub'-bling-ly
bub'-bly
bu-bon'-ic
buc'-ca-neer
buc-ci-na-tor
bu'-cen-taur
bu-ceph'-a-lus
Bu-chan'-an
Bu'-cha-rest
buck'-a-roo
buck'-board
buck'-et
buck'-et-ful
buck'-eye
buck'-hound
Buck'-ing-ham
buck'-le
buck'-ler
buck'-ling
Buck-nell'
buck'o
buck'-ram
buck'-saw
buck'-shot
buck'-skin
buck'-thorn
buck'-tooth
buck'-wheat
bu-col'-ic
bu-col'-i-cal-ly
Bu'-da-pest
Bud'-dha
Bud'-dhism
Bud'-dhist
bud'-dle
bud'-dy
budge
bud'-ger-i-gar
bud'-get
bud'-get-ar:y†
bud'-get-ed
bud'-ge-teer
bud'-get-er

bud'-get-ing
bud'-less
Bu'-ell
Bue'-na Vis'-ta
Bue'-nos Ai'-res
buf'-fa-lo
buff'-er†
buf'-fet (blow)
buf-fet' (furniture)
buff'-ing
buf-foon'
buf-foon'-er:y
bug'-a-boo
bug'-bear
bu'-gle
bu'-gler
bu'-gling
bug'-proof
buhr'-stone
build'-er
build'-ing
build'-up
built'=in
bul-ba'-ceous
bul'-bar*
bul'-bil
bul'-bous*
bul'-bul
Bul'-gar
Bul-gar'-i:a†
Bul-gar'-i-an†
bulge
bulg'-er
bulg'-ing
bu-lim'-i:a
bulk'-head
bulk'-i-er
bulk'-i-ness
bulk·y
bul'-late
bull'-dog
bull'-doze
bull'-doz-er
bull'-doz-ing
bul'-let
bul'-le-tin
bul'-let-proof
bull'-fight
bull'-fight-er
bull'-finch
bull'-frog
bull'-head
bull'-head-ed
bul'-lied
bul'-lion
bull'-ish

bul'-lock*
bull'-pen
bull'-pout
Bull Run
bull's'=eye
bull'-whip
bul'-ly
bul'-ly-ing
bul'-ly-rag
bul'-rush
bul'-wark
bum'-ble-bee
bum'-bling
bum'-boat
bump'-er
bump'-i-er
bump'-kin
bump'-tious
bump'-tious-ly
bump·y
bunch
bunch'-i-er
bunch·y
bun'-co
bun'-combe
bun'-der
Bun'-des-rat
bun'-dle
bun'-dling
bun'-ga-low
bun'-gle
bun'-gled
bun'-gler
bun'-gling
bun'-gling-ly
bun'-ion
bun'-ker*
bunk'-house
bun'-ko
bun'-ny
Bun'-sen
bunt'-er (one who bunts)
bun'-ter (of a geologic time period)
bun'-ting (bird)
bunt'-ing (fabric)
Bun'-yan
buoy
buoy'-age
buoy'-an-cy
buoy'-ant
bu-pres'-tid
bu-ran'
Bur'-bank
bur'-den
bur'-den-some
bur'-dock

53

bu'-reau
bu-reauc'-ra-cy†
bu'-reau-crat
bu-reau-crat'-ic
bu-rette'
bur'-gage*
bur-gee'
bur'-geon
bur'-gess
bur'-gher*†
bur'-glar
bur'-gla-ries
bur-glar'-i-ous†
bur'-glar-ize
bur'-glar-proof
bur'-gla-ry
bur'-go-mas-ter
Bur-goyne'
Bur-gun'-di-an
Bur'-gun-dy
bur'-i-al
bur'-i-al ground
bur'-ied
bur'-ies
bu'-rin
bur'-lap
Bur'-leigh
bur-lesque'
bur-lesqued'
bur-lesqu'-er
bur'-ley
bur'-li-ness
Bur'-ling-ton
bur'-ly
Bur'-ma
Bur-mese'
burned
burn'-er
bur-net'
Bur'-ney
burn'-ing
burn'-ish*†
bur-noose'
burn'-sides
burnt
bur'-ring
bur'-ro
Bur'-roughs
bur'-row
bur'-row-er
bur'-sa
bur'-sar
bur-sar'-i-al†
bur'-sa-ry
bur-ser-a'-ceous
bur-si'-tis
burst
burst'-ing

bur'-then
Bur'-ton
bur'-weed
bur'y
bur'y-ing
bur'y-ing ground
bus'-es
bush'-el
bush'-i-er
bush'-ing
Bush'-man
bush'-mas-ter
bush'-rang-er
bush'-whack-er
bush'y
bus'-ied
bus'-i-er
bus'-i-est
bus'-i-ly
bus'-i-ness
bus'-i-ness col'-lege
bus'-i-ness-like
bus'-i-ness-man
bus'-kin
bus'-ses (n., pl.)
buss'-es (v.)
bus'-tard
bust'-er
bus'-tle
bus'-tled
bus'-tler
bus'-tling
bus'-tling-ly
bus'y
bus'y-bod:y
bus'y-ness
bus'y-work
bu-ta-di'-ene
bu'-tane
butch'-er
butch'-er:y
bu'-te-nyl
but'-ler
butte
but'-ter (spread)
butt'-er (one who butts)
but'-ter-cup
but'-ter-fat
but'-ter-fin-ger
but'-ter-fish
but'-ter-fly
but'-ter-milk
but'-ter-nut
but'-ter-scotch
but'-ter-weed
but'-ter:y
but'-tocks
but'-ton

but'-ton-hole
but'-ton-mold
but'-ton-wood
but'-tress
bu'-tyl
bu'-tyl-ene†
bu-tyr-a'-ceous†
bu'-tyr-ate†
bu-tyr'-ic
bu'-tyr-in
bux'-om
bux'-om-ness
buy'-er
buy'-ing
buz'-zard
buzz'-er
buzz'-ing
buzz saw
by'=and=by'
by'=e:lec'-tion
by'-gone
by'-law
by'=line
by'-pass
by'-path
by'-play
by'=prod-uct
Byrd
byre
byr'-nie
by'-road
By'-ron
bys'-sus
by'-stand-er
by'-way
by'-word
Byz'-an-tine*†
By-zan'-tin-ism
By-zan'-tium

C

ca-bal'
cab'-a-la
cab-a-lis'-tic
cab-a-lis'-ti-cal
ca-balled'
ca-bal-le'-ro
ca-ban'a*†
ca-bane'
cab-a-ret'
cab'-bage
cab'-by
Cab'-ell
ca'-ber
ca-ber-net'

cab'-e-zone
cab'-in
cab'-in boy
cab'-i-net
cab'-i-net-mak-er
cab'-i-net-work
ca'-ble
ca'-ble-gram
ca'-blet
ca'-bling
cab'-man
cab'-o-chon*†
ca-boose'
Cab'-ot
cab'-o-tage
ca-bri'-lla*†
cab'-ri-ole
cab-ri-o-let'
cab'-stand
ca-bu'-ya
ca-ca'o
cach'-a-lot
cache
ca-chec'-tic
cached
ca-chet'
ca-chex'-i:a
cach'-in-nate
cach-in-na'-tion
ca-chou'
ca-cique'
cack'-le
cack'-ling
cac'o-de'-mon
cac'-o-dyl
cac-o-ë'-thes
cac:o-gen'-ics
ca-cog'-ra-phy
ca-coph'-o-nous
ca-coph'-o-ny
cac-ta'-ceous
cac'-ti
cac'-tus
ca-das'-tral
ca-das'-tre
ca-dav'-er†
ca-dav'-er-ous
cad'-die
cad'-dis
cad'-dish
cad'-dy
ca-delle'
ca'-dence
ca'-den-cy
ca-den'-za
ca-det'
ca-det'-ship
Cad'-il-lac

55

Ca-diz′
Cad′-me-an
cad′-mi-um
Cad′-mus
cad′-re*†
ca-du′-ca-ry
ca-du′-ce-us
ca-du′-ci-ty
ca-du′-cous
cae-cil′-i-an
Caen
Cae′-sar
Cae-sa-re′a†
Cae-sar′-e-an†
cae′-si-ous
caes′-pi-tose
cae-su′-ra
ca-fe′
caf-e-te-te′-ri:a
caf′-feine*†
caf′-tan
Ca-ga-yan′†
cage′-ling
ca′-gey*
ca′-gi-er*
ca′-gi-ly*
cai′-man
ca-ique′
cairn
cairn′-gorm
Cai′-ro
cais′-son
cai′-tiff
Ca′-ius
caj′-e-put
ca-jole′
ca-jol′-er:y
Ca′-jun
cake′-box
cake mix′-er
cake pan
cake′-walk
cal′-a-bash
cal′-a-boose
Ca-la′-bri:a
Ca-la′-bri-an
ca-la′-di-um
Ca-lais′
cal′-a-man-der
cal′-a-mar:y†
cal′-a-mine
cal′-a-mite
ca-lam′-i-tous
ca-lam′-i-ty
cal′-a-mus
ca-lash′
cal′-a-thos
cal-a-ver′-ite*†

cal-ca′-ne-us
cal′-car
cal-car′-e-ous†
cal′-ca-rine
cal′-ce-i-form
cal-ce-o-lar′-i:a*†
cal-cif′-er-ol
cal-cif′-er-ous
cal-ci-fi-ca′-tion
cal′-ci-fy
cal-cim′-e-ter
cal′-ci-mine
cal-ci-na′-tion
cal′-cine
cal′-cin-er
cal′-cite
cal′-ci-um
cal′-cu-la-ble
cal′-cu-late
cal′-cu-lat-ing
cal-cu-la′-tion
cal′-cu-la-tive
cal′-cu-la-tor
cal′-cu-li
cal′-cu-lus
Cal-cut′-ta
Cal-de-ron′
cal′-dron
Ca′-leb
Cal′-e-don
Cal-e-do′-ni:a
Cal-e-do′-ni-an
cal-e-fa′-cient
cal′-e-fac-to-ry
cal-en-dar′
cal′-en-der
Cal′-ends
ca-len′-du-la
cal′-en-ture
calf
calf′-skin
Cal′-ga-ry
Cal-houn′
Cal′-i-ban
cal′-i-ber
cal′-i-brate
cal-i-bra′-tion
cal′-i-bra-tor
ca′-li-ces†
cal′-i-co
Cal-i-for′-nia
Cal-i-for′-ni-an
ca-lig′-i-nous
Ca-lig′-u-la
cal′-i-per
ca′-liph
ca′-liph-ate*†
cal-i-sa′-ya

cal-is-then′-ics
ca′-lix
calk
calk′-ing
cal′-la
call′-a-ble
Cal-la′o
call′-er
Cal′-les
cal-lig′-ra-pher
cal-li-graph′-ic
cal-lig′-ra-phy
call′-ing
cal-li′-o-pe
cal-li-op′-sis
cal-li-pyg′-i-an
Cal-lis′-to
cal-los′-i-ty
cal′-lous
cal′-low
cal′-lus
cal′-lus-es
calm
calm′-a-tive*†
calm′-ly
calm′-ness
cal′-o-mel
cal-o-res′-cence
ca-lor′-ic
cal-o-ric′-i-ty
cal′-o-rie
cal′-o-ries
cal-o-rif′-ic
cal-o-rim′-e-ter
cal′-o-rize
cal-o-so′-ma
ca-lotte′
ca-loy′-er*†
cal′-trop
cal′-u-met
ca-lum′-ni-ate
ca-lum-ni-a′-tion
ca-lum′-ni-a-tor
cal′-um-nies
ca-lum′-ni-ous
ca-lum′-ni-ous-ly
cal′-um-ny
Cal′-va-ry
calve
Cal′-vert
calves
Cal′-vin
Cal′-vin-ism
Cal′-vin-ist
Cal-vin-is′-tic
cal-vi′-ti-es
calx
ca′-ly-coid†

ca-lyc′-u-lus
Cal′-y-don
ca-lyp′-so
ca-lyp′-tra
ca′-lyx
ca-ma-ra′-de-rie
cam-a-ril′-la
ca-ma′-ta
cam′-ber
cam′-bist
cam′-bi-um
Cam-bo′-di:a
Cam-bo′-di-an
Cam-brai′
Cam′-bri:a
Cam′-bri-an
cam′-bric
Cam′-bridge
Cam′-den
cam′-el
cam′-el-eer′
ca-mel′-lia
ca-mel′-o-pard
Cam′-e-lot
Cam′-em-bert†
cam′-e:o
cam′-e-os
cam′-er:a
cam′-er-al
cam′-er:a-man
Cam′-er-oon
Cam′-er-oun
Ca-mil′-la
Ca-mille′
ca-mion′
cam-i-sard′
cam′-i-sole
cam′-o-mile
Ca-mor′-ra
cam′-ou-flage†
Cam-pa′-gna
cam-paign′
cam-paign′-er
cam-pa-ni′-le
cam-pa-nol′-o-gy
cam-pan′-u-la
Camp′-bell
Camp′-bell-ite†
camp′-er
camp′-fire
camp′-ground
cam′-phor
cam′-phor-at-ed
cam-phor′-ic
cam′-pi-on
cam′-po
cam′-pus
Ca′-naan

57

Ca'-naan-ite
Can'-a-da
Ca-na'-di-an
ca-naille'
ca-nal'
ca-nal'-boat
can-a-lic'-u-lar
ca-nal-i-za'-tion
ca-nal'-ize
ca'-na-pé
ca-nard'
ca-nar'-ies†
ca-nar'y†
ca-nas'-ta
can'-can
can'-cel
can'-celed
can'-cel-er
can'-cel-ing
can-cel-la'-tion
can'-cer
can'-cer-ous
can-de-la'-bra
can-de-la'-brum
can-de-li'-lla*†
can'-dent
can-des'-cence
can-des'-cent
can'-did
can-di-da-cy
can'-di-date
can-di-da-ture
can'-did-ly
can'-did-ness
can'-died
can'-dies
can'-dle
can-dle-ber-ry
can'-dle-fish
can'-dle-grease
can'-dle-light
Can'-dle-mas
can'-dle-nut
can'-dle-pin
can'-dle-pow-er
can'-dler
can'-dle-shade
can'-dle-stick
can'-dle-wood
can'-dor
can'-dy
can'-dy-tuft
cane'-brake
can'-e-phore
ca-nes'-cent
Can'-field
ca-nic'-u-lar
ca'-nine

Ca'-nis
can'-is-ter
can'-ker
can'-ker-ous
can'-ker-worm
can'-na
canned
can'-nel
can'-ner
can'-ner:y
Cannes
can'-ni-bal
can'-ni-bal-ism
can-ni-bal-is'-tic
can'-ni-bal-ize
can-ni-kin
can'-ni-ly
can'-ni-ness
can'-ning
can'-non
can'-non-ade'
can'-non-ball
can'-non-eer
can'-not
can'-nu-la
can'-ny
ca-noe'
ca-noe'-ing
ca-noe'-ist
ca-noes'
can'-on
ca'-ñon
can'-on-ess
ca-non'-i-cal
can-on-ic'-i-ty
can-on-i-za'-tion
can'-on-ize
can'-on-ry
can' o'pen-er
can'-o-pies
Ca-no'-pus
can'-o-py
ca-no'-rous
Ca-no'-va
can-ta'-bi-le
Can-ta-brig'-i-an
can'-ta-loupe
can-tan'-ker-ous
can-ta'-ta
can-teen'
cant'-er (one who cants)
can'-ter (n., a gait; v., to lope)
Can'-ter-bur:y
can-thar'-i-des
can'-tha-ris
can'-thus
can'-ti-cle

58

Can-ti-gny'
can'-ti-le-ver†
can'-tile
can'-to
Can'-ton
can'-ton-al
Can'-ton-ese'
can-ton'-ment
can'-tor
Ca-nuck'
Ca-nute'
can'-vas
can'-vas-back
can'-vass
can'-vass-er
can'-yon
caou-tchouc'†
ca-pa-bil'-i-ties
ca-pa-bil'-i-ty
ca'-pa-ble
ca'-pa-bly
ca-pa'-cious
ca-pa'-cious-ly
ca-pac'-i-tance
ca-pac'-i-ty
cap'=a=pie'
ca-par'-i-son
cap'-e-lin
Ca-pel'-la
ca'-per
Ca-per'-na-um
Ca-pet'
Ca-pe'-tian
cap'-ful
ca'-pi-as
cap-il-la'-ceous
cap-il-lar'-i-ty
cap-il-lar:y†
cap'-i-ta
cap'-i-tal
cap-i-tal-ism
cap-i-tal-ist
cap-i-tal-is'-tic
cap-i-tal-i-za'-tion
cap'-i-tal-ize
cap'-i-tan'
cap'-i-tate
cap-i-ta'-tion
cap'-i-tol
Cap'-i-to-line
ca-pit'-u-lar
ca-pit'-u-late
ca-pit-u-la'-tion
ca'-pon
ca-pote'
Cap-pa-do'-cia
ca-pre'-o-line†
Ca-pri'

cap'-ric
ca-pric'-cio
ca-price'
ca-pri'-cious
Cap'-ri-corn
cap-ri-fi-ca'-tion
cap-ri-ole
ca-pro'-ic
cap'-ry-late*†
ca-pryl'-ic
cap-sa'-i-cin
cap'-si-cum
cap'-size
cap'-siz-ing
cap'-stan
cap'-stone
cap'-su-lar
cap'-sule
cap'-tain
cap'-tain-cy
cap'-tion
cap'-tious
cap'-ti-vate
cap'-ti-vat-ing
cap-ti-va'-tion
cap'-ti-va-tor
cap'-tive
cap-tiv'-i-ty
cap'-tor
cap'-ture
cap'-tur-ing
cap'-u-chin
cap'-u-cine
Cap'-u-let
ca'-put†
cap-y-bar'a*†
car'-a-ba'o†
car'-a-bi-neer'†
car'-a-cal
Car'-a-cal'-la
car-a-car'a*†
Ca-ra'-cas†
car'-a-cole
car'-a-cul
ca-rafe'
car'-a-mel
car'-a-pace
car'-at
car'-a-van
car-a-van'-sa-ry
car'-a-vel
car'-a-way
car-bam'-ic
car-bam'-ide
car-ba-nil'-ic
car-ba-nil'-ide*†
car'-bide
car'-bine

car'-bi-nol†
car-bo-hy'-drate
car-bol'-ic
car'-bo-lize
car'-bon
car-bo-na'-ceous†
car'-bon-ate
car-bon-a'-tion
car'-bon di-ox'-ide
car-bon'-ic
car-bon-if'-er-ous
car'-bon-ize
car'-bon-yl
car-bo-run'-dum
car-box'-yl
car-box-yl'-ic
car'-boy
car'-bun-cle
car-bun'-cu-lar
car'-bu-ret
car'-bu-ret-or
car-bu-ri-za'-tion
car'-bu-rize
car'-ca-jou
car'-ca-net
car'-cass
car-cin'-o-gen
car-ci-no'-ma
car-ci-nom'-a-tous
car'-da-mom
card'-board
card'-case
Car'-de-nas
car'-di-ac
car-di-al'-gi:a
Car'-diff
car'-di-gan
car'-di-nal
car'-di-nal-ate
card'-ing
car'-di:o-gram
car-di-og'-ra-phy
car'-di-oid
car-di'-tis
Car-do'-zo
card'-play-er
card'-room
card ta'-ble
car-du-a'-ceous
card writ'-er
ca-reen'
ca-reer'
ca-reer'-ist
care'-free
care'-ful
care'-ful-ly
care'-ful-ness
care'-less

care'-less-ly
care'-less-ness
ca-ress'
ca-ress'-ing-ly
ca-ress'-ive*
ca-ress'-ive-ly*
car'-et
care'-tak-er
Ca-rew'
care'-worn
car'-fare
car'-go
car'-goes
Car'-ib
Ca'-ri-ban*†
Car'-ib-be'-an
car'-i-bou
car'-i-ca-ture
car'-i-ca-tur-ist
car'-ies*†
car'-il-lon
car'-il-lon-neur'†
ca-ri'-na
car'-i-nate
car-i-o'-ca
car'-i-ous†
cark'-ing
Car-lisle'
Car'-list†
car'-load
Car-lot'-ta
Car-lo-vin'-gi-an
Car-lyle'
car'-ma-gnole'
car'-man
Car'-mel
Car-mel'a
Car'-mel-ite
car-min'-a-tive
car'-mine
car'-nage
car'-nal
car-nal'-i-ty
car'-nall-ite†
car'-nal-ly
car-na'-tion
Car'-ne-gie†
car-ne-'lian*
car'-ni-fy
car'-ni-val
car-niv'-o-ra
car-niv'-o-rous
car'-ob
ca-roche'
car'-ol
car'-ol-er
Car-o-li'-na

Car'-o-line
Car-o-lin'-ian
car'-om
car'-o-tene
ca-rot'-id
ca-rous'-al†
ca-rouse'
ca-rous'-ing
car'-pal
car-pa'-le
Car-pa'-thi-an
car'-pel
car'-pen-ter
car'-pen-try
car'-pet
car'-pet-bag
car'-pet-bag'-ger
car'-pet-beat-er
car'-pet clean'-ing
car'-pet-ing
car-po-go'-ni-um
car-pol'-o-gy
car-poph'-a-gous
car'-pus
car-ra-geen
Car-ran'-za
Car-ra'-ra
Car-rel'
car'-riage
car'-ri-er
car'-ri-on
Car'-roll
car'-ron-ade
car'-rot
car'-rot:y
car-rou-sel'
car'-ried
car'-ry
car'-ry-all
car'-ry=back
car'-ry=o'ver
cart'-age
Car-ta-ge'-na
carte blanche
car-tel'
car-tel-i-za'-tion
cart'-er
Car'-ter
Car-te'-sian
Car'-thage
Car-tha-gin'-i-an
Car-thu'-sian
Car-tier'
car'-ti-lage
car-ti-lag'-i-nous
cart'-load
car-tog'-ra-pher
car-to-graph'-ic

car-tog'-ra-phy
car'-ton
car-toon'
car-toon'-ist
car-touche'
car'-tridge
cart'-wheel
car'-un-cle
ca-run'-cu-late
Ca-ru'-so
car'-va-crol
car'-vel=built
carv'-en†
car'-vene
carv'-er
carv'-ing
Car'y†
car-y-at'-id
car-y-at'-id-al*†
car-y-o-phyl-la'-ceous
car-y-op'-sis
ca-sa'-ba
Ca-sa-blan'-ca
Cas-a-no'-va†
cas'-ca-bel
cas-cade'
cas-car'a†
cas-ca-ron'
ca'-se-ate
case' hard'-en
ca-sein*†
ca-sein'-ate*†
case'-mate
case'-ment
ca'-se-ous
ca-sern'
ca-shaw'
cash'-book
cash'-ew†
cash-ier'
cash'-mere
cas'-ing
ca-si'-no
cask
cas'-ket
Cas'-per
Cas'-pi-an
casque
Cas-san'-dra
cas-sa'-tion
cas-sa'-va
cas'-se-role
cas'-si:a
cas'-si-mere
Cas-si-o-pe'-ia
cas-sit'-er-ite†
Cas'-sius
cas'-sock

61

cas'-so-war:y†
cast
cas-ta-net'
cast'-a-:way
caste
caste'-less
cas'-tel-lan
cas'-tel-lat-ed
cas-tel-la'-tion
cast'-er
cas'-ti-gate
cas-ti-ga'-tion
Cas-ti-glio'-ne
Cas-tile'
Cas-til'-ian
cast'-ing
cast iron
cas'-tle
cas'-tling
cast'=off
cas'-tor
cas-to'-re-um
cas-tra-me-ta'-tion
cas'-trate
cas-tra'-tion
ca'-su-al*†
ca'-su-al-ly*†
ca'-su-al-ness*†
ca'-su-al-ty*†
ca'-su-ist*†
ca'-su-is'-tic*†
ca-su-is'-ti-cal-ly*†
ca'-su-is-try*†
ca'-sus
cat-a-bol'-ic
cat-a-bol'-i-cal-ly
ca-tab'-o-lism
cat-a-chre'-sis
cat-a-chres'-tic
cat'-a-clysm
cat-a-clys'-mic
cat'-a-comb
ca-tad'-ro-mous
cat'-a-falque
Cat'-a-lan
cat-a-lec'-tic
cat'-a-lep-sy
cat-a-lep'-tic
Cat-a-li'-na
cat'-a-log
cat'-a-log-er
cat'-a-log-ing
Cat-a-lo'-ni-an
ca-tal'-pa
ca-tal'-y-sis
cat'-a-lyst
cat-a-lyt'-ic
cat'-a-lyze

cat'-a-lyz-er
cat-a-ma-ran'
cat-a-me'-ni:a
cat'-a-mite
cat'-a-mount
cat:a-pho-re'-sis†
cat:a-pla'-si:a
cat'-a-pult
cat'-a-ract
ca-tarrh'
ca-tarrh'-al
ca-tarrh'-ous
ca-tas'-ta-sis
ca-tas'-tro-phe
cat-a-stroph'-ic
cat:a-ton'-ic
Ca-taw'-ba
cat'-bird
cat'-boat
cat'-call
catch'-all
catch'-er
catch'-i-er
catch'-pen-ny
catch'=up
catch'-word
catch'y
cat-e-che'-sis
cat'-e-chism
cat-e-chis'-mal
cat'-e-chist
cat-e-chis'-tic
cat-e-chi-za'-tion
cat'-e-chize
cat'-e-chol
cat'-e-chu
cat-e-chu'-men
cat-e-chu'-men-al†
cat-e-gor'-i-cal
cat-e-gor'-i-cal-ly
cat'-e-go-rize
cat'-e-go-ry
ca-te'-na
cat'-e-nar:y†
cat'-e-nate
ca'-ter
cat'-er-an
cat'-er-cor-ner
cat'-er=cor-nered
ca'-ter-er
cat'-er-pil-lar
cat'-er-waul
cat'-er-waul-ing
cat'-fish
cat'-gut
Cath'-ar
ca-thar'-sis
ca-thar'-tic

Ca-thay'
ca-thec'-tic
ca-the'-dral
Cath'-er
Cath'-er-ine†
cath'-e-ter
cath'-e-ter-ize
cath'-ode
Cath'-o-lic
Ca-thol'-i-cism
cath-o-lic'-i-ty
ca-thol'-i-cize
Cat'-i-line
cat'-i:on
cat'-kin
cat'-like
cat'-nap
cat'-nip
Ca'-to
cat=o'=nine=tails
ca-top'-tric
cat's=eye
Cats'-kill
cat's=paw
cat'-sup
cat'-tail
cat'-ta-lo
cat'-tle
cat'-tle-man
cat'-ty
Ca-tul'-lus
cat'-walk
Cau-ca'-sia
Cau-ca'-sian
Cau'-ca-sus
cau'-cus
cau'-dal
cau'-dal-ly
cau'-dex
cau'-dle
caught
cau-les'-cent
cau'-li-cle
cau'-li-flow-er
cau'-line
caus'-al
cau-sal'-gi:a
cau-sal'-i-ty
cau-sa'-tion
caus'-a-tive
cause'-less
caus'-er
cau-se-rie'†
cause'-way
caus'-ing
caus'-tic
caus-ti-cal-ly
cau-ter-i-za'-tion

cau'-ter-ize
cau'-ter:y
cau'-tion
cau-tion-ar:y†
cau'-tious
cau'-tious-ly
cav'-al-cade'
cav'-a-lier'
ca-val'-la
cav'-al-ry
cav'-al-ry-man
cav-a-ti'-na*†
ca'-ve-at
Cav-ell'
cave'-man
Cav-en-dish
cav'-ern
cav'-ern-ous
cav'-i-ar
cav'-il
cav-i-ta'-tion
Ca-vi'-te
cav'-i-ties
cav'-i-ty
ca-vort'
ca-vort'-ing
Ca-vour'
ca'-vy
Cax'-ton
cay'-enne'
cay'-man
cay'-use
cease
ceased
cease'-less
cease'-less-ly
ceas'-ing
Ce'-cil†
Ce-cil'-i:a
ce-cro'-pi:a
ce'-cum
ce'-dar
cede
ced'-ed
ce-dil'-la
ced'-ing
ce'-drat
ce-du-la*†
ceil
ceil'-ing
ceil-om'-e-ter
cel'-an-dine
Cel'-a-nese
Cel'-e-bes
cel'-e-brant
cel'-e-brate
cel'-e-brat-ed
cel-e-bra'-tion

63

cel'-e-bra-tor
ce-leb'-ri-ty
ce-ler'-i-ty
cel'-er:y
ce-les'-ta
ce-les'-tial
Ce-les'-tine
cel'-es-tite
cel'-i-ba-cy
cel'-i-bate
ce'-lite
cel'-lar
cel'-lar-age
cel'-lar-er
cel'-lar-ette'
Cel-li'-ni
cel'-list
cel'-lo
cel'-lo-phane
cel'-lu-lar
cel'-lule
cel-lu-li'-tis
cel'-lu-loid
cel'-lu-lose
cel'-lu-los'-ic*†
Cel'-si-us
Celt'-ic
Celt'-i-cism
cel'-ti-um
cel'-tuce
ce-ment'
ce-men-ta'-tion†
ce-ment'-ite
ce-men-ti'-tious†
cem'-e-ter-ies
cem'-e-ter:y
ce-no'-bi-an
cen'-o-bite
cen'-o-bit'-ic
ce-no-ge-net'-ic†
cen'-o-taph
Ce-no-zo'-ic
cen'-ser
cen'-sor
cen-so'-ri-al
cen-so'-ri-ous
cen'-sor-ship
cen-sur-a-ble
cen'-sure
cen'-sured
cen'-sur-ing
cen'-sus
cen'-tare
cen'-taur
cen'-tau-ry
cen-ta'-vo
cen-te-nar'-i-an†
cen-ten'-a-ry*†

cen-ten'-ni-al
cen'-ter
cen'-ter-board
cen'-ter-piece
cen-tes'-i-mal
cent'-ge-ner
cen'-ti-grade
cen'-ti-gram
cen-ti-li'-ter
cen'-time
cen'-ti-me-ter
cen'-ti-pede
cen'-tral
cen-tral-i-za'-tion
cen'-tral-ize
cen-trif'-u-gal
cen'-tri-fuge
cen-trip'-e-tal
cen'-trist
cen'-tro-bar'-ic
cen-troi'-dal
cen'-trum
cen'-tu-ple
cen-tu'-pli-cate
cen-tu'-ri-al
cen-tu'-ri-on
cen'-tu-ry
ce-phal'-ic
ceph'-a-lin
ceph-a-li-za'-tion
ceph'-a-lo-pod
ceph'-a-lo-tho'-rax
Ce'-phe-id*
ce-ram'-ic
ce-ram'-ics
ce-ram'-ist*
ce-rar'-gy-rite
ce-ras'-tes
ce'-rate
Cer-be'-re-an
Cer'-ber-us†
cer-car'-i:a*†
ce'-re-al
cer-e-bel'-lar
cer-e-bel'-lum
cer:e'-bral
cer:e-bro-spi'-nal
cer:e'-brum
cere'-ment
cer-e-mo'-ni-al
cer'-e-mo-nies
cer-e-mo'-ni-ous
cer'-e-mo-ny
Ce'-res
ce'-re-us
ce'-ric
ce-rise'
ce'-rite

ce'-ri-um
cer'-met
ce-rog'-ra-phy
ce-ro'-tic*†
ce'-rous
cer'-tain
cer'-tain-ly
cer'-tain-ties
cer'-tain-ty
cer-ti-fi-a-ble
cer-tif'-i-cate
cer-ti-fi-ca'-tion
cer'-ti-fied
cer'-ti-fies
cer'-ti-fy
cer'-ti-fy-ing
cer-ti:o-ra'-ri
cer'-ti-tude
ce-ru'-le-an
ce-ru'-men
ce-rus'-site
Cer-van'-tes
cer-van'-tite
cer'-ve-lat
cer-vi-cal
cer'-vix
ce-sar'-e-an†
ce-sar'-e-vich
ce'-si-um
ces-sa'-tion
ces'-sion
cess'-pit
cess'-pool
ce-ta'-cean
ce'-tene
ce'-tyl*
Cey-lon'
Cey'-lon-ese'*
Ce-zanne'
Cha'-blis
chac'-ma
Cha'-co
chae'-to-pod
chafed
cha-fer*† (beetle)
chaf'-er (one that chafes)
chaf-fer (bargain)
chaff'-er† (n., a sieve; v. to remove chaff)
chaf'-finch
chaf'-ing
chaf'-ing dish
Cha'-gres
cha-grin'
cha-grined'
chain' gang
chain mail
chain-o-mat'-ic

chain re-ac'-tion
chain'=smoke
chain stitch
chain store
chain'-work
chair'-man
chair'-man-ship
chaise longue
cha-la'-za
Chal'-ce-don
chal-ced'-o-ny
chal'-cid
chal-co-lith'-ic
chal-co-py'-rite
Chal-da'-ic
Chal-de'a
Chal-de'-an
chal'-dron
cha'-let
chal'-ice
chalk'-i-ness
chalk'y
chal'-lenge
chal'-lenge-a-ble
chal'-leng-er
chal'-leng-ing
chal'-lis
cha-lyb'-e-ate
cha-made'
cham'-ber
cham'-bered
cham'-ber-lain
cham'-ber-maid
cham'-bray
cha-me'-leon*†
cham'-fer
cham'-ois
cham-pagne'
cham'-per-tous
cham'-per-ty
cham'-pi-gnon
cham'-pi-on
cham'-pi-on-ship
Cham-plain'
Champs E:ly-sées
chance'-ful
chan'-cel
chan'-cel-ler:y
chan'-cel-lor
chan'-cel-lor-ship
Chan-cel-lors-ville
chan'-cer:y
chan'-cre
chancy
chan-de-lier'
chan'-dler
chan'-dler:y
change-a:bil'-i-ty

65

change'-a:ble
changed
change'-ful
change'-less
change'-ling
chang'-er
chang'-ing
chan'-nel
chan'-neled
chan'-nel-ing
Chan'-ning
chan-son'
chant'-er
chan-te-relle'
chan'-tey*†
chan'-ti-cleer
chan'-try†
cha'-os
cha-ot'-ic
chap-a-ra'-jos*†
chap'-ar-ral'
chap'-book
cha-peau'
cha-peaux'
chap'-el
chap'-er-on
chap'-fall-en
chap'-i-ter
chap'-lain
chap'-lain-cy
chap'-let
Chap'-lin
chap'-man
chap'-ter
char'-a-banc
char'-ac-ter
char-ac-ter-is'-tic
char-ac-ter-is'-ti-cal-ly
char-ac-ter-i-za'-tion
char'-ac-ter-ize
char'-ac-ter:y
cha-rade'
char'-coal
charge'-a:ble
char'-gé d'af-faires'
charged
charg'-er
charg'-ing
char'-i-ly
char'-i-ness
char'-i-ot
char'-i-o-teer'*†
cha-ris'-ma
char'-is-mat'-ic
char'-i-ta-ble
char'-i-ties
char'-i-ty
cha-ri-va-ri'

char'-la-tan
Char'-le-magne
Charles'-ton
Charles'-town
Char'-ley
Char'-lotte
Char'-lottes-ville
Char'-lotte-town
charm'-er
char-meuse'
charm'-ing
charm'-ing-ly
char'-nel
Char'-on*†
char'-ter (a deed)
chart'-er (one that charts)
Char'-tism*†
Char'-tist*†
Chartres
char-treuse'
chart room
char'-tu-lar:y†
char'-wom-an†
char'y
Cha-ryb'-di-an
Cha-ryb'-dis
chased
chas'-er
chas'-ing
chasm
chas'-mal
chasm'y†
chasse'-pot
chas-seur'
chas'-sis
chaste
chas'-ten†
chas-tise'
chas-tise'-ment
chas-tis'-er
chas'-ti-ty
chas'-u-ble
châ-teau'
châ-teaux'
Cha-teau-bri-and'
Châ-teau=Thier'-ry
cha'-te-lain*
cha-te-laine*†
Chat'-ham
cha-toy'-ance
cha-toy'-ant
Chat-ta-hoo'-chee
Chat-ta-noo'-ga
chat'-tel
chat'-ter
chat'-ter-box
chat'-ter-er
Chat'-ter-ton

chat'-ti-ly
chat'-ting
chat'-ty
Chau'-cer
chauf'-fer
chauf'-feur
chaul-moo'-gra
Chau-tau'-qua
chau'-vin-ism
chau'-vin-ist
chau-vin-is'-ti-cal-ly
cheap'-en
cheap'-ened
cheap'-ly
cheap'-ness
cheat'-er
check'-book
check'-er
check'-er-ber-ry
check'-er-board
check'-ered
check'-ers
check girl
check'-mate
check'=out
check'-rein
check'-room
check'-up (n.)
ched'-dar
chedd'-ite
cheek'-bone
cheek'y
cheer'-er
cheer'-ful
cheer'-ful-ly
cheer'-ful-ness
cheer'-i-ly
cheer'-less
cheer'y
cheese'-cake
cheese'-cloth
cheese knife
cheese'-par-ing
chees'-i-ness
chees'y
chee'-tah
chef
chef d'oeu'-vre
Che'-ka
Che'-khov
che'-late
che-lic'-er:a†
che'-li-form†
che-lo'-ni-an
Chel'-sea
Chel'-ten-ham
chem-i-at'-ric
chem'-ic

chem'-i-cal
che-mise'
chem-i-sette'
chem'-ist
chem'-is-try
chem:o-ther'-a-py
chem'-ur-gy
che-nille'
che-no-po'-di-um
Cheops†
che'-quer*†
Cher'-bourg
cher'-ish
cher'-no-zem'
Cher'-o-kee
che-root'
cher'-ries
cher'-ry
cher'-so-nese
cher'-ub
che-ru'-bic
che-ru'-bi-cal-ly
cher'-u-bim
cher-vo'-nets
Ches'-a-peake
Chesh'-ire
chess'-board
chess'-man
Ches'-ter
Ches'-ter-field
Ches'-ter-ton
chest'-nut
chest'y
che-va-lier'
Chev'-i-ot
Chev'-ro-let'
chev'-ron
chew'-ing
che-wink'
Chey-enne'
Cheyne
Chiang' Kai-shek'
Chi-an'-ti
chia'-ro-scu'-ro*
chi-as'-ma
Chi-ca'-go
Chi-ca'-go-an
chi-cane'
chi-ca'-ner:y*†
chick'-a-dee
Chick-a-hom'-i-ny
Chick-a-mau'-ga
chick'-a-ree
Chick'-a-saw
chick'-en
chick'-en-heart'-ed
chick'en pox
chick'-pea

chick'-weed
chi'-cle*†
chic'-o-ry
chide
chid'-ing
chief'-ly
chief'-tain
chief'-tain-ship
chif-fon'
chif'-fo-nier'
chif'-fo-robe
chig'-ger
chi'-gnon
Chi-hua'-hua
chil'-blain
child'-bear-ing
child'-bed
child'-birth
child'-hood
child'-ish
child'-ish-ly
child'-ish-ness
child'-less
child'-like
chil'-dren
Chil'e†
Chil'-e:an
chil'i
chil'-i-ad
chill'-i-ness
chill'-ing
Chil-lon'
chill'y
chi-mae'-roid
chimed
chim'-er
chi-me'-ra
chi-mer'-i-cal
chi-mer'-i-cal-ly
chim'-ing
chim'-ney
chim'-ney-piece
chim'-ney pot
chim'-ney sweep
chim'-pan-zee
Chi'-na
chi'-na-ber-ry
Chi'-na-man
Chi'-na-town
chi'-na-ware
chin-chil'-la
Chi-nese'
Chin-kiang†
chinned
chin'-ning
chi-nook'
chin'-qua-pin
chintz

Chi'-os
chip'-munk
chipped
Chip'-pen-dale
chip'-per
Chip'-pe-wa
chip'-ping
chi'-ro-graph
chi-rog'-ra-pher
chi'-ro-graph'-ic
chi-rog'-ra-phy
chi'-ro-man-cy
Chi'-ron
chi-rop'-o-dist
chi-rop'-o-dy
chi'-ro-prac'-tic
chi'-ro-prac'-tor
chir'-rup
chir'-ruped
chir'-rup-ing
chis'-el
chis'-eled
chis'-el-er
chis'-el-ing
chit'-chat
chi'-tin
chi'-tin-ous†
chi'-ton
chi-val'-ric*†
chiv'-al-rous
chiv'-al-ry
chlam'-ys*†
Chlo'e
chlo'-ral
chlor-am'-ide
chlor-am'-ine*
chlo'-rate
chlo'-dane
chlo'-ric
chlo'-ride
chlo'-ri-dize*†
chlo'-ri-nate*†
chlo-rin-a'-tion
chlo'-rine
chlo'-rite
chlo'-ro-form
chlo'-ro-my-ce'-tin
chlo'-ro-phyll
chlo-ro'-sis
chlo'-rous
chock'=full'
choc'-o-late
Choc'-taw
choice'-ly
choic'-est
choir
choke'-ber-ry
choke'-bore

choke'-cher-ry
choked
choke'-damp
chok'-er
chok'-ing
chol-an'-threne*†
chol'-er
chol'-er:a
chol'-er-ic
cho-les'-ta-nol
cho-les'-ter-ol
cho'-line
cho-lin-es'-ter-ase
chon-dro'-ma
chon'-drule
choose
choos'-ing
chop'-house
Cho'-pin
chop'-per
chop'-ping
chop'-py
chop'-stick
chop su'-ey
cho-ra'-gus
cho'-ral
chord
chord'-al
chor'-date
chore
cho-re'a
chore'-man
cho-re-og'-ra-pher†
cho-re-og'-ra-phy†
cho'-ri-amb
cho'-ric
cho'-ri-on
cho'-ris-ter*†
cho-rog'-ra-phy
cho'-roid
chor'-tle
chor'-tling
cho'-rus
chose
cho'-sen
chow'-der
chres-tom'-a-thy
chrism
chris'-mal
chris'-ma-to-ry
chris'-om
Chris'-ta-bel
chris'-ten
chris'-ten-dom
chris'-ten-ing
Chris'-tian
chris-ti-an'-ia†
Chris-ti:an'-i-ty

chris'-tian-ize
Christ'-like
Christ'-ly
Christ'-mas
Christ'-mas-tide
Chris'-to-pher
chro'-ma
chro'-mate
chro-mat'-ic
chro-mat'-i-cal-ly
chro'-ma-tin
chro'-ma-tism
chro-mat'o-gram*
chro-ma-tog'-ra-phy
chro-mat'o-scope*
chrome
chro'-mic
chro'-mite
chro'-mi-um
chro'-mo
chro'-mo-gen
chro-mom'-e-ter
chro'-mo-some
chro'-mo-sphere
chro'-mous
chron'-ic
chron'-i-cal-ly
chron'-i-cle
chron'-i-cler
chron'-i-cling
chron'-o-graph
chro-nog'-ra-pher
chron-o-log'-ic
chron-o-log'-i-cal
chro-nol'-o-gist
chro-nol'o-gy
chro-nom'-e-ter
chron-o-met'-ric
chrys'-a-lid
chrys'-a-lis
chry-san'-the-mum*†
chrys-el-e-phan'-tine
chry'-sene*†
chrys'o-ber-yl
chrys'-o-lite
chrys'-o-prase
chtho'-ni-an
chub'-by
chuck'-le
chuck'-led
chuck'-le-head
chuck'-ling
chuff'y†
chuk'-ker
chum'-mi-ly
chum'-my
Chung-king
chunk'y

church'-go-er
Church'-ill
church'-ly
church'-man
church'-ward-en†
church'-yard
churl'-ish
churl'-ish-ly
churl'-ish-ness
churn'-er
chute
chut'-ney
chy-la'-ceous
chyle
chyme
chy'-mi-fy
chy'-mous
ci-bo'-ri-um
ci-ca'-da
ci-ca'-la
cic'-a-tri-ces
cic-a-tri'-cial
cic'-a-trix
cic-a-tri'-zant
cic-a-tri-za'-tion
cic'-a-trize
cic'-e-ly
Cic'-e-ro
cic-e-ro'-ne† (n.)
cic'-e-rone† (v.)
Cic-e-ro'-ni-an
ci-cho-ri-a'-ceous
ci'-der
ci'=de-vant'
ci-gar'
cig-a-rette' (cig-a-ret')
ci-gar'=shaped
cil'-i-a
cil'-i-ar;y†
cil'-i-ate
Ci-li'-cia
Ci-li'-cian
Ci-ma-bu'e
cim'-ar-ron*†
Ci'-mex
ci'-mi-coid†
Cim-me'-ri-an
cin-cho'-na
cin-chon'-i-dine
cin'-cho-nism
cin'-cho-phen
Cin-cin-nat'i†
Cin-cin-nat'-us†
cinc'-ture
cin'-der
Cin-der-el'-la
cin'-e-ma
cin-e-mat'-o-graph

cin-e-ma-tog'-ra-pher
cin-e-ma-tog'-ra-phy
cin-e-rar'-i:a*†
cin'-er-ar:y†
cin'-er-a-tor
ci-ne'-re-ous
cin'-er-ous
cin'-gu-late
cin-na-bar
cin-nam'-ic
cin'-na-mon
cin-que-cen'-tist
cin-que-cen'-to
cinque'-foil
ci'-on
ci'-pher
cip'o-lin
cir'-ca
Cir-cas'-sian
Cir'-ce
cir'-cle
cir'-cled
cir'-clet
cir'-cling
cir'-cuit
cir-cu'-i-tous
cir'-cu-lar
cir-cu-lar-i-za'-tion
cir'-cu-lar-ize
cir'-cu-late
cir-cu-la'-tion
cir'-cu-la-tive
cir'-cu-la-tor
cir-cu-la-to-ry
cir-cum-am'-bi-ent
cir'-cum-cise
cir-cum-ci'-sion
cir-cum'-fer-ence
cir-cum-fer-en'-tial
cir'-cum-flex
cir-cum'-flu-ent
cir-cum-lo-cu'-tion
cir-cum-loc'-u-to-ry
cir-cum-nav'-i-gate
cir-cum-nav-i-ga'-tion
cir-cum-nu-ta'-tion
cir'-cum-po'-lar
cir'-cum-scis'-sile
cir'-cum-scribe
cir-cum-scrip'-tion
cir'-cum-spect
cir-cum-spec'-tion
cir'-cum-stance
cir'-cum-stanced
cir'-cum-stan'-tial
cir-cum-stan'-tial-ly
cir-cum-stan'-ti-ate
cir'-cum-vent

cir'-cum-vent-er
cir-cum-ven'-tion
cir-cum-vo-lu'-tion
cir'-cus
cirque
cir-rho'-sis
cir-rhot'-ic
cir'-ri
cir'-ri-pede
cir-ro-cu'-mu-lus
cir-ro-stra'-tus
cir'-rous
cir'-rus
cir'-soid
cis-al'-pine
cis-pa-dane'
cis-ta'-ceous
Cis-ter'-cian
cis'-tern
cit'-a-del
ci-ta'-tion
ci'-ta-to-ry
cite
cith'-a-ra
cit'-ies
cit'-i-fy
cit'-ing
cit'-i-zen
cit'-i-zen-ess
cit'-i-zen-ry
cit'-i-zen-ship
cit'-ral
cit'-rate
cit'-re-ous
cit'-ric
cit'-rin
ci-tri'-nin*
cit'-ron
cit-ro-nel'-la*†
cit'-rous
cit'-rus
cit'y
cit'y=state
civ'-et
civ'-ic
civ'-ics
civ'-il
ci-vil'-ian
ci-vil'-i-ty
civ-i-li-za'-tion
civ'-i-lize
civ'-i-lized
civ'-i-liz-ing
civ'-il-ly
civ-il serv'-ice†(1)

civ'-ism
clab'-ber
claim'-ant
claim'-er
clair-voy'-ance
clair-voy'-ant
cla'-mant†
clam-a-to'-ri-al
clam'-bake
clam'-ber
clam'-mi-ness
clam'-my
clam'-or
clam'-or-ous
clam'-shell
clan-des'-tine
clang'-or†
clang'-or-ous†
clan'-nish
clans'-man
clap'-board
clapped
clap'-per
clap'-ping
clap'-trap
claque
cla-queur'
Clar'a
Clar'-ence
Clar'-en-don
clar'-et
Clar'-ice
clar-i-fi-ca'-tion
clar'-i-fied
clar'-i-fy
clar'-i-fy-ing
clar'-i-net'
clar'-i-on
clar'-i-ty
clas'-sic
clas'-si-cal
clas'-si-cal-ly
clas'-si-cism
clas'-si-cist
clas'-si-fi-a-ble
clas'-si-fi-ca'-tion
clas'-si-fi-ca-to-ry
clas'-si-fied
clas'-si-fy
clas'-si-fy-ing
clas'-sis
class'-mate
class'-room
clas'-tic
clat'-ter

(1) preferred to ser'-vice, given by *Webster's 3rd New International Dictionary*

clat'-tered
clau-di-ca'-tion
Clau'-di-us
claus'-al
clause
claus'-tral
claus-tro-pho'-bi:a
clav'-a-cin
cla'-vate
clav'-i-chord
clav'-i-cle
cla-vic'-u-lar
cla-vier'*†
clav'-i-form
claw'-like
clay'-ey
clay'-more
clean=cut
clean'-er
clean'-li-ness
clean'-ly
clean'-ness
cleanse
cleansed
cleans'-er
cleans'-ing
clean'-up
clear'-ance
clear=cut
clear=eyed
clear'-head-ed
clear'-ing
clear'-ing-house
clear'-ly
clear'-ness
clear=sight-ed
cleav'-a-ble
cleav'-age
cleaved
cleav'-er
cleav'-ing
cleis-tog'-a-mous
cleis-tog'-a-my
clem'-a-tis
Cle-men-ceau'
clem'-en-cy
Clem'-ens
clem'-ent
Clem'-en-tine
Cle-om'-e-nes
Cle'-on
Cle-o-pat'-ra†
clep'-sy-dra
clere'-sto:ry
cler'-gy
cler'-gy-man
cler'-ic
cler'-i-cal

cler'-i-sy
clerk'-ship
Cler'-mont
Cleve'-land
clev'-er
clev'-er-ly
clev'-er-ness
clev'-is
clew
cli-an'-thus
cli-ché'
click
click'-er
cli'-ent
cli'-ent-age
cli-en'-tal†
cli-en-tele'
Clif'-ford
cliff'y
Clif'-ton
cli-mac'-ter-ic
cli-mac'-tic
cli'-mate
cli-mat'-ic
cli-ma-to-log'-i-cal
cli-ma-tol'-o-gy
cli'-max
climbed
climb'-er
climb'-ing
cli-nan'-dri-um
clinch'-er
cling'-ing
cling'-stone
cling'y
clin'-ic
clin'-i-cal
cli-ni'-cian
clink'-er
cli-nom'-e-ter
cli-no-met'-ric
clin'-quant
Clin'-ton
clin-to'-ni:a
Cli'o
clipped
clip'-per
clip'-ping
clique
cli'-quey†
cli'-quish†
clit'-o-ris*†
clo-a'-ca
cloak'-room
clob'-ber
cloche
clock'-mak-er
clock tow'-er

clock'-wise
clock'-work
clod'-hop-per
clog'-ging
cloi-son-né'
clois'-ter
clois'-tral
clo'-nic*†
clo'-nus
closed
close'=fist-ed
close'=fit-ting
close'=hauled
close'=lipped
close'-ly
close'-mouthed
close'-ness
clos'-est
clos'-et
close'=up
clo'-sure
cloth
clothe
clothes
clothes'-line
cloth'-ier
Clo-thil'-da
cloth'-ing
cloth' yard
clo'-ture
cloud'-burst
cloud'=capped
cloud cham'-ber
cloud'-i-ness
cloud'-less
cloud'-let
cloud'y
clough
clo'-ven
clo'-ven=foot-ed
clo'-ver
Clo'-vis
clown'-ish
cloy'-ing
cloy'-ing-ly
club'-ba-ble
clubbed
club'-bing
club'-foot
club'-house
club'-man
club'-room
club'-wom-an†
clum'-si-er
clum'-si-ly
clum'-si-ness
clum'-sy
Clu'-ny

clu'-pe-id
clus'-ter
clut'-ter
Clydes'-dale
clyp'-e-ate
Cnos'-sus
coach'-man
co-ad'-ju-tant
co-ad-ju'-tor
co-ad'-u-nate
co-ag'-u-la-ble
co-ag'-u-late
co-ag-u-la'-tion
co-ag'-u-la-tive
co-ag'-u-la-tor
coal barge
coal bin
coal box
coal car
coal cel'-lar
coal chute
coal deal'-er
co-a-lesce'
co-a-les'-cence
co-a-les'-cent
co-a-lesc'-ing
coal'-field
coal gas
coal hod
coal'-hole
co-a-li'-tion
coal mine
coal scut'-tle
coal shov'-el
coal tar
coal yard
coarse
coarse'-ly
coars'-en
coarse'-ness
coast'-al
coast'-er
coast guard
coast'-line
coast'-wise
coat-ee'
co-a'-ti
coat'-ing
coat of arms
coat of mail
coat'-room
coat'-tail
co'-au'-thor
coax
co-ax'-i-al
coax'-ing
coax'-ing-ly
co'-balt

co-bal'-tous†
cob'-ble
cob'-bler
cob'-ble-stone
Cob'-den
Cobh
Cob'-ham
co'-ble†
co'-bra
Co'-burg
cob'-web
co-caine'†
co-cain'-ism†
coc'-ci
coc'-cus
coc-cyg'-e-al
coc'-cyx
Co'-chin
coch'-i-neal
coch'-le:a
cock-ade'
cock'-a-too
cock'-a-trice
cock-boat
cock-cha-fer*†
cock'-crow
cock'-er
cock'-er-el
cock'-eyed
cock'-horse'
cock'-le
cock'-le-bur
cock'-le-shell
Cock'-ney
Cock'-ney-ism
cock'-pit
cock'-roach
cock'-spur
cock'-sure
cock'-tail
cock'y
co'-co
co'-coa
co-co-bo'-lo
co'-co-nut
co-coon'
co'-da
cod'-dle
cod'-ed
co-de-fend'-ant†
co'-deine†
co'-dex
cod'-fish
codg'-er
cod'-i-cil
cod-i-fi-ca'-tion
cod'-i-fied
cod'-i-fy

cod'-ling
co'=ed'
co-ed-u-ca'-tion
co-ed-u-ca'-tion-al
co'-ef-fi'-cient
coe-len'-ter-ate
coe'-li-ac
coe'-lom
coe-nes-the'-sia†
coe-nu'-rus
co-e'qual
co-erce'
co-erc'-i-ble*
co-erc'-ing
co-er'-cion
co-er'-cive
co-e-ta'-ne-ous
co-e-ta'-ne-ous-ly
co-e'-val
co-ex-ist'
co-ex-is'-tence*
co-ex-is'-tent*
co-ex-ten'-sive
cof'-fee
cof'-fee-house
cof'-fee-pot
cof'-fer
cof'-fer-dam
cof'-fin
co'-gen-cy
co'-gent
cog'-i-ta-ble
cog'-i-tate
cog'-i-tat-ing
cog-i-ta'-tion
cog'-i-ta-tive
co'-gnac†
cog'-nate
cog-ni'-tion
cog'-ni-za-ble
cog'-ni-zance
cog'-ni-zant
cog-no'-men
cog-nos'-ci-ble
cog'-way
cog'-wheel
co-hab'-it
co-hab'-i-tant*
co'-heir
co-here'
co-her'-ence
co-her'-ent
co-her'-er
co-he'-sion
co-he'-sive
co-he'-sive-ness
co'-hort
coif-feur'

coif-fure'
coign
coin
coin'-age
co-in-cide'
co-in'-ci-dence
co-in'-ci-dent
co-in-ci-den'-tal
co-in-cid'-ing
coin'-er
co-in-sure'
cois'-trel
co-i'-tion
co'-i-tus
coked
cok'-ing
col'-an-der
Col'-bert
Col'-by
Col'-ches-ter
col'-chi-cine
Col'-chi-cum
col'-chis
col'-co-thar
cold'=blood-ed
cold cream
cold chis'-el
cold'-heart-ed
cold'-ly
cold'-ness
cold'-proof
cole'-man-ite
co-le-op'-te-rous*†
Cole'-ridge
cole'-slaw
co'-le-us
Col'-gate
col'-ic
col'-ick:y
col'-ic-root
col'-ic-weed
col-i-se'-um
co-li'-tis
col-lab'-o-rate
col-lab'-o-rat-ing
col-lab-o-ra'-tion
col-lab'-o-ra-tor
col-lage'
col-lapse'
col-lapsed'
col-laps'-i-ble
col-laps'-ing
col'-lar
col'-lar-band
col'-lar-bone
col'-lar but-ton
col-late'
col-lat'-er-al

col-lat'-ing
col-la'-tion
col-la'-tor
col'-league
col-lect' (v.)
col'-lect (n.)
col-lec-ta'-ne:a
col-lect'-ed
col-lect'-i-ble
col-lec'-tion
col-lec'-tive
col-lec'-tive-ly
col-lec'-tiv-ist
col-lec'-tor
col'-leen
col'-lege
col'-leg-er
col-le'-gi-al
col-le'-gian†
col-le'-giate†
col-len'-chy-ma
col-lide'
col-lid'-ing
col'-lie
col'-lier
col'-lier:y
col'-li-gate
col'-li-ma-tor
col-lin'-e:ar
Col'-lins
col-li'-sion
col'-lo-cate
col-lo-ca'-tion
col-lo'-di-on
col'-loid
col-loi'-dal
col'-lop
co-lo'-qui-al
co-lo'-qui-al-ism
co-lo'-qui-al-ly
col'-lo-quy
col-lude'
col-lud'-ing
col-lu'-sion
col-lu'-sive
col-lu'-sive-ly
col-lyr'-i-um
col'-o-cynth
co-logne'
Co-lom'-bi:a
Co-lom'-bi-an
Co-lom'-bo
co'-lon
co-lon'
col'-o-nel*†
col'-o-nel-cy*†
co-lo'-ni-al
co-lon'-ic

75

col'-o-nies
col'-o-nist
col-o-ni-za'-tion
col'-o-nize
col-on-nade'
col'-o-ny
col'-o-phon
col'-o-pho-ny
col'-or
Col-o-rad'-an*†
Col-o-rad'o*†
col-or-a'-tion
col-or-a-tu'-ra*
col'-or=blind
col'-or-cast
col'-ored
col'-or-ful
col-or-im'-e-ter
col-or-im'-e-try
col'-or-ing
col'-or-ist
col'-or-less
co-los'-sal
Col-os-se'-um
Co-los'-si-an*†
co-los'-sus
co-los'-trum
col'-por'-teur
col'-ter
colt'-ish
col'-u-brine
co-lu'-go
Co-lum'-ba
col-um-ba'-ri-um
col'-um-bar:y†
Co-lum'-bi:a
col'-um-bine
co-lum'-bi-um
Co-lum'-bus
col-u-mel'-la
col'-umn
co-lum'-nar
co-lum-ni-a'-tion
col'-um-nist†
co-lure'
co'-ma
Co-man'-che
co'-ma-tose*
co'-ma-tose-ly*
co-mat'-u-lid
com'-bat (n., v.)
com-bat' (v.)
com-bat'-ant
com-bat'-ing
com-bat'-ive*†
com-bat'-ive-ness†
comb'-er
com-bi-na'-tion

com'-bi-na-tive
com-bi'-na-to'-ri-al*
com-bine' (to join)
com'-bine (n.; to harvest)
com-bin'-ing
com-bus'-ti-ble
com-bus'-tion
come'-back
co-me'-di-an
co-me'-di-enne
com'-e-dies
com'-e-dy
come'-li-ness
come'-ly
com'-er
co-mes'-ti-ble
com'-et
com'-fit
com'-fort
com'-fort-a:ble
com'-fort-a:bly
com'-fort-er
com'-fort-less
com'-ic
com'-i-cal
Com'-in-form
com'-ing
Com'-in-tern
co-mi'-tia
co-mi'-tial
com'-i-ty
com'-ma
com-mand'
com'-man-dant
com'-man-deer'
com-mand'-er
com-mand'-ing
com-mand'-ment
com-man'-do
com-man'-dos
com-mea'-sure*
com-mem'-o-rate
com-mem'-o-rat-ing
com-mem-o-ra'-tion
com-mem'-o-ra-tive
com-mence'
com-mence'-ment
com-menc'-ing
com-mend'
com-mend'-a:ble
com-men-da'-tion
com-men'-da-to-ry*†
com-men'-sal
com-men'-sal-ism
com-men-su-ra-bil'-i-ty
com-men'-su-ra-ble
com-men'-su-rate
com-men'-su-rate-ly

com-men-su-ra'-tion
com'-ment
com'-men-tar:y†
com'-men-ta-tor
com'-merce
com-mer'-cial
com-mer'-cial-ism
com-mer'-cial-ize
com-mer'-cial-ized
com-mer'-cial-ly
com-mi-na'-tion
com-min'-gle
com-min'-gling
com'-mi-nute
com-mi-nu'-tion
com-mis'-er-a-ble
com-mis'-er-ate
com-mis-er-a'-tion
com'-mis-sar
com-mis-sar'-i-at†
com'-mis-sar:y†
com-mis'-sion
com-mis'-sion-aire
com-mis'-sion-ed
com-mis'-sion-er
com'-mis-sur-al*†
com'-mis-sure
com-mit'
com-mit'-ment
com-mit'-tal
com-mit'-ted
com-mit'-tee
com-mit'-tee-man
com-mit'-ting
com-mode'
com-mo'-di-ous
com-mod'-i-ties
com-mod'-i-ty
com'-mo-dore
com'-mon
com'-mon-a:ble
com'-mon-al-ty
com'-mon-er
com'-mon-ly
com'-mon-place
com'-mon sense
com'-mon-weal
com'-mon-wealth
com-mo'-tion
com-mu'-nal
com-mune' (v.)
com'-mune (n.)
com-mu'-ni-ca-ble
com-mu'-ni-cant
com-mu'-ni-cate
com-mu'-ni-cat-ing
com-mu'-ni-ca'-tion
com-mu'-ni-ca-tive

com-mu'-ni-ca-tor
com-mu'-nion*
com-mu'-ni-qué
com'-mu-nism
com'-mu-nist
com'-mu-nis'-tic
com-mu'-ni-ties
com-mu'-ni-ty
com-mut'-a:ble
com'-mu-tate
com-mu-ta'-tion
com'-mu-ta-tor
com-mute'
com-mut'-er
com-mut'-ing
Co'-mo
co'-mose
com'-pact (n.)
com-pact' (adj., v.)
com'-pa-nies
com-pan'-ion
com-pan-ion-a:ble
com-pan'-ion-ate
com-pan'-ion-less
com-pan'-ion-ship
com-pan'-ion-way
com'-pa-ny
com'-pa-ra-ble
com-par'-a-tive
com-par'-a-tive-ly
com-par'-a-tor*†
com-pare'
com-par'-ing
com-par'-i-son
com-part'-ment
com'-pass
com'-pass-es
com-pas'-sion
com-pas'-sion-ate
com-pat-i-bil'-i-ty
com-pat'-i-ble
com-pa'-tri-ot
com'-peer
com-pel'
com-pelled'
com-pel'-ling
com-pen'-di-ous
com-pen'-di-ous-ly
com-pen'-di-um
com-pen'-sa-ble
com'-pen-sate
com'-pen-sat-ing
com-pen-sa'-tion
com-pen'-sa-tive
com-pen'-sa-tor
com-pen'-sa-to-ry
com-pete'
com'-pe-tence

com'-pe-tent
com'-pet'-ing
com-pe-ti'-tion
com-pet'-i-tive
com-pet'-i-tive-ly
com-pet'-i-tor
com-pi-la'-tion
com-pile'
com-pil'-er
com-pil'-ing
com-pla'-cence
com-pla'-cen-cy
com-pla'-cent
com-pla'-cent-ly
com-plain'
com-plain'-ant
com-plaint'
com-plai'-sance
com-plai'-sant
com'-ple-ment
com-ple-men'-tal
com-ple-men'-ta-ry
com-plete'
com-plete'-ly
com-plete'-ness
com-ple'-tion
com'-plex
com-plex'-ion
com-plex'-ioned
com-plex'-i-ty
com-pli'-a-ble
com-pli'-ance
com-pli'-ant
com'-pli-cate
com'-pli-cat-ed
com-pli-ca'-tion
com-plic'-i-ty
com-plied'
com'-pli-ment
com-pli-men'-ta-ry
com-ply'
com-ply'-ing
com-po'-nent
com-port'
com-port'-ment
com-pose'
com-posed'
com-pos'-ed-ly
com-pos'-er
com-pos'-ite
com-pos'-ite-ly
com-po-si'-tion
com-pos'-i-tor
com-pos-i-to'-ri-al
com'-post
com-po'-sure
com-po-ta'-tion
com'-pote

com'-pound (n., adj.)
com-pound' (v., adj.)
com'-pra-dor'
com-pre-hend'
com-pre-hend'-i:ble
com-pre-hen'-si-ble
com-pre-hen'-sion
com-pre-hen'-sive
com'-press (n.)
com-press' (v.)
com-pressed'
com-press'-i:ble
com-press'-ing
com-pres'-sion
com-pres'-sive
com-pres'-sor
com-prise'
com-pris'-ing
com'-pro-mise
comp-tom'-e-ter
comp-trol'-ler
com-pul'-sion
com-pul'-sive
com-pul'-so-ri-ly
com-pul'-so-ry
com-punc'-tion
com-pur-ga'-tion
com-put'-a:ble
com-pu-ta'-tion
com-pute'
com-put'-er
com-put'-ing
com-put'-ist†
com'-rade
com'-rade-ship
Comte
Comt'-i:an*†
Comt'-ism†
Co'-mus
Co'-nant
co-na'-tion
co'-na-tive*
con-cat-e-na'-tion
con'-cave
con-cav'-i-ty
con-ceal'
con-ceal'-ment
con-cede'
con-ced'-ed
con-ced'-er
con-ced'-ing
con-ceit'
con-ceit'-ed
con-ceit'-ed-ly
con-ceiv-a:bil'-i-ty
con-ceiv'-a:ble
con-ceiv'-a:bly
con-ceive'

con-ceiv'-ing
con-cen'-ter
con'-cen-trate
con'-cen-trat-ing
con'-cen-tra'-tion
con'-cen-tra-tor
con-cen'-tric
con-cen'-tri-cal
con-cen-tric'-i-ty
con'-cept
con-cep'-ta-cle
con-cep'-tion
con-cep'-tu-al
con-cern'
con-cerned'
con-cern'-ing
con-cern'-ment
con'-cert (n.)
con-cert' (v.)
con-cert'-ed
con-cer-ti'-na
con-cer'-to
con-ces'-sion
con-ces'-sion-aire'
con-ces'-sion-ar:y†
con-ces'-sive
conch
con'-cha
conch-if'-er-ous*†
conch'-i-form*†
con'-choid
con'-choi-dal
con-chol'-o-gy
con-cierge'*
con-cil'-i-a-ble
con-cil'-i-ate
con-cil'-i-at-ing
con-cil-i-a'-tion
con-cil'-i-a-tor
con-cil'-ia-to-ry*†
con-cise'
con-cise'-ly
con-cise'-ness
con-ci'-sion
con'-clave
con'-clav-ist
con-clude'
con-clud'-ing
con-clu'-sion
con-clu'-sive
con-clu'-sive-ly
con-coct'
con-coct'-er
con-coc'-tion
con-com'-i-tance
con-com'-i-tant
con'-cord (n.)
con-cord' (v.)

con-cor'-dance*
con-cor'-dant
con-cor'-dat
con'-course
con-cres'-cence
con'-crete (con-crete')
con-crete'-ly
con-cre'-tion
con-cre'-tion-ar:y†
con-cu'-bi-nage
con-cu'-bi-nar:y†
con'-cu-bine
con-cu'-pis-cence
con-cu'-pis-cent
con-cur'
con-curred'
con-cur'-rence
con-cur'-rent
con-cur'-ring
con-cus'-sion
Con-dé'
con-demn'
con-dem-na'-tion
con-dem'-na-to-ry
con-demned'
con-demn'-er
con-demn'-ing
con-dens'-a:ble*
con-den'-sate
con-den-sa'-tion
con-dense'
con-dens'-er
con-dens'-ing
con-de-scend'
con-de-scend'-ence†
con-de-scend'-ing
con-de-scend'-ing-ly
con-de-scen'-sion
con-dign'
Con-dil-lac'
con'-di-ment
con-di'-tion
con-di'-tion-al
con-di'-tion-al-ly
con-di'-tioned
con-dole'
con-do'-lence
con-dol'-ing
con-do-min'-i-um
con-don'-ance†
con-do-na'-tion
con-done'
con'-dor
con-duce'
con-du'-cive
con'-duct (n.)
con-duct' (v.)
con-duct'-ance†

con-duct'-ed
con-duc'-tion
con-duc'-tive
con-duc-tiv'-i-ty
con-duc'-tor
con'-duit
con-du'-pli-cate
con'-dy-lar
con'-dyle
con-dy-lom'-a-tous
Con'-el-rad
cone'=shaped
co'-ney
con-fab'-u-late
con-far-re-a'-tion
con-fec'-tion
con-fec'-tion-ar:y†
con-fec'-tion-er
con-fec'-tion-er:y
con-fed'-er-a-cy
con-fed'-er-ate
con-fed-er-a'-tion
con-fer'
con'-fer-ee
con'-fer-ence
con-ferred'
con-fer'-ring
con-fer'-va
con-fess'
con-fessed'
con-fess'-ed-ly
con-fes'-sion
con-fes'-sion-al
con-fes'-sor
con-fet'-ti
con'-fi-dant
con'-fi-dante
con-fide'
con-fid'-ed
con'-fi-dence
con'-fi-dent
con-fi-den'-tial
con-fi-den'-tial-ly
con'-fi-dent-ly
con-fid'-ing
con-fig-u-ra'-tion†
con-fine' (v.)
con'-fine (n.)
con-fine'-ment
con-fin'-er
con-fin'-ing
con-firm'
con-firm'-a:ble
con-fir-ma'-tion
con-fir'-ma-to-ry*†
con-firmed'
con-fis'-ca-ble
con'-fis-cate

con'-fis-cat-ing
con-fis-ca'-tion
con-fis'-ca-to-ry
con-fit'-e-or
con-fla-gra'-tion
con'-flict (n.)
con-flict' (v.)
con-flic'-tion
con-flic'-tive
con'-flu-ence
con'-flu-ent
con'-flux
con-form'
con-form'-a:ble
con-form'-ance
con-for-ma'-tion
con-form'-ist
con-form'-i-ty
con-found'
con-found'-ed-ly
con-fra-ter'-ni-ty
con-frere'
con-front'
con-fron-ta'-tion
Con-fu'-cian
Con-fu'-cian-ism
Con-fu'-cius
con-fuse'
con-fused'
con-fus'-ed-ly
con-fus'-ing
con-fu'-sion
con-fu-ta'-tion
con-fu'-ta-tive*
con-fute'
con'-ga
con-geal'
con-geal'-ment
con-ge-la'-tion
con'-ge-ner
con-ge'-nial*
con-ge-ni:al'-i-ty
con-gen'-i-tal
con'-ger
con'-ger eel
con'-ge-ries*†
con-gest'
con-gest'-ed
con-ges'-tion
con'-gi-us
con-glo-ba'-tion
con-glom'-er-ate
con-glom-er-a'-tion
con-glu-ti-na'-tion
Con'-go
con-grat'-u-lant
con-grat'-u-late
con-grat'-u-lat-ing

con-grat-u-la′-tion
con-grat′-u-la-tor
con-grat′-u-la-to-ry
con′-gre-gate
con-gre-ga′-tion
con-gre-ga′-tion-al
Con-gre-ga′-tion-al-ist
con′-gress
con-gres′-sio-nal*†
con′-gress-man
con′-gress-wom-an†
Con′-greve
con-gru′-ence
con-gru′-en-cy
con-gru′-ent
con-gru′-i-ty
con′-gru-ous
con′-ic
con′-i-cal
con′-i-cal-ly
con′-ics
co-nid′-i-al
con′-i-fer*‡
co-nif′-er-ous
co′-ni-ine
con-jec′-tur-al
con-jec′-tur-al-ly
con-jec′-ture
con-join′
con-joint′
con′-ju-gal
con′-ju-gal-ly
con′-ju-gate
con-ju-ga′-tion
con′-ju-ga-tor
con-junc′-tion
con-junc-ti′-va
con-junc′-tive
con-junc-ti-vi′-tis
con-junc′-ture
con-ju-ra′-tion
con′-jure (con-jure′)
con′-jur-er
con′-ju-ror*†
Con′-naught
con-nect′
con-nect′-ed
con-nect′-ed-ly
con-nect′-er
Con-nect′-i-cut
Con-nect′-i-cut-er
con-nec′-tion
con-nec′-tive
con-nec-tiv′-i-ty
con-nec′-tor
con-nex′-ion-al-ism
conn′-ing†
conn′-ing tow-er†

con-niv′-ance
con-nive′
con-niv′-ent†
con′-nois-seur′
con-no-ta′-tion
con′-no-ta-tive*
con′-no-ta-tive-ly*
con-note′
con-not′-ing
con-nu′-bi-al
co′-noid
co-noi′-dal
co′-no-scope
con′-quer
con′-quered
con′-quer-ing
con′-quer-or
con′-quest
con-quis′-ta-dor
Con′-rad
con-san′-guine
con-san-guin′-e:ous
con-san-guin′-i-ty
con′-science
con′-science-less
con′-science=strick′-en
con-sci-en′-tious
con-sci-en′-tious-ly
con′-scious
con′-scious-ly
con′-scious-ness
con′-script (n.)
con-script′ (v.)
con-scrip′-tion
con′-se-crate
con′-se-crat-ing
con-se-cra′-tion
con-se-cu′-tion
con-sec′-u-tive
con-sec′-u-tive-ly
con-sen′-su-al
con-sen′-sus
con-sent′
con-sen-ta′-ne-ous
con-sent′-er
con-sen′-tient
con′-se-quence
con′-se-quent
con-se-quen′-tial
con′-se-quent-ly
con-serv′-an-cy†
con-ser-va′-tion†
con-serv′-a-tism†
con-serv′-a-tive†
con-ser-va-toire′
con-ser′-va-tor
con-serv′-a-to-ry†
con-serve′

con-serv'-ing
con-sid'-er
con-sid'-er-a-ble
con-sid'-er-a-bly
con-sid'-er-ate
con-sid'-er-ate-ly
con-sid-er-a'-tion
con-sid'-ered
con-sid'-er-ing
con-sign'
con-sig-na'-tion
con'-sign-ee'
con-sign'-ment
con-sign'-or
con-sist'
con-sist'ence†
con-sist'-en-cy†
con-sist'-ent†
con-sist'-ent-ly†
con'-sis-to'-ri-al
con-sis'-to-ry
con-so-la'-tion
con-sol'-a-to-ry
con-sole' (v.)
con'-sole (n.)
con-sol'-i-date
con-sol'-i-dat-ing
con-sol-i-da'-tion
con-sol'-ing
con-sol'-ing-ly
con'-som-mé'
con'-so-nance
con'-so-nan-cy
con'-so-nant
con'-so-nan'-tal
con'-so-nant-ly
con-sort' (v.)
con'-sort (n.)
con-sor'-ti-um
con-spec'-tus
con-spic'-u-ous
con-spic'-u-ous-ly
con-spir'-a-cy
con-spir'-a-tor
con-spir'-a-to'-ri-al
con-spire'
con-spir'-ing
con'-sta-ble
con-stab'-u-lar:y†
Con'-stance
con'-stan-cy
con'-stant
Con'-stan-tine
Con'-stan-ti-no'-ple
con'-stel-late
con'-stel-la'-tion
con'-ster-nate

con-ster-na'-tion
con'-sti-pate
con'-sti-pat-ed
con-sti-pa'-tion
con-stit'-u-en-cy
con-stit'-u-ent
con'-sti-tute
con-sti-tu'-tion
con-sti-tu'-tion-al
con-sti-tu-tion-al'-i-ty
con-sti-tu'-tion-al-ly
con'-sti-tu-tive
con-strain'
con-strained'
con-strain'-ing
con-straint'
con-strict'
con-stric'-tion
con-stric'-tive
con-stric'-tor
con-strin'-gent
con-struct' (v.)
con'-struct (n.)
con-struc'-tion
con-struc'-tive
con-struc'-tive-ly
con-struc'-tor
con-strue'
con-strued'
con-stru'-ing
con'-sue-tude
con-sue-tu'-di-nar:y†
con'-sul
con'-sul-ar*†
con'-sul-ate*†
con'-sul-ship
con-sult'
con-sul'-tant*
con-sul-ta'-tion
con-sul'-ta-tive*†
con-sum'-a:ble
con-sume'
con-sumed'
con-sum'-ed-ly
con-sum'-er
con-sum'-ing
con-sum'-mate (adj.)
con'-sum-mate (v., adj.)
con-sum-ma'-tion
con-sump'-tion
con-sump'-tive
con'-tact
con'-tac-tor
con-ta'-gion
con-ta'-gious
con-ta'-gious-ly
con-tain'
con-tain'-er

con-tain'-ing
con-tain'-ment
con-tam'-i-nant
con-tam'-i-nate
con-tam'-i-nat-ed
con-tam'-i-nat-ing
con-tam-i-na'-tion
con-tang'o*†
con-temn'
con-temn'-er†
con-tem'-nor
con-tem'-per
con-tem'-pla-ble
con'-tem-plate
con'-tem-plat-ing
con-tem-pla'-tion
con-tem'-pla-tive
con-tem-po-ra'-ne-ous
con-tem'-po-rar-y†
con-tem'-po-rize
con-tempt'
con-tempt'-i:ble
con-tempt'-i:bly
con-temp'-tu-ous
con-temp'-tu-ous-ly
con-tend'
con-tend'-er
con-tent' (adj., v., n.)
con'-tent (n.)
con-tent'-ed
con-tent'-ed-ly
con-ten'-tion
con-ten'-tious
con-ten'-tious-ly
con-tent'-ment
con'-tents
con-ter'-mi-nous
con-ter'-mi-nous-ly
con'-test (n.)
con-test' (v.)
con-test'-a:ble
con-tes'-tant*
con-tes-ta'-tion
con'-text
con-tex'-tu-al
con-tex'-ture
con-ti-gu'-i-ty
con-tig'-u-ous
con-tig'-u-ous-ly
con'-ti-nence
con'-ti-nent
con-ti-nen'-tal
con-tin'-gen-cy
con-tin'-gent
con-tin'-u-al
con-tin'-u-al-ly
con-tin'-u-ance
con-tin-u-a'-tion

con-tin'-u-a-tive
con-tin'-ue
con-tin'-u-ing
con-ti-nu'-i-ty
con-tin'-u-ous
con-tin'-u-ous-ly
con-tin'-u-um
con-tort'
con-tor'-tion
con-tor'-tion-ist
con-tor'-tive
con'-tour
con'-tra-band
con'-tra-band-ist
con'-tra-bass
con'-tra-cep'-tion
con'-tra-cep'-tive
con'-tract (n., v.)
con-tract' (v.)
con-tract'-ed
con-tract'-ile*†
con-trac-til'-i-ty
con-trac'-tion
con-trac'-tor
con-trac'-tu-al
con-tra-dict'
con-tra-dic'-tion
con-tra-dic'-to-ri-ly
con-tra-dic'-to-ry
con-tra-dis-tinc'-tion
con-tra-in'-di-cate
con-tral'-to
con-trap'-tion
con-tra-pun'-tal
con-tra-ri'-e-ty
con'-trar-i-ness*†
con'-trar:i-wise*†
con'-trar:y*†
con-trast' (v.)
con'-trast (n.)
con-tra-vene'
con-tra-ven'-tion
con-tre-danse'
con'-tre-temps
con-trib'-ute
con-trib'-ut-ing
con-tri-bu'-tion
con-trib'-u-tor
con-trib'-u-to-ry
con-trite'
con-trite'-ly
con-tri'-tion
con-triv'-ance†
con-trive'
con-triv'-er
con-triv'-ing
con-trol'
con-trol'-la-ble

83

con-trolled'
con-trol'-ler
con-trol'-ling
con-tro-ver'-sial
con'-tro-ver-sy
con'-tro-vert
con-tro-vert'-i:ble
con-tu-ma'-cious
con'-tu-ma-cy
con-tu-me'-li-ous
con'-tu-me-ly
con-tuse'
con-tu'-sion
co-nun'-drum
con-va-lesce'
con-va-les'-cence
con-va-les'-cent
con-va-lesc'-ing
con-vect'
con-vec'-tion
con-vec'-tor
con-vene'
con-ve'-nience*
con-ve'-nient*
con-ve'-nient-ly*
con-ven'-ing
con'-vent
con-ven'-ti-cle
con-ven'-tion
con-ven'-tion-al
con-ven'-tion-al'-i-ty
con-ven'-tu-al
con-verge'
con-ver'-gence
con-ver'-gent
con-verg'-ing
con-vers'-a:ble
con-ver'-sant
con-ver-sa'-tion
con-ver-sa'-tion-al
con-ver-sa'-tion-al-ist
con'-verse (n., adj.)
con-verse' (v., adj.)
con-verse'-ly
con-vers'-ing
con-ver'-sion
con-ver'-sive
con'-vert (n.)
con-vert' (v.)
con-vert'-er
con-vert'-i:ble
con-ver'-tor†
con'-vex
con-vex'-i-ty
con-vey'
con-vey'-ance
con-vey'-anc-er
con-vey'-ing

con'-vict (n.)
con-vict' (v.)
con-vic'-tion
con-vince'
con-vinc'-ing
con-vinc'-ing-ly
con-viv'-i-al
con-viv-i-al'-i-ty
con-vo-ca'-tion
con-voke'
con-vok'-ing
con'-vo-lute
con-vo-lu'-tion
con-vol-vu-la'-ceous
con-vol'-vu-lus
con'-voy
con'-voyed
con'-voy-ing
con-vulse'
con-vul'-sion
con-vul'-sion-ar:y†
con-vul'-sive
con-vul'-sive-ly
coo'-ing
cook'-book
cook'-er
cook'-er:y
cook'-ie
cook'-stove
cool'-er
cool=head-ed
Coo'-lidge*
coo'-lie
cool'-ly
cool'-ness
coon'-skin
coop'-er†
coop'-er-age†
co-op'-er-ate
co-op-er-a'-tion
co-op'-er-a-tive
co-op'-er-a-tor
coop'-er:y
co=opt'
co-or'-di-nate
co-or-di-na'-tion
co-or'-di-na-tor
coot'-ie
co-pai'-ba
co'-pal
co-part'-ner-ship
Co-pen-ha'-gen
co'-pe-pod
Co-per'-ni-can
Co-per'-ni-cus
cop'-i-er
cop'-ies
co-pi'-lot

cop'-ing
co'-pi-ous
co'-pi-ous-ly
co'-pi-ous-ness
cop'-per
cop'-per-as
cop'-per=col'-ored
cop'-per-head
cop'-per-plate
cop'-per-smith
cop'-per-ware
cop'-per:y
cop'-pice
co'-pra*†
copse
Cop'-tic
cop'-u-la
cop'-u-late
cop-u-la'-tion
cop'-u-la-tive
cop'y
cop'y-book
cop'y-hold-er
cop'y-ing
cop'y-ist
cop'y-right
coque'-li-cot
co-quet'
co'-quet-ry
co-quette'
co-quet'-ting
co-quett'-ish†
co-qui'-na
Co'-ra
cor-a-cid'-i-um
cor'-a-cite
cor'-a-cle
cor'-al
cor'-al-ine
cor'-al-loid
cor'-ban
cor'-bel
cord
cord'-age
cor'-date
cord'-ed
Cor-de'-lia*
cor'-dial
cor-dial'-i-ty
cor'-dial-ly
cor-dil-le'-ra
cord'-ite
Cór'-do-ba
cor'-don
cor'-do-van
cor'-du-roy
cord'-wood

core
co-re-la'-tion
co-re-op'-sis
cor'-er
Cor'-fu
co-ri-a'-ceous
co-ri-an'-der
Cor'-inth
Co-rin'-thi-an
Co-ri-o'-lis*
co'-ri-um
cork'=lined
cork'-screw
cork'-wood
corm
cor'-mo-phyte
cor'-mo-rant
cor'-mose
cor'-mus
cor-na'-ceous
corn bread
corn'-cob
cor'-ne:a
cor'-ne-al
corned
Cor-neille'
cor'-nel
Cor-ne'-lia*
cor-ne'-lian*
Cor-ne'-lius*
cor'-ne-ous
cor'-ner (angle)
corn'-er (one who corns)
cor'-ner-stone
cor'-ner-wise
cor-net'
cor-net'-ist
corn'-field
corn'-flow-er
corn'-husk-ing
cor'-nice
Cor'-nish
corn pone
corn'-stalk
corn'-starch
cor-nu-co'-pi:a
Corn'-wall
Corn-wal'-lis
co-rol'-la
cor'-ol-lar:y†
co-ro'-na
cor'-o-nach
Cor-o-na'-do
cor'-o-nal*
cor'-o-nar:y†
cor-o-na'-tion
cor'-o-ner

85

cor'-o-net'
Co-rot'
cor'-po-ral
cor-po-ral'-i-ty
cor'-po-rate
cor-po-ra'-tion
cor-po'-re-al
cor-po-re'-i-ty
corps
corpse
cor'-pu-lence
cor'-pu-lent
cor'-pus
Cor'-pus Chris'-ti
cor'-pus-cle
cor-pus'-cu-lar
cor'-pus de-lic'-ti
cor-ral'
cor-rect'
cor-rec'-tant*
cor-rec'-tion
cor-rec'-tion-al
cor-rec'-ti-tude*
cor-rec'-tive
cor-rect'-ly
cor-rec'-tor
Cor-reg'-gio
Cor-reg'-i-dor
cor'-re-late
cor-re-la'-tion
cor-rel'-a-tive
cor-re-spond'
cor-re-spon'-dence*
cor-re-spon'-dent*
cor-re-spond'-ing
cor-re-spon'-sive
cor'-ri-dor
cor-ri-gen'-dum
cor'-ri-gi-ble
cor-rob'-o-rate
cor-rob-o-ra'-tion
cor-rob'-o-ra-tive
cor-rob'-o-ra-tor
cor-rob'-o-ra-to-ry
cor-rob'-o-ree
cor-rode'
cor-rod'-i-ble
cor-rod'-ing
cor-ro'-sion
cor-ro'-sive
cor'-ru-gate
cor'-ru-gat-ed
cor-ru-ga'-tion
cor-rupt'
cor-rupt'-er
cor-rupt'-i:ble
cor-rup'-tion
cor-rup'-tive

cor-sage'
cor'-sair
corse'-let (piece of armor)
cor-se-let'† (foundation garment)
cor'-set
Cor'-si-ca
Cor'-si-can
cor'-tege
cor'-tes
cor'-tex
cor'-ti-cal
cor'-ti-cate
cor-ti-cos'-ter-one
cor'-ti-sone
co-run'-dum
co-rus'-cant
cor'-us-cate
cor-us-ca'-tion
cor'-vée
cor-vette'
cor'-vine
Cor'-y-bant
co-ryd'-a-lis
Cor'-y-don
cor'-ymb
cor'-ym-bose*†
cor-y-phae'-us
cor'-y-phée'*†
co-ry'-za
co-se'-cant
co-seis'-mal
Cos'-grave
co-sig'-na-to-ry
co'-sine
cos-met'-ic
cos'-mic
cos'-mi-cal-ly
cos-mog'-o-ny
cos-mog'-ra-pher
cos-mog'-ra-phy
cos-mo-log'-i-cal
cos-mol'-o-gy
cos'-mo-naut
cos-mo-pol'-i-tan
cos-mop'-o-lite
cos-mo-ra'-ma
cos'-mos
Cos'-sack
cos'-set
cos'-tal
cos'-tard
Cos'-ta Ri'-ca
cos'-ter (street seller)
cost'-er (one who finds costs)
cos'-ter-mong-er*†
cos'-tive

cost'-li-ness
cost'-ly
cos'-trel
cos'-tume
cos'-tum-er
cos-tum-ier'†
co-tan'-gent
co-tan-gen'-tial
co-ten'-an-cy
co'-te-rie
co-ter'-mi-nous
co-thur'-nus
co-til'-lion
Cots'-wold
cot'-tage
cot'-tag-er
cot'-ter
cot'-ti-er
cot'-ton
cot'-ton-seed
cot'-ton-tail
cot'-ton-wood
cot'-ton:y
cot-y-le'-don
couch'-ant
cou'-gar
cou'-lee
cou-lisse'
cou'-lomb
cou'-ma
cou'-ma-rin
cou'-ma-rone
coun'-cil
coun'-cil-man
coun'-sel
coun'-sel-or*
coun'-te-nance
coun'-ter (against)
count'-er (computer)
coun'-ter-act'
coun'-ter-at-tack'
coun'-ter-bal-ance
coun'-ter-check
coun'-ter-claim
coun'-ter-clock'-wise
coun'-ter-es-pi-o-nage
coun'-ter-feit
coun'-ter-feit-er
coun'-ter-foil
coun'-ter-ir'-ri-tant
coun'-ter-mand
coun'-ter-march
coun'-ter-mine
coun'-ter-pane
coun'-ter-part
coun'-ter-plot
coun'-ter-point
coun'-ter-poise

coun'-ter-rev-o-lu'-tion
coun'-ter-shaft
coun'-ter-sign
coun'-ter-sink
coun'-ter-weight
count'-ess
coun'-ties
count'-ing-house
count'-less
coun'-tries
coun'-tri-fied
coun'-try
coun'-try house
coun'-try-man
coun'-try-seat
coun'-try-side
coun'-try-wom-an†
count'-ship
coun'-ty
coup' d'e:tat'
cou-pé'
coupe
cou'-ple†
cou'-pler†
cou'-plet†
cou'-pling†
cou'-pon
cour'-age
cou-ra'-geous
cou-rante'
cou'-ri-er*
course
cours'-er
cour'-te-ous
cour'-te-san
cour'-te-sy
court'-house
cour'-tier*†
court'-li-ness
court'-ly
court'=mar-tial
court'-room
court'-ship
court'-yard
cous'-in
cous'-in=ger'-man
cous'-in-ry
cou-ture'
cou-tu'-rier
co-var'-i-ance†
co-var'-i-ant†
cov'-e-nant
cov'-e-nan-ter*†
cov'-e-nan-tor
Cov'-en-try
cov'-er
cov'-er-age
cov'-ered

87

cov'-er-let
cov'-ert
cov'-er-ture
cov'-et
cov'-e-tous*†
cov'-e-tous-ness*†
cov'-ey
cow'-ard
cow'-ard-ice
cow'-bane
cow'-bell
cow'-bird
cow'-boy
cow'-catch-er
cow'-er
cow'-herd
cow'-hide
Cow'-ley
cow'-lick
cowl'-ing
co'=work'-er
cow'-path
Cow'-per
cow'-pox
cow'-punch-er
cow'-rie
cow'-shed
cow'-slip
cox'a
cox-al'-gia
cox'-comb
cox-comb'-i-cal
cox'-comb-ry
cox'-swain
coy'-ness
coy'-ote†
co-yo-til'-lo
coy'-pu
coz'-en
coz'-en-age
co'-zi-est
co'-zi-ly
co'-zy
crab ap'-ple
crab'-bed
crab'-bing
crab'-by
crab'-grass
crack'-down
crack'-er
crack'-ing
crack'-le
crack'-ling
crack'=up
Cra'-cow
cra'-dle
cra'-dling
craft'-i-ly

craft'-i-ness
crafts'-man
crafts'-man-ship
craft'y
crag'-gi-ness
crag'-gy
cram
crammed
cram'-ming
cramped
cram'-pon
cran'-ber-ry
craned
cra'-ni-al
cran'-ing
cra-ni-ol'-o-gy
cra-ni-om'-e-ter
cra'-ni-um
crank'-case
crank'-i-ness
crank'y
Cran'-mer
cran'-nied
cran'-ny
crap'-pie
crap'-u-lous
crashed
cra'-sis
crass'-ly
cras-su-la'-ceous
Cras'-sus
cra'-ter (volcano)
crat'-er (one who crates)
crat'-ing
cra-vat'
cra'-ven
Cra-ven-ette'
crav'-ing
craw'-fish
crawl'-ing
crawl'y
cray'-fish
cray'-on
crazed
cra'-zi-ly
cra'-zi-ness
craz'-ing
cra'-zy
creak
creak'y
cream'=col-ored
cream'-er
cream'-er-y
cream'y
creased
creas'-ing
cre-ate'
cre'-a:tine

cre-at'-ing
cre-a'-tion
cre-a'tive
cre-a'tive-ly
cre-a'tor
crea'-tur-al
crea'-ture
crèche
Cré-cy
cre'-dence
cre-den'-tial
cred-i-bil'-i-ty
cred'-i-ble
cred'-it
cred'-it-a:ble
cred'-i-tor
cre'-do
cre'-dos
cre-du'-li-ty
cred'-u-lous
creek
creep'-er
creep'-ing
creep'y
cre'-mate
cre-ma'-tion
cre'-ma-to-ry
Cre-mo'-na
cre'-nate
cre-na'-tion
cren'-a-ture
cren'-el-late
cren'-el-lat-ed
cren'-u-lat-ed
cren-u-la'-tion
Cre'-ole
cre'-o-sol
cre'-o-sote
crepe
crepe de chine
crep'-i-tant
crep'-i-tate
cre-pus'-cu-lar
cre-pus'-cule
cre-scen'-do†
cres'-cent
cres'-sol
cres'-set
Cres'-si-da
cres'-sy
crest'-ed
crest'-fall-en
cres'-yl†
cre-syl'-ic
cre-ta'-ceous
Cre'-tan
cre'-tin
cre'-tin-ism

cre'-tonne
cre-vasse'
crev'-ice
crew'-el
crib'-bage
crib'-bing
crib'-work
Crich'-ton
crick'-et
crick'-et-er
cri'-coid
cried
cri'-er
Cril'-lon
Cri-me'a
Cri-me'-an
crim'-i-nal
crim-i-nal'-i-ty
crim'-i-nate
crim-i-no-log'-i-cal
crim-i-nol'-o-gist
crim-i-nol'-o-gy
crim'-son
cringe
cringed
cring'-ing
crin'-gle
cri'-nite
crin'-kle
crin'-kly
cri'-noid
crin'-o-line
cri'-num
crip'-ple
crip'-pled
crip'-pling
cri'-ses
cri'-sis
cris'-pate
Cris'-pin
crisp'-ing
crisp'-ly
crisp'-ness
crisp'y
criss'-cross
cris'-tate
Cris-to'-bal
cri-te'-ri-on
crit'-ic
crit'-i-cal
crit'-ic-as-ter
crit'-i-cism
crit'-i-cize
crit'-i-ciz-ing
cri-tique'
croak'-er
Croat*†
Cro-a'-tia

Cro-a′-tian
cro-chet′
cro-cheted′
cro-chet′-er
cro-chet′-ing
cro-cid′-o-lite
crock′-er:y
Crock′-ett
croc′-o-dile
croc′-o-dil′-i:an
croc′-o-ite*†
cro′-cus
Croe′-sus
Croix de guerre
Cro=Mag′-non†
Cro′-mer
crom′-lech
Crom′-well
Cro′-nus
cro′-ny
crook′-ed
crooked
croon′-er
crop′-per
crop′-ping
cro-quet′
cro-quette′
cro′-qui-gnole
cro′-sier
cross′-bar
cross′-bill (bird)
cross=bill (bill of
  exchange)
cross′-bones
cross′-bow
cross′-bow-man
cross′-bred
cross′-breed
cross=coun′-try
cross′-cut
cross=ex-am-i-na′-tion
cross=ex-am′-ine
cross=eyed
cross=grained
cross′=ing
cross=leg-ged
cross′-let
cross′-ly
cross-o:ver
cross′-piece
cross=pol′-li-nate
cross=pol-li-na′-tion
cross=ques′-tion
cross=ref′-er-ence
cross′-road
cross sec′-tion
cross=stitch
cross′-tree

cross′-walk
cross′-ways
cross′-wise
cross′-word
crotch′-et
crotch′-et:y
cro′-ton
crou′-pi-er
croup′-ous
crou′-ton
crow′-bar
crowd′-ed
crow′-foot
crow′-ing
crowned
Croy′-don
croz′-er
cru′-ces
cru′-cial
cru′-ci-ate
cru′-ci-ble
cru′-ci-fer
cru-cif′-er-ous
cru′-ci-fied
cru′-ci-fix
cru-ci-fix′-ion
cru′-ci-form
cru′-ci-fy
crude′-ly
cru′-di-ty
cru′-el
cru′-el-ly
cru′-el-ty
cru′-et
cruised
cruis′-er
cruis′-ing
crul′-ler
crum′-ble
crum′-bling
crum′-bly
crum′-pet
crum′-ple
crum′-pling
crunch′-ing
crup′-per
cru′-ral
cru-sade′
cru-sad′-er
cru-sad′-ing
cruse
Cru′-soe
Crus-ta′-cea
crus-ta′-cean
crus-ta′-ceous
crust′-ed
crust′y
crux

cru-zei'-ro
cry
cry'-ing
cry'-o-gen
cry-o-gen'-ics
cry'-o-lite
cry'-o-phil'-ic
cry'-o-tron
crypt-a:nal'-y-sis†
cryp'-tic
cryp'-to-gam
cryp'-to-gram
cryp-tog'-ra-pher
cryp-tog'-ra-phy
crys'-tal
crys'-tal-line
crys-tal-lin'-i-ty
crys'-tal-lite
crys-tal-li-za'-tion
crys'-tal-lize
crys'-tal-loid
cten'-oid*
cte-tol'-o-gy
Cu'-ba
Cu'-ban
cub'-by-hole
cu'-beb
cubed
cu'-bic
cu'-bi-cal
cu'-bi-cal-ly
cu'-bi-cle
cu-bic'-u-lum
cub'-ism
cub'-ist
cu'-bit
cu'-bi-tal
cu'-bi-tus
cuck'-old
cuck'-oo
cu'-cul-late
cu'-cum-ber
cud'-dle
cud'-dled
cud'-dling
cud'-gel*†
cud'-gel-er*†
cui-rass'
cui'-ras-sier'
cui-sine'
cuisse
cul'=de=sac
Cu-le'-bra
cu'-let
Cu'-lex
cul'-i-nar:y*†
cull'-ing
cul'-lion

cul-mif'-er-ous
cul'-mi-nate
cul-mi-na'-tion
cu-lotte'
cul-pa-bil'-i-ty
cul'-pa-ble
cul'-prit
cul'-ti-va-ble
cul'-ti-vate
cul'-ti-vat-ed
cul-ti-va'-tion
cul'-ti-va-tor
cul'-tur-al
cul'-ture
cul'-tured
cul'-ve-rin*†
cul'-vert
cum'-ber
Cum'-ber-land
cum'-ber-some
cum'-brous
cu'-mene
cu'-me-nyl
cu'-mic
cu'-mi-dine
cum'-in
cum lau'-de
cum'-mer-bund
Cum'-mings
cu'-mu-late
cu-mu-la'-tion
cu'-mu-la-tive
cu'-mu-lus
cunc-ta'-tion
cu'-ne-al
cu-ne'-i-form
cun'-ning
cup'-bear-er
cup'-board
cup'-cake
cu-pel'
cup'-ful
Cu'-pid
cu-pid'-i-ty
cup'-like
cu'-po-la
cup'-ping
cu-pram-mo'-ni-um
cu'-pre-ous
cu'-pric
cu-prif'-er-ous
cu'-pro-cy'-a-nide
cu'-pro-nick'-el
cu-prous
cup'=shaped
cur-a:bil'-i-ty
cur'-a:ble
Cu'-ra-cao'

91

cu'-ra-cy
cu-ra'-re
cu'-rate
cu'-ra-tive*†
cu-ra'-tor
curb'-ing
curb'-stone
cur-cu'-li:o
cur'-cu-ma
cur'-dle
cur'-dling
curd'y
cure
cure'=all
cure'-less
cu-rett'-age*†
cur'-few
cu'-ri:a
Cu-rie'
cur'-ing
cu'-ri:o
cu-ri-o'-sa
cu-ri-os'-i-ty
cu'-ri-ous
cu'-ri-um
cur'-lew
cur'-li-cue*†
curl'-i-ness
curl'-ing
curl'y
cur-mud'-geon*†
cur'-rant
cur'-ren-cy
cur'-rent
cur'-ri-cle
cur-ric'-u-lar
cur-ric'-u-lum
cur'-ried
cur'-ri-er
cur'-ri-er:y
cur'-ry
cur'-ry-comb
cur'-ry-ing
cursed
curs'-ing
cur'-sive
cur'-so-ry
cur-tail'
cur-tail'-ment
cur'-tain
cur'-tal
Cur'-ti-us
curt'-ly
curt'-sy
cu'-rule
cur-va'-ceous
cur'-va-ture

curved
cur'-vet'
cur-vet'-ted
cur'-vi-lin'-e:ar
curv'-ing
cur-vom'-e-ter*
cu-shaw'
Cush'-ing
cush'-ion
cus'-pate
cus'-pi-dal
cus'-pi-date
cus'-pi-dor
cuss'-ed-ness
cus'-tard
Cus'-ter
cus-to'-di-al
cus-to'-di-an
cus'-to-dy
cus'-tom
cus'-tom-ar'-i-ly†
cus'-tom-ar:y†
cus'-tom-er
cus'-tom-house
cus'-tom=made
cus'-tu-mal†
cu-ta'-ne-ous
cut'-a:way
cut glass
cu'-ti-cle
cu-tic'-u-lar
cu'-tin
cu'-tis
cut'-lass
cut'-ler
cut'-ler:y
cut'-let
cut'-off
cut'-out
cut'-purse
cut=rate
cut'-ter
cut'-throat
cut'-ting
cut'-tle
cut'-tle-fish
cut'-wa-ter
cut'-worm
Cu-vier'
cy-an'-a-mide*
cy-an'-ic
cy-a-ni-da'-tion
cy'-a-nide
cy-an'-o-gen
cy-a-nom'-e-try
cy-a-no'-sis
cy-a-not'-ic
cy-a-nu'-ric†

Cyb'-e-le
cy-ber-net'-ics
cy-ca-da'-ceous*†
Cyc'-la-des
cy'-cla-men*†
cy'-cle
cy'-clic†
cy'-cli-cal†
cy'-cling
cy'-clist
cy'-cloid
cy-cloi'-dal
cy-clom'-e-ter
cy'-clone
cy-clon'-ic
cy'-clo-pe'-an
cy-clo-pe'-di:a
Cy'-clops
cy-clo-ra'-ma
cy-clo-thy'-mi:a
cy'-clo-tron
cyg'-net
cyl'-in-der
cy-lin'-dri-cal
cy'-ma-rose
cy-ma'-ti-um
cym'-bal
Cym'-be-line
cyme
cy'-mo-gene
cy'-mo-graph
cy'-mose
cy-mot'-ri-chous
Cym'-ry
cyn'-ic
cyn'-i-cal
cyn'-i-cism
cy'-no-sure
Cyn'-thi:a
cyp-er-a'-ceous*†
cy pres
cy'-press
Cyp'-ri-an
cy-prin'-o-dont
cyp'-ri-noid
Cyp'-ri-ot
cyp-ri-pe'-di-um
Cy'-prus
Cy'-ra-no
Cyr-e-na'-ic*†
Cy-re'-ne
Cyr'-il
cy-ril'-lic
Cy'-rus
cyst
cys'-tic*
cys-ti-cer'-cus
cys'-tine

cys-ti'-tis
cys'-toid
cys-to'-ma
cy-tas'-ter
Cyth-er-e'a†
cy-to-ge-net'-ics
cy'-to-ki-ne'-sis
cy-tol'-o-gy
cy'-to-plasm
czar
czar'-e-vitch
cza-rev'-na
cza-ri'-na
czar'-ism
Czech
Czech'-o-slo'-vak
Czech'-o-slo-va'-ki:a
Czech'-o-slo-va'-ki-an*

D

dab'-bing
dab'-ble
dab'-bling
dab'-ster
da ca'-po
dachs'-hund
Da'-cia
Da'-cian
da-coit'
da-coit'y
Da'-cron
dac'-tyl
dac-tyl'-ic
dac-ty-li'-tis
dac-tyl'-o-gram*†
dac-ty-log'-ra-phy
dac-ty-lol'-o-gy
dad'-dy
da'-do
Daed'-a-lus
dae'-mon
dae-mon'-ic
daf'-fo-dil
dag'-ger
Da'-ghe-stan'†
Da'-go
Da'-gon
da-guerre'-o-type
da-ha-be'-ah
dahl'-ia†
Da-ho'-mey
dai'-lies
dai'-ly
dain'-ties
dain'-ti-ly
dain'-ti-ness

dain'-ty
Dai-ren'
dair'-ies†
dairy'y†
dairy'y-ing†
dairy'y-man†
da'-is
dai'-sies
dai'-sy
Da-kar'†
Da'-kin
Da-ko'-ta
Da-la-dier'
Dal-e-car'-li-an*†
Dal'-las
dal'-li-ance
dal'-lied
dal'-ly
dal'-ly-ing
Dal-ma'-tia
Dal-ma'-tian
dal-mat'-ic
Dal'-ton
dam
dam'-age
dam'-ag-ing-ly
dam'-an
dam'-a-scene†
Da-mas'-cus
dam'-ask
dam'-mar
dammed
dam'-ming
damn
dam'-na-ble
dam-na'-tion
damned
damn'-ing†
damn'-ing-ly†
Dam'-o-cles
Da'-mon
damp'-en
damp'-en-er
damp'-er
damp'-ing
damp'-ish
dam'-sel
dam'-son
Da'-na
Dan'-a:e†
danced
danc'-er
danc'-ing
dan'-de-li-on
dan'-der
dan'-di-fied
dan'-di-fy
dan'-dle

dan'-druff
dan'-dy
dan'-ger
dan'-ger-ous
dan'-ger-ous-ly
dan'-gle
dan'-gled
dan'-gler
dan'-gling
Dan'-iel
Dan'-ish
dank'-ness
dan-seuse'
Dan'-te
Dan'-te-an
Dan-tesque'
Dan'-ube
Da-nu'-bi-an
Dan'-ville
Dan'-zig
Daph'-ne
dap'-per
dap'-ple
Dar-da-nelles'
dare'-dev-il
dar'-ic
Dar-i-en'†
dar'-ing
Da-ri'-us
Dar-jee'-ling
dark'-en
dark horse
dar'-kle
dark'-ly
dark'-ness
dark'-room
dark'y
dar'-ling
Darm'-stadt
dar'-nel
Dart'-mouth
Dar'-win
Dar-win'-i-an
dash'-board
dashed
da-sheen'
dash'-er
dash'-ing
das'-tard
das'-tard-ly
da'-ta
da'-ta-ry
dat'-ed
date'-less
dat'-ing
da'-tive
da'-tum
Da-tu'-ra

daub'-er
daub'-er:y
Dau-det'
daugh'-ter
daugh'-ter=in=law
daunt'-less
daunt'-less-ly
dau'-phin
Dav'-e-nant
dav'-en-port
Da'-vid
Da'-vis
da'-vi-son-ite
da'-vit*†
daw'-dle
daw'-dler
daw'-dling
Daw'-son
day'-book
day'-break
day coach
day'-dream
day la'-bor-er
day let'-ter
day'-light
day'-spring
day'-star
day'-time
Day'-ton
Day-to'-na
dazed
daz'-ed-ly
daz'-ing
daz'-zle
daz'-zling
daz'-zling-ly
dea'-con
dea'-con-ate
dea'-con-ess
dead'-en
dead'-eye
dead'-fall
dead'-head
dead'-li-er
dead'-light
dead'-line
dead'-li-ness
dead'-lock
dead'-ly
dead reck'-on-ing
dead'-wood
deaf'-en
deaf'-en-ing
deaf'-en-ing-ly
deaf'=mute
deaf'-ness
deal'-er
deal'-ing

dealt
dean'-er:y
Dear'-born
dear'-ie
dear'-ly
dear'-ness
dearth
death'-bed
death'-blow
death'=deal-ing
death'-less
death'-like
death'-ly
death mask
death rate
death's'=head
death war'-rant
death'-watch
de-ba'-cle†
de-bar'
de-bar-ka'-tion
de-bar'-ment
de-bar'-ring
de-base'
de-based'
de-base'-ment
de-bas'-ing
de-bat'-a:ble
de-bate'
de-bat'-er
de-bat'-ing
de-bauch'
de-bauch'-ee*†
de-bauch'-er
de-bauch'-er:y
de-ben'-ture
de-bil'-i-tate
de-bil'-i-tat-ed
de-bil-i-ta'-tion
de-bil'-i-ty
deb'-it
deb'-o-nair'
Deb'-o-rah
dé-bou-ché'
de-bris'
debt'-or
de-bunk'
de'-but
deb'-u-tante†
dec'-ade
dec'-a-dence*†
dec'-a-dent*†
dec'-a-gon
dec'-a-gram
dec'-a-he'-dron
de-cal-co-ma'-ni:a
de-ca-les'-cence
dec'a-li-ter

95

dec'-a-logue
De-cam'-er-on
de-cam'-e-ter† (verse form)
dec'a-me-ter (10 meters)
de-camp'
de-camp'-ment
de-ca-nal† (of a dean)
dec'-a-nal (chemical compound)
dec'-ane
de-cant'
de-can-ta'-tion
de-cant'-er
de-cap'-i-tate
de-cap-i-ta'-tion
dec'-a-pod
De-cap'-o-lis
dec'-are
dec'a-stere
de-cath'-lon†
De-ca'-tur
de-cay'
de-cayed'
de-cay'-ing
Dec'-can
de-cease'
de-ceased'
de-ce'-dent
de-ceit'
de-ceit'-ful
de-ceit'-ful-ness
de-ceive'
de-ceiv'-er
de-ceiv'-ing-ly
de-cel'-er-ate
de-cel-er-a'-tion
De-cem'-ber
de-cem'-vir
de'-cen-cy
dec'-ene†
de-cen'-na-ry
de-cen'-ni-al
de-cen'-ni-al-ly
de'-cent
de'-cent-er (adj., comp. of decent)
de-cen'-ter (to place off center)
de'-cent-ly
de-cen-tral-i-za'-tion
de-cen'-tral-ize
de-cep'-tion
de-cep'-tive
dec'-i-bel
de-cide'
de-cid'-ed-ly
de-cid'-u:a

de-cid'-u-ous
de-cid'-u-ous-ly
dec'i-gram
dec'-ile
dec'-i-mal
dec'-i-mate
dec-i-ma'-tion
dec'-i-me-ter
de-ci'-pher
de-ci'-pher-a:ble
de-ci'-sion
de-ci'-sive
de-ci'-sive-ly
dec'-i-stere
deck'-le
de-claim'
dec-la-ma'-tion
de-clam'-a-to-ry
dec-la-ra'-tion
de-clar'-a-tive
de-clar'-a-to-ry
de-clare'
de-clas'-si-fy
de-clen'-sion
de-clin'-a:ble
dec-li-na'-tion
de-clin'-a-to-ry†
de-cline'
de-clined'
de-clin'-ing
dec-li-nom'-e-ter
de-cliv'-i-tous
de-cliv'-i-ty
de-cli'-vous†
de-coc'-tion
de-code'
de-cod'-ing
dé-col-le-tage'
dé-col-le-té'
de-col'-or-ize
de-com-pose'
de-com-po-si'-tion
de-con-tam'-i-nate
de-con-tam-i-na'-tion
de-cor'
dec'-o-rate
dec-o-ra'-tion
dec'-o-ra-tive
dec'-o-ra-tor
dec'-o-rous†
de-co'-rum
de-coy'
de-coyed'
de-coy'-ing
de'-crease (n.)
de-crease' (v.)
de-cree'
de-creed'

de-cree'-ing
dec'-re-ment
de'-crem-e-ter
de-crep'-it
de-crep'-i-tate
de-crep'-i-tude
de'-cre-scen'-do
de-cres'-cent
de-cre'-tal
de-cre'-tive-ly
dec'-re-to-ry
de-cried'
de-cry'
dec'-u-man
de-cum'-bent
dec'-u-ple
de-cu'-ri-on
dec'-u-ry
dec'-us-sate*†
dec'-yl-ene†
ded'-i-cate
ded-i-ca'-tion
ded'-i-ca-to-ry
de-duce'
de-duced'
de-duc'-i-ble
de-duc'-ing
de-duct'
de-duct'-i:ble
de-duc'-tion
de-duc'-tive
deem'-ster
deep'-en
deep'=laid
deep'=root-ed
deep'=sea
deep'=seat-ed
deep'=set
deer'-hound
deer'-meat
deer'-skin
de-face'
de-faced'
de-fac'-ing
de fac'-to
de-fal'-cate
de-fal-ca'-tion†
def-a-ma'-tion
de-fam'-a-to-ry
de-fame'
de-fat'-i-ga-ble
de-fault'
de-fault'-er
de-fea'-sance
de-fea'-si-ble
de-feat'
de-feat'-ed
de-feat'-ist

def'-e-cate
def-e-ca'-tion
de'-fect (n.)
de-fect' (v.)
de-fect'-ed
de-fec'-tion
de-fec'-tive
de-fend'
de-fend'-ant†
de-fend'-er
de-fen-es-tra'-tion
de-fense'
de-fense'-less
de-fen-si-bil'-i-ty
de-fen'-si-ble
de-fen'-sive
de-fer'
def'-er-ence
def'-er-ent
def-er-en'-tial
de-fer'-ra-ble
de-ferred'
de-fer'-ring
de-fer-ves'-cence†
de-fi'-ance
de-fi'-ant
de-fi'-ant-ly
de-fi'-cien-cy
de-fi'-cient
def'-i-cit
de-fied'
def'-i-lade
de-file'
de-file'-ment
de-fil'-ing
de-fin'-a:ble
de-fine'
de-fin'-ing
def'-i-nite
def'-i-nite-ly
def-i-ni'-tion
de-fin'-i-tive
def'-la-grate
de-flate'
de-fla'-tion
de-fla'-tion-ar:y
de-flect'
de-flec'-tion
de-flec'-tive
de-flec'-tor
de-flo-ra'-tion
de-flow'-er
def'-lu-ent
De-foe'
de-fo'-li-ate
de-for'-ciant
de-for'-est
de-for-est-a'-tion†

de-form'
de-form-a:bil'-i-ty
de-form'-a:ble
de-for-ma'-tion†
de-for'-ma-tive*†
de-formed'
de-for'-mi-ty*
de-fraud'
de-frau-da'-tion†
de-fraud'-ed
de-fray'
de-frayed'
de-fray'-ing
de-frost'
de-frost'-er
deft'-ly
deft'-ness
de-funct'
de-fy'
de-fy'-ing
De-gas'
de-gen'-er-a-cy
de-gen'-er-ate
de-gen-er-a'-tion
de-gen'-er-a-tive
de-glu-ti'-tion
deg-ra-da'-tion
de-grade'
de-grad'-ed
de-grad'-ing
de-gree'
de-gus-ta'-tion
de-his'-cence
de-his'-cent
de-hor-ta'-tion
de-hu'-man-ize
de-hu-mid'-i-fi-er
de-hy'-drate
de-hy-dra'-tion
de-hyp'-no-tize
de-ic'-er
de'-i-cide
deic'-tic
de-if'-ic
de-i-fi-ca'-tion
de'-i-fied
de'-i-fy
deign
de'ism
de'-ist
de'-i-ties
de'-i-ty
de-ject'-ed
de-ject'-ed-ly
de-jec'-tion
de-jeu-ner'
de ju'-re
De Ko'-ven

De-la-croix'
Del-a-go'a
de-laine'
De'-land
Del'-a-ware
Del'-a-war'-e-an
de-lay'
de-layed'
de-lay'-ing
de'-le
de-lec'-ta-ble
de-lec-ta'-tion
del'-e-ga-cy
del'-e-gate
del-e-ga'-tion
de'-le-ing
de-lete'
de-let'-ed
del-e-te'-ri-ous
de-le'-tion
delft
delft'-ware
Del'-hi
De'-li:a
De'-li-an
de-lib'-er-ate
de-lib-er-a'-tion
de-lib'-er-a-tive
del'-i-ca-cies
del'-i-ca-cy
del'-i-cate
del'-i-cate-ly
del-i-ca-tes'-sen
de-li'-cious
de-light'
de-light'-ed
de-light'-ful
De-li'-lah
de-lim'-it
de-lim-i-ta'-tion
de-lin'-e-ate
de-lin-e-a'-tion
de-lin'-e-a-tor
de-lin'-quen-cy
de-lin'-quent
del-i-quesce'
del-i-ques'-cent
del-i-ra'-tion
de-lir'-i-ous
de-lir'-i-um
del'-i-tes'-cent
de-liv'-er
de-liv'-er-a:ble
de-liv'-er-ance
de-liv'-er-er
de-liv'-er-ies
de-liv'-er:y
de-lo-cal-iz:a'-tion*

98

De'-los
Del'-phi
Del'-phi-an
Del'-phic
del'-phi-nine
del-phin'-i-um
Del-phi'-nus
Del-sarte'
Del-sar'-ti-an
del'-ta
del'-toid
de-lude'
de-lud'-ed
de-lud'-ing
del'-uge
del'-uged
de-lu'-sion
de-lu'-sive
de-lu'-so-ry
de-luxe'
delve
delved
delv'-er
delv'-ing
de-mag'-net-ize
dem'-a-gog'-ic
dem'-a-gogue
dem'-a-gogu-er:y*
dem'-a-gog:y
de-mand'
de-mand'-ant†
de-mand'-ed
de-mar-ca'-tion
de-mean'
de-mean'-or
de-ment'-ed
de-men'-tia
de-mer'-it
de-mesne'
De-me'-ter
De-me'-tri-us
dem'i-bas'-tion
dem'i-god
dem'i-john
de-mil-i-ta-ri-za'-tion
de-mil'-i-ta-rize
dem'i-lune
dem'i-monde
de-mise'
dem'i-tasse
de-mo-bi-li-za'-tion†
de-mo'-bi-lize†
de-moc'-ra-cy
dem'-o-crat
dem'-o-crat'-ic
de-moc'-ra-tize
De-moc'-ri-tus
De-moc'-ri-te'-an

De-mo-gor'-gon
de-mog'-ra-pher
de'-mo-graph'-ic
de-mog'-ra-phy
dem-oi-selle'
de-mol'-ish
dem-o-li'-tion
de'-mon
de-mon-e-ti-za'-tion
de-mon'-e-tize
de-mo'-ni-ac
de'-mo-ni'-a-cal
de-mon'-ic
de'-mon-ism
de-mon-ol'-a-try
de-mon-ol'-o-gy
de-mon'-stra-ble
de-mon'-stra-bly
dem'-on-strate
dem'-on-strat'-ing
dem-on-stra'-tion
de-mon'-stra-tive
dem'-on-stra-tor
de-mor-al-i:za'-tion
de-mor'-al-ize
de-mor'-al-iz-ing
de'-mos
De-mos'-the-nes
de-mote'
de-mot'-ed
de-mot'-ic
de-mo'-tion
de-mount'-a:ble
de-mul'-cent
de-mur'
de-mure'
de-mur'-rage
de-mur'-ral
de-murred'
de-mur'-rer
de-mur'-ring
dem'y*†
de-nar'-i-us†
de'-na-ry*†
de-na'-ry-a-lize*†
de-nat'-u-ral-ize
de-na'-tur-ant†
de-na'-tured
den'-dri-form
den'-drite
den'-dro-lite
den-drol'-o-gy
Den'-eb
den-e-ga'-tion
den'-gue
de-ni'-al
de-nied'
de-ni'-er   (one who denies)

de-nier' (yarn measure)
de-nies'
den'-i-grate
den'-im
Den'-is
den'-i-zen
Den'-mark
Den'-nis
de-nom'-i-nate
de-nom-i-na'-tion
de-nom-i-na'-tion-al
de-nom-i-na'-tion-al-ism
de-nom'-i-na-tive
de-nom'-i-na-tor
de-no-ta'-tion
de-note'
de-not'-ing
de-noue-ment'
de-nounce'
de-nounced'
de-nounce'-ment
de-nounc'-ing
dense
dense'-ly
den-sim'-e-ter
den'-si-ty
den'-tal
den-ta'-tion
den'-ti-cle
den-tic'-u-late
den'-ti-frice
den-tig'-er-ous
den'-til
den'-tin
den'-tist
den'-tis-try*†
den-ti'-tion
den'-ture
de'-nu-date*
de-nu-da'-tion*†
de-nude'
de-nun'-ci-ate
de-nun-ci-a'-tion
de-nun'-ci-a-tive
de-nun'-ci-a-to-ry
Den'-ver
de-ny'
de-ny'-ing
de'-o-dand
de'-o-dar
de-o'dor-ant
de-o'dor-ize
de-o'dor-iz-er
de-on-tol'-o-gy
de-part'
de-part'-ed
de-part'-ment
de-part-men'-tal

de-par'-ture
de-pend'
de-pend-a:bil'-i-ty
de-pend'-a:ble
de-pen'-dence*
de-pen'-den-cy*
de-pen'-dent*
de-phleg'-ma-tor
de-pict'
de-pic'-tion
dep'-i-late
de-pil'-a-to-ry
de-plete'
de-plet'-ed
de-ple'-tion
de-plor'-a-ble
dep-lo-ra'-tion†
de-plore'
de-plored'
de-plor'-ing
de-ploy'
de-ploy'-ment
de-po'-lar-ize
de-po'-nent
de-pop'-u-late
de-pop-u-la'-tion
de-port'
de-por-ta'-tion
de-port'-ed
de-port-ee'*†
de-port'-ment
de-pos'-al
de-pose'
de-posed'
de-pos'-ing
de-pos'-it
de-pos'-i-tar:y†
de-pos'-it-ed
dep-o-si'-tion
de-pos'-i-tor
de-pos'-i-to-ry
de'-pot
dep-ra-va'-tion
de-prave'
de-praved'
de-prav'-i-ty
dep'-re-cate
dep'-re-cat-ing
dep-re-ca'-tion
dep'-re-ca-to-ry
de-pre'-cia-ble
de-pre'-ci-ate
de-pre-ci-a'-tion
dep'-re-date
dep-re-da'-tion
dep'-re-da-tor
dep'-re-da-to-ry
de-press'

de-pres'-sant
de-pressed'
de-press'-i:ble†
de-press'-ing
de-pres'-sion
de-pres'-sor
de-priv'-al
dep-ri-va'-tion
de-prive'
de-prived'
de-priv'-ing
depth
dep'-u-rate
dep-u-ta'-tion
de-pute'
dep'-u-ties
dep'-u-tize
dep'-u-ty
De Quin'-cey
de-rac'-i-nate
de-rail'
de-rail'-ment
de-range'
de-range'-ment
de-rang'-ing
der'-by
Der'-by-shire
de-re'-cho
der'-e-lict
der-e-lic'-tion
de-ride'
de-rid'-ing
de ri-gueur'
de-ris'-i-ble
de-ri'-sion
de-ri'-sive
de-ri'-sive-ly
de-ri'-so-ry
der-i-va'-tion
de-riv'-a-tive
de-rive'
de-rived'
de-riv'-ing
der-ma-ti'-tis
der'-mat'-o-gen
der'-ma-toid
der-ma-tol'-o-gist
der-ma-tol'-o-gy
der'-mis
der'-nier'
der'-o-gate
der-o-ga'-tion
de-rog'-a-to'-ri-ly
de-rog'-a-to-ry
der'-rick
der'-rin-ger
der'-vish
Der'-went

des'-cant
Des-cartes'
de-scend'
de-scend'-ant†
de-scend'-ed
de-scend'-er
de-scend'-i:ble
de-scent'
de-scrib'-a:ble
de-scribe'
de-scribed'
de-scrip'-tion
de-scrip'-tive
des-cry'*†
des-cry'-ing*†
Des-de-mo'-na
des'-e-crate
des-e-cra'-tion
des'-e-cra-tor
de-seg'-re-gate
de-seg-re-ga'-tion
de-sen'-si-tize
des'-ert (wasteland)
de-sert' (to abandon)
de-sert'-er
de-ser'-tion
de-serve'
de-served'
de-serv'-ed-ly
de-serv'-ing
des'-ha-bille'
des'-ic-cate
des-ic-ca'-tion
des'-ic-ca-tor
de-sid-er-a'-ta
de-sid-er-a'-tum
de-sign'
de-sign'-a:ble (can be designed)
des'-ig-na-ble (can be designated)
des'-ig-nate
des-ig-na'-tion
des'-ig-na-tive
des'-ig-na-tor
de-sign'-ed-ly
des'-ig-nee'
de-sign'-er
de-sign'-ing
de-sip'-i-ence
de-sir-a:bil'-i-ty
de-sir'-a:ble
de-sire'
de-sir'-ous
de-sist'
de-sis'-tance*
Des Moines
des'-o-late

des-o-la´-tion	de-tail´
De So´-to	de-tain´
de-spair´	de-tect´
de-spaired´	de-tect´-a:ble
de-spair´-ing	de-tec´-ta-phone
des-per-a´-do	de-tec´-tion
des-per-a´-does	de-tec´-tive
des´-per-ate	de-tec´-tor
des´-per-ate-ly	de-ten´-tion
des-per-a´-tion	de-ten´-tive
de-spic´-a-ble*†	de-ter´
de-spis´-a:ble	de-ter´-gent
de-spise´	de-te´-ri-o-rate
de-spised´	de-te´-ri-o-ra´-tion
de-spis´-er	de-ter´-min-a:ble*†
de-spis´-ing	de-ter´-mi-nant
de-spite´	de-ter´-mi-nate
de-spite´-ful	de-ter-mi-na´-tion
de-spit´-e-ous-ly*†	de-ter´-mine
de-spoil´	de-ter´-mined
de-spoil´-er	de-ter´-mined-ly
de-spoil´-ing	de-ter´-mi-nism*†
de-spo-li-a´-tion	de-ter´-mi-nist*†
de-spond´	de-terred´
de-spon´-dence*	de-ter´-rent
de-spon´-den-cy*	de-ter´-ring
de-spon´-dent*	de-ter´-sive
des´-pot	de-test´
des-pot´-ic	de-test´-a:ble
des-pot´-i-cal	de-tes-ta´-tion
des´-po-tism*†	de-throne´
des´-pu-mate*	de-throne´-ment
des-pu-ma´-tion	det´-i-nue
des´-qua-mate	det´-o-na-ble
des-qua-ma´-tion	det´-o-nate
des-sert´	det-o-na´-tion
des´-sia-tine´	det´-o-na-tor
des-ti-na´-tion	de´-tour
des´-tine	de-tract´
des´-ti-nies	de-trac´-tion
des´-ti-ny	de-trac´-tor
des´-ti-tute	de-trac´-to-ry
des-ti-tu´-tion	det´-ri-ment
de-stroy´	det-ri-men´-tal
de-stroyed´	de-tri´-tion
de-stroy´-er	de-tri´-tus
de-struc´-ti-ble*	De-troit´
de-struc´-tion	de-trun´-cate
de-struc´-tive	Deu-ca´-li-on
de-struc´-tive-ness	deuc´-ed*†
des´-ue-tude	deu´-ter-ide
de-sul´-fu-rize†	deu-te´-ri-um
des´-ul-to-ry	deu-ter-og´-a-my
de-syn-ap´-sis	deu´-ter-on
de-tach´	Deu-ter-on´o-my
de-tach´-a:ble	Deutsch´-land
de-tached´	de´-va
de-tach´-ment	

De Va-le'-ra
de-val'-u-ate
de-val-u-a'-tion
dev'-as-tate
dev'-as-tat-ed
dev'-as-tat-ing
dev-as-ta'-tion
de-vel'-op
de-vel'-oped
de-vel'-op-er
de-vel'-op-ing
de-vel'-op-ment
de-vel'-op-men'-tal
de'-vi
de-vi'-ate
de-vi-a'-tion
de-vice'
dev'-il
dev'-il-fish
dev'-il-ish
dev'-il-ment
dev'-il-ry
dev'-il-try
de'-vi-ous
de'-vi-ous-ly
de-vis'-a:ble
de-vise'
dev'-i-see*
dev'-i-sor*†
de-vi-tal-i:za'-tion
de-vit'-ri-fy
de-vo'-cal-ize
de-void'
de-voir'
dev-o-lu'-tion
de-volve'
de-volve'-ment
de-volv'-ing
Dev'-on
De-vo'-ni-an
Dev'-on-shire
de-vote'
de-vot'-ed
de-vot'-ed-ly
dev'-o-tee'
de-vo'-tion
de-vo'-tion-al
de-vour'
de-vout'
de-vout'-ly
De Vries'
Dew'-ar
dew'-ber-ry
dew'-drop
Dew'-ey
dew'-i-ness
De Witt'

dew'-lap
dew'-point
dew'y
dex'-ter
dex-ter'-i-ty
dex'-ter-ous
dex'-ter-ous-ly
dex'-tral
dex'-trin
dex'-trose
dex'-trous
dhar'-ma
dhar'-na
dhow
di-a-be'-tes
di'-a-bet'-ic
dia-ble-rie'
di-a-bol'-ic
di-a-bol'-i-cal
di-ab'-o-lism
di'a-caus'-tic
di-a:ce'-tyl*†
di-ach'-y-lon
di-ac'-id
di-ac'-o-nal
di-a-crit'-ic
di-a-crit'-i-cal
di-a-del'-phous
di'-a-dem
di-aer'-e-sis
di'-ae-ret'-ic
di'-ag-nose
di-ag-no'-sis
di-ag-nos'-tic
di-ag-nos-ti'-cian
di-ag'-o-nal
di-ag'-o-nal-ly
di'-a-gram
di'-a-gram-mat'-ic
di'-a-gram-mat'-i-cal
di:a-ki-ne'-sis
di'-al
di'-a-lect
di'-a-lec'-tal
di-a-lec'-tal-ly
di-a-lec'-tic
di-a-lec'-ti-cal
di-a-lec'-ti-cism
di'-aled
di'-al-ing
di'-a-log
di-al'-o-gism
di'-a-logue
di-al'-y-sis
di-a-lyt'-ic
di-a-lyt'-i-cal-ly
di:a-mag-net'-ic
di-am'-e-ter

103

di-am'-e-tral
di-a-met'-ric
di-a-met'-ri-cal
di'-a:mine'†
di'-a-mond
Di-an'a
di-an'-drous
di-a-net'-ic
di'-an'-thus
di-a-pa'-son
di'-a-per
di-aph'-a-nous
di-a-pho-re'-sis
di'-a-phragm
di'-a-phrag-mat'-ic
di-aph'-y-se'-al
di-aph'-y-sis
di-a:poph'-y-sis
di'-a-ries
di'-a-rist
di-ar-rhe'a
di-ar-thro'-sis
di'-a-ry
Di'-as
di-as'-po-ra
di'-a-spore
di'-a-stase
di-a-sta'-sic†
di'-as-ta-sis
di'-a-stat'-ic
di-as'-ter
di-as'-to-le
di'-a-stol'-ic*†
di'-a-sto-mat'-ic
di-a-tes'-sa-ron
di-a-ther'-man-cy
di'-a-ther'-mic
di'-a-ther-my
di-ath'-e-sis
di'-a-thet'-ic
di'-a-tom
di'-a-to-ma'-ceous
di-a:tom'-ic
di-at'-om-ite
di'-a-ton'-ic
di'-a-tribe
di-at'-ro-pism
Di-az'
di-a'zo*†
di'-a-zole†
di-az'-o-tize
dib'-ble
di-bran'-chi-ate
di'-cast
di-cas'-ter:y
di-cas'-tic
di-ce'-tyl*

di-cha'-si-um
di-chlo'-ride
di-chot'-o-mous
di-chot'-o-my
di-chro-mat'-ic
dick-cis'-sel
Dick'-ens
Dick-en'-si-an
dick'-er
dick'-ey
Dick'-in-son
di-cli'-nous
di'-cot-y-le'-don
di'-cot-y-le'-don-ous†
di-cou'-ma-rin
di-crot'-ic
dic'-ta
Dic'-ta-phone
dic'-tate
dic'-tat-ing
dic-ta'-tion
dic'-ta-tor
dic-ta-to'-ri-al
dic-ta'-tor-ship
dic'-tion
dic'-tio-nar-ies*†
dic'-tio-nar:y*†
Dic'-to-graph
dic'-tum
di-dac'-tic
di-dac'-ti-cism
did'-dle
Di-de-rot'
Di'-do
di-dym'-i-um
did'-y-mous
die=cut
die cut'-ter
died
Di-e'-go
diel'-drin
di-e:lec'-tric
die'-mak-er
di'-ene
Dieppe*†
di-er'-e-sis
di'-et
di'-e-tar:y†
di'-et-er
di-e-tet'-ic
di-e-ti'-tian
dif'-fer
dif'-fered
dif'-fer-ence
dif'-fer-ent
dif-fer-en'-tia
dif-fer-en'-tia-ble
dif-fer-en'-tial

dif-fer-en'-ti-ate
dif-fer-en-ti-a'-tion
dif'-fi-cult
dif'-fi-cul-ties
dif'-fi-cul-ty
dif'-fi-dence
dif'-fi-dent
dif-fract'
dif-frac'-tion
dif-fuse'
dif-fus'-i:ble
dif-fu'-sion
dif-fu'-sive
dig'-a-my
di-gas'-tric
di'-gest (n.)
di-gest' (v.)
di-gest-i:bil'-i-ty
di-gest'-i:ble
di-ges'-tion
di-ges'-tive
dig'-ger
dig'-ging
dig'-it
dig'-i-tal*
dig-i-tal'-in†
dig-i-tal'-is†
dig'-i-ta-lize*
di'-glot
dig'-ni-fied
dig'-ni-fied-ly
dig'-ni-fy
dig'-ni-fy-ing
dig'-ni-tar-ies†
dig'-ni-tar:y†
dig'-ni-ties
dig'-ni-ty
di-gress'
di-gres'-sion
di-he'-dral
di-lap'-i-date
di-lap'-i-dat-ed
di-lap-i-da'-tion
di-la'-tant*
dil-a-ta'-tion
di-late'
di-lat'-ing
di-la'-tion
dil'-a-to-ry
di-lem'-ma
dil-et-tante'*
dil-et-tant'-ism
dil'-i-gence
dil'-i-gent
dil'-u-ent
di-lute'
di-lut'-ing
di-lu'-tion

di-lu'-vi-al
di-men'-sion
dim'-er-ous
di-me'-ter
di-min'-ish
di-min-u-en'-do
dim-i-nu'-tion
di-min'-u-tive
dim'-is-so-ry
dim'-i-ty
dim'-ly
dimmed
dim'-ming
dim'-ness
di-mor'-phism
di-mor'-phous
dim'-ple
dim'-pling
di-nar'
dined
din'-er
di-ner'-ic
di-nette'
dingh'y*†
din'-gi-ly
din'-gi-ness
din'-gle
din'-gy
din'-ing
din'-ing room
din'-ner
din'-ner-time
din'-ner-ware
di-noc'-er-as
di'-no-saur
di'-no-sau-ri-an
di'-no-there
di-oc'-e-san
di'-o-cese
Di-o-cle'-tian
di-oe'-cious
Di-og'-e-nes
Di-o-me'-des
Di'-on
Di'-o-nys'-i-ac
Di'-o-nys'-i-an*
Di-o-ny'-si-us†
Di-o-ny'-sus
Di'-o-phan'-tine
di-op'-side
di-op'-ter
di-op-tom'-e-ter
di-o-ram'a*†
di'-o-rite
Di-os-cu'-ri
di-ox'-ide
di'-phase
di-phen'-yl†

diph-the'-ri:a
diph'-the-rit'-ic
diph'-the-roid
diph'-thong
diph'-thong'-al*†
diph'-thong-ize
di-ple'-gia
dip-lo-coc'-cus
di-plod'-o-cus†
di-plo'-ma
di-plo'-ma-cy
dip'-lo-mat
dip-lo-mat'-ic
dip-lo-mat'-i-cal-ly
di-plo'-ma-tist
di-plo'-pi:a
di-plop'-ic
di-plo'-sis
dip'-no-an
dip'-o-dy
di'-pole
dipped
dip'-per
dip-so-ma'-ni:a
Dip'-ter:a
dip'-ter-ous
di-rect'
di-rec'-tion
di-rect'-ly
di-rect'-ness
di-rec'-tor
di-rec'-tor-ate*
di-rec'-to-ry
dire'-ful
dire'-ly
dirge
dir'-i-gi-ble
dir'-i-ment
dirn'-dl
dirt'-i-er
dirt'-i-ly
dirt'-i-ness
dirt'y
dis-a:bil'-i-ty
dis-a'ble
dis-a'bled
dis-a'bling
dis-a:buse'
di-sac'-cha-ride
dis-ad-van'-tage
dis-ad-van-ta'-geous
dis-af-fect'-ed
dis-af-fec'-tion
dis-af-firm'-ance
dis-af-fir-ma'-tion
dis-a:gree'
dis-a:gree'-a:ble
dis-a:gree'-ment

dis-al-low'
dis-al-low'-ance
dis-ap-pear'
dis-ap-pear'-ance
dis-ap-peared'
dis-ap-point'
dis-ap-point'-ed
dis-ap-point'-ment
dis-ap-pro-ba'-tion
dis-ap-prov'-al
dis'-ap-prove'
dis'-ap-prov'-ing
dis'-ap-prov'-ing-ly
dis-arm'
dis-ar'-ma-ment
dis-ar-range'
dis-ar-range'-ment
dis-ar-ray'
dis-ar-tic'-u-late
dis-as-so'-ci-ate
di-sas'-ter*†
di-sas'-trous*†
di-sas'-trous-ly*†
dis-a:vow'
dis-a:vow'-al
dis-band'
dis-bar'
dis-bar'-ment
dis-bar'-ring
dis-be-lief'
dis-be-lieve'
dis-be-liev'-er
dis-bur'-den
dis-burse'
dis-burse'-ment
dis-burs'-ing
disc
dis'-card (n.)
dis-card' (v.)
dis-cern'
dis-cern'-i:ble
dis-cern'-i:bly
dis-cern'-ing
dis-cern'-ment
dis'-charge (n.)
dis-charge' (n., v.)
dis-ci'-ple
dis-ci-plin'-a:ble
dis'-ci-plin-al*
dis'-ci-plin-ant
dis'-ci-pli-nar'-i-an†
dis'-ci-pli-nar:y†
dis'-ci-pline
dis'-ci-plin-er
dis-claim'
dis-claim'-er
dis-cla-ma'-tion
dis-close'

dis-clo'-sure
dis-cob'-o-lus
dis-cog'-ra-phy
dis'-coid
dis-coi'-dal
dis-col'-or
dis-col-or-a'-tion
dis-com'-fit
dis-com'-fi-ture
dis-com'-fort
dis-com'-fort-a:ble
dis'-com-mode'
dis-com-pose'
dis-com-po'-sure
dis'-con-cert'
dis-con-nect'
dis-con-nect'-ed
dis-con-nec'-tion
dis-con'-so-late
dis-con'-so-late-ly
dis-con-tent'
dis-con-tent'-ed
dis-con-tent'-ment
dis-con-tin'-u-ance
dis-con-tin-u-a'-tion
dis-con-tin'-ue
dis-con-ti-nu'-i-ty
dis-con-tin'-u-ous
dis'-cord
dis-cor'-dance*
dis-cor'-dant*
dis'-count
dis-coun'-te-nance
dis-cour'-age
dis-cour'-age-ment
dis-cour'-ag-er
dis-cour'-ag-ing
dis'-course (n.)
dis-course' (v.)
dis-cour'-sive
dis-cour'-te-ous
dis-cour'-te-sy
dis-cov'-er
dis-cov'-er-er
dis-cov'-er-ies
dis-cov'-ert
dis-cov'-er:y
dis-cred'-it
dis-cred'-it-a:ble
dis-creet'
dis-creet'-ly
dis-crep'-an-cy
dis-crep'-ant
dis-crete'
dis-cre'-tion
dis-cre'-tion-ar:y†
dis-crim'-i-nate
dis-crim'-i-nat-ing

dis-crim-i-na'-tion
dis-crim'-i-na-to:ry
dis-crown'
dis-cur'-sive
dis-cur'-sive-ly
dis'-cus
dis-cuss'
dis-cussed'
dis-cuss'-i:ble
dis-cus'-sion
dis-dain'
dis-dain'-ful
dis-dain'-ful-ly
dis-ease'
dis-eased'
dis-eas'-es
dis-em-bark'
dis-em-bar-ka'-tion
dis-em-bar'-rass
dis-em-bod'-i-ment
dis-em-bod'y
dis-em-bogue'
dis-em-bow'-el
dis-en-a'ble
dis-en-chant'
dis-en-chant'-ment
dis-en-cum'-ber
dis-en-gage'
dis-en-tan'-gle
dis-es-tab'-lish
dis-es-tab'-lish-ment
dis-es-teem'
dis-fa'-vor
dis-fig-u-ra'-tion
dis-fig'-ure
dis-fig'-ure-ment
dis-fig'-ur-ing
dis-fran'-chise
dis-gorge'
dis-grace'
dis-grace'-ful
dis-grun'-tle
dis-grun'-tled
dis-guise'
dis-guis'-ed-ly
dis-gust'
dis-gust'-ed
dis-gust'-ed-ly
dis-gust'-ing
dis-gust'-ing-ly
dis-ha-bille'
dis-har-mo'-ni-ous
dis-har'-mo-ny
dish'-cloth
dish-heart'-en
di-shev'-el
di-shev'-eled
dish'-mop

dis-hon'-est
dis-hon'-es-ty
dis-hon'-or
dis-hon'-or-a:ble
dish'-pan
dish rack
dish tow'-el
dish'-wash-er
dish'-wa:ter
dis-il-lu'-sion
dis-il-lu'-sion-ment
dis-in-cli-na'-tion
dis-in-clined'
dis-in-fect'
dis-in-fec'-tant*
dis-in-fec'-tion
dis-in-gen'-u-ous
dis-in-her'-it
dis-in'-te-grate
dis-in-te-gra'-tion
dis-in-ter'
dis-in'-ter-est-ed
dis-in'-ter-est-ed-ness
dis-join'
dis-joint'
dis-joint'-ed
dis-junct'
dis-junc'-tion
dis-junc'-tive
disk
dis-like'
dis'-lo-cate
dis-lo-ca'-tion
dis-lodge'
dis-loy'-al
dis-loy'-al-ty
dis'-mal
dis'-mal-ly
dis-man'-tle
dis-man'-tling
dis-mast'
dis-may'
dis-mem'-ber
dis-mem'-ber-ment
dis-miss'
dis-mis'-sal*
dis-mis'-sion
dis-mount'
dis-o:be'-di-ence
dis-o:be'-di-ent
dis-o:bey'
dis-o:beyed'
dis-o:blige'
dis-o:blig'-ing
dis-o:blig'-ing-ly
dis-or'-der
dis-or'-dered
dis-or'-der-li-ness

dis-or'-der-ly
dis-or-ga-ni-za'-tion*†
dis-or'-ga-nize*†
dis-own'
dis-par'-age
dis-par'-age-ment
dis-par'-ag-ing-ly
dis-par'-ate*†
dis-par'-i-ty
dis-part'
dis-pas'-sion-ate
dis-patch'
dis-patch'-er
dis-pel'
dis-pelled'
dis-pel'-ling
dis-pens'-a:bil'-i-ty*†
dis-pens'-a:ble
dis-pen'-sa-ry
dis-pen-sa'-tion
dis-pen'-sa-to-ry
dis-pense'
dis-pens'-er
dis-peo'-ple
dis-per'-sal
dis-per'-sant*
dis-perse'
dis-pers'-i:ble
dis-per'-sion
dis-per'-sive
dis-per'-soid*
di-spir'-it*†
di-spir'-it-ed*†
dis-place'
dis-placed'
dis-place'-ment
dis-play'
dis-please'
dis-pleas'-ing
dis-plea'-sure'
di-sport'*†
dis-pos'-a:ble
dis-pos'-al†
dis-pose'
dis-pos'-er
dis-po-si'-tion
dis-pos-sess'
dis-praise'
dis-proof'
dis-pro-por'-tion
dis-pro-por'-tion-al
dis-pro-por'-tion-ate
dis-prove'
dis-put-a:bil'-i-ty*†
dis-put'-a:ble*†
dis-pu'-tant
dis-pu-ta'-tion
dis-pu-ta'-tious

dis-pu'-ta-tive
dis-pute'
dis-qual-i-fi-ca'-tion
dis-qual'-i-fied
dis-qual'-i-fy
dis-qui'-et
dis-qui'-e-tude
dis-qui-si'-tion
Dis-rae'-li
dis-re-gard'
dis-re-pair'
dis-rep'-u-ta-ble
dis-rep'-u-ta-bly
dis-re-pute'
dis-re-spect'
dis-re-spect'-a-ble
dis-re-spect'-ful
dis-robe'
dis-rupt'
dis-rup'-tion
dis-sat-is-fac'-tion
dis-sat'-is-fied
dis-sat'-is-fy
dis-sect'
dis-sect'-ed
dis-sec'-tion
dis-sec'-tor
dis-seis'-ee'*
dis-sei'-sin
dis-sem'-blance
dis-sem'-ble
dis-sem'-bler
dis-sem'-i-nate
dis-sem-i-na'-tion
dis-sem'-i-na-tor
dis-sen'-sion
dis-sent'
dis-sent'-er
dis-sen'-tient
dis-sen'-tious
dis'-ser-tate
dis-ser-ta'-tion
dis'-ser-ta-tive
dis-serv'-ice† (1)
dis-sev'-er
dis'-si-dence
dis'-si-dent
dis-sil'-ien-cy
dis-sil'-ient
dis-sim'-i-lar
dis-sim-i-lar'-i-ty
dis-sim-i-la'-tion
dis-sim'-i-la-tive
dis-si-mil'-i-tude
dis-sim'-u-late
dis-sim-u-la'-tion

dis'-si-pate
dis'-si-pat-ed
dis-si-pa'-tion
dis'-si-pa-tor
dis-so'-ci-ate
dis-so'-ci-a'-tion
dis-sol-u-bil'-i-ty†
dis-sol'-u-ble†
dis'-so-lute
dis-so-lu'-tion
dis-solv'-a-ble
dis-solve'
dis-sol'-vent
dis-solv'-ing
dis'-so-nance
dis'-so-nan-cy
dis'-so-nant
dis-suade'
dis-sua'-sion
dis-sua'-sive
dis-sua'-sive-ly
dis'-taff
dis-tain'
dis'-tal
dis'-tance
dis'-tant
dis'-tant-ly
dis-taste'
dis-taste'-ful
dis-tem'-per
dis-tend'
dis-ten'-si-ble
dis-ten'-sion
dis-ten'-tion
dis'-tich
dis'-ti-chous*
dis-till'
dis-till'-a:ble†
dis'-til-late
dis-til-la'-tion
dis-till'-er†
dis-till'-er:y†
dis-till'-ing†
dis-tinct'
dis-tinc'-tion
dis-tinc'-tive
dis-tinct'-ly
dis-tinct'-ness
dis'-tin-gué'
dis-tin'-guish
dis-tin'-guish-a:ble
dis-tin'-guish-a:bly
dis-tin'-guished
di-stom'a-tous†
dis-tort'
dis-tort'-ed

(1) preferred to ser'-vice, given by *Webster's 3rd New International Dictionary*.

dis-tor'-tion
dis-tor'-tive
dis-tract'
dis-tract'-i:ble
dis-trac'-tion
dis-trac'-tive
dis-train'
dis-trait'
dis-traught'
dis-tress'
dis-tress'-ful
dis-tress'-ing
dis-trib'u-u-tar:y†
dis-trib'-ute
dis-tri-bu'-tion
dis-trib'-u-tive
dis-trib'-u-tor
dis'-trict
dis-trust'
dis-trust'-ful
dis-turb'
dis-tur'-bance*
dis-turb'-er
di-sul'-fide
dis-un'-ion†
dis-u:nite'
dis-use'
di'-the-ism
dith'-er
di-thi-on'-ic
dith'-y-ramb
dith'-y-ram'-bic
di-tol'-yl
dit-tan'-der
dit'-ta-ny
dit'-to
dit-tog'-ra-phy
dit'-ty
di-u:re'-sis
di-u:ret'-ic
di-ur'-nal
di'-va
di'-va-gate
di-va'-lent
di-van'
di-var'-i-cate
di-var-i-ca'-tion
div'-er
di-verge'
di-ver'-gence
di-ver'-gen-cy
di-ver'-gent
di-ver'-gent-ly
di'-vers (different)
div'-ers (those who dive)
di-verse'
di-verse'-ly
di-ver-si-fi-ca'-tion

di-ver'-si-fied
di-ver'-si-fy
di-ver'-sion
di-ver'-si-ty
di-vert'
di'-ver-tic'-u-lar
di-ver-tic'-u-lum
di-ver'-tise-ment
di-ver'-tisse-ment
di-ver'-tive
Di'-ves
di-vest'
di-vide'
di-vid'-ed
div'-i-dend
di-vid'-er
di-vid'-u-al
div-i-na'-tion
di-vin'-a-to-ry
di-vine'
di-vine'-ly
di-vin'-er
div'-ing
di-vin'-i-ty
di-vis-i-bil'-i-ty
di-vis'-i-ble
di-vi'-sion
di-vi'-sion-al
di-vi'-sive
di-vi'-sor
di-vorce'
di-vor'-cee'
di-vorce'-ment
div'-ot
di-vul'-gate
di-vulge'
di-vulge'-ment
di-vulg'-ing
Dix'-ie
Dix'-on
di'-zen*†
diz'-zi-ly
diz'-zi-ness
diz'-zy
Dnie'-per
Dnies'-ter
do'-a:ble
dob'-bin
Do'-ber-man pin'-scher
do-blon'
do'-bra
doc'-ile
doc'-ile-ly
do-cil'-i-ty
dock'-et
dock fore'-man
dock'-hand
dock house

110

dock'-man
dock'-mas-ter
dock rent
dock'-side
dock'-yard
doc'-tor
doc'-tor-al
doc'-tor-ate
doc'-tri-naire'
doc'-tri-nal
doc'-trine
doc'-u-ment
doc'-u-men'-ta-ry
doc-u-men-ta'-tion
dod'-der
do-dec'-a-gon
do-de-cag'-o-nal
Do-dec-a-nese'
do'-de-cyl*
dodg'-er
dodg'-ing
do'-er
doe'-skin
does'-n't
dog'-ber-ry
dog'-bite
dog'-cart
dog'-catch-er
dog col'-lar
dog days
doge
dog'=ear
dog'=eared
dog'-fight
dog'-fish
dog'-ged
dog'-ged-ly
dog'-ger-el
dog'-ger:y
dog'-ging
dog'-gy
dog'-house
do'-gie
dog'-ma
dog-mat'-ic
dog-mat'-i-cal
dog-mat'-i-cal-ly
dog'-ma-tism
dog'-ma-tist
dog'-ma-tize
dog rose
dog'=tired
dog'-trot
dog'-watch
dog'-wood
doi'-lies
doi'-ly
do'-ing

dol'-ce
dol'-drum
dole'-ful
dole'-ful-ly
dol'-er-ite
dol'-ing
dol'-lar
dol'-ly*
dol'-man
dol'-men
do'-lo-mite*†
do'-lor
Do-lo'-res
do'-lo-rous*†
dol'-phin
dolt'-ish
do-main'
Domes'-day
do-mes'-tic
do-mes'-ti-cate
do-mes-ti-ca'-tion
do-mes-tic'-i-ty
dom'-i-cal†
dom'-i-cile
dom-i-cil'-i-ar
dom-i-cil'-iar:y†
dom'-i-nance
dom'-i-nant
dom'-i-nate
dom-i-na'-tion
do'-mi-ne'*
dom'-i-neer'
dom'-i-neer'-ing
Dom'-i-nic
Dom-i-ni'-ca
do-min'-i-cal
Do-min'-i-can
dom'-i-nie
do-min'-ion
Dom'-i-nique
do-min'-i-um
dom'-i-no
dom'-i-noes
Do-mi'-tian
do'-na
Don'-ald
do-nate'
Don-a-tel'-lo
do-nat'-ing
do-na'-tion
Don'-a-tism
do'-na-tive*†
do-nee'
Don'-e-gal
don'-jon
Don Ju'-an
don'-key
don'-na

Donne
do'-nor
Don Qui-xo'-te*
don't
doo'-dle
doo'-dling
dooms'-day
door'-bell
door'-keep-er
door'-knob
door'-man
door'-nail
door'-plate
door'-post
door'-sill
door'-step
door'-stone
door'-way
door'-yard
doped
dop'-ey*†
dop'-ing
Do'-ra
Dor'-cas
Dor'-ches-ter
Do-ré'
Do'-ri-an
Dor'-ic
Dor'-is†
Dor'-king
dor'-man-cy
dor'-mant
dor'-mer
dor'-mi-ent
dor'-mi-to-ries
dor'-mi-to-ry
dor'-mouse
Dor-o-the'a
Dor'-o-thy
dor'-sal
dor-sa'-lis
Dor'-set
Dor'-set-shire
dor'-sum
Dort'-mund
do'-ry
dos'-age
dosed
do-sim'-e-try
dos'-ing
dos'-ser (basket)
doss'-er (in doss houses)
dos'-sier*
Dos-to-ev'-ski
dot'-age†
do'-tal
dot'-ard*†
dot'-ed

dot'-ing
dot'-ish†
dot'-ted
dot'-ter-el
dot'-ty
dot'y†
dou'-ble†
dou'-ble=bar'-reled†
dou'-ble cross (n.)†
dou'-ble=cross' (v.)†
dou'-ble en-ten'-dre
dou'-ble-head'-er†
dou'-ble=quick'†
dou'-blet†
dou'-bling†
dou-bloon'†
dou'-bly†
doubt
doubt'-a:ble
doubt'-ful
doubt'-ful-ly
doubt'-less
douche
douch'-ing
dough'-boy
Dough'-er-ty
dough'-nut
dough'-ty
dough'y
Doug'-las
doused
dous'-ing
dove'-cote
Do'-ver
dove'-tail
dow'-a:ble
dow'-a-ger
dowd'-i-ness*†
dowd'y*†
dow'-el
dow'-er
down'-cast
down'-fall
down'-heart-ed
down'-hill'
down'-i-ness
down'-pour
down'-right
down'-stairs'
down'-stream
down'-throw
down'-town'
down'-trod'-den
down'-ward
down'y
dow'-ries
dow'-ry
dows'-er

dox-o-log'-i-cal
dox-ol'-o-gy
dox'y
doy-en'
doz'-en
doz'-ing
drab'-ness
drach'-ma
Dra'-co
Dra-co'-ni-an
draft
draft-ee'
draft'-i-ly
drafts'-man
draft'y
dragged
drag'-ging
drag'-gle
drag'-net
drag'-o-man
drag'-on
drag'-on-et'
drag'-on-fly
dra-goon'
drag'-rope
drain'-age
drain cock
drain'-er
drain'-pipe
drain pump
drain valve
dra'-ma
dra-mat'-ic
dra-mat'-i-cal-ly
dra'-ma-tis per-so'-nae*†
dram'-a-tist
dram-a-ti-za'-tion
dram'-a-tize
dram'-a-tur-gy
dram'-shop
drap'-er (type of worker)
dra'-per (type of machine)
drap'-er:y*
drap'-ing
dras'-tic
dras'-ti-cal-ly
draught
draughts'-man
draught'y
Dra-vid'-i-an
draw'-back
draw'-bar
draw'-bridge
draw-ee'
draw'-er
draw'-ing
drawl'-ing
dray'-age

dray'-man
Dray'-ton
dread'-ful
dread'-ful-ly
dread'-nought
dream'-er
dream'-i-ly
dream'-i-ness
dream'-ing
dream'-land
dream'-less
dreamt
dream'y
drear'-i-ly
drear'-i-ness
drear'y
dredg'-er
dredg'-ing
Drei'-ser
Dres'-den
dress'-er
dress'-ing
dress'-ing gown
dress'-ing room
dress'-mak-er
dress'-mak-ing
dress'y
Drey'-fus
drib'-ble
drib'-bled
drib'-let
dri'-er
drift'-age
drift'-er
drift'-ing
drift'-wood
drift'y
drilled
drill'-er
drill'-ing
drill'-mas-ter
drill'-stock
dri'-ly
drink'-a:ble
drink'-er
Drink'-wa-ter
dripped
drip'-ping
drive'=in
driv'-el
driv'-el-er
driv'-en
driv'-er
drive'-way
driv'-ing
driz'-zle
driz'-zly
Dro'-ghe-da

113

droll'-er:y
drom'-e-dar:y†
drom'-ond†
dron'-ing
dron'-ish
droop'-ing
droop'y
drop'-let
dropped
drop'-per
drop'-ping
drop'-si-cal
drop'-sied
drop'-sy
drosh'-ky
Dro-soph'-i-la
drought
dro'-ver
drowned
drows'-i-ly*†
drows'-i-ness*†
drows'y*†
drub'-bing
drudge
drudg'-er:y
drudg'-ing
drug clerk
drugged
drug'-get
drug'-ging
drug'-gist
drug'-store
dru'-id
dru'-id-ism
drum'-lin
drummed
drum'-mer
drum'-ming
Drum'-mond
drum'-stick
drunk'-ard
drunk'-en
drunk'-en-ness
dru-pa'-ceous
Dru'-se-an
dry'-ad
Dry'-den
dry-dock (n.)
dry=dock (v.)
dry'-er
dry' goods
dry'-ing
dry'-ly
dry'-ness
dry=shod
du'-al
du'-al-ism
du-al'-i-ty

du'-al-ly
dub'-bing
du-bi'-e-ty
du-bi-os'-i-ty
du'-bi-ous
du'-bi-ous-ly
du'-bi-ta-ble
Dub'-lin
Du-buque'
du'-cal
duc'-at
duch'-ess
du-chesse'
duch'y
duck'-bill
duck'-ling
duck'-weed
duck'y
duc'-tile
duc-til'-i-ty
duct'-less
du-deen'
dud'-geon*†
Dud'-ley
due bill
du'-el
du'-el-ist
du-el'-lo
du-en'-na
du-et'
duf'-fel
duf'-fer*
du'-gong
dug'-out
duke'-dom
dul'-cet
dul-ci-an'a
dul'-ci-fy
dul'-ci-mer
Dul-ci-ne'a*†
du-li'a
dul'-lard*†
dull'-ness
dul'-ly
Du-luth'
du'-ly
Du'-ma
Du-mas'
Du Mau-rier'
dumb'-bell
dumb'-found
dumb'-ly
dumb'-wait-er
dum'-dum
dum'-found
dum'-my
dump'-i-ness
dump'-ling

114

dump'y
Dun'-bar
Dun'-can
dunce
Dun'-ci-ad
Dun'-das
Dun-dee'
Dun-e'-din
dun-ga-ree'
Dun'-ge-ness'
dun'-geon
dung'-hill
du'-nite*†
Dun'-kard*
Dun'-ker*
dunk'-er
Dun'-kerque
Dun'-kirk
dun'-nage
dunned
dun'-ning
Dun'-sa-ny
Dun'-si-nane
Dun'-stan
du'o
du'-o-dec'-i-mal
du'-o-dec'-i-mo
du'-o-de'-nal
du'-o-den'-ar:y*†
du-o-de'-num
du-op'-o-ly
du-op'-so-ny
dup'-a:ble
duped
dup'-er:y
dup'-ing
du'-plex
du-plex'-i-ty
du'-pli-cate
du'-pli-ca'-tion
du'-pli-ca-tive
du'-pli-ca-tor
du-plic'-i-ty
Du-quesne'
du-ra-bil'-i-ty
du'-ra-ble
Du-ral'-u-min†
du'-ra ma'-ter
du-ra'-men
du'-rance*†
du-ra'-tion
dur'-bar
Dü'-rer
Dur'-ham
du'-ri-an
dur'-ing
dusk'-i-ness

dusk'y
Dus'-sel-dorf
dust'-bin
dust bowl
dust brush
dust cap
dust'-cloth
dust cov'-er
dust'-er
dust'-heap
dust'-i-ly
dust'-less
dust'-man
dust'-pan
dust'-proof
dust'=tight
dust'y
Dutch'-man
du'-te-ous
du'-te-ous-ly
du'-ti-a:ble
du'-ties
du'-ti-ful
du'-ty
du'-ve-tyn
Dvo'-rak
dwarf'-ish
dwell'-er
dwell'-ing
dwell'-ing place
dwelt
dwin'-dle
dwin'-dling
dy'-ad
Dy'-ak
dyed
dye'-ing
dy'-ing
dyke
dy'-na-graph
dy-nam'-ic
dy-nam'-i-cal
dy-nam'-ics
dy'-na-mism
dy-na-mis'-tic
dy'-na-mite
dy'-na-mit-ed
dy'-na-mit-er
dy'-na-mo
dy'-na-mos
dy-na-mom'-e-ter
dy'-na-mo-tor
dy'-nast
dy-nas'-tic
Dy-nel'
dys'-en-ter'-ic
dys'-en-ter:y
dys-func'-tion

115

dys'-lo-gis'-tic
dys-pep'-sia
dys-pep'-tic
dysp'-ne:a
dys-pro'-si-um

E

ea'-ger
ea'-ger-ly
ea'-ger-ness
ea'-gle
ea'-gle=eyed
ea'-glet
ea'-gre
ear'-ache
ear'-drop
ear'-drum
earl'-dom
ear'-li-er
ear'-li-est
ear'-ly
ear'-mark
ear'-muff
earn'-er
ear'-nest
ear'-nest-ly
ear'-nest-ness
earn'-ing
ear'-phone
ear'-ring
ear'-shot
earth'-born
earth'-en
earth'-en-ware
earth'-i-er
earth'-i-ness
earth'-li-ness
earth'-ly
earth'-quake
earth'-ward
earth'-work
earth'-worm
earth'y
ear trum'-pet
ear'-wax
ear'-wig
eased
ea'-sel
ease'-ment
eas'-i-er
eas'-i-est
eas'-i-ly
eas'-i-ness
eas'-ing
Eas'-ter*†
east'-er (type of storm)
east'-er-ly

east'-ern
east'-ern-er
Eas'-ter-tide*†
Eas'-ton
east'-ward
eas'y
eas'y chair
eas'y-go-ing
eat'-a-ble
eat'-en
eat'-er
eat'-ing
eaves
eaves'-drop
eaves'-drop-per
eaves'-drop-ping
ebbed
ebb'-ing
Eb-e-ne'-zer*
eb'-on
eb'-on-ite†
eb'-o-ny*
e:brac'-te-ate
E'bro
e:bul'-lience
e:bul'-lient
e:bul-li-om'-e-ter
e:bul-li-o-scop'-ic
e:bul-li-os'-co-py
eb-ul-li'-tion
eb-ur-na'-tion*
Ec-bat'-a-na
ec'-ce ho'-mo
ec-cen'-tric
ec-cen'-tri-cal
ec-cen'-tri-cal-ly
ec-cen-tric'-i-ty
ec-chy-mo'-sis
ec-cle'-si:a
Ec-cle-si-as'-tes
ec-cle-si-as'-tic
ec-cle-si-as'-ti-cal
ec-cle-si-ol'-a-try
ec-cle-si-ol'-o-gy
ec-dys'-i-al
ec-dys'-i-ast
ec'-dy-sis
ec'-go-nine
E:che-ga-ray'
ech'-e-lon
e:chid'-na
e:chi'-nate*†
e:chi'-no-derm
e:chi'-noid
e:chi'-nus
ech'o
ech'-oed
ech'-oes

e:cho'-ic†
ech'o-ing
ech'o-ism
ech'o-me-ter
é'clair
ec-lamp'-si:a
é:clat'
ec-lec'-tic
ec-lec'-ti-cal
ec-lec'-ti-cism
e:clipse'
e:clips'-ing
e:clip'-tic
ec'-lo-gite
ec'-logue
e:clo'-sion
é:cole'
ec-o-log'-i-cal
e:col'-o-gist
e:col'-o-gy
e:con'-o-met'-ric
ec-o-nom'-ic*
ec-o-nom'-i-cal*
ec-o-nom'-i-cal-ly*
e:con'-o-mies
e:con'-o-mist
e:con'-o-mize
e:con'-o-miz-ing
e:con'-o-my
ec'-o-sphere
ec'-ru†
ec'-sta-sies
ec'-sta-sy
ec-stat'-ic
ec-stat'-i-cal-ly
ec'-to-derm
ec'-to-der'-mal
ec'-to-der-moi'-dal
ec-tog'-e-nous
ec-to-par'-a-site
ec'-to-plasm
ec'-to-plas-mic
ect'-os-to'-sis*†
ec'-typ-al*†
Ec'-ua-dor
Ec'-ua-dor'-an*
Ec'-ua-dor'-i-an*†
ec-u-men'-i-cal
ec-u-me-nic'-i-ty*
ec-ze'-ma
ec-ze'-ma-tous*†
e:da'-cious
e:dac'-i-ty
E'dam
Ed'-da
Ed'-die
ed'-died

ed'-dies
ed'-dy
ed'-dy-ing
Ed'-dy-stone
e'del-weiss
e:de'-ma
e:dem'-a-tous
E'den
e:den'-tate
Ed'-gar
edge'-ways
edge'-wise
Edge'-worth
edg'-ing
edg'y
ed-i-bil'-i-ty
ed'-i-ble
e'dict
e'dic'-tal
ed-i-fi-ca'-tion
ed'-i-fice
ed'-i-fied
ed'-i-fies
ed'-i-fy
ed'-i-fy-ing
Ed'-in-burg (Tex.)
Ed'-in-burgh (Scot.)
Ed'-i-son
ed'-it
E'dith
e:di'-tion
ed'-i-tor
ed-i-to'-ri-al
ed-i-to'-ri-al-ize
ed-i-to'-ri-al-ly
ed'-i-tor-ship
Ed'-mond
Ed'-mund
Ed'-na
E'dom
E'dom-ite
ed'-u-ca-ble
ed'-u-cate
ed'-u-cat-ing
ed-u-ca'-tion
ed-u-ca'-tion-al
ed-u-ca'-tion-al-ist
ed-u-ca'-tion-al-ly
ed'-u-cat-ive*†
ed'-u-ca-tor
ed'-u-ca-to-ry
e:duce'
e:duc'-i:ble
e:duc'-tion
e:duc'-tive
e:duc'-tor
e:dul'-co-rate
Ed'-ward

117

Ed'-win
Ed-wi'-na
eel'-grass
eel'y
ee'-rie
ee'-ri-ly
ee'-ri-ness
ef-face'
ef-face'-a:ble
ef-face'-ment
ef-fac'-ing
ef-fect'
ef-fect'-i:ble
ef-fec'-tive
ef-fec'-tive-ly
ef-fec'-tive-ness
ef-fec'-tu-al
ef-fec-tu-al'-i-ty
ef-fec'-tu-al-ly
ef-fec'-tu-ate
ef-fec-tu-a'-tion
ef-fem'-i-na-cy
ef-fem'-i-nate
ef'-fer-ent
ef-fer-vesce'
ef-fer-ves'-cence
ef-fer-ves'-cent
ef-fer-vesc'-i:ble*
ef-fer-vesc'-ing
ef-fete'
ef-fi-ca'-cious
ef'-fi-ca-cy
ef-fi'-cien-cy
ef-fi'-cient
ef-fi'-cient-ly
ef-fig'-ial
ef'-fi-gy
ef'-flo-resce'
ef-flo-res'-cence
ef-flo-res'-cent
ef-flu-ence
ef'-flu-ent
ef-flu'-vi-um
ef-fo'-di-ent
ef'-fort
ef-fron-ter'-y:y†
ef-ful'-gence
ef-ful'-gent
ef-fuse'
ef-fu-si-om'-e-ter
ef-fu'-sion
ef-fu'-sive
ef-fu'-sive-ly
eft-soon'
e:gad'
e:gal-i-tar'-i-an†
Eg'-bert
E:ge'-ri:a

e:ges'-tive
egg'-head
egg'-nog
egg'-plant
egg'-shaped
egg'-shell
e'gis
eg'-lan-tine
e'go†
e'go-cen'-tric†
e:go-cen-tric'-i-ty†
e:go-cen'-trism
e'go-ism†
e'go-ist†
e'go-is'-tic†
e'go-is'-ti-cal†
e'go-tism†
e'go-tist†
e'go-tis'-tic†
e'go-tis'-ti-cal†
e'go-tis'-ti-cal-ly†
e:gre'-gious
e'gress
e:gres'-sion
e'gret
E'gypt
E:gyp'-tian
E:gyp-tol'-o-gist†
E:gyp-tol'-o-gy†
ei'-co-sane
ei'-der
ei'-der-down
ei'-do-graph
ei'-do-lon
ei-dou-ra'-ni-on
Eif'-fel
ei'-gen-func-tion
ei'-gen-val-ue
eight
eigh-teen'*†
eigh-teenth'*†
eight'-fold
eighth
eight'-i-eth
eight'y
ei-ko-nom'-e-ter
Ein'-stein
Ein'-stein-i-an
ein'-stei-ni-um
eis-e-ge'-sis*†
ei'-ther
e:jac'-u-late
e:jac'-u-lat-ing
e:jac'-u-la'-tion
e:jac'-u-la-tive
e:jac'-u-la-to-ry
e:ject'

e:jec'-ta
e:jec'-tion
e:jec'-tive
e:jec'-tor
eked
ek'-ing
e:lab'-o-rate
e:lab'-o-rate-ly
e:lab'-o-rate-ness
e:lab'-o-rat-ing
e:lab-o-ra'-tion
e:lab'-o-ra-tive
el-ae-op'-tene
el-a-gab'-a-lus
E:laine'
E'lam
é:lan'
e'land
e:lapse'
e:laps'-ing
e:las'-mo-branch
e:las'-tic
e:las'-ti-cal-ly
e:las-tic'-i-ty
e:las'-to-mer
e:las-tom'-e-ter
e:las-to'-sis
e:late'
e:lat'-ed
el'-a-ter
e:lat'-er-id
e:lat'-er-in
el-a-te'-ri-um
e:la'-tion
El'-ba
El-ber'-ta
el'-bow
el'-bow-room
el'-der*†
el'-der-ber-ry
el'-der-ly*†
el'-dest*†
El Do-ra'-do
El'-ea-nor
El-ea-nor'a†
El-e-a'-zar
el-e-cam-pane'
e:lect'
e:lec'-tion
e:lec'-tion-eer'
e:lec'-tive
e:lec'-tor
e:lec'-tor-al†
e:lec'-tor-ate†
E:lec'-tra
e:lec'-tric
e:lec'-tri-cal
e:lec'-tri-cal-ly

e:lec-tri'-cian
e:lec-tric'-i-ty
e:lec-tri-fi-ca'-tion
e:lec'-tri-fied
e:lec'-tri-fy
e:lec'-tro
e:lec-tro-a:nal'-y-sis
e:lec-tro-car'-di:o-gram
e:lec-tro-car'-di:o-graph
e:lec-tro-chem'-i-cal
e:lec-tro-chem'-is-try
e:lec'-tro-cute
e:lec-tro-cu'-tion
e:lec'-trode
e:lec-tro-dy-nam'-ics
e:lec-tro-graph'-ic
e:lec-trog'-ra-phy
e:lec-trol'-y-sis
e:lec'-tro-lyte
e:lec-tro-lyt'-ic
e:lec-tro-lyt'-i-cal
e:lec'-tro-lyze
e:lec'-tro-mag-net
e:lec-tro-mag-net'-ic
e:lec-tro-mag'-net-ism
e:lec-trom'-e-ter
e:lec-tro-met'-ric
e:lec'-tro-mo-tive
e:lec'-tron
e:lec-tron'-ic
e:lec-tro-os-mo'-sis
e:lec-troph'-o-rus
e:lec'-tro-plate
e:lec'-tros
e:lec'-tro-scope
e:lec-tro-scop'-ic
e:lec-tro-stat'-ic
e:lec-tro-ther'-a-py
e:lec-tro-ton'-ic
e:lec-trot'-o-nus
e:lec'-tro-type
e:lec'-tro-typ-er
e:lec'-trum
e:lec'-tu-ar:y†
el-ee-mos'-y-nar:y†
el'-e-gance
el'-e-gan-cy
el'-e-gant
el'-e-gant-ly
el'-e-gi'-ac†
el'-e-gist
el'-e-gize
el'-e-gy
el'-e-ment
el-e-men'-tal
el-e-men-tar'-i-ly*
el-e-men'-ta-ry
el'-e-mi

El'-e-na
e:len'-chus
e:lenc'-tic
el'-e-phant
el-e-phan-ti'-a-sis
el'-e-phan'-tine
El-eu-sin'/-i-an
E:leu'-sis
el'-e-vate
el'-e-vat-ed
el-e-va'-tion
el'-e-va-tor
e:lev'-en
e:lev'-enth
el'-e-von
elf'-in
elf'-ish
El'-gin
E'li
E:li'-as
e:lic'-it
e:lic-i-ta'-tion
e:lic'-i-tor
e:lide'
e:lid'-i-ble
e:lid'-ing
el-i-gi-bil'-i-ty
el'-i-gi-ble
E:li'-hu
E:li'-jah
e:lim'-i-nant
e:lim'-i-nate
e:lim-i-na'-tion
e:lim'-i-na-tor
El'-i-ot
E'lis
E:li'-sha
e:li'-sion
e:lite'
e:lix'-ir
E:li'-za
E:liz'-a-beth
E:liz-a-be'-than†
Elk'-hart
El'-la
El'-len
El'-li-ot
el-lipse'
el-lips'-es (pl. of ellipse)
el-lip'-ses (pl. of ellipsis)
el-lip'-sis
el-lip'-soid*
el-lip'-soi'-dal
el-lip-som'-e-ter
el-lip'-tic
el-lip'-ti-cal
el-lip-tic'-i-ty

El'-lis
El'-mer
El-mi'-ra
e-lo-cu'-tion
e-lo-cu'-tion-ar:y†
e-lo-cu'-tion-ist
e:loge'
e:lo'-gi-um
El-o-him'
El-o-his'-tic
e:loign'-er
e:lon'-gate
e:lon-ga'-tion
e:lope'
e:lope'-ment
e:lop'-er
e:lop'-ing
el'-o-quence
el'-o-quent
el'-o-quent-ly
El Pas'o†
El'-sa
else'-where
El'-sie
e:lu'-ci-date
e:lu-ci-da'-tion
e:lu'-ci-da-tive
e:lude'
e:lud'-i-ble
e:lud'-ing
el'-u-ent
E:lul'
e:lu'-sion
e:lu'-sive
e:lu'-so-ry
e:lu'-tri-ate
e:lu'-vi-um
El'-vis
el'-vish*†
El'-wood
E'ly
E:ly'-ri:a†
E:ly-see'
E:ly'-sian†
E:ly'-si-um†
El'-ze-vir
e:ma'-ci-ate
e:ma-ci-a'-tion
em'-a-nate
em-a-na'-tion
em'-a-na-tive
e:man'-ci-pate
e:man-ci-pa'-tion
e:man'-ci-pa-tor
em-a-nom'-e-ter
e:mar'-gi-nate
e:mas'-cu-late

e:mas-cu-la'-tion
em-balm'
em-balm'-er
em-balm'-ment
em-bank'
em-bank'-ment
em-bar-ca-de'-ro
em-bar'-go
em-bar'-goed
em-bar'-goes
em-bark'
em-bar-ka'-tion
em'-bar-ras'
em-bar'-rass
em-bar'-rassed
em-bar'-rass-es
em-bar'-rass-ing
em-bar'-rass-ing-ly
em-bar'-rass-ment
em'-bas-sage
em'-bas-sies
em'-bas-sy
em-bat'-tle
em-bed'
em-bed'-ded
em-bel'-lish
em-bel'-lish-ment
em'-ber
em-bez'-zle
em-bez'-zled
em-bez'-zle-ment
em-bez'-zler
em-bit'-ter
em-bla'-zon
em-bla'-zon-ment
em-bla'-zon-ry
em'-blem
em'-blem-at'-ic
em-blem-at'-i-cal
em-blem-at'-i-cal-ly
em-blem'-a-tize
em'-ble-ment
em-bod'-i-ment
em-bod'y
em-bold'-en
em-bo-lec'-to-my
em-bol'-ic
em'-bo-lism
em-bo-lis'-mic
em'-bo-lus
em-bon-point'
em-bos'-om†
em-boss'
em-bossed'
em-boss'-er
em-boss'-ing
em-bou-chure'

em-bow'-el
em-bow'-er
em-brace'
em-brace'-a:ble
em-brace'-or
em-brac'-er
em-brac'-er:y
em-brac'-ing
em-bran'-gle-ment
em-bra'-sure
em'-bro-cate
em-bro-ca'-tion
em-broi'-der
em-broi'-der-er
em-broi'-der:y
em-broil'
em-broil'-ment
em-brown'
em-bry-ec'-to-my
em'-bry:o
em-bry:o-ge-net'-ic
em-bry-og'-e-ny
em-bry-o-log'-i-cal
em-bry-ol'-o-gist
em-bry-ol'-o-gy
em'-bry-o-nal
em-bry-on'-ic
em'-bry-os
e:mend'
e:mend'-a:ble
e-men-da'-tion
e'men-da-tor†
e:men'-da-to-ry*†
em'-er-ald
em'-er-al-dine*
e:merge'
e:mer'-gence
e:mer'-gen-cies
e:mer'-gen-cy
e:mer'-gent
e:merg'-ing
e:mer'-i-tus
e:mer'-sion
Em'-er-son
em'-er:y
em'-e-sis
e:met'-ic
em'-e-tine
em'-i-grant
em'-i-grate
em'-i-grat-ing
em-i-gra'-tion
e:mi-gre'
E'mil
E:mile'
Em'-i-ly
em'-i-nence

em'-i-nen-cy
em'-i-nent
em'-i-nent-ly
e:mir'
em'-is-sar-ies†
em'-is-sar:y†
e:mis'-sion
e:mis'-sive
e:mis-siv'-i-ty*†
e:mit'
e:mit'-ted
e:mit'-ter
e:mit'-ting
Em'-ma
Em-man'-u-el
em'-mer
em'-met
Em'-mett
em-me-tro'-pi:a
em'-o-din
e:mol'-lient
e:mol'-u-ment
e:mote'
e:mot'-er
e:mot'-ing
e:mo'-tion
e:mo'-tion-al
e:mo'-tion-al-ism
e:mo'-tion-al-ize
e:mo'-tion-al-ly
e:mo'-tive
e:mo-tiv'-i-ty
em-pan'-el
em-pan'-el-ing
em-path'-ic
em'-pa-thy
Em-ped'-o-cles
em-pen'-nage
em'-per-or
em'-per:y
em'-pha-ses
em'-pha-sis
em'-pha-size
em'-pha-siz-ing
em-phat'-ic
em-phat'-i-cal-ly
em-phy-se'-ma
em'-pire
em-pir'-ic
em-pir'-i-cal
em-pir'-i-cism
em-pir'-i-cist
em'-pi-ris'-tic
em-place'-ment
em-ploy'
em-ploy-ee'
em-ploy'-er
em-ploy'-ment

em-po-reu'-tic
Em-po'-ri:a
em-po'-ri-um
em-pow'-er
em'-press
em-prise'
emp'-tied
emp'-ti-er
emp'-ties
emp'-ti-ness
emp'-ty
emp'-ty=hand-ed
emp'-ty=head-ed
emp'-ty-heart-ed
emp'-ty-ing
em-pur'-pled
em-py-e'-ma
em'-py-re'-al*†
em-py-re'-an
em-py-reu'-ma
e'mu
em'-u-late
em-u-la'-tion
em'-u-la-tive
em'-u-la-tive-ly
em'-u-la-tor
em'-u-la-to-ry
em'-u-lous
em'-u-lous-ly
e:mul-si-fi-ca'-tion
e:mul-si-fied'
e:mul'-si-fi-er
e:mul'-si-fy
e:mul'-sion
e:mul'-sive
e:mul'-sold
e:munc'-to-ry
en-a'ble
en-a'bling
en-act'
en-ac'-tive
en-act'-ment
en-ac'-to-ry
en-am'-el
en-am'-eled
en-am'-el-er
en-am'-el-ware
en-am'-or
en-am'-ored
e:nan-thal'-de-hyde
e:nan'-thic
en-an'-ti-o-morph
en-ar'-gite
en-ar-thro'-sis
en-cae'-nia
en-camp'
en-camp'-ment
en-cap'-su-late

en-car'-nal-ize
en-case'
en-cas'-ing
en-caus'-tic
en-ceinte'
en'-ce-phal'-ic
en-ceph'-a-lit'-ic
en-ceph-a-li'-tis
en-ceph'-a-lo-cele
en-ceph'-a-lo-coele
en-ceph'-a-lo-gram
en-ceph'-a-lo-graph'-ic
en-ceph-a-log'-ra-phy
en-ceph'-a-loid
en-ceph'-a-lon
en-ceph-a-lop'-a-thy
en-chain'
en-chant'
en-chant'-er
en-chant'-ing
en-chant'-ment
en-chant'-ress
en-chase'
en-chi-la'-da
en-chi-rid'-i-on
en-chon-dro'-ma
en-chon-drom'-a-tous
en-cho'-ri-al
en-chym'-a-tous
en-ci'-na
en'-ci-nal'
en-cir'-cle
en-cir'-cle-ment
en-cir'-cling
en'-clave
en-clit'-ic
en-close'
en-clos'-er
en-clos'-ing
en-clo'-sure
en-coi'-gnure
en-co'-mi-ast
en-co'-mi-as'-tic
en-co'-mi-um
en-com'-pass
en'-core
en-coun'-ter
en-cour'-age
en-cour'-age-ment
en-cour'-ag-ing
en-crat'-ic
en-cri'-nal
en-crin'-ic
en'-cri-nite
en-croach'
en-croach'-ment
en-crust'
en-crus-ta'-tion

en-cum'-ber
en-cum'-brance
en-cyc'-lic*
en-cyc'-li-cal*
en-cy-clo-pe'-di:a
en-cy-clo-pe'-dic
en-cy-clo-pe'-dism
en-cy-clo-pe'-dist
en-cyst'
en-cys-ta'-tion
en-cyst'-ment
end'-a:moe'-ba*†
en-dan'-ger
end-ar-te-ri'-tis*†
en-dear'
en-dear'-ing
en-dear'-ment
en-deav'-or
en-deav'-ored
en-de'-mi-al
en-dem'-ic
en-dem'-i-cal-ly
en-de-mic'-i-ty
en-de-mi-ol'-o-gy
en'-de-mism
En'-der-by
end'-er-gon'-ic
en-der'-mic
En'-di-cott
end'-ing
en'-dive
end'-less
end'-less-ly
end'-long
end man
end'-most
en'-do-blas'-tic
en'-do-car-di'-tis
en-do-car'-di-um
en'-do-carp
en'-do-cri'-nal
en'-do-crine
en'-do-crin-o-log'-ic
en-do-cri-nol'-o-gy
en'-do-crin'-o-path'-ic
en-do-cri-nop'-a-thy
en-doc'-ri-nous†
en'-do-der'-mal
en'-do-gam'-ic
en-dog'-a-mous
en-dog'-a-my
en-do-ge-net'-ic
en-do-ge-nic'-i-ty
en-dog'-e-nous
en-dog'-e-nous-ly
en-do-me-tri'-tis
en-do-me'-tri-um
en'-do-mor'-phic

123

en'-do-plasm
en'-do-plas'-ma
en'-do-plas'-mic
en-dors'-a:ble
en-dorse'
en-dors'-ee*
en-dorse'-ment
en-dors'-er
en-dors'-ing
en-dos'-co-py
end'-os-mo'-sis*†
en'-do-sperm
en-do-spo'-ri-um
en'-do-spor'-ous*†
end-os'-te-um*†
end-os-to'-sis*†
en-do-the'-ci-um
en'-do-the'-li-al
en-do-the-li-o'-ma
en-do-the'-li-um
en'-do-the'-loid*
en'-do-ther'-mic
en-dow'
en-dow'-ment
en'-drin
en-due'
en-dur'-a:ble
en-dur'-ance
en-dure'
en-dur'-ing
end'-ways
end'-wise
En-dym'-i-on
ene'-di'-ol
en'-e-ma
en'-e-mies
en'-e-my
en-er-gei'a
en-er-get'-ic
en-er-get'-i-cal
en-er-get'-i-cal-ly
en'-er-gies
en'-er-gism
en'-er-gize
en'-er-giz-er
en'-er-gu'-men
en'-er-gy
en'-er-vate
en-er-va'-tion
en'-er-va-tor
en-face'
en-fant'
en-fee'-ble
en-fee'-bling
en-feoff'-ment
en-fet'-ter
en'-fi-lade
en'-fleu-rage'

en-fold'
en-force'
en-force'-a:ble
en-forc'-ed-ly*
en-force'-ment
en-forc'-er
en-forc'-ing
en-fran'-chise
en-fran'-chise-ment
en-gage'
en-gaged'
en-gage'-ment
en-gag'-ing
En'-gels†
en-gen'-der
en'-gine
en-gi-neer'
en-gi-neer'-ing
en'-gine room
en'-gine-ry
En'-gland*
En'-gland-er*
En'-glish*
En'-glish-ism*
En'-glish-man*
En'-glish-wom-an*†
en-graft'
en-grain'
en-grave'
en-grav'-er
en-grav'-ing
en-gross'
en-gross'-ing
en-gross'-ment
en-gulf'
en-hance'
en-hance'-ment
en-hanc'-ing
en-har-mon'-ic
E'nid
e:nig'-ma
e:nig-mat'-ic
e:nig-mat'-i-cal
e:nig-mat'-i-cal-ly
e:nig'-ma-tize
En-i-we'-tok
en-join'
en-join'-der
en-joy'
en-joy'-a:ble
en-joy'-a:bly
en-joy'-ment
en-kin'-dle
en-kin'-dling
en-lace'
en-large'
en-large'-ment
en-light'-en

en-light'-en-ment
en-list'
en-list-ee'
en-list'-ment
en-liv'-en†
en-mesh'
en'-mi-ties
en'-mi-ty
en'-ne-ad
en-no'-ble
en-no'-bler
en-no'-bling
en-nui'
en'-nuy:é'
E'noch
e:nor'-mi-ty
e:nor'-mous
e:nor'-mous-ly
E'nos
e:no'-sis
e:nough'
e:now'
en-phy-tot'-ic
en-quire'
en'-quir:y
en-rage'
en rap-port'
en-rapt'
en-rap'-ture
en-rav'-ish
en-rich'
en-rich'-ment
en-robe'
en-roll'
en-rolled'
en-roll'-ee'
en-roll'-ing
en-roll'-ment
en-rol'-ment
en route
en-sam'-ple
en-san'-guine
en-sconce'
en-sconce'-ing
en-sem'-ble
en-shrine'
en-shroud'
en'-si-form
en'-sign (n.)
en-sign' (v.)
en'-sign-cy
en'-si-lage
en-slave'
en-slave'-ment
en-slav'-er
en-slav'-ing
en-snare'
en-sor'-cell

en-sue'
en-su'-ing
en-su'-ing-ly
en-sure'
en-tab'-la-ture
en-tail'
en-tail'-ment
en-tan'-gle
en-tan'-gle-ment
en-tan'-gler
en-tan'-gling
en'-ta-sis
en-tel'-e-chy
en-tente'
en'-ter
en-ter-al'-gi:a
en-ter'-ic
en-ter-i'-tis
en-ter-o-cri'-nin
en'-ter-on
en-ter-os'-to-my
en'-ter-prise
en'-ter-pris-ing
en'-ter-pris-ing-ly
en-ter-tain'
en-ter-tain'-er
en-ter-tain'-ing
en-ter-tain'-ment
en'-thal-py
en-thet'-ic
en-thrall'
en-thrall'-ing
en-thrall'-ing-ly
en-throne'
en-thron-i:za'-tion†
en-thuse'
en-thu'-si-asm
en-thu'-si-ast
en-thu-si-as'-tic
en-thu-si-as'-ti-cal-ly
en'-thy-meme
en-tice'
en-tice'-ment
en-tic'-ing
en-tire'
en-tire'-ly
en-tire'-ty
en'-ti-ties
en-ti'-tle
en-ti'-ty
en-tomb'
en-tomb'-ment
en-to-mo-log'-i-cal
en-to-mol'-o-gist
en-to-mol'-o-gy
en-to-mos'-tra-can
en'-tou-rage'
en'-tr'acte

125

en'-trails
en-train'
en'-trance (n.)
en-trance' (v.)
en'-trance-way
en-tranc'-ing
en-tranc'-ing-ly
en'-trant
en-trap'
en-trap'-ment
en-trap'-ping
en'-tre
en-treat'
en-treat'-ies
en-treat'-ing
en-treat'-ing-ly
en-treat'y
en'-trée
en'-tre-mets'
en-trench'
en-trench'-ment
en'-tre nous
en'-tre-pre-neur'
en-tre-pre-neur'-i-al
en'-tre-sol
en'-tries
en'-tro-py
en-trust'
en'-try
en'-try-way
en-twine'
e:nu'-cle-ate
e:nu'-mer-ate
e:nu-mer-a'-tion
e:nu'-mer-a-tive
e:nu'-mer-a-tor
e:nun'-cia-ble
e:nun'-ci-ate
e:nun-ci-a'-tion
e:nun'-cia-tive
e:nun'-ci-a-tor
en-vel'-op
en-ve-lope
en-vel'-oped
en-vel'-op-ing
en-vel'-op-ment
en-ven'-om
en'-vi-a:ble
en'-vi-a:bly
en'-vied
en'-vies
en'-vi-ous
en'-vi-ous-ly
en-vi'-ron
en-vi'-ron-ment
en-vi'-ron-men'-tal
en-vi'-rons
en-vis'-age

en-vi'-sion
en'-voy
en'-vy
en'-vy-ing
en'-vy-ing-ly
en-wrap'
en-zo-ot'-ic
en'-zy-mat'-ic
en'-zyme
en-zy-mol'-o-gy
E'o-cene
e:o-hip'-pus
e'o-lith
e'o-lith'-ic
e'on
E'os
e'o-sin
e:o-sin'-o-phil
e:os'-pho-rite
E'o-zo'-ic
e'pact†
ep'-a-go-ge
E:pam-i-non'-das
ep'-arch
ep-ar'-chi-al
ep'-au-let'
é'pée
é'pée-ist
e:pei'-ro-gen'-ic†
ep-ei-rog'-e-ny
ep'-en-ceph'-a-lon
ep-en'-dy-ma
ep-en'-the-sis
ep'-ex-e-ge'-sis
e'phah
e:phe'-bic
e:phed'-rine†
e:phem'-er:a
e:phem'-er-al
e:phem'-er-id
e:phem'-er-is
e:phem'-er-on
E:phe'-sian
Eph'-e-sus
eph'-od
eph'-or
E'phra-im
Eph'-ra-ta
ep'-i-bol'-ic
e:pib'-o-ly
ep'-ic
ep'-i-cal
ep'-i-cal-ly
ep'-i-ca'-lyx
ep'-i-can'-thic
ep'-i-can'-thus
ep-i-car'-di-um
ep'-i-carp

ep'-i-cede
ep-i-ce'-di-um
ep'-i-cene
ep-i-cen-ism
ep'-i-cen'-ter
ep'-i-cen'-trum
ep'-i-cot-yl
ep'-i-crit'-ic
Ep-ic-te'-tus
ep'-i-cure
Ep'-i-cu-re'-an
ep'-i-cur-ism
Ep'-i-cu-rus
ep'-i-cy-cle
ep'-i-cy'-cloid
ep-i-cy'-cloi'-dal
ep'-i-dem'-ic
ep-i-dem'-i-cal
ep-i-de-mic'-i-ty
ep-i-de-mi-o-log'-i-cal
ep-i-de-mi-ol'-o-gy
ep'-i-der'-mal
ep'-i-der'-mic
ep'-i-der'-mis
ep-i-der'-moid
ep-i-der-moi'-dal
ep'-i-did'-y-mis
ep'-i-dote
ep'-i-dot-ite
ep-i-du'-ral
ep'-i-fo'-cal
ep-i-gas'-tric
ep-i-gas'-tri-um
ep'-i-ge'-al
ep-i-gen'-e-sis
ep'-i-ge-net'-ic
e:pig'-e-nous
ep'-i-glot'-tis
ep'-i-gone
ep'-i-gram
ep'-i-gram-mat'-ic
ep'-i-gram-mat'-i-cal
ep-i-gram'-ma-tist
ep'-i-graph
e:pig'-ra-pher
ep'-i-graph'-ic
e:pig'-ra-phy
e:pig'-y-nous
ep-i-la'-tion
ep'-i-la-tor
ep'-i-lep-sy
ep'-i-lep'-tic
ep'-i-logue
ep'-i-mer
ep-i-mer-i-za'-tion
ep'-i-mer-ize
Ep-i-me'-theus
ep'-i-nas-ty

ep-i-neph'-rine
ep-i-neu'-ri-um
ep'-i-nine
E:piph'-a-ny
ep-i-phe-nom'-e-non
e:piph'-y-se'-al*†
e:piph'-y-sis
ep'-i-phyte
ep'-i-phy-tot'-ic
ep'-i-pter'-ic
E:pi'-rote
E:pi'-rus
e:pis'-co-pa-cy
e:pis'-co-pal
E:pis'-co-pa'-lian
e:pis'-co-pal-ism
e:pis'-co-pate
ep-i-sco-tis'-ter
ep'-i-sode
ep-i-sod'-ic
ep'-i-sod'-i-cal
ep'-i-sod'-i-cal-ly
ep'-i-spas'-tic
e:pis'-ta-sis
ep-i-stat'-ic
ep-i-stax'-is
ep-i-ste'-me
e:pis'-te-mo-log'-i-cal†
e:pis'-te-mol'-o-gy†
ep'-i-ster'-num
e:pis'-tle
e:pis'-to-lar:y†
ep'-i-stome
ep'-i-taph
e:pit'-a-sis
ep-i-tha-la'-mi-on
ep-i-tha-la'-mi-um
ep-i-the'-li-al
ep-i-the-li-o'-ma
ep'-i-the-li-om'-a-tous
ep-i-the'-li-um
ep'-i-them
e:pith'-e-sis
ep'-i-thet
ep:it'-o-me
ep'-i-tom'-i-cal
ep:it'-o-mize
e:pit'-ro-phy
ep-i-zo'-on
ep'-i-zo-ot'-ic
ep-i-zo'-o-ty
e plu'-ri-bus u'num
ep'-och
ep'-och-al
ep'-ode
ep'-o-nym
ep'-o-nym'-ic
e:pon'-y-mous

127

e:pon'-y-my
ep'-o-pee
ep'-os
ep-ox'y
ep'-si-lon
Ep'-som
Ep'-stein
eq-ua-bil'-i-ty†
eq'-ua-ble†
e'qual
e'qualed
e'qual-ing
e:qual'-i-tar'-i-an†
e:qual'-i-ty
e'qual-i-za'-tion
e'qual-ize
e'qual-iz-er
e'qual-ly
e:qua-nim'-i-ty
e:quate'
e:qua'-tion
e:quat'-ive
e:qua'-tor
e:qua-to'-ri-al
eq'-uer-ry
e:ques'-tri-an
e:ques'-tri-enne'
e'qui-an'-gu-lar
e:qui-an-gu-lar'-i-ty
e'qui-dis'-tant
e'qui-lat'-er-al
eq-ui-len'-in†
e:quil'-i-brant†
e:quil'-i-brate*†
e:quil-i-bra'-tion*†
e:qui-lib'-ri-rist*†
e:qui-lib'-ri-stat
e:qui-lib'-ri-um
eq'-ui-lin
e'quine
e'qui-noc'-tial
e'qui-nox
e:quip'
eq'-ui-page
e:quip'-ment
eq'-ui-poise*†
e:qui-pol'-lence
e:qui-pol'-lent
e:qui-pon'-der-ate
e'qui-po-ten'-tial
e:quipped'
e:quip'-ping
eq-ui-se'-tum
eq'-ui-ta-ble
eq'-ui-tes
eq'-ui-ties
eq'-ui-ty
e:quiv'-a-lence

e:quiv'-a-len-cy
e:quiv'-a-lent
e:quiv'-o-cal
e:quiv'-o-cate
e:quiv'-o-ca'-tion
e:quiv'-o-ca-tor
eq'-ui-voque
e'ra
e:ra-di-a'-tion
e:rad'-i-ca-ble
e:rad'-i-cate
e:rad-i-ca'-tion
e:rad'-i-ca-tive
e:rad'-i-ca-tor
e:ras'-a:ble
e:rase'
e:rased'
e:ras'-er
e:ras'-ing
E:ras'-mus
E:ras'-tian
E:ras'-tus
e:ra'-sure
Er'-a-to
Er-a-tos'-the-nes
er'-bi-um
Er'-e-bus
Er-ech-the'-um
e:rect'
e:rec'-tile
e:rec-til'-i-ty
e:rec'-tion
e:rect'-ly
e:rec'-tor
e:rect'-ness
er-e-ma-cau'-sis
er'-e-mite
er-e-mit'-i-cal
er'-e-thism
Er'-e-whon
Er'-furt
er'-ga-tive
er'-go
er-god'-ic
er-go-gen'-ic
er-gom'-e-ter
er'-gone
er-go-no'-vine
er-gos'-ter-ol†
er'-got
er-got'-a-mine
er-got'-ic
er'-go-tism (logical reasoning)
er'-got-ism (toxic condition)
er'-go-tize (to argue logically)

er'-got-ize (to treat with
    ergot)
Er'-ic
er'-i-ca'-ceous
Er'-ic-son
E'rie
e:rig'-er-on
Er'-in†
e:rin'-e-um
er'-in-ite*
e:rin-i-nose
er-i-o-dic'-ty-ol*
er-i-om'-e-ter*
E'ris
e:ris'-tic*
Er-i-tre'a†
Er'-len-mey-er
Er'-ma
er'-mine
Er'-nest
e:rode'
e:rod'-i-ble
e:rog'-e-nous
Er'-os
e:ro'-sion
e:ro'-sive
e:rot'-ic
e:rot'-i-cism
er'-o-tism
err-a:bil'-i-ty*
er'-rand
er'-rant
er'-rant-ry
er-ra'-ta
er-rat'-ic
er-rat'-i-cal-ly
er-ra'-tum
erred
er'-rhine
err'-ing
err'-ing-ly
er-ro'-ne-ous
er-ro'-ne-ous-ly
er'-ror
er'-ror=proof
er'-satz
erst'-while'
er-u-bes'-cence
er-u-bes'-cent
e:ru'-cic
e:ruct'
e:ruc'-tate
e:ruc-ta'-tion
er'-u-dite
er-u-di'-tion
e:rum'-pent
e:rupt'
e:rup'-tion

e:rup'-tive
e:rup-tiv'-i-ty
er-y-sip'-e-las
er'-y-si-pel'-a-tous
er-y-the'-ma
er'-y-them'-a-tous
er'-y-thrine
er'-y-thrism*†
er'-y-thrite*†
e:ryth'-ri-tol
e:ryth'-ro-blast
e:ryth'-ro-cyte
e:ryth-ro-cy-tom'-e-ter
er-y-thro'-i-dine
e:ryth-ro-my'-cin
er-y-thro'-pi:a
e:ryth'-ro-scope
er'-y-throse
e:ryth'-ro-sin
er-y-thro'-sis
e:ryth'-ru-lose
E'sau
es'-ca-drille
es'-ca-lade
es'-ca-la-tor
es-cal'-lop
es-cal'-loped
es-cam'-bi:o
es-cap'-a:ble
es'-ca-pade
es-cape'
es-caped'
es'-cap-ee'*†
es-cape'-ment
es-cap'-ing
es-ca'-pism*
es-cap'-ist
es'-ca-role
es-carp'-ment
es'-char
es'-cha-rot'-ic
es-cha-tol'-o-gist
es-cha-tol'-o-gy
es-cheat'
es-chew'
es-chew'-al
es'-chy-nite
Es-co'-ri-al
es'-cort (n.)
es-cort' (v.)
es'-cri-toire
es'-crow
es-cu-age
es'-cu-do
es-cu'-dos
es'-cu-lent
es'-cu-lin
es-cutch'-eon

129

es'-er-o-line
Es'-ki-mo
Es'-ki-mos
e:soph'-a-ge'-al*†
e:soph-a-gi'-tis
e:soph-a-go-scope
e:soph-a-gos'-co-pist
e:soph'-a-gus
es'-o-ter'-ic
es-o-ter'-i-cal-ly
es-pal'-ier
es-par'-to
es-pe'-cial
es-pe'-cial-ly
Es-pe-ran'-to
cs-pi'-al
es'-pi-o-nage
es'-pla-nade
es-plees'
es-pous'-al†
es-pouse'
es-pous'-er
es-pous'-ing
es-prit'
es-py'
e:squam'-u-lose
Es'-qui-line
es'-quire
es'-say (n.)
es-say' (v.)
es'-say-ist
Es'-sen
es'-sence
Es-sene'
Es-se'-ni-an
es-sen'-tial
es-sen-ti-al'-i-ty
es-sen'-tial-ly
Es'-sex
es'-so-nite
es-tab'-lish
es-tab'-lished
es-tab'-lish-ment
es-ta-mi-net'
es-tate'
es-teem'
es'-ter
es'-ter-ase
es-ter-i-fi-ca'-tion
es-ter'-i-fy
es'-ter-ize
Es'-ther
es-the'-sia
es-the'-sis
es'-thete
es-thet'-ic
es-thet'-ics
Es-tho'-ni:a

Es-tho'-ni-an
es'-ti-ma-ble
es'-ti-mate
es-ti-ma'-tion
es'-ti-ma-tor
es'-ti-va-tor
Es-to'-ni:a
Es-to'-ni-an
es-top'
es-topped'
es-top'-pel
es-top'-ping
es-to'-vers
es-tra-di-ol'
es-trange'
es-trange'-ment
es-trang'-ing
es-tray'
es'-tro-gen
es'-tro-gen'-ic
es'-trone
es'-trous
es'-tu-a-rine
es'-tu-ar:y†
e:su'-ri-ent
e'ta
e'ta-mine*†
et cet'-er:a
etch'-ing
e:ter'-nal
e:ter'-nal-ly
e:ter'-ni-ty
e:te'-sian
E'than
eth'-ane
eth'-a-nol
eth-a-nol-a:mine'
eth-a-nol'-y-sis
Eth'-el
Eth'-el-bert
eth'-ene
e'ther
e:the'-re-al
e:the-re-al'-i-ty
e:the'-re-al-ize
e:the'-re-ous
e:ther-i-fi-ca'-tion
e:ther'-i-fy
e:ther-i:za'-tion
e'ther-ize
eth'-ic
eth'-i-cal
eth'-ics
eth-i-on'-ic
e:thi'-o-nine
E:thi-o'-pi:a
E:thi-o'-pi-an
E:thi-o'-pic

eth'-moid
eth-moi'-dal
eth-moid-i-'tis
eth'-nic
eth'-ni-cal
eth'-ni-cal-ly
eth-nic'-i-ty
eth'-no-cen'-tric
eth'-no-cen'-trism
eth-nog'-e-ny
eth-no-graph'-ic
eth-no-graph'-i-cal
eth-nog'-ra-phy
eth-no-log'-i-cal
eth-nol'-o-gist
eth-nol'-o-gy
e'thos
eth-ox'-y-line
eth'-yl
eth'-yl-a:mine'†
eth'-yl-ate
eth'-yl-ene
eth'-yl-e'-nic
eth'-yl-e:phed'-rine
e:thyl'-ic
e:thyl'-i-dene*
e:thy'-nyl*
e:thy-nyl-a'-tion
E:tienne'
e'ti-o-late
e'ti-o-log'-i-cal
e:ti-ol'-o-gy
e:ti:o-phyl'-lin
et'-i-quette
Et'-na
E'ton
E:to'-ni-an
E:tru'-ri:a
E:trus'-can
é'tude
et-y-mo-log'-i-cal
et-y-mol'-o-gist
et-y-mol'-o-gy
et'-y-mon
Eu-boe'a
eu'-ca-lypt
eu'-ca-lyp'-tic
eu-ca-lyp'-tole
eu-ca-lyp'-tus
eu'-cha-ris
Eu'-cha-rist
Eu-cha-ris'-tic
eu'-chre
eu'-chred
eu'-chro-ite
eu'-clase
Eu'-clid
Eu-clid'-e-an

eu-dae'-mon
eu'-dae-mon'-ic
eu'-dae-mon-ism
eu'-da-lene
eu-di-om'-e-ter
eu'-di-o-met'-ric
Eu-do'-ra
Eu'-gene
eu-gen'-ic
eu-gen'-i-cal
eu-gen'-i-cist
eu-gen'-ics
Eu-ge-nie'
eu-gen'-ist*
eu'-ge-nol
Eu-gle'-na
eu-he'-mer-ism
Eu'-ler
eu-lo'-gi:a
eu'-lo-gies
eu'-lo-gist
eu-lo-gis'-tic
eu-lo-gis'-ti-cal
eu'-lo-gize
eu'-lo-gy
Eu-nice' (feminine name)
Eu-ni'-ce (worm)
eu'-nuch
eu-on'-y-mous
eu-on'-y-my
eu-pa-to'-rin
eu-pa-to'-ri-um
eu-pat'-rid
eu-pat'-ri-dae
eu-pav'-er-ine
eu-pep'-sia
eu-pep'-tic
eu'-phe-mism
eu'-phe-mis'-tic
eu'-phe-mize
eu-phon'-ic
eu-pho'-ni-ous
eu-pho'-ni-um
eu'-pho-ny
eu-phor'-bi:a
eu-phor'-bi-a'-ceous
eu-pho'-ri:a
eu-phor'-ic
eu'-phra-sy
Eu-phra'-tes
eu'-phroe
Eu-phros'-y-ne
Eu'-phu-es
eu'-phu-ism
eu'-phu-is'-tic
eup'-ne:a
Eur-a'sia

Eur-a'sian
Eu-re'-ka
Eu-rip'-i-des
eu-ri'-pus
Eu-ro'-pa
Eu'-rope
Eu-ro-pe'-an
eu-ro'-pi-um
Eu'-rus
Eu-ryd'-i-ce
eu'-ryg-nath'-ic
eu-ryth'-mics
eu-ryth'-my
Eu-se'-bi-an
Eu-sta'-chian
eu'-sta-cy
eu'-tax:y
eu-tec'-tic
eu-tec'-toid
Eu-ter'-pe
eu-tha-na'-sia
eu-then'-ics
eux'-e-nite
Eux'-ine
E'va
e:vac'-u-ate
e:vac-u-a'-tion
e:vac'-u-ee'*
e:vade'
e:vad'-ing
E:vad'-ne
e:vag'-i-nate
e:val'-u-ate
e:val-u-a'-tion
ev'-a-nesce'
ev-a-nes'-cence
ev'-a-nes'-cent
e:van'-gel
e:van-gel'-ic†
e:van-gel'-i-cal†
E:van'-ge-line
e:van'-ge-lism†
e:van'-ge-list†
e:van'-ge-lis'-tic†
e:van'-ge-lize†
Ev'-ans
Ev'-ans-ton
Ev'-ans-ville
e:vap'-o-ra-ble
e:vap'-o-rate
e:vap'-o-rat-ing
e:vap-o-ra'-tion
e:vap'-o-ra-tive
e:vap'-o-ra-tor
e:vap-o-rim''-e-ter
e:va'-si-ble
e:va'-sion
e:va'-sive

e:vec'-tion
Ev-e-li'-na
Ev'-e-lyn
e'ven
e'ven-fall
e'ven-hand-ed
e'ven-ing (making even)
eve'-ning (nightfall)
e'ven-ly
e'ven-ness
e'ven-song
e:vent'
e:vent'-ful
e'ven-tide
e:ven'-tu-al
e:ven'-tu-al'-i-ty
e:ven'-tu-al-ly
e:ven'-tu-ate
ev'-er
Ev'-er-est
Ev'-er-ett
Ev'-er-glades
ev'-er-green
ev-er-last'-ing
ev-er-last'-ing-ly
ev-er-more'
e:ver'-si-ble
e:ver'-sion
e:vert'
e:ver'-tor
ev'-er:y
ev'er:y-bod:y
ev'er:y-day
ev'-er:y-one
ev'-er:y-thing
ev'-er:y-where
e:vict'
e:vic'-tion
e:vic'-tor
ev'-i-dence
ev'-i-denc-ing
ev'-i-dent
ev'-i-den'-tial
ev'-i-dent-ly
e'vil
e'vil-do-er
e'vil-ly
e'vil=mind-ed
e'vil-ness
e:vince'
e:vinc'-i:ble
e:vinc'-ing
e:vin'-cive
e:vis'-cer-ate
e:vis-cer-a'-tion
e:vis'-cer-a-tor
ev'-i-ta-ble
ev'-o-ca-ble

e:vo·ca'·tion*†
e:voc'·a·tive†
e'vo·ca·tor*†
e:voc'·a·to·ry
e:voke'
e:vok'·ing
ev'·o·lute
ev·o·lu'·tion
ev·o·lu'·tion-ar:y†
ev·o·lu'·tion·ist
e:volve'
e:volve'·ment
e:volv'·ing
e:vul'·sion
ev'·zone
ewe
ew'·er
ex-ac'·er·bate
ex-ac'·er·bat·ing
ex-ac·er·ba'·tion
ex-act'
ex-act'·a:ble
ex-act'·ing
ex-ac'·tion
ex-ac'·ti·tude*†
ex-act'·ly
ex-act'·ness
ex-ag'·ger·ate
ex-ag'·ger·at·ed
ex-ag·ger·a'·tion
ex-ag'·ger·a·tive
ex-ag'·ger·a·tor
ex-alt'
ex-al·ta'·tion
ex-alt'·ed
ex-alt'·er
ex-am'
ex-a'·men
ex-am'·in·a:ble†
ex-am·i·na'·tion
ex-am'·ine
ex-am'·in·er
ex-am'·ple
ex-an'·i·mate
ex-an·the'·ma
ex'·an·them'·a·tous
ex'·arch
ex-as'·per·ate
ex-as'·per·at·ing
ex-as'·per·at·ing·ly
ex-as·per·a'·tion
Ex-cal'·i·bur
ex ca·the'·dra
ex'·ca·vate
ex-ca·va'·tion
ex'·ca·va·tor
ex-ceed'
ex-ceed'·ing

ex-ceed'·ing·ly
ex-cel'
ex-celled'
ex'·cel·lence
ex'·cel·len·cy
ex'·cel·lent
ex'·cel·lent·ly
ex-cel'·ling
ex-cel'·si·or
ex-cept'
ex-cept'·a:ble
ex-cept'·ing
ex-cep'·tion
ex-cep'·tion·a:ble
ex-cep'·tion·al
ex-cep'·tion·al·ly
ex'·cerpt' (n.)
ex-cerpt' (v.)
ex-cerpt'·er
ex-cerpt'·i:ble
ex-cess' (n.)
ex'·cess (adj.)
ex-ces'·sive
ex-ces'·sive·ly
ex-change'
ex-change'·a:ble
ex-chang'·ing
ex'·che-quer*†
ex-cip'·i-ent
ex'·cis·a:ble
ex'·cise (n., tax)
ex-cise' (v., to cut out)
ex-ci'·sion
ex-cit·a:bil'·i·ty
ex-cit'·a:ble
ex-cit'·ant
ex-ci·ta'·tion
ex-cit'·a·tive†
ex-cit'·a·to·ry†
ex-cite'
ex-cit'·ed·ly
ex-cite'·ment
ex-cit'·er
ex-cit'·ing
ex-ci'·tor
ex-claim'
ex-cla·ma'·tion
ex-clam'·a·to·ry
ex-clud'·a:ble
ex-clude'
ex-clud'·ing
ex-clu'·sion
ex-clu'·sive
ex-clu'·sive·ly
ex-clu'·sive·ness
ex-clu'·so·ry
ex-cog'·i-tate
ex-com-mu'·ni-cate

133

ex-com-mu-ni-ca'-tion
ex=con'-vict
ex-co'-ri-ate
ex-co-ri-a'-tion
ex'-cre-ment
ex-cres'-cence
ex-cres'-cen-cy
ex-cres'-cent
ex-cre'-ta
ex-crete'
ex-cre'-tion
ex'-cre-to-ry
ex-cru'-ci-ate
ex-cru'-ci-at-ing
ex-cru-ci-a'-tion
ex'-cul-pate
ex-cul-pa'-tion
ex-cul'-pa-to-ry
ex-cur'-rent
ex-cur'-sion
ex-cur'-sion-ist
ex-cur'-sive
ex-cus'-a:ble
ex-cu'-sa-to-ry
ex-cuse'
ex-cus'-ing
ex-e-cra-ble
ex'-e-crate
ex-e-cra'-tion
ex'-e-cra-to-ry
ex-e-cut-a:ble
ex-ec'-u-tant
ex'-e-cute
ex-e-cu'-tion
ex-e-cu'-tion-er
ex-ec'-u-tive
ex-ec'-u-tor
ex-ec-u-to'-ri-al
ex-ec'-u-to-ry
ex-ec'-u-trix
ex'-e-dra
ex-e-ge'-sis
ex'-e-gete
ex-e-get'-ic
ex'-e-get'-i-cal
ex-em'-plar
ex-em'-pla-ry
ex-em'-pli-fi-ca'-tion
ex-em'-pli-fy
ex-empt'
ex-empt'-i:ble
ex-emp'-tion
ex-emp'-tive
ex-en'-ter-ate
ex-e-qua'-tur
ex'-e-quy
ex'-er-cis-a:ble
ex'-er-cise

ex'-er-cis-er
ex-er'-e-sis
ex'-ergue
ex-ert'
ex-er'-tion
ex-ert'-ive
Ex'-e-ter
ex'-e-unt
ex-fo-li-a'-tion
ex'-hal'-ant†
ex-ha-la'-tion
ex'-hale
ex-haust'
ex-haust'-ed
ex-haust'-er
ex-haust'-i:ble
ex-haus'-tion
ex-haus'-tive
ex-haus'-tive-ly
ex-haust'-less
ex-hib'-it
ex-hi-bi'-tion
ex-hi-bi'-tion-er
ex-hi-bi'-tion-ism
ex-hi-bi'-tion-ist
ex-hib'-i-tive
ex-hib'-i-tor
ex-hib'-i-to-ry
ex-hil'-a-rant
ex-hil'-a-rate
ex-hil-a-ra'-tion
ex-hil'-a-ra-tive
ex-hil'-a-ra-to-ry
ex-hort'
ex-hor-ta'-tion
ex-hort'-a-to-ry*
ex-hu-ma'-tion
ex-hume'
ex'-i-gen-cies
ex'-i-gen-cy
ex'-i-gent
ex'-i-gi-ble
ex-i-gu'-i-ty
ex-ig'-u-ous
ex'-ile
ex-il'-ic
ex-in-a-ni'-tion
ex-ist'
ex-is'-tence*
ex-is'-tent*
ex-is-ten'-tial
ex-is-ten'-tial-ism
ex-is-ten'-tial-ist
ex'-it
ex li'-bris
ex'-o-derm
ex-o-don'-tia
ex-o-don'-tist

ex'-o-dus
ex of-fi'-ci:o†
ex'-o-gam'-ic
ex-og'-e-nous
ex-og'-a-my
ex-og'-e-nous
ex-on'-er-ate
ex-on-er-a'-tion
ex:o-pep'-ti-dase
ex-oph'-a-gy
ex-oph-thal'-mi:a
ex-oph-thal'-mic
ex-or'-bi-tance
ex-or'-bi-tant
ex-or-ci-sa'-tion
ex'-or-cise
ex'-or-cis-er
ex'-or-cism
ex'-or-cist
ex-or'-di-um
ex:o-skel'-e-tal
ex:o-skel'-e-ton
ex-os-to'-sis
ex'-o-ter'-ic
ex-ot'-i-cal-ly
ex-ot'-i-cism
ex'o-ther'-mic
ex:o-ther-mic'-i-ty
ex-ot'-ic
ex-pand'
ex-pand'-a:ble
ex-pand'-er
ex-panse'
ex-pan-si-bil'-i-ty
ex-pan'-si-ble
ex-pan'-sile
ex-pan'-sion
ex-pan'-sive
ex par'-te
ex-pa'-ti-ate
ex-pa-ti-a'-tion
ex-pa'-tri-ate
ex-pa-tri-a'-tion
ex-pect'
ex-pect'-a:ble
ex-pect'-an-cy†
ex-pect'-ant†
ex-pect'-ant-ly†
ex-pec-ta'-tion
ex-pect'-a-tive†
ex-pec'-to-rant
ex-pec'-to-rate
ex-pec-to-ra'-tion
ex-pec'-to-ra-tor
ex-pe'-di-en-cy
ex-pe'-di-ent
ex-pe'-di-ent-ly
ex'-pe-dite

ex'-pe-dit-er
ex'-pe-dit-ing
ex-pe-di'-tion
ex-pe-di'-tion-ar:y†
ex-pe-di'-tious
ex-pe-di'-tious-ly
ex-pel'
ex-pel'-la-ble
ex-pel'-lant
ex-pelled'
ex-pel-lee'
ex-pel'-ling
ex-pend'
ex-pend'-a:ble
ex-pend'-i-ture†
ex-pense'
ex-pen'-sive
ex-pen'-sive-ly
ex-pe'-ri-ence
ex-pe'-ri-enced
ex-pe'-ri-enc-ing
ex-pe'-ri-en'-tial
ex-per'-i-ment
ex-per'-i-men-tal
ex-per'-i-men-tal-ly
ex-per'-i-men-ta'-tion
ex-per'-i-ment-er
ex-pert' (*adj.*)
ex'-pert (*n., adj.*)
ex-per-tise' (expert
  opinion)
ex'-pert-ize (to pass
  judgment)
ex'-pert-ly
ex'-pert-ness
ex'-pi-a-ble
ex'-pi-ate
ex-pi-a'-tion
ex'-pi-a-tor
ex'-pi-a-to-ry
ex-pi-ra'-tion
ex-pir'-a:to-ry
ex-pire'
ex-pired'
ex-pir'-ing
ex-pi'-ry
ex-plain'
ex-plain'-a:ble
ex-pla-na'-tion
ex-plan'-a-tive
ex-plan'-a-to-ry
ex'-ple-tive
ex-plic'-a-ble*†
ex'-pli-cate
ex-pli-ca'-tion
ex-plic'-a-tive*†
ex'-pli-ca-tor
ex-plic'-a-to-ry*†

ex-plic'-it
ex-plic'-it-ly
ex-plode'
ex-plod'-ed
ex-plod'-ing
ex-ploit' (v.)
ex'-ploit (n.)
ex-ploit'-a:ble
ex-ploi-ta'-tion
ex-ploit'-a:tive
ex-ploit'-er
ex-plo-ra'-tion
ex-plor'-a:tive
ex-plor'-a-to-ry
ex-plore'
ex-plor'-er
ex-plor'-ing
ex-plo'-si-ble
ex-plo-sim'-e-ter
ex-plo'-sion
ex-plo'-sive
ex-plo'-sive-ly
ex-po'-nent
ex-po-nen'-tial
ex-po-nen'-tial-ly
ex-po'-ni-ble
ex'-port (n., v.)
ex-port' (v.)
ex-port'-a:ble
ex-por-ta'-tion
ex-port'-er
ex-pose'
ex-po-sé'
ex-posed'
ex-pos'-er
ex-pos'-ing
ex-po-si'-tion
ex-pos'-i-tive
ex-pos'-i-tor
ex-pos'-i-to-ry
ex post fac'-to
ex-pos'-tu-late
ex-pos-tu-la'-tion
ex-pos'-tu-la-to-ry
ex-po'-sure
ex-pound'
ex-pound'-er
ex=pres'-i-dent
ex-press'
ex-press'-age
ex-press'-er
ex-press'-i:ble
ex-press'-ing
ex-pres'-sion
ex-pres'-sion-ism
ex-pres'-sion-less
ex-pres'-sive
ex-pres'-sive-ly

ex-press'-ly
ex-press'-man
ex-pres'-sor
ex-press'-way
ex-pro'-pri-ate
ex-pro-pri-a'-tion
ex-pro'-pri-a-tor
ex-pug'-na-to-ry
ex-pul'-sion
ex-pul'-sive
ex-punge'
ex-pung'-ing
ex'-pur-gate
ex-pur-ga'-tion
ex'-pur-ga'-tor
ex-pur'-ga-to'-ri-al
ex-pur'-ga-to-ry
ex-quis'-ite*†
ex-quis'-ite-ly*†
ex-san'-gui-nate
ex-sert'
ex-sert'-ed
ex-ser'-tile
ex-ser'-tion
ex'-sic-cate
ex-sic-ca'-tion
ex-stip'-u-late
ex'-tant
ex-tem'-po-ral
ex-tem-po-ra-ne'-i-ty
ex-tem-po-ra'-ne-ous
ex-tem'-po-rar:y†
ex tem'-po-re
ex-tem-po-ri-za'-tion
ex-tem'-po-rize
ex-tem'-po-riz-er
ex-tend'
ex-tend'-ed
ex-tend'-er
ex-tend'-i:ble
ex-ten-si-bil'-i-ty
ex-ten'-si-ble
ex-ten'-sion
ex-ten'-si-ty
ex-ten'-sive
ex-ten'-sive-ly
ex-ten-som'-e-ter
ex-ten'-sor
ex-tent'
ex-ten'-u-ate
ex-ten'-u-at-ing
ex-ten-u-a'-tion
ex-ten'-u-a-tor
ex-ten'-u-a-to-ry
ex-te'-ri-or
ex-te'-ri-or-ize
ex-ter'-mi-nate
ex-ter-mi-na'-tion

ex-ter'-mi-na-tive
ex-ter'-mi-na-tor
ex-ter'-mi-na-to-ry
ex-ter'-nal
ex-ter-nal'-i-ty
ex-ter'-nal-ize
ex-ter'-nal-ly
ex'-ter-o-cep'-tive
ex'-ter-o-cep'-tor
ex-tinct'
ex-tinc'-tion
ex-tinc'-tive
ex-tin'-guish
ex-tin'-guish-a:ble
ex-tin'-guish-er
ex'-tir-pate
ex-tir-pa'-tion
ex'-tir-pa-tor
ex-tol'
ex-tolled'
ex-tol'-ling
ex-tor'-sion
ex-tort'
ex-tort'-ed
ex-tor'-tion
ex-tor'-tion-ate
ex-tor'-tion-er
ex-tor'-tion-ist
ex-tort'-ive*†
ex'-tra
ex-tra-ca-non'-i-cal
ex'-tract (n.)
ex-tract' (v.)
ex-tract'-a:ble
ex-tract'-ant
ex-trac'-tion
ex-trac'-tive
ex-trac'-tor
ex'-tra-cur-ric'-u-lar
ex'-tra-dit-a:ble
ex'-tra-dite
ex'-tra-dit-ing
ex-tra-di'-tion
ex'-tra-dos
ex-tral'-i-ty
ex'-tra-mar'-i-tal
ex'-tra-mun'-dane'
ex'-tra-mu'-ral
ex-tra-ne'-i-ty
ex-tra'-ne-ous
ex-traor'-di-nar'-i-ly†
ex-traor'-di-nar:y†
ex-trap'-o-late†
ex-trap'-o-lat-ed†
ex-trap-o-la'-tion†
ex-trap'-o-la-to-ry
ex'-tra-sen'-so-ry

ex-tra-ter-ri-to'-ri-al
ex-tra-ter-ri-to-ri-al'-i-ty
ex-trav'-a-gance
ex-trav'-a-gant
ex-trav-a-gan'-za
ex-trav-a-sa'-tion
ex-treme'
ex-treme'-ly
ex-tre'-mism*†
ex-trem'-ist
ex-trem'-i-ty
ex-tre'-mum
ex-tric'-a-ble*†
ex'-tri-cate
ex-tri-ca'-tion
ex-trin'-sic
ex-trin'-si-cal-ly
ex-tro-ver'-sion
ex'-tro-vert
ex-tro-vert-ish
ex-tro-ver'-tive
ex-trude'
ex-trud'-er
ex-trud'-ing
ex-tru'-si-ble
ex-tru'-sion
ex-tru'-sive
ex-tu'-ber-ance
ex-u'-ber-ance
ex-u'-ber-ant
ex-u'-ber-ate
ex'-u-date
ex-u-da'-tion
ex-ude'
ex-ult'
ex-ult'-ance†
ex-ult'-ant†
ex-ul-ta'-tion
ex-ult'-ing-ly
ex'-urb
ex-ur'-ban-ite
ex-ur'-bi:a
ex-u'-vi-ae
ex-u'-vi-al
ex-u'-vi-ate
ey'-as
eye'-ball
eye'-bright
eye'-brow
eye'-cup
eyed
eye'-glass
eye'-hole
eye'-ing
eye'-lash
eye'-let
eye'-le-teer'*†
eye'-lid

eye'-piece
eye'-shade
eye'-sight
eye'-sore
eye'-spot
eye'-strain
eye'-strings
eye'-tooth
eye'-wash
eye'-wa-ter
eye'-wink
eye'-wit-ness
ey'-rir
E:ze-ki-el
Ez'-ra

F

fa-ba'-ceous
Fa'-bi-an
Fa'-bi-us
fa'-ble
fa'-bled
fab'-li-au
Fa'-bre
fab'-ric
fab'-ri-cant
fab'-ri-cate
fab-ri-ca'-tion
fab'-ri-ca-tor
Fab'-ri-koid
fab'-u-list
fab'-u-lous
fab'-u-lous-ly
fa-çade'
face'-a:ble
faced
face'=hard-en
fac'-er
fac'-et
fac'-et-ed
fa-ce'-tious
fa'-cial
fa-ci-end
fa'-cient
fa-ci-es
fac'-ile
fac'-ile-ness
fa-cil'-i-tate
fa-cil'-i-ties
fa-cil'-i-ty
fac'-ing
fa-cin'-o-rous
fa-con-ne'
fac-sim'-i-le
Fac'-tice
fac-tic'-i-ty
fac'-tion

fac'-tion-al
fac'-tion-al-ism
fac'-tious
fac'-tious-ly
fac-ti'-tious
fac-ti'-tious-ly
fac'-ti-tive
fac'-tor
fac'-tor-age
fac-to'-ri-al
fac-to-ries
fac-tor-i-za'-tion
fac'-tor-ize
fac'-to-ry
fac-to'-tum
fac'-tu-al
fac'-tu-al-ly
fac'-u-la
fac'-ul-ta-tive
fac'-ul-ties
fac'-ul-ty
fa-cun'-di-ty
fad
fad'-dist
fade
Fade=Om'-e-ter
fade'=out
fad'-er
fa-e'-na
Fa-en'-za
fa'-er-ie
fa'-ery*
fa-ga'-ceous
Fa'-gin
fa'-gine
fag'-ot
fag'-ot-ing
Fahr'-en-heit†
fa-ience'
fail'-ing
fail'-ing-ly
faille
fail'-ure
fai-naigue'
fai'-ne-ance
fai'-ne-an-cy
fai'-ne-ant
faint
faint'-ed
faint'-heart-ed
faint'-ish
faint'-ly
faint'-ness
Fair'-fax
fair=haired
fair'-ies
fair'-lead
fair'-ly

138

fair′=mind-ed
fair′-ness
fair′-sized
fair′=spo-ken
fair′-way
fair′y
fair′y-hood
fair′y-land
fair′y-like
fair′y tale
fait ac-com-pli′
faith′-ful
faith′-ful-ly
faith′-ful-ness
faith′-less
fai′-tour
fak′-er
fa-kir′
Fa-lan′-gist
fal′-ba-la
fal′-cate
fal′-chion
fal-ci-form
fal-cip′-a-rum
fal′-con
fal′-con-er
fal′-con-et′*†
fal′-con-ry
fal′-de-ral
Falk′-land
fal′-la-cies
fal-la′-cious
fal-la′-cious-ly
fal-la′-cy
fall′-en
fal-li-bil′-i-ty
fal′-li-ble
fall′-ing
Fal-lo′-pi-an
fall′-out
fal′-low
Fal′-mouth
false′-heart-ed
false′-hood
false′-ly
false′-ness
fal-set′-to
fal-set′-tos
false′-work
fal-si-fi-ca′-tion
fal′-si-fied
fal′-si-fi-er
fal′-si-fy
fal′-si-fy-ing
fal′-si-ty
Fal′-staff
Fal-staff′-i-an
fal′-ter

fal′-ter-ing
famed
fa-mil′-ial
fa-mil′-iar
fa-mil-iar′-i-ty
fa-mil-iar-i:za′-tion
fa-mil′-iar-ize
fa-mil′-iar-ly
fam′-i-lies
fam′-i-ly
fam′-ine
fam′-ish
fa′-mous
fa′-mous-ly
fam′-u-lus
fa-nat′-ic
fa-nat′-i-cal
fa-nat′-i-cism
fan′-cied
fan′-ci-er
fan′-cies
fan′-ci-ful
fan′-ci-ful-ly
fan′-cy
fan′-cy=free
fan′-cy-ing
fan′-cy-work
fan-dan′-go
fa-ne′-ga
fa-ne-ga′-da
Fan′-euil
fan′-fare
fan-far-o-nade′*†
fanged
fan′-gled
fanned
fan′-ning
Fan′-ny
fan′-on
fan′-tail
fan′=tan
fan-ta′-sia
fan′-ta-size
fan-tas′-tic
fan-tas′-ti-cal
fan-tas′-ti-cal-ly
fan′-ta-sy
fan′-tod
fan′-wise
far′-ad
Far′-a-day
fa-rad′-ic
far′-a-dism
far′-an-dole†
far′-a:way
farce
far′-cial
far′-ci-cal

far-ci-cal'-i-ty
far'-cy
far'-del
fare-well'
far=famed
far'-fetched
far=flung
Far'-go
fa-ri'-na
far-i-na'-ceous
far'-i-nose
farm'-er
farm-er-ette'
farm'-house
farm'-ing
farm'-stead
farm'-yard
Far-ne'-se
far'o
far=off
Fa-rouk'
far-rag'-i-nous
far-ra'-go
Far'-ra-gut
far=reach'-ing
far'-ri-er
far'-ri-er:y
far'-row
far-see'-ing
far'-sight-ed
far'-ther
far'-ther-most
far'-thest
far'-thing
far'-thin-gale
fas'-ces
fas'-ci:a
fas'-ci-ate
fas'-ci-a'-tion
fas'-ci-cle
fas-cic'-u-lar
fas-cic'-u-late
fas'-ci-nate
fas'-ci-nat-ed
fas'-ci-nat-ing
fas'-ci-nat-ing-ly
fas-ci-na'-tion
fas'-ci-na-tor
fas-cine'
fas-ci-o-li'-a-sis
fas'-cism
Fas'-cist
Fa-scis'-ta
Fa-scis'-ti
fash'-ion
fash'-ion-a:ble
fash'-ion-a:bly

fas'-ten†
fas'-ten-er†
fas'-ten-ing†
fas-tid'-i-ous
fas-tid'-i-ous-ness
fas-tig'-i-ate
fas-tig'-i-at-ed
fas-tig'-i-um
fast'-ing
fast'-ness
fa'-tal
fa'-tal-ism
fa'-tal-ist
fa-tal-is'-tic
fa-tal-is'-ti-cal-ly
fa-tal'-i-ty
fa'-tal-ly
fat'-ed
fate'-ful
fa'-ther
fa'-ther-hood
fa'-ther=in=law
fa'-ther-land
fa'-ther-less
fa'-ther-like
fa'-ther-li-ness
fa'-ther-ly
fath'-om
fath'-om-a:ble
Fa-thom'-e-ter
fath'-om-less
fa-tid'-ic
fa-tid'-i-cal
fat'-i-ga-ble
fa-tigue'
fa-tigued'
fa-tigu'-ing*
fa-tigu'-ing-ly*
Fat'-i-ma
Fat'-i-mid
fat'-ling
fat'-ness
fat'-ten
fat'-ten-er
fat'-ter
fat'-tish
fat'-ty
fa-tu'-i-tous
fa-tu'-i-ty
fat'-u-old
fat'-u-ous
fat'-u-ous-ly
fau-bourg'
fau'-cal
fau'-cal-ize
fau'-ces
fau'-cet

fau'-cial
fault'-find-ing
fault'-i-er
fault'-i-ly
fault'-i-ness
fault'-less
fault'y
faun
fau'-na
fau'-nal
fau'-vism
faux pas
fa-ve'-o-late
fa-ve'-o-lus
fa'-vism
fa-vo'-ni-an
fa'-vor
fa'-vor-a:ble
fa'-vor-a:bly
fa'-vored
fa'-vor-er
fa'-vor-ite
fa'-vor-it-ism
Fa-vrile'
fa'-vus
fawn
fa-yal'-ite*†
faze
fe'-al-ty
fear'-ful
fear'-ful-ly
fear'-less
fear'-less-ly
fear'-less-ness
fear'-some
fea'-sance
fea-si-bil'-i-ty
fea'-si-ble
feath'-er
feath'-er-bed-ding
feath'-er-brain
feath'-ered
feath'-er-edge
feath'-er-head
feath'-er-ing
feath'-er-less
feath'-er=veined
feath'-er-weight
feath'-er-y
fea'-ture
fea'-tured
fea'-ture-less
feb'-ri-cide
fe-bric'-i-ty
fe-bric'-u-la
feb-ri-fa'-cient
fe-brif'-er-ous

fe-brif'-ic
fe-brif'-u-gal
feb'-ri-fuge
fe-brif'-u-gine
feb'-rile*
fe-bril'-i-ty
Feb'-ru-ar:y†
fe'-cal
fe'-ces
feck'-less
fec'-u-la
fec'-u-lence
fec'-u-lent
fe'-cund†
fec'-un-date*
fec-un-da'-tion*
fe-cun'-da-tive
fe-cun'-di-ty
fed'-er-a-cy
fed'-er-al
fed'-er-al-ese
fed'-er-al-ism
fed'-er-al-ist
fed-er-al-is'-tic
fed-er-al-i:za'-tion
fed'-er-al-ize
fed'-er-ate
fed-er-a'-tion
fed'-er-a-tive
fe-do'-ra
fee'-ble
fee'-ble-heart-ed
fee'-ble-mind-ed
fee'-ble-ness
fee'-blish
fee'-bly
feed'-bin
feed'-er
feed'-ing
feed pipe
feed'-stuff
feed valve
feel'-er
feel'-ing
feel'-ing-ly
Feh'-ling
feign
feigned
feign'-er
feint
feld'-spar
feld'-spath-ic
feld-spath-oi'-dal
Fe-li'-cia
fe'-li-cide
fe-li-cif'-ic
fe-lic'-i-tate

141

fe-lic-i-ta'-tion
fe-lic'-i-tous
fe-lic'-i-ty
fe'-lid
fe'-line
fe-lin'-i-ty
Fe'-lix
fell'-er
fell'-ness
fel'-loe
fel'-low
fel'-low-ship
fel'-ly
fel'-on
fe-lo'-ni-ous
fe-lo'-ni-ous-ly
fel'-o-ny
felt'-er
felt'-ing
fe-luc'-ca
fe'-male
fe-mal'-i-ty
fem'-i-na-cy
fem-i-nal'-i-ty
fem-i-ne'-i-ty
fem'-i-nine
fem-i-nin'-i-ty
fem'-i-nism
fem'-i-nist
fe-min'-i-ty
fem'-i-nize
femme fa-tale'
fem'-o-ral
fe'-mur
fence
fenced
fence'-less
fenc'-er
fen'-chene
fen'-chone
fen'-chyl
fen'-ci-ble†
fenc'-ing
fend'-er
Fé-ne-lon'
fen-es-tel'-la
fe-nes'-tra
fen'-es-trat-ed*†
fen-es-tra'-tion
Fe'-ni-an
fen'-nec
fen'-nel
feoff'-ee
feof'-for†
fe-ra'-cious
fe-rac'-i-ty
fe'-ral
Fer'-ber

fer'=de=lance'
Fer'-di-nand
fer'-e-to-ry
fe-ri:a
fe'-rine
fer'-i-ty
fer-ment'
fer-ment'-a:ble
fer-men-ta'-tion
fer-ment'-a-tive†
fer-ment'-er
fer-men'-tive
fer'-mi-um
Fer-nan'-dez
fern'-er:y
fe-ro'-cious
fe-ro'-cious-ness
fe-roc'-i-ty
Fer-ra'-ra
fer'-ret
fer'-ret-er
fer'-ri-age
fer'-ric
fer-ri-cy-an'-ic
fer-ri-cy'-a-nide
fer'-ried
fer'-ries
fer-rif'-er-ous
fer-ri-na'-trite
Fer'-ris wheel
fer'-rite
fer-rit'-ic
fer'-ri-tin
fer-ro-cal'-cite
fer'-ro-cene
fer-ro-cy'-a-nide
fer-ro-mag-net'-ic
fer-ro-mag'-net-ism
fer-rom'-e-ter
fer'-rous
fer-ru'-gi-nous
fer'-rule
fer'-ry
fer'-ry-boat
fer'-ry-ing
fer'-ry-man
fer'-tile
fer-til'-i-ty
fer'-til-iz-a:ble*
fer-til-i:za'-tion*
fer'-til-ize*
fer'-til-iz-er*
fer'-u-la
fer-u-la'-ceous
fer'-ule
fe-ru'-lic
fer'-va-nite
fer'-ven-cy

fer'-vent
fer'-vent-ly
fer'-vid
fer'-vor
fes'-cue
fes'-tal
fes'-ter
fes'-ti-val
fes'-tive
fes-tiv'-i-ty
fes-toon'
fe'-tal
fe-ta'-tion
fetch'-ing
fete
fet-er-i'-ta*†
fe'-tial
fe'-ti-ci'-dal*†
fe'-ti-cide†
fet'-id
fe-tid'-i-ty
fe-tip'-a-rous
fet'-ish*†
fet'-ish-ism*†
fet'-lock
fe'-tor
fet'-ter
fet'-tle
fe'-tus
feud
feu'-dal
feu'-dal-ism
feu-dal-i:za'-tion
feu'-dal-ize
feu'-dal-ly
feu'-da-to-ry
feud'-ist
feuil-le-ton'†
fe'-ver
fe'-vered
fe'-ver-ish
fe'-ver-ish-ly
fe'-ver-ous
fe'-ver-weed
few'-ness
fez'-zes
fi-an-cé'
fi-an-cée'
fi-an-chet'-to
fi-as'-co
fi'-at
fib'-bing
fi'-ber
fi'-ber-board
Fi'-ber-glas
fi'-ber-ize
fi'-bril
fi'-bril-lar:y†

fib-ril-la'-tion*†
fi'-bril-lous
fi'-brin
fi-brin'-o-gen
fi-bri-nog'-e-nous†
fi'-brin-ous†
fi'-broid
fi-bro-in
fi-bro'-ma
fi-brom'-a-tous†
fi-bro'-sis
fi-bro-si'-tis
fi'-brous
fib'-u-la
fib'-u-lar
Fich'-te
fich'u
fick'-le
fick'-le-ness
fic'-tile
fic'-tion
fic'-tion-al
fic-ti'-tious
fic-ti'-tious-ly
fid'-dle
fid'-dler
fid'-dle-sticks
fid'-dling
fi'-de-ism
fi-del'-i-ty
fid'-get*†
fid'-get:y*†
Fi'-do
fi-du'-cial
fi-du'-cial-ly
fi-du'-ci-ar:y†
field day
field'-er
field glass
Field'-ing
field mar'-shal
field'-piece
field'-work-er
fiend
fiend'-ish
fierce
fierce'-ly
fierce'-ness
fierc'-er
fi'-er:i-ness†
fi'-er:y†
fi-es'-ta*
fif-teen'
fif-teenth'
fif'-ti-eth
fif'-ty
Fig'-a-ro†
fight'-er

fight'-ing
fig'-ment
fig'-u-line
fig'-ur-al†
fig'-u-rant
fig'-u-rate*†
fig'-u-rate-ly*†
fig-u-ra'-tion†
fig'-u-ra-tive*†
fig'-u-ra-tive-ly*†
fig'-ure
fig'-ured
fig'-ure-head
fig'-u-rine'
Fi'-ji
Fi'-ji-an
fil'-a-ment
fil-a-men'-ta-ry
fil'-a-men'-tous
fi'-lar
fi-lar'-i:a*†
fi-lar'-i-al†
fil-a-ri'-a-sis†
fil'-a-ture
fil'-bert
fil'-er
filch'-er
fi-let'
fi-let' mi-gnon'
fil'-i-al
fil-i-a'-tion
fil'-i-bus-ter
fil-i-ci'-dal*
fil'-i-cide
fil'-i-gree
fil'-ing
fil-i-o'-que
Fil-i-pi'-no
fill'-er (one who fills)
fil'-ler (Hungarian coin)
fil'-let
fill'-ing
fil'-lip
Fill'-more
fil'-ly
film'-i-er
film'y
fi'-lose
fil'-o-selle'
fil'-ter
fil-ter-a:bil'-i-ty
fil'-ter-a:ble
fil'-ter-er
filth'-i-er
filth'-i-ly
filth'-i-ness
filth'y
fil-tra-bil'-i-ty

fil'-tra-ble
fil'-trate
fil-tra'-tion
fim-bri-a'-tion
fin'-a:ble
fi-na'-gle
fi-na'-gling
fi'-nal
fi'-nal'e*†
fi'-nal-ist
fi-nal'-i-ty
fi'-nal-ly
fi-nance'
fi-nan'-cial
fi-nan'-cial-ly
fin-an-cier'
fi-nanc'-ing
fin'-back
find'-er
find'-ing
fine'=grained'
fine'-ly
fine'-ness
fin'-er
fin'-er:y
fine'-spun'
fi-nesse'
Fin'-gal
fin'-gent
fin'-ger
fin'-ger-nail
fin'-ger-print
fin'-ger-tip
fin'-i-al
fin'-i-cal
fin'-ick-ing
fin'-ick:y
fin'-is*†
fin'-ish
fin'-ished
fin'-ish-er
fi'-nite
fin'-i-tude
Fin'-land
fin'-nan had'-die
Finn'-ish
fin'-ny
fiord
fire ant
fire'-arm
fire'-ball
fire'-bird
fire'-box
fire'-brand
fire'-brick
fire'-bug
fire'-crack-er

fire'-dog
fire'=eat-er
fire en'-gine
fire'-fly
fire'-less
fire'-light
fire'-man
fire'-place
fire'-plug
fire'-pow-er
fire'-proof
fire'=re-sist'-ant
fire'-side
fire'-stone
fire tow'-er
fire'-trap
fire wall
fire'-wa-ter
fire'-wood
fire'-works
fir'-ing
fir'-kin
fir'-ma-ment
fir-ma-men'-tal
fir-man'
firm'-er
firm'-ly
firm'-ness
fir'-ry
first aid
first'-born
first'=class (adj.)
first'-hand
first'-ling
first'-ly
first'=rate
first wa'-ter
fis'-cal
fis'-cal-ly
fisch'-er-ite
fish'-er
fish'-er-man
fish'-er-y
fish'-hook
fish'-i-ly
fish'-i-ness
fish'-ing
fish'-line
fish'-mon-ger
fish'-tail
fish'-wife
fish'-worm
fish'y
fis'-sile
fis-sil'-i-ty
fis'-sion
fis'-sion-a:ble
fis-sip'-a-rous

fis-si-ros'-tral
fis'-sure
fis'-sur-ing
fist'-ic
fist'-i-cuff
fis'-tu-la
fis'-tu-lous
fitch'-et
fit'-ful
fit'-ful-ly
fit'-ly
fit'-ness
fit'-ted
fit'-ter
fit'-ting
fit'-ting-ly
Fitz-ger'-ald
Fitz-pat'-rick
Fiu'-me†
five'-fold
fiv'-er
fix'-a:ble
fix'-ate
fix-a'-tion
fix'-a-tive
fixed
fix'-ed-ly
fix'-ed-ness
fix'-ing
fix'-i-ty
fix'-ture
fizz'-er
fiz'-zle
fiz'-zling
fizz'y
fjord
flab'-ber-gast
flab'-bi-er
flab'-bi-ness
flab'-by
fla-bel'-late
fla-bel'-lum
flac'-cid
flac-cid'-i-ty
flac'-cid-ly
flac'-on*‡
flag'-el-lant
flag'-el-late
flag-el-la'-tion
flag-el-la-tor
fla-gel'-lum
flag'-eo-let'
flagged
flag'-ging
fla-gi'-tious
fla-gi'-tious-ly
flag'-man
flag'-on

145

flag'-pole
fla'-grance
fla'-gran-cy
fla'-grant
fla'-grant-ly
flag'-ship
flag'-staff
flag'-stone
flail
flair
flaked
flak'-i-er
flak'-ing
flak'y
flam'-beau
flam-boy'-ance
flam-boy'-an-cy
flam-boy'-ant
flamed
fla'-men
fla-men'-co
flame'-proof
flam'-ing
fla-min'-go
fla-min'-gos
flam'-ma-ble
flam'y
Flan'-ders
flange
flanged
flang'-er
flang'-ing
flank'-er
flan'-nel
flan-nel-ette'
flap'-er-on
flap'-jack
flapped
flap'-per
flap'-ping
flare
flare'=up
flar'-ing
flash'-board
flash'-i-ly
flash'-i-ness
flash'-ing
flash'-light
flash'y
flat'-boat
flat'=bot'-tomed
flat'=foot
flat'=foot-ed
flat'-head
flat'-i:ron
flat'-ness
flat'-ten
flat'-ter

flat'-ter-er
flat'-ter-ing
flat'-ter:y
flat'-top
flat'-u-lence
flat'-u-lent
fla'-tus
flat'-ware
flat'-worm
Flau-bert'
flaunt
flaunt'-er
flaunt'-ing
flau'-tist†
flav'-a-none
fla-van'-throne
fla-ves'-cence
fla-ves'-cent
Fla'-vi:a
fla-vi-an'-ic
fla'-vin
fla'-vone
fla'-vo-nol
fla-vo-pur'-pu-rin
fla'-vor
fla'-vor-ing
flaw'-less
flax'-en
flax'-seed
flax'y
flay'-er
flea'-bite
flea'=bit-ten
flec'-tion
flec'-tion-al
fledged
fledg'-ing
fledg'-ling
fleece
fleec'-i-er
fleec'-i-ness
fleec'y
flee'-ing
fle'-er (one who flees)
fleer (to scoff)
fleet'-ing
fleet'-ly
fleet'-ness
Flem'-ing
Flem'-ish
flesh'=col-ored
flesh'-i-ness
flesh'-less
flesh'-ly
flesh'-pot
flesh'y
fletch'-er
fletch'-er-ize

146

fleur=de=lis'
Fleur-ry'
flew
flex-i-bil'-i-ty
flex'-i-bi-lize
flex'-i:ble
flex'-ion
flex-om'-e-ter
flex'-or
flex-u-os'-i-ty
flex'-u-ous
flex'-ur-al†
flex'-ure
flib'-ber-ti-gib-bet
flick'-er
flick'-er-ing-ly
flick'-er:y
fli'-er
flight
flight'-i-ness
flight'-less
flight'y
flim'-si-ly
flim'-si-ness
flim'-sy
flinched
flinch'-ing
flin'-ders
fling'-ing
flint'-i-er
flint'-lock
flint'y
flip'-pan-cy
flip'-pant
flipped
flip'-per
flip'-ping
flir-ta'-tion
flir-ta'-tious
flirt'-er
flirt'-ing-ly
flit'-ter
flit'-ting
fliv'-ver
float'-a:ble
float'-er
float'-ing
floc-cil-la'-tion
floc'-cu-lant
floc-cu-la'-tion
floc'-cu-la-tor
floc'-cu-lence
floc'-cu-lent
floc'-cu-lus
flocked
flock'y
flogged
flog'-ging

flood'-gate
flood'-light
flood-om'-e-ter
flood'-proof
floor'-ing
floor'-walk-er
flopped
flop'-pi-er
flop'-ping
flop'-py
Flo'-ra
flo'-ral
Flor'-ence
flor'-enc-ite
Flor'-en-tine
flo-res'-cence
flo-res'-cent
flo'-ret
flo'-ri-at-ed
flo-ri-cul'-tur-al
flo'-ri-cul-ture
flor'-id
Flor'-i-da
Flo-rid'-i-an
flo-rid'-i-ty
flor'-id-ly
flor'-id-ness
flo-rif'-er-ous
flo'-ri-gen
flor'-in
flo'-rist
flo-riv'-o-rous
flor'-u-lent
floss'y
flo'-tage
flo-ta'-tion
flo-til'-la
flot'-sam
flounce
flounced
flounc'-ing
floun'-der
floun'-dered
floun'-der-ing
flour'-ish
flour'-ished
flour'-ish-ing
flour'y
flout'-ed
flout'-ing
flow'-er
flow'-ered
flow'-er-et
flow'-er-i-ly
flow'-er-ing
flow'-er-pot
flow'-er:y
flown

fluc'-tu-ant
fluc'-tu-ate
fluc'-tu-at-ed
fluc'-tu-at-ing
fluc-tu-a'-tion
flu'-en-cy
flu'-ent
fluff'-i-er
fluff'-i-ly
fluff'-i-ness
fluff'y
flu'-id
flu-id'-ic
flu-id'-i-ty
fluk'y
flu'-mer-in
flum'-mer:y
flun'-ky*†
flu:o-bo'-rate
flu:o-bo'-rite
flu:o-chlo'-ride
flu-o-ran'-thene*†
flu-or-ap'-a-tite
flu'-o-rene†
flu'-o-re-nyl
flu-o-resce'
flu-o-res'-ce-in
flu-o-res'-cence
flu-o-res'-cent
flu-o-resc'-ing
flu-or'-ic
flu-o-ri-date
flu-o-ri-da'-tion
flu'-o-ride
flu'-o-ri-dize
flu'-o-ri-nate
flu'-o-rine
flu'-o-rite†
flu-o-ro-a:ce'-tic
flu'-o-ro-graph'-ic
flu-o-rog'-ra-phy*†
flu-o-rom'-e-ter*†
flu'-o-ro-scope†
flu-o-ros'-co-py*†
flu-o-ro'-sis
flu'-or-spar
flu:o-sil'-i-cate
flu:o-si-lic'-ic
flur'-ried
flur'-ries
flur'-ry
flur'-ry-ing
Flush'-ing
flus'-ter
flus-ter-a'-tion
flus-tra'-tion
flut'-ed
flut'-er

flut'-ing
flut'-ist
flut'-ter
flut'-tered
flut'-ter-ing
flut'-ter:y
flut'y
flu'-vi-al
flu-vi-a-tile
flu-vi-ol'-o-gy
flux'-i:ble
flux'-ion
flux'-ion-al
flux'-ion-ar:y†
flux'-me-ter
fly'-a:way
fly'-catch-er
fly'-er
fly'-ing
fly'-ing fish
fly'-leaf
fly'-speck
fly'-trap
fly'-weight
fly'-wheel
foamed
foam'-i-er
foam'-ing
Foam'-ite
foam'y
fo'-cal
fo-cal-i:za'-tion
fo'-cal-ize
fo-com'-e-ter
fo'-cus
fo'-cused
fo'-cus-er
fo'-cus-ing
fod'-der
foe'-man
fog'-gi-er
fog'-gi-ly
fog'-gy
fog'-horn
fo'-gram†
fo'-gy
foi'-ble
foiled
foil'-ing
foist'-ed
fold'-ed
fold'-er
fol'-de-rol
fold'-ing
fo-li-a'-ceous
fo'-li-age
fo'-li-ate
fo'-li-at-ed

fo-li-a'-tion
fo'-lic
fo-lin'-ic
fo'-li:o
fo'-li-o-late
fo'-li-ose
fo'-li-um
folk'-lore
folks:y*
folk'-way
fol'-li-cle
fol-lic'-u-lar
fol-lic'-u-lin
fol-lic-u-li'-tis
fol'-low
fol'-lowed
fol'-low-er
fol'-low-ing
fol'-low=through
fol'-low=up
fol'-ly
fo-ment'
fo-men-ta'-tion
fo-ment'-er
fon'-dant
fon'-dle
fon'-dled
fon'-dler
fon'-dling
fond'-ly
fond'-ness
fon-du'
fon-due'
Fon-taine-bleau'
fon-ta-nel'
Foo'-chow'
food'-stuff
fool'-er:y
fool'-har-di-ness
fool'-har-dy
fool'-ing
fool'-ish
fool'-ish-ly
fool'-ish-ness
fool'-proof
fools'-cap
foot'-age
foot'-ball
foot'-bath
foot'-board
foot'-bridge
foot'-can-dle
foot'-ed
foot'-fall
foot'-hill
foot'-hold
foot'-ing
foo'-tle†

foot'-less
foot'-light
foot'-ling (wood strip)
foo'-tling (silly)
foot'-loose
foot'-man
foot'-mark
foot'-note
foot'-pad
foot'-path
foot'=pound
foot=pound'-al
foot'-print
foot'-room
foot' rule
foot'-sore
foot'-step
foot'-stool
foot'-walk
foot'-wear
foot'-work
foot'-worn
foo'-zle
fop'-per:y
fop'-pish
for'-age
for'-aged
for'-ag-er
for'-ag-ing
fo-ra'-men
for-a-min'-i-fer†
Fo-ram-i-nif'-er:a
fo-ram-i-nif'-er-al
fo-ram-i-nif'-er-ous
fo-ram'-i-nous
for-as-much
for'-ay
for-bade'
for-bear' (to refrain)
for-bear'-ance
for-bid'
for-bid'-dance
for-bid'-den
for-bid'-der
for-bid'-ding
for-bore'
forced
force'-ful
force'-meat
for'-ceps
forc'-er
forc'-i:ble*†
forc'-i:bly*†
forc'-ing
ford'-a:ble
for-do'
fore'-arm

149

fore'-bear (ancestor)
fore-bode'
fore-bod'-ing
fore'-cast
fore'-cast-er
fore'-cas-tle
fore-close'
fore-clo'-sure
fore-doom'
fore'-fa-ther
fore'-fin-ger
fore'-foot
fore'-front
fore'-go-ing
fore'-gone'
fore'-ground
fore'-hand
fore'-hand-ed
fore'-head
for'-eign
for'-eign-er
for'-eign-ness
fore-judge'
fore'-know'
fore'-knowl-edge
fore'-la-dy
fore'-land
fore'-leg
fore'-lock
fore'-man
fore'-mast
fore'-most
fore'-name
fore'-noon
fo-ren'-sic
fo-ren'-si-cal
fo-ren'-si-cal-ly
fore-or-dain'
fore-or'-di-nate
fore-or-di-na'-tion
fore'-part
fore'-paw
fore'-quar-ter
fore-run' (v.)
fore'-run (n.)
fore'-run-ner
fore'-sail
fore-saw'
fore-see'
fore-see'-a:ble
fore-see'-ing
fore-seen'
fore-shad'-ow
fore-short'-en
fore'-sight
fore'-skin
fore'-est
fore-stall'

for-est-a'-tion
fore'-stay
for'-est-ed
for'-est-er
for'-est-ry
fore'-taste
fore-tell'
fore-tell'-er
fore-tell'-ing
fore'-thought
fore'-to-ken
fore-told'
for-ev'-er
for-ev-er-more'
fore-warn'
fore'-wom-an†
fore'-word
for'-feit
for'-feit-er
for'-feit-ure*†
for-fend'
for'-fi-cate
for-gath'-er
for-gave'
forge
forge'-a:ble
forg'-er
for'-ger:y
for-get'
for-get'-ful
for-get'-ful-ness
for-ge'-tive
for-get'=me=not
for-get'-ta-ble
for-get'-ting
forg'-ing
for-give'
for-giv'-en
for-give'-ness
for-giv'-ing
for-go'
for-go'-ing
for-gone'
for-got'
for-got'-ten
fo'-rint
forked
fork'-ed-ly
for-lorn'
for-lorn'-ly
for'-mal
form-al'-de-hyde†
For'-ma-lin
for'-mal-ism
for'-mal-ist
for-mal-is'-tic
for-mal'-i-ty
for'-mal-ize

for'-mal-iz-er
for'-mal-iz-ing
form-am'-ide
form-am'-i-dine
for'-mant*
for'-mate
for-ma'-tion
form'-a-tive
form'-a-zan
form'-er (one who forms)
for'-mer (previous)
for'-mer-ly
for'-mic
For-mi'-ca
for'-mi-car:y†
for'-mi-cate
for'-mi-cide
for-mi-da-bil'-i-ty
for'-mi-da-ble
form'-less
for'-mol-ize
For-mo'-sa
For-mo'-san
for'-mu-la
for'-mu-la-ri-i:za:ble
for'-mu-lar-i:za'-tion
for'-mu-lar-ize
for'-mu-lar:y†
for'-mu-late
for-mu-la'-tion
for'-mu-la-tor
for-mu-lis'-tic
for'-myl
for'-myl-ate
for-nent'
for'-ni-cate
for-ni-ca'-tion
for'-ni-ca-tor
for'-nix
for-sake'
for-sak'-en
For'-se-ti†
for-sook'
for-sooth'
for-swear'
for-sworn'
for-syth'-i:a†
fort
for'-ta-lice†
forte (strong point)
for'-te (loud, in music)
forth
forth'-com-ing
forth'-right
forth-with'
for'-ti-eth

for-ti-fi-ca'-tion
for'-ti-fied
for'-ti-fi-er
for'-ti-fy
for-tis'-si-mo
for'-ti-tude
for-ti-tu'-di-nous
fort'-night
fort'-night-ly
for'-tress
for-tu'-i-tism
for-tu'-i-tous
for-tu'-i-ty
For-tu'-na
for'-tu-nate
for'-tu-nate-ly
For-tu-na'-tus
for'-tune
for-tune=tell-er
for'-ty
fo'-rum
for'-ward
for'-ward-er
for'-ward-ly
for'-ward-ness
for-zan'-do
fos'-sa
fos'-sick
fos'-sil
fos-sil-if'-er-ous
fos-sil-i-za'-tion
fos'-sil-ize
fos-so'-ri-al
fos'-ter
Fou-cault'
fou-droy'-ant
foul
fou-lard'
foul'-ly
foul'-ness
foun-da'-tion
found'-er (one who founds)
foun'-der (to collapse, to sink)
foun'-der-ous
found'-ling
found'-ries†
found'-ry†
foun'-tain
foun'-tain-head
foun'-tain pen
Four-drin'-i-er
four'-fold
four'=foot-ed
Fou'-ri-er
Fou'-ri-er-ism
four'=post-er
four-ra-gère'

151

four'-score
four'-some
four'-square
four-teen'
four-teenth'
fourth
fou'-ter
fo'-ve:a
fo'-ve-ate
fo'-ve-o-la
fo'-ve-o-late
fo'-ve-o-let
fowl
Fow'-ler*
fowl'-er
fox'-glove
fox'-hole
fox'-hound
fox'-i-ness
fox'-tail
fox ter'-ri-er
fox'=trot
fox'y
foy'-er
fra'-cas
frac'-tion
frac'-tion-al
frac'-tion-ar:y
frac'-tion-ate
frac-tion-a-'tion
frac'-tious
frac-tog'-ra-phy
frac'-tur-al
frac'-ture
frag'-ile
fra-gil'-i-ty
frag'-ment
frag-men'-tal
frag'-men-tar:y†
frag-men-ta'-tion
frag'-ment-ed
frag'-ment-ize
fra'-grance
fra'-gran-cy
fra'-grant
frail
frail'-ties
frail'-ty
fram-be'-si:a
framed
fram'-er
frame'=up
frame'-work
fram'-ing
franc
fran-çais'
Fran'-ces
fran'-chise

Fran'-cis
Fran-cis'-can
Fran-cis'-co
fran'-ci-um
Fran-çois'
fran'-co-lin
Fran-co'-ni:a
Fran'-co-phile
Fran-co-pho'-bi:a
fran-gi-bil'-i-ty
fran'-gi-ble
fran-gi-pan'i
frank
Frank'-en-stein
Frank'-fort
frank'-furt-er
fran-kin-cense*†
Frank'-ish
Frank'-lin
frank'-lin-ite
frank'-ly
frank'-ness
fran'-tic
fran'-ti-cal-ly
frap-pé'
fra'-ter
fra-ter'-nal
fra-ter'-ni-ty
frat-er-ni-za'-tion
frat'-er-nize
frat'-ri-ci-dal*
frat'-ri-cide
frau
fraud'-u-lence
fraud'-u-len-cy
fraud'-u-lent
fraud'-u-lent-ly
fräu-lein
Fraun'-ho-fer
frax-i-nel'-la
frayed
Fra'-zer
fra'-zil
fraz'-zle
fraz'-zling
freak'-ish
freck'-le
freck'-led
Fred-er-i'-ca
Fred'-er-ick
Fred'-er-icks-burg
Fred'-er-ic-ton
free'-board
free'-boot-er
free'-born
freed'-man
free'-dom
free'-hand (*adj.*)

free'-hand-ed
free'-hold
free'-ly
free'-man
free'-mar-tin
Free'-ma-son
Free'-ma-son-ry
fre'-er
free'-si:a
fre'-est
free'-stone
free'-think-er
free'-way
free-wheel'-ing
free'-will (*adj.*)
freez'-er
freez'-ing
Frei'-burg
freight'-age
freight'-er
frem'-i-tus
Fre'-mont
fre'-nal
French'-man
Fre-neau'
fre-net'-ic
fre-net'-i-cal
fre-net'-i-cal-ly
fren'-u-lum
fre'-num
fren'-zied
fren'-zy
Fre'-on
fre'-quen-cy
fre'-quent
fre-quen-ta'-tion
fre-quen'-ta-tive
fre'-quent-er
fre'-quent-ly
fres'-co
fres'-co-er
fres'-coes
fresh'-en
fresh'-et
fresh'-ly
fresh'-man
fresh'-ness
fresh-wa'-ter
Fres-nel'
Fres'-no
fret'-ful
fret'-ful-ly
fret'-saw
fret'-ted
fret'-ty
fret'-work
Freud'-i-an†

fri-a-bil'-i-ty
fri'-a-ble
fri'-ar
fri'-ar:y
Fri'-bourg
fric'-an-deau
fric-as-see'
fric'-a-tive
fric'-tion
fric'-tion-al
Fri'-day
fried'-cake
friend'-less
friend'-li-er
friend'-li-ly
friend'-li-ness
friend'-ly
friend'-ship
Frie'-sian
Fries'-ic
Fries'-land
frieze
frig'-ate
fright
fright'-en
fright'-ened
fright'-en-ing
fright'-ful
fright'-ful-ly
fright'-ful-ness
frig'-id
Frig'-i-daire*
fri-gid'-i-ty
frig-o-rif'-ic
frig-o-rim'-e-ter
fri'-jol
fri-jo'-les
frill'-ing
frill'y
fringed
frin-gil'-line
fring'-ing
fring'y
frip'-per:y
Fris'-co
fri-sette'
Fri'-sian†
fris'-ket
frisk'-i-er
frisk'-i-ly
frisk'y
frit'-il-lar:y†
frit'-ter
friv'-ol
fri-vol'-i-ty
friv'-o-lous
frizz'-ing
friz'-zle

153

friz'-zling
friz'-zly†
Fro'-bish-er†
frock
Froe'-bel
frog'-bit
frog'-man
frol'-ic
frol'-icked
frol'-ick-ing
frol'-ic-some
fron-des'-cence
front'-age
fron'-tal
fron-ta'-lis
fron-tier'
fron-tiers'-man
fron'-tis-piece
front'-less
front'-let
fron-to-gen'-e-sis
front-ol'-y-sis*†
fron-to-pa-ri'-e-tal
front=page
frost'-bite
frost'-bit-ten
frost'-i-ness
frost'-ing
frost'-proof
frost'y
froth'-i-er
froth'-i-ly
froth'y
fro'-ward
frowned
frown'-ing
frow'-zi-er*
frow'-zi-ness*
frow'-zy*
froze
fro'-zen
fruc-tes'-cence
fruc-tif'-er-ous
fruc-ti-fi-ca'-tion
fruc'-ti-fied
fruc'-ti-fy
fruc-tiv'-o-rous
fruc-tol'-y-sis
fruc'-tose
fruc'-to-side
fruc-tu-ous
fru'-gal
fru-gal'-i-ty
fru'-gal-ly
fru'-gal-ness
fru-giv'-o-rous
fruit'-age
fruit'-er

fruit'-er-er
fruit'-ful
fruit'-ful-ness
fruit'-i-ness
fru-i'-tion
fruit'-less
fruit'y
fru-men-ta'-ceous
fru-men-ty
frump'-ish
frump'y
frus'-trate
frus'-trat-ed
frus'-trat-er
frus'-trat-ing
frus-tra'-tion
frus'-tule
frus'-tum
fru-tes'-cence
fru-tes'-cent
fru'-ti-cose
fry'-er
fu-ca'-ceous
fuch'-sia
fuch'-sin
fuch-sin'-o-phil
fu'-coid
fu-coi'-dal
fu-cos'-ter-ol
fu'-cu-lose
fu'-cus
fud'-dle
fud'-dling
fudge
Fu-e-e'-gi-an
fu'-el
fu-el-er
fu-ga'-cious
fu-ga'-cious-ly
fu-gac'-i-ty
fu'-gi-tive
fu'-gle
fu'-gle-man
fugue
Füh'-rer
Fu-ji-ya'-ma
ful'-crum
ful-fill'
ful-fill'-ing
ful-fill'-ment
ful-gen'-ic
ful'-gide
ful'-gu-rant
ful-gu-ra'-tion
ful'-gu-rite
ful'-gu-rous
fu-lig'-i-nous
full'-back

full′=blown′
full′=dress′ (*adj.*)
Ful′-ler
full′-er (*adj.*)
ful′-ler (hammer)*†
full′=fledged′
full′=grown′
full′=length′
full′-ness
full′=sized′
ful′-ly†
ful′-mar
ful′-mi-nate
ful′-mi-nat-ing
ful-mi-na′-tion
ful′-mi-na-tor
ful′-mi-na-to-ry
ful-min′-ic
ful′-mi-nous
ful-min-u′-ric*†
ful′-some
ful′-some-ness
Ful′-ton
ful′-vous
fu′-ma-rase
fu-mar′-ic
fu′-ma-role
fu-mar′-o-yl
fu-ma-to′-ri-um
fu′-ma-to-ry
fum′-ble
fum′-bler
fum′-bling
fumed
fu′-met
fu-mig′-a-cin
fu′-mi-gate
fu′-mi-gat-ing
fu-mi-ga′-tion
fu′-mi-ga-tor
fum′-ing
fu′-mi-to-ry
fu′-mu-lus
fum′y
fu-nam′-bu-list
func′-tion
func′-tion-al
func′-tion-ar:y†
func′-tion-ate
fun-da-men′-tal
fun-da-men′-tal-ism
fun-da-men′-tal-ist
fun-da-men′-tal-ly
fun′-dus
fun-dus′-co-py
Fun′-dy
fu′-ner-al

fu′-ner-ar:y†
fu-ne′-re-al
fu-nest′
fun′-gal
fun′-gi
fun-gi-bil′-i-ty
fun′-gi-ble
fun′-gi-ci-dal*
fun-gi-cide
fun-gif′-er-ous
fun-giv′-o-rous
fun′-goid
fun-gos′-i-ty
fun′-gous
fun′-gus
fun′-gus=proof
fu′-ni-cle
fu-nic′-u-lar
fun′-nel
fun′-neled
fun′-nel-ing
fun′-ni-er
fun′-ni-ly
fun′-ny
fur
fu′-ran
fu′-ra-nose*†
fu-ran′-o-side
fur-be-low′
fur′-bish
fur′-bish-er
fur′-cal
fur′-cu-lum
fur-fu-ra′-ceous
fur′-fu-ral*
fur-fu-ryl′-i-dene*
fu′-ri-bund
fu′-ri-ous
fu′-ri-ous-ly
fur′-long
fur′-lough
fur′-nace
fur′-nish
fur′-nish-er
fur′-nish-ings
fur′-ni-ture
Fur′-ni-vall
fu-ro′-ic
fu′-ror
fu′-rore
furred
fur′-ri-er
fur′-ri-ness
fur′-ring
fur′-row
fur′-ry
fur′-ther
fur′-ther-ance

155

fur'-ther-more
fur'-ther-most
fur'-thest
fur'-tive
fur'-tive-ly
fu-run'-cle
fu-run-cu-lo'-sis
fu'-ry
fu'-ryl
furze
fu'-sain
fu-sar'-i-um*†
fus'-cous
fuse
fused
fu-see'
fu'-sel
fu'-se-lage
fu-si-bil'-i-ty
fu'-si-ble
fu'-sil
fu'-si-lier*
fu'-sil-lade
fus'-ing
fu'-sion
fu-so-spi'-ro-chete
fuss'-i-ly
fuss'y
fus'-tian
fus'-tic
fus'-ti-er*†
fus'-ti-ly*†
fus'-ty*†
fu'-thark
fu'-tile
fu'-tile-ly
fu-til-i-tar'-i-an†
fu-til'-i-ty
fut'-tock
fut'-ur-al*
fu'-tu-ram'-ic
fu'-ture
fu'-tur-ism
fu'-tur-ist
fu-tu'-ri-ty
fuze
fuzz'-i-ness
fuzz'y
fyl'-fot
fyn'-chen-ite

G

gab'-ar-dine
ga'-ba-rit'
gab'-bing
gab'-ble
gab'-bro

gab'-by
ga-belle'
gab'-er-dine
ga'-bi-on
ga'-ble
ga'-bled
ga'-bling
Ga-bon'
Ga'-bri-el
Ga-bri-lo'-witsch
ga'-by
gach'-u:a
gad'-a:bout
gad'-ding
gad'-fly
gad'-get*†
gad'-ge-teer'
gad'-get-ry
ga-did†
Gad'-ite
ga'-doid
gad-o:le'-ic
gad'-o-lin-ite
gad-o-lin'-i-um
ga-droon'
Gael'-ic
gaf'-fer (old man)
gaff'-er (spear-fisher)
gage
gag'-er
gagged
gag'-ging
gahn'-ite
gai'-e:ty
gail-lar'-di:a
gai'-ly
gain'-er (one who gains)
gai'-ner† (high dive)
gain'-ful
gain'-said
gain'-say
Gains'-bor-ough
gait
gait'-ed
gai'-ter (footwear)
gait'-er (pacer)
Ga'-ius
ga-la
ga-lac'-ta-gogue
ga-lac'-tic
ga-lac'-to-lip'-id
gal-ac-tom'-e-ter
gal-ac-tom'-e-try
gal'-ac-ton'-ic
ga-lac-to-poi-e'-sis
ga-lac-tos'-a:mine
ga-lac'-tose
ga-lac-to-sid'-ase

gal-ac-to'-sis
ga-lac'-tu-ron'-ic
Gal'-a-had
gal'-an-tine
ga-lan'-ty
Ga-la'-pa-gos
Ga-la-te'a
Ga-la'-ti:a
Ga-la'-tian
ga'-lax
ga-lax'-i-al
gal'-ax:y
gal'-ba-num
ga'-le:a
ga'-le-ate
ga-le'-gine
ga-le'-i-form
Ga'-len
ga-le'-na
ga-len'-ic (of Galen)
ga-le'-nic† (of galena)
ga-len'-i-cal
ga-le'-no-bis'-mut-ite
Ga-le'-ri-us
Ga-li'-cia
Ga-li'-cian
Gal-i-le'-an
Gal'-i-lee
Gal-i-le'o
gal-i-ma'-ti-as
gal'-in-gale
gal'-lant
gal'-lant-ly
gal'-lant-ries
gal'-lant-ry
gal'-le-ass
gal'-le-on
gal'-ler:y
gal'-ley
gal'-leys
gal'-liard
Gal'-lic
Gal'-li-can
Gal'-li-cize
Gal'-li=Cur'-ci
Gal-lie-ni'
Gal-li-e'-nus
gal-li-na'-ceous
gall'-ing
gal'-li-nule
gal'-li-ot
Gal-lip'-o-li
gal'-li-um
gal'-li-vant
gal'-lon
gal-loon'
gal'-lop

gal'-loped
gal'-lop-er
gal'-lop-ing
Gal'-lo-way
gal'-lows
gall'-stone
gal'-op
ga-lore'
ga-losh'
ga-losh'-es
Gals'-wor-thy
gal-van'-ic
gal'-va-nism
gal-va-ni-za'-tion
gal'-va-nize
gal'-va-niz-ing
gal-va-no-mag-net'-ic
gal-va-nom'-e-ter
gal-va-no-met'-ric
gal-va-nom'-e-try
gal-van'o-scope*†
gal-va-not'-ro-pisn:
Gal'-ves-ton
Gal'-way
Gal-we'-gian
gal'-yak
ga-mash'-es
gam-ba'-do
gam'-be-son
gam'-bier
gam'-bit
gam'-ble
gam'-bler
gam'-bling
gam-boge'
gam'-bol
gam'-boled
gam'-bol-ing
gam'-brel
Gam-bri'-nus
game'-cock
game'-keep-er
game'-ness
game'-some
game'-ster
ga-mete*†
ga-met'-ic
ga-met'-i-cal-ly
ga-me'-to-cide
ga-me-to-gen'-e-sis*†
gam'-e-toid
ga-me'-to-phore†
ga-me'-to-phyte†
gam'-ic
gam'-i-ly
gam'-in
gam'-i-ness
gam'-ing

gam'-ma
gam-ma'-di-on
gam'-ma glob'-u-lin
gam'-mer
gam'-mon
gam'-o-pet'-a-lous*
gam'-o-sep'-a-lous*
gam'-ut
gam'y
gan'-der
Gan'-dha'-ra
Gan'-dhi
gan'-dy danc-er
Gan'-ges
gan'-gli:a
gan-gli-ec'-to-my
gan-gli-i'-tis
gan'-gling†
gan'-gli-on
gan-gli-on-at-ed
gan-gli-on'-ic
gan-gli-o-side
gan'-gly†
gang'-plank
gan'-grene
gan'-gre-nous
gang'-ster
gangue
gang'-way
gan'-is-ter
gan'-net
gan'-oid
ga-nom'-a-lite
gant'-let
Gan'-tri-sin
gan'-try
Gan'-y-mede
gaol
gaped
gap'-er
gap'-ing
gapped
gap'-ping
ga-rage'
Gar'-a-mond
gar'-an-cine'
Ga-rand'*†
gar'-bage
gar'-ble
gar'-bled
gar'-bling
gar-çon'
gar'-den
gar'-den-er
gar-de'-nia
Gar'-di-ner (Me.)
gar'-di-nol
Gard'-ner (Mass.)

Gar'-eth
Gar'-field
gar'-fish
Gar-gan'-tu:a
gar-gan'-tu-an
gar'-gle
gar'-gled
gar'-gling
gar'-goyle
Gar-i-bal'-di
gar'-ish
gar'-land
gar'-lic
gar'-lick:y
gar'-ment
gar'-ner
gar'-net
gar'-nish
gar-nish-ee'
gar-nish-ee'-ing
gar'-nish-er
gar'-nish-ment
gar'-ni-ture
gar'-ret
Gar'-rick
gar'-ri-son
gar'-ron-ite
gar-rote'
gar-rot'-ed
gar-rot'-ing
gar-ru'-li-ty
gar'-ru-lous
gar'-ru-lous-ly
gar'-ter
Gar'y†
Gas'-con
gas'-con-ade'
Gas'-co-ny
gas'-e-ous
gashed
gas'-house
gas'-i-fi-a:ble
gas-i-fi-ca'-tion
gas'-i-fy
gas'-ket
gas'-light
gas mask
gas-o-line'
gas-om'-e-ter
gas'-o-met'-ric
gas'-ser
gas'-sing
gas sta'-tion
gas'-sy
gas-ter-o-sto'-ma-ta
gas'-tight
gas-tral'-gia

158

gas-tra'-li-um
gas-trec'-to-my
gas'-tric
gas-tri'-tis
gas-tro-cne'-mi-us
gas-tro-en-ter-i'-tis
gas-tro-en-ter-os'-to-my
gas-tro-in-tes'-ti-nal
gas-trol'-o-ger
gas-tro-nom'-ic
gas-tro-nom'-i-cal
gas-tron'-o-my
gas'-tro-pod
Gas-trop'-o-da
gas-trop'-o-dous
gas-tros'-co-py
gas-tros'-to-my
gas'-tru-la
gas-tru-la'-tion
gas'-works
gate
gate'-post
gate'-way
gath'-er
gath'-ered
gath'-er-ing
gat'-ing
Gat'-ling
Ga-tun'
gauche
gauche'-ly
gau'-che-rie'
gau'-cho
gau'-chos
gau-de-a'-mus
gaud'-er:y
gaud'-i-er
gaud'-i-ly
gaud'-i-ness
gaud'y
gauge
gauged
gaug'-er
gaug'-ing
Gau-guin'
gau'-lei-ter
Gaull'-ist
gaul-the'-ri:a
gaunt'-let
gaunt'-ly
gauss
Gauss'-i-an
Gau-tier'
gauze
gauz'-i-ness
gauz'y
ga-vage'
gav'-el

gav'-el-er
ga'-vi-al
ga-votte'
Ga-wain'
gawk'-i-ly
gawk'-i-ness
gawk'y
gay'-ness
Ga'-za
ga-ze'-bo
gazed
ga-zelle'
gaz'-er
ga-zette'
gaz'-et-teer'
gaz'-ing
ge'-an'-ti-cli'-nal
gear'-ing
gear'-shift
gear' wheel
geck'o
gee'-zer
Ge'-gen-schein
Ge-hen'-na
Gei'-ger
gei'-sha
Geiss'-ler
gel
gel'-a-tin
gel'-a-tin-ase†
ge-lat'-i-nate
ge-lat-i-ni-za'-tion
ge-lat'-i-nize
ge-lat'-i-niz-er
ge-lat'-i-no-chlo'-ride†
ge-lat'-i-nous
ge-la'-tion
geld'-ed
geld'-ing
gel'-id
ge-lid'-i-ty†
gel'-ig-nite
gelled
gel'-ling
gel'-ose†
gel-se'-mic†
gel-se'-mi-um
Ge-ma'-ra
gem'-i-nate
gem-i-na'-tion
gem'-i-na-tive
Gem'-i-ni
gem'-ma
gem'-mate
gem-ma'-tion
gemmed
gem-mif'-er-ous
gem-mip'-a-rous

gem'-mule
ge-mot'
gen'-darme
gen-dar'-mer-ie*†
gen-dar'-mer:y*
gen'-der
gen:e-a-log'-i-cal
gen:e-a-log'-i-cal-ly
gen:e-al'-o-gist
gen:e-al'-o-gy
gen-e:col'-o-gy
gen'-er:a
gen'-er-al
gen-er-a-lis'-si-mo*†
gen-er-al'-i-ty
gen-er-al-i:za'-tion
gen'-er-al-ize
gen'-er-al-ly
gen'-er-al-ship
gen'-er-ate
gen'-er-a-ting
gen-er-a'-tion
gen'-er-a-tive
gen'-er-a-tor
gen'-er-a'-trix
ge-ner'-ic
ge-ner'-i-cal
ge-ner'-i-cal-ly
gen-er-os'-i-ty
gen'-er-ous
gen'-er-ous-ly
gen'-e-sis
gen'-et† (mammal)
ge-net' (plant)
ge-neth'-li-ac
gen-eth-li'-a-cal†
ge-net'-ic
ge-net'-i-cal
ge-net'-i-cist
ge-net'-ics
Ge-ne'-va
Ge-ne'-van
Gen'-e-vese'
Gen'-e-vieve
Gen'-ghis Khan
ge'-nial* (pleasant)
ge-ni'-al (of the chin)
ge-ni-al'-i-ty
ge'-nial-ly*
gen'-ic
ge-nic'-u-late
ge'-nie
gen'-in
ge'-ni:o-plas-ty
ge-nis'-te-in
gen'-i-tal
gen'-i-ti'-val
gen'-i-tive

gen'-i-to-u'ri-nar:y†
gen'-i-ture
ge'-nius*
Gen-nes'-a-ret
Gen-o:a
gen'-o-ci'-dal*
gen'-o-cide
Gen'-o-ese'
ge'-nome*†
ge'-no-mere
ge'no-type*†
ge'no-typ'-ic*
gen're
gen-teel'
gen-teel'-ly
genth'-ite†
gen'-tian
gen-tia-na'-ceous†
gen-tia-nel'-la*†
gen'-tian-in
gen'-tian-ose
gen'-tile
gen-til'-i-ty
gen-ti-o-bi'-ose
gen-tis'-ic
gen'-ti-sin
gen'-tle
gen'-tle-man
gen'-tle-ness
gen'-tle-wom-an†
gen'-tlest
gent'-ly*†
gen'-trice
gen'-try
gen-u-flect
gen-u-flec'-tion
gen'-u-flec'-to-ry
gen'-u-ine
gen'-u-ine-ly
gen'-u-ine-ness
ge'-nus
ge-o-bo-tan'-i-cal
ge'-o-cen'-tric
ge-o-cen'-tri-cal
ge-o-ce'-rite
ge-o-chem'-i-cal
ge-o-chem'-is-try
ge-och'-ro-ny
ge-oc'-ro-nite
ge'-ode
ge'-o-des'-ic
ge-od'-e-sist
ge-od'-e-sy
ge'-o-det'-ic
ge'-o-det'-i-cal
ge-od'-ic
Ge-o-dim'-e-ter
ge'o-duck

Geoff'-rey
ge-og'-e-nous
ge-og'-nos'-tic
ge-og'-no-sy
ge-og'-o-ny
ge-og'-ra-pher
ge-o-graph'-ic
ge-o-graph'-i-cal
ge-o-graph'-i-cal-ly
ge-og'-ra-phy
ge'-oid
ge-oi'-dal
ge-o-log'-ic
ge-o-log'-i-cal
ge-ol'-o-gist
ge-ol'-o-gy
ge-o-mag-net'-ic
ge-o-mag'-net-ism
ge-om'-a-lism
ge'-o-man-cy
ge'-ome
ge-om'-e-ter
ge-o-met'-ric
ge-o-met'-ri-cal
ge-om-e-tri'-cian
ge-om'-e-trid
ge-om'-e-triz-er
ge-om'-e-try
ge'-on
ge-oph'-a-gy
ge-o-phys'-i-cal
ge-o-phys'-i-cist
ge-o-phys'-ics
ge-o-po-lit'-i-cal
ge-o-pol-i-ti'-cian
ge-o-pol'-i-tics
ge-o-pon'-ics
George'-town
Geor-gette'
Geor'-gia
Geor'-gian
ge-os'-co-py
ge-o-syn'-cline
ge-o-tech-no-log'-i-cal
ge-o-tech-nol'-o-gy
ge-o-tec-ton'-ic
ge-ot-ri-cho'-sis
ge'-o-trop'-ic
ge-ot'-ro-pism
ge'-rah
Ge-raint'
Ger'-ald
Ger'-al-dine
ge-ra-ni-a'-ceous
ge-ran'-ic
ge-ra'-ni-ol
ge-ra'-ni-um
ge-ra'-nyl

Ge-rard'
ge-rat'-ic
ger-a-tol'-o-gy
ge'-rent
ger'-fal-con
Ger'-hard
ger-i-a-tri'-cian
ger-i-at'-rics
Ger'-man
ger-man'-der
ger-mane'
Ger-man'-ic
ger'-ma-nite*
ger-ma'-ni-um
Ger'-ma-ny
ger'-mi-ci'-dal*
ger'-mi-cide
ger'-mi-nal
ger'-mi-nant
ger'-mi-nate
ger-mi-na'-tion
ger'-mi-na-tor
germ'-proof
Ge-ron'-i-mo
ger-on-toc'-ra-cy
ge-ron-to-log'-i-cal
ger-on-tol'-o-gist
ger-on-tol'-o-gy
ger'-ry-man-der
Ger'-trude
ger'-und
ge-run'-di-al
ger'-un-di'-val†
ge-run'-dive
Ge'-ry-on
Ge-sell'-schaft
ges'-so
Ge-stalt'
ge-sta'-po†
ges'-tate
ges'-tat-ing
ges-ta'-tion
ges'-tic
ges-tic'-u-late
ges-tic'-u-la'-tion
ges-tic'-u-la-tive
ges-tic'-u-la-to-ry
ges'-ture
ges'-tur-ing
get'-a:way
Geth-sem'-a-ne
get'-ta-ble
get'-ting
Get'-tys-burg
get'-up
gew'-gaw
gey'-ser
gey'-ser-ite

161

Gha'-na
Gha'-na-ian
ghar'-ry
ghast'-li-ness
ghast'-ly
gha'-zi
Ghent
gher'-kin
ghet'-to
Ghib'-el-line
Ghi-ber'-ti
ghost
ghost'-like
ghost'-li-ness
ghost'-ly
ghost'-write
ghost'-writ-ten
ghoul'-ish
gi'-ant
gi'-ant-ess
gi'-ant-ism
giaour
gib'-ber
gib-ber-el'-lic
gib-ber-el'-lin
gib'-ber-ish
gib'-bet
gib'-bon
Gib'-bons
gib-bos'-i-ty
gib'-bous
gibbs'-ite
gibe
Gib'-e-on-ite
gib'-ing
gib'-let
Gi-bral'-tar
Gib'-son
gi'-bus
gid'-di-ly
gid'-di-ness
gid'-dy
Gid'-e-on
gift'-ed
gi-gan-te'-an
gi-gan-tesque'
gi-gan'-tic
gi-gan'-tism
gi-gan-tom'-a-chy
gig'-gle
gig'-gling
gig'-o-lo†
gig'-ot
Gi'-la
Gil'-bert
gild
gil'-der† (coin)
gild'-er† (one who gilds)

gild'-ing
Gil'-e-ad
gilled
gil'-ly-flow-er
Gil'-son-ite
gilt
gilt'=edged
gim'-bal
gim'-baled
gim'-let
gim'-mal
gim'-mick
gin'-ger
gin'-ger-bread
gin'-ger-li-ness
gin'-ger-ly
gin'-ger-snap
gin'-ger:y
ging'-ham
gin-gi'-val
gin-gi-vi'-tis
gink'-go
gin'-seng
Giot'-to
Gio-van'-ni
gi-pon'
gi-raffe'
gir'-an-dole
Gi-rard'
gir'-a-sol
gird'-er
gird'-ing
gir'-dle
gir'-dler
gir'-dling
girl'-hood
girl'-ish
girl'-ish-ly
Gi-ron'-dist
girth
gi-sarme'
gist
gi-tal'-in*†
gi-tox-i-gen'-in*
git'-tern
give'-a:way
giv'-en
giv'-er
giv'-ing
giz'-zard
gla-bel'-la
gla'-brate
gla-bres'-cent
gla'-brous
gla-cé'
gla'-cial
gla'-cial-ist
gla'-cial-ly

gla'-ci-ate
gla-ci-a'-tion
gla'-cier
gla-ci-ol'-o-gy
gla-ci-om'-e-ter
gla'-cis
glad'-den
glad'-i-ate
glad'-i-a-tor
glad'-i-a-to'-ri-al
gla-di-o'-lus*
glad'-ly
glad'-ness
glad'-some
Glad'-stone
Glad'-ys
glair
glair'-e-ous
glam'-o-rous*†
glam'-our
glance
glanc'-ing
glan'-ders
glan'-du-lar
glan'-du-lous
glare
glar'-ing
glar'y
Glas'-gow
glass'-es
glass'-ful
glass'-i-ly
glass'-ine'
glass'-i-ness
glass'-ware
glass'y
Glas-we'-gian
Glau'-ber
glau-ber-ite
glau-co-cer'-i-nite
glau-co'-ma
glau-co'ma-tous
glau'-co-nite
glau'-cous
glazed
glaz'-er
gla'-zier
glaz'-ing
gleam
gleam'-ing
gleam'y
glean'-er
glean'-ing
glebe
glee'-ful
glee'-man
Gleich'-schal-tung
Glen-gar'-ry

glen'-oid*†
gli'-al
glib'-best
glib'-ly
glide
glid'-er
glid'-ing
glim'-mer
glim'-mer-ing
glim'-mer-ing-ly
glimpse
glimps'-ing
gli-o'-ma
gli-om'a-tous
glis-sade'
glis-san'-do
glis'-ten
glis'-ter
glit'-ter
glit'-ter-ing
glit'-ter:y
gloam'-ing
gloat'-ing
glob'-al†
glob'-al-ism
glo-bal'-i-ty
glob'-al-ly†
glo'-bate
globe'=trot-ter
glo-big-e-ri'-na*†
glo'-bin
glo'-boid
glo'-bose
glo-bos'-i-ty
glob'-u-lar
glob-u-lar'-i-ty
glob'-ule
glob-u-lif'-er-ous
glob'-u-lin
glock'-en-spiel
glom'-er-ate
glom-er-a'-tion
glo-mer'-u-lar
glom'-er-ule
glo-mer'-u-lus
glon'-o-in
gloom'-i-ly
gloom'-i-ness
gloom'-ing
gloom'y
glo'-ri:a
glo-ri-fi-ca'-tion
glo'-ri-fied
glo'-ri-fi-er
glo'-ri-fy
glo'-ri-fy-ing
glo'-ri-ole
glo'-ri-ous

163

glo'-ri-ous-ly
glo'-ry
glos'-sal
glos-sar'-i-al†
glos'-sa-rist
glos'-sa-ry
glos'-sa-tor
gloss'-er
gloss'-si-ly*
gloss'-si-ness*
gloss'-me-ter
glos-sog'-ra-pher
glos-sol'-o-gy
gloss'y
glot'-tal
glot'-tis
glot-tol'-o-gy
Glouces'-ter
Glouces'-ter-shire
gloved
glov'-er
glov'-ing
glow'-er
glow'-er-ing
glow'-er-ing-ly
glow'-ing
glow'-worm
glox-in'-i:a
glu'-ca-mine
glu-car'-ic
glu-cin'-i-um
glu'-ci-num
glu'-ci-tol
glu'-ci-tyl
glu'-co-nate
glu'-con'-ic
glu-co-pro'-tein
glu-co-py-ran'-o-side
glu-co'-sa-mine*†
glu'-cose
glu-co'-si-dase
glu'-co-side
glu-cu-ron'-ic
glu-cu-ron'-i-dase
glu-cu-ro'-nide
glue
glued
glu'-ey*
glu'-i-ness
glu'-ing
glu-ma'-ceous
glum'-ly
glum'-ness
glut'-a:con'-ic*†
glu'-ta-mate
glu-tam'-ic
glu'-ta-min-ase
glu'-ta-mine†

glu'-ta-min'-ic
glu-tam'-o-yl
glu-ta-thi'-one
glu'-te-al
glu'-ten
glu'-te-nin
glu'-ten-ous* (of gluten)
glu'-ti-nous (sticky)
glu'-ti-nous-ly
glut'-ted
glut'-ton
glut'-ton-ous
glut'-ton:y
gly-ce'-mi:a
gly-ce'-mic
glyc'-er-al'-de-hyde
glyc'-er-ate
gly-cer'-ic†
glyc'-er-ide
glyc'-er-in
glyc'-er-ol
glyc'-er:o-phos-phor'-ic
glyc'-er-yl
gly-cid'-ic
glyc'-i-dol
gly'-cine†
gly-co-cy'-a-mine†
gly'-co-gen
gly-co-gen'-ic
gly-co-gen-ol'-y-sis
gly-co-gen-o-lyt'-ic
gly'-col
gly-col'-y-sis
gly-co-lyt'-ic
gly-co-pro'-tein*
gly-co'-si-dase
gly-cos-u'ri:a*†
glyc:u-re'-sis
gly'-cyl
gly-ox-yl'-ic
glyph'-ic
Glyp'-tal
glyp'-tic
glyp'-to-dont
glyp-tog'-ra-phy
glyp-tol'-o-gy
gnarl
gnarled
gnarl'y
gnash
gnat
gna-thon'-ic†
gnat'-like
gnaw
gnawed
gnaw'-ing
gneiss
gneiss'-oid

gnome
gno'-mic
gnom'-ish
gno-mol'-o-gy
gno'-mon
gno-mon'-ic
gno-se-ol'-o-gy
gno'-sis
gnos'-tic
gnos'-ti-cism
gno-to-bi-ot'-ics
gnu
Go'a
goad'-ed
go'=a:head
goal'-keep-er
goa-tee'*
goat'-herd
goat'-skin
goat'-suck-er
gob'-bet
gob'-ble
gob'-ble-dy-gook
gob'-bler
gob'-bling
Go'be-lin
go'=be-tween
Go'-bi
go'-bies
gob'-let
gob'-lin
go'-by (a fish)
go'=cart
Go-da'-va-ri
god'-child
god'-daugh-ter
god'-dess
god'-fa-ther
god'=fear-ing
god'=giv-en
god'-head
Go-di'-va
god'-less
god'-less-ness
god'-like
god'-li-ness
god'-ly
god'-moth-er
Go-dol'-phin
god'-par-ent
go-droon'
god'-send
god'-ship
god'-son
God'-speed'
God'-win
Goeb'-bels
go'-er

Goe'-thals
Goe'-the
goe'-thite
go-et'-ic
gog'-gle
gog'-gle=eyed
gog'-gling
gog'-let
Goi-del'-ic*
go'-ing
goi'-ter
goi'-tro-gen'-ic
goi-tro-ge-nic'-i-ty
goi'-trous
Gol-con'-da
gold'-beat-er
gold'-brick
gold'-en
gold'-en=haired
gold'-en-rod
gold'=filled
gold'-finch
gold'-fin-ny
gold'-fish
gold'-i-locks
gold'-smith
gold stick
golf'-er
Gol'-gi
Gol'-go-tha
gol'-iard†
gol-iar'-dic†
Go-li'-ath
gol'-li-wog
gom'-bo
gom-broon'
gom'-er-al
Go-mor'-rah
Gom'-pers
gom-pho'-sis
go-mu'-ti
go'-nad*†
go-nad'-al*
go-nad-ec'-to-my
go-na'-di-al
go-nad-o-tro'-phin*
gon'-do-la
gon-do-lier'
Gon'-er-il
gon'-fa-lon
gon-fa-lon-ier'
gon'-fa-non
Gon'-go-rism
go-nid'-i-al
go-nid'-i-um
go-ni-om'-e-ter
go-ni-o-met'-ric

165

go-ni-om'-e-try
go'-ni-on
go'-ni-um
gon-o-coc'-ci
gon-o-coc'-cus
gon'-of
gon'-o-phore
gon-or-rhe'a
gon-or-rhe'-al
goo'-ber
good=by'
good=for=noth'-ing
good'=heart-ed
good hu'-mor
good=hu'-mored
good'-ies
good'-ish
good'-li-ness
good'=look'-ing
good'-ly
good'-man
good'=na'-tured
good'-ness
good night
good'=tem-pered
good'-wife
good will
good'y
Good'-year
goof'y
goo'-gly
goo'-gol
goo'-gol-plex
goo-san'-der*
goose
goose'-ber-ry
goose'-flesh
goose'-foot
goose'-herd
goose'-neck
goose'=step
go'-pher
go'-ral
Gor'-cha-kov'
gor'-cock
Gor'-di-an
Gor'-don
gored
gorge
gor'-geous
gor'-geous-ly
gorg'-er
gor'-ger-in
gor'-get
gorg'-ing
Gor'-gon
Gor-go'-ni-an
gor'-gon-ize

Gor-gon-zo'-la
gor'-hen
go-ril'-la
gor'-ing
Gor'-ki
gor'-lic
gor'y
gos'-hawk
Go'-shen
gos'-ling
gos'-pel
gos'-pel-er
gos'-sa-mer
gos'-san
gos'-sip
gos'-sip-ing
gos'-sip-red
gos'-sip:y
gos-soon'
gos-syp'-i-trin
Go'-te-borg
Goth'-am†
Goth'-am-ite†
Goth'-ic
Goth'-i-cism
Goth'-i-cize
got'-ten
goug'-ing
gou'-lash
Gou-nod'
gou-ra'-mi
gourd
gour'-mand
gour'-mand-ism
gour'-man-diz-er
gour'-met
gout
gout'-i-ly
gout'y
gov'-ern
gov'-ern-a:ble
gov'-ern-ance
gov'-er-nante
gov'-er-ness*†
gov'-ern-ment
gov-ern-men'-tal
gov'-er-nor
gov'-er-nor=gen'-er-al
gov'-er-nor-ship
gow'-an
gowned
goy'-a-zite*†
Graaf'-i:an
grab'-bing
grab'-ble
Grac'-chi
Grac'-chus
grace'-ful

grace'-ful-ly
grace'-ful-ness
grace'-less
grac'-ile
gra-cil'-i-ty
grac'-ing
gra-ci-o'-so
gra'-cious
gra'-cious-ly
grack'-le
gra'-date
gra-da'-tion
gra-da'-tion-al
grad'a-to-ry
grad'-ed
grad'-er
gra'-di-ent
gra'-dine
grad'-ing
gra-di-om'-e-ter
grad'-u-al
grad'-u-al-ism
grad'-u-al-ist
grad'-u-al-ly
grad'-u-ate
grad'-u-at-ing
grad-u-a'-tion
grad'-u-a-tor
gra'-dus
Grae'-ae
graf-fi'-to
graft'-age
graft'-er
graft'-ing
gra'-ham
Grain'-ger
grain'-ing (*adj.*)
grai'-ning*† (type of fish)
grain'y
gral-la-to'-ri-al
gram
gram'a*†
gra-mer'-cy
gram-i-ci'-din
Gram-i-na'-les
gram'-ine
gra-min'-e-ous
gram'-mar
gram-mar'-i-an†
gram'-mar school
gram-mat'-i-cal
Gram'-o-phone
Gram'-pi-an
gram'-pus
Gra-na'-da
gran-a-dil'-la
gra'-na-ry*†
gran'-dam

grand'-aunt
grand-child
grand'-chil-dren
grand-daugh-ter
gran-dee'
gran'-deur
grand'-fa-ther
gran-dil'-o-quence
gran-dil'-o-quent
gran-di-ose
gran-di-os'-i-ty
gran-di-o'-so
grand'-ly
grand'-ma
grand'-moth-er
grand'-neph-ew
grand'-niece
grand'-pa
grand'-par-ent
Grand Rap'-ids
grand'-sire
grand'-son
grand'-stand
grand'-un-cle
grang'-er
gran'-ger-ize*
gran'-ite
gran'-ite-ware
gra-nit'-ic
gran'-it-ite
gran'-i-vore
gra-niv'-o-rous
gran'-ny
gran'-o-blas'-tic
gran'-o-phyre
grant-ee'*
Gran'-tha
grant'-or
grants'-ite
gran'-u-lar
gran-u-lar'-i-ty
gran'-u-late
gran'-u-lat-ed
gran'-u-lat-er
gran'-u-lat-ing
gran-u-la'-tion
gran'-u-la-tor
gran'-ule
gran-u-lit'-ic
gran-u-lo-ma-to'-sis
gran'-u-lous
grape'-fruit
grape juice
grap'-er:y
grape'-shot
grape'-skin
grape'-vine

graph'-eme
gra-phe'-mic
graph'-ic
graph'-i-cal
graph'-i-cal-ly
graph'-ite
gra-phit'-ic
graph'-i-tize
gra-phol'-o-gy*†
graph'-o-met'-ric
grap'-nel
grap'-ple
grap'-pling
grap'y
grasped
grasp'-er
grasp'-ing
grasp'-ing-ly
grass'-hop-per
grass'-land
grass'y
grate
grate'-ful
grate'-ful-ly
grat'-er
Gra'-tian
grat'-i-cule
grat-i-fi-ca'-tion
grat'-i-fied
grat'-i-fi-er
grat'-i-fy
grat'-i-fy-ing
grat'-in*†
grat'-i-nate
grat'-ing
gra'-tis
grat'-i-tude
gra-tu'-i-ties
gra-tu'-i-tous
gra-tu'-i-ty
grat'-u-lant
grat'-u-late
grat-u-la'-tion
grat'-u-la-to-ry
grau'-pel
gra-va'-men
grave'-clothes
grave'-dig-ger
grav'-el
grav'-eled
grav'-el-ly
grave'-ly
grav'-en
grave'-ness
Gra'-ven-stein
grav'-er
grave'-stone
grave'-yard

grav:i-cep'-tor
grav'-id
gra-vid'-i-ty
gra-vim'-e-ter
grav-i-met'-ric
gra-vim'-e-try
grav'-i-sphere
grav'-i-tate
grav'-i-tat-er
grav'-i-tat-ing
grav-i-ta'-tion
grav-i-ta'-tion-al
grav'-i-ta-tive
grav-i-tom'-e-ter
grav'-i-ton
grav'-i-ty
gra-vure'
gra'-vy
gray
gray'-beard
gray'=haired
gray'=head-ed
gray'-ish
gray'-ling
gray'-ness
graze
graz'-er†
gra'-zier
graz'-ing
greas'-er
grease'-wood
greas'-i-ly
greas'-i-ness
greas'y
great
Great Brit'-ain
great'-coat
great gross
great'-heart-ed
great'-ly
great'-ness
greave
grebe
Gre'-cian
Gre'-co=Ro'-man
greed'-i-ly
greed'-i-ness
greed'y
Gree'-ley
green'-back
green'-bri-er
green'-er:y
green'=eyed
green'-gage
green'-gro-cer
green'-horn
green'-house
green'-ing

green'-ish
Green'-land
green'-ling
green'-ness
gree'-nock-ite*
Gree'-nough
green'-room
green'-sward
Green'-wich
green'-wood
greet'-ing
greg'-a-rine
gre-gar'-i-ous†
gre-gar'-i-ous-ness†
Gre-go'-ri-an
Greg'-o-ry
grei'-sen
gre'-mi-al
grem'-lin
Gre-na'-da
gre-nade'
gren'-a-dier
gren'-a-dine'
Gren'-fell
Gre-no'-ble
Gresh'-am
gres-so'-ri-al
Gre'-ta
Gret'-chen
Gret'-na
grey
grey'-hound
grib'-ble
grid'-dle
grid'-dle cake
grid'-i-ron
grief
grief'-strick-en
griev'-ance
grieve
griev'-ing
griev'-ing-ly
griev'-ous
griev'-ous-ly
grif'-fin
grif'-fon
grift'-er
Gri-gnard'
grill (in cooking)
gril'-lage
grille (a screen)
grill'-room
grim'-ace*†
gri-mal'-kin
grime
grim'-i-er
grim'-ly
grim'-mer

grim'-ness
grim'y
grin
grin-de'-li:a
grind'-er
grind'-er:y
grind'-ing
grind'-stone
grin'-go
grin'-gos
grinned
grin'-ning
grip
gripe
griph'-ite
grip'-ing
grippe
grip'-ping
gri-saille'
Gri-sel'-da
gris-e:o-ful'-vin
gris'-e-ous
gri-sette'
gris'-kin
gris'-li-er
gris'-li-ness
gris'-ly
gris'-tle
gris'-tly
grist'-mill
grit'-ting
grit'-ty
griz'-zle
griz'-zled
griz'-zly
groaned
groan'-ing-ly
gro'-cer
gro'-cer-ies
gro'-cer:y
grog'-ger:y
grog'-gi-ness
grog'-gy
grog'-ram
grog'-shop
groin
Gro'-li-er
grom'-met
grom'-well
grooms'-man
groove
groov'-ing
grope
grop'-er (one who gropes)
gro'-per (type of fish)*†
grop'-ing
gros'-beak
gro'-schen

169

gros'-grain
gross'-ly
gross'-ness
gro-tesque'
gro-tesque'-ly
gro-tes'-que-rie*†
Gro'-ti-us
grot'-to
grouch'-i-ness
grouch'y
ground'-age
ground crew
ground'-er
ground floor
ground'-hog
ground'-less
ground'-ling
ground plan
ground'-sill
ground'-work
group'-er (one who groups)
grou'-per*† (type of fish)
grouse
grous'-er (complainer)
grou'-ser† (cleat)
grout'-er
grov'-el
grov'-eled
grov'-el-er
grov'-el-ing
grow'-er
grow'-ing
growl'-er
grown'=up
growth
grubbed
grub'-bi-er
grub'-bing
grub'-by
grub'-stake
grudge
grudg'-ing
grudg'-ing-ly
gru'-el
gru'-el-ing
grue'-some
gruff'-ly
grum'-ble
grum'-bler
grum'-bling
gru'-mose
gru'-mous
grump'-i-ness
grumpy
Grun'-dy
grun'-ion
grunt'-er
grunt'-ing

Gru-yère'
gry'-phon*†
gua-ca-mo'-le
gua'-cha-ro
gua'-co
Gua-dal-ca-nal'
Gua-dal-qui-vir'†
Gua'-de-loupe'
guai'-ac
guai'-a-col
guai'-a-cum
Guam
Gua-ma'-ni-an
gua-na'-co
gua'-na-mine†
gua'-nase
gua'-ni-dine*
gua-nif'-er-ous
gua'-nine
gua'-no
gua'-no-sine
gua-nyl'-ic
Gua'-ra-ni'
guar'-an-tee'
guar-an-tee'-ing
guar'-an-ties
guar'-an-tor
guar'-an-ty
guard'-ed
guard'-ed-ly
guard'-house
guard'-i-an
guard'-i-an-ship
guard'-room
guards'-man
Gua-te-ma'-la
Gua-te-ma'-lan
gua'-va
gua-yu'-le
gu'-ber-na-to'-ri-al
gu-ber'-ni-ya
gud'-geon*†
Gud'-run
guel'-der rose
Guelph
gue-non'
guer'-don
Guern'-sey
guer-ril'-la
guess'-ing
guess'-work
guest
guest' room
guf-faw'
Gui-an'a*†
Gui'-a-nese'
gui-chet'
guid'-a:ble

guid'-ance†
guide'-book
guide'-post
guid'-ing
Gui'-do
gui'-don
gui-gnol'
guild
guil'-der
guild'-hall
guild'-mas-ter
guile'-ful
guile'-less
Guil'-ford
guil'-le-mot
guil-loche'
guil'-lo-tine
guilt
guilt'-i-ly
guilt'-i-ness
guilt'-less
guilt'y
guimpe
guin'-ea
Guin'-e-vere
gui-pure'
guise
gui-tar'
Gu'-ja-ra'-ti
gu'-lar
gul'-den
gul'-let
gull-i:bil'-i-ty†
gull'-i:ble†
gul'-lies
Gul'-li-ver
gul'-ly
gu'-lose
gu-los'-i-ty
gulped
gulp'-ing
gum'-bo
gum'-drop
gum'-ma
gum'-ma-tous
gummed
gum'-mi-ness
gum-mo'-sis
gum'-mous
gum'-my
gump'-tion
gum'-shoe
gun'-boat
gun'-cot-ton
gun'-fire
gun'-flint
Gun'-ite
gun'-lock

gun'-man
gun'-met-al
gun'-nel
gun'-ner
gun'-ner:y
gun'-ning
gun'-ny
gun'-pow-der
gun'-room
gun'-run-ner
gun'-shot
gun'-smith
gun'-stock
Gun'-ther
gun'-wale
gup'-py
gur-gi-ta'-tion
gur'-gle
gur'-glet
gur'-gling
gur'-nard
gush'-er
gush'-ing
gush'y
gus'-set
gus-ta'-tion
gus'-ta-to-ry
Gus-ta'-vus
gust'-i-ly
gus'-to
gust'y
Gu'-ten-berg (printer)
gut'-ta
gut'-ta=per'-cha
gut'-ted
Gut'-ten-berg (N.J. town)
gut'-ter
gut'-ter-snipe
gut'-ting
gut'-tur-al
gut-tur-al'-i-ty
guy'-ing
guz'-zle
guz'-zling
gym-kha'-na
gym-na'-si-arch
gym-na'-si-ast
gym-na'-si-um
gym'-nast
gym-nas'-tic
gym-nas'-tics
gym-nog'-e-nous
gym-nos'-o-phist
gym'-no-sperm
gym'-no-sper'-mous
Gym-no-sto'-ma-ta
gym-no-stom'a-tous†
gy-nae-ce'-um*†

gyn-an'-drous*†
gyn-an'-dry*
gyn'-arch:y†
gy-ne-coc'-ra-cy*†
gy-ne'-co-crat
gy-ne-co-log'-i-cal*†
gy-ne-col'-o-gist*†
gy-ne-col'-o-gy*†
gy-ne-co-mor'-phous*†
gy-ne-ol'-a-try†
gyn-i-at'-rics
gyn'-ics
gy-noe'-ci-um
gy'-no-phore*†
gypped
gyp'-ping
gyp'-se-ous
gyp'-se-ous
gyp-soph'-i-la
gyp'-sum
gyp'-sy
gy'-ral
gy'-rate
gy-ra'-tion
gy'-rat-ing
gy'-ra-tor
gy'-ra-to-ry
gyr-fal-con
gy'-ro-com-pass
gy-roi'-dal
gy-rom'-e-ter
gy'-ro-plane
gy'-ro-scope
gy'-ro-scop'-ic
gy'-rose
gy-ro-sta'-bi-liz-er
gy-ro-stat'-ics
gy'-rus

H

Haar'-lem
Hab'-ak-kuk†
ha'-be-as
ha'-be-as cor'-pus
ha-ben'-dum
hab'-er-dash-er
hab'-er-dash-er:y
hab'-er-geon
hab'-ile
ha-bil'-i-ment
ha-bil'-i-tate
ha-bil-i-ta'-tion
hab'-it
hab'-it-a:bil'-i-ty
hab'-it-a:ble
hab'-i-tant*
hab'-i-tat

ha-bit-a'-tion
ha-bit'-u-al
ha-bit'-u-al-ly
ha-bit'-u-ate
ha-bit-u-a'-tion
hab'-i-tude
ha-bit'-u:é
ha-chure'†
ha-ci-en'-da*
hack'-a-more
hack'-ber-ry
hack'-le
hack'-ler
hack'-ly
hack'-man
hack'-ney
hack'-neyed
hack'-saw
had'-dock
Ha'-des
Ha'-dri-an
haem- (see hem-)
ha'-fiz
haf'-ni-um
Ha-ga'-nah
Ha'-gar
Ha'-gen
hag'-fish
hag-ga'-da
hag-ga-dis'-tic
Hag'-ga:i
hag'-gard
hag'-gis
hag'-gle
hag'-gling
Hag-i-oc'-ra-cy†
hag-i-og'-ra-pha†
hag-i-og'-ra-pher†
hag-i-ol'-a-ter†
hag-i-ol'-a-trous
hag-i-o-log'-ic†
hag-i-ol'-o-gy†
hag'=rid-den
Hague
hai'-duk
Hai'-fa
hai'-kwan'
Hai-le Se-las'-sie
hail'-stone
hail'-storm
hair'-breadth
hair'-brush
hair'-cloth
hair'-cut
hair'-dress-er
hair'-i-ness
hair'-like
hair'-line

hair net
hair oil
hair'-pin
hair'=rais-ing
hair'-split-ter
hair'-split-ting
hair'-spring
hair ton'-ic
hair'y
Hai'-ti
Hai'-tian
haj'i
ha'-ken-kreuz
ha'-kim (ha-kim')
Hak'-luyt
Ha-la'-kah
ha-la'-tion
hal'-a-zone
hal'-berd
hal'-berd-ier'†
hal'-cy-on
half
half'-back
half=baked'
half=breed
half broth'-er
half=caste'
half=heart-ed
half hour
half=mast'
half=moon'
half note
half'-pence
half'-pen-ny
half step
half ti'-tle
half'-tone
half=truth'
half'-way
half=wit'-ted
hal'-i-but
Hal-i-car-nas'-sus
hal'-ide
hal'-i-dom
hal-i-eu'-tics
Hal'-i-fax
hal-i-ste-re'-sis*†
hal'-ite
hal-i-to'-sis
hal'-i-tus
hal'-lan
hal-lel'
hal-le-lu'-jah
Hal'-ley
hal'-ling*†
hall'-mark
hal-loo'
hal'-low

hal'-lowed
hal'-lowed-ness
Hal'-low-een'
Hall'-statt
hal-lu'-ci-nate
hal-lu-ci-na'-tion
hal-lu'-ci-na-to-ry
hal-lu-ci-no'-sis
hal'-lux
hall'-way
ha'-lo
hal'-o-gen
hal'-o-gen-ate
hal-o-gen-a'-tion
ha-log'-e-nous
hal-o-hy'-drin
ha-lom'-e-ter
hal'-o-phyte
ha-lot'-ri-chite
halt'-er (one who halts)
hal'-ter (rope)
hal'-tere
halt'-ing
halt'-ing-ly
halve
halves
halv'-ing
hal'-yard
ham-a-dry'-ad
ha-mal'†
ham-a-mel'-i-da'-ceous*†
Ha'-man
ha-mar-ti'a
ha-mar-ti-ol'-o-gy
Ham-ble-to'-ni-an
Ham'-burg
ham'-burg-er
Ham'-e-lin
Ham'-il-ton
Ham-il-to'-ni-an
Ham'-ite
Ham-it'-ic†
ham'-let
Ham'-mar-skjöld
ham'-mer
ham'-mer-head
ham'-mer-less
ham'-mock
Ham'-mond
Ham-mu-ra'-bi
Hamp'-den
ham'-per
Hamp'-shire
Hamp'-ton
ham'-ster
ham'-string
ham'-strung
Ham'-tramck

ham'-u-lus
han'-a-per
Han'-cock
hand'-bag
hand'-ball
hand'-bill
hand'-book
hand'-cart
hand'-cuff
hand'-ed
Han'-del
hand'-ful
hand'-hold
hand'-i-cap
hand'-i-capped
hand'-i-cap-ping
hand'-i-craft
hand'-i-crafts-man
hand'-i-ly
hand'-i-ness
hand'-i-work
hand'-ker-chief
han'-dle
han'-dle-a:ble
han'-dle-bar
han'-dler
hand'-less
han'-dling
hand'-made'
hand'-maid
hand'-maid-en
hand'-out
hand'-picked'
hand'-rail
hand'-saw
hand'-sel
hand'-shake
hand'-some
hand'-some-ly
hand'-som-est
hand'-spike
hand'-spring
hand'=to=mouth
hand'-work
hand'-worked'
hand'-writ-ing
hand'y
handy'-man
han'-gar*
hang'-dog
hang'-er
hang'-ing
hang'-man
hang'-nail
hang'-out
hang'-o:ver
han'-ker
han'-ker-ing

Han'-kow'
Han'-na
Han'-nah
Han'-ni-bal
Ha-noi'
Han'-o-ver
Han-o-ve'-ri-an
Han'-sard
Han-se-at'-ic
han'-sel
han'-som
Ha'-nuk-kah
hap'-haz'-ard
hap'-less
hap'-loid
hap-lo'-sis
hap'-ly
hap'-pen
hap'-pen-ing
hap'-pi-ly
hap'-pi-ness
hap'-py
hap'-py=go=luck'y
Haps'-burg
hap'-tene
hap'-to-glo'-bin
hap'-to-phore
har'a=kir'i†
ha-rangue'
ha-rangued'
ha-rangu'-er
ha-rangu'-ing
ha-rass'*†
ha-rassed'*†
ha-rass'-ing*†
ha-rass'-ment*†
Har'-bin
har'-bin-ger
har'-bor
har'-bor-age
hard'=bit'-ten
hard'=boiled'
hard'-en
hard'-en-er
hard'=eyed
hard'=faced
hard'=fist-ed
hard'=hand-ed
hard'-head
hard'-head-ed
hard'=heart-ed
har'-di-hood
har'-di-ly
har'-di-ness
Har'-ding
hard'=look-ing
hard'-ly
hard'-ness

hard'-pan
hard'=shell'
hard'-ship
hard'-tack
hard'-top
hard'-ware
hard'-wood
har'-dy
hare'-bell
hare'=brained
hare'-lip
ha'-rem
har'-i-cot
Har'-le-ian
Har'-lem
har'-le-quin
har-le-quin-ade'
Har'-ley
har'-lot
har'-ma-line
har-mat-tan'
harm'-ful
harm'-ful-ly
harm'-less
harm'-less-ly
harm'-less-ness
har-mo'-ni-al
har-mon'-ic
har-mon'-i-ca
har-mon'-ics
har-mo'-ni-ous
har'-mo-nist
har-mo'-ni-um
har-mo-ni-za'-tion
har'-mo-nize
har'-mo-niz-ing
har'-mo-ny
har'-ness
Har'-old
harp'-er
harp'-ing
harp'-ist
har-poon'
harp'-py
harp'-si-**chord**
har'-que-bus
har-que-bus-ier'
har'-ri-dan
har'-ri-er
Har'-ri-et
Har'-ris-burg
Har'-ri-son
Har-ro'-vi-an
har'-row
har'-ry
harsh'-ly
harsh'-ness
har'-tal

har'-te-beest
Hart'-ford
Hart'-ley
harts-horn
har'-um=scar'-um
ha-rus'-pi-cal
Har'-vard
har'-vest
har'-vest-er
Har'-vey
Har'-vey-ize
has'=been
Has'-dru-bal
ha'-sen-pfef-fer
hash'-ish
has'-sle
has'-sled
has'-sock
has'-tate
has'-ten†
hast'-i-ly
hast'-i-ness
hast'-ing
Has'-tings
hast'y
hat'-band
hat'-box
hat'-brush
hatch'-er
hatch'-er:y
hatch'-et
hatch'-ing
hatch'-ment
hatch'-way
hate'-ful
hate'-ful-ly
hat'-er
Hath'-or†
Ha-thor'-ic
hat'-ing
hat' rack
ha'-tred
hat'-stand
hat'-ter
Hat'-ter-as
hau'-berk
haugh'-ti-ly
haugh'-ti-ness
haugh'-ty
haul'-age
haul'-er
haunch
haunt'-ed
Haupt'-mann
Hau'-sa
haut'-boy
hau-teur'
Ha-va'-na*†

175

have'-lock
ha'-ven
have'=not
Ha'-ver-hill
hav'-er-sack
Ha-ver'-sian
hav'-er-sine
hav'-oc
hav'-ocked
hav'-ock-ing
Ha-wai'i
Ha-wai'-ian
hawk'-er
hawk'=eyed
Haw'-kins
haw'-ser
haw'-thorn
Haw'-thorne
hay'-cock
Hay'-dn
hay fe'-ver
hay'-field
hay'-loft
hay'-mak-er
Hay'-mar-ket
hay'-mow
hay'-rack
hay'-rick
hay'-seed
hay'-stack
hay'-ward
hay'-wire
haz'-ard
haz'-ard-ous
ha'-zel
ha'-zel-nut
ha'-zi-ly†
ha'-zi-ness†
haz'-ing
Haz'-litt
ha'-zy†
head'-ache
head'-band
head'-dress
head'-ed
head'-er
head'-first'
head-fore'-most
head'-gear
head'-i-ly
head'-i-ness
head'-ing
head'-land
head'-less
head'-light
head'-line
head'-long
head'-man

head'-mas-ter
head'=on'
head'-piece
head'-quar-ters
head'-room
head'-ship
heads'-man
head'-spring
head'-stone
head'-strong
head'-wait'-er
head'-wa-ters
head'-way
head'-work
head'y
heal'-er
heal'-ing
health'-ful
health'-ful-ness
health'-i-er
health'-i-est
health'-i-ly
health'-i-ness
health'y
heaped
heard
hear'-er
hear'-ing
hark'-en
hear'-say
hearse
heart'-ache
heart'-beat
heart'-break
heart'-break-ing
heart'-bro-ken
heart'-burn
heart'-ed
heart'-en
heart'-felt
hearth
hearth'-stone
heart'-i-ly
heart'-i-ness
heart'-land
heart'-less
heart'-rend-ing
hearts'-ease
heart'=shaped
heart'-sick
heart'-string
heart'y
heat'-ed
heat'-ed-ly
heat'-er
heath
hea'-then
hea'-then-dom

hea'-then-ish
hea'-then-ism
heath'-er
heath'y
heat'=proof
heaved
heav'-en
heav'-en-ly
heav'-en-ward
heav'-er
heav'-i-er
heav'-i-ly
heav'-i-ness
heav'-ing
Heav'-i-side
heav'y
heav'y=du'-ty
heav'y=eyed
heav'y=fist-ed
heav'y=foot-ed
heav'y=hand-ed
heavy'-heart-ed
heav'y-set
heav'y-weight
heb'-do-mad
heb-dom'-a-dal
He'-be
he-be-phre'-ni:a
He'-ber
heb'-e-tate
he-bet'-ic
heb'-e-tude
He-bra'-ic
He-bra'-i-cal-ly
He'-bra-ism
He'-bra-ist
He'-brew
Heb'-ri-des
He'-bron
Hec'-a-te
hec'-a-tomb
heck'-le
heck'-ler
heck'-ling
hec-o-gen'-in
hec'-tare
hec'-tic
hec-ti-cal-ly
hec-to-cot'-y-lus
hec'-to-graph
hec'-to-graph'-ic
hec'-to-li-ter
hec'-to-me-ter
hec'-tor
Hec'-u-ba
hed'-er-in
hedge'-hog
hedg'-er

hedge'-row
hedg'-ing
he-don'-ic
he-don'-ics
he'-do-nism*†
he'-do-nist*†
he-do-nis'-tic†
he-do-nis'-ti-cal†
he-do-nom'-e-ter
he'-dral
heed'-ful
heed'-less
heed'-less-ness
heel'-er
heft'-i-er
heft'-i-est
heft'y
He'-gel
He-ge'-li-an
He-ge'-li-an-ism
heg'-e-mon'-ic†
he-gem'-o-ny†
He-gi'-ra†
he-gu'-men
Hei'-del-berg
heif'-er
Hei'-fetz
height
height'-en
hei'-li-gen-schein
Heim'-dall
Hei'-ne
hei'-nous
hei'-nous-ly
heir
heir'-ess
heir'-loom
Hei'-sen-berg
Hel'-e-na
hel-e-nal'-in
hel'-e-nin
he-li'-a-cal
he-li-an'-the-mum
he-li-an'-thus
hel'-i-cal
hel'-i-ces
he-lic'-i-ty
hel'-i-coi'-dal
hel'-i-con
hel'-i-cop-ter
he'-li-o-cen'-tric
he'-li-o-graph
he-li-og'-ra-phy
he'-li-o-gra-vure'
he-li-om'-e-ter
he'-li-o-met'-ric
he-li-om'-e-try
he'-li-o-pho'-bic

He-li-op'-o-lis
He'-li-os
he'-li:o-scope
he'-li:o-ther'-a-py
he'-li:o-trope
he-li-ot'-ro-pism
he'-li:o-ty-pog'-ra-phy
hel'-i-port
he'-li-um
he'-lix
he-lix-om'-e-ter
Hel'-las
hell'=bent
hell'-cat
hel'-le-bore
hel-le-bo-rine'
Hel'-len
Hel'-lene
Hel-len'-ic
Hel'-le-nism*
Hel-le-nis'-tic*†
Hel'-les-pont
hell'-fire
hell'-gram-mite
hel'-lion
hell'-ish
hel'-lo'
hel'-met
hel'-met-ed
hel'-minth
hel-min'-thic
hel-min-thol'-o-gy
hel-min-tho-spo'-rin
helms'-man
He-lo-ise'
hel'-ot
hel'-ot-ism
help'-er
help'-ful
help'-less
help'-less-ly
help'-less-ness
help'-mate
help'-meet
Hel'-sin-ki
hel'-ter=skel'-ter
Hel-ve'-tia
Hel-ve'-tian
Hel-vet'-ic
Hel-ve'-ti:i
hel'-vite
hel-vol'-ic
he-ma-cy-tom'-e-ter†
he-ma-fi'-brite*†
he-mag-glu'-ti-nin†
he'-mal
he-mal-bu'-men†
he-man-gi-o-ma-to'-sis

he-ma-poi-e'-sis†
he-mar-thro'-sis†
he'-ma-tal
he-ma-te'-in†
he-mat'-ic
hem-a-tin-om'-e-ter†
hem'-a-tite
hem'-a-tit'-ic
hem'-a-to-cele
hem'-a-to-crit
hem'-a-tog'-e-nous
he'-ma-toid†
hem'-a-to-lite
he-ma-tol'-o-gy*†
he-ma-to'-ma†
he-ma-tom'-e-ter†
hem'-a-to-por'-phy-rin
hem'-a-tose
he-ma-to'-sis†
he-ma-tox'-y-lin†
hem'-a-to-zo'-on
hem-el'-y-tron
hem'i-ac'-e-tal
he'-mic
hem'i-cy'-clic†
hem'i-he'-dral
hem'i-kar'-y-on
he'-min
Hem'-ing-way
He-mip'-ter:a
he-mip'-ter-al
he-mip'-ter-oid
hem'-i-sphere
hem'-i-spher'-ic
hem'-i-spher'-i-cal
hem'-i-spher'-i-cal-ly
hem'-i-sphe'-roid
hem'-i-stich
hem'-i-stich'-al*
hem'-lock
he-mo-chro'-mo-gen†
he-mo-chro-mom'-e-ter†
he-mo-co-ni-o'-sis†
he-mo-cy'-a-nin†
he'-mo-cyte†
he-mo-cy-tol'-y-sis†
he'-mo-glo-bin†
he-mo-glo-bi-nom'-e-ter†
he'-moid
he'-mo-lymph†
he-mol'-y-sin*†
he-mol'-y-sis
he'-mo-lyt'-ic†
he-mom'-e-ter†
he-mo-phil'-i:a†
he-mo-phil'-i:ac†
he-mop'-ty-sis†

hem'-or-rhage
hem'-or-rhag'-ic
hem'-or-rhoid
hem'-or-rhoi'-dal
hem'-or-rhoids
he-mo-sid'-er-in†
he-mo-sid-er-o'-sis†
he-mo-stat'-ic†
hemp'-en
hemp'-seed
hem'-stitch
hence'-forth'
hence-for'-ward
hench'-man
hen'-coop
hen-dec'-a-gon
hen-de-cag'-o-nal
hen-dec:a-syl-lab'-ic
Hen'-der-son
hen-di'-a-dys
hen'-e-quen
hen'-house
Hen'-ley
hen'-na
hen'-naed
hen'-na-ing
hen'-ner:y
hen'-o-the-ism
hen'-peck
Hen'-ri'
Hen-ri-et'-ta
hen'-ry
he'-par
hep'-a-rin
he-pat'-ic
he-pat'-i-ca
hep-a-ti'-tis
hep-a-ti-za'-tion
hep-a-to-cu'-pre-in
hep-a-to-fla'-vin
hep-a-tos'-co-py
He-phaes'-tus
Hep'-ple-white
hep-ta-dec'-yl
hep-ta-gon
hep-tag'-o-nal
hep-tam'-e-ter
hep'-tar-chy*
Hep'-ta-teuch
hep'-tu-lose
hep'-tyl-ene
He'-ra
Her-a-cle'a
Her'-a-cles
Her-a-cli'-tus
her'-ald
he-ral'-dic
her'-ald-ry

her-ba'-ceous
herb'-age
herb'-al
her-bar'-i-um†
Her-bar'-ti-an
Her'-bert
her'-bi-ci'-dal
her'-bi-cide
her-biv'-o-rous
Her-cu-la'-ne-um
Her'-cu-le'-an
Her'-cu-les
Her'-der
herd'-er
her'-dic
herds'-man
here'-a:bouts
here-af'-ter*
here'-by
he-red-i-ta-bil'-i-ty
he-red'-i-ta-ble
her-e-dit'-a-ment
he-red-i-tar'-i-ly†
he-red'-i-tar:y†
he-red'-i-ty
Her'-e-ford
here'-in'
here'-in-af'-ter*
here-in-be-fore'
here-of'
he-re'-si-arch†
her'-e-sy
her'-e-tic
he-ret'-i-cal
here'-to-fore'
here'-u:pon'
here-with'
Her'-ges-hei-mer
her'-i-ot
her-i-ta-bil'-i-ty†
her'-i-ta-ble*
her'-i-tage*
her'-i-tance*
her'-i-tor
Her'-man
her-maph'-ro-dite
her-maph'-ro-dit-ism
Her-maph-ro-di'-tus
her-me-neu'-tics
Her'-mes
her-met'-ic
her-met'-i-cal
her-met'-i-cal-ly
Her-mi'-o-ne
her'-mit
her'-mit-age
her-ni:a
her-ni-ar'-in†

179

her-ni-ot'-o-my
he'-ro
Her'-od
He-ro'-di-as
He-rod'-o-tus
he'-roes
he-ro'-ic
he-ro'-i-cal
her'-o-in†
her'-o-ine
her'o-ism
her'-on
He'-ront†
her'-pes
her'-pe-to-log'-i-cal
her-pe-tol'-o-gy
Her'-rick
her'-ring
her'-ring-bone
Her'-schel
her-self'
Hert'-ford
Hert'-ford-shire
hertz'-i:an
Her-ze-go-vi'-na
Her-ze-go-vin'-i:an
her'-zog
Hesh'-van
He'-si-od
hes'-i-tan-cy
hes'-i-tant
hes'-i-tant-ly
hes'-i-tate
hes'-i-tat-er
hes'-i-tat-ing
hes'-i-tat-ing-ly
hes-i-ta'-tion
hes'-i-ta-tive
Hes'-per
Hes-pe'-ri-an
Hes-per'-i-des
hes-per'-i-din
Hes'-per-is
Hes'-per-us
Hes'-se
Hes'-sian
hess'-ite
Hes'-y-chast
he-tae'-ra
he-tae'-rism
het-er:o-al-lele'
het'-er:o-aux'-in
het'-er:o-chro-mat'-ic†
het'-er:o-cy'-clic†
het'-er-o-dox
het'-er-o-dox:y
het'-er:o-dyne

het'-er-oe'-cious
het-er:o-ga-mete'†
het-er-og'-a-mous
het-er-o-ge-ne'-i-ty
het-er-o-ge-ne:ous
het-er-og'-e-nous
het-er-og'-e-ny
het-er-og'-o-ny
het-er-og'-ra-phy
het-er:o-ki-ne'-sis
het-er-ol'-o-gy
het-er-ol'-y-sis
het'-er-om'-er-ous
het-er-on'-o-mous
het-er-on'-y-mous
het-er:o-ou'-si:a
het'-er-o-pol'y
het-er:o-sce-das'-tic
het-er:o-sce-das-tic'-i-ty
het-er-os'-co-py
het-er-o'-sis
het'-er:o-tax'-is
het-er:o-to-pi:a
het'-er:o-top'-ic
het'-er:o-troph'-ic
het-er:o-zy-go'-sis
het-er:o-zy'-gote
het-er:o-zy'-gous
heu-ris'-tic
hew'-ing
hex-a-chlo'-ro-eth'-ane
hex-a-dec'-ane
hex-a-em'-er-on
hex'-a-gon
hex-ag'-o-nal
hex'-a-gram
hex-a-he'-dral
hex-a-he'-dron
hex-am'-e-ter
hex-a-met'-ric
hex'-ane
hex'-a-no'-ic
hex'-a-no'-yl
hex'-a-pod
hex-a-stan'-nite
Hex'-a-teuch
hex-es'-trol
hex-os'-a:mine'
hex'-u-lose
hex'-u-ron'-ic
hex'-yl-ene†
hey'-day
Hez-e-ki'-ah
hi-a'-tus
Hi-a-wa'-tha
hi-ber-nac'-u-lum
hi-ber'-nal

180

hi'-ber-nate
hi'-ber-nat-ing
hi-ber-na'-tion
hi'-ber-na-tor
Hi-ber'-ni:a
Hi-ber'-ni:an
hi-bis'-cus
hic'-cough
hic'-cup
hick'-o-ry
hi-dal'-go
hid'-den
hide'-bound
hid'-e-ous
hid'-e-ous-ly
hid'-e-ous-ness
hid'-ing
hi-dro'-sis
hi-drot'-ic
hi'-er-arch
hi'-er-ar'-chal
hi'-er-ar'-chi-cal
hi'-er-ar-chy*
hi'-er-at'-ic
hi'-er-o-crat'-i-cal
hi'-er-o-dule
hi'-er-o-glyph'-ic
hi'-er-o-glyph'-i-cal
hi'-er-o-glyph'-i-cal-ly
hi'=fi
hig'-gle-dy=pig'-gle-dy
high'-ball
high'-born
high'-boy
high'-bred
high'-brow
high chair
High Church
high-fa-lu'-tin
high fi-del'-i-ty
high'=flown'
high'=fre'-quen-cy (adj.)
high'=grade (v., adj.)
high'=hand-ed
high'=hat' (v., adj.)
high'=heeled'
high'=jack
high'=jack-er
High'-land
High'-land-er
high'-lev'-el
high'-light
high'-ly
high'=mind-ed
high'-ness
high'=pitched'
high'=pow'-ered

high'-road
high school
high seas
high'=sound-ing
high'=spir'-it-ed
high'=strung'
high'=ten'-sion (adj.)
high'=test'
high'=toned'
high'-way
high'-way-man
hi'-jack
hi'-jack-er
hik'-er
hik'-ing
hi-lar'-i-ous†
hi-lar'-i-ty
Hil'-a-ry
Hil'-de-brand
hil'-ding
hill'-bill'y†
hill'-i-ness
hill'-ock
hill'-ocked
hill'-side
hill'-top
hill'y
hi'-lum
hi'-lus
Him'a-lay'a*†
Him'a-lay'-an*†
hi-mat'-i-on
him-self'
Hin'-den-burg
hin'-der (to obstruct)
hind'-er (rear)
hind'-most
hind'-quar-ter
hin'-drance
hind'-sight
Hin'-du
Hin'-du-stan'
Hin-du-stan'i*†
hinge
hing'-ing
hint'-er
hin'-ter-land
hint'-ing-ly
hip'-bone
hip-po-cam'-pus
hip'-po-cras
Hip-poc'-ra-tes
Hip'-po-crat'-ic
hip'-po-drome
Hip-pol'-y-tus
hip-po-pot'-a-mus
hip-pu'-ric

181

Hi′-ram
hir′-cine
hire′-ling
hir′-ing
Hi-ro-hi′-to
Hir′o-shi′-ma†
hir′-su′-tal
hir′-sute
hir′-u-din′-e-an
hi-run′-dine
His-pa′-ni:a
His-pan′-ic
His-pan′-i-cism
his-pan′-i-dad
His-pan-i-o′-la†
hiss′-ing
his-tam′-i-nase
his′-ta-mine
his′-ti-dine
his′-to-log′-i-cal
his-tol′-o-gy
his-tol′-y-sis
his-to′-ri-an
his-tor′-ic
his-tor′-i-cal
his-tor′-i-cal-ly
his-to-ric′-i-ty
his′-to-ries
his-to-ri-og′-ra-pher
his′-to-ry
his-tri-on′-ic
his-tri-on′-i-cal
his-tri-on′-ics
hitch′-hike
hitch′-hik-er
hith′-er
hith′-er-to′
Hit′-ler
Hit′-ler-ism
Hit′-ler-ite
hit′-ting
Hit′-tite
hoard
hoard′-ing
hoar-frost
hoar′-i-ness
hoarse
hoarse′-ly
hoarse′-ness
hoar′y
hoax
hoax′-er
hob′-ble
hob′-bler
hob′-bling
hob′-by
hob′-by-horse
hob′-gob-lin

hob′-nail
hob′-nob
hob′-nob-bing
ho′-bo
ho′-boes
ho′-bo-ism
Ho′-bo-ken
hock′-ey
ho′-cus
ho′-cus=po′-cus
hodge′-podge
Hodg′-kin′s
hod′-o-graph
hoe′-cake
Hoff′-mann
Ho′-garth
hog′-back
hog′-ging
hog′-gish
hogs′-head
hog′-tie
Ho′-hen-stau-fen
Ho′-hen-zol-lern
hoi pol-loi′
hoist′-ed
hoist′-er
ho′-kum
Hol′-bein
hold′-back (n.)
hold′-er
hold′-fast (n.)
hold′-ing
hold′-o:ver (n.)
hold′-up (n.)
hole′-proof
hole′y
hol′-i-day
ho′-li-ness
Hol′-ins-hed
ho′-lism
Hol′-land
hol′-lan-daise′
Hol′-land-er
hol′-low
hol′-low-ness
hol′-ly
hol′-ly-hock
Hol′-ly-wood
hol′-mi-um
hol′o-caust
hol′-o-graph
hol′-o-graph′-ic
hol′-o-he′-dral
hol′-o-pho′-tal
ho-loph′-ra-sis
hol-o-plank′-ton
Hol′-stein
Hol′-stein=Frie′-sian

182

hol'-ster
ho'-ly
Hol'-yoke
ho'-ly-stone
hom'-age
hom'-ag-er
hom'-bre
Hom'-burg
home'-bred'
home brew
home'-land
home'-less
home'-like
home'-li-ness
home'-ly
home'-made'
home'-mak-er
ho-me-ol'-o-gy
ho'-me:o-path
ho'-me:o-path'-ic
ho-me-op'-a-thist
ho-me-op'-a-thy
ho-me:o-sta'-sis
ho'-me:o-typ'-ic
home'-own-er
home'=own-ing
ho'-mer (measure)
hom'-er (home run)
Ho'-mer
Ho-mer'-ic
home'-sick
home'-sick-ness
home'-spun
home'-stead
home'-stead-er
home town
home'-ward
home'-work
hom'-ey*†
hom'i-ci-dal*
hom'i-cide
hom-i-let'-ics
hom'-i-est
hom'-i-lies
hom'-i-ly
hom'-i-nid
hom'-i-ny
hom'-ish
Ho'-mo
ho-mo-al-lele'
ho'-mo-cys-teine
ho'-mo-er'-o-tism
ho-mo-ga'-my
ho-mo-ge-ne'-i-ty
ho-mo-ge-ne:ous
ho-mo-ge-ni-za'-tion
ho-mog'-e-nize
ho-mog'-e-niz-er†

ho-mog'-e-niz-ing
ho-mog'-e-nous
ho-mog'-e-ny
ho-mog'-o-ny
hom'o-graph†
ho'-mo-log*†
ho-mol'-o-gate
ho-mo-log'-i-cal†
ho-mol'-o-gize
ho-mol'-o-gous
ho'-mo-logue*†
ho-mol'-o-gy
ho-mol'-y-sis
hom'o-nym
hom'o-nym'-ic*
ho-mon'-y-mous
hom'o-phone
ho-moph'-o-nous
ho-moph'-o-ny
ho-mop'-ter-ous
Ho'-mo sap'i-ens*
ho-mo-sce-das'-tic
ho-mo-sce-das-tic'-i-ty
ho-mo-sex'-u-al
ho-mo-sex-u-al'-i-ty
ho'-mo-spor'-ous*†
ho-mo-tax'-is
ho'-mo-thet'-ic
ho-mo-zy-go'-sis
ho-mo-zy'-gote†
ho-mo-zy'-gous
ho-mun'-cu-lus
Hon-du'-ran
Hon-du'-ras
honed
hon'-est
hon'-est-ly
hon'-es-ty
hon'-ey
hon'-ey-bee
hon'-ey-comb
hon'-ey-dew
hon'-eyed
hon'-ey-moon
hon'-ey-suck-le
hon'-ing
Hon'-i-ton
honk'y=tonk†
Hon'o-lu'-lu
hon'-or
hon'-or-a:ble
hon'-or-a:bly
hon-o-rar'-i-um†
hon'-or-ar:y†
Ho-no-ri'a
hon-or-if'-ic
Ho-no'-ri-us

183

hood'-ed	ho-rol'-o-gist
hood'-lum	ho-rol'-o-gy
hoo'-doo	hor'-o-scope
hood'-wink	ho-ros'-co-py
hoofed	hor-ren'-dous
hoof'-print	hor'-ri-ble
hoo-kah*	hor'-ri-bly
hook'-er	hor'-rid
hook'-up (n.)	hor-rif'-ic
hook'-worm	hor'-ri-fied
hook'y	hor'-ri-fy
hoo'-li-gan	hor-rip-i-la'-tion
hoo'-poe	hor'-ror
hoo-ray'	hor'-ror=struck
hoose'-gow	hors d'oeuvre
Hoo'-sier	horse
Hoo'-ver	horse'-back
hope'-ful	horse'-car
hope'-ful-ly	horse chest'-nut
hope'-ful-ness	horse'-flesh
hope'-less	horse'-fly
hope'-less-ly	horse'-hair
Ho'-pi	horse'-hide
Hop'-kins	horse'-laugh
hop'-lite	horse'-leech
hop'-per	horse'-less
hop'-scotch	horse'-man
ho'-ra	horse'-man-ship
Hor'-ace	horse op'-er-a
Ho'-rae	horse pis'-tol
ho'-ral	horse'-play
ho'-ra-ry	horse'-pow-er
Ho-ra'-tian	horse'-rad-ish
Ho-ra'-tio	horse sense
Ho-ra'-tius	horse'-shoe
horde	horse'-sho-er
Ho'-reb	horse'-tail
hore'-hound	horse'-whip
ho-ri'-zon	horse'-wom-an†
hor'-i-zon'-tal	hors'-ey*
hor'-i-zon'-tal-ly	hor'-ta-tive
hor'-mo'-nal	hor'-ta-to-ry
hor'-mone	Hor'-tense
hor-mon'-ic	hor-ti-cul'-tur-al
horn'-beam	hor'-ti-cul-ture
horn'-bill	hor'-ti-cul'-tur-ist
horn'-blende	Ho'-rus
horn'-book	ho-san'-na
hor'-net	Ho-se'a
hor-ni'-to	ho'-sier
horn'-less	ho'-sier-y
horn'-pipe	hos'-pice
horn'-swog-gle	hos-pit'a-ble*†
horn'y	hos-pit'a-bly*†
hor'-o-loge	hos'-pi-tal
ho-rol-o-ger	hos-pi-tal'-er
hor'-o-log'-ic	hos-pi-tal'-i-ty
	hos-pi-tal-i-za'-tion

hos'-pi-tal-ize
hos-pi'-ti-um
hos'-po-dar
hos'-tage
host'-al
hos'-tel
hos'-tel-ry
host'-ess
hos'-tile
hos-til'-i-ty
hos'-tler
hot'-bed
hot'-box
hot dog
ho-tel'
hot'-foot
hot'-head
hot'-head-ed
hot'-house
hot'-ly
hot'-ness
hot'-spur
hot'=tem'-pered
Hot'-ten-tot
Hou'-dan
Hou-di'-ni
Hou'-dry
hound
hour'-glass
hou'-ri
hour'-ly
house'-boat
house'-break-ing
house'-bro-ken
house'-coat
house flag
house'-fly
house'-ful
house'-hold
house'-hold-er
house'-keep-er
house'-keep-ing
house'-less
house'-line
house'-maid
house or'-gan
house'-room
house'-top
house'-warm-ing
house'-wife
house'-wife-ry*
house'-work
hous'-ing
Hous'-ton
Hou-yhn'-hnm
hov'-el
hov'-er
hov'-er-ing

How'-ard
how-be'-it
how'-dah
How'-ells
how-ev'-er
how'-it-zer*
howl'-er
how'-lite
how-so-ev'-er
hoy'-den
hua-ra'-che
Hub'-bard
hub'-bub
Hu'-bert
huck'-le-ber-ry
huck'-ster
hud'-dle
hud'-dling
Hu'-di-bras
Hu-di-bras'-tic
Hud'-son
Hue'-ne-me
Huer'-ta
huff'-i-ly
huff'-i-ness
huff'-ish
huff'y
huge'-ly
huge'-ous
hugged
hug'-ging
Hu'-gue-not
hu'-la
hu'-la=hu'-la
hulk'-ing
hul'-la-ba-loo
hu'-man
hu-mane'
hu-mane'-ly
hu'-man-ism
hu'-man-ist
hu-man-is'-tic
hu-man-i-tar'-i-an†
hu-man-i-tar'-i-an-ism†
hu-man'-i-ty
hu'-man-ize
hu'-man-kind
hu'-man-ly
Hum'-ber
Hum'-bert
hum'-ble
hum'-ble-ness
hum'-bling
hum'-bly
Hum'-boldt
hum'-bug
hum'-drum
hu-mec'-tant

185

hu'-mer-al
hu'-mer-us
hu'-mic
hu'-mid
hu-mid-i-fi-ca'-tion
hu-mid'-i-fied
hu-mid'-i-fy
hu-mid'-i-ty
hu'-mi-dor
hu-mi-fi-ca'-tion
hu-mil'-i-ate
hu-mil'-i-at-ing
hu-mil-i-a'-tion
hu-mil'-i-ty
hu'-min
hu'-mit
hum'-ite
hu'-mi-ture
hummed
hum'-ming
hum'-ming-bird
hum'-mock
hu'-mor
hu'-mor-esque'
hu'-mor-ist
hu'-mor-ous
hu'-mor-ous-ly
hu'-mous (adj.)
hump'-back
hump'-backed
Hum'-phrey
humpy
hu'-mu-lene
hu'-mus (n.)
hunch'-back
hunch'-backed
hun'-dred
hun'-dred-fold
hun'-dredth
hun'-dred-weight
Hun-gar'-i-an†
Hun'-ga-ry
hun'-ger
hun'-ger-ing
hun'-gri-er
hun'-gri-ly
hun'-gri-ness
hun'-gry
hun'-ker
Hun'-nish
hunt'-er
hunt'-ing
Hun'-ting-don*†
Hun'-ting-ton†
hunt'-ress
hunts'-man
hur'-dle
hur'-dler

hur'-dy=gur'-dy
hurl'-er
hur'-ly=bur'-ly*
Hu'-ron
hur-rah'
hur'-ri-cane
hur'-ried
hur'-ried-ly
hur'-ry
hur'-ry=scur'-ry
hurt'-er (one who hurts)
hur'-ter* (artillery
   bumper)
hurt'-ful
hurt'-ing
hur'-tle
hur'-tling
hus'-band
hus'-band-man
hus'-band-ry
hush pup'-py
husk'-er
husk'-i-ly
husk'-i-ness
husk'-ing
husk'y*†
hus-sar'
Huss'-ite
hus'-sy
hus'-ting†
hus'-tle
hus'-tler
hus'-tling
Hutch'-ins
Hutch'-in-son
Hux'-ley
Huy'-gens
Hwang Ho
hy'-a-cinth
hy'-a-cin'-thine
Hy-a-cin'-thus
Hy'-a-des
hy-a-les'-cence
hy'-a-line
hy-a-lin-i:za'-tion
hy-a-li-no'-sis
hy-al'-o-gen
hy-al'-o-phane
hy-a-lu'-ro-nate
hy-a-lu-ron'-i-dase
hy'-brid
hy-brid-i:za'-tion
hy'-brid-ize
hy-dan'-to-in
hy'-da-tid
hy'-da-to-gen'-ic
Hy'-der-a-bad
hyd'-no-car'-pic

hy'-dra
hy-drac'-id
hy-drac'-ry-late*
hy-dra-cryl'-ic
hy-dral'-a-zine
Hy'-dra=Mat'-ic
hy'-dra-mine†
hy-dran'-gea
hy'-drant
hy-drar'-gy-rism
hy-dras'-ti-nine
hy'-drate
hy-dra'-tion
hy'-dra-tor
hy-drau'-lic
hy-drau'-li-cal-ly
hy'-dra-zide
hy-draz'-i-dine
hy'-dra-zine
hy-dra-zin'-i-um
hy-dra-zo'-ate
hy-dra-zo'-ic
hy'-dra-zone
hy-dre'-mi:a
hy'-dride
hy-dri-od'-ic
hy-dri'-o-dide
hy'-dro-ab-i'-e-tyl
hy-dro-a:cous'-tic
hy-dro-cal'-u-mite
hy'-dro-car'-bon
hy'-dro-cele
hy-dro-ce-phal'-ic
hy-dro-ceph'-a-lous
hy-dro-ceph'-a-lus
hy-dro-chlo'-ric
hy-dro-chlo'-ride
hy-dro-cin-nam'-ic
hy-dro-cor'-ti-sone
hy-dro-cy-an'-ic
hy-dro-e:lec'-tric
hy-dro-dy-nam'-ics
hy-dro-flu-or'-ic
hy-dro-flu'-or-ide
hy'-dro-foil
hy-dro-form'-ate
hy'-dro-gen
hy'-dro-gen-ate
hy-dro-gen-a'-tion
hy-dro-gen-a-tor
hy'-dro-gen-ize
hy-drog'-e-nous
hy-drog'-no-sy
hy-drog'-ra-pher
hy-dro-graph'-ic
hy-drog'-ra-phy
hy'-droid
hy-dro-ki-net'-ics

hy'-dro-lase
hy-drol'-o-gy
hy-drol'-y-sate
hy-drol'-y-sis
hy-dro-lyt'-ic
hy'-dro-lyze
hy-dro-me-chan'-i-cal
hy-drom'-e-ter
hy'-dro-met'-ric
hy-drom'-e-try
hy-dro'-ni-um
hy-drop'-a-thy
hy'-dro-phane
hy-dro-pho'-bi:a
hy-dro-pho'-bic
hy'-dro-phone
hy'-dro-phyte
hy-drop'-ic
hy'-dro-plane
hy-dro-pon'-ics
hy-dro-qui-none'†
hy'-dro-scope
hy-dro-scop'-ic
hy-dro-so'-da-lite
hy'-dro-some
hy'-dro-sphere
hy'-dro-stat
hy-dro-stat'-ics
hy-dro-sul'-fide
hy-dro-ther-a-peu'-tics
hy-dro-ther'-a-py
hy-drot'-ro-pism
hy'-drous
hy-drox'-ide
hy-drox-im'-i-no
hy-drox'y-am'-i-no
hy-drox'y-bu-tyr'-ic
hy-drox'-yl
hy-drox'-yl-a:mine'†
hy-drox'y-late
hy-drox'y-my'-cin
hy-drox'y-zine
hy'-dro-zo'-an
hy'-dryl
hy-e'-na
hy-e-tog'-ra-phy
hy-e-tol'-o-gy
hy-e-tom'-e-ter
Hy-ge'-ia
hy'-ge-ist
hy'-giene
hy-gi-en'-ic
hy-gi-en'-i-cal-ly
hy'-gien'-ist*
hy-grom'-e-ter
hy'-gro-met'-ric
hy-grom'-e-try
hy-gro-my'-cin

hy'-gro-scope
hy'-gro-scop'-ic
Hyk'-sos
hy-lo-zo'-ist
hy'-men
hy'-me-ne'-al
hy-me-no-cal'-list†
Hy-me-nop'-ter:a†
hy-me-nop'-ter-ous†
Hy-met'-tus
hymn
hym'-nal
hym'-no-dy
hym-nol'-o-gy
hy'-oid
hyp-a:cu'-sic
hy-pae'-thral†
hyp-al-ge'-sia
hy'-per-ac'-id
hy-per-a:cid'-i-ty
hy'-per-bo-la
hy'-per-bo-le
hy'-per-bol'-ic
hy'-per-bol'-i-cal
hy'-per-bol'-i-cal-ly
hy-per'-bo-lize
hy-per'-bo-loi'-dal
Hy-per-bo-re'-an
hy'-per-crit'-i-cal
hy-per-du'-li:a
hy-per-e'-mi:a
hy'-per-gol
hy-per-go-lic'-i-ty
hy-per'-i-cin
hy'-per-in
Hy-pe'-ri-on
hy-per-met'-ric
hy-per-me-tro'-pi:a
hy'-per-on
hy-per-o'pi:a
hy-per-os-to'-sis
hy-per-phys'-i-cal
hy-per-pi-e'-sia
hy-per-pla'-sia
hy-per-pne'a*
hy-per-sen'-si-tive
hy-per-son'-ic
hy'-per-sthene
hy-per-ten'-sion
hy-per-ten'-sive
hy-per-thy'-roid
hy-per'-tro-phic*†
hy-per'-tro-phy
hyp-es-the'-sia
hy'-pha
hy'-phen
hy'-phen-ate
hy-phen-a'-tion

hyp'-noid
hyp-nol'-o-gy
hyp-no'-sis
hyp-not'-ic
hyp-not'-i-cal-ly
hyp'-no-tism
hyp'-no-tist
hyp'-no-tize
hyp'-no-tiz-ing
hy'-po-bro'-mous
hy'-po-caust†
hy-po-chlo'-rite
hy-po-chlo'-rous
hy-po-chon'-dri:a
hy-po-chon'-dri-ac
hy'-po-chon-dri'-a-cal
hy-poc'-ri-sy
hyp'-o-crite
hyp-o-crit'-i-cal
hyp-o-crit'-i-cal-ly
hy'-po-der'-mal
hy'-po-der'-mic
hy-po-der'-mi-cal-ly
hy-po-der'-mis
hy'-po-eu-tec'-tic
hy-pog'-a-my
hy-po-gas'-tric
hyp'-o-gene
hy-po-gen'-ic
hy-pog'-e-nous
hy-po-ge'-um*†
hy-pog'-y-nous
hy'-poid
hy'-po-i:o'-dous
hy-po-mor'-pho-sis
hy-po-phos'-phite
hy-poph'-y-se'-al*†
hy-poph'-y-sis
hy-po-pla'-sia
hy-pos'-ta-sis
hy'-po-style*†
hy-po-sul'-fite
hy-pot'-e-nuse
hy-po-thal'-a-mus
hy-poth'-ec
hy-poth'-e-car:y†
hy-poth'-e-cate
hy-poth-e-ca'-tion
hy-poth'-e-ca-tor
hy-poth'-e-ses
hy-poth'-e-sis
hy-poth'-e-size
hy-po-thet'-i-cal
hy-po-thet'-i-cal-ly
hy-pox-e'-mi:a
hy-pox'-i:a
hyp-sog'-ra-phy
hyp-som'-e-ter

hyp-som'-e-try
hy'-son
hys'-sop
hys-taz'-a-rin
hys-ter-ec'-to-my
hys-ter-e'-sis
hys-ter-et'-ic
hys-te-re'-ri:a
hys-ter'-ic
hys-ter'-i-cal
hys-ter'-i-cal-ly
hys-ter'-ics
hys-ter-or'-rha-phy
hys-ter-os'-co-py
hys-ter-ot'-o-my
hy'-ther-graph

I

I:a'-go
i'amb
i:am'-bic
i:am'-bus
i:at'-ri-cal
i:at'-ro-chem'-is-try†
i:at'-ro-gen'-ic
i:at-ro-ge-nic'-i-ty
I:be'-ri:a
I:be'-ri-an
i'bex
ib:i-dem*
i'bis
Ib'-sen
I:car'-i-an†
Ic'-a-rus
ice' bag
ice'-berg
ice'-boat
ice'-bound
ice'-box
ice'-break-er
ice'-cap
ice cream
iced
Ice'-land
Ice'-land-er
Ice'-lan'-dic
ice'-man
I:ce'-ni-an
ice plant
Ich'-a-bod
ich-neu'-mon
ich-nog'-ra-phy
i'chor
i'chor-ous
ich'-thus
ich'-thy-oid
Ich'-thy-ol

ich-thy-o-log'-i-cal
ich-thy-ol'-o-gist
ich-thy-ol'-o-gy
ich-thy-oph'-a-gous
ich-thy-oph'-a-gy
ich'-thy:o-saur
ich-thy-o'-sis
ich'-thy-ot'-ic
ic'i-cle
ic'-i-ly*
ic'-i-ness*
ic'-ing
i'con
i:con'-ic
i:con'-o-clasm
i:con'-o-clast
i:con'-o-clas'-tic
i:co-nog'-ra-pher
i:co-nog'-ra-phy
i:co-nol'-a-try
i:co-nol'-o-gy
i:co-nom'-e-ter
i:con'-o-scope
i:co-nos'-ta-sis
i:co'sa-he'-dron
ic-ter'-ic
ic'-ter-us
icy*
I'da-ho
I'da-ho'-an
i:de'a
i:de'-al
i:de'-al-ism
i:de'-al-ist
i:de'-al-is'-tic
i:de'-al-i:za'-tion
i:de'-al-ize
i:de'-al-ly
i'de-ate
i:de-a'-tion
i'dem
i:den'-tic
i:den'-ti-cal
i:den-ti-fi-a-ble
i:den-ti-fi-ca'-tion
i:den'-ti-fied
i:den'-ti-fies
i:den'-ti-fy
i:den'-ti-ty
i:de-oc'-ra-cy
i'de:o-gram*
i'de:o-graph*
i:de-og'-ra-phy*
i:de-o-log'-i-cal*
i:de-ol'-o-gist*
i:de-ol'-o-gy*
Ides

id-i-oc′-ra-cy
id′-i-o-cy
id′-i:o-gram
id′-i-o-lect
id′-i-om
id-i-o-mat′-ic†
id-i-om′-e-ter
id′-i-o-path′-ic
id-i-op′-a-thy
id-i-o-syn′-cra-sy
id′-i-ot
id-i-ot′-ic
id-i-ot′-i-cal
id-i-ot′-i-cal-ly
id′-i-ot-ism
id′-i-tol
i′dle
i′dled
i′dle-ness
i′dler
i′dling
i′dly
i′dol
i:dol′-a-ter
i:dol′-a-trize
i:dol′-a-trous
i:dol′-a-try
i′dol-ism
i:dol-i-za′-tion
i′dol-ize
i:do′-ne-ous
i′dyll
i:dyl′-lic
i′dyll-ist†
ig′-loo
Ig-na′-tian
Ig-na′-ti-us
ig′-ne-ous
ig-nes′-cent
ig′-nis fat′-u-us
ig-nit′-a:ble
ig-nite′
ig-nit′-er
ig-nit′-ing
ig-ni′-tion
ig′-ni-tron
ig-no-bil′-i-ty
ig-no′-ble
ig-no-min′-i-ous
ig-no-min′-i-ous-ly
ig′-nom:i-ny*†
ig-no-ra′-mus
ig′-no-rance
ig′-no-rant
ig′-no-rant-ly
ig-nore′
Ig-o-rot′*†
i:gua′-na

i:gua′-no-don*
i′kon
il′-e-al
il-e-i′-tis
il-e-os′-to-my
il′-e-um
i′lex
il′-i-ac
Il′-i-ad
il′-i-um
ilk
ill′=ad-vised′
il-lapse′
il-la′-tion
il′-la-tive
ill′=bred
ill′=dis-posed′
il-le′-gal
il-le-gal′-i-ty
il-leg-i-bil′-i-ty
il-leg′-i-ble
il-le-git′-i-ma-cy
il-le-git′-i-mate
ill′=fat′-ed
ill′=fa′-vored
ill′=fit′-ting
ill′=got′-ten
ill′=hu′-mored
il-lib′-er-al
il-lic′-it
il-lim′-it-a:ble
il-lin′-i-um
Il′-li-nois′
Il′-li-nois′-an
il′-lite
il-lit′-er-a-cy
il-lit′-er-ate
ill′=man′-nered
ill′=na′-tured
ill′-ness
il-log′-i-cal
ill′=o′mened
ill′=starred′
ill′=tem′-pered
ill′=timed′
ill′=treat′
ill′=treat′-ment
il-lude′
il-lume′
il-lu′-mi-nant
il-lu′-mi-nate
Il-lu-mi-na′-ti
il-lu′-mi-nat-ing
il-lu-mi-na′-tion
il-lu′-mi-na-tive
il-lu′-mi-na-tor
il-lu′-mine
il-lu′-min-er

190

il-lu′-min-ing
il-lu-mi-nom′-e-ter
ill′=us′-age
ill′=use′ (v.)
il-lu′-sion
il-lu′-sive
il-lu′-so-ri-ly
il-lu′-so-ry
il′-lus-trate
il′-lus-trat-ing
il-lus-tra′-tion
il-lus′-tra-tive
il′-lus-tra-tor
il-lus′-tri-ous
il-lu′-vi-al
il-lu′-vi-ate
il-lu-vi-a′-tion
Il-lyr′-i-a
Il-lyr′-i-an
il′-men-ite
I:lo-ca′-no
I′lo-i′lo
im′-age
im′-ag-e:ry*†
im:ag′-in-a:ble*†
im:ag′-i-nal (of an image)
im:a′-gi-nal*† (of an
   imago)
im:ag′-i-nar:y†
im:ag′-i-na′-tion
im:ag′-i-na-tive
im:ag′-ine
im:ag′-in-ing
im′-ag-ism
im′-ag-ist
im′-ag-is′-tic
i:ma′-go
I:mam′
I:mam′-ate
i:ma′-ret
im-bal′-ance
im′-be-cile
im-be-cil′-i-ty
im-bed′
im-bibe′
im-bib′-er
im-bi-bi′-tion
im′-bri-cate
im′-bri-cat-ed
im-bri-ca′-tion
im-bro′-glio
im-brue′
im-bru′-ing
im-bue′
im-bu′-ing
im-id-az′-ole
im-id-az′-o-line
im-id-az′-o-lyl

im′-ide
im′-i-do*
i:mid′-o-gen
im-in-az′-ole*
im′-ine*
im′-i-no*
im-i-ta-bil′-i-ty
im′-i-ta-ble
im′-i-tate
im-i-ta′-tion
im′-i-ta-tive
im′-i-ta-tor
im-mac′-u-la-cy
im-mac′-u-late
im′-ma-nence
im′-ma-nent
Im-man′-u-el
im-mar′-gin-ate†
im-ma-te′-ri-al
im-ma-te-ri-al′-i-ty
im-ma-ture′
im-ma-tur′-i-ty*
im-mea′-sur-a:ble*
im-mea′-sur-a:bly*
im-me′-di-a-cy
im-me′-di-ate
im-me′-di-ate-ly
im-med′-i-ca-ble
Im′-mel-mann
im-mem′-o-ra-ble
im-me-mo′-ri-al
im-mense′
im-mense′-ly
im-men′-si-ty
im-men′-su-ra-ble†
im-merge′
im-merse′
im-mersed′
im-mers′-i:ble
im-mers′-ing
im-mer′-sion
im′-mi-grant
im′-mi-grate
im-mi-gra′-tion
im′-mi-nence
im′-mi-nent
im-mis′-ci-ble
im-mit′-i-ga-ble
im-mo′-bile
im-mo-bil′-i-ty
im-mo-bi-li-za′-tion
im-mo′-bi-lize†
im-mod′-er-a-cy
im-mod′-er-ate
im-mod-er-a′-tion
im-mod′-est
im′-mo-late
im-mo-la′-tion

im-mor'-al
im-mo-ral'-i-ty
im-mor'-al-ly
im-mor'-tal
im-mor-tal'-i-ty
im-mor-tal-i:za'-tion
im-mor'-tal-ize
im-mo'-tile
im-mov-a-bil'-i-ty
im-mov'-a:ble
im-mov'-a:bly
im-mune'
im-mu'-ni-ty
im-mu-ni-za'-tion†
im'-mu-nize†
im-mu'-no-gen
im-mu-nol'-o-gy
im-mure'
im-mur'-ing
im-mu-ta-bil'-i-ty
im-mu'-ta-ble
Im'-o-gen
im'-pact
im-pac'-tion
im-pac'-tive
im-pair'
im-pair'-ment
im-pale'
im-pal'-ing
im-pal-pa-bil'-i-ty
im-pal'-pa-ble
im-pa-na'-tion
im-pan'-el
im-pan'-eled
im-par'-i-ty
im-park'
im-par'-lance
im-part'
im-par-ta'-tion
im-par'-tial
im-par-ti:al'-i-ty
im-par'-tial-ly
im-part'-i:ble
im-pass-a:bil'-i-ty
im-pass'-a:ble
im'-passe
im-pas-si-bil'-i-ty
im-pas'-si-ble
im-pas'-sion
im-pas'-sion-ate
im-pas'-sioned
im-pas'-sive
im-pas'-sive-ly
im-pas-siv'-i-ty
im-pas'-to
im'-pa-ter'-nate
im-pa'-tience
im-pa'-tiens

im-pa'-tient
im-pa'-tient-ly
im-pav'-id
im-peach'
im-peach-a:bil'-i-ty
im-peach'-a:ble
im-peach'-ment
im-pearl'
im-pec-ca-bil'-i-ty
im-pec'-ca-ble
im-pe-cu-ni:os'-i-ty
im-pe-cu'-ni:ous
im-ped'-ance†
im-pede'
im-ped'-i:ble
im-pe'-di-ent
im-ped'-i-ment
im-ped-i-men'-ta
im-ped-i-men'-tal
im-ped-i-men'-ta-ry
im-ped'-ing
im-ped'-i-tive
im-pe-dom'-e-ter
im-pe'-dor
im-pel'
im-pelled'
im-pel'-lent
im-pel'-ler
im-pel'-ling
im-pend'
im-pend'-ent†
im-pend'-ing
im-pen-e-tra-bil'-i-ty
im-pen'-e-tra-ble
im-pen'-i-tence
im-pen'-i-tent
im-pen'-nate
im-per'-a-tive
im-per'-a-tive-ly
im'-pe-ra'-tor
im-per-a-to'-ri-al
im-per-cep'-ti-ble
im-per-cep'-ti-bly
im-per'-fect
im-per-fec'-tion
im-per'-fect-ly
im-per'-fect-ness
im-per'-fo-rate
im-per'-fo-rat-ed
im-per-fo-ra'-tion
im-pe'-ri-al
im-pe'-ri-al-ism
im-pe'-ri-al-ist
im-pe'-ri-al-is'-tic
im-pe'-ri-al-ly
im-per'-il
im-per'-iled
im-per'-il-ing

im-pe'-ri-ous
im-pe'-ri-ous-ly
im-per'-ish-a:ble
im-pe'-ri-um
im-per'-ma-nence
im-per'-ma-nent
im-per-me-a:bil'-i-ty
im-per'-me-a:ble
im-per-scrip'-ti-ble
im-per'-son-al
im-per'-son-al-ly
im-per'-son-ate
im-per-son-a'-tion
im-per'-son-a-tor
im-per-sua'-si-ble
im-per'-ti-nence
im-per'-ti-nen-cy
im-per'-ti-nent
im-per-turb-a:bil'-i-ty
im-per-turb'-a:ble
im-per-tur-ba'-tion
im-per'-vi-ous
im-pe-ti'-go
im'-pe-trate
im-pet-u-os'-i-ty
im-pet'-u-ous
im-pet'-u-ous-ly
im'-pe-tus
im-pi'-e-ty
im-pig-no-ra'-tion
im-pinge'
im-pinge'-ment
im-ping'-er
im-ping'-ing
im'-pi-ous
imp'-ish
im-plac:a-bil'-i-ty
im-plac'a-ble
im-plant'
im-plan-ta'-tion
im-plas-tic'-i-ty
im-plau'-si-ble
im'-ple-ment
im-ple-men'-tal
im'-pli-cate
im-pli-ca'-tion
im'-pli:ca-tive
im-plic'-it
im-plic'-it-ly
im-plied'
im-pli'-ed-ly
im-plor'-a-to-ry
im-plore'
im-plor'-ing
im-plor'-ing-ly
im-plo'-sion
im-plo'-sive
im-ply'

im-po-lite'
im-pol'-i-tic
im-pon'-der-a:ble
im-port' (v.)
im'-port (n., v.)
im-port'-a:ble
im-por'-tance
im-por'-tant
im-por'-tant-ly
im-por-ta'-tion
im-port'-er
im-por'-tu-na-cy
im-por'-tu-nate
im'-por-tune
im'-por-tun'-ing
im-por-tu'-ni-ty
im-pose'
im-pos'-ing
im-po-si'-tion
im-pos-si-bil'-i-ty
im-pos'-si-ble
im'-post
im-pos'-tor
im-pos'-tume
im-pos'-ture
im'-po-tence
im'-po-ten-cy
im'-po-tent
im-pound'
im-pov'-er-ish
im-pov'-er-ish-ment
im-pow'-er
im-prac-ti-ca-bil'-i-ty
im-prac'-ti-ca-ble
im-prac'-ti-cal
im-prac-ti-cal'-i-ty
im'-pre-cate
im-pre-ca'-tion
im'-pre-ca-tor
im'-pre:ca-to-ry
im-pre-cise'
im-preg-na-bil'-i-ty
im-preg'-na-ble
im-preg'-nate
im-preg-na'-tion
im-preg-na'-tor
im'-pre-sar'-i-al
im-pre-sar'-i:o*†
im-pre-scrip'-ti-ble
im-press' (v.)
im'-press (n.)
im-press'-a:ble
im-press'-i:bil'-i-ty
im-press'-i:ble
im-pres'-sion
im-pres'-sion-a:ble
im-pres'-sion-ism
im-pres-sion-is'-tic

im-pres'-sive
im-pres'-sive-ly
im-press'-ment
im-pri-ma'-tur
im-pri'-mis
im'-print (n.)
im-print' (v.)
im-pris'-on
im-pris'-on-ment
im-prob-a-bil'-i-ty
im-prob'-a-ble
im-pro'-bi-ty†
im-promp'-tu
im-prop'-er
im-prop'-er-ly
im-pro-pri'-ate
im-pro-pri'-e-ty
im-prov'-a:ble
im-prove'
im-prove'-ment
im-prov'-er
im-prov'-i-dence
im-prov'-i-dent
im-prov'-ing
im-prov:i-sa'-tion
im-prov'i-sa-tor
im'-pro-vise
im'-pro-vis-ing
im-pru'-dence
im-pru'-dent
im-pru'-dent-ly
im'-pu-dence
im'-pu-dent
im-pu-dic'-i-ty
im-pugn'
im-pugn'-a:ble (can be
   impugned)
im-pug'-na-ble
   (unconquerable)
im-pugn:a'-tion
im-pugn'-er
im-pu'-is-sant
im'-pulse
im-pul'-sion
im-pul'-sive
im-pul'-sive-ly
im-pu'-ni-ty
im-pure'
im-pu'-ri-ty
im-put'-a:ble
im-pu-ta'-tion
im-pu'-ta-tive*
im-pute'
im-put'-ing
in-a:bil'-i-ty
in ab-sen'-tia
in-ac-ces-si-bil'-i-ty
in-ac-ces'-si-ble

in-ac'-cu-ra-cy
in-ac'-cu-rate
in-ac'-tion
in-ac'-ti-vate
in-ac-ti-va'-tion
in-ac'-tive
in-ac-tiv'-i-ty
in-ad'-e-qua-cy
in-ad'-e-quate
in-ad-mis'-si-ble
in-ad-ver'-tence*
in-ad-ver'-tent*
in-ad-ver'-tent-ly*
in-ad-vis'-a:ble
in-a'lien-a:ble
in-al'-ter-a:ble
in-am-o-ra'-ta
in-ane'
in-an'-i-mate
in-a-ni'-tion
in-an'-i-ty
in-ap-peas'-a:ble
in-ap'-pe-tence
in-ap'-pli-ca-ble
in-ap'-po-site
in-ap-pre'-cia-ble
in-ap-pre'-cia-tive
in-ap-proach'-a:ble
in-ap-pro'-pri-ate
in-apt'
in-ap'-ti-tude*†
in-ar-tic'-u-late
in-ar-ti-fi'-cial
in-ar-tis'-tic
in-as-much'
in-at-ten'-tion
in-at-ten'-tive
in-au'-di-ble
in-au'-gu-ral
in-au'-gu-rate
in-au'-gu-rat-ing
in-au-gu-ra'-tion
in-aus-pi'-cious
in-aus-pi'-cious-ly
in'-board
in'-born
in'-bred
in'-breed-ing
in'-built
In'-ca
in-cal'-cu-la-ble
in-cal'-cu-la-bly
in-ca-les'-cent
in-can-desce'
in-can-des'-cence
in-can-des'-cent
in-can-ta'-tion
in-ca-pa-bil'-i-ty

in-ca'-pa-ble
in-ca-pa'-cious
in-ca-pac'-i-tate
in-ca-pac-i-ta'-tion
in-ca-pac'-i-ty
in-car'-cer-ate
in-car-cer-a'-tion
in-car'-di-nate
in-car'-na-dine
in-car'-nate
in-car-na'-tion
in-case'
in-cau'-tious
in-cen'-di-a-rism
in-cen'-di-ar:y†
in'-cense (n.)
in-cense' (v.)
in-cens'-ing
in-cen'-tive
in-cep'-tion
in-cep'-tive
in-cep'-tor
in-cer'-ti-tude
in-ces'-san-cy
in-ces'-sant
in-ces'-sant-ly
in'-cest
in-ces'-tu-ous
in-cho'-ate
in-cho'-ate-ly
in-cho'-a-tive
inch'-worm
in'-ci-dence
in-ci-dent
in-ci-den'-tal
in-ci-den'-tal-ly
in-cin'-er-ate
in-cin-er-a'-tion
in-cin'-er-a-tor
in-cip'-i-ence
in-cip'-i-ent
in-cise'
in-ci'-sion
in-ci'-sive
in-ci'-sor
in-cit'-ant†
in-ci-ta'-tion
in-cite'
in-cite'-ment
in-cit'-er
in-cit'-ing
in-ci'-to-ry
in-ci-vil'-i-ty
in-civ'-ism*†
in-clem'-en-cy
in-clem'-ent
in-clin'-a:ble
in-cli-na'-tion

in-cli'-na-to-ry
in-cline' (v., n.)
in'-cline (n.)
in-clined'
in-clin'-ing
in-cli-nom'-e-ter
in-close'
in-clud'-a:ble
in-clude'
in-clud'-ed
in-clud'-ing
in-clu'-sion
in-clu'-sive
in-co-erc'-i-ble*
in-cog-ni'-to
in-co-her'-ence
in-co-her'-ent
in-com-bus'-ti-ble
in'-come
in'-com-ing
in-com-men'-su-ra-ble
in-com-men'-su-rate
in-com-mode'
in-com-mo'-di-ous
in-com-mu'-ni-ca-ble
in-com-mu-ni-ca'-do
in-com'-pa-ra-ble
in-com-pat-i-bil'-i-ty
in-com-pat'-i-ble
in-com'-pe-tence
in-com'-pe-ten-cy
in-com'-pe-tent
in-com-plete'
in-com-plete'-ly
in-com-pli'-ant
in-com-pre-hen'-si-ble
in-com-pre-hen'-sion
in-com-press'-i-ble
in-com-put'-a:ble
in-con-ceiv'-a:ble
in-con-ceiv'-a:bly
in-con-clu'-sive
in-con-cus'-si-ble
in-con'-dite
In'-co-nel
in-con-gru'-i-ty
in-con'-gru-ous
in-con-sec'-u-tive
in-con'-se-quence
in-con'-se-quent
in-con-se-quen'-tial
in-con-sid'-er-a-ble
in-con-sid'-er-ate
in-con-sid-er-a'-tion
in-con-sist'-en-cy†
in-con-sist'-ent†
in-con-sol'-a-ble

195

in-con'-so-nance
in-con'-so-nant
in-con-spic'-u-ous
in-con'-stan-cy
in-con'-stant
in-con-test-a:bil'-i-ty
in-con-test'-a:ble
in-con'-ti-nence
in-con'-ti-nent
in-con-tro-vert'-i-ble
in-con-ve'-ni-ence*
in-con-ve'-nien-cy*
in-con-ve'-ni-ent*
in-con-vert'-i-ble
in-con-vin'-ci-ble†
in-cor'-po-ra-ble
in-cor'-po-rate
in-cor'-po-rat-ed
in-cor-po-ra'-tion
in-cor'-po-ra-tive
in-cor'-po-ra-tor
in-cor-po'-re-al
in-cor-po-re'-i-ty
in-cor-rect'
in-cor-ri-gi-bil'-i-ty
in-cor'-ri-gi-ble
in'-cor-rupt'
in-cor-rupt-i-bil'-i-ty
in-cor-rupt'-i-ble
in-creas'-a:ble
in-crease' (v.)
in'-crease (n.)
in-creas'-er
in-creas'-ing
in-cred-i-bil'-i-ty
in-cred'-i-ble
in-cred'-i-bly
in-cre-du'-li-ty
in-cred'-u-lous
in-cred'-u-lous-ly
in'-cre-ment
in'-cre-men'-tal
in-cre'-to-ry
in-crim'-i-nate
in-crim-i-na'-tion
in-crim'-i-na-to-ry
in-crust'
in-crus-ta'-tion
in'-cu-bate
in'-cu-ba'-tion
in'-cu-ba-tor
in'-cu-bous (adj.)
in'-cu-bus (n.)
in-cul'-cate
in-cul-ca'-tion
in-cul'-ca-tor
in-cul'-pate
in-cul-pa'-tion

in-cul'-pa-to-ry
in-cum'-ben-cy
in-cum'-bent
in-cum'-ber
in-cum'-brance
in-cu-nab'-u-la
in-cu-nab'-u-lum
in-cur'
in-cur'-a-ble
in-cu'-ri-ous
in-cur'-ra-ble
in-curred'
in-cur'-rence
in-cur'-ring
in-cur'-sion
in-cur'-sive
in'-cur-vate
in'-cur-va'-tion
in'-da-ga-tor
in'-da-mine†
in'-da-zole
in-debt'-ed
in-debt'-ed-ness
in-de'-cen-cy
in-de'-cent
in-de-ci'-pher-a:ble
in-de-ci'-sion
in-de-ci'-sive
in-de-clin'-a:ble
in'-de-com-pos'-a:ble
in-dec'-or-ous*†
in-de-co'-rum
in-deed'
in-de-fat-i-ga-bil'-i-ty
in-de-fat'-i-ga-ble
in'-de-fea'-si-ble
in-de-fen'-si-ble
in-de-fin'-a-ble
in-def'-i-nite
in-def'-i-nite-ly
in-de-his'-cent
in-de-lib'-er-ate
in-del-i-bil'-i-ty
in-del'-i-ble
in-del'-i-ca-cy
in-del'-i-cate
in-dem-ni-fi-ca'-tion
in-dem'-ni-fied
in-dem'-ni-fies
in-dem'-ni-fy
in-dem'-ni-tor
in-dem'-ni-ty
in'-dene
in-dent'
in-den-ta'-tion
in-dent'-ed
in-dent'-er
in-den'-tion

in-den'-ture
in-de-pen'-dence*
in-de-pen'-den-cy*
in-de-pen'-dent*
in-de-pen'-dent-ly*
in-de-scrib'-a:ble
in-de-struc-ti-bil'-i-ty*
in-de-struc'-ti-ble*
in-de-ter'-min-a:ble*†
in-de-ter'-mi-nate
in-de-ter-mi-na'-tion
in'-dex
in'-dex-er
in'-dex-es
In'-di:a
In'-di-an
In-di-an'a
In-di-an'-an
In-di-an-ap'-o-lis
in'-di-can
in'-di-cate
in-di-ca'-tion
in'-di-ca-tor
in-dic'-a-tive
in-dic'-a-to-ry*†
in'-di-ces
in-di'-cia
in-dic'-o-lite
in-dict'
in-dict'-a:ble
in-dic'-tion
in-dict'-ment
in-dict'-or
In'-dies
in-dif'-fer-ence
in-dif'-fer-ent
in-dif'-fer-ent-ly
in'-di-gen
in'-di-gence
in-dig'-e-nous
in'-di-gent
in-di-gest'-i:ble
in-di-ges'-tion
in-dig'-nant
in-dig'-nant-ly
in-dig-na'-tion
in-dig'-ni-ty
in'-di-go
in-dig'-o-lite†
In'-di-go-sol
in-dig'-o-tin†
in-di-rect'
in-di-rec'-tion
in-di-rect'-ly
in-di-rect'-ness
in-di-ru'-bin
in-dis-cern'-i:ble

in-dis-creet'
in'-dis-crete'
in-dis-cre'-tion
in-dis-crim'-i-nate
in-dis-crim'-i-nate-ly
in-dis-crim-i-na'-tion
in-dis-pens'-a:ble*†
in-dis-pose'
in-dis-posed'
in-dis-po-si'-tion
in-dis-put'-a:ble*†
in-dis-sol'-u-ble*†
in-dis-tinct'
in-dis-tinc'-tive
in-dis-tinct'-ly
in-dis-tinct'-ness
in-dis-tin'-guish-a:ble
in-dite'
in-dite'-ment
in'-di-um
in-di-vert'-i:ble
in-di-vid'-u-al
in-di-vid'-u-al-ism
in-di-vid'-u-al-ist
in-di-vid-u-al-is'-tic
in-di-vid-u-al'-i-ty
in-di-vid-u-al-ize
in-di-vid'-u-al-ly
in-di-vis-i-bil'-i-ty
in-di-vis'-i-ble
In'-do=Chi'-na
In'-do=Chi-nese'
in-doc'-ile
in-doc'-tri-nate
in-doc-tri-na'-tion
in-doc'-tri=na-tor
In'-do=Eu-ro-pe'-an
in'-dole-a:ce'-tic
in'-do-lence
in'-do-lent
in'-do-line
in'-do-lyl
in-dom'-i-ta-ble
In'-do-ne'-sia
In'-do-ne'-sian
in'-door
in'-doors'
in-do-phe'-nin
in-do-phe'-nol
in-dorse'
in-dors-ee'†
in-dorse'-ment
in-dors'-er
in-dox'-yl
in'-drawn
in-du'-bi-ta-ble
in-duce'
in-duce'-ment

in-duc'-er
in-duc'-i:ble
in-duc'-ing
in-duct'
in-duc'-tance*
in-duct-ee'†
in-duc'-tile
in-duc-til'-i-ty
in-duc'-tion
in-duc'-tive
in-duc-tiv'-i-ty
in-duc-tom'-e-ter
in-duc'-tor
in-duc-to'-ri-um
in-due'
in-dulge'
in-dul'-gence
in-dul'-gent
in-dul'-gent-ly
in-dulg'-er
in-dulg'-ing
in'-du-line
in-du'-pli-cate
in'-du-rate
in-du-ra'-tion
in'-du-ra-tive
In'-dus
in-du'-si-um
in-dus'-tri-al
in-dus'-tri-al-ism
in-dus'-tri-al-ist
in-dus-tri-al-i:za'-tion
in-dus'-tri-al-ize
in'-dus-tries
in-dus'-tri-ous
in-dus'-tri-ous-ly
in'-dus-try
in'-dwell-ing
in-e'bri-ant
in-e'bri-ate
in-e:bri-a'-tion
in-e:bri'-e:ty
in-ed-i-bil'-i-ty
in-ed'-i-ble
in-ef-fa-bil'-i-ty
in-ef'-fa-ble
in-ef-face'-a:ble
in-ef-fec'-tive
in-ef-fec'-tive-ly
in-ef-fec'-tu-al
in-ef-fec-tu-al'-i-ty
in-ef-fi-ca'-cious
in-ef'-fi-ca-cy
in-ef-fi'-cen-cy
in-ef-fi'-cient
in-e:las'-tic
in-e:las-tic'-i-ty
in-el'-e-gance

in-el'-e-gant
in-el-i-gi-bil'-i-ty
in-el'-i-gi-ble
in-el'-o-quent
in-e:luc'-ta-ble
in-e:lud'-i:ble
in-ept'
in-ep'-ti-tude*
in-e:qual'-i-ty
in-eq'-ui-ta-ble
in-eq'-ui-ty
in-e:rad'-i-ca-ble
in-e:ras'-a:ble
in-err'-a:ble*†
in-er'-rant
in-ert'
in-ert'-ance
in-er'-tia
in-er'-tial
in-es-cap'-a-ble
in-es-sen'-tial
in-es'-ti-ma-ble
in-ev-i-ta-bil'-i-ty
in-ev'-i-ta-ble
in-ev'-i-ta-ble-ness
in-ev'-i-ta-bly
in-ex-act'
in-ex-ac'-ti-tude*†
in-ex-cus'-a:ble
in-ex-haust-a-bil'-i-ty
in-ex-haust'-i:ble
in-ex-is-tence*
in-ex-is'-tent*
in-ex-o-ra-bil'-i-ty
in-ex'-o-ra-ble
in-ex'-o-ra-bly
in-ex-pe'-di-en-cy
in-ex-pe'-di-ent
in-ex-pen'-sive
in-ex-pe'-ri-ence
in-ex-pe'-ri-enced
in-ex'-pert
in-ex'-pi-a-ble
in-ex-plain'-a:ble
in-ex-plic-a-bil'-i-ty
in-ex-plic'a-ble
in-ex-plic'-it
in-ex-press'-i-ble
in-ex-pres'-sive
in-ex-pug'na-ble
in-ex-pung-i:ble
in-ex-ten'-si-ble
in-ex-tin'-guish-a:ble
in-ex'-tir-pa-ble
in ex-tre'-mis
in-ex-tric-a-bil'-i-ty
in-ex-tric'a-ble
in-ex-tric'a-bly

in-fal-li-bil′-i-ty
in-fal′-li-ble
in′-fa-mous
in′-fa-my
in′-fan-cy
in′-fant
in-fan′-ta
in-fan′-te
in-fan′-ti-cide
in′-fan-tile
in′-fan-ti-lism†
in′-fan-tine
in′-fan-try
in′-fan-try-man
in′-farct
in-farc′-tion
in-fat′-u-ate
in-fat′-u-at-ed
in-fat-u-a′-tion
in-fect′
in-fect′-ant†
in-fect′-i:ble
in-fec′-tion
in-fec′-tious
in-fec′-tive
in-fec′-tor
in-fe′-cund
in-fe-cun′-di-ty
in-fe-lic′-i-tous
in-fe-lic′-i-ty
in-fer′
in-fer′-a:ble
in′-fer-ence
in-fer-en′-tial
in-fe′-ri-or
in-fe-ri-or′-i-ty
in-fer′-nal
in-fer′-no
in-ferred′
in-fer′-ring
in-fer′-tile
in-fer-til′-i-ty
in-fest′
in-fes′-tant
in-fes-ta′-tion
in-fest′-er (one who infests)
in-fes′-ter (to cause to fester)
in-feu-da′-tion
in′-fi-del
in-fi-del′-i-ty
in′-field
in-fil′-trate
in′-fil-tra′-tion
in′-fil-tra-tive
in′-fil-tra-tor
in-fil-trom′-e-ter

in′-fi-nite
in′-fi-nite-ly
in-fin-i-tes′-i-mal
in-fin′-i-ti′-val
in-fin′-i-tive
in-fin′-i-tude
in-fi-ni′-tum
in-fin′-i-ty
in-firm′
in-fir′-ma-ry
in-fir′-mi-ty
in-flame′
in-flam′-ing
in-flam-ma-bil′-i-ty
in-flam′-ma-ble
in-flam-ma′-tion
in-flam′-ma-to-ry
in-flat′-a:ble
in-flate′
in-flat′-ed
in-flat′-er
in-flat′-ing
in-fla′-tion
in-fla′-tion-ar:y
in-fla′-tion-ist
in-fla′-tor
in-flect′
in-flect′-i:ble
in-flec-tion
in-flec′-tor
in-flex-i-bil′-i-ty
in-flex′-i-ble
in-flict′
in-flict′-er
in-flic′-tion
in-flo-res′-cence
in-flo-res′-cent
in′-flow
in′-flu-ence
in′-flu-enc-er
in′-flu-en′-tial
in-flu-en′-za
in′-flux
in-fold′
in-form′
in-for′-mal
in-for-mal′-i-ty
in-for′-ma-lize*
in-for′-mal-ly
in-for′-mant*†
in-for-ma′-tion
in-form′-a-tive
in-form′-er
in-fract′-i:ble
in-frac′-tion
in-fran′-gi-ble
in′-fra-red′
in-fra-son′-ics

199

in'-fra-sound
in'-fra-struc-ture
in-fre'-quen-cy
in-fre'-quent
in-fre'-quent-ly
in-fringe'
in-fringe'-ment
in-fring'-er
in-fring'-ing
in-fun-dib'-u-lar
in-fun-dib'-u-lum
in-fu'-ri-ate
in-fu'-ri-at-ing
in-fu-ri-a'-tion
in-fuse'
in-fu'-si-ble†
in-fu'-sion
in-fu-so'-ri-al
in-gem'-i-nate
in-gen'-er-ate
in-ge'-nious*
in-ge'-nious-ly*
in-ge-nue
in-ge-nu'-i-ty
in-gen'-u-ous
In'-ger-soll
in-gest'
in-ges'-tant
in-ges'-tion
in'-gle
in-glo'-ri-ous
in'-got
in-grained'
in'-grate
in-gra'-ti-ate
in-gra'-ti-at-ing
in-gra-ti-a'-tion
in-gra'-tia-to-ry
in-grat'-i-tude
in-gra-ves'-cence
in'-gra-ves'-cent
in-grav'-i-date
in-gre'-di-ent
In'-gres
in'-gress
in-gres'-sion
in'-grown
in'-growth
in'-gui-nal
in-gur'-gi-tate
in-hab'-it
in-hab-it-a:bil'-i-ty
in-hab'-i-tant*
in-hab-i-ta'-tion
in-hab'-it-er
in-hal'-ant†
in-ha-la'-tion
in'-ha-la-tor

in-hale'
in-hal'-er
in-hal'-ing
in-har-mon'-ic
in-har-mo'-ni-ous
in-here'
in-her'-ence
in-her'-ent
in-her'-it
in-her'-it-a:ble
in-her'-i-tance*
in-her'-i-tor
in-her'-i-tress
in-he'-sion
in-hib'-it
in-hib'-it-er
in-hi-bi'-tion
in-hib'-i-tor
in-hib'-i-to-ry
in-hos-pit'a-ble
in-hos-pi-tal'-i-ty
in-hu'-man
in-hu-mane'
in-hu-man'-i-ty
in-hu-ma'-tion
in-im'-i-cal
in-im'-i-cal-ly
in-im'-i-ta-ble
in-i-on
in-iq'-ui-tous
in-iq'-ui-ty
in-i'-tial
in-i'-tial-ly
in-i'-ti-ate
in-i-ti-a'-tion
in-i'-ti:a-tive
in-i'-ti:a-to-ry
in-ject'
in-jec'-tion
in-jec'-tor
in-ju-di'-cious
in-junc'-tion
in-junc'-tive
in'-jure
in'-ju-ries
in'-jur-ing
in-ju'-ri-ous
in'-ju-ry
in-jus'-tice
ink bot-tle
ink'-horn
ink'-i-er
in'-kle
in'-kling*†
ink'-stain
ink'-stand
ink'-well
ink'y

in'-laid
in'-land
in'=law
in'-lay
in'-let
in'-li-er
in'-ly
in'-mate
in me-mo'-ri-am
in'-most
in-nas'-ci-ble
in'-nate'
in-nate'-ly
in'-nel-ite
in'-ner
in'-ner-most
in-ner'-vate
in-ner-va'-tion
in'-ning
inn'-keep-er
in'-no-cence
in'-no-cent
in'-no-cent-ly
in-noc'-u-ous
in-nom'-i-nate
in'-no-vate
in-no-va'-tion
in'-no-va-tor
in'-no-va-to-ry
in-nox'-ious
in-nu-en'-do
in-nu-en'-dos
in-nu'-mer-a-ble
in-nu-tri'-tion
in-oc'-u-la-ble
in-oc'-u-late
in-oc'-u-lat-ing
in-oc-u-la'-tion
in-oc'-u-la-tor
in-oc'-u-lum
in-of-fen'-sive
in-of-fi'-cious
in-op'-er-a-ble
in-op'-er-a-tive
in-op-por-tune'
in-op-por-tune'-ness
in-or'-di-na-cy
in-or'-di-nate
in-or'-di-nate-ly
in-or-gan'-ic
in-or-gan'-i-cal-ly
in-os'-cu-late
in:o'-si-tol
in-ox'-i-diz-a:ble
in per-so'-nam
in'-put
in'-quest
in-qui'-e-tude

in'-qui-line
in-quire'
in-quir'-er
in-quir'-ies
in-quir'-ing
in-quir'-ing-ly
in-quir'y
in-qui-si'-tion
in-quis'-i-tive
in-quis'-i-tive-ly
in-quis'-i-tive-ness
in-quis'-i-tor
in-quis-i-to'-ri-al
in'-road
in'-rush
in-sa-lu'-bri-ous
in-sane'
in-san'-i-tar:y†
in-san'-i-ty
in-sa-tia-bil'-i-ty
in-sa'-tia-ble
in-sa'-tiate*†
in-scrib'-a:ble
in-scribe'
in-scrib'-er
in-scrib'-ing
in-scrip'-tion
in-scru'-ta-ble
in'-sect
in-sec-ti-ci'-dal*
in-sec'-ti-cide
in'-sec-ti'-val
In-sec-tiv'-o-ra
in-sec-tiv'-o-rous
in-sec-tol'-o-gy†
in-se-cure'
in-se-cur'-i-ty*†
in-sem'-i-nate
in-sem-i-na'-tion
in-sen'-sate
in-sen-si-bil'-i-ty
in-sen'-si-ble
in-sen'-si-tive
in-sen'-tient
in-sep'-a-ra-ble
in-sert' (v.)
in'-sert (n.)
in-ser'-tion
in-ser'-tive
in'-ses-so'-ri-al
in'-set
in-shore
in-side'
in-sid'-er
in-sid'-i-ous
in-sid'-i-ous-ly
in'-sight

in-sig'-ne
in-sig'-ni:a
in-sig-nif'-i-cance
in-sig-nif'-i-cant
in-sin-cere'
in-sin-cere'-ly
in-sin-cer'-i-ty
in-sin'-u-ate
in-sin-u-a'-tion
in-sin'-u-a-tor
in-sip'-id
in-si-pid'-i-ty
in-sip'-i-ence
in-sist'
in-sis'-tence*
in-sis'-tent*
in-sis'-tent-ly*
in-sist'-er
in-so-bri'-e-ty
in'-so-late
in-so-la'-tion
in'-sole
in'-so-lence
in'-so-lent
in-sol-u-bil'-i-ty
in-sol'-u-ble
in-solv'-a:ble
in-sol'-ven-cy
in-sol'-vent
in-som'-ni:a
in'-so-much'
in-sou'-ci-ance
in-sou'-ci-ant
in-spect'
in-spec'-tion
in-spec'-tor
in-spec'-to-scope
in-spir'-a:ble
in-spi-ra'-tion
in-spi-ra'-tion-al
in-spir'a-tive
in-spir'-a-to-ry
in-spire'
in-spir'-er
in-spir'-ing
in-spir'-it
in-spis'-sate
in-spis'-sa-tor
in-sta-bil'-i-ty
in-sta'-ble
in-stall'
in-stal-la'-tion
in-stalled'
in-stall'-ing
in-stall'-ment
in'-stance
in'-stan-cy
in'-stant

in-stan-ta'-ne:ous
in-stan-ta'-ne:ous-ly
in-stan'-ter
in'-stant-ly
in'-star
in-stau-ra'-tion
in-stead'
in'-step
in'-sti-gate
in'-sti-gat-ing
in-sti-ga'-tion
in'-sti-ga-tor
in-still'
in-stilled'
in-still'-ing
in'-stinct (n.)
in-stinct' (adj.)
in-stinc'-tive
in-stinc'-tive-ly
in'-sti-tute
in-sti-tu'-tion
in-sti-tu'-tion-al
in'-sti-tu-tor
in-struct'
in-struct'-ed
in-struct'-i:ble
in-struc'-tion
in-struc'-tion-al
in-struc'-tive
in-struc'-tor
in-stru-ment
in-stru-men'-tal
in-stru-men-tal'-i-ty
in-stru-men-ta'-tion
in-sub-or'-di-nate
in-sub-or-di-na'-tion
in-sub-stan'-tial
in-suf'-fer-a:ble
in-suf-fi'-cien-cy
in-suf-fi'-cient
in'-suf-fla-tor
in'-su-lar
in-su-lar'-i-ty
in'-su-late
in'-su-la'-tion
in'-su-la-tor
in'-su-lin
in'-sult (n.)
in-sult' (v.)
in-sul-ta'-tion
in-su'-per-a:ble
in-sup-port'-a:ble
in-sup-press'-i:ble
in-sur'-a:ble
in-sur'-ance
in-sure'
in-sured'
in-sur'-er

in-sur'-gence
in-sur'-gen-cy
in-sur'-gent
in-sur'-ing
in-sur-mount'-a:ble
in-sur-rec'-tion
in-sus-cep'-ti-ble
in-tact'
in-ta'-glio*
in'-take
in-tan-gi-bil'-i-ty
in-tan'-gi-ble
in-tar'-si:a
in'-te-ger
in'-te-gra-ble
in'-te-gral
in'-te-grate
in-te-gra'-tion
in'-te-gra-tive
in'-te-gra-tor
in-teg'-ri-ty
in-teg'-u-ment
in-teg'-u-men-tal
in-teg'-u-men'-ta-ry
in'-tel-lect
in-tel-lec'-tu-al
in-tel-lec'-tu-al-ism
in-tel-lec'-tu-al-ly
in-tel'-li-gence
in-tel'-li-genc-er
in-tel'-li-gent
in-tel-li-gen'-tial
in-tel'-li-gent-ly
in-tel-li-gen'-tsi:a*†
in-tel-li-gi-bil'-i-ty
in-tel'-li-gi-ble
in-tem'-er-ate
in-tem'-per-ance
in-tem'-per-ate
in-tend'
in-tend'-ance†
in-tend'-an-cy†
in-tend'-ant†
in-ten'-er-ate
in-tense'
in-tense'-ly
in-ten-si-fi-ca'-tion
in-ten'-si-fied
in-ten'-si-fies
in-ten'-si-fy
in-ten'-sion
in-ten-si-tom'-e-ter
in-ten'-si-ty
in-ten'-sive
in-ten'-sive-ly
in-tent'
in-ten'-tion
in-ten'-tion-al

in-ten'-tion-al-ly
in-tent'-ly
in-tent'-ness
in-ter'
in-ter-act'
in-ter-ac'-tion
in-ter'-ca-lar:y†
in-ter'-ca-late
in-ter-ca-la'-tion
in-ter-cede'
in-ter-ced'-ing
in-ter-cel'-lu-lar
in'-ter-cept (n.)
in-ter-cept' (v.)
in-ter-cep'-tion
in-ter-cep'-tor
in-ter-ces'-sion
in-ter-ces'-sor
in-ter-ces'-so-ry
in'-ter-change (n.)
in-ter-change' (v.)
in-ter-change'-a:ble
in-ter-clav'-i-cle
in-ter-col-le'-giate
in-ter-co-lo'-ni-al
in'-ter-com
in-ter-com-mu'-ni-cate
in-ter-com-mu-ni-ca'-tion
in-ter-cos'-tal
in'-ter-course
in-ter-den'-tal
in-ter-de-pen'-dence
in-ter-de-pen'-dent
in-ter-dict'
in-ter-dic'-tion
in-ter-dic'-tor
in'-ter-est
in'-ter-est-ed
in'-ter-est-ing
in-ter-fere'
in-ter-fer'-ence
in-ter-fe-ren'-tial
in-ter-fer'-ing
in-ter-fer-om'-e-ter†
in-ter-fer-om'-e-try
in-ter-fer'-on
in-ter-fuse'
in-ter-fu'-sion
in-ter-gla'-cial
in'-ter-grade
in'-ter-im
in-te'-ri-or
in-ter-ject'
in-ter-jec'-tion
in-ter-jec'-tor
in-ter-jec'-tur-al
in-ter-knit'
in-ter-lace'

In'-ter-la'-ken
in-ter-lam'-i-nate
in-ter-lay'
in-ter-leave'
in-ter-lin'-e-al
in-ter-lin'-e-ar
In-ter-lin'-gua
in'-ter-lin-ing
in'-ter-lock
in-ter-lo-cu'-tion
in-ter-loc'-u-tor
in-ter-loc'-u-to-ry
in-ter-loc'-u-tress
in'-ter-lop-er
in'-ter-lude
in-ter-lu'-nar
in'-ter-mar'-riage
in'-ter-mar'-ry
in-ter-med'-dle
in-ter-med'-dler
in-ter-me'-di-ar:y
in-ter-me'-di-ate
in-ter'-ment
in-ter-mez'-zo
in-ter-mi'-na-ble
in-ter-mi'-na-bly
in-ter-min'-gle
in-ter-min'-gling
in-ter-mis'-sion
in'-ter-mit'
in-ter-mit'-tent
in-ter-mit'-tent-ly
in-ter-mix'
in-ter-mix'-ture
in-tern' (v.)
in'-tern (n.)
in-ter'-nal
in-ter'-nal-ly
in-ter-na'-tion-al
in-ter-na'-tion-al-ism
in-ter-na'-tion-al-ist
in-ter-na'-tion-al-ize
in-ter-na'-tion-al-ly
in-ter-nec'-ine*†
in'-terned'
in-ter'-nist†
in'-tern-ship
in-ter-nun'-ci:o
in'-ter-o-cep'-tive
in-ter-pel'-late
in-ter-pel-la'-tion
in-ter-pen'-e-trate
in-ter-plan'-e-tar:y†
in'-ter-play
in-ter'-po-late
in-ter'-po-lat-er
in-ter-po-la'-tion
in-ter'-po-la-tor

in-ter-pose'
in-ter-pos'-ing
in-ter-po-si'-tion
in-ter'-pret
in-ter'-pret-a:ble
in-ter'-pre-ta'-tion
in-ter'-pre-ta-tive
in-ter'-pret-er
in-ter'-pre-tive
in-ter-ra'-cial
in-ter-ra'-di-al
in-terred'
in-ter-reg'-num
in-ter-re-late'
in-ter-re-lat'-ed
in-ter-re-la'-tion
in-ter-re-la'-tion-ship
in-ter'-ring
in-ter'-ro-gate
in-ter-ro-ga'-tion
in-ter-rog'-a-tive
in-ter-rog'-a-tor
in-ter-rog'-a-to-ry
in-ter-rupt'
in-ter-rupt'-ed
in-ter-rupt'-er
in-ter-rupt'-i:ble
in-ter-rupt'-ing
in-ter-rup'-tion
in-ter-sect'
in-ter-sec'-tion
in'-ter-space
in-ter-sperse'
in-ter-sper'-sion
in'-ter-state'
in-ter-stel'-lar
in-ter-stice'
in-ter-stic-es
in-ter-sti'-tial
in'-ter-twine
in'-ter-twist
In'-ter-type
in-ter-ur'-ban
in'-ter-val
in'-ter-vene'
in-ter-ven'-er
in-ter-ve'-nor
in-ter-ven'-tion
in-ter-ven'-tion-ist
in'-ter-view
in'-ter-view-er
in'-ter-weave
in-ter-wo'-ven
in-tes'-ta-cy
in-tes'-tate
in-tes'-ti-nal
in-tes'-tine
in'-ti-ma

in'-ti-ma-cy
in'-ti-mate
in'-ti-mate-ly
in'-ti-mat-er
in-ti-ma'-tion
in-tim'-i-date
in-tim-i-da'-tion
in-tim'-i-da-tor
in-tit'-ule
in-tol'-er-a:ble
in-tol'-er-a:bly
in-tol'-er-ance
in-tol'-er-ant
in'-to-nate
in-to-na'-tion
in-tone'
in-ton'-ing
in-tox'-i-cant
in-tox'-i-cate
in-tox'-i-cat-ing
in-tox-i-ca'-tion
in-tox-im'-e-ter
in-tra-cel'-lu-lar
in-trac-ta-bil'-i-ty
in-trac'-ta-ble
in'-tra-dos
in-tra-mo-lec'-u-lar
in-tra-mu'-ral
in-tran'-si-gent
in-tran'-si-tive
in'-tra-state'
in-tra-tel-lu'-ric
in-trav-a-sa'-tion†
in-tra-ve'-nous
in-treat'
in-trep'-id
in-tre-pid'-i-ty
in'-tri-ca-cy
in'-tri-cate
in'-tri-gant'
in-trigue'
in-trigued'
in-trigu'-er*
in-trigu'-ing*
in-trigu'-ing-ly*
in-trin'-sic
in-trin'-si-cal
in-trin'-si-cal-ly
in-tro-duce'
in-tro-duc'-tion
in-tro-duc'-to-ry
in'-tro-it
in-tro-jec'-tion
in'-tro-mit'-tent
in'-tro-spect'
in-tro-spec'-tion
in-tro-spec'-tive
in-tro-ver'-si-ble

in-tro-ver'-sion
in'-tro-vert
in-trude'
in-trud'-er
in-tru'-sion
in-tru'-sive
in-trust'
in-tu-ba'-tion
in-tu-i'-tion
in-tu'-i-tive
in-tu-mes'-cence
in-tus-sus-cep'-tion
in'-u-lase
in'-u-lin
in-unc'-tion
in-un'-dant
in'-un-date
in-un-da'-tion
in'-un-da-tor
in-un'-da-to-ry
in-ure'
in-ur'-ing
in-u'tile
in-u:til'-i-ty
in-vade'
in-vad'-er
in-vad'-ing
in-vag'-i-nate
in-vag-i-na'-tion
in-val'-id (not valid)
in'-va-lid (ill)
in'-val'-i-date
in-val-i-da'-tion
in'-va-lid-ism
in-va-lid'-i-ty
in-val'-u-a:ble
in-var'-i-a:ble†
in-var'-i-a:bly†
in-var'-i-ant†
in-va'-sion
in-vec'-tive
in-veigh'
in-vei'-gle
in-vei'-gling
in-vent'
in-vent'-a:ble
in-ven'-tion
in-ven'-tive
in-ven'-tor
in-ven-to'-ri-al
in'-ven-to-ries
in'-ven-to-ry
in-ve-rac'-i-ty
In'-ver-ness
in-verse'
in-ver'-sion
in-vert'
in-vert'-ase†

INVERTEBRATE

in-ver'-te-brate
in-vert'-er
in-vert'-i:ble
in-ver'-tor
in-vest'
in-ves'-ti-gate
in-ves-ti-ga'-tion
in-ves'-ti-ga-tor
in-ves'-ti-ture
in-vest'-ment
in-ves'-tor
in-vet'-er-a-cy
in-vet'-er-ate
in-vid'-i-ous
in-vig'-i-late
in-vig'-o-rate*†
in-vig'-o-rat-ing*†
in-vig-o-ra'-tion*†
in-vin-ci-bil'-i-ty
in-vin'-ci-ble
in-vi-o-la-bil'-i-ty
in-vi'-o-la-ble
in-vi'-o-la-cy
in-vi'-o-late
in-vis-i-bil'-i-ty
in-vis'-i-ble
in-vi-ta'-tion
in-vi'-ta-to-ry
in-vite'
in-vit'-er
in-vit'-ing
in-vit'-ing-ly
in'-vo-cate
in-vo-ca'-tion
in'-vo-ca-tor
in-voc'-a-to-ry
in'-voice
in'-voic-ing
in-voke'
in-vok'-ing
in-vol'-u-cel
in'-vo-lu'-cral
in'-vo-lu-cre
in-vo-lu'-crum
in-vol-un-tar'-i-ly†
in-vol'-un-tar:y†
in'-vo-lute
in'-vo-lut-ed
in-vo-lu'-tion
in-volve'
in-volve'-ment
in-volv'-ing
in-vul-ner-a-bil'-i-ty
in-vul'-ner-a-ble
in-vul-tu-a'-tion
in'-ward
in'-ward-ly

in'-weave'
in'-wo-ven*
in'-wrought
I'o
i'o-date
i:od'-ic
i'o-dide
i'o-di-nate†
i'o-dine
i'o-din-oph'-i-lous
i'o-do-a:ce'-tic
i:o'-do-form
i:o-do-hy'-drin
i:o-dom'-e-try
i:o-do'-ni-um
i:o-do-phthal'-e-in
i:o-do-pyr'-a-cet
i:o-dox'y-ben-zene'
i:od'-y-rite
i'on
I:o'-ni:a
I:o'-ni-an
I:on'-ic
i:o'-ni-um
i:on-i:za'-tion
i'on-ize
i:o-nom'-e-ter
I'o-none
i:on'-o-sphere
i:on'-o-spher'-ic
i:o'-ta
i:o'-ta-cism
I'o-wa
I'o-wan
ip'-e-cac
Iph-i-ge-ni'a
ip-o-me'a
ip'-so fac'-to
Ips'-wich
I'ra
i:ra-cun'-di-ty
i:ra'-de
I:ran'
I:ra'-ni-an
I:raq'
I:raq'i
i:ras-ci-bil'-i-ty
i:ras'-ci-ble
i:ra'-ser
i:rate'
ire'-ful
ire'-ful-ly
Ire'-land
I:rene'
i:ren'-ic
Ir:i-an'
ir:i-da'-ceous
ir:i-dec'-to-my

206

ir-i-des'-cence
ir-i-des'-cent
i:rid'-ic
i:rid'-i-um
ir:i-di-za'-tion
i'ris
i:ris-a'-tion*
I'rish
I'rish-man
I'rish-wom-an
i:ri'-tis
irk'-some
Ir'-ma
i'ron
i'ron-bound
i'ron-clad
i:ron'-ic
i:ron'-i-cal
i:ron'-i-cal-ly
i'ron-ing
i'ron-mas-ter
i'ron-mon-ger
i'ron-side
I'ron-sides
i'ron-stone
i'ron-ware
i'ron-wood
i'ron-work
i'ron-work-er
i'ron:y (of iron)
i'ro-ny (ridicule)
Ir'-o-quoi'-an
Ir'-o-quois
ir-ra'-di-ate
ir-ra-di-a'-tion
ir-rad'-i-ca-ble
ir-ra'-tio-nal*‡
ir-re-claim'-a:ble
ir-rec'-on-cil-a:ble
ir-re-cov'-er-a:ble
ir-re-deem'-a:ble
ir-re-den'-ta
ir-re-den'-tist
ir-re-duc-i:bil'-i-ty
ir-re-duc'-i:ble
ir-re-frag'-a-ble*‡
ir-re-fran'-gi-ble
ir-re-fut-a:bil'-i-ty
ir-re-fut'-a:ble*
ir-reg'-u-lar
ir-reg-u-lar'-i-ty
ir-reg'-u-lar-ly
ir-rel'-e-vance
ir-rel'-e-vant
ir-re-li'-gion†
ir-re-li'-gious†

ir-re'-me-a:ble*
ir-re-me'-di-a:ble
ir-re-mov'-a:ble
ir-rep'-a-ra-ble
ir-re-place'-a:ble
ir-re-press'-i:ble†
ir-re-proach'-a:ble
ir-re-sist'-i:ble†
ir-re-sist'-i:bly†
ir-re-sol'-u-ble*‡
ir-res'-o-lute
ir-res'-o-lute-ly
ir-res-o-lu'-tion
ir-re-solv'-a:ble
ir-re-spec'-tive
ir-re-spon-si-bil'-i-ty
ir-re-spon'-si-ble
ir-re-triev'-a:ble
ir-rev'-er-ence
ir-rev'-er-ent
ir-re-vers-i:bil'-i-ty
ir-re-vers'-i:ble
ir-rev-o-ca-bil'-i-ty
ir-rev'-o-ca-ble
ir-rev'-o-ca-bly
ir'-ri-ga-ble
ir'-ri-gate
ir-ri-ga'-tion
ir'-ri-ga-tor
ir-rig'-u-ous
ir-ri'-sion
ir-ri-ta-bil'-i-ty
ir'-ri-ta-ble
ir'-ri-ta-bly
ir'-ri-tan-cy
ir'-ri-tant
ir'-ri-tate
ir'-ri-tat-ing
ir-ri-ta'-tion
ir-rup'-tion
ir-rup'-tive
Ir'-ving
I'saac
Is'-a-bel
Is-a:cous'-tic
Is-a-do'-ra
i'sa-go-ge
i:sa-gog'-ics
I:sa'-iah
i'sa-tin
i'sa-tin'-ic
Is-car'-i-ot
is-che'-mi:a
is'-chi-al
is'-chi-at'-ic
is'-chi-um
Ish'-ma-el
Ish'-ma-el-ite

Ish'-tar
i'sin-glass
I'sis
Is-lam'
Is-lam'-ic
Is-lam'-ism
is'-land
is'-land-er
is'-let
i:so-am'-yl-ene
i'so-bar
i'so-bar'-ic
i'so-bath
i'so-bath'y-therm
i'so-chro-mat'-ic
i:soch'-ro-nal
i'so-chrone
i:soch'-ro-nism
i:soch'-ro-nous
i:so-cla'-site
i:so-cli'-nal
I'soc'-ra-tes
i'so-drin
i:sog'-a-mous
i:sog'-e-nous
i:so-gloss'-al*
i:sog'-o-nal
i:so-gon'-ic
i'so-la-ble†
i'so-lat-a:ble
i'so-late†
i'so-la'-tion†
i:so-la'-tion-ist†
I:solde'
i:so-leu'-cine
i:sol'-o-gous
i:so-mag-net'-ic
i'so-mer
i:so-mer'-ic
i:som'-er-ism
i:som'-er-ize
i:so-met'-ric
i:so-met'-ri-cal-ly
i:so-me-tro'-pi:a
i:so-mor'-phic
i:so-mor'-phism
i:so-ni'-a-zid
i:son'-o-my
i:so-oc'-tane
i:so-phthal'-ic*
i:so-pi-es'-tic
i'so-pleth
i'so-pod
i:so-pol'-i-ty
i'so-prene
i:so-pre'-noid
i:so-pro'-pa-nol
i'so-pro'-pyl

i:sos'-ce-les
i:so-seis'-mal
i:so'-ta-sy
i:so-stat'-ic
i'so-ther'-al*†
i'so-there
i'so-therm
i:so-ther'-mal
i:so-ton'-ic
i:so-to-nic'-i-ty
i'so-tope
i'so-top'-ic
i:so-to-py*
i'so-tron
i:so-trop'-ic
i:sot'-ro-pous
i:sot'-ro-py
i'so-zyme
Is'-ra-el
Is-rae'-li
Is'-ra-el-ite
Is'-ra-el-it-ish
is-sei'
is'-su-a:ble
is'-su-ance
is'-sue
is'-su-ing
Is'-tan-bul'
isth'-mi-an
isth'-mus
is'-tle
Is'-tri-an
it-a-col'-u-mite
it'-a-con'-ic
I:tal'-ian
i:tal'-ic
i:tal'-i-cize
i:tal'-i-ciz-ing
i:tal'-ics
It'-a-ly
itch'-i-ness
itch'y
i'tem
i'tem-i:za'-tion
i'tem-ize
it'-er-ance
it'-er-ate
it-er-a'-tion
it'-er-a-tive
Ith'-a-ca
ith:y-phal'-lic
i:tin'-er-an-cy
i:tin'-er-ant
i:tin'-er-ar:y†
i:tin'-er-ate
its (possessive)
it's (contr. for it is)
it-self'

I'van
i'vied
i'vo-ry
i'vy
Iz-mir'

J

jabbed
jab'-ber
jab'-bing
jab'-i-ru'
jab-o-ran'-di
ja-bot'
ja'-ca-na†
jac-a-ran'-da
ja'-cinth
jack'-al
jack'-a-napes
jack'-ass
jack'-boot
jack'-daw
jack'-et
jack'-knife
jack'=o'=lan-tern
jack plane
jack'-pot
jack'-rab-bit
Jack'-son
Jack'-son-ville
jack'-straw
Ja'-cob
Jac:o-be'-an
Ja-co'-bi-an
Jac'o-bin
Jac'o-bite
Ja-co'-bus
jac'-o-net
Jac'quard
Jac'-que-line
jacque'-mi-not
Jac-que-rie'†
jac-ta'-tion
jac-ti-ta'-tion
jac'-u-late
jad'-ed
jade'-ite
jae'-ger
Jaf'-fa
ja'-ger
jag'-ged
jag'-ger:y
jag'-uar
jai a:lai'
jail'-bird
jail'-break
jail'-er
Jain'-ism

Jai-pur'
Ja'-i-rus
jal'-ap
jal'a-pin
ja-lop'y
jal'-ou-sie†
Ja-mai'-ca
Ja-mai'-can
jam-ba-lay'a
jam'-bo-ree'
James'-town
jam'-ming
jam'=packed'
Jan'-et†
jan'-gle
jan'-gling
Jan'-ice
jan'-is-sar:y†
jan'-i-tor
jan'-i-tress
Jan'-sen
Jan'-sen-ism
Jan'-u-ar:y†
Ja'-nus
Ja-pan'
Jap'-a-nese'
ja-panned'
Ja'-pheth
Ja-phet'-ic
ja-pon'-i-ca
ja-ra'-be
jar'-di-niere'
Ja'-red
jar'-gon
jar'-gon-ize
jar-goon'
ja-ro-'site*
jar:o-vi-za'-tion
jar'o-vize
jar'-rah
jarred
jar'-ring
jas'-mine
jas'-mone
Ja'-son
jas'-per
jas-pid'-e-an
jaun'-dice
jaun'-ti-ly†
jaun'-ty†
Jav'a
Jav'a-nese'
jav'-e-lin
jaw'-bone
jay'-walk-er
jeal'-ous
jeal'-ous-ly
jeal'-ou-sy*†

209

Jean-nette'
Jeb'-u-site
jec'-o-rize
jeer'-ing-ly
Jef'-fer-son
Jef-fer-so'-ni-an
Jef'-frey
Je-ho'-vah
Je-ho-vis'-tic
Je'-hu
je-ju'-nal
je-june'
je-ju-nos'-to-my
je-ju'-num
Jek'-yll*†
jell
jel'-lied
jel'-li-fy
jel'-ly
jel'-ly-fish
jem'-a-dar
Je-mi'-mah
Je'-na
Jen'-kins
Jen'-ner
jen'-net
Jen'-nie
Jen'-ni-fer
jen'-ny
jeop'-ard
jeop'-ar-dize*†
jeop'-ar-diz-ing*†
jeop'-ar-dy*†
Jeph'-thah
je-quir'-i-ty
jer-bo'a
jer-e-mi'-ad
Jer-e-mi'-ah
Jer'-i-cho
jerk'-i-ly
jer'-kin
jerk'y (*adj.*, with a jerk)
jer'-ky*† (*n.* jerked meat)
Jer-o-bo'-am
Je-rome'
Jer'-ry
jer'-ry=built
jer'-sey
Je-ru'-sa-lem
jes'-sa-mine
Jes'-se
Jes'-sie
jest'-er
jest'-ing-ly
Jes'u-it
Je'-sus
jet'-lin-er
jet'-sam

jet'-ties
jet'-ting
jet'-ti-son
jet'-ty
Jev'-ons
jew'-el
jew'-eled
jew'-el-er
jew'-el-ry
jew'-el-weed
jew'-fish
Jew'-ish
Jew's harp
Jez'-e-bel
jib'-bing
jib'-boom
jif'-fy
jig'-ger
jig'-gle
jig'-gling
jig'-saw
jilt'-ed
jim'-mied
jim'-my
jim'-son-weed
jin'-gle
jin'-gling
jin'-go
jin'-goes
jin'-go-ism
jin-rik'-i-sha
jit'-ney
jit'-ter-bug
jit'-ters
jit'-ter:y
Jo'-ab
Jo'-a-chim
Job
job'-ber
job'-ber:y
job'-bing
job'-hold-er
job'-less
jo'-cism
jock'-ey
jock'-eys
jo-cose'
jo-cos'-i-ty
joc'-u-lar
joc-u-lar'-i-ty
joc'-und
jo-cun'-di-ty
jodh'-pur
Jo'-el
jog'-ging
jog'-gle
jog'-gling
Jo'-hann

Jo-han'-nes
Jo-han'-nes-burg
Jo-han'-nine
Jo-hans'-son
joh'-nin
john'-ny-cake
John'-son
John'-son-ese'
John-so'-ni-an
John'-ston
Johns'-town
join'-der
join'-er
join'-er:y
joint'-ed
joint'-er
joint'-ly
joint'-ress
join'-ture
Join'-ville
joist
joked
jok'-er
joke'-ster
jok'-ing
jok'-ing-ly
Jo-li-et'
jol-li-fi-ca'-tion
jol'-li-fy
jol'-li-ly
jol'-li-ty
jol'-ly
jol'-ly-boat
Jo'-nah
Jon'-a-than
jon-gleur'
jon'-quil
Jon'-son
Jop'-lin
Jop'-pa
Jor'-dan
Jor-da'-ni-an
jo'-rum
Jo-se'
jo-se'-ite
Jo'-seph
Jo'-se-phine†
Jo-se'-phus
Josh'-u:a
Jo-si'-ah
jos'-tle
jos'-tled
jos'-tling
jot'-ted
jot'-ting
jounce
jounc'-ing
jour'-nal

jour-nal-ese'
jour'-nal-ism
jour'-nal-ist
jour-nal-is'-tic
jour-nal-is'-ti-cal-ly
jour'-nal-ize
jour'-ney
jour'-neyed
jour'-ney-man
jour'-neys
joust
joust'-er
jo'-vi:al
jo-vi:al'-i-ty
jo'-vi:al-ly
Jo'-vi-an
joy'-ance
joy'-ful
joy'-ful-ly
joy'-ous
joy'-ous-ly
joy'-ous-ness
joy'-ride
Jua'-rez
ju'-ba
ju'-bate
ju'-bi-lance
ju'-bi-lant
ju'-bi-late
Ju-bi-la'-te
ju-bi-la'-tion
ju'-bi-lee
Ju'-dah
Ju-da'-ic
Ju'-da-ism
Ju'-das
Ju-de'a
Ju-de'-an
Judg'-es
judge'-ship
judg'-ing
judg'-ment
ju'-di-ca-tive
ju'-di-ca-to-ry
ju'-di-ca-ture
ju-di'-cial
ju-di'-ciar:y†
ju-di'-cious
ju-di'-cious-ly
Ju'-dith
ju'-do
Ju'-dy
ju'-gal
jug'-ger-naut
jug'-gle
jug'-gler
jug'-gler:y
jug'-gling

ju'-glone
Ju-go-slav'-i:a
jug'-u-lar†
jug'-u-late†
Ju-gur'-tha
juic'-i-ly
juic'-i-ness
juic'y
ju-jit'-su
ju'-jube
juke'-box
ju'-lep
Ju'-lia*
Ju'-lian*
Ju-li-an'a
ju-li:enne'
Ju'-liet
Ju'-lius*
Ju-ly'
jum'-ble
jum'-bled
jum'-bling
jum'-bo
jump'-er
jump'-ing
jump'y
jun'-co
junc'-tion
junc'-tur-al
junc'-ture
Ju'-neau
Jung'-frau
jun'-gle
jun'-gly
jun'-ior
ju-nior'-i-ty*†
ju'-ni-per
Ju'-nius
Jun'-ker
junk'-er
jun'-ket
jun'-ke-teer'
junk'-man
Ju'-no
jun'-ta
jun'-to
Ju'-pi-ter
Ju'-ra
ju'-ral
ju'-rane
Ju-ras'-sic
ju'-rat
ju-rel'
ju-rid'-i-cal
ju'-ries
ju-ris-dic'-tion
ju-ris-pru'-dence
ju'-rist

ju-ris'-tic
ju'-ror
ju'-ry
ju'-ry-man
jus'-tice
jus-ti'-cia-ble
jus-ti'-ci-ar
jus-ti-fi-a:ble
jus-ti-fi-ca'-tion
jus-tif'-i-ca-to-ry*
jus'-ti-fied
jus'-ti-fi-er
jus'-ti-fy
jus'-ti-fy-ing
Jus'-tin
Jus-tin'-i-an
Jus-tin'-i-a'-ni-an
just'-ly
just'-ness
Jut'-land
jut'-ting
Ju'-ve-nal
ju-ve-nes'-cence
ju-ve-nes'-cent
ju'-ve-nile
ju-ve-nil'-i-ty
jux'-ta-pose
jux-ta-po-si'-tion

K

Kaa'-ba
ka-bu'-ki
Ka-bul'
Ka-byle'
ka-chi'-na
Kaf'-fir
kai'-nite
kai-nos-ite†
kai'-ser
ka'-ka
ka-ke-mo'-no†
Kal-a-ma-zoo'
ka-lei'-do-scope
ka-lei'-do-scop'-ic
Ka-le-va'-la
kal-i-bo'-rite
ka-lic'-i-nite
ka-lig'-e-nous
Kal'-i-spel'
kal'-mi:a
Kal'-muck
ka'-long
ka-ma-la
Kam-chat'-ka
ka-me-rad'
ka-mi-ka'-ze
Ka-nak'a*

Kan-a-rese'*
kan'-ga-roo'
Kan'-san
Kan'-sas
kan-tar'
Kant'-i:an
kao'-li:ang'
ka'-o:lin
ka-o:lin'-ic
ka'-o:lin-ite
Ka-pell'-meis-ter
ka'-pok
kap'-pa
Ka-ra'-chi
kar'-a-kul†
kar'-at
Ka-ren'
kar'-ma
Kar'-nak
ka-roo'-ite
kar-roo'
kar-y:o-gam'-ic
kar-y:og'-a-my
kar-y:o-ki-ne'-sis
kar-y:ol'-o-gy
kar-y:ol'-y-sis
kar-y:o-mi'-tome*†
kar-y:o-mi-to'-sis
kar-y:o-some
Kash'-mir
Kashmir'-i:an†
ka-tab'-a-sis
kat'-a-bat'-ic
Ka-tan'-ga
Ka-tan'-gan
Kath'-a-rine
ka'-ty-did
kau'-ri
ka'-va
kay'-ak
Ka-zan'
Kear'-ney
Kear'-ny
ked'-dah
keel'-haul
keel'-son
keen'-ly
keen'-ness
keep'-er
keep'-ing
keep'-sake
ke-fir'*†
keit'-lo:a
Kel'-ler
Kel'-logg
Kel'-ly
ke'-loid
kel'-pie

Kel'-vin
Ke-mal' A:ta-turk'
Ken'-il-worth
Ken'-ne-bec
Ken'-ne-dy
ken'-nel
ke-no'-sis
ken'-o-tron
Ken'-sing-ton
Kent'-ish
Ken-tuck'-i-an
Ken-tuck'y
Ke'-nya
Ken'-yon
Ke'-o-kuk
Kep'-ler
ker'-a-tin
ke-rat'-i-nous
ker-a-ti'-tis
ker'-a-tog'-e-nous
ker'-a-toid
Ker'-a-tol
ker-a-tol'-y-sis
ker-a-to'-sis
ker'-a-tot'-ic
ker'-chief
ker'-chiefed
Ke-ren'-sky†
kerf
ker'-mes
ker'-mes-ite†
ker'-mis
kerned
ker'-nel
ker'-neled
ker'-o-gen
ker'-o-sene
Ker'-ry
ker'-sey
kes'-trel
ke'-ta-zine
ke'-tene
ke'-ti-mine
ke-to-gen'-e-sis
ke-to-gen'-ic
ke-to-glu-tar'-ic
ke-to-hex'-ose
ke-tol'-y-sis
ke'-to-lyt'-ic
ke'-tone
ke-ton'-ic
ke-to-nu'-ri:a
ke'-to-side
ke-to'-sis
ket'-tle
ket'-tle-drum
kev'-el
Ke-wee-naw'-an

key'-board
keyed
key'-hole
Keynes'-i-an
key'-note
key'-stone
khad'-dar
khak'i
kham-sin'
Khar'-toum'
khe-dive'
Khmer
Khru'-shchev
Khy'-ber
kib'-itz
kib'-itz-er
ki'-bosh
kick'-back
kick'-off (n.)
kick'-shaw
kid'-ded
kid'-ding
kid'-nap
kid'-naped
kid'-nap-er
kid'-nap-ing
kid'-napped
kid'-nap-per
kid'-nap-ping
kid'-ney
kier
Kier'-ke-gaard
kie'-sel-guhr
kie'-ser-ite
kil'-der-kin
kil'-hig
Kil-i-man-ja'-ro
Kil-ken'-ny
Kil-lar'-ney
kill'-deer
kill'-er
kil'-lick
kil'-li-fish
kill'-ing
kill'-joy
kiln
ki'-lo†
kil'o-cy-cle
kil'o-gram
kil'o-li-ter
ki-lom'-e-ter*†
kil:o-met'-ric
kil'o-ton
kil'o-watt
kil'o-watt=hour
Kil-pat'-rick
kilt'-ed
kil'-ter

Kim'-ber-ley
ki-mo'-no
ki-mo'-nos
kim'-zey-ite
ki'-nase†
kin'-der-gar-ten
kin'-der-gart-ner
kind'-heart-ed
kin'-dle
kind'-less
kind'-li-ness
kin'-dling
kind'-ly
kind'-ness
kin'-dred
kin-e-mat'-ics
kin-e-mat'-o-graph
kin'-e-scope
ki-ne-si-at'-rics
ki-ne'-sics
kin-e-sim'-e-ter
ki-ne-si-o-log'-ic
ki-ne-si-ol'-o-gy
kin-es-the'-sia
kin-es-the'-sis
kin'-es-thet'-ic
ki-net'-ic
kin'-e-tin
ki-ne'-to-graph†
ki-ne'-to-graph'-ic†
ki-ne'-to-phone†
Ki-ne'-to-scope†
kin-e-to'-sis
ki-ne'-to-some
kin'-folk
king'-bird
king'-dom
king'-fish
king'-fish-er
king'-less
king'-let
king'-li-ness
king'-ly
king'-pin
king'-ship
Kings'-ley
Kings'-ton*†
kin'-in
kin'-ka-jou
kin'-kled
kink'y
kin'-ni-kin-nick'
ki'-no
kin'-ship
kins'-man
kins'-wom-an†
ki'-osk
Kip'-ling

Ki'-o-wa
kip'-per
Kirch'-hoff
Kir-ghiz'
Kirsch'-ner
kir'-tle
kis'-met
kiss'-a:ble
kitch'-en
kitch'-en-ette'
kitch'-en-maid
kitch'-en-ware
kit'-ten
kit'-ten-ish
kit'-ti-wake
kit'-ty
ki'-va
Ki-wa'-ni-an
Ki-wa'-nis
ki'-wi
Kjel'-dahl
Klam'-ath†
Klee'-nex
klep-to-ma'-ni:a
klep-to-ma'-ni-ac
Kling'-sor
Klon'-dike
klys'-tron
knack'-er
knag'-gy
knap'-sack
knav'-er:y
knav'-ish
knead
knee'-cap
kneed
knee'=deep'
knee'=high'
kneel'-ing
knick'-er-bock-er
knick'-ers
knick'-knack
knife
knight=er'-rant
knight=er'-rant-ry
knight'-hood
knight'-li-ness
knight'-ly
knit
knit'-ter
knit'-ting
knives
knobbed
knob'-by
knob'-ker-rie
knock'-a:bout
knock'-down (n., adj.)
knock'-er

knock'-out (n., adj.)
knoll
knot'-hole
knot'-ted
knot'-ter
knot'-ting
knot'-ty
know'-a:ble
know'=how
know'-ing
know'-ing-ly
knowl'-edge
knowl'-edge-a:ble
Knox'-ville
knuck'-le
knuck'-led
knuck'-ling
knurl'y
ko-a'la
ko'-bold
Ko'-dak
Ko'-di-ak
ko'-el
ko-gas'-in
Koh'-i-noor
kohl-rab'i†
koi'-ne
koi-no-ni'a
ko'-jic
kok=so-ghyz'
ko'-la
ko-lin'-sky
kol-khoz'
kom-man-da-tu'-ra
ko-nim'-e-ter*
kȯ-ni-ol'z-o-gy
koo'-doo
kook'-a-bur-ra
Koo'-te-nai
ko'-peck
Ko-ran'
Ko-re'a
Ko-re'-an
Kor'-sa-koff
ko'-ru-na
ko'-sher
Kous-se-vitz'-ky
kow'-tow
kra'-ken
Kreis'-ler
Krem'-lin
kreu'-zer
krim'-mer
Krish'-na
kro'-na
kro'-ne
Kro-pot'-kin
kryp'-ton

215

Ksha'-tri-ya*†
Ku'-blai Khan
ku'-du
kud'-zu
Ku'-fic
ku'-gel-blitz
ku-lak'
kum'-quat
Kunst'-lied
kunz'-ite
Kuo-min-tang
kur'-bash
Kur'-di-stan'
kur-to'-sis
Kwa'-ja-lein
kwa'-shi-or'-kor
ky'-ack
ky'-a-nize†
kym'-ber-lite
ky'-mo-graph
ky-mog'-ra-phy
kyn-u:ren'-ine
ky-pho'-sis
ky-phot'-ic

L

laa'-ger
lab'-a-rum
lab'-da-num
lab-e-fac'-tion
la'-bel
la'-beled
la'-bel-er
la'-bel-ing
la'-bi:a
la'-bi-al
la'-bi-al-ize
la'-bi-ate
la'-bile†
la-bil'-i-ty
la'-bi-lize†
la'-bi:o-den'-tal
la'-bi-um
la'-bor
lab'-o-ra-to-ry
la'-bored
la'-bor-er
la-bo'-ri-ous
la-bo'-ri-ous-ly
la'-bor-ite
Lab'-ra-dor
lab'-ra-dor-ite
la'-bret
la'-broid*
la'-brum
La Bru-yère'
la-bur'-num

lab'-y-rinth
lab-y-rin'-thi-an
lab-y-rin'-thine
lac'-co-lith
Lac-e-de-mo'-ni-an
lac'-er-ate
lac'-er-at-ing
lac-er-a'-tion
lac-er-til'-i-an
lac'-er-tine*†
lace'-work
lach'-es
Lach'-e-sis
lach'-ry-mal
lach'-ry-ma-to-ry
lach'-ry-mose
lac'-ing
la-cin'-i-ate
lack-a-dai'-si-cal
Lack-a-wan'-na
lack'-ey
lack'-ing
lack'-lus-ter
La-co'-ni:a
la-con'-ic
la-con'-i-cal-ly
lac'-o-nism
lac'-quer
lac'-ri-mal
lac'-ri-ma-to-ry
la-crosse'
lact-al-bu'-min*
lac'-ta-ry
lac'-tase
lac'-tate
lac-ta'-tion
lac'-te-al
lac'-te-ous
lac-tes'-cence
lac-tes'-cent
lac'-tic
lac-tif'-er-ous
lac-to-ba-cil'-lus
lac'-to-fla'-vin
lac-tom'-e-ter
lac-to-pro'-tein
lac'-tose
la-cu'-na
lacu'u-nar:y†
la-cu'-nu-lose
la-cus'-trine
lac'y
lad'-der
lad'-die
lad'-en
lad'-en-ing
la'-dies
lad'-ing

La-di'-no
la'-dle
la'-dle-ful
la'-dler
la'-dy
la-drone'
la'-dy-bird
la'-dy-bug
la'-dy-fin-ger
la'-dy=kill-er
la'-dy-like
la'-dy-ship
la'-dy's maid
la'-dy's slip-per
La-er'-tes
La-fay-ette'*
La Fol'-lette
La Fon-taine'
lag'-an†
la'-ger
lag'-gard
lag'-ging
la'-gniappe
la-goon'
la-goon'-al
La-hore'
la'-ic
la'-i-cal
lais'-sez=faire
lai'-tance
la'-i-ty
lake'-side
lal-la'-tion
la-lop'-a-thy
la'-ma
La-marck'-i:an
La-marck'-ism
La-mar-tine'
la'-ma-ser:y
lam-baste'
lamb'-da
lamb'-doid
lam'-ben-cy
lam'-bent
lam'-bert
Lam'-beth
lamb'-kin
lam'-bre-quin
lamb'-skin
la-mé'
la-mel'-la
la-mel'-lar†
lam'-el-late
la-mel-li-bran'-chi-ate
la-mel'-li-corn
la-mel'-li-ros'-tral

la-mel'-lose†
lame'-ly
lame'-ness
la-ment'
lam'-en-ta-ble
lam'-en-ta-bly
lam-en-ta'-tion
la-ment'-ed
la'-mi:a
la-mi-a'-ceous
lam'-i-na
lam'-i-na-graph
lam-i-nag'-ra-phy
lam'-i-nal
lam'-i-nar
lam-i-nar'-i-a'-ceous*†
lam-i-nar'-in
lam'-i-nate
lam-i-na'-tion
lam'-i-na-tor
lam-i-ni'-tis
lam'-pad
lamp'-black
lam'-pi-on
lamp'-light
lam-poon'
lamp'-post
lam'-prey
lamp'-stand
Lan'-ark
la'-nate
la-nat'-o-side
Lan'-ca-shire
Lan'-cas-ter
Lan-cas'-tri-an
Lan'-ce-lot
lan'-ce-o-lar
lan'-ce-o-late
lanc'-er
lan'-cet
lan'-cet-ed
lance'-wood
lan'-ci-nate
lanc'-ing
lan'-dau
lan'-dau-let'
land'-ed
land'-fall
land'-grave
land'-hold-er
land'-ing
land'-ing craft
land'-ing field
land'-ing gear
land'-ing strip
land'-la-dy
land'-less
land'-locked

land'-lop-er
land'-lord
land'-lub-ber
land'-mark
Lan'-dor
land'-own-er
land'=poor
land'-scape
land'-slide
land'-slip
lands'-man
Land'-sturm
land'-ward
Lang'-land
lan'-grage
Lang'-shan
lang'-spiel
lan'-guage
lan'-guet
lan'-guid
lan'-guid-ly
lan'-guish
lan'-guished
lan'-guish-ing
lan'-guor
lan'-guor-ous
la'-ni-ar:y†
La-nier'
lank'-i-er
lank'y
lan'-o-ce'-ric
lan'-o-lin
la'-nose
la-nos'-ter-ol
Lan'-sing
lans'-que-net'
Lan'-ston
lan-ta'-na
lan'-tern
lan'-tha-nide
lan'-tha-num
lan-thi'-o-nine
la-nu'-gi-nous
la-nu'-go
lan'-yard
La-oc'-o-on
La-od'-i-ce'-an
lap-a-rot'-o-my
lap'-dog
la-pel'
la-pel'-er
lap'-i-dar:y†
lap-i-da'-tion
la-pid'-i-fy
la-pil'-lus
lap'-in*
lap'-is la'-zu-li*†
La-place'

Lap'-land
Lap'-land-er
lap'-pet
lap'-ping
laps'-a:ble
lapsed
laps'-ing
La-pu'-ta
lap'-wing
Lar'-a-mie
lar'-board
lar'-ce-nist
lar'-ce-nous
lar'-ce-ny
lar-da'-ceous
lar'-der*
La'-res
large'-ly
large'-ness
larg'-er
lar-gess'
larg'-est
lar-ghet'-to
lar'-go
lar'-i-at
lar'-ine
lark'-spur
La Roche-fou-cauld'
lar'-ri-kin
lar'-rup
lar'-va
lar'-vae
lar'-val
lar'-vi-cid-al†
lar'-vi-cide
lar-vic'-o-lous
lar-viv'-o-rous*
la-ryn'-gal
la-ryn'-ge-al
la-ryn-gec'-to-my
la-ryn'-ges
lar'-yn-git'-ic
la-ryn-gi'-tis
la-ryn'-go-log'-i-cal
lar-yn-gol'-o-gist
lar-yn-gol'-o-gy
la-ryn'-go-scope
la-ryn-gos'-co-py
la-ryn'-go-spasm
lar'-ynx
La Salle
las'-car
las-civ'-i-ous
la'-ser
lash'-ing
las'-sie
las'-si-tude
las'-so

las'-so-er
last'-ing
last'-ly
lat-a-ki'a†
latch'-et
latch'-key
latch'-string
la-teen'
late'-ly
la'-ten-cy
late'-ness
la'-tent
la'-tent-ly
lat'-er
lat'-er-al
lat'-er-al-ly
Lat'-er-an
lat'-er-ite
lat'-er-i'-tious
lat-er-i-za'-tion
lat'-est
la'-tex
lath
lathe
lath'-er
lath'-er-ing
lath'-ing
lath'-work
lat'-i-ces
lat-i-cif'-er-ous
lat-i-fun'-di:a
lat-i-fun'-di-um
Lat'-i-mer
Lat'-in
Lat'-in-ist
La-tin'-i-ty
Lat'-in-ize
lat'-ish
la'-tite
lat'-i-tude
lat-i-tu'-di-nal
lat-i-tu-di-nar'-i-an†
lat-i-tu'-di-nous
La'-tium
La-to'-na
la-tri'a
la-trine
la'-tron
lat'-ter
lat'-tice
lat'-tice-work
lat'-tic-ing
Lat'-vi:a
Lat'-vi-an
laud-a:bil'-i-ty
laud'-a:ble
lau-dan'-i-dine
lau'-da-nine

lau-dan'-o-sine
lau'-da-num
lau-da'-tion
laud'-a-tive
lau'-da-to-ry*
Lau'-der
Laud'-i:an
laugh'-a:ble
laugh'-ing
laugh'-ing-stock
laugh'-ter
launched
launch'-er
laun'-der
Laun-der-Om'-e-ter
laun'-dress
laun'-dries
Laun'-dro-mat
laun'-dry
laun'-dry-man
Lau'-ra
lau-ra'-ceous
lau'-rate
lau-re-ate
lau'-rel
lau'-reled
Lau'-rence
Lau-ren'-tian
Lau-ren-tide
lau'-ric
Lau'-ri-er
lau'-rus-tine
lau'-ryl
Lau-sanne'
lau'-ter
la'-va
la-va'-bo
la-vage'*
lav'a-liere'
la-va'-tion
lav'-a-to-ry
lav'-en-der
la'-ver
lav'-ing
La-vin'-i:a
lav'-ish
La-voi-sier'
law'=a:bid'-ing
law'-break-er
law'-ful
law'-giv-er
law'-less
law'-less-ness
law'-mak-er
law'-mak-ing
Law'-rence
law'-renc-ite†
law-ren'-ci-um

Law'-son
law'-suit
law'-yer
lax-a'-tion
lax'-a-tive
lax'-i-ty
lay'-er
lay-ette'†
lay'-man
lay'-off (n.)
lay'-out (n.)
laz'-ar*†
laz-a-ret'
laz-a-ret'-to
Laz'-a-rus
la'-zi-er
la'-zi-ly
la'-zi-ness
laz'-u-lite
laz'-u-rite
la'-zy
leach
lead'-en
lead'-er
lead'-er-ship
lead'-ing
leads'-man
lead'y
leaf'-age
leaf'-less
leaf'-let
leaf'y
league
lea'-guer (camp, siege)
leagu'er* (league
    member)
leak'-age
leak'-proof
leak'y
lean
Le-an'-der
lean'-ing
lean'-ness
lean'=to
leap'-frog
leap'-ing
leap year
learned (acquired
    knowledge)
learn'-ed (erudite)
learn'-er
learn'-ing
leased
lease'-hold
leas'-ing
leath'-er
leath'-er-ine'

leath'-ern
Leath'-er-neck
leath'-er-work
leath'-er:y
leav'-en
Leav'-en-worth
leav'-ing
Leb'-a-nese'
Leb'-a-non
le'-bens-raum
lech'-er-ous
lech'-er:y
lec'-i-thin
lec'-i-thin-ase
lec'-tern
lec'-tion
lec'-tor
lec'-ture
lec'-tured
lec'-tur-er
lec'-tur-ing
Le'-da
ledg'-er
le'-dol
lee'-board
leech
leer'-ing
leer'-ing-ly
leer'y
lee'-ward
lee'-way
left=hand'-ed
left'-ist
left'-o:ver
leg-a-cies
leg'-a-cy
le'-gal
le'-gal-is'-tic
le-gal'-i-ty
le-gal-i:za'-tion
le'-gal-ize
le'-gal-ly
leg'-ate (emissary)
le-gate' (to will)
leg'-a-tee'
le-ga'-tion
le-ga'-to
leg'-end
leg'-end-ar:y†
leg'-er-de-main'
le-ger'-i-ty
leg'-ged
leg'-gings
Leg'-horn
leg-i-bil'-i-ty
leg'-i-ble
le'-gion

220

le'-gion-ar:y†
le'-gion-naire'
leg'-is-late
leg-is-la'-tion
leg'-is-la-tive
leg'-is-la-tor
leg-is-la-to'-ri-al
leg'-is-la-ture
le'-gist
le-git'-i-ma-cy
le-git'-i-mate
le-git'-i-ma-tize
le-git'-i-mist
le-git'-i-mize
le-git'-i-miz-ing
leg'-man
leg'-ume
le-gu'-min
le-gu'-mi-nous
Le'-high
Leib'-nitz
Leices'-ter
Leip'-zig
leish-ma-ni'-a-sis*†
leis'-ter
leis'-ter-er
lei'-sure
lei'-sure-ly
leit'-mo-tiv'
lem'-an†
lem'-ma
lem'-ming
lem-nis'-cus
lem'-on
lem'-on-ade'
le'-mur
lem'-u-res
Le'-na
lend'-er
lend'-ing
length
length'-en
length'-i-er
length'-wise
length'y
le'-nience
le'-nien-cy
le'-nient
le'-nient-ly
Len'-in†
Len'-in-grad†
Len'-in-ism†
len'-i-tive
len'-i-ty
Len'-ox
len-ta-men'-te
len-tan'-do

Lent'-en
len'-ti-cel
len-tic'-u-lar
len-tig'-i-nous
len-ti'-go
len'-til
Leom'-in-ster
Leon'-ard
Le'-o-nar-desque'
Le-on'-i-das
le'-o-nine
le'-o-nite†
Le'-o-no'-ra
leop'-ard
Le'-o-pold
le'-o-tard
Le-pan'-to
lep'-er
lep-i-do-cro'-cite†
le-pid'-o-lite†
Lep-i-dop'-ter:a
lep-i-dop'-ter-ous
lep-i-do'-sis
lep'-i-dote
lep'-o-rid
lep'-re-chaun
lep-rol'-o-gy
lep-ro-sar'-i-um†
le-pro'-sis*
lep'-ro-sy
lep-rot'-ic
lep'-rous
lep'-to-ceph'-a-lous
lep-to-ceph'-a-ly
lep-to-kur'-tic
lep-to-kur-to'-sis
lep'-to-mat'-ic
lep'-ton
lep-to-spi-ro'-sis
lep'-tus
Ler-nae'-an
Les'-bi-an
Les'-bos
lese maj'-es-ty
le'-sion
les-pe-de'-za
less-see'
less'-en
less'-er
les'-son
les'-sor
let'-down (n.)
le'-thal
le-thal'-i-ty
le-thar'-gic
le-thar'-gi-cal-ly
leth'-ar-gize

221

leth'-ar-gy
Le'-the
le-thif'-er-ous
Le-ti'-tia
let'-ter
let'-ter box
let'-ter car'-ri-er
let'-tered
let'-ter-head
let'-ter-ing
let'-ter=per'-fect
let'-ter-press
Lett'-ish*†
let'-tre de ca-chet'
let'-tuce
let'-up (n.)
leu'-cine
leu'-cite
leu-co-cy-the'-mi:a
leu-co'-ma
leu'-co-maine*†
leu'-co-noid
leu-cop'-te-rin
leu'-co-sin
leu-co-sphe'-nite
leu-cot'-o-my
leu-cov'-o-rin
leu-ke'-mi:a
leu'-ker-gy
leu'-ko-cyte
leu'-ko-cyt'-ic
leu-ko-cy-to'-sis
leu-ko-pe'-ni:a
leu'-ko-poi-e'-sis
leu'-ko-poi-et'-ic
leu-kor-rhe'a
leu-ko'-sis
lev'-an
Le-vant'-er
Lev'-an-tine*†
le-va'-tor
le'-vee*† (reception)
lev'-ee (river bank)
lev'-el
lev'-eled
lev'-el-er
lev'-el-ing
lev'-el-ly
lev'er*
lev'er-age*
lev'-er-et
Le'-vi
levi'i-a:ble
le-vi'-a-than
lev'-i-gate
lev'-i-ga-tor

lev'i-rate
lev'i-rat'-ic
lev'-i-tate
lev'-i-tat-ing
lev-i-ta'-tion
Le'-vite
le-vit'-i-cal
Le-vit'-i-cus
lev'-i-ty
le-vo-glu'-co-san
le'-vo-gy'-rate
le-vo-ro-ta'-tion
le-vo-ro'-ta-to-ry
lev'-u-li-nate
lev-u-lin'-ic
lev'-u-lose
lev'y
lev'y-ing
lewd'-ness
Lew'-is
Lew'-i-sohn
lew'-is-ite
lew'-is-son
Lew'-is-ton
Lew'-is-town
lex'-i-cal
lex-i-cog'-ra-pher
lex'-i-co-graph'-ic
lex-i-co-graph'-i-cal
lex-i-cog'-ra-phy
lex'-i-con
lex-ig'-ra-phy
Lex'-ing-ton
Ley'-den
li-a-bil'-i-ty
li'-a-ble
li'-ai-son
li-a'-na†
li'-ar
li-ba'-tion
li'-bel
li'-bel-ant
li'-beled
li'-bel-ee'
li'-bel-er
li'-bel-ing
li'-bel-lee'
li'-bel-ous
lib'-er-al
lib'-er-al-ism
lib'-er-al-is'-tic
lib-er-al'-i-ty
lib-er-al-i:za'-tion
lib'-er-al-ize
lib'-er-al-ly
lib'-er-ate
lib-er-a'-tion
lib'-er-a-tor

Li-be′-ri:a
lib-er-tar′-i-an†
li-ber′-ti-cide†
lib′-er-tine
lib′-er-ty
li-bid′-i-nal
li-bid′-i-nous
li-bi′-do
Li′-bra
li-brar′-i-an†
li′-brar:y†
li-bra′-tion
li′-bra-to-ry
li-bret′-tist
li-bret′-to
li-bret′-tos
li′bri-form
Lib′-y:a
Lib′-y-an
li-can′-ic
li′-cens-a:ble
li′-cense
li′-censed
li′-cens-ee′*†
li′-cens-er
li′-cens-ing
li′-cen-sor
li-cen′-ti-ate
li-cen′-tious
li-cen′-tious-ness
li′-chen
li′-chen-in
lic′-it
lic′-o-rice
lic′-tor
lid′-o-caine
Lieb′-frau-milch
Lie′-der-kranz
liege
liege man
lien
lien-ee′
lien′-or
li-en-ter′-ic
li′-en-ter:y
li-erne′
lieu-ten′-an-cy
lieu-ten′-ant
life
life belt
life′-blood
life′-boat
life buoy
life′-guard
life′-less
life′-like
life′-line
life′-long

life net
life raft
life′-sav-er
life′-sav-ing
life′-time
lift′-er
lig′-a-ment
lig′-a-men′-ta-ry
lig′-a-men′-tous
lig′-and
li′-gate
li-ga′-tion
lig′-a-ture
li′-geance
light′-ed
light′-en
light′-ened
light′-en-ing (making lighter)
light′-er
light′-er-age
light′=fin-gered
light′-heart-ed
light′-house
light′-ing
light′-ness
light′-ning (electric discharge)
light′-proof
light′-ship
light′-tight
light′-weight
light′=year
lign-al′-oe†
lig′-ne-ous
lig-nes′-cent
lig′-ni-fy
lig′-nin
lig′-nite
lig′-num vi′-tae
lig′-ro-in
lig′-u-la
lig′-u-late
lig′-ure
Li-gu′-ri-an
lik′-a:ble
like′-li-hood
like′-ly
lik′-en
like′-ness
like′-wise
lik′-ing
li′-lac
li-la′-ceous
lil-i-a′-ceous
Lil′-i-an
Lil′-ien-thal
lil′-ies

223

Lil'-ith
Lille
Lil'-li-put
Lil'-li-pu'-tian
lil'y
Li'-ma
lim'-a-cine
lim'-bate
lim'-ber (flexible)
limb'-er* (logger)
lim'-bo
Lim'-burg-er
lim'-bus
lime'-ade
lime'-kiln
lime'-light
lim'-er-ick
lime'-stone
lime'-wa-ter
li-mic'-o-line
li-mic'-o-lous
li'-min-al*†
lim'-it
lim'-i-tar:y†
lim-i-ta'-tion
lim'-it-ed
lim'-it-less
li-miv'-o-rous
lim'-ner
lim-nim'-e-ter
lim-nol'-o-gy
Li-moges'
lim'-o-nene
li'-mo-nite
lim'-ou-sine†
lim'-pet
lim'-pid
lim-pid'-i-ty
lim'-pid-ly
limp'-ly
lim'-u-lus
lim'y
lin'-a:ble
lin'-age
lin-al-a'-o-ol
lin-a-mar'-in*†
linch'-pin
Lin'-coln
lin'-dane
Lind'-bergh
lin'-den
lin'-e:age
lin'-e:al
lin'-e:a-ment
lin'-e:ar
lin-e:ar'-i-ty
lin'-e:ate
lin-e:a'-tion

line'-man
lin'-en
lin'-e:o-late
lin'-er
line'-up (n.)
lin'-ger
lin-ge-rie'
lin'-go
lin'-gua
lin'-gual
lin'-guist
lin-guis'-tic
lin-guis'-ti-cal-ly
lin-guis-ti'-cian
lin-guis'-tics
lin'-guis-try
lin'-gu-late
ling'y
lin'-i-ment
lin'-ing
link'-age
link'-ing
Lin-nae'-us
lin'-net
li-no'-le-ate
lin'-o-le'-ic†
li-no'-le-in
lin'-o-le'-nic
li-no'-le-um
Li'-no-type*
li-nox'-yn
lin'-seed
lin'-sey
lin'-sey=wool'-sey
lin'-tel
lint'-er
li'-on
Li'-o-nel
li'-on-ess
li'-on-heart-ed
li-on-i:za'-tion
li'-on-ize
li'-on-like
lip'-a-rid
li'-pase†
li-pe'-mi:a
lip'-ide
lip-o-chon'-dri-on
lip-o-fus'-cin
li-pog'-e-nous
li-po'-ic
lip'-oid
lip-oi-do'-sis
li-pol'-y-sis
lip'-o-lyt'-ic
li-po'-ma
li-po-ma-to'-sis

lip-o-pro'-tein*†
li-po'-si-tol
lip'-o-trop'-ic
lip'-stick
li'-quate
li-qua'-tion
liq-ue-fa'-cient
liq-ue-fac'-tion
liq'-ue-fied
liq'-ue-fy
liq'-ue-fy-ing
li-ques'-cence
li-ques'-cent
li-queur'
liq'-uid
liq'-uid-am'-bar
liq'-ui-date
liq-ui-da'-tion
liq'-ui-da-tor
liq-uid'-i-ty
liq'-ui-dus
li'-quor*
li'-ra
lir-i-o-den'-dron
lir'-i-pipe
li-roc'-o-nite
Li'-sa
Lis'-bon
lis'-e-ran
lisp'-er
lisp'-ing
lisp'-ing-ly
lis'-some
lis'-ten
lis'-ten-er
Lis'-ter
list'-er
lis-ter-el-lo'-sis
Lis-te'-ri:a
Lis'-ter-ize
list'-less
list'-less-ness
lit'-a-ny
li'-tchi'
li'-ter
lit'-er-a-cy
lit'-er-al
lit'-er-al-ly
lit'-er-ar:y†
lit'-er-ate
lit-e-ra'-ti
lit-e-ra'-tim
lit'-er-a-tor
lit'-er-a-ture
lith'-arge
li-the'-mi:a†
lithe'-some
lith'-i:a

li-thi'-a-sis†
li-thid'-i-o-nite
lith'-i-um
lith'-o-cho'-lic*
lith'-o-graph
li-thog'-ra-pher†
lith'-o-graph'-ic
li-thog'-ra-phy†
lith'-oid
lith'-o-log'-ic
li-thol'-o-gy†
lith'-o-mor'-phic
lith'-o-pone
lith'-o-sere
lith'-o-sol
lith'-o-sphere
lith'-o-tome
li-thot'-o-my†
li-thot'-ri-ty†
Lith'u-a'-ni:a
Lith'u-a'-ni-an
li-thu'-ri:a†
lit'-i-ga-ble
lit'-i-gant
lit'-i-gate
lit-i-ga'-tion
lit'-i-ga-tor
li-ti'-gious†
li-ti'-gious-ly†
lit'-mus
li'-to-tes†
lit'-ter
lit'-ter-a-teur'*
lit'-tle
lit'-to-ral
li-tur'-gi-cal
li-tur'-gi-cal-ly
lit'-ur-gist
lit'-ur-gy
liv'-a:ble
live'-li-hood
live'-li-ness
live'-long
live'-ly
liv'-en
liv'-er
liv'-er-ied
Liv'-er-pool
liv'-er-wort
liv'-er-wurst
liv'-er:y
liv'-er:y-man
live'-stock
liv'-id
li-vid'-i-ty
liv'-ing
liv'-ing room
Liv'-ing-ston

Li-vo'-ni-an
li'-vre
Liv'y
lix-iv'-i-ate
liz'-ard
lla'-ma
lla'-no
Llew-el'-lyn
load'-er
Load-om'-e-ter
loaf
loaf'-er
loam'y
loath (*adj.*)
loathe (*v.*)
loath'-er
loath'-ing
loath'-some
loaves
lo'-bar
lo'-bate
lo-ba'-tion
lobbed
lob'-bied
lob'-bing
lob'-by
lob'-by-ing
lob'-by-ist
lo-bec'-to-my
lo-be'-lia
lo'-be-line
lo-bot'-o-my
lob'-ster
lob'-u-lar
lob'-ule
lob'-u-lose
lo'-cal
lo-cale'
lo-cal'-i-ty
lo-cal-i:za'-tion
lo'-cal-ize
lo'-cal-iz-er
lo'-cal-ly
lo'-cant
Lo-car'-no
lo'-cate
lo-cat'-er
lo-cat'-ing
lo-ca'-tion
loc'-a-tive
lo'-ca-tor
lo-chet'-ic*
Loch'-in-var
lock'-age
lock'-er
lock'-et
lock'-jaw
lock'-out (*n.*)

lock'-smith
lock'-step
lock'-stitch
lock'-up (*n.*)
lo'-co
lo-co-mo'-tion
lo-co-mo'-tive
lo-co-mo'-tor
lo'-co-weed
loc'-u-lar
loc'-u-late
lo'-cus
lo'-cust
lo-cu'-tion
lode'-star
lode'-stone
lodg'-er
lodg'-ing
lodg'-ment
loess
loft'-i-ly
loft'-i-ness
loft'y
lo'-gan-ber-ry
lo-ga-ni-a'-ceous
lo'-ga-nin*
log'-a-oe'-dic
log'-a-rithm
log-a-rith'-mic
log-a-rith'-mi-cal
log-a-rith'-mi-cal-ly
log'-book
log'-gia
log'-ging
lo'-gi:a*†
log'-ic
log'-i-cal
log'-i-cal-ly
lo-gi'-cian
lo'-gi-on*†
lo-gis'-tic
lo-gis-ti'-cian
lo-gis'-tics
log'-o-gram
log'-o-gram-mat'-ic
lo-gog'-ra-phy
log'-o-pe'-dic
log-or-rhe'a
Lo'-gos*†
log'-o-thete
log'o-type
log'o-roll-ing
log'-wood
lo'-gy
Lo'-hen-grin
loin'-cloth

Lo'-is
loi'-ter
loi'-ter-er
Lol'-lard
loll'-ing
lol'-li-pop
Lom'-bard
Lom'-bar-dy*
lo'-ment
Lo'-mond
Lon'-don
Lon'-don-der-ry
Lon'-don-er
lone'-li-ness
lone'-ly
lone'-some
lon-ga-nim'-i-ty
long'-boat
long'-bow
long=dis'-tance (*adj., adv., v.*)
longe
longe'-ing
long'-er (*adj.*)
lon'-ger† (row of barrels)
lon'-ge-ron
long'-est
lon-gev'-i-ty
lon-ge'-vous
Long'-fel-low
long=haired' (*adj.*)
long'-hand
long'-head-ed
long'-horn
lon'-gi-corn
lon-gi-fo'-lene
long'-ing
Lon-gi'-nus
lon'-gi-tude
lon-gi-tu'-di-nal
long=lived'
long=range' (*adj.*)
long'-shore-man
long=suf'-fer-ing (*adj.*)
long=term' (*adj.*)
long=wind-ed
loo'-by
look'-er
look'-ing
look'-ing glass
look'-out (*n.*)
loo'-ny*†
loop'-hole
loop'y
loose'=leaf (*adj.*)
loose'-ly
loos'-en
loot'-er

Lo'-pez
lo'-phine†
loph'-o-phore*†
lop'-per
lop'-sid-ed
lo-qua'-cious
lo-quac'-i-ty
lo'-quat
lo'-qui-tur†
lo'-ran
lord'-li-ness
lor-do'-sis
lord'-ship
Lor'e-lei
Lo-ren'-zo
Lo-ret'-ta
lor-gnette'
lo-ri'-ca
lor'-i-cate
lo'-ris
Lor-raine'
lor'-ries
lor'-ry
lo'-ry
los'-a:ble
Los An'-ge-les
los'-er
los'-ing
Los'-sen
loss'-er
Lo-thar'-i:o†
lo'-tion
lot'-ter:y
lot'-to
lo'-tus
loud'-ness
loud'-speak-er
Lou'-is
Lou-i'-sa
Lou-ise'
Lou-i-si-an'a
Lou-i-si-an'-i-an
Lou'-is-ville
lounged
loung'-er
loung'-ing
louse
lous'-i-ness
lous'y
lout'-ish
lou'-ver
Lou'-vre
lov'-a:ble
lov'-age
love'-bird
love'-less
love'-li-er
love'-li-ness

love'-lorn
love'-ly
lov'-er
love'-sick (adj.)
lov'-ing=kind'-ness
low'-born
low'-boy
low'-bred
low'-brow
Low Church
low'=cut' (adj.)
low'-down (n.)
Low'-ell
low'-er
low'-er case (n.)
low'-er=case (adj.)
low'-er-ing
low'=grade' (adj.)
low'-land
low'-li-ness
low'-ly
low'=pres-sure (adj.)
low'=rate' (adj.)
low'=spir-it-ed (adj.)
lox
lox'-o-drome
lox'-o-drom'-ic
loy'-al
loy'-al-ist
loy'-al-ly
loy'-al-ty
Loy-o-'la†
loz'-enge
lub'-ber
Lub'-bock
Lu'-beck
lu'-bri-cal
lu'-bri-cant
lu'-bri-cate
lu-bri-ca'-tion
lu'-bri-ca-tor
lu-bri'-cious
lu-bric'-i-ty
lu'-bri-cous
lu'-cen-cy
lu'-cent
Lu-cerne'
Lu'-cia
Lu'-cian
lu'-cid
lu-cid'-i-ty
lu'-cid-ness
lu'-ci-fer
lu-cif'-er-ase†
lu-cif'-er-in
lu-cif'-er-ous
Lu-cin'-da
Lu'-cite

Lu'-cius
luck'-i-er
luck'-i-est
luck'-i-ly
luck'-less
luck'y
lu'-cra-tive
lu'-cre
Lu-cre'-tia
Lu-cre'-tius
lu-cu-brate
lu-cu-bra'-tion
lu'-cu-bra-tor
lu'-cu-lent
Lu-cul'-lan
Lu'-cy
Ludd'-ism*†
Ludd'-ite*†
lu'-di-crous
lu'-di-crous-ness
lu-di-fi-ca'-tion
Lud'-low
Lud'-wig
lu'-es
lug'-gage
lug'-ger
lug'-ging
lu-gu'-bri-ous
lug'-worm
luke'-warm
lull'-a-by
lum-ba-'go
lum'-bar
lum'-ber
lum'-ber-jack
lum'-ber-man
lum'-ber-yard
lum'-bri-coid
lu'-men
lu-miere'
lu-mi-fla'-vin
lu-mi-naire'
lu'-mi-nar:y†
lu-mi-nesce'
lu-mi-nes'-cence
lu-mi-nes'-cent
lu-mi-nif'-er-ous
lu-mi-nom'-e-ter
lu-mi-nos'-i-ty
lu'-mi-nous
lu-mis'-ter-ol
lum'-mox
lump'-i-er
lump'-i-ly
lump'-ish
lump'y
lu'-na
lu'-na-cy

lu'-nar
lu-nar'-i-an†
lu'-nate
lu'-na-tic
lu-na'-tion
lunch'-eon
lunch'-eon-ette'
lunch'-room
lu-nette'
lunged'
lung'-er
lung'-ing
lu'-nik
lu'-ni-tid'-al†
lu'-nu-late
lu'-nule
lu'-pine
lu'-pin-ine
lu'-pu-lin
lu'-pu-lone
lu'-pus
lurch
lurched
lurch'-ing
lured
lu'-rid
lu'-rid-ly
lur'-ing
lurk'-er
lurk'-ing
lus'-cious
lush'-ly
Lu-si-ta'-ni:a
lus'-ter (shine)
lust'-er (one who lusts)
lus'-ter-ware
lust'-ful
lust'-i-er
lust'-i-ly
lus'-tral
lus'-trate
lus-tra'-tion
lus'-tring
lus'-trous
lus'-trum
lust'y
lu'-ta-nist
lu-te'-in
lu-te'-in-ize
lu-te'-o-lin
lu-te'-ous
lu-te:o-vi-res'-cent
lu-te'-tium
Lu'-ther
Lu'-ther-an
Lu'-ther-an-ism

lu'-ti-din'-ic
lut'-ist
lux'-ate
lux-a'-tion
Lux'-em-bourg
lux-u'-ri-ance
lux-u'-ri-ant
lux-u'-ri-ate
lux-u'-ri-at-ing
lux-u'-ries
lux-u'-ri-ous
lux'-u-ry
ly'-can-thrope
ly'-can-throp'-ic
ly-can'-thro-py
ly-cée'
ly-ce'-um
Lyc'-i-das
ly'-co-pene
ly-co-po'-di-um
Ly-cur'-gus
lydd'-ite†
Lyd'-i:a
Lyd'-i-an
ly'-ing
ly'-ing=in' (n.)
Lyl'y
lymph
lymph-ad-e-ni'-tis*
lymph-ad-e-nop'-a-thy*
lym-phan'-gi-al†
lym-phat'-ic
lym'-pho-cyte†
lymph'-oid
lym-pho-ma-to'-sis
lym'-pho-sar-co'-ma†
lyn-ce'-an
lynch
lynch'-ing
lynx
lynx'=eyed (adj.)
ly'-on-naise
Ly-on-nesse'
Ly'-ons
ly'-o-phil'-ic
ly-oph'-i-lize
ly'-rate
lyr'-ic
lyr'-i-cal
lyr'-i-cal-ly
ly'-ri-form†
Ly-sen'-ko-ism
ly-ser'-gic
Lys'-i-as
ly-sim'e-ter
ly'-sin
ly'-sine
ly'-so-gen'-ic

229

Ly'-sol
ly'-so-some
lyt'-ic

M

Ma'-bel
ma-ca'-bre
ma-ca'-co
mac-ad'-am
mac-ad-am-i:za'-tion
mac-ad'-am-ize
Ma-ca'o
ma-caque'
mac-a-ro'-ni
mac'-a-ron'-ic
mac'-a-roon'
ma-cas'-sar
Ma-caul'-ay
ma-caw'
Mac-beth'
Mac'-ca-be'-an
Mac-Dow'-ell
ma'-cé-doine'*
Mac'-e-don
Mac-e-do'-ni:a
Mac-e-do'-ni-an
mac'-er-al'
mac'-er-ate
mac-er-a'-tion
mac'-er-a-tor
ma-chet'e*†
Ma-chia-vel'-li†
mach-i-a-vel'-li-an
ma-chic-o-la'-tion†
ma-chi'-nal*†
mach-i-na'-tion
mach'-i-na-tor
ma-chine'
ma-chine' gun
ma-chin'-er:y
ma-chine' shop
ma-chine' tool
ma-chin'-ist
ma-chree'
Mac-ken'-zie
mack'-er-el
Mack'-i-nac
mack'-i-naw
mack'-in-tosh
ma'-cle†
Mac-Mil'-lan
Ma'-con
mac'-ra-me'
mac-ro-bi-o'-sis
mac'-ro-cosm
mac'-ro-cos'-mic
mac'-ro-cy'-clic†

mac-ro-cy-to'-sis
mac-rog'-ra-phy*†
mac'-ro-mol'-e-cule
ma'-cron
mac'-ro-phys'-ics
mac-rop'-si:a*†
mac'-ro-scop'-ic
ma-cru'-ral
ma-cru'-rous
mac'-u-la
mac-u-la'-tion
mac'-u-la-ture
mac'-ule
Mad'-a-gas'-car
mad'-am
ma-dame'*
Ma-da-ri'-a-ga
mad'-cap
mad'-den
mad'-den-ing
mad'-der
mad'-dest
Ma-dei'-ra
Mad'-e-line
ma-de-moi-selle'
mad'-house
Mad'-i-son
mad'-ly
mad'-man
mad'-ness
Ma-don'-na
ma-dras'
mad'-re-pore
Ma-drid'
mad'-ri-gal
ma-dro'-na
ma-du'-ro
Mae-ce'-nas
mael'-strom
mae'-nad
mae-nad'-ic
mae-stro†
Mae'-ter-linck
Maf'-e-king†
maf'-fick
Ma'-fi:a
maf'-ic
mag-a-zine'
mag'-a-zin'-ist
Mag-da-len
Mag'-de-burg
Ma-gel'-lan
Mag'-el-lan'-ic
ma-gen'-ta
Mag-gio'-re
mag'-got
ma'-gi
mag'-ic

mag'-i-cal
mag'-i-cal-ly
ma-gi'-cian
Ma'-gi-not'
ma-gis'-ter
mag-is-te'-ri-al
mag'-is-ter:y
mag'-is-tra-cy
mag'-is-trate
mag'-is-tra-ture
mag'-ma
Mag'-na Car'-ta
mag'-na cum lau'-de
Mag'-na-flux
mag-na-nim'-i-ty
mag-nan'-i-mous
mag'-nate
mag-ne'-sia
mag-ne'-si:o-chro'-mite
mag'-ne-site
mag-ne'-si:um
mag'-net
mag-net'-ic
mag-net'-i-cal-ly
mag'-net-ism
mag'-net-ite
mag-net-iz-a:ble
mag-net-i:za'-tion
mag'-net-ize
mag-ne'-to
mag'-ne-to-graph
mag-ne-to-hy-dro-dy-
  nam'-ics
mag-ne-tom'-e-ter†
mag-ne-tom'-e-met'-ric†
mag-ne'-tom'-e-try†
mag'-ne-ton
mag-ne'-tos
mag-ne-to-stric'-tion†
mag'-ne-tron
Mag-nif'-i-cat
mag-nif-i-ca'-tion
mag-nif'-i-cence
mag-nif'-i-cent
mag-nif'-i-co
mag'-ni-fied
mag-ni-fi-er
mag'-ni-fy
mag'-ni-fy-ing
mag-nil'-o-quence
mag-nil'-o-quent
mag'-ni-tude
mag-no'-lia
mag-no-li-a'-ceous
mag'-num
mag'-pie
ma-guey'*

ma'-gus
Mag'-yar
Ma-ha'-bha'-ra-ta
Ma-han'
ma-ha-ra'-ja
ma-ha-ra'-ni
ma-hat'-ma
mah'-di
Ma-hi'-can
Mah'=Jongg'
ma-hog'-a-ny
Ma-hom'-et
ma-hout'
Mah-rat'-ta
maid'-en
maid'-en-hair
maid'-en-head
maid'-en-hood
maid'-en-ly
maid'-ser-vant*
ma-ieu'-tic
mai'-gre
mail'-a:ble
mail'-bag
mail'-box
mail'-er
mail-lot'
mail'-man
Mai-mon'-i-des
Maine
Main'-er
main'-land
main'-ly
main'-mast
main'-sail
main'-spring
main'-stay
main-tain'
main'-te-nance
mai'-so-nette'
mai'-tre d'hô-tel'
maize
ma-jes'-tic
ma-jes'-ti-cal
ma-jes'-ti-cal-ly
maj'-es-ty
ma-jol'-i-ca
ma'-jor
Ma-jor'-ca
ma-jor-do'-mo
ma'-jor gen'-er-al
ma-jor'-i-ties
ma-jor'-i-ty
ma-jus'-cu-lar
maj'-us-cule*†
Ma-kas'-sar
make'=be-lieve (n., adj.)
make'-fast

231

mak'-er
make'-shift
make'-up (n.)
make'-weight
mak'-ing
Mal'-a-bar
Ma-lac'-ca
Mal'-a-chi
mal'-a-chite
ma-la'-cia
mal-a-col'-o-gy
mal-a-cos'-tra-can
mal'-ad-just'-ed
mal'-ad-just'-ment
mal-ad-min'-is-ter
mal-ad-min-is-tra'-tion
mal'-a-droit'
mal'-a-droit'-ly
mal'-a-dy
Mal'-a-ga
Mal'-a-gas'y
ma:la-gue'-na
mal-aise'*
mal'-an-ders
mal'-a-pert'
mal'-a-prop-ism
mal-ap-ro-pos'
ma'-lar
ma-lar'-i:a†
ma-lar'-i-al†
ma-lar-i-om'-e-try
mal-as-sim-i-la'-tion
mal'-ate
Mal-a-thi'-on
Ma-lay'
Ma-lay'a
Mal-a-ya'-lam
Ma-lay'-an
Ma-lay'-sia
Ma-lay'-sian
Mal'-colm
mal'-con-tent
mal' de mer'
ma-le'-ate
mal-e-dic'-tion
mal'-e-fac'-tion
mal'-e-fac'-tor
ma-lef'-ic
ma-lef'-i-cence
ma-lef'-i-cent
ma-le'-ic
ma-lev'-o-lence
ma-lev'-o-lent
mal-fea'-sance
mal'-for-ma'-tion
mal'-formed'
Ma'-li
mal'-ic†

mal'-ice
ma-li'-cious
ma-li'-cious-ly
ma-lif'-er-ous
ma-lign'
ma-lig'-nan-cy
ma-lig'-nant
ma-lig'-ni-ty
Ma-lines'
ma-lin'-ger
ma-lin'-ger-er
mal'-i-son
mal'-lard
mal-le-a-bil'-i-ty
mal'-le:a-ble
mal-le'-o-lar
mal-le'-o-lus
mal'-let
mal'-le-us
Mal'-linck-rodt
Mal'-lo-ry
mal'-low
malm'-sey
mal-nu-tri'-tion
mal'-o:dor
mal-o'dor-ous
mal-o'dor-ous-ly
mal'-o-nate
ma-lo'-nic†
mal'-o-nyl
Mal'-o-ry
mal'-pigh-i-a'-ceous
Mal-pigh'-i-an
mal'-po-si'-tion
mal'-prac-tice
Mal'-ta
malt'-ase
Mal-tese'
mal'-tha
Mal'-thus
Mal-thu'-sian
malt'-ose
mal'-treat'
mal'-treat'-ment
malt'-ster
malt'y
mal-va'-ceous
mal-va'-sia
mal-ver-sa'-tion
mam'-ba
mam'-bo
Mam'-e-luke
mam'-ma
mam-ma'-li-an
mam-ma-lif'-er-ous
mam-mal'-o-gy
mam'-ma-ry

mam-mif'-er-ous
mam'-mil-lar:y†
mam'-mil-late
mam'-mon
mam'-moth
man'-a-cle
man'-a-cling
man'-age
man'-age-a:bil'-i-ty
man'-age-a:ble
man'-age-ment
man'-ag-er
man'-a-ge'-ri-al
man'-ag-ing
Ma-na'-gua
man'-a-kin
ma-ña'-na
Ma-nas'-sas
Ma-nas'-seh
man=at=arms
man'-a-tee
Man'-ches-ter
man-chi-neel'
Man'-chu'
Man'-chu-kuo'
Man-chu'-ri:a
Man-chu'-ri-an
man'-ci-ple
Man-dae'-an
Man'-da-lay'
man-da'-mus
man'-da-rin
man'-da-rin-ate
man'-da-tar:y†
man'-date
man-da'-tor
man'-da-to-ry
man'=day'
man'-del-ate
man-del'-ic
Man'-de-ville
man'-di-ble
man-dib'-u-lar
man'-do-lin'
man'-do-lin'-ist
man-drag'-o-ra
man'-drake
man'-drel
man'-drill
man'-du-cate
man'=eat-er
ma-nege'
ma'-nes
Ma-net'
ma-neu'-ver
ma-neu'-ver-a:bil'-i-ty
ma-neu'-ver-er
man'-ful

man'-ful-ly
man'-ga-nate
man'-ga-nese
man-gan'-ic
man-ga-nif'-er-ous
man'-ga-nite
man-ga-no'-site
man'-ga-nous
man'-gel=wur'-zel
man'-ger
man'-gi-er
man'-gi-ly
man'-gi-ness
man'-gle
man'-gler
man'-gling
man'-go
man'-goes
man'-go-nel
man'-grove
man'-gy
man'-han-dle
Man-hat'-tan
man'-hole
man'-hood
man'=hour'
ma'-ni:a
ma'-ni-ac
ma-ni'-a-cal
man'-ic*†
man'-ic=de-pres'-sive*†
Man-i-che'-an
man-i-co'-ba
man'-i-cure
man'-i-cur-ist
man'-i-fest
man-i-fes'-tant
man-i-fes-ta'-tion
man'-i-fest-ly
man'-i-fes'-to
man-i-fes'-tos
man'-i-fold
man'-i-fold-er
man'-i-kin
Ma-nil'a
ma-nil'-la
man'-i-oc
man'-i-ple
ma-nip'-u-late
ma-nip-u-la'-tion
ma-nip'-u-la-tive
ma-nip'-u-la-tor
ma-nip'-u-la-to-ry
Man-i-to'-ba
Man'-i-to'-ban
man'-i-tou
man'-kind'
man'-like

man'-li-ness
man'-ly
man'-na
man'-ne-quin
man'-ner
man'-ner-ism
man'-ner-less
man'-ner-ly
man'-ni-kin
man'-nish
man'-ni-tol
man'-nose
man'-nu-ron'-ic
man=of=war
ma-nom'-e-ter
man'-o-met'-ric
ma-nom'-e-try
man'-or
ma-no'-ri-al
man'-o-stat
man'-pow-er
man'-rope
man'-sard
man'-ser-vant*
man'-sion
man'-slaugh-ter
man'-slay-er
man'-stop-per
man'-sue-tude
man'-ta
man-teau'
man'-tel
man'-tel-et
man'-tel-piece
man'-tel-shelf
man'-tic
man-til'la
man'-tis
man-tis'-sa
man'-tle
man'-tling
man'-tra
Man'-tu:a
man'-u-al
man'-u-al-ly
ma-nu'-bri-um
man'-u-duc'-tive
Man'-u-el
man-u-fac'-to-ry
man-u-fac'-ture
man-u-fac'-tur-er
man-u-fac'-tur-ing
man-u-mis'-sion
man-u-mit'
ma-nure'
ma'-nus
man'-u-script
Manx

man'y
man-za-ni'-ta
Mao'-ri
ma'-ple
ma-quette'
ma-quis'
mar'-a-bou
mar'-a-bout
ma-ra'ca
Mar'-a-cai'-bo
mar-a-schi'-no
ma-ras'-mus
Ma-ra'-tha
mar'-a-thon
ma-raud'
ma-raud'-er
ma-raud'-ing
mar-a-ve'-di
mar'-ble
mar'-bled
Mar'-ble-head
mar'-ble-ize
mar'-bling
Mar'-burg
marc
mar'-ca-site
mar-cel'
mar-celled'
mar-ces'-cent
march'-er
mar-che'-sa
mar-che'-se
mar'-chio-ness*†
Mar'-cia
Mar'-cion-ite
Mar-co'-ni
mar-co'-ni-gram
Mar'-co Po'-lo
Mar'-di Gras
ma-rem'-ma
Ma-ren'-go
mare's nest
mare's tail
mar'-ga-rate
Mar'-ga-ret
mar-gar'-ic
mar'-ga-rin
mar'-ga-rine
mar'-ga-rite
mar-ga-ro'-san-ite
Mar'-ger:y
mar'-gin
mar'-gin-al†
mar-gi-na'-li:a
mar'-gin-ate
Mar'-got
mar'-grave
mar'-gue-rite'

Ma-ri′a
ma-ri-a′-chi
Mar′-i-an (fem. name)
Mar′-i-an† (adj., of Mary)
Mar-i-co′-pa
Ma-rie′
Mar-i-et′-ta†
mar′-i-gold
mar-i-hua′-na
mar-i-jua′-na
ma-rim′-ba
ma-ri′-na
mar′-i-nade′
mar′-i-nate
mar′-i-nat-ing
mar-i-na′-tion
ma-rine′
mar′-i-ner
Ma-ri′-nist
ma-rin′-ist
ma-ri-no-ra′-ma
Mar-i-ol′-a-try†
Mar′-i-on
mar′-i-o-nette′
mar′-i-tage
mar′-i-tal
mar′-i-tal-ly
ma-rit′-i-cide
mar′-i-time
Mar′-i-us†
mar′-jo-ram
Mar′-jo-ry
mark′-ed-ly
mark′-er
mar′-ket
mar-ket-a:bil′-i-ty
mar′-ket-a:ble
mar′-ket-er
mar′-ket-ing
mar′-ket-place
Mark′-ham
marks′-man
marks′-man-ship
mar-la′-ceous
Marl′-bor-ough
mar′-lin (fish)
mar′-line (rope)
mar′-line-spike
marl′-ite
mar-lit′-ic
Mar′-lowe
mar′-ma-lade
Mar′-mi-on
mar-mo-ra′-ceous
mar-mo′-re-al
mar′-mo-set
mar′-mot
ma-roon′

marque
mar-quee′
Mar-que′-san
mar′-quess
mar′-quess-ate
mar′-que-te-rie
mar-que-try†
Mar-quette′
mar′-quis
mar-quise′
mar′-qui-sette′
mar′-riage
mar′-riage-a:ble
mar′-ried
mar-ron′ gla-cé′
mar′-row
mar′-row-bone
mar′-ry
Mar-seil-laise′
Mar-seilles′
mar′-shal
mar′-shal-cy
mar′-shaled
mar′-shal-er
Mar′-shall
marsh gas
marsh′-i-ness
marsh′-mal-low
marsh′y
mar-su′-pi-al
mar-su′-pi-al-ize
mar-su′-pi-um
Mar-tel′
Mar-tel′-lo
mar′-ten
mar′-tens-ite
Mar′-tha
mar′-tial
mar′-tial-ly
Mar′-tian
mar′-tin
Mar-ti-neau′
mar′-ti-net′
mar′-tin-gale
mar-ti′-ni
Mar-ti-nique′
Mar′-tin-mas
mar′-tite
mar′-tyr
mar′-tyr-dom
mar′-tyr-ize
mar-tyr-o-log′-i-cal
mar-tyr-ol′-o-gist
mar-tyr-ol′-o-gy
mar′-vel
mar′-veled
mar′-vel-ing
mar′-vel-ous

mar'-vel-ous-ly
Marx'-i:an
Marx'-ism
Mar'y†
Mar'y-land†
Mar'y-land-er†
mar'-zi-pan
Ma-sa-ryk'
Ma:sca'-gni
mas-car'a
mas'-cle
mas'-cot
mas'-cu-line
mas-cu-lin'-i-ty
ma'-ser
mash'-er
mash'-ie
mask'-er
mas'-och-ism
mas'-och-ist
mas'-och-is'-tic†
ma'-son
ma-son'-ic
Ma'-son-ite
ma'-son-ry
Mas'-o-rete
Mas'-o-ret'-ic
masqu'-er*
mas'-quer-ade'
Mas'-sa-chu'-setts
mas'-sa-cre
mas'-sa-cred
mas'-sa-crer
mas'-sa-cring
mas-sage'
mas-sag'-er
mas-sag'-ing
mas'-sa-sau'-ga
mas-sé'
mas-se'-ter
mas-seur'
mas-seuse'
mas'-si-cot
mas-sif'
mass'-i-ness
mas'-sive†
mass meet-ing
mas'-so-ther'-a-py
mass'y
mas'-ta-ba
mas'-ter (head)
mast'-er (ship with masts)
mas'-ter=at=arms
mas'-ter-dom
mas'-ter-ful
mas'-ter-ful-ly
mas'-ter-ly
mas'-ter-piece

mas'-ter-ship
mas'-ter-work
mas'-ter:y
mast'-head
mas'-tic
mas'-ti-cate
mas-ti-ca'-tion
mas'-ti-ca-tor
mas'-ti-ca-to-ry
mas'-tiff
mas-tit'-ic
mas'-ti-tis
mas'-to-don
mas'-to-don'-toid
mas'-toid
mas-toi'-dal
mas-toid-i'-tis†
mas-toid-ot'-o-my
mas-tur-ba'-tion
ma-su'-ri-um
mat'-a-dor
match'-a:ble
match'-board
match'-less
match'-lock
match'-mak-er
match'-mak-ing
match'-mark
match'-wood
ma'-té (herb)
mate'-lot
ma'-ter (mother)
mat'-er (matcher)
ma-te'-ri-al
ma-te'-ri-al-ism
ma-te'-ri-al-ist
ma-te'-ri-al-is'-tic
ma-te'-ri-al-is'-ti-cal-ly
ma-te'-ri-al-ism
ma-te'-ri-al'-i-ty
ma-te-ri-al-i:za'-tion
ma-te'-ri-al-ly
ma-te'-ri:a med'-i-ca
ma-te-ri-el'
ma-ter'-nal
ma-ter'-nal-ly
ma-ter'-ni-ty
math-e-mat'-i-cal
math-e-mat'-i-cal-ly
math-e-ma-ti'-cian
math-e-mat'-ics
Math'-er
ma-thet'-ic
Ma-til'-da
mat'-in
mat'-in-al†
mat'-i-nee'
mat'-ing

ma'-tri-arch
ma'-tri-ar'-chal
ma'-tri-arch-ate†
ma'-tri-ar-chy*
ma'-tri-ces
ma'-tri-ci'-dal*
ma'-tri-cide
ma-tric'-u-lant
ma-tric'-u-late
ma-tric-u-la'-tion
ma-tri-lin'-e:al
mat'-ri-mo'-ni-al
mat'-ri-mo-ny
ma'-trix
ma-tro-cli'-nous*†
ma'-tron
ma'-tron-age
ma'-tron-ize
ma'-tron-li-ness
ma'-tron-ly
mat-ro-nym'-ic
mat'-ted
mat'-ter
Mat'-ter-horn
mat'-ter=of=fact' (adj.)
Mat'-thew
Mat-thi'-as
mat'-ting
mat'-tock
mat'-toid
mat'-toir'
mat'-tress
mat-u-rate
mat-u-ra'-tion
mat'-u-ra-tive*
ma-ture'
ma-ture'-ly
ma-ture'-ness
ma-tur'-i-ty*†
ma-tu'-ti-nal
mat'-zoth*
maud'-lin
Maugham
maul'-er
maund'-er*
Maun'-dy
Mau-pas-sant'
Mau-re-ta'-ni:a
Mau-re-ta'-ni-an
Mau-rice'
Mau-ri'-ti-us
Mau-rois'
Mau'-ser
mau-so-le'-um
mauve
mau'-vine*†
mav'-er-ick
ma'-vis

ma-vour'-neen
mawk'-ish
max-il'-la
max'-il-lar:y†
max-il'-lo=pal'-a-tal
max'-im
max'-i-mal
max'-i-mal-ist
Max-i-mil'-ian
max'-im-ite
max'-i-mize
max'-i-miz-er
max'-i-mum
Max'-well
Ma'ya
may'-be
May Day
may'-fish
May'-flow-er
may'-hap
may'-hem
May'o
may'-on-naise
may'-or
may'-or-al-ty
may'-pole
May'-time
Ma-za-rin'†
maze
ma'-zer
maz'-i-ly*
ma-zur'-ka
ma-zut'
maz'y
maz'-zard
Mc:Car'-thy
Mc:Clel'-lan
Mc:Cor'-mick
Mc:Kin'-ley
me'a cul'-pa
mead'-ow
mead'-ow-sweet
mead'-ow:y
mea'-ger
mea'-ger-ly
meal'-i-ness
meal'-time
meal'-worm
meal'y
meal'y-mouthed
mean
me-an'-der
me-an'-drous
mean'-ing
mean'-ing-ful
mean'-ing-less
mean'-ly

237

mean'-ness
meant
mean'-time
mean'-while
mea'-sles
mea'-sly
mea-sur-a:bil'-i-ty*
mea'-sur-a:ble*
mea'-sure*
mea'-sured*
mea'-sure-less*
mea'-sure-ment*
mea'-sur-er*
me-a'-tus
meat'y
Mec'-ca
me-chan'-ic
me-chan'-i-cal
me-chan'-i-cal-ly
mech-a-ni'-cian
me-chan'-ics
mech'-a-nism
mech'-a-nist
mech-a-nis'-tic
mech-a-ni-za'-tion
mech'-a-nize
mech-a-no-mor'-phic
mech-a-no-ther'-a-py
Mech'-lin
Meck'-len-burg
me-com'-e-ter
me-con'-ic
mec'-o-nin
me-co'-ni-um
med'-al
med'-aled
med'-al-ist
me-dal'-lic
me-dal'-lion
med'-dle
med'-dler
med'-dle-some
Me-de'a
me'-di:a
me'-di-al
me'-di-an
me-di-as-ti-ni'-tis
me-di-as-ti'-num
me'-di-ate
me'-di-ate-ly
me-di-a'-tion
me'-di-a-tive
me'-di-a-tize
me'-di-a-tor
me'-di-a-to'-ri-al
me'-di-a-to-ry
me'-di-a-tress
med'-ic

med'-i-ca-ble
med'-i-cal
med'-i-cal-ly
me-dic'-a-ment†
med'-i-cate
med-i-ca'-tion
med'-i-ca-tive
Med'-i-ce'-an
Med'-i-ci
me-dic'-i-na-ble
me-dic'-i-nal
med'-i-cine
med'-i-cine bag
med'-i-cine man
med'-i-co
med'-i-co-le'-gal
me-di'-e-ty
me:di:e'-val
me:di:e'-val-ism
me:di:e'-val-ist
Me-di'-na
me'di-o'-cre
me:di-oc'-ri-ty
med'-i-tate
med-i-ta'-tion
med'-i-ta-tive
med'-i-tat-or*‡
Med'-i-ter-ra'-ne-an
me'-di-um
me'-di-um-is'-tic
med'-lar
med'-ley
me-dul'-la
me-dul'-la ob-lon-ga'-ta
med'-ul-lar:y†
me-du'-sa
meek'-ly
meek'-ness
meer'-schaum
meet'-ing
meet'-ing-house
meet'-ly
meg'a-ce-phal'-ic
meg'a-ceph'-a-lous
meg'a-cy-cle
meg'a-ga-mete'†
meg'a-lith'-ic
meg'-a-lo-ce-phal'-ic
meg'-a-lo-ceph'-a-ly
meg-a-lo-ma'-ni:a
meg-a-lop'-o-lis
meg'-a-lo-pol'-i-tan
meg'-a-lo-saur
meg'a-phone
meg'a-pod
meg'a-scop'-ic
meg'a-spo-ran'-gi-um
meg'a-spore

238

meg:a-spo-ro-gen'-e-sis
meg'a-ton
me-gilp'
meg'-ohm-me-ter
me'-grim
mei'-o-nite
mei-o'-sis
mei-ot'-ic
mei'-ster*†
Mei'-ster-sing-er*†
me-lac'-o-nite
mel'-a-mine†
mel-an-cho'-li:a
mel-an-cho'-li-ac
mel'-an-chol-ic
mel'-an-chol:y
Me-lanch'-thon
Mel-a-ne'-sia
Mel-a-ne'-sian
me-lange'
me-lan'-ger*†
me-lan-geur'
me-lan'-ic
mel'-a-nin
mel'-a-nism
mel'-a-no
mel'-a-no-cyte
mel'-a-noid
mel-a-no'-ma
mel-a-no-ma-to'-sis
mel-a-no'-sis
mel-a-no-stib'-i-an
me-lan'-ter-ite
mel-an-tha'-ceous
mel'-a-phyre
Mel'-bourne
Mel'-chi-or
Mel-chiz'-e-dek
meld'-er
Mel-e-a'-ger
me'-lee
me-le'-na
me-lez'-i-tose
me-li-a'-ceous
mel-i-bi'-ose†
mel'-ic
Mel'-i-cent
mel'-i-lite
mel'-i-lot
me'-lio-rate*
me-lio-ra'-tion*
me'-lio-ra-tive*
me'-lio-rism*
me'-lio-rist*
me-lior'-i-ty*†
mel'-is-mat'-ic
Me-lis'-sa
mel'-i-tose

mel-lif'-er-ous
mel-lif'-lu-ence
mel-lif'-lu-ent
mel-lif'-lu-ous
mel'-li-tate
mel-lit'-ic
mel'-low
mel'-low-ness
me-lo'-de-on
me-lo'-di:a
me-lod'-ic
me-lod'-i-cal-ly
me-lo'-di-on
me-lo'-di-ous
me-lo'-di-ous-ly
mel'-o-dist
mel'-o-dize
mel'o-dra-ma
mel'o-dra-mat'-ic
mel'o-dram'-a-tist
mel'-o-dy
mel'-oid
mel:o-ma'-ni:a
mel'-on
mel'-o-nite
mel'-o-plas-ty
Me'-los
Mel-pom'-e-ne
Mel'-rose
melt-a:bil'-i-ty
melt'-a:ble
melt'-er
mel'-ton
Mel'-ville
mem'-ber
mem'-ber-ship
mem-bra-na'-ceous
mem'-bra-nate
mem'-brane
mem'-bra-nous
me-men'-to
me-men'-tos
Mem'-non
mem'-oir
mem-o-ra-bil'i:a
mem-o-ra-bil'-i-ty
mem'-o-ra-ble
mem-o-ran'-da
mem-o-ran'-dum
me-mo'-ri-al
me-mo'-ri-al-ist
me-mo'-ri-al-ize
me-mo'-ri-al-iz-ing
me-mo'-ri-am
mem'-o-ries
mem-o-ri-za'-tion
mem'-o-rize
mem'-o-riz-er

MEMORIZING

mem'-o-riz-ing
mem'-o-ry
Mem'-phis
men'-ace
men'-ac-ing
men'-ac-ing-ly
men-a-di'-one
mé-nage'
me-nag'-er-ie
me-naph'-thone
men-ar'-che*†
Menc'-ken
men-da'-cious
men-da'-cious-ly
men-dac'-i-ty
Men'-del
men-de-le'-vi-um
Men-de'-lian
Men'-dels-sohn
men-de-lye'-ev-ite
mend'-er
men'-di-can-cy
men'-di-cant
men-dic'-i-ty
Men-e-la'-us
men'-folk
men-ha'-den
men'-hir
me'-nial
Mé'-ni-ère'
men'-i-lite
me-nin'-ge-al
me-nin'-ges
me-nin-gi-o'-ma
men'-in-git'-ic
men-in-gi'-tis
me-nin'-go-cele
me-nin-go-coc'-cus
me-nin-go-my-e-li'-tis
me-nis'-cus
Men'-no-nite*
me-nol'-o-gy
Me-nom'-i-nee
men-o-pau'-sal*
men'-o-pause
Me-no'-rah
men-or-rha'-gia
men'-ses
men'-stru-al
men'-stru-ate
men-stru-a'-tion
men'-stru-um
men-su-ra-bil'-i-ty*
men'-su-ra-ble*
men'-su-ral
men-su-ra'-tion
men'-su-ra-tive
men'-tal

men-tal'-i-ty
men'-tal-ly
men-tha'-ceous
men-tha-di'-ene
men'-thane
men'-tha-nol
men'-the-none
men'-thol
men'-tho-lat-ed
men'-thyl
men'-ti-cide
men'-tion
men'-tion-a:ble
men'-tion-er
men'-tor
men'u
me-per'-i-dine
me-phen'-e-sin
Meph:is-toph'-e-les
meph'is-to-phe'-lian
me-phit'-ic
me-phi'-tis
me-pro'-ba-mate
mer-al'-lu-ride
mer'-can-tile
mer'-can-til-ism
mer-cap'-tan
mer-cap'-to
mer-cap-tom'-er-in
mer'-cap-tu'-ric
Mer-ca'-tor
mer'-ce-nar:y†
mer'-cer
mer'-cer-ize
mer'-cer-iz-ing
mer'-cer:y
mer'-chan-dise
mer'-chan-dis-er
mer'-chan-dis-ing
mer'-chant
mer'-chant-a:ble
mer'-chant-man
Mer'-cia
mer'-cies
mer'-ci-ful
mer'-ci-ful-ly
mer'-ci-ful-ness
mer'-ci-less
mer'-cu-rate
mer-cu'-ri-al
mer-cu'-ri-al-ism
mer-cu-ri-al'-i-ty
mer-cu'-ric
mer-cu'-ro-chrome
mer-cu'-rous
mer'-cu-ry
mer'-cy
Mer'-e-dith

mere'-ly
me-ren'-gue
me-re-ol'-o-gy
mer'-est
mer-e-tri'-cious
mer-gan'-ser
merge
mer'-gence
Mer'-gen-tha-ler
merg'-er
Mer'-i-den
me-rid'-i-an
me-rid'-i-o-nal
me-ringue'
me-ri'-no
me-ri'-nos
mer'-i:on
mer'-ism
mer'i-stem
mer'i-ste-mat'-ic
mer'-it
mer'-it-ed
mer-i-to'-ri-ous
mer'-lin
mer'-maid
mer'-man
mer'o-blas'-tic
mer'-o-crine
mer-o-gon'-ic
me-rog'-o-ny
mer-o-he'-dral
Mer'-o-pe
me-ro'-pi:a
me-rot'-o-mize
Mer'-o-vin'-gian
me-rox'-ene
mer'-ri-ly
Mer'-ri-mac
mer'-ri-ment
mer'-ri-ness
mer'-ry
mer'-ry=an'-drew
mer'-ry=go=round
mer'-ry-mak-er
mer'-ry-mak-ing
mer-sal'-yl
Mer'-sey
Mer-thi'-o-late
me'-sa
mes:a-con'-ic
mes'-al-li-ance'*†
mes'-ar-te-ri'-tis†
mes-cal'
mes'-ca-line*
mes-dames'
mes-en-ce-phal'-ic
mes-en-ceph'a-lon
me-sen'-chy-ma*†

mes-en'-chy-mal
mes-en-chym'-a-tous
mes'-en-chyme
mes-en-ter'-ic
mes-en-ter-i'-tis
mes-en'-ter-on
mes'-en-ter:y
mesh'-work
mesh'y
me'-si-al†
mes'-ic*
mes'-i-dine
mes'-i-tyl
me-sit'-y-lene
mes-mer'-ic
mes'-mer-ism
mes-mer-i:za'-tion
mes'-mer-ize
mes'-mer-iz-ing
mes'-nal-ty*†
mesne
mes'o-blast
mes:o-car'-di:a
mes'o-carp
mes'o-ce-phal'-ic
mes'o-derm
mes'o-der'-mal
me-sog'-na-thous†
mes'o-lite
mes'o-mer'-ic
me-som'-er-ism
mes'-on
mes'o-neph'-ric
mes'o-neph'-ros
mes'o-phyll
Mes-o-po-ta'-mi:a
mes'o-sphere
mes'o-the'-li-um
mes'o-tron
mes'-ox-al'-ic
mes-ox'-a-lyl
Mes'o-zo'-ic
mes-quite'
mes'-sage
mes'-sa-line'
mes'-sen-ger
Mes-si'-ah
Mes'-si-an'-ic
mes-sieurs'
mess'-i-ness
mess'-mate
messy
mes-ti'-zo
mes-ti'-zos
mes'-yl
me-tab'-a-sis
met:a-bi'-o-sis
met:a-bi-ot'-ic

241

met'a-bol'-ic
me-tab'-o-lism
me-tab'-o-lite
me-tab'-o-liz-a:ble
me-tab'-o-lize
met'a-bo'-rate
met'a-car'-pus
met'-age
met'a-ge-net'-ic
me-tag'-na-thous
me-tag'-no-my
me-tag'-ra-phy
met'-al
met'al-de-hyde
met'al-ing
met'-al-ist
me-tal'-lic
met-al-lif'-er-ous
met'-al-line
met'-al-lize
me-tal'-lo-graph'-ic
met-al-log'-ra-phy
met'-al-loid
met-al-lur'-gic
met'al-lur'-gi-cal
met-al-lur'-gist
met'-al-lur-gy
met-al-os'-co-py
met'-al-ware
met'-al-work
met'-al-work-ing
met'a-mer
met'a-mer'-ic
me-tam'-er-ism†
me-tam'-er-ized†
met:a-mor'-phic
met:a-mor'-phism
met:a-mor'-phose
met:a-mor'-pho-ses
met:a-mor'-pho-sis
met'-a-phor
met-a-phor'-i-cal
met'-a-phrase
met:a-phys'-i-cal
met:a-phy-si'-cian
met'a-phys-ics
met'a-pro'-tein
met-ar-te'-ri-ole
met:a-so-ma-to'-sis
met'a-sta-ble
me-tas'-ta-sis
met'a-stat'-ic
met:a-tar'-sal
met:a-tar'-sus
me-tath'-e-sis
met:a-tho'-rax
Met:a-zo'a

me-tem-psy-cho'-sis*†
met-en-ceph'-a-lon
me'-te-or
me-te-or'-ic
me'-te-or-ite
me-te-or'-it-ics
me-te-or'-o-graph
me-te-o-rog'-ra-phy*†
me'-te-or-oid
me-te-or:o-log'-i-cal
me-te-o-rol'-o-gist*†
me-te-o-rol'-o-gy*†
me-te-or-om'-e-ter
me'-te-or-o-scope
me-te-or-os'-co-py
me'-ter
meth-ac'-ry-late
meth-a:cryl'-ic
meth'a-done
meth-al'-lyl
meth'-ane
meth'-a-nol†
meth-a-no'-lic
meth-a-nol'-y-sis
meth-a-nom'-e-ter
meth-an'-the-line
me-theg'-lin
me-the'-na-mine
meth'-ene
meth'-ide
meth'-i:on'-ic
me-thi'-o-nine
me'-thi-um
meth'-od
me-thod'-i-cal
me-thod'-i-cal-ly
Meth'-od-ism
Meth'-od-ist
meth'-od-ize
meth-od-ol'-o-gy
me-tho'-ni-um
me-thox'y-car'-bon-yl*†
meth-ox'-yl
Me-thu'-se-lah
meth'-yl
meth-yl-al'
meth'-yl-a:mine'†
meth'-yl-ate†
meth'-yl-ene†
meth-yl-en'-i:mine
meth'-yl-eth'-yl-pyr'-i-dine
me-thyl'-ic
me-thyl'-i-dyne
meth-yl-naph'-tha-lene
meth'-yl-ol-u:re'a
me-tic-u-los'-i-ty
me-tic'-u-lous

mé-tier'
me-ton'-y-my
met'-ope*†
me-top'-ic
met'-o-pon*
met-o-pos'-co-py
Met'-ra-zol
met'-ric
met'-ri-cal
me-tri'-cian
met'-ri-cize
met'-ri-fy
me-tri'-tis
me-trol'-o-gist
me-trol'-o-gy
met'-ro-nome
met'-ro-nom'-ic
me:tro-nym'-ic
met'-ro-pole
me-trop'-o-lis
met'-ro-pol'-i-tan
Met'-ter-nich
met'-tle
met'-tled
met'-tle-some
mev'-a-lon'-ic
Mex'-i-can
Mex'-i-co
Mey'-er-beer
me-zer'e-um
mez'-za-nine'
mez'-zo
mez'-zo=so-pra'no
mez'-zo-tint
mho'-me-ter
Mi-am'i
mi-ar'-gy-rite
mi-as'-ma
mi'-ca
mi-ca'-ceous
Mi'-cah
mi-cel'-lar
mi-celle'
Mi'-chael
Mich'-ael-mas
Mi-chel-an'-ge-lo
Mi-chele'
Mich'-i-gan
Mich'-i-gan-ite
mi'-cren-ceph'-a-lous
mi'-cri-nite
mi'-cro-a:nal'-y-sis
mi'-cro-an-a-lyt'-ic
mi'-crobe
mi-cro'-bi-al
mi-cro'-bic
mi-cro'-bi-cide
mi'-cro-ceph'-a-ly

mi'-cro-cop:y
mi'-cro-cosm
mi'-cro-cos'-mic
mi'-cro-film
mi'-cro-graph
mi'-cro-graph'-ic
mi-crog'-ra-phy
mi'-cro-groove
mi'-cro-lite
mi-cro-me-rit'-ics
mi-crom'-e-ter
mi-cro-met'-ri-cal
mi-crom'-e-try
mi'-cro-mho
mi'-cron
mi'-cron-ize†
mi-cro-or'-ga-nism*†
mi'-cro-phone
mi'-cro-phon'-ic
mi'-cro-phyte
mi-crop'-si:a
mi-cro-py-rom'-e-ter
mi'-cro-scope
mi'-cro-scop'-ic
mi-cro-scop'-i-cal-ly
mi-cros'-co-py
mi'-cro-seism
mi'-cro-some
mi'-cro-spe'-cies
mi'-cro-spore
mi'-cro-stom'-a-tous
mi'-cro-tome
mi-crot'-o-my
mi'-cro-wave
mic'-tu-rate
mic-tu-ri'-tion
mid'-af'-ter-noon'*
Mi'-das
mid'-brain
mid'-day'
mid'-den
mid'-dle
mid'-dle=aged'
mid'-dle-man
mid'-dle=of=the=road'
  (adj.)
mid'-dle-weight
mid'-dling
mid'-dy
midg'-et
mi-di'
Mid'-i-an
mid'-i:ron
mid'-land
Mid-lo'-thi-an
mid'-most
mid'-night
mid'-rib

mid'-riff
mid'-ship-man
mid'-ships
mid'-stream'
mid'-sum'-mer
mid=Vic-to'-ri-an
mid'-way
mid-week'-ly
mid'-west'
mid'-west'-ern
Mid-west'-ern-er
mid'-wife
mid'-wife-ry
mid'-win'-ter
mid'-year'
mien
might
might'-i-er
might'-i-ly
might'-i-ness
might'y
mi-gnon'
mi'-gnon-ette'
mi'-graine
mi-grain'-oid
mi'-grant
mi'-grate
mi-gra-tet'-ics
mi'-grat-ing
mi-gra'-tion
mi'-gra-to-ry
mi-ka'-do
mi-la'-dy
Mi-lan'
Mil-a-nese'†
milch
mil'-dew
mil'-dew-proof
mil'-dew:y
mild'-ly
mild'-ness
Mil'-dred
mile'-age
mile'-post
mile'-stone
mil-i-a'-ri:a
mil'-i-ar:y†
mi-lieu'
mil'-i-tan-cy
mil'-i-tant
mil'-i-tant-ly
mil'-i-tar'-i-ly†
mil'-i-ta-rism†
mil'-i-ta-rist
mil'-i-ta-ris'-tic
mil-i-ta-ri-za'-tion
mil'-i-ta-rize
mil'-i-ta-riz-ing

mil'-i-tar:y†
mil'-i-tate
mil'-i-tat-ing
mi-li'-tia
mi-li'-tia-man
mil'-i-um
milk bar
milk'-er
milk'=fed
milk'-i-ness
milk' leg
milk'=liv-ered
milk'-man
milk run
milk shake
milk'-sop
milk'-weed
milk'-wood
milk'y
Mil-lay'
mill'-board
mill'-dam
mil-le-nar'-i-an†
mil'-le-nar:y†
mil-len'-ni-al
mil-len'-ni-um
mil'-le-pede
mill'-er
mil-les'-i-mal
mil'-let
mil'-li-am'-me-ter
mil'-li-am'-pere
mil'-liard
mil'-li-ar:y†
mil'-li-gram
Mil'-li-kan
mil'-li-me-ter
mil'-li-mi'-cron
mil'-li-ner
mil'-li-ner:y
mill'-ing
mil'-lion
mil-lion-aire'
mil'-lionth
mil'-li-pede
mill'-pond
mill'-race
mill'=run' (adj.)
mill'-stone
mill'-stream
mill wheel
mill'-wright
Milne
mi'-lo
mi-lord'
Milque'-toast
mil-reis'
Mil-ti'-a-des

Mil-ton'-ic
Mil-wau'-kee
mim'-e-o-graph
mim'-er
mi-me'-sis
mi-met'-ic
mim'-e-tite
mim'-ic
mim'-icked
mim'-ick-er
mim'-ick-ing
mim'-ic-ry
mim'-ing
mi-mo'-sa
mim'-o-sa'-ceous
mi-mo'-sine
mim'-o-type
min'-a:ble
mi-na'-cious
min'-a-ret'
min'a-to-ri-ly
min'a-to-ry
mince'-meat
mince' pie'
minc'-er
minc'-ing
minc'-ing-ly
Min'-del
mind'-er
mind'-ful
mind'-less
mind read'-ing
mi'-nen-wer'-fer
min'-er
min-er-ag'-ra-phy
min'-er-al
min'-er-al-ize
min'-er-al-iz-er
min'-er-al-og'-i-cal
min-er-al'-o-gist
min-er-al'-o-gy
Mi-ner'-va
min-e-stro'-ne*
mi-nette'
min'-gle
min'-gling
min'-i-a'-ceous
min'-i-a-ture
min'-i-a-tur-ist
Min'-i:é
min'-i-fy
min'-i-kin
min'-im
min'-i-mal
min-i-mi-za'-tion
min'-i-mize
min'-i-miz-er
min'-i-mum

min'-ing
min'-ion
min'-is-ter
min'-is-te'-ri-al
min-is-te'-ri-um
min'-is-trant
min-is-tra'-tion
min'-is-tries
min'-is-try
min'-i-track
min'-i-um
min'-i-ver
Min-ne-ap'-o-lis
min'-ne-sing-er
Min-ne-so'-ta
Min-ne-so'-tan
min'-now
Mi-no'-an
mi-nom'-e-ter
mi'-nor
Mi-nor'-ca
mi-nor'-i-ty
Mi'-nos
Min'-o-taur
min'-ster
min'-strel
min'-strel-sy
mint'-age
mint'-er
min'-u-end
min-u-et'
Min'-u-it
mi'-nus
mi-nus'-cu-lar
min'us-cule
min'-ute (60 seconds)
mi-nute' (small)
min'-ute hand
min'-ute-ly (every minute)
mi-nute'-ly (small)
min'-ute-man
mi-nute'-ness
mi-nu'-tia
mi-nu'-ti-ae
Mi'-o-cene
mi-o'-sis
mi-ot'-ic
mir'-a-belle'
mi-rab'-i-lite
mir'-a-cle
mi-rac'-u-lous
mi-rac'-u-lous-ly
mir'-a-dor
mi-rage'
Mi-ran'-da
mired
Mir'-i-am

mir'-ing
mir'-ror
mirth'-ful
mirth'-less
mir'y
mir'-za
mis-ad-ven'-ture
mis-al-li'-ance
mis'-an-thrope
mis'-an-throp'-ic
mis'-an-throp'-i-cal-ly
mis-an'-thro-pist
mis-an'-thro-py
mis-ap-pli-ca'-tion
mis'-ap-plied'
mis'-ap-ply'
mis'-ap-pre-hend'
mis-ap-pre-hen'-sion
mis-ap-pro'-pri-ate
mis-ap-pro-pri-a'-tion
mis-ar-range'-ment
mis-be-com'-ing
mis-be-got'-ten
mis-be-have'
mis-be-hav'-ing
mis-be-hav'-ior†
mis-be-lief'
mis-be-lieve'
mis-be-liev'-er
mis-cal'-cu-late
mis-cal-cu-la'-tion
mis-call'
mis-car'-riage
mis-car'-ried
mis-car'-ry
mis-car'-ry-ing
mis'-ceg:e-na'-tion
mis-cel-la-ne'-i-ty
mis-cel-la'-ne:ous
mis'-cel-la-ny
mis-chance'
mis'-chief
mis'-chief=mak-er
mis'-chie-vous
mis'-chie-vous-ly
mis-ci-bil'-i-ty
mis'-ci-ble
mis-con-ceive'
mis-con-cep'-tion
mis-con'-duct
mis-con-struc'-tion
mis'-con-strue'
mis'-cre-ance
mis'-cre-an-cy
mis'-cre-ant
mis'-cre-ate
mis-cre-a'-tion
mis-cue'

mis-deal'
mis-deed'
mis-de-mean'-ant
mis'-de-mean'-or
mis-di-rect'
mis-di-rec'-tion
mis-do'-er
mis-do'-ing
mi'-ser
mis'-er-a-ble
mis'-er-a-bly
Mi-se-re're*†
mi-ser'-i-cord*†
mi'-ser-li-ness
mi'-ser-ly
mis'-er:y
mis-fea'-sance
mis-fea'-sor
mis-fire'
mis'-fit'
mis-for'-tune
mis-gave'
mis-give'
mis-giv'-ing
mis-gov'-ern
mis-gov'-ern-ment
mis-guid'-ance†
mis-guide'
mis-guid'-ed
mis-han'-dle
mis-han'-dling
mis'-hap
mis'-hear'
mis'-in-form'
mis'-in-for-ma'-tion
mis-in-ter'-pret
mis'-in-ter-pre-ta'-tion
mis-judge'
mis-judg'-ment
mis-laid'
mis-lay'
mis-lay'-ing
mis-lead'
mis-lead'-ing
mis-led'
mis-like'
mis-man'-age
mis-man'-age-ment
mis-match'
mis-mate'
mis-mat'-ing
mis-name'
mis-no'-mer
mi-sog'-a-mist†
mi-sog'-a-my†
mi-sog'-y-nist†
mi-sog'-y-ny†
mi-sol'-o-gy†

mis:o-ne'-ism
mis-place'
mis-place'-ment
mis'-print
mis-pri'-sion
mis'-pro-nounce'
mis-pro-nounc'-ing
mis-pro-nun-ci-a'-tion
mis-quo-ta'-tion
mis'-quote'
mis'-quot'-ing
mis'-read'
mis'-rep-re-sent'
mis-rep-re-sen-ta'-tion
mis-rule'
mis-rul'-ing
mis'-sal
mis-shape'
mis-shap'-en†
mis'-sile
mis'-sil-eer'
mis'-sile-ry
miss'-ing
mis'-sion
mis'-sion-ar-ies†
mis'-sion-ar:y†
Mis-sis-sip'-pi
Mis-sis-sip'-pi-an
mis'-sive
Mis-sou'-ri
Mis-sou'-ri-an
mis-speak'
mis-spell'
mis-spelled'
mis-spell'-ing
mis-spelt'
mis-spend'
mis-spent'
mis-state'
mis-state'-ment
mis-step'
mis-tak'-a:ble
mis-take'
mis-tak'-en
mis-tak'-en-ly
mis-tak'-ing
mis'-ter
mist'-i-ness
mis'-tle-toe
mis-took'
mis'-tral
mis-treat'
mis-treat'-ment
mis'-tress
mis-tri'-al
mis-trust'
mis-trust'-ful
mist'y

mis-un-der-stand'
mis-un-der-stand'-ing
mis-un-der-stood'
mis-us'-age†
mis-use'
mis-us'-ing
Mitch'-ell
mi'-ter
Mith-ra'-ic
Mith'-ra-ism
Mith-ri-da'-tes
mith-ri-da'-tism†
mit'-i-ga-ble
mit'-i-gate
mit'-i-gat-ing
mit-i-ga'-tion
mit'-i-ga-tive
mit'-i-ga-tor
mit'-i-ga-to-ry
mi'-tis
mi-to-chon'-dri:a
mi-to'-sis
mi-tot'-ic
mi'-trail-leuse'†
mi'-tral
mi'-trate
mit'-ten
mit'-ti-mus
mix'-er
mix'-ture
mix'=up
Miz'-pah
miz'-zen
miz'-zen-mast
mne-mon'-ic
Mne-mos'-y-ne
mo'a
Mo'-ab-ite
moan'-ing
mobbed
mob'-bing
mob'-cap
mo'-bile
mo-bil'-i-ty
mo-bi-li-za'-tion†
mo'-bi-lize†
mo-bil-om'-e-ter
Mö'-bi-us
mob-oc'-ra-cy
moc'-ca-sin
mo'-cha
mo-chi'-la
mock'-er
mock'-er:y
mock'-ing
mock'-ing-bird
mock'-ing-ly
mod'-al†

mod'-al-ism†
mo-dal'-i-ty
mod'-el
mod'-eled
mod'-el-ing
mod'-er-ate
mod'-er-ate-ly
mod'-er-at-ing
mod-er-a'-tion
mod'-er-a'-to*†
mod'-er-a-tor
mod'-ern
mod'-ern-ism
mod'-ern-ist
mod'-ern-is'-tic
mo-der'-ni-ty
mod-ern-i:za'-tion
mod'-ern-ize
mod'-ern-iz-ing
mod'-ern-ly
mod'-ern-ness
mod'-est
mod'-est-ly
mod'-es-ty
mod'-i-cum
mod'-i-fi'-a:ble
mod-i-fi-ca'-tion
mod'-i-fi-ca-to-ry
mod'-i-fied
mod'-i-fi-er
mod'-i-fy
mod'-i-fy-ing
mo-dil'-lion
mo-di'-o-lus
mod'-ish
mo-diste'
Mo'-dred
mod-u-la-bil'-i-ty
mod'-u-lar
mod'-u-late
mod-u-la'-tion
mod'-u-la-tor
mod'-u-la-to-ry
mod'-ule
mod'-u-lus
mo'-dus op:e-ran'-di
mo'-dus vi-ven'-di
mo'-gul
mo'-hair
Mo-ham'-med
Mo-ham'-med-an
Mo-ha'-ve
Mo'-hawk
Mo-hi'-can
mo'-hole
Mo-ho-ro'-vi-cic
moi'-dore
moi'-e-ty

moil'-ing
moi'-ra
moi-ré'
moist'-en*†
moist'-en-er*†
moist'-ly
moist'-ness
mois'-ture
mois'-ture-proof
mo'-lal
mo-lal'-i-ty
mo'-lar
mo-lar'-i-ty
mo'-la-ry
mo-las'-ses
mold
mold'-a:ble
Mol-da'-vi:a
mold'-board
mold'-er
mold'-i-ness
mold'-ing
mold'y
mo-lec'-u-lar
mol'-e-cule
mole'-hill
mole'-skin
mo-lest'
mo-les-ta'-tion
mo-lest'-er
Mo-lière'
Mo-li'-na
Mo'-li-nism†
mol-les'-cent
mol-li-fi-ca'-tion
mol'-li-fied
mol'-li-fy
mol'-li-fy-ing
mol'-li-sol
mol-lus'-coid
mol'-lusk
Mol'-ly
mol'-ly-cod-dle
mo'-loch
Mo-lo-kai'
Mo'-lo-tov
mol'-ten
molt'-er
Mo-luc'-ca
mo-lyb'-date
mo-lyb'-de-nite
mo-lyb'-de-num
mo-lyb'-dic
mo-lyb-do-me'-nite
mo-lyb'-dous
mol'-y-site
mo'-ment
mo'-men-tar'-i-ly†

mo'-men-tar:y†
mo'-ment-ly
mo-men'-tous
mo-men'-tum
mom'-ism
Mon'a-can
mon'-a-chal
mon'-a-chism
Mon'a-co
mo'-nad*†
mon-a-del'-phous
mo-nad'-ic†
mon-ad-is'-tic†
mo-nad'-nock
mo-nan'-drous
mo-nan'-dry
mon'-arch
mo-nar'-chal
mo-nar'-chi-al
mo-nar'-chi-an-ism
mo-nar'-chic
mo-nar'-chi-cal
mon'-ar-chism*†
mon'-ar-chist*†
mon'-ar-chy*
mon-ar-tic'-u-lar
mon'-as-te'-ri-al
mon'-as-ter:y
mo-nas'-tic
mo-nas'-ti-cism
mon'-a:tom'-ic
mon-ax'-i-al
mon'-a-zite
Mon'-day
Mo-nel'
mo-ne'-sia
Mo-net'
mon-e-tar'-i-ly†
mon'-e-tar:y†
mon'-e-tite
mon-e-ti-za'-tion
mon'-e-tize
mon'-ey
mon'-ey-bags
mon'-ey-eyed
mon'-ey-mak-er
mon'-ey-mak-ing
mon'-ey or-der
mon'-eys
mon'-ey-wort
mon'-ger
Mon'-gol
Mon-go'-li:a
Mon-go'-li-an
mon'-gol-ism
Mon'-gol-oid†
mon'-goose
mon'-grel

Mon'-i-ca
mon'-i-ker
mo-nim'-o-lite
mon'-ism
mon'-ist
mo-nis'-tic
mo-ni'-tion
mon'-i-tor
mon-i-to'-ri-al
mon'-i-tor-ship
mon'-i-to-ry
mon'-i-tress
monk'-er:y
mon'-key
mon'-key-ish
mon'-key-pod
mon'-key pot
mon'-keys
mon'-key-shine
mon'-key wrench
monk'-hood
monk'-ish
monks'-hood
Mon'-mouth
mon:o-ac'-e-tin
mon'o-ac'-id
mon-o-a:cid'-ic
mon'o-am'-ide
mon'o-a:mine'
mon'o-ba'-sic*
mon'o-car'-pous
mon'o-chord
mon'o-chro-mat'-ic
mon:o-chro'-ma-tor
mon'o-chrome
mon'o-chro'-mous
mo-noch'-ro-nous
mon'-o-cle
mon'o-coque
mon'o-cot-y-le'-don
mo-noc'-ra-cy
mon'o-crot'-ic
mo-noc'-u-lar
mon:o-dac'-tyl-ism*
mon:o-dac'-ty-lous
mo-nod'-ic
mo-nod'-i-cal-ly
mon'o-dra'-ma
mon'-o-dy
mo-noe'-cious
mon'o-gam'-ic
mo-nog'-a-mist
mo-nog'-a-mous
mo-nog'-a-my
mon'o-gen'-e-sis
mon'o-ge-net'-ic
mon'o-gen'-ic
mo-nog'-e-nism

mo-nog'-e-ny
mo-nog'-o-ny
mon'o-gram
mon'o-gram-mat'ic
mon'o-grammed
mon'o-graph
mo-nog'-ra-pher
mon'o-graph'ic
mo-nog'-y-ny
mo-nol'-a-try
mon'o-lith
mon'o-lith'-ic
mon'o-log
mo-nol'-o-gist
mon'o-logue
mo-nol'-o-gy
mon'o-ma'-chy
mon'o-ma'-ni:a
mon'o-ma'-ni-ac
mon'o-ma-ni'-a-cal
mon'o-mer
mo-nom'-er-ous
mon'o-me-tal'-lic
mon'o-met'-al-lism
mon'-om'-e-ter
mo-no'-mi-al
Mo-non-ga-he'-la
mon'o-nu-cle-o'-sis
mon'o-plane
mon'o-ple'-gi:a
mon:o-po'-di-um
mo-nop'-o-list
mo-nop'-o-lis'-tic
mo-nop'-o-li-za'-tion
mo-nop'-o-lize
mo-nop'-o-ly
mo-nop'-so-ny
mon'o-rail
mon:o-sep'-al-ous
mon'o-spor'-ous*†
mon'o-stome
mon'o-strophe*†
mon'o-syl-lab'-ic
mon'o-syl'-la-ble
mon'o-the-ism
mon'o-the-ist
mon'o-the-is'-tic
mon'o-tone
mo-not'-o-nous
mo-not'-o-ny
mon'o-treme
mo-not'-ri-chous
mo-not'-ro-py
Mon'o-type
mon'o-typ'-ic
mon'o-va'-lent
mon-ox'-ide
Mon-roe' Doc'-trine

Mon-ro'-vi:a
mon-sei-gneur'
mon-sieur'
mon-si'-gnor
mon-soon'
mon'-ster
mon'-strance
mon-stros'-i-ty
mon'-strous
mon-tage'
Mon-taigne'
Mon-tan'a†
Mon-tan'-an
Mon'-te Car'-lo
Mon'-te-ne'-grin
Mon'-te-ne'-gro
Mon'-te-rey'
Mon'-ter-rey'
Mon'-tes-quieu'
Mon'-tes-so'-ri
Mon-te-vi-de'o†
Mon-te-zu'-ma
Mont-gol-fier'
Mont-gom'-er:y
month'-ly
Mon-ti-cel'-lo
mon-tic'-u-late
mon'-ti-cule
Mont-mar'-tre
mont-mo-ril'-lon-ite*†
Mont-pe'-lier
Mon'-tre-al'
mon-troy'-dite†
mon'-u-ment
mon-u-men'-tal
mon'-zo-nite
mood'-i-ly
mood'-i-ness
mood'y
mooed
moo'-ing
moon'-beam
moon=blind
moon'-calf
moon'-eye
moon'-fish
moon'-less
moon'-light
moon'-lit
moon'-rise
moon'-shine
moon'-shin-er
moon'-stone
moon'-struck
moor'-age
moor'-hen
moor'-ing
Moor'-ish

moor'-land
moped
mop'-ing
mop'-pet
mop'-ping
mo-quette'
mo'-ra
mo-ra'-ceous
mo-raine'
mo-rain'-ic
mor'-al
mo-rale'
mor'-al-ism
mor'-al-ist
mor'-al-is'-tic
mo-ral'-i-ty
mor-al-i:za'-tion
mor'-al-ize'
mor'-al-ly
mo-rass'
mor-a-to'-ri-um
mor'-a-tor:y†
Mo-ra'-vi-an
mo-ra'-vite
mo-ray'
mor'-bid
mor-bid'-i-ty
mor'-bid-ly
mor-bif'-ic
mor-bose'
mor-da'-cious
mor-dac'-i-ty
mor'-dan-cy
mor'-dant (chemical for
    dyeing; *adj.*)
Mor'-de-cai
mor'-dent (musical grace)
mo-reen'
mo-rel'-lo
mo-ren'-cite
more-o'ver
mo'-res
Mor'-gan
mor'-ga-nat'-ic
Mor'-gan-ton
Mor'-gan-town
Mor'-gen-thau
morgue
mor'-i-bund
mor-i-bun'-di-ty
mo-rin'-done
mo'-ri-on
Mor'-ley
Mor'-mon
Mor'-mon-ism
Mor'-mon-ite
morn'-ing

morn'-ing glo'-ry
morn'-ing star
Mo'-ro
Mo-roc'-can
Mo-roc'-co
mo'-ron
mo-ron'-ic
mo-rose'
mo-rose'-ly
mo-rose'-ness
mo-ros'-i-ty
mor'-pheme
mor-phe'-mics
Mor'-phe:us
mor'-phine
mor-phog'-ra-phy
mor'-pho-line
mor-pho-log'-ic
mor-pho-log'-i-cal
mor-phol'-o-gist
mor-phol'-o-gy
mor-phom'-e-try
mor-pho'-sis
mor-phot'-o-my
mor'-ris
mor'-row
mor'-sal
mor'-sel
mor'-tal
mor-tal'-i-ty
mor'-tal-ly
mor'-tar
mor'-tar-board
mort'-gage
mort'-ga-gee'
mort'-gag-ing
mort'-ga-gor'
mor-ti'-cian
mor-ti-fi-ca'-tion
mor'-ti-fied
mor'-ti-fy
mor'-ti-fy-ing
Mor'-ti-mer
mor'-tise
mor'-tis-er
mor'-tis-ing
Mor'-ton
mor'-tu-ar:y†
mor'-u-la
mo-sa'-ic
mo-sa'-i-cism
mos'-cha-tel'
Mos'-cow
Mo-selle'
Mo'-ses
mo'-ses-ite
Mos'-lem
mosque

251

mos-qui'-to
mos-qui'-toes
moss'-back
moss'=grown
moss'-i-er
moss'-i-ness
moss'y
most'-ly
Mo'-sul
mo-tel'
mo-tet'
moth'=eat-en
moth'-er
moth'-er-hood
moth'-er=in=law
moth'-er-land
moth'-er-less
moth'-er-li-ness
moth'-er-ly
moth'-er=of=pearl
moth'-proof
mo-tif'
mo'-tile
mo-til'-i-ty
mo'-tion
mo'-tion-less
mo'-ti-vate
mo'-ti-vat-ing
mo-ti-va'-tion
mo'-tive
mo'-tive-less
mo-tiv'-i-ty
mot'-ley
mo'-tor
mo'-tor-boat
mo'-tor-bus
mo'-tor-cade
mo'-tor-car
mo'-tor-cy-cle
mo'-tor-cy-clist
mo-to'-ri-al
mo'-tor-ist
mo-tor-i:za'-tion
mo'-tor-ize
mo'-tor-man
mot'-tle
mot'-tled
mot'-tling
mot'-to
mot'-toes
mouf'-lon
mou-jik'
mou-lage'
mou-lin'
mount'-a:ble
moun'-tain
moun'-tain-eer'
moun'-tain-ous

moun'-te-bank
mount'-ed
mount'-er
mount'-ing
Mount Ver'-non
mourn'-er
mourn'-ful
mourn'-ful-ly
mourn'-ing
mous'-er
mouse'-tail
mouse'-trap
mous'-que-taire'
mousse-line'
Mous-sorg'-sky
mous'-tache
mous'y
mouth'-ful
mouth'-piece
mou'-ton
mov-a-bil'-i-ty
mov'-a:ble
mov'-ant
move'-ment
mov'-er
mov'-ie
mov'-ies
mov'-ing
mowed
mow'-er
mow'-ing
mown
Mo-zam-bique'
Mo'-zart
moz-zet'-ta
mu'-ce-dine
mu-ced'-i-nous
mu'-cic
mu'-cid
mu-cif'-er-ous
mu'-ci-lage
mu'-ci-lag'-i-nous
mu-cin'-o-gen
mu'-cin-oid
mu'-ci-no-lyt'-ic
mu'-ci-nous*†
muck'-er
muck'-rake
muck'y
mu'-coid
mu-coi'-dal
mu-co'-i-tin
mu'-co-lyt'-ic
mu-con'-ic
mu-co'-sa
mu-cos'-i-ty
mu'-cous (adj.)
mu'-cus (n.)

mud'-di-ly	mul'-ti-pli-a:ble
mud'-di-ness	mul'-ti-plic'-a-ble*†
mud'-dle	mul-ti-pli-cand'
mud'-dled	mul-ti-pli-ca'-tion
mud'-dy	mul-ti-pli-ca'-tive
mud'-fish	mul-ti-plic'-i-ty
mud'-guard	mul'-ti-plied
mu-ez'-zin	mul'-ti-pli-er
muf'-fin	mul'-ti-ply
muf'-fin-eer'	mul'-ti-ply-ing
muf'-fle	mul'-ti-tude
muf'-fler	mul-ti-tu'-di-nous
muf'-fling	mul'-ti-va'-lent
muf'-ti	mum'-ble
mug'-ger	mum'-bling
mug'-gi-ness	mum'-mer
mug'-ging	mum'-mer:y
mug'-gy	mum'-mi-fy
mu'-gi-ent	mum'-my
mug'-wump	Mun'-chau-sen
Muh'-len-berg	mun'-dane'
Muk'-den	mun'-go
mu-lat'-to	Mu'-nich
mu-lat'-toes	mu-nic'-i-pal
mul'-ber-ry	mu-nic-i-pal'-i-ty
mulch'-er	mu-nic'-i-pal-ize
mulct	mu-nif'-i-cence
mu'-le-teer'	mu-nif'-i-cent
mu-li-eb'-ri-ty	mu'-ni-ment
mul'-ish	mu-ni'-tion
mul'-lah	mu'-ral
mul'-lein	mu-rar'-i-um
mull'-er	Mu-rat'
mul'-let	mur'-der
mul'-li-gan	mur'-der-er
mul'-li-ga-taw'-ny	mur'-der-ess
mul'-lion	mur'-der-ous
mull'-ite	mu'-ri-at'-ic
mult-an'-gu-lar	Mu-ril'-lo
mul-ti-cel'-lu-lar	mu'-rine
mul'-ti-col'-ored	mu'-ri-um
mul'-ti-far'-i-ous†	murk'-i-er
mul'-ti-fid	murk'-i-ly
mul'-ti-form	murk'y
mul-ti-form'-i-ty*†	mur'-mur
Mul'-ti-graph	mur'-mur-ing
mul-ti-lat'-er-al	mur'-mur-ous
Mul'-ti-lith	Mur'-phy
mul-til'-o-quent	mur'-ra
Mul-tim'-e-ter	mur'-rain
mul-tim'-e-try	mur'-rhine
mul-ti-mil'-lion-aire'	mu-sa'-ceous
mul-tip'-a-ra	mus'-ca-dine
mul-tip'-a-rous	mus'-ca-rine
mul-ti-par'-tite	mus'-cat
mul'-ti-ped	mus'-ca-tel'
mul'-ti-ple	mus'-cle
mul'-ti-plex	mus'-cle=bound

mus-co-va'-do
Mus'-co-vite
Mus'-co-vy
mus'-cu-lar
mus-cu-lar'-i-ty
mus'-cu-la-ture
mus'-cu-lo-trop'-ic
mused
mu-se-og'-ra-phy
mu-se-ol'-o-gy
mus'-er
mu-sette'
mu-se'-um
mush'-room
mush'y
mu'-sic
mu'-si-cal
mu'-si-cale'
mu'-si-cal-ly
mu-si'-cian
mu-si-col'-o-gy
mus'-ing
musk deer
Mus-ke'-gon
mus'-kel-lunge
mus'-ket
mus-ke-teer'*†
mus'-ket-ry
musk'-mel-on
Mus-ko'-gee
musk'=ox
musk'=ox-en
musk'-rat
musk'y
mus'-lin
mus'-sel
Mus-so-li'-ni
muss'y
mus'-tache
mus'-tang
mus'-tard
mus'-te-line
mus'-ter
must'-i-ness*
must'y*
mu-ta-bil'-i-ty
mu'-ta-ble
mu'-ta-gen'-ic
mu'-tant
mu-ta-ro-ta'-tion
mu'-tase
mu'-tate
mu'-tat-ing
mu-ta'-tion
mu'-ta-tive
mut'-ed
mute'-ly
mute'-ness

mu'-ti-late
mu-ti-la'-tion
mu'-ti-la-tor
mu'-ti-neer'
mut'-ing
mu'-ti-nied
mu'-ti-nous
mu'-ti-ny
mu'-ti-ny-ing
mut'-ism
mut'-ter
mut'-ter-ing
mut'-ton
mut'-ton-head
mu'-tu-al
mu-tu-al'-ism
mu-tu-al'-i-ty
mu-tu-al-i:za'-tion
mu'-tu-al-ly
mu'-tu-el
mu'-tule
mu-zhik'
muz'-zle
muz'-zle=load-er
muz'-zling
my-al'-gia
My-an'-e-sin
my-as-the'-ni:a
my'-as-then'-ic
my-ce'-li-oid
my-ce'-li-um
My-ce'-nae
My-ce-nae'-an
my-ce-to'-ma
my-col'-o-gist
my-col'-o-gy
my-co-my'-cin
my-co'-sis
myc-ter'-ic
my-dri'-a-sine
my-dri'-a-sis
myd'-ri-at'-ic
my'-e-lin
my-e-li'-tis
my'-e-lo-cyte
my'-e-loid
my-e-lo-ma-to'-sis
my-e-lom'-a-tous
my-e-lop'-a-thy
my-e-lo'-sis
my'-na
my-o-car-di'-tis
my-o'-ma
my-op'-a-thy
my-o'-pi:a
my-op'-ic
my'-o-sin
my-o-si'-tis

my-os'-mine
my-ot'-o-my
myr'-i-ad
myr'-i-am-e-ter†
myr'-i-a-pod
my-ric'-e-tin
my-ric'-i-trin
myr'-i-cyl
myr-in-gi'-tis
myr-in-got'-o-my
my-ris'-tate
my-ris'-tic
myr-me-col'-o-gy
Myr'-mi-don
my-rob'-a-lan
My'-ron
myrrh
myrrh'-ic†
myr-ta'-ceous
myr'-tle
my-self'
My'-sore
mys-ta-gog'-ic
mys'-ter-ies
mys-te'-ri-ous
mys-te'-ri-ous-ly
mys-ter:y
mys'-tic
mys'-ti-cal
mys'-ti-cism
mys-ti-fi-ca'-tion
mys'-ti-fied
mys'-ti-fy
mys'-ti-fy-ing
mys'-ti-fy-ing-ly
mys-tique'
myth'-ic
myth'-i-cal
myth'-i-cal-ly
myth'-i-cist
myth'-i-cize
my-thog'-ra-pher
myth-o-log'-i-cal
my-thol'-o-gist
my-thol'-o-gy
myth-o-ma-'ni:a
myth'-o-poe'-ic
myx-e:dé'-ma
myx'-o-bac-te'-ri-al
myx-o-ma-to'-sis

N

nab'-bing
nab'-la
na'-bob
na-celle'
na'-cre

na'-cre-ous
na'-crite
na'-dir
nad'-or-ite
na-ga'-na
Na'-ga-sa'-ki
nag'-ging
Na-go'-ya
nah'-co-lite
Na'-hum
na'-iad*
nail'-er
nail'-wort
nain'-sook
Nai-ro'-bi
na-ive'
na-ive-té'
na'-ked
na'-ked-ness
nam'-by=pam'-by
name'-a:ble
name'-less
name'-ly
nam'-er
name'-sake
nam'-ing
Na-mur'
Na-nai'-mo
Nan'-cy
na'-nism
na-ni-za'-tion
nan-keen'
Nan'-king
na'-no-gram
na'-noid
Nan'-sen
Nantes
Nan-tuck'-et
na-ol'-o-gy
Na-o'-mi
na'-palm
nape
na'-per:y
na-phaz'-o-line
naph'-tha
naph'-tha-lene
naph'-tha-len'-ic
naph-thal'-ic
naph'-thene
naph'-the-nic
naph'-thi-o-nate
naph'-thi-on'-ic
naph'-thol
naph'-thol-sul-fon'-ic
naph'-tho-qui-none'†
naph-thox:y-a:ce'-tic
naph'-tho-yl

255

naph'-thyl
naph'-thyl-a:mine'†
naph'-thy-lene*
Na'-pi-er
na'-pi-form
nap'-kin
Na'-ples
Na-po'-le:on
Na-po-le-on'-ic
nap'-per
nap'-ping
nap'-ra-path
na-prap'-a-thy†
nar'-ce-ine
nar'-cis-sism
nar-cis-sist
nar-cis'-sus
nar'-co-lep-sy
nar-co-lep'-tic
nar-co'-ma
nar-co'-sis
nar-co-syn'-the-sis
nar-co-ther'-a-py
nar-cot'-ic
nar'-co-tism
nar'-co-tize
nar'-co-tol-ine
nard
nar-es†
nar'-gi-leh
nar'-i-al†
nar-in-gen'-in†
na-rin'-gin
nar-is†
Nar-ra-gan'-sett
nar-rat'-a:ble
nar'-ra-tage
nar-ra'-tion
nar'-ra-tive
nar'-ra-tor
nar'-row=gage' (adj.)
nar'-row-ly
nar'-row=mind'-ed
nar'-row-ness
nar'-thex
Nar-va'-ez
nar'-whal
na'-sal
na-sa'-lis
na-sal'-i-ty
na'-sal-ize
na'-sal-ly
nas'-cen-cy
nas'-cent
Nash'-ville
na'-si-on

na'-so-scope
Nas'-sau
nas'-tic
nas'-ti-ly
nas'-ti-ness
nas-tur'-tium
nas'-ty
na'-tal
Na-tal'
na'-tant
na-ta'-tion
na-ta-to'-ri-al
na-ta-to'-ri-um
na'-ta-to-ry
Natch'-ez
Na'-than
Na-than'-iel
na'-tion
na'-tion-al
na'-tion-al-ism
na'-tion-al-ist
na-tion-al-is'-tic
na-tion-al'-i-ty
na-tion-al-i:za'-tion
na'-tion-al-ize
na'-tion-al-ly
na'-tion-wide'
na'-tive
na'-tive=born'
na'-tive-ly
na'-tive-ness
na'-tiv-ism
na-tiv-is'-tic
na-tiv'-i-ty
na'-tri-um
na'-tro-lite†
na'-tron
na-troph'-i-lite
nat'-ti-ly
nat'-ty
nat'-u-ral
nat'-u-ral-ism
nat'-u-ral-ist
nat-u-ral-is'-tic
nat-u-ral-i:za'-tion
nat'-u-ral-ize
nat'-u-ral-ly
nat'-u-ral-ness
na'-ture
na'-tur-o-path
na-tur-op'-a-thy
naught
naugh'-ti-ly
naugh'-ti-ness
naugh'-ty
nau-ma'-chi:a
nau'-pli-us
Na-u'-ru

nau'-se:a
nau'-se-ate
nau'-se-at-ed
nau'-seous
nau'-ti-cal
nau'-ti-cal-ly
nau'-ti-lus
nau'-to-phone
Nav'a-ho (Nav'a-jo)
na'-val
nav'-ar†
Na-varre'
na'-vel
na-vic'-u-lar
na'-vies
nav-i-ga-bil'-i-ty
nav'-i-ga-ble
nav'-i-gate
nav'-i-ga'-tion
nav'-i-ga-tor
na'-vite
nav'-vy
na'-vy yard
Naz'-a-rene
Naz'-a-reth
Na'-zi
na'-zi-ism
na'-zism
Ne-an'-der-thal
Ne-a-pol'-i-tan
neap tide
near'-by'
Ne-arc'-tic
near'-est
near'-ly
near'-ness
near'-sight-ed
ne-ar-thro'-sis
neat'-herd
neat'-ly
neat'-ness
Ne'-bo
Ne-bras'-ka
Ne-bras'-kan
neb'-ris
Neb-u-chad-nez'-zar
neb'-u-la
neb'-u-lae
neb'-u-lar
ne-bu'-li-um
neb'-u-lize
neb-u-los'-i-ty
neb'-u-lous
nec'-es-sar'-i-ly†
nec'-es-sar:y†
ne-ces-si-tar'-i-an†
ne-ces-si-tar'-i-an-ism†

ne-ces'-si-tate
ne-ces'-si-ties
ne-ces'-si-tous
ne-ces'-si-tous-ly
ne-ces'-si-ty
neck'-band
neck'-cloth
Neck'-er
neck'-er-chief
neck'-ing
neck'-lace
neck'-line
neck'-piece
neck'-tie
neck'-wear
nec'-ro-bi-o'-sis
nec'-ro-log'-i-cal
ne-crol'-o-gist
ne-crol'-o-gy
nec'-ro-man-cer
nec'-ro-man-cy
ne-croph'-a-gous
ne-crop'-o-lis
ne'-crop-sy*‡
ne-cros'-co-py
nec'-ro-sin
ne-cro'-sis
ne-crot'-ic
nec'-ro-tize
ne-crot'-o-my
nec'-tar
nec-tar'-e-ous†
nec'-tar-ine'
nec'-ta-ry
need'-ful
need'-i-er
need'-i-est
need'-i-ness
nee'-dle
nee'-dle-fish
nee'-dle-ful
nee'-dle-like
nee'-dle-point
nee'-dler
need'-less
need'-less-ly
need'-less-ness
nee'-dle-wom-an†
nee'-dle-work
need'y
ne'er'=do=well
ne-far'-i-ous†
ne-gate'
ne-ga'-tion
neg'-a-tive
neg'-a-tive-ly
neg'-a-tiv-ism
neg'-a-tiv-is'-tic

257

neg-a-tiv'-i-ty
neg'-a-to-ry
neg'-a-tron
ne-glect'*†
ne-glect'-er*†
ne-glect'-ful*†
neg-li-gee'
neg'-li-gence
neg'-li-gent
neg'-li-gent-ly
neg-li-gi-bil'-i-ty
neg'-li-gi-ble
ne-go-tia-bil'-i-ty
ne-go'-tia-ble
ne-go'-ti-ate
ne-go'-ti-at-ing
ne-go-ti-a'-tion
ne-go'-ti-a-tor
Ne-grit'-ic
Ne'-gro
Ne'-groes
Ne'-groid
ne'-gus
Ne-he-mi'-ah
Neh'-ru
neigh
neigh'-bor
neigh'-bor-hood
neigh'-bor-ing
neigh'-bor-li-ness
neigh'-bor-ly
nei'-ther
nek'-ton
Nel'-son
ne-mat'-ic
nem'-a-to-ci'-dal
nem'-a-tode
nem-a-to-di'-a-sis
nem-a-tol'-o-gy
Nem'-bu-tal
Ne'-me-an
nem'-er-tine*†
ne-mes'-ic
nem'-e-sis
ne-moph'-i-ly
nem'-o-ral
Ne'o-Ant-er'-gan
ne'o-ars-phen'-a-mine†
ne'o-blast
Ne'-o-cene
ne'o-clas'-si-cal
ne:o-dym'-i-um
ne-og'-a-my
Ne'-o-lith'-ic
ne'-o-log'-i-cal
ne-ol'-o-gism
ne-ol'-o-gist
ne-ol'-o-gy

ne'-o-my'-cin
ne'-on
ne-on-tol'-o-gy
ne'-o-phyte
ne-o-pla'-sia
ne'-o-plasm
ne'-o-prene
ne'o-stig'-mine
Ne:o-sy-neph'-rine
ne'-o-ter'-ic
ne-ot'-er-ism
ne-ot'-o-cite
Ne-pal'
Nep'-a-lese'
ne-pen'-the
ne-pen'-the-an
neph'-e-line
neph'-e-lin-ite
neph'-e-lite
neph-e-lom'-e-ter
neph'-e-lo-scope
neph'-ew
ne-phol'-o-gy
neph'-o-scope
ne-phrec'-to-my
neph'-ric
ne-phrid'-i-al
ne-phrid'-i-um
neph'-rite
ne-phrit'-ic
ne-phri'-tis
ne-phrol'-o-gy
neph'-ron
neph-ro:pto'-sis
ne-phro'-sis
ne-phrot'-ic
ne-phrot'-o-my
nep:i-on'-ic
ne-pot'-ic
nep'-o-tism
Nep'-tune
nep-tu'-ni-um
Ne'-re-id
ne-rit'-ic
Ne'-ro
ner'-o-li
ne-rol'-i-dol
Ne-rol'-ni-an
ner-ter-ol'-o-gy
ner'-vate*
ner-va'-tion
nerve'-less
ner'-vine*
nerv'-ing
ner-von'-ic
ner-vos'-i-ty
ner'-vous*
ner'-vous-ly*

ner'-vous-ness*
ner'-vule
ner'-vure
nerv'y
ne'-science*†
ne'-scient*†
nest'-er
nes'-tle
nes'-tling (snuggling)
nest'-ling (baby bird)†
Nes'-tor
Nes-to'-ri-an
neth'-er
Neth'-er-land-er
Neth'-er-lands
neth'-er-most
Ne-trop'-sin
net'-ting
net'-tle
net'-tled
net'-work
Neuf'-châ-tel'
neu'-ral
neu-ral'-gia
neu-ral'-gic
neur-as-the'-ni:a†
neur-as-then'-ic†
neu-rec'-to-my
neu'-rine
neu-rit'-ic
neu-ri'-tis
neu-ro-blas-to'-ma
neu-ro-coele
neu-ro-crine
neu-ro-gen'-ic
neu-rog'-li:a
neu-rog'-ra-phy
neu'-roid
neu-ro-log'-i-cal
neu-rol'-o-gist
neu-rol'-o-gy
neu-rol'-y-sis†
neu-ro'-ma
neu'-ron
neu'-ro-nal
neu-ron'-ic
neu'-ro-path'-ic
neu'-ro-path'-i-cal-ly
neu-rop'-a-thy
neu-rop'-ter-ous
neu-ro'-ses
neu-ro'-sis
neu-rot'-ic
neu-rot'-i-cism
neu-rot'-o-my
neu'-ro-trop'-ic
neu-rot'-ro-pism
neu'-ter

neu'-tral
neu'-tral-ism
neu-tral'-i-ty
neu-tral-i-za'-tion
neu'-tral-ize
neu'-tral-iz-er
neu'-tral-ly
neu-tri'-no
Neu'-tro-dyne
neu'-tron
Ne-vad'a†
Ne-vad'an†
nev'-er
nev'-er-more'
nev'-er-the-less'
ne'-vus
New'-ark
new'-born
New'-burgh
New'-cas-tle
new'-com-er
new'-el
new'-fan'-gled
New'-found-land
New'-gate
New Guin'-ea
New Hamp'-shire
New Ha'-ven
New Jer'-sey
new'-ly
New'-man
New'-mar-ket
New Mex'-i-co
new'=mown
new'-ness
New Or'-leans
New'-port
news'-boy
news'-cast
news'-cast-er
news' deal-er
news'-let-ter
news'-man
news'-mon-ger
news'-pa-per
news'-pa-per-man
news'-print
news'-reel
news'-room
news'-stand
news'y
New'-ton
New-to'-ni-an
New Zea'-land
New Zea'-land-er
next=door
nex'-us
ni'-a-cin

259

ni-a-cin'-a-mide
Ni-ag'-a-ra
nib'-ble
nib'-bling
Ni-be-lung'en-lied
nib'-lick
Nic'-a-ra'-gua
Nic-a-ra'-guan
nice'-ly
Ni'-cene
nice'-ness
nic'-est
ni'-ce-ty
niche
Nich'-o-las
nick'-el
nick-el-if'-er-ous
nick'-el-ine'
nick-el-o'de-on
nick'-el=plate
nick'-el-type
nick'-er
nick'-name
nic-o-tin'-a:mide
nic-o-tin'-ate
nic'-o-tine
nic'-o-tin'-ic
nic'-o-tin-ism
nic-o-ti'-no-yl
nic'-o-tin-u'ric
nic'-ti-tate
nic-ti-ta'-tion
ni-dic'-o-lous
nid'-i-fi-cate
nid-i-fi-ca'-tion
nid'-i-fy
ni-dol'-o-gy
ni'-dor
ni'-dus
Nie'-buhr
niece
ni-el'-lo
Nietz'sche†
Nietz'-sche-ism*
nif'-ty
Ni'-ger
Ni-ge'-ri:a
ni'-ger-ite
nig'-gard
nig'-gard-li-ness
nig'-gard-ly
nig'-gle
nig'-gling
night'-cap
night'-club
night'-fall
night'-gown

night'-hawk
night'-in-gale
night'-long
night'-ly
night'-mare
night'-shade
night'-shirt
night'-time
ni-gres'-cence
ni-gres'-cent
ni'-grine
nig'-ri-tude
ni-grom'-e-ter
ni'-gro-sine
ni'-grous
ni'-hi-lism*†
ni'-hi-list*†
ni'-hi-lis'-tic*†
ni-hil'-i-ty
Ni'ke
Ni-lom'-e-ter
nim'-ble
nim'-ble-ness
nim'-bly
nim'-bo-stra'-tus
nim'-bus
ni-mi'-e-ty
Nim'-rod
nin'-com-poop
nine'-fold
nine'-pins
nine'-teen'
nine'-teenth'
nine'-ti-eth
nine'-ty
Nin'-e-veh
Nin-hy'-drin
nin'-ny
ninth
ninth'-ly
Ni'-o-be
ni-o'-bic
ni-o'-bi-um
ni-o-bo=es'-chy-nite
ni'-pa
nip'-e-cot'-ic
nip'-per
nip'-ping
nip'-ple
Nip'-pon
Nip'-pon-ese'
nip'-py
Nir-va'-na
Ni-sei'
ni'-si
ni'-sin
ni'-si pri'-us

Nis'-sen
Nissl*†
ni'-sus
ni'-ter
nit'-id
ni-tid'-i-ty
ni-tra-mine'†
ni'-trate
ni'-tra-tor
ni'-tric
ni'-tride
ni'-trid-ize
ni-tri-fi-ca'-tion
ni'-tri-fy
ni'-trile
ni'-trite
ni-tro-an'-i-line
ni-tro-fu'-ra-zone
ni'-tro-gen
ni'-tro-gen-ate
ni'-tro'-gen-ize
ni-trog'-en-ous
ni-tro-glyc'-er-in
ni-tro'-lic*†
ni-trom'-e-ter
ni-tro'-ni-um
ni-tros-a:mine'†
ni'-tro-sate
ni-tro'-so
ni-tro-tol'-u-ene
ni-tro-tol'-u-ol
ni'-trous
ni-trox'-yl
ni'-tryl
ni'-val
ni-va'-tion
niv'-e-ous
ni-zam'
No-a'-chi-an
no'-a-chite
No'-ah
No-bel'
no-bel'-i-um
no-bil'-i-ar:y†
no-bil'-i-ty
no'-ble
no'-ble-man
no'-ble-ness
no-blesse' o:blige'
no'-ble-wom-an†
no'-bly
no'-bod:y
no-car-di-o'-sis
no'-cent
no'-cer-ite
no-ci-cep'-tive

no'-ci-cep'-tor
noc-tam-bu-la'-tion
noc-tam'-bu-lism
noc-tam'-bu-list
noc-ti-lu'-ca
noc-ti-lu'-cine
noc-tiv'-a-gant
noc'-to-vi-sion
noc'-tu-id
noc-tur'-nal
noc'-turne
noc'-u-ous
nod'-al†
no-dal'-i-ty
nod'-ding
nod'-dle
nod'-dy
nod'-i-cal
nod'-u-lar
nod'-ule
no-e-gen'-e-sis
no-e-ge-net'-ic
No-el'
no-e-ma-ta-chom'-e-ter
no-e'-sis
no-et'-ic
nog'-gin
No-gu'-chi
no'-how
noise'-less
noise'-less-ly
nois'-i-ly
nois'-i-ness
nois'-ing
noi'-some
nois'y
No-ko'-mis
no-li'-tion
no'-lo con-ten'-de-re
no'-mad†
no-mad'-ic
no-mad'-i-cal
no'-mad-ism†
nom'-arch
nom'-ar:chy*
nom de plume
no'-men-cla-tor
no'-men-cla-ture
nom'-ic
nom'-i-nal
nom'-i-nal-ly
nom'-i-nal-ism
nom'-i-nal-ist
nom'-i-nal-ize
nom'-i-nate
nom'-i-nat-ed
nom-i-na'-tion

NOMINATIVE

nom'-i-na-tive
nom'-i-na-tor
nom'-i-nee'
no'-mism
no-moc'-ra-cy
nom'-o-gram†
nom'-o-graph'-ic†
no-mog'-ra-phy
no-mol'-o-gy
nom-o-thet'-ic
non-ac-cept'-ance†
non-a-co'-sane
non-a-dec'-ane
non'-age (youth)
no'-nage (ninth)
non:a-ge-nar'-i-an†
non-ag-gres'-sion
non'-a-gon
no'-nane†
non'-a-no'-ic
no'-na-nol
non-ap-pear'-ance
non'-cha-lance'
non'-cha-lant'
non'-cha-lant-ly
non-com-bat'-ant†
non-com-mis'-sioned
non-com-mit'-tal
non com'-pos men'-tis
non-con-duc'-tor
non-con-form'-ist
non-con-form'-i-ty
non-co-op-er-a'-tion
non'-de-script'
no'-nene
non-en'-ti-ty
non-es-sen'-tial
none'-such
non-ex-is'-tence*
non-ex-is'-tent*
non-fea'-sance
non'-fic'-tion
non-ful-fill'-ment
non-in-ter-ven'-tion
non-join'-der
non-me-tal'-lic
non-ni-trog'-e-nous
no-no'-ic
non'-pa-reil'
non'-par'-ous
non-par-tic'-i-pat-ing
non'-par'-ti-san
non'-pay'-ment
non'-plus'
non-plussed'
non-plus'-sing
non-pro-duc'-tive
non-prof'-it

non pro-se'-qui-tur†
non-res'-i-dence
non-res'-i-dent
non-sec-tar'-i-an†
non'-sense
non-sen'-si-cal
non se'-qui-tur†
non'-skid'
non'-stop'
non'-suit'
non-sup-port'
non-un'-ion†
non'-yl-ene
no-nyl'-ic†
noo'-dle
no-ol'-o-gy
noon'-day
noon'-tide
noon'-time
no'-pal
no'-pi-nene
No'-ra
Nor'-dic
Nor-di-ca
nor-di-hy'-dro-guai'-a-
ret'-ic
Nor'-folk
no'-ri:a
nor'-mal
nor'-mal-cy
nor-mal'-i-ty
nor'-mal-ize
nor'-mal-iz-er
nor'-mal-ly
Nor'-man
Nor'-man-dy
nor'-ma-tive
Nor'-ris
Norse
Norse'-man
North A:mer'-i-ca
North-amp'-ton
North Car-o-li'-na
North Car-o-lin'-i-an
North Da-ko'-ta
North Da-ko'-tan
north'-east'
north-east'-er
north-east'-er-ly
north-east'-ern
north-east'-ward
north'-er
north'-er-ly
north'-ern
north'-ern-er
north'-ern-most
north'-land
North-um'-ber-land

North-um´-bri-an
north´-ward
north´-ward-ly
north´-west´
north´-west´-er-ly
north-west´-ern
Nor´-way
Nor-we´-gian
Nor´-wich
nose bag
nose´-band
nose´-bleed
nose´=dive
nose´-gay
no´-se-lite
nose´-piece
nos´-ing
no-sog´-ra-phy
nos-o-log´-i-cal
no-sol´-o-gist
no-sol´-o-gy
nos-tal´-gia
nos-tal´-gic
nos-tol´-o-gy
nos´-tril
nos´-trum
nos´y
no´-ta be´-ne
no-ta-bil´-i-ty
no´-ta-ble
no´-ta-ble-ness
no´-ta-bly
no´-tam
no-tar´-i-al†
no´-ta-ries
no´-ta-rize
no´-ta-ry
no´-ta-ry pub´-lic
no-ta´-tion
notched
notch´-er
note´-book
not´-ed
note´-less
note´-pa-per
note´-wor-thi-ly
note´-wor-thi-ness
note´-wor-thy
noth´-ing
noth´-ing-ness
no´-tice
no´-tice-a:ble
no´-tice-a:bly
no´-tic-ing
no´-ti-fi-ca´-tion
no´-ti-fied
no´-ti-fi-er
no´-ti-fy

no´-ti-fy-ing
not´-ing
no´-tion
no´-tion-al
No-to-gae´-an
no-to-ri´-e-ty
no-to´-ri-ous
no-to´-ri-ous-ly
no-to-un´-gu-late
Not´-ting-ham
Not´-ting-ham-shire
not-with-stand´-ing
nou´-gat
nou´-me-nal-ism
nou´-me-non
nour´-ish
nour´-ish-ing
nour´-ish-ment
nou-veau´ riche
no-vac´-u-lite
No´-va Sco´-tia
No´-va Sco´-tian
No-va´-tian-ism
no-va´-tion
nov´-el
nov´-el-ette
nov´-el-ist
nov-el-is´-tic
nov´-el-ize
no-vel´-la
nov´-el-ties
nov´-el-ty
No-vem´-ber
no-ve´-na
no-ver´-cal
Nov´-go-rod
nov´-ice
no-vi´-tiate
No´-vo-cain†
now´-a-days
no´-way
no´-ways
no´-where
no´-wise
nox´-ious
Noyes
noz´-zle
nu´-ance
nub´-bin
nu´-bi:a
Nu´-bi-an
nu´-bile
nu-bil´-i-ty
nu´-bi-lous
nu´-chal
nu´-ci-form
nu´-cle-ar
nu´-cle-ate

nu-cle-a'-tion
nu'-cle-a-tor
nu'-cle:i
nu-cle'-ic
nu-cle-in-a'-tion
nu-cle-og'-o-ny
nu'-cle:o-his'-tone
nu-cle'-o-lar
nu-cle'-o-lus
nu-cle-ol'-y-sis
nu-cle-om'-e-ter
nu'-cle-on
nu-cle-on'-ics
nu'-cle:o-plasm
nu'-cle-o-tid-ase
nu-cle-us
nu'-clide
nu-clid'-ic
nude'-ness
nudged
nudg'-er
nudg'-ing
nud'-ism†
nud'-ist†
nu'-di-ty
nu'-ga-to-ry
nug'-get
nui'-sance
nul-li-fi-ca'-tion
nul'-li-fied
nul'-li-fi-er
nul'-li-fy
nul'-li-fy-ing
nul'-li-ty
Nu'-ma
num'-ber
num'-bered
num'-ber-er
num'-ber-less
numb'-fish
numb'-ing
numb'-ing-ly
num'-bles
numb'-ly
numb'-ness
nu'-men
nu'-mer-a-ble
nu'-mer-al
nu'-mer-ar:y†
nu'-mer-ate
nu-mer-a'-tion
nu'-mer-a-tive
nu'-mer-a-tor
nu-mer'-i-cal
nu-mer'-i-cal-ly
nu-mer-ol'-o-gy
nu'-mer-ous

Nu-mid'-i:a
nu'-mi-nous
nu-mis-mat'-ics
nu-mis'-ma-tist
num'-skull
nun'-ci-a-ture
nun'-ci:o
nun'-cu-pa-tive
nun'-like
nun'-ner:y
nup'-tial
nup-ti-al'-i-ty
Nur'-em-berg†
nurse'-maid
nurs'-er
nur'-sery*†
nur'-sery-man*†
nurs'-ing
nurs'-ling
nur'-tur-al
nur'-ture
nur'-tur-ing
nu'-tant
nu-ta'-tion
nut=brown
nut'-crack-er
nut'-hatch
nut'-meg
nu'-tri:a
nu'-tri-ent
nu'-tri-lite
nu'-tri-ment
nu-tri'-tion
nu-tri'-tion-al
nu-tri'-tion-ist
nu-tri'-tious
nu'-tri-tive
nut'-shell
nut'-ter
nut'-ti-er
nut'-ti-ness
nut'-ting
nut'-ty
nuz'-zle
Ny-an'-za
nyc'-ta-gi-na'-ceous
nyc-ta-lo'-pi:a
nyc-ti-trop'-ic
nyc-tit'-ro-pism
ny'-lon
nymph
nym'-pha
nym-phae-a'-ceous
nymph'-al
nymph'-a-lid*†
nym-pho-ma'-ni:a
nys-tag'-mic

nys-tag'-mus
nys'-ta-tin
ny'-tril

O

O:a'-hu
oak'-en
Oak'-land
oa'-kum†
oar'-fish
oar'-lock
oars'-man
oars'-man-ship
o:a'-ses
o:a'-sis
oat'-cake
oat'-en
oat'-meal
O:ba-di'-ah
ob-bli-ga'-to
ob'-du-ra-cy
ob'-du-rate
O'be-ah
o:be'-di-ence
o:be'-di-ent
o:be'-di-ent-ly
o:bei'-sance
o:bei'-sant
o:be'-li-al
ob'-e-lisk
ob'-e-lus
O:ber-am'-mer-gau
O'ber-lin
O'ber-on
o:bese'
o:be'-si-ty*†
o:bey'
o:bey'-ing
ob-fus'-cate
ob-fus-ca'-tion
ob-fus'-ca-tor
ob-fus'-ca-to-ry
o'bi-ter dic'-tum*†
o:bit'-u-ar-ies†
o:bit'-u-ar:y†
ob'-ject (n.)
ob-ject' (v.)
ob-jec-tee'
ob-jec-ti-fi-ca'-tion
ob-jec'-ti-fy
ob-ject'-ing
ob-jec'-tion
ob-jec'-tion-a:ble
ob-jec'-tive
ob-jec'-tive-ly
ob-jec'-tive-ness

ob-jec'-tiv-ism
ob-jec-tiv'-i-ty
ob-jec'-tor
ob'-jet d'art
ob-ju-ra'-tion
ob'-jur-gate
ob-jur-ga'-tion
ob'-jur-ga-tor
ob'-last†
ob'-late
ob-la'-tion
ob'-la-to-ry
ob'-li-gate
ob'-li-gat-ing
ob-li-ga'-tion
ob'-li-ga-tor
o:blig'-a-to-ry†
o:blige'
ob'-li-gee'
o:blig'-er
o:blig'-ing
o:blig'-ing-ly
ob'-li-gor'
o:blique'
o:blique'-ly
o:blique'-ness
ob-liq'-ui-tous
ob-liq'-ui-ty
ob-lit'-er-ate
ob-lit-er-a'-tion
ob-lit'-er-a-tive
ob-lit'-er-a-tor
ob-li-ves'-cence
ob-liv'-i-on
ob-liv'-i-ous
ob'-long
ob'-long-at-ed
ob'-lo-quy
ob-mu-tes'-cence
ob-nox'-ious
ob-nu-bi-la'-tion
o'boe
o'bo-ist
ob'-o-lus
O:bre-gon'
ob-scene'
ob-scene'-ly
ob-scen'-i-ty
ob-scu'-rant*†
ob-scu'-ran-tism*†
ob-scu-ra'-tion
ob-scure'
ob-scure'-ly
ob-scure'-ness
ob-scur'-ing
ob-scu'-ri-ty
ob-se-cra'-tion

ob'-se-quies
ob-se'-qui-ous
ob-se'-qui-ous-ness
ob'-seq-ui-ty†
ob'-se-quy
ob-serv'-a:ble
ob-serv'-ance†
ob-serv'-ant†
ob-ser-va'-tion
ob-serv'-a-tive†
ob-serv'-a-to-ry†
ob-serve'
ob-serv'-er
ob-serv'-ing
ob-sess'
ob-ses'-sion
ob-ses'-sive
ob-ses'-sor
ob-sid'-i-an
ob-so-les'-cence
ob-so-les'-cent
ob'-so-lete'
ob'-so-lete'-ness
ob'-sta-cle
ob-stet'-ri-cal
ob-ste-tri'-cian
ob-stet'-rics
ob'-sti-na-cy
ob'-sti-nance
ob'-sti-nate
ob'-sti-nate-ly
ob-strep'-er-ous
ob-struct'
ob-struct'-er
ob-struc'-tion
ob-struc'-tion-ism
ob-struc'-tion-ist
ob-struc'-tive
ob-struc'-tor
ob-tain'
ob-tain'-a:ble
ob-tain'-ment
ob-test'
ob-tes-ta'-tion
ob-trude'
ob-trud'-er
ob-trud'-ing
ob-tru'-sion
ob-tru'-sive
ob-tru'-sive-ly
ob-tund'
ob-tund'-ent†
ob'-tu-rate
ob-tu-ra'-tion
ob'-tu-ra-tor
ob-tuse'
ob-tu'-si-ty
ob-verse' (adj.)

ob'-verse (n.)
ob-verse'-ly
ob-ver'-sion
ob'-ver-tend
ob'-vi-ate
ob'-vi-at-ing
ob-vi-a'-tion
ob'-vi-a-tor
ob'-vi-ous
ob'-vi-ous-ly
ob'-vi-ous-ness
ob'-vo-lute
oc-a-ri'-na
oc-ca'-sion
oc-ca'-sion-al
oc-ca'-sion-al-ism
oc-ca'-sion-al-ly
Oc'-ci-dent
oc'-ci-den'-tal
Oc-ci-den'-tal-ism
oc-ci-den'-tal-ize
oc-cip'-i-tal
oc-cip-i-ta'-lis
oc-cip'-i-to-pa-ri'-e-tal
oc'-ci-put
oc-clude'
oc-clud'-ent†
oc-clud'-ing
oc-clu'-sal
oc-clu'-sion
oc-clu'-sive
oc-cult'
oc-cul-ta'-tion
oc-cult'-ism
oc-cult'-ist
oc'-cu-pan-cy
oc'-cu-pant
oc-cu-pa'-tion
oc-cu-pa'-tion-al
oc'-cu-pa-tive
oc'-cu-pied
oc'-cu-pi-er
oc'-cu-py
oc'-cu-py-ing
oc-cur'
oc-curred'
oc-cur'-rence
oc-cur'-rent
oc-cur'-ring
o'cean
o:cean-nar'-i-um
O:ce-an'-i:a
o:ce-an'-ic
o:cean-og'-ra-pher*
o:cean-o-graph'-ic
o:cean-og'-ra-phy*
o:cel'-late*†
o:cel'-lus

o'ce-lot
o'cher
o'cher-ous
och-loc'-ra-cy
och'-lo-crat
o:chro-no'-sis*
Ock'-ham
o':clock'
o:co-ti'-llo*†
oc-ta-co'-sane
oc'-ta-dec'-a-di-e-no'-ic
oc'-ta-dec'-ane
oc'-ta-dec'-a-no'-ic
oc-ta-dec'-yl
oc'-ta-gon
oc-tag'-o-nal
oc-ta-he'-dral
oc-ta-he'-dron
oc'-tal
oc'-ta-mer
oc-tam'-er-ous
oc-tam'-e-ter
oc'-tane
oc-tan'-gu-lar
oc-ta-no'-ate
oc'-ta-nol
oc'-ta-no'-yl
oc'-tant
oc-tan'-tal†
oc'-ta'-val
oc'-ta-va'-lent
oc'-tave
Oc-ta'-vi-us
oc-ta'-vo
oc-ta'-vos
oc-ten'-ni-al
oc-tet'
Oc-to'-ber
oc-to-ge-nar'-i-an†
oc-tog'-e-nar:y†
oc-to'-ic
oc'-to-nar:y†
Oc-top'-o-da
oc'-to-pus
oc'-to-roon'
oc'-tose
oc'-troi
oc-tu-ple
oc-tup'-let*†
oc'-tyl-ene
oc'-u-lar
oc'-u-list
oc'-u-lo-gy'-ric
o'da-lisque
odd'-i-ty
odd'-ly
odd'-ment
odd'-ness

O:des'-sa
od'-ic†
o:dif'-er-ous
O'din
o:di-om'-e-ter
o'di-ous
od'-ist
o'di-um
O'do-a'-cer
o'do-graph
o:dom'-e-ter
o:don-e'-ter
o:don-tal'-gia
o:don-ti'-tis
o:don-to-gen'-ic
o:don-tol'-o-gy
o:don-tom'-e-ter
o:don-tot'-o-my
o'dor
o'dor-ant
o:dor-if'-er-ous
o'dor-ize
o'dor-less
o:dor-om'-e-ter
o'dor-ous
O:dys'-seus
Od'-ys-sey
oed'-i-pal
Oed'-i-pus
oe-nan'-thic
oe-nol'-o-gist
oer'-sted
of'-fal
off'-beat
off'-cast
off'=cen'-ter
off'=col'-or
of-fend'
of-fend'-er
of-fend'-ing
of-fense'
of-fen'-sive
of-fen'-sive-ness
of'-fer
of'-fer-ing
of-fer-to'-ri-al
of'-fer-to-ry
off'-hand'-ed
of'-fice
of'-fice-hold-er
of-fi'-cer
of-fi'-cial
of-fi'-cial-dom
of-fi'-cial-ese'
of-fi'-cial-ly
of-fi'-ci-ant
of-fi'-ci-ar:y†
of-fi'-ci-ate
of-fi-ci-a'-tion

267

of-fi'-ci-a-tor
of-fic'-i-nal
of-fi'-cious
of-fi'-cious-ly
off'-ing
off'-ish
off'-print
off'-scour-ing
off'-set (*n., adj.*)
off-set' (*v.*)
off-set'-ting
off'-shoot
off-shore'
off'-side'
off'-spring
off'-stage'
off=the=face
of'-ten†
of'-ten-times†
Og'-den
o'gee'
og'-ham
o:gi'-val
o'give
o'gle
O'gle-thorpe
o'gling
o'gre
o'gre-ish
o'gress
O:hi'o
O:hi'o-an
ohm
ohm'-age
ohm'-ic
ohm'-me-ter
oil cake
oil'-cloth
oil'-er
oil field
oil'-i-ness
oil'-man
oil paint'-ing
oil'-skin
oil slick
oil'-stone
oil well
oil'y
oint'-ment
oi-ti-ci'-ca
O:jib'-way (O:jib'-wa)
o:ka'-pi
o:kay'
o'ken-ite
O'ki-na'-wa
O'ki-na'-wan
O:kla:ho'-ma
O:kla-ho'-man

o:ko-le-hao'
ok'-o-nite†
o'kra
O'laf
old'-en
old=fash'-ioned
old'-ish
old=line'
old'-ness
old'-ster
old'=time'
old=tim'-er
Ol'-du-vai
old=world' (*adj.*)
o'le-a'-ceous
o:le-ag'-i-nous
o:le-an'-der
o:le-an'-drin
o'le-ate
o:lec'-ra-non†
o'le-fin
o'le-fin'-ic
o:le'-ic
o'le-in
o'le:o
o'le-o-graph
o:le-og'-ra-phy
o'le-o-mar'-ga-rine
o:le-om'-e-ter
o:le-o-res'-in
o:le'-o-yl
ol-fac'-tion
ol-fac'-tive
ol-fac-tom'-e-ter
ol-fac'-to-ry
ol'-i-garch
ol'-i-gar'-chic
ol'-i-gar-chy*
ol-i-ge'-mi:a
Ol'-i-go-cene
ol'-i-go-chaete
ol-i-go-chro-me'-mi:a
ol'-i-go-clase
ol'-i-go-dy-nam'-ic
ol'-i-go-nite†
ol-i-gop'-o-ly
ol-i-gop'-so-ny
ol'-i-va'-ceous
ol'-i-var†
ol'-ive
o:liv'-en-ite†
Ol'-i-ver
ol-i-ves'-cent
Ol'-i-vet
ol'-i-vine
ol'-la
o:lym'-pi-ad

O:lym'-pi-an
O:lym'-pic
O:lym'-pus
O'ma-ha
O:man'
O'mar Khay-yam'
om'-bro-graph
om-brom'-e-ter
o:meg'a*‡
om'-e-let
o:men
o:men-ol'-o-gy
o:men'-tum
o'mer
om'-i-cron
om'-i-nous
om'-i-nous-ly
o:mis'-si-ble
o:mis'-sion
o:mis'-sive
o:mit'
o:mit'-ted
o:mit'-ting
om'-ni-bus
om'-ni-far'-i-ous†
om-nif'-ic
om-nif'-i-cence
om-nif'-i-cent
om-nim'-e-ter
om-nip'-o-tence
om-nip'-o-tent
om-ni-pres'-ence
om-ni-pres'-ent
om'-ni-range
om-ni'-science*‡
om-ni'-scient*‡
om-niv'-o-rous
o:mo-pho'-ri-on
om-phal'-ic
om-pha-li'-tis
om'-pha-los
on'-a-ger
on'-a-gra'-ceous
o'nan-ism
o'nan-ist
once=o'ver
on'-co-gen'-ic
on-cog'-e-ny
on-col'-o-gy
on-col'-y-sis
on-com'-e-ter
on'-com-ing
on-cot'-o-my
on'-do-graph
on-dom'-e-ter
on'-du-le'
one'=armed'
one'=celled'

one'=eyed
one'=horse'
O:nei'-da
o:nei'-ric
o:nei'-ro-crit'-i-cal
o:nei'-ro-crit'-i-cism
o:nei'-ro-man-cy
one'=leg'-ged
one'-ness
one'=piece'
on'-er-ous
one-self'
one'=sid'-ed
one'=step
one'-time
one'=track'
one'=way'
one'=world'-er
on'-ion
on'-ion-skin
on'-look-er
on'-ly
on-o-ma-si-ol'-o-gy
on-o-mas'-ti-con
on-o-mat-o-poe'-ia
on-o-mat-o-poe'-ic
on-o-mat-o-po-et'-ic
On-on-da'-ga
on'-rush
on'-set
on'-shore'
on'-slaught
On-tar'-i-an†
On-tar'-i:o†
on'-to
on-tog'-e-ny
on'-to-log'-i-cal
on-tol'-o-gist
on-tol'-o-gy
o'nus
on'-ward
on-y-chol'-y-sis
on-y-cho-my-co'-sis
on-y-choph'-a-gy
on-y-cho'-sis
on'yx
o'o-lite
o:o-lit'-ic
o:ol'-o-gy
oo'-long
o:om'-e-ter
o:o-the'-ca
oozed
ooz'-ing
ooz'y*†
o:pa-cim'-e-ter
o:pac'-i-ty
o'pal

o:pal-esce'
o:pal-es'-cence
o:pal-es'-cent
o'pal-ine
o'pal-oid
o:paque'
o:paque'-ly
o:paqu'-er
o:paqu'-ing*
o:pei'-do-scope
o:pen
o:pen=air' (adj.)
o:pen=door' (adj.)
o'pen-er
o:pen=eyed'
o:pen=faced'
o'pen-hand'-ed
o'pen-heart-ed
o:pen=hearth (adj.)
o'pen house'
o'pen-ing
o'pen-ly
o:pen=mind'-ed
o:pen-mouthed'
o'pen-ness
o'pen-work
op'-er:a (music drama)
o'pe-ra (pl. of opus)
op'-er-a-ble
op'-er:a glass
op'-er-and'
op'-er-at-a:ble
op'-er-ate
op-er-at'-ic
op-er-at'-i-cal-ly
op-er-a'-tion
op-er-a'-tion-al
op'-er-a-tive
op'-er-a-tor
o:per'-cu-lar
o:per'-cu-lum
op-er-et'-ta†
op'-er-on
op'-er-ose
O:phe'-lia*
oph'i-cleide
o:phid'-i-an
o:phi-ol'-a-try
o:phi-ol'-o-gy
O'phir
o:phit'-ic
oph-thal-mi:a
oph-thal'-mic
oph-thal-mi'-tis
oph-thal'-mo-log'-ic
oph-thal-mo-log'-i-cal
oph-thal-mol'-o-gist
oph-thal-mol'-o-gy

oph-thal-mom'-e-ter
oph-thal'-mo-met'-ric
oph-thal'-mo-scope
oph-thal-mos'-co-py
o'pi-an'-ic
o'pi-ate
o'pi-at'-ic
o:pine'
o:pin'-ion
o:pin'-ion-at-ed
o:pin'-ion-a-tive
o:pin'-ion-a-tor
op-i-som'-e-ter
o:pis'-tho-gas'-tric
op'-is-thog'-na-thous
op-is-thot'-o-nos
o'pi-um
o'pi-um-ism
o:pop'-a-nax
O:por'-to
o:pos'-sum
op'-pi-dan
op-pi-la'-tion
op-po'-nent
op'-por-tune'
op'-por-tune'-ly
op-por-tune'-ness
op-por-tun'-ism†
op-por-tun'-ist‡
op-por-tun-is'-tic†
op-por-tu'-ni-ty
op-pos-a:bil'-i-ty
op-pos'-a:ble
op-pose'
op-pos'-ing
op'-po-site
op-po-si'-tion
op-press'
op-press'-i:ble
op-pres'-sion
op-pres'-sive
op-pres'-sor
op-pro'-bri-ate
op-pro'-bri-ous
op-pro'-bri-um
op-pugn'
op-pug'-nan-cy
op-pug-na'-tion
op-pugn'-er
op'-si-math
op-son-i-fi-ca'-tion
op'-so-nin
op'-ta-tive
op'-tic
op'-ti-cal
op-ti'-cian
op'-tics
op'-ti-mal

op'-ti-mal-ize
op'-ti-me
op-tim'-e-ter
op'-ti-mism
op'-ti-mist
op'-ti-mis'-tic
op-ti-mis'-ti-cal-ly
op'-ti-mum
op'-tion
op'-tion-al
op-tom'-e-ter
op'-to-met'-ric
op-tom'-e-trist
op-tom'-e-try
op'-u-lence
op'-u-len-cy
op'-u-lent
o:pun'-tia
o'pus
or'-a-cle
o:rac'-u-lar
o:rac-u-lar'-i-ty
o'ral
o'ral-ly
O:ran'
or'-ange
or'-ange-ade'
o:ran'-ge-lo
or'-ange-ry
or'-ange-wood
o:rang'-u:tan
o:rate'
o:ra'-tion
or'-a-tor
or-a-tor'-i-cal
or-a-tor'-i-cal-ly
or-a-to'-ri-o
or'-a-to-ry
or-bic'-u-lar
or-bic-u-lar'-i-ty
or-bic'-u-late
or'-bit
or'-bit-al†
or'-bit-ed
or'-bit-er
or'-bit-ing
or'-chard
or'-chard-ist
or'-ches-tra
or-ches'-tral
or'-ches-trate
or-ches-tra'-tion
or'-chid
or-chi-da'-ceous
or-chid-ol'-o-gy†
or-dain'
or'-deal†

or'-der
or'-dered
or'-der-li-ness
or'-der-ly
or'-di-nal
or'-di-nance
or-di-nar'-i-ly†
or'-di-nar:y†
or'-di-nate
or-di-na'-tion
ord'-nance
or'-don-nance
Or'-do-vi'-cian
or'-dure
O're-ad
o:rec'-tic
o:reg'-a-no*†
Or'-e-gon
Or-e-go'-ni-an
O:res'-tes
or'-gan
or'-gan-dy
or-gan'-ic
or-gan'-i-cal-ly
or-gan'-i-cism
or-gan'-i-cist
or'-ga-nism*†
or'-gan-ist
or-ga-niz'-a:ble*†
or-ga-ni-za'-tion*†
or'-ga-nize*†
or'-ga-niz-er*†
or'-ga-niz-ing*†
or-gan'o-gel
or-ga-no-gen'-e-sis
or-ga:no-gen'-ic
or-ga-nog'-ra-phy
or'-ga:no-lep'-tic
or-ga-non
or-ga-nos'-co-py
or-gan'o-sol
or-ga:no-ther'-a-py
or'-ga-num
or'-gasm
or-gas'-tic
or'-geat
or'-gi-ast
or'-gi-as'-tic
or'-gies
or'-gone
or-gu-lous
or'-gy
o'ri-el
o'ri-ent
o:ri-en'-tal
o:ri-en-ta'-lia
O:ri-en'-tal-ism

271

O:ri-en'-tal-ist
o'ri-en-tate
o'ri-en-ta'-tion
o'ri-en-ta'-tor
o:ri-en-tite
or'-i-fice
or'-i-fi'-cial
or'-i-flamme
o:rig'-a-num
Or'-i-gen
or'-i-gin
o:rig'-i-nal
o:rig'-i-nal'-i-ty
o:rig'-i-nal-ly
o:rig'-i-nate
o:rig'-i-na'-tion
o:rig'-i-nat-ing
o:rig'-i-na'-tive
o:rig'-i-na-tor
o'ri-na'-sal
O'ri-no'-co
o'ri-ole
O:ri'-on
or-is-mol'-o-gy*
or'-i-son
Ork'-ney
Or-lan'-do
Or'-le:an-ist
Or'-leans
Or'-lon
or'-mo-lu
or'-na-ment
or'-na-men'-tal
or-na-men-ta'-tion
or'-nate'
or-nate'-ness
or'-ner:y†
or-nith'-ic
or'-ni-thine
or-nith'o-log'-i-cal
or-ni-thol'-o-gist
or-ni-thol'-o-gy
or'-ni-thop-ter
or-nith:o-rhyn'-chus
or-ni-tho'-sis
or-ni-thot'-o-my
or'-nith-u'ric*
o'ro-ban-cha'-ceous*†
o:rog'-e-ny
or'o-graph'-ic
o:rog'-ra-phy
o'ro-ide
o:rol'-o-gy
o:rom'-e-ter
or'-o-met'-ric
o'ro-tund
o:ro-tun'-di-ty
or'-phan

or'-phan-age
or'-phan-hood
Or'-phe-um
Or'-pheus
or'-phic
or'-phism
or'-phrey
or'-pi-ment
or'-pine
Or'-ping-ton
or'-rer:y†
or'-ris
or'-ris-root
Or'-sat
or'-sel-lin'-ic
or'-tha-nil'-ic
or'-thi-con
or'-tho-ar'-se-nate
or'-tho-ben'-zo-qui-none'
or'-tho-ce-phal'-ic
or-tho-ceph'-a-ly
or'-tho-clase
or-tho-don'-tia
or'-tho-don'-tic
or'-tho-don'-tist
or'-tho-dox
or'-tho-dox:y
or'-tho-ep'-ic
or'-tho-ep'-i-cal-ly
or-tho-ep'ist
or-tho-ep:y
or-tho-for'-mic
or-thog'-a-my
or-tho-gen'-e-sis
or-thog'-na-thous
or-thog'-o-nal
or-thog'-ra-pher
or-tho-graph'-ic
or-thog'-ra-phy
or-thom'-e-try
or'-tho-pe'-dic
or-tho-pe'-dist
or-thop'-ne:a
Or-thop'-ter:a
or-thop'-ter-al
or-thop'-tics
or'-tho-scop'-ic
or-tho'-sis
or-thos'-ti-chy
or-thot'-ro-pism
or'-tho-typ'-ic
or-to-lan
Or-vie'-to
o:ryc-tog'-no-sy*†
o:ryc-tol'-o-gy*†
o'ryx
O'sage'
O:sa'-ka

o'sa-zone†
Os'-car
Os-ce-o'-la
os'-cil-late
os-cil-la'-tion
os'-cil-la-tor
os'-cil-la-to-ry
os-cil'-lo-graph
os-cil'-lo-scope
os'-ci-tan-cy
os'-ci-tant
os'-cu-lant
os'-cu-lar
os'-cu-late
os-cu-la'-tion
os'-cu-la-to-ry
os-cu-lom'-e-ter
Osh'-kosh
o'sier
O:si'-ris
Os'-lo
os'-mic
os-mi-dro'-sis
os-mi-rid'-i-um
os'-mi-um
os-mom'-e-ter
os'-mo-met'-ric
os-mom'-e-try
os-mo'-sis
os-mot'-ic
os-phre'-sis
os'-prey
Os'-sa
os'-se-ous
os'-si-cle
os-sic'-u-lar
os-si-cu-lec'-to-my
os-si-fi-ca'-tion
os-sif'-i-ca-to-ry†
os'-si-fied
os'-si-fy
os'-si-fy-ing
Os'-si-ning
os'-su-ar:y†
os'-te-al
os-te-ec'-to-my
os'-te-it'-ic
os-te-i'-tis
os-tend'
Ost'-end†
os-ten'-si-ble
os-ten'-si-bly
os-ten'-sive
os-ten'-sive-ly
os-ten-ta'-tion
os-ten-ta'-tious
os-ten-ta'-tious-ly

os-te-o-chon-dro'-sis
os-te-oc'-la-sis†
os-te-ol'-o-gist
os-te-ol'-o-gy
os-te-ol'-y-sis
os-te-o'-ma
os'-te-o'-ma-tous
os-te-om'-e-try
os'-te:o-my-e-li'-tis
os'-te-o-path
os'-te-o-path'-ic
os-te-op'-a-thy
os-te-o-plas-ty
os-te-ot'-o-my
os'-ti-ar:y†
os'-ti-ole
os-to'-sis
os'-tra-cism
os'-tra-cize
os'-tra-ciz-ing
os'-trich
Os'-tro-goth
Os'-wald
Os-we'-go
o:tal'-gi:a
O:thel'-lo
o'the-o-scope
oth'-er
oth'-er-wise
o'ti-ose
o:ti-os'-i-ty
o:ti'-tis
o:ti'-tis me'-di:a
o:tog'-e-nous
o'to-la-ryn'-go-log'-i-cal
o'to-lar-yn-gol'-o-gy
o'to-log'-ic
o:tol'-o-gy
o:tos'-co-py
o:to'-sis
O:tran'-to
ot-ta'-va
Ot'-ta-wa
ot'-ter
Ot'-to
ot'-to-man
oua-ba'-in
ou-bli-ette'
ought
Oui'-da
Oui'-ja
ounce
ou'-ri-cu-ry'
our-self'
our-selves'
oust'-er
out-bal'-ance
out-bid'

out'-board
out'-bound'
out'-break
out'-build
out'-build-ing
out'-burst
out'-cast
out'-class'
out'-come
out'-crop
out'-crop-ping
out'-cry
out'-curve
out'-did
out'-dis'-tance
out-do'
out-done'
out'-door'
out-doors'
out'-er
out'-er-most
out'-face'
out'-field
out'-field-er
out'-fit
out'-fit-ter
out'-flank
out'-flow
out-gen'-er-al
out'-go
out'-go'-ing
out'-grew'
out'-grow'
out'-growth
out'-house
out'-ing
out'-land
out'-land-er
out-land'-ish
out'-last'
out'-law
out'-law-ry
out'-lay
out'-let
out-line'
out-live'
out'-look
out'-ly-ing
out-ma-neu'-ver
out'-mod'-ed
out-num'-ber
out=of=date
out=of=doors
out=of=the=way
out'-pa-tient
out'-play'
out'-point'
out'-post

out'-pour
out'-pour-ing
out'-put
out'-rage
out-ra'-geous
out-ra'-geous-ly
out'-rag-er
out'-ran'
ou-trance'
out'-rank'
ou-tré'
out'-reach
out'-rid-er
out'-rig-ger
out'-right
out'-root'
out'-run'
out'-run-ner
out'-sell'
out'-set
out'-shine
out'-shone
out-side'
out-sid'-er
out'-sit'
out'-size
out'-skirts
out-smart'
out'-soar'
out'-speak'
out'-spo'-ken
out'-spread'
out-stand'
out-stand'-ing
out'-stay'
out'-stretch'
out-stretched'
out'-strip'
out-stripped'
out'-ward
out'-ward-ly
out'-wear'
out-weigh'
out'-wit'
out'-wit'-ted
out'-work'
out-worn'
ou-zel
o'va
o'val
o:val'-i-form
o:val'-i-ty
o:var'-i-an†
o:var'-i-ec'-to-my†
o:var'-i-ole†
o:var'-i-ot'-o-my†
o:va-ri'-tis
o'va-ry

274

o'vate
o:va'-tion
ov'-en
ov'-en-bird
ov'-en-ware
o'ver
o'ver-act'
o'ver-ac-tiv'-i-ty
o'ver-all (n.)
o'ver-all' (adj.)
o'ver-arm'
o:ver-awe'
o:ver-bal'-ance
o'ver-bear'
o:ver-bear'-ing
o'ver-bid'
o'ver-blown'
o'ver-board
o'ver-bold'
o'ver-bore'
o'ver-borne'
o'ver-build'
o'ver-bur'-den
o:ver-came'
o:ver-cap'-i-tal-ize
o'ver-cast'
o:ver-charge'
o:ver-cloud'
o'ver-coat
o:ver-come'
o'ver-crowd'
o:ver-did'
o:ver-do'
o:ver-done'
o'ver-dose
o'ver-draft
o:ver-draw'
o:ver-drawn'
o:ver-dress'
o'ver-drive'
o'ver-due'
o'ver-eat
o:ver-es'-ti-mate
o:ver-fed'
o'ver-feed'
o'ver-flow'
o:ver-grown'
o'ver-growth
o'ver-hand'
o'ver-haul'
o'ver-head'
o:ver-hear'
o'ver-hung'
o'ver-joy'
o'ver-joyed'
o'ver-laid'
o'ver-land

o'ver-land-er
o'ver-lap'
o:ver-lap'-ping
o'ver-lay'
o'ver-load'
o'ver-look'
o'ver-lord
o'ver-ly
o'ver-match'
o'ver-much'
o:ver-night'
o'ver-pass
o:ver-pay'
o:ver-play'
o:ver-pop-u-la'-tion
o:ver-pow'-er
o:ver-pro-duc'-tion
o:ver-ran'
o:ver-rate'
o:ver-reach'
o:ver-ride'
o:ver-rule'
o:ver-run'
o:ver-seas'
o:ver-see'
o'ver-seer†
o'ver-set'
o:ver-shad'-ow
o'ver-shoe
o'ver-shoot'
o:ver-shot'
o'ver-sight'
o'ver-size'
o:ver-sleep'
o:ver-slept'
o:ver-spread'
o:ver-state'
o:ver-stay'
o:ver-step'
o:ver-stock'
o'ver-sup-ply'
o:ver-stuffed'
o:vert'
o:ver-take'
o:ver-tak'-en
o:ver-tax'
o:ver-threw'
o:ver-throw'
o:ver-thrown'
o'ver-time
o'ver-tired'
o:vert'-ly
o'ver-tone
o:ver-took'
o'ver-ture
o:ver-turn'
o'ver-wear'
o'ver-wea'-ry

275

o:ver-ween'-ing
o'ver-weight
o:ver-whelm'
o:ver-whelm'-ing
o:ver-whelm'-ing-ly
o:ver-work'
o:ver-worked'
o'ver-wrought'
o'vi-ci'-dal*
o'vi-cide
o:vic'-u-lar
Ov'-id
O:vid'-i-an
o'vi-duct
o'vi-form
o:vig'-er-ous
o'vi-na'-tion
o'vine
o'vip'-a-ra
o:vi-par'-i-ty
o'vip'-a-rous
o'vi-pos-i-tor
o'void
o'vo-vi-vip'-a-rous
o'vu-lar
o'vu-late
o:vu-la'-tion
o'vu-la-to-ry
o'vule
o'vum
Ow'-en†
Ow'-ens-bor:o
ow'-ing
owl'-et
owl'-ish
own'-er
own'-er-ship
ox'-a-late
ox-al'-ic
ox-al'is*†
ox'-al-u'-ric*†
ox'-a-lyl
ox-am'-ic
ox-am'-ide
ox-am'-i-dine
ox-an'-i-late
ox'-a-nil'-ic
ox'-a-zine†
ox-a-zol'-i-dine
ox'-bow
ox'-cart
ox'-en
ox'-eye
ox'=eyed
Ox'-ford
ox'-heart
ox'-i-dant
ox'-i-dase

ox'-i-da'-tion
ox'-i-da-tive
ox'-ide
ox-i-dim'-e-try
ox'-i-diz-a:ble
ox-i-di-za'-tion
ox'-i-dize
ox'-i-diz-er
ox-id'-u-lat-ed
ox-im'-e-ter
ox'-i-met'-ric
ox'-in-dole
Ox-o'-ni-an
ox-o'-ni-um
ox:o-phen-ar'-sine
ox'-tail
ox'-tongue
Ox'-us
ox:y-a:can'-thine
ox:y-a:cet'-y-lene
ox'y-bi'-o-tin
ox'-y-gen
ox'-y-gen-ate
ox-y-gen-a'-tion
ox'-y-gen'-ic
ox'-y-gen-ize
ox:y-he'-mo-glo-bin†
ox:y-lu-cif'-er-in
ox:y-sul'-fide
ox:y-tet-ra-cy'-cline
ox-y-to'-cic†
ox-y-to'-cin
oy'-er*†
oy'-ez*†
oys'-ter
oys'-ter bed
oys'-ter-man
oys'-ter rake
oys'-ter-shell
Oz'-a-lid
O'zark
O:zark'-i:an
o:zo-ke'-rite
o'zon-ate*
o'zone
o'zon-ide*†
o'zon-if'-er-ous*†
o'zon-iz-er*†
o:zon-ol'-y-sis
o:zo'-no-sphere
o'zon-ous*†

P

pab'-u-lum
paced
pace'-mak-er
pac'-er

pa-chi′-si
pach′-no-lite
pach′y-derm
pach′y-der′-ma-tous
pa-chym′-e-ter
pach:y-san′-dra
pach′y-tene
pac′-i-fi-a:ble
pa-cif′-ic
pac′-if-i-cate
pa-cif′-i-cal-ly
pac-i-fi-ca′-tion
pac′-i-fi-ca-tor*
pa-cif′-i-ca-to-ry
pac′-i-fied
pac′-i-fi-er
pac′-i-fism
pac′-i-fist
pac′-i-fis′-tic
pac′-i-fy
pac′-i-fy-ing
pac′-ing
pack′-age
pack′-ag-er
pack′-ag-ing
Pack′-ard
pack′-er
pack′-et
pack′-ing
pack′-ing-house
pack′-man
pack rat
pack′-sack
pack′-sad-dle
pack′-thread
pac′-tion
pad′-ding
pad′-dle
pad′-dle-fish
pad′-dler
pad′-dle wheel
pad′-dling
pad′-dock
pad′-dy
Pad-e-rew′-ski†
pad′-lock
pa′-dre
pa-dro′-ne
Pad′-u:a
Pad′-u-an
pad′-u-a-soy
Pa-du′-cah
pae′-an
pae′-do-gen′-e-sis
pae-do-mor′-pho-sis
pae′-on
pa′-gan
Pa:ga-ni′-ni

pa′-gan-ish
pa′-gan-ism
pa′-gan-ize
pag′-eant
pag′-eant-ry
paged
pag′-er
Pag′-et
pag′-i-nal
pag′-i-nate
pag-i-na′-tion
pag′-ing
pa-go′-da
pa-gu′-ri-an
pail′-ful
pain′-ful
pain′-ful-ly
pain′-less
pain′-less-ly
pains′-tak-ing
pains′-tak-ing-ly
paint box
paint′-brush
paint′-er
paint′-ing
paint′-work
pai-sa′-no
Pais′-ley
pa-ja′-ma
Pak′i-stan†
Pak:i-stan′i
pal′-ace
pa-la′-ceous
pal′-a-din
pal-an-quin′
pal-at-a:bil′-i-ty
pal′-at-a:ble
pal′-a-tal
pal-a-tal-i:za′-tion
pal′-a-tal-ize
pal′-ate
pa-la′-tial
pa-lat′-i-nate
pal′-a-tine
pal-a-ti′-tis
pal-a-to-gram
pa-lav′-er
pa′-le:a
pa-le-a′-ceous
pa′-le-eth-nol′-o-gy
pale′-face
pale′-ness
pa-le-og′-ra-pher
pa′le:o-graph′-ic
pa-le-og′-ra-phy
Pa′le:o-lith′-ic
pa-le-ol′-o-gy
pa-le-on-tol′-o-gist

277

pa-le-on-tol'-o-gy
Pa'-le:o-zo'-ic
Pa-ler'-mo
Pal'-es-tine
Pal-es-tin'-i-an
Pa-les-tri'-na
pal'-ette
pal'-frey
pa-lil'-o-gy
pal'-imp-sest
pal'-in-drome
pal'-ing
pal-in-gen'-e-sis
pal-i-sade'
Pal-la'-di-an
pal-la'-di-um
Pal'-las
pall'-bear-er
pal'-let (platform)
pal'-let-ize
pal-lette' (piece of armor)
pal'-li-ate
pal'-li-at-ing
pal-li-a'-tion
pal'-li:a-tive
pal'-li:a-tor
pal'-li:a-to-ry
pal'-lid
pal'-li-um
pall'=mall'
pal'-lor
pal:mar'-i-an†
pal'mate
pal:ma'-tion
palm'-er
palm'-ist
palm'-is-try
pal'mi-tate
pal:mit'-ic
pal'mi-tin
pal-mit-o:le'-ic*
palm leaf
palm'y
Pal-my'-ra
pal-o-mi'-no
Pa'-los
pal-pa-bil'-i-ty
pal'-pa-ble
pal'-pa-bly
pal'-pate
pal-pa'-tion
pal'-pi-tant
pal'-pi-tate
pal'-pi-tat-ing
pal-pi-ta'-tion
pal'-pus

pal'-sied
pal'-sy
pal'-ter
pal'-tri-ness
pal'-try
pa-lu'-dal
pal'-u-dism
pal'-u-drine
pa-lus'-trine
pal-y-nol'-o-gy
pam'-a-quine
Pam'-e-la
pam'-pa
pam'-pe-an
pam'-per
pam-pe'-ro
pamph'-let*†
pam'-phleteer*†
pam'-phlet-ize
pan-a-ce'a
pa-nache' (head dress)
pa-na-ché' (food)
Pan'-a-ma
Pan-a-ma'-ni-an
Pan=A:mer'-i-can
pan'-a-ry
pan-a-tel'a
pan'-cake
pan-car-di'-tis
pan-chro-mat'-ic
pan-cra'-ti-um
pan'-cre-as
pan-cre-a-tec'-to-my
pan'-cre-at'-ic
pan'-cre-a-tin
pan-cre-a-ti'-tis
pan-cre-a-tot'-o-my
pan-cre-o-zy'-min
pan'-da
pan-dem'-ic
pan-de-mo'-ni-um
pan'-der
Pan-do'-ra
pan-dow'-dy
pan'-du-rate
pan-du'-ri-form
pan-e-gyr'-ic
pan'-e-gyr'-i-cal
pan'-e-gyr'-ist
pan'-e-gy-rize
pan'-el
pan'-el-board
pan'-eled
pan'-el-ing
pan'-el-ist
pan-gen'-e-sis
pan'-ge-net'-ic
pan'-go-lin

pan'-han-dle
pan'-han-dling
pan'=Hel-len'-ic
pan'-ic
pan'-icked
pan'-ick-ing
pan'-ick-y
pan'-i-cle
pan'-ic=strick-en
pa-nic'-u-late
pan-mne'-sia
pan-nic-u-li'-tis
pan'-nier
pan'-ni-kin
pan'-ning
pa-no'-cha
pan'-o-ply
pan-o-ram'a*†
pan'-o-ram'-ic
pan-soph'-ic
pan'-so-phism
pan'-sies
pan'-sy
pan-tag'-a-my
Pan'-ta-gru'-el*†
pan-ta-lets'
pan-ta-loon'
pan'-tar-chy*
pan-te-the'-ine
pan'-the-ism
pan'-the-ist
pan'-the-is'-tic
pan'-the-is-lism
pan'-the-on
pan'-the-on'-ic
pan'-ther
pant'-ing
pant-i-soc'-ra-cy†
pan'-to-chro-mism
pan'-to-graph
pan-tog'-ra-pher
pan-to'-ic
pan-tol'-o-gy
pan-tom'-e-ter
pan'-to-mime
pan'-to-mim'-ic
pan'-to-mim:ist
pan'-to-then'-ic
pan'-to-yl
pan'-tries
pan'-try
pan'-zer
pa'-pa-cy
pa-pa'-in
pa-pa'-in-ase
pa'-pal
Pa-pa-ni'-co-laou
pa'-par-chy*

pa-pav'-er-a'-ceous'
pa-pav'-er-ine
pa-paw'
pa-pay'a†
pa'-per
pa'-per-back
pa'-per-board
pa'-per boy
pa'-per chase
pa'-per cut-ter
pa'-per-hang-er
pa'-per knife
pa'-per-like
pa'-per=thin'
pa'-per-weight
pa'-per work
pa'-per:y
pap'-e-teries†
pa-pier=mâ-ché'
pa-pil'-la
pap'-il-lar:y†
pap-il-lo'-ma
pap-il-lo'-ma-to'-sis
pap-il-lom'a-tous
pap'-il-lose
pap-il-los'-i-ty
pa'-pism
pa'-pist
pa-poose'
pa-pri'-ka
Pap'-u:a†
Pap'-u-an
pap'-u-lar
pap'-y-ra'-ceous
pap'-y-rin
pa:py'-rus
par'a-a:mi'-no-ben-zo'-ic†
par'-a-ban'-ic
par'-a-ba'-sic*
pa-rab'-a-sis
par:a-bi-o'-sis
par'-a-ble
pa-rab'-o-la
par'-a-bol'-ic
par'-a-bol'-i-cal
pa-rab'-o-lize
pa-rab'-o-loid
pa-rab'-o-loi'-dal
Par:a-cel'-sus
par'-a-chor
par'a-chord-al*†
pa-rach'-ro-nism*†
par'a-chute
par'a-chut-ist
Par'-a-clete
pa-rade'
pa-rad'-er
pa-rad'-ing

279

par'-a-digm
par'-a-di-sa'-ic
par'-dise
par'-a-di-si'-a-cal
par'-a-dox
par'-a-dox'-i-cal
par'-af-fin
par'-af-fin'-ic
par:a-gen'-e-sis
par'a-gly'-co-gen
par'-a-go-ge
par'-a-gog'-ic
par'-a-gon
pa-rag'-o-nite
par'-a-graph
par'-a-graph-er
par'-a-graph'-i-cal-ly
Par'-a-guay
Par'-a-guay'-an
par'-a-keet
par-al'-de-hyde
par-al-lac'-tic
par'-al-lax
par'-al-lel
par'-al-leled
par-al-lel-e:pi'-ped
par'-al-lel-e-pip'-e-dal
par-al-lel-ing
par'-al-lel-ism
par-al-lel'o-gram
par-al-lel-om'-e-ter
pa-ral'-o-gism
pa-ral'-o-gize
pa-ral'-y-sis
par'-a-lyt'-ic
par-a-ly-za'-tion
par'-a-lyze
par'-a-lyzed
par'-a-lyz-ing
Par-a-mar'-i-bo
par-a-me'-ci:um
pa-ram'-e-ter
par'a-met'-ric (of a
  parameter)
par'a-me'-tric (near the
  womb)
par'-a-mide†
par'-a-mor'-phism
par'-a-mount
par'-a:mour
par:a-neph'-ros
par'-a-noi'a
par'-a-noi'-ac
par'-a-noid
par'-ant-he'-li-on
par'-a-pet
par'-a-pet-ed
par'aph

par'-a-pha'-sia
par-a-pher-na'-lia
par'a-phrase
par'a-phras-er
par'a-phras-ing
pa-raph'-ra-sis
par'a-phrast
par'a-phras'-tic
pa-raph'-y-sis
par:a-ple'-gia
par'a-ple'-gic*
par-ap'-sis
par'a-se-le'-ne
par'-a-site
par-a-sit-e'mi:a
par'-a-sit'-ic
par'-a-sit'-i-cal
par-a-sit'-i-ci'-dal*
par-a-sit'-i-cide
par'-a-sit-ism
par'-a-si-tize*†
par-a-si:to'-sis
par'-a-sol
par:a-syn'-the-sis
par:a-tax'-is
par:a-thi'-on
par'a-thy'-roid
par'a-troop-er
pa-rat'-ro-phy
par'a-vane
par'-boil
par'-cel
par'-celed
par'-cel-ing
par'-cel post
par-ce-nar:y†
Par-chee'-si
parch'-ment
par'-don
par'-don-a:ble
par'-don-er
pared
par'-e-gor'-ic
par'-e-gor'-i-cal
pa-ren'-chy-ma
par'-en-chym'-a-tous
par'-ent
par'-ent-age
pa-ren'-tal
par-en'-ter-al
par-en'-the-ses
pa-ren'-the-sis
pa-ren'-the-size
par'-en-thet'-ic
par'-en-thet'-i-cal
par'-en-thet'-i-cal-ly
par'-ent-hood
par-er'-ga

par-er'-gon
pa-re'-sist†
par-es-the'-si:a
pa-ret'-ic
par ex-cel-lence'
par-fait'
par-he'-lion
pa-ri'-ah
Par'-i-an†
pa-ri'-e-tal
pa-ri'-e-to-fron'-tal
par:i-mu'-tu-el†
par'-i-nar'-ic
par'-ing
Par'-is
par'-ish
pa-rish'-io-ner*†
Pa-ri'-sian
Pa-ri-si-enne'
par'-i-son
par'-i-ty
par'-ka
Par'-ker
park'-er
Par'-kin-son
Park'-man
park'-way
par'-lance
par'-lay
par'-ley
par'-lia-ment
par-lia-men-tar'-i-an†
par-lia-men'-ta-ry
par'-lor
par'-lor car
par'-lous
Par'-ma
Par-men'-i-des
Par'-me-san
Par-nas'-sian
Par-nas'-sus
Par-nell'
pa-ro'-chi:al
par'-o-died
par'-o-dist
par'-o-dis'-tic
par'-o-dy
par'-o-dy-ing
pa-roe'-mi:a
pa-roe-mi-og'-ra-pher
pa-rol'
pa-role'
pa-roled'
pa-rol-ee'
pa-rol'-ing
par-o-no-ma'-sia
par-o-nych'-i:a
par'-o-nym

pa-ron'-y-mous
Par'-os†
pa-ro'-tic†
pa-rot'-id
pa-rot-i-dec'-to-my
par'-o-tit'-ic
par-o-ti'-tis
par'-ous
par'-ox-ysm
par'-ox-ys'-mal
par-quet'
par'-que-try*†
par'-ri-ci'-dal*
par'-ri-cide
par'-ried
par'-rot
par'-ry
par'-ry-ing
parse
Par'-si
Par'-si-fal
par-si-mo'-ni:ous
par'-si-mo-ny
pars'-ing
pars'-ley
pars'-nip
par'-son
par'-son-age
par-tage'†
par-take'
par-tak'-en
par-tak'-er
part'-ed
part'-er
par-terre'
par'-the-no-gen'-e-sis
par'-the-no-ge-net'-ic
Par'-the-non
Par-then'-o-pe
Par'-thi-an
par'-tial
par-ti:al'-i-ty
par'-tial-ly
par-ti-bil'-i-ty†
par-tic'-i-pant
par-tic'-i-pate
par-tic'-i-pa'-tion
par-tic'-i-pa-tor
par-tic'-i-cip'-i-al
par'-ti-ci-ple
par'-ti=col-ored
par-tic'-u-lar
par-tic-u-lar'-i-ty
par-tic'-u-lar-ize
par-tic'-u-lar-ly
par-tic'-u-late
par'-ties
part'-ing

par'-ti-san
par'-ti-san-ship
par-ti-'tion
par-ti'-tion-er
par-ti'-tion-ing
par'-ti-tive
part'-ly
part'-ner
part'-ner-ship
par-took'
par'-tridge
part'=time'
par-tu'-ri-ent
par-tu-ri'-tion
par'-ty
pa-ru'-lis
par'-ve-nu
par'-vis
par'-vo-line
par'-vule
Pas'-a-de'-na
Pas-cal'
pas'-chal
pa'sha
pas'-i-graph'-ic
pa-sig'-ra-phy
pas-quin-ade'
pass'-a:ble
pass'-a:bly
pas-sa-ca'-glia
pas'-sage
pas'-sage-way
Pas-sa'-ic
pass'-book
pas-sé'
passe-men'-terie
pas'-sen-ger
pass'-er
pass'-er-by
pas'-si-ble
pas'-sim
pas-sim'-e-ter
pass'-ing
pas'-sion
pas'-sion-ate
pas'-sion-ate-ly
Pas'-sion-ist
pas'-sion-less
pas'-si-va-tor
pas'-sive
pas'-sive-ly
pas'-sive-ness
pas'-siv-ism
pas'-siv-ist
pas-siv'-i-ty
pass'-key
pas-som'-e-ter
Pass'-o:ver

pass'-port
pass'-word
paste'-board
past'-ed
pas-tel'
past'-er
pas'-tern
Pas-teur'
pas-teur-i:za'-tion
pas'-teur-ize
pas-tiche'
pas-tille'
pas'-time
past'-i-ness
past'-ing
pas'-tor
pas'-tor-age
pas'-to-ral†
pas-to-rale'*†
pas'-to-ral-ism†
pas'-to-ral-ist†
pas'-to-ral-ize†
pas'-tor-ate
pas-to'-ri-um
pas'-tor-ship
pas-tra-mi'
pas'-tries†
pas'-try†
pas'-try-cook†
pas'-tur-a:ble
pas'-tur-age
pas'-ty*† (n.)
past'y (adj.)
pa-ta'-gi-um
Pat-a-go'-ni:a
Pat-a-go'-ni-an
Pa-taps'-co
patch'-er
patch'-er:y
patch'-i-ness
patch'-ou-li†
patch test
patch'-work
patch'y
pâ-té' de foie gras'
pa-tel'-la
pat'-en
pat'-en-cy*
pat'-ent
pat-ent-a:bil'-i-ty
pat'-ent-a:ble
pat'-en-tee*
pat'-ent-ly
pat'-en-tor
pa'-ter
pa-ter-fa-mil'-i-as
pa-ter'-nal
pa-ter'-nal-ism

pa-ter'-nal-is'-tic
pa-ter'-nal-ly
pa-ter'-ni-ty
pa'-ter-nos-ter
Pat'-er-son (N.J.)
pa-thet'-ic
pa-thet'-i-cal-ly
path'-find-er
path'-less
path-o-don'-tia
path'-o-gen
path'-o-ge-net'-ic
path'-o-gen'-ic
path-o-ge-nic'-i-ty
pa-thog'-e-ny
pa-thog'-no-my
pa-thol'-o-gist
pa-thol'-o-gy
pa-thom'-e-ter
pa'-thos
pa-tho'-sis
path'-way
pat'-i-ble
pa-tib'-u-lar:y†
pa'-tience
pa'-tient
pa'-tient-ly
pat'-i-na
pat-i-na'-tion
pat'-i:o*†
pa-tis'-se-rie†
pa'-tois*
pa'-tri-arch
pa'-tri-ar'-chal
pa'-tri-arch-ate
pa'-tri-ar:chy*†
Pa-tri'-cia
pa-tri'-cian
pa-tri'-ci-ate
pat'-ri-cid'-al†
pat'-ri-cide
Pat'-rick
pat'-ri-lin'-e:al
pat'-ri-mo'-ni-al
pat'-ri-mo-ny
pa'-tri-ot
pa'-tri-ot'-ic
pa'-tri-ot'-i-cal-ly
pa'-tri-ot-ism
pat'-ri-pas'-si-an*†
pa-tris'-tic
pa-trol'
pa-trolled'
pa-trol'-ler
pa-trol'-ling
pa-trol'-man
pa'-tron

pa'-tron-age†
pa'-tron-ess
pat'-ro-nite†
pa'-tron-ize†
pa'-tron-iz-ing†
pat-ro-nym'-ic
pat-ro-nym'-i-cal-ly
pa-troon'
pat'-ten
pat'-ter
pat'-tern
pat'-terned
pat'-tern-mak-er
Pat'-ter-son
pat'-ting
pat'-ty
pat'-u-lous
pau'-ci-ty
Pau'-li
Pau-li'-na
Pau-line' (feminine name)
Paul'-ine (of St. Paul)
Paul'-ist
pau'-lo-post
paunch'-i-ness
paunch'y
pau'-per
pau'-per-ism
pau'-per-ize
paus'-al
paus'-ing
pave'-ment
pav'-er
pa-vil'-ion
pav'-ing
Pav'-lov
Pav-lov'-i-an
pav'-o-nine
pav'-o-nite
pawn'-bro-ker†
pawn'-brok-ing*
Paw-nee'
pawn-ee'
pawn'-er
pawn'-shop
Paw-tuck'-et
pay'-a:ble
pay'-day
pay-ee'
pay'-er
pay'-ing
pay'-mas-ter
pay'-ment
pay-o'-la
pay'-roll
Pea-bod'y
peace'-a:ble
peace'-a:bly

283

peace'-ful
peace'-ful-ly
peace'-ful-ness
peace'-mak-er
peace of'-fer-ing
peace pipe
peace'-time
peach'-blos'-som (peach-colored)
peach'-blow
peach'y
pea'-cock
pea'-hen
pea jack'-et
peaked (pointed)
peak'-ed (worn)
pea'-nut
pearl ash
pearl'-er
pearl-es'-cent
pearl'-i-ness
pearl'-ite
pearl'y
pear'=shaped
Pear'-son
Pea'-ry
peas'-ant
peas'-ant-ry
peat'y
pea'-vey
peb'-ble
peb'-bled
peb'-bling
peb'-bly
pe-can'
pec'-ca-ble
pec-ca-dil'-lo
pec-ca-dil'-loes
pec'-can-cy
pec'-cant
pec'-ca-ry
peck'-er
peck'-ing
pec'-tase
pec'-tate
pec'-ten
pec'-tic
pec'-tin
pec'-tin-ase
pec'-ti-nate
pec-tin'-ic
pec'-to-lyt'-ic
pec'-to-ral
pec-to-ril'-o-quy
pec'-tous (jellied)
pec'-tus (chest)
pec'-u-late
pec'-u-lat-ing

pec-u-la'-tion
pec'-u-la-tor
pe-cu'-liar*
pe-cu'-liar-i-ty
pe-cu'-liar-ly*
pe-cu'-li-um
pe-cu'-ni-ar'-i-ly†
pe-cu'-ni-ar;y†
ped'-a-gog'-ic
ped'-a-gog'-i-cal
ped'-a-gogue
ped'-a-gog;y*†
ped'-al
ped'-aled
pe-dal'-fer†
ped'-al-ine
ped'-ant
pe-dan'-tic
pe-dan'-ti-cal-ly
pe-dan'-ti-cism
ped'-ant-ry
ped'-ate
ped'-dle
ped'-dler
ped'-dler;y
ped'-dling
ped'-er-ast
ped'-er-as-ty
Pe'-der-sen
ped'-es-tal
pe-des'-tri-an
pe-des'-tri-an-ism
pe'-di-a'-tric
pe-di-a-tri'-cian
pe-di-at'-rics
ped'-i-cel
ped'-i-cle
pe-dic'-u-lar
pe-dic-u-lo'-sis
pe-dic'-u-lous
ped'-i-cure
ped'-i-form
ped'-i-gree
ped'-i-ment
ped'-i-men'-tal
ped-i-men-ta'-tion
ped'-i-palp
ped-i-pla-na'-tion
ped'-o-cal
pe-dol'-o-gy
pe-dom'-e-ter
ped:o-met'-ri-cal
Pe'-dro
pe'-dun-cle
pe-dun'-cu-lar
pe-dun'-cu-late
peel'-er
peel'-ing

284

peep'-er
peep'-hole
peer'-age
peer'-ess
peer'-less
pee'-vish
pee'-vish-ness
Peg'-a-se'-an
Peg'-a-sus
peg'-ging
peg'-ma-tite
peg-ma-tit'-ic
peign-oir'†
Pei'-ping'
pei-ram'-e-ter
pej'-o-ra-tive*†
Pe'-kin-ese'
Pe'-king'
Pe'-king-ese'
pe'-koe
pel'-age
Pe-la'-gi:an
Pe-la'-gian-ism
pe-lag'-ic
pel-ar'-go-nate
pel-ar-gon'-ic
pel-ar-gon'-i-din
pel-ar-go'-nin
pel-ar-go'-ni-um
pel-er-ine'
Pel'-ham
pel'-i-can
Pe'-li-on
pe-lisse'
pel-la'gra
pel-la'-grous
pel'-let
pel'-let-er
pel'-let-ize
pel'-li-cle
pel-lic'-u-lar
pel'-li-to-ry
pell'=mell'
pel-lu'-cid
pel-lu-cid'-i-ty
pel-mat'-o-gram
Pel-o-pon-ne'-sian
Pel-o-pon-ne'-sus
Pe'-lops
pe-lor'-ic†
pe-lo'-rus
pel'-tast
pelt'-er
pel'-try*†
pel'-vic
pel-vim'-e-ter
pel'-vis
pem'-mi-can

pem'-phi-gus
pe'-nal
pe-nal-i:za'-tion
pe'-nal-ize
pe'-nal-iz-ing
pen'-al-ties
pen'-al-ty
pen'-ance
pe-na'-tes
pench'-ant*†
pen'-cil
pen'-ciled
pen'-cil-ing
pen'-cil-ler
pen'-dant (ornament
pen-de-loque'
pen'-den:cy*
pen'-dent (hanging)*
pen-den'-tive
pend'-ing
pen-drag'-on
pen-du-los'-i-ty
pen'-du-lous
pen'-du-lum
Pe-nel'-o-pe
pe'-ne-plain'
pe-ne-pla-na'-tion
pen-e-tra-bil'-i-ty
pen'-e-tra-ble
pen-e-tra'-lia
pen-e-tram'-e-ter
pen'-e-trance
pen'-e-trate
pen'-e-trat-ing
pen-e-tra'-tion
pen'-e-tra-tive
pen'-e-tra-tor
pen-e-trom'-e-ter
pen'-guin
pen'-hold-er
pen-i-cil'-lin
pen-i-cil'-lin-ase
pen-i-cil-li-o'-sis
pen-i-cil'-li-um
pe-nin'-su-la*
pe-nin'-su-lar*
pe'-nis
pen'-i-tence
pen'-i-tent
pen'-i-ten'-tial
pen-i-ten'-tia-ry
pen'-i-tent-ly
pen'-knife
pen'-man
pen'-man-ship
pen name
pen'-nant
pen'-nate

285

pen'-nies
pen'-ni-less
pen'-ning
pen'-ni-nite
pen'-non
Penn-syl-va'-nia
Penn-syl-va'-nian
pen'-ny
pen'-ny-roy'-al
pen'-ny-weight
pen'-ny=wise'
pen'-ny-worth
Pe-nob'-scot
pe'-no-log'-i-cal
pe-nol'-o-gist
pe-nol'-o-gy
pen point
Pen-sa-co'-la
pen'-sile
pen'-sion
pen'-sion-ar:y†
pen'-sion-er
pen'-sive
pen'-sive-ly
pen'-stock
pent-ac'-id†
pen'-ta-cle
pen'-tad
pen'-ta-dec'-ane
pen'-ta-dec'-yl
pen'-ta-e:ryth'-ri-tol
pen'-ta-gon
pen'-tag'-o-nal
pen'-tag'-o-nal-ly
pen'-ta-he'-dral
pen-ta-hy'-drite
pen'-ta-mer
pen-tam'-er-al
pen-tam'-er-ous
pen-tam'-e-ter
pent-am'-i-dine
pen'-tane
pen'-ta-no'-ic
pen'-ta-none
pen'-ta-ploid
pen'-tar:chy*
Pen'-ta-teuch
pen-tath'-lon
pen'-ta-tom'-ic
pen'-ta-va'-lent
Pen'-te-cost
Pen-te-cos'-tal
pen'-tene
pent'-house
pen'-ti-tol
pen'-to-bar'-bi-tal
pen'-tode
pen-tom'-ic

pen'-to-san
pen'-tose
Pen'-to-thal
pent-ox'-ide†
pen'-tryl
pen'-tu-lose
pent'=up'
pen'-tyl
pen'-tyl-ene
pen-tyl'i-dene
pe-nu'-che
pe'-nult
pe-nul'-ti-mate
pe-num'-bra
pe-nu'-ri-ous
pen'-u:ry
pen'-writ-ten
Pen-zance'
pe'-on
pe'-on-age
pe'-o-nies
pe'-o-ny
peo'-ple
peo'-pling
Pe-o'-ri:a
pe-pi'-no
pep'-lum
pep'-per
pep'-per-box
pep'-per-corn
pep'-per-mint
pep'-per:y
pep'-py
pep'-si-gogue
pep'-sin
pep-sin-if'-er-ous
pep-sin'-o-gen
pep'-tic
pep'-ti-dase
pep'-to-nate
pep'-tone
pep-to-niz-a'-tion*†
pep'-to-nize
Pepys
Pe'-quot
per-a:ce'-tic
per'-ad-ven'-ture
per-am'-bu-late
per-am'-bu-lat-ing
per-am'-bu-la'-tion
per-am'-bu-la-tor
per-am'-bu-la-to-ry
per an'-num
per-bo'-rate
Per'-bu'-nan
per-cale'
per'-ca-line
per cap'-i-ta

per-ceiv′-a:ble
per-ceiv′-a:bly
per-ceive′
per-ceiv′-er
per-cent′
per-cent′-age
per-cent′-ile*†
per′-cept
per-cep-ti-bil′-i-ty
per-cep′-ti-ble
per-cep′-ti-bly
per-cep′-tion
per-cep′-tive
per-cep′-tu-al
per-chance′
perch′-er
Per′-che-ron
per-chlo′-rate
per-chlo′-ryl
per-cip′-i-ence
per-cip′-i-en-cy
per-cip′-i-ent
Per′-ci-val
per′-coid
per-coi′-de-an
per′-co-late
per-co-la′-tion
per′-co-la-tor
per cu′-ri-am
per-cuss′
per-cus′-sion
per-cus′-sive
Per′-cy
per di′-em
per-di′-tion
per′-e-gri-nate
per-e-gri-na′-tion
per′-e-gri-na-tor
per′-e-grine
pe-rei′-ra
pe-rei′-rine
pe-remp′-tive
pe-remp′-to-ri-ly*†
pe-remp′-to-ri-ness*†
pe-remp′-to-ry*†
pe-ren′-ni:al*†
per′-fect (adj.)
per-fect′ (v.)
per-fect′-er
per-fect′-i:bil′-i-ty
per-fect′-i:ble
per-fec′-tion
per-fec′-tion-ism
per-fec′-tive
per-fect′-ly
per-fec′-to
per-fec′-tor
per-fec′-tos

per-fer′-vid
per-fid′-i-ous
per-fid′-i-ous-ly
per-fid′-i-ous-ness
per′-fi-dy
per′-fo-rate
per′-fo-rat-ed
per-fo-ra′-tion
per′-fo-ra-tive
per′-fo-ra-tor
per-force′
per-form′
per-form′-a:ble
per-form′-ance
per-form′-er
per′-fume
per-fum′-er
per-fum′-er:y
per-func′-to-ri-ly
per-func′-to-ry
per-fu′-sion
per-fu′-sive
per′-go-la
per-haps′
pe′-ri
peri′-anth
peri′-ar-thri′-tis
peri′-as′-tron
peri-car′-di-al
peri:i-car-di′-tis
peri:i-car′-di-um
peri:i-chon′-dri-um
peri:i-cho-re′-sis
peri′-clase
Per′-i-cle′-an
Per′-i-cles
pe-ric′-o-pal
pe-ric′-o-pe
peri-cop′-ic
peri:i-cra′-ni-um
pe-rid′-i-um
pe-rid′-o-tite*†
peri-ge′-an
peri-gee
pe-rig′-y-nous
peri-he′-lion
per′-il
per′-iled
per′-il-ing
per′-il-ous†
per′-il-ous-ly†
pe-rim′-e-ter*
peri-met′-ric
peri-met′-ri-cal
pe-rim′-e-try*
peri-morph
per-i-ne′-al
per-i-ne-or′-rha-phy

287

per:i-neph'-ri-um
per-i-ne'-um
per:i-neu'-ri-um
pe-rin'-i-um
pe'-ri-od
pe'-ri:od'-ic (cyclic)
per'-i:od'-ic (acid of
  iodine)
pe-ri-od'-i-cal
pe-ri-od'-i-cal-ly
pe-ri-o-dic'-i-ty
peri'-os'-te-al
per:i-os'-te-um
per:i-os-ti'-tis
peri'-o'-tic
per:i-pa-tet'-ic
per:i-pe-tei'a*
pe-rip'-e-ty
pe-riph'-er-al
pe-riph'-er-al-ly
pe-riph'-er:y
peri'-phrase
pe-riph'-ra-sis
peri'-phras'-tic
peri'-plus
pe-rip'-ter-al
pe-rip'-ter:y
pe-rique'
pe-ris'-ci:an
pe-ris'-ci:i
peri'-scope
peri'-scop'-ic
per'-ish
per'-ish-a:ble
peri'-som'-al*†
pe-ris'-sad
per-is-sol'-o-gy
pe-ris'-ta-lith
per:i-stal'-sis
peri'-stal'-tic
peri'-ste:le
peri'-sty'-lar
peri'-style
per'-it
per:i-the'-ci-um
peri'-the-li-o'-ma
peri'-to-ne'-al
per:i-to-ne-os'-co-py
per:i-to-ne'-um
peri'-to-nit'-ic
per:i-to-ni'-tis
per:i-vis'-cer-al
peri'-wig
peri'-win-kle
per'-jure
per'-jur-er
per'-jur-ing
per-ju'-ri-ous

per'-ju-ry
perk'-i-ness
Per'-kins
perk'y
per'-lite
per'-ma-frost
Perm'-al-loy
per'-ma-nence
per'-ma-nen-cy
per'-ma-nent
per'-ma-nent-ly
per'man'-ga-nate
per-me-a:bil'-i-ty
per'-me-a:ble
per'-me:a:me-ter*
per'-me-ance
per'-me-ant
per'-me-ate
per-me-a'-tion
per'-me-a:tive
Per'-mi-an
per-mis-si-bil'-i-ty
per-mis'-si-ble
per-mis'-sion
per-mis'-sive
per-mit' (v., n.)
per'-mit (n.)
per-mit'-ted
per'-mit-tee'
per-mit'-ting
per-mit-tiv'-i-ty
per-mut'-a:ble
per-mu-ta'-tion
per'-mu-ta-tor
per-mute'
per-ni'-cious
per-nick'-e-ty*
per-ni-o'-sis
Pe-ron'
per'-o-ne'-al
Pe:ro'-nism
Pe:ro'-nist
Pe-ro-nis'-ta
per'-o:rate'
per-o-ra'-tion
pe-ro'-sis
per-ox'-i-dase
per-ox'-ide
per-ox'y-a:ce'-tic
per-ox'y-di-sul'-fate
per-pen-dic'-u-lar
per'-pe-trate
per-pe-tra'-tion
per'-pe-tra-tor
per-pet'-u-al
per-pet'-u-al-ly
per-pet'-u-ate
per-pet-u-a'-tion

per-pet'-u-a-tor
per-pe-tu'-i:ty
Per-pi-gnan'
per-plex'
per-plexed'
per-plexed'-ness*†
per-plex'-ing
per-plex'-i-ty
per'-qui-site
per'-ron
per'-ry
per'-se-cute
per-se-cu'-tion
per'-se-cu-tor
per'-se-cu-to-ry
Per'-se-id
per-se-i-tol
per-se'-i-ty
Per-seph'-o-ne
Per-sep'-o-lis
Per'-seus
per-se-ver'-ance
per-sev'-er-a-tive
per'-se-vere'
per'-se-ver'-ing
Per'-shing
Per'-sia
Per'-sian
per'-si-enne'
per'-si-flage
per-sim'-mon
per-sist'
per-sist'-ence†
per-sist'-en-cy†
per-sist'-ent†
per-sist'-ent-ly†
per-sist'-er
per-snick'-e-ty*
per'-son
per-so'na
per'-son-a:ble
per'-son-age
per'-son-al
per-son-al'-i-ty
per'-son-al-ize
per'-son-al-ly
per'-son-al-ty
per-so'na non gra'ta
per'-son-ate
per-son-a'-tion
per-son-i-fi-ca'-tion
per-son'-i-fi-er
per-son'-i-fy
per-son'-i-fy-ing
per'-son-nel'
per-spec'-tive
per-spec-tom'-e-ter
per-spi-ca'-cious

per-spi-cac'-i-ty
per-spi-cu'-i:ty
per-spic'-u-ous
per-spir'-a:ble
per-spi-ra'-tion
per-spi'ra-tive
per-spir'-a-to-ry
per-spire'
per-spir'-ing
per-suad'-a:ble
per-suade'
per-suad'-er
per-suad'-ing
per-sua-si-ble
per-sua'-sion
per-sua'-sive
per-sua'-sive-ly
per-tain'
perth'-ite
Perth'-shire
per'-ti-na'-cious
per'-ti-na'-cious-ly
per-ti-nac'-i-ty
per'-ti-nence
per'-ti-nen-cy
per'-ti-nent
pert'-ly
per-turb'
per-turb'-a:ble
per-tur-ba'-tion
per-turb'-ed-ly
per-turb'-er
per-tus'-sal
per-tus'-sis
Pe-ru'
pe-ruke'
pe-rus'-a:ble
pe-rus'-al†
pe-ruse'
pe-rus'-er
pe-rus'-ing
Pe-ru'-vi-an
per-vade'
per-vad'-ing
per-va'-sion
per-va'-sive
per-va'-sive-ly
per-verse'
per-verse'-ly
per-verse'-ness
per-ver'-sion
per-ver'-si-ty
per-ver'-sive
per-vert' (v.)
per'-vert (n.)
per-vert'-ed
per-vert'-er
per-vert'-i-ble

289

per-vi-ca'-cious
per-vi-cac'-i-ty
per'-vi-ous
per'-y-lene
Pe'-sach
pe-se'-ta
Pe-sha'-war†
pes'-ky
pe'-so
pes'-sa-ry
pes-si-mism
pes'-si-mist
pes-si-mis'-tic
pes-si-mis'-ti-cal-ly
Pes'-ta-loz'-zi
pes'-ter
pes'-tered
pest'-house
pes'-ti-ci'-dal*
pes-tif'-er-ous
pes'-ti-lence
pes'-ti-lent
pes'-ti-len'-tial
pes'-tle
pes-tol'-o-gy
pet'-al
pet'-aled
pet-al-if'-er-ous†
pet'-al-ine†
pet'-al-ism
pet'-al-ite†
pet'-a-lo-dy
pet'-al-ous†
pe-tard'
pet'-cock
pe-te'-chi-al†
Pe'-ter
pe'-tered
Pe'-ters-burg
pet'-i-o-lar*
pet'-i-o-late
pet'-i-ole
pe-tit' (small)
pet'-it (jury)
pe-tite'
pe-ti'-tion
pe-ti'-tion-ar:y†
pe-ti'-tion-er
pe-tits' fours
Pe'-trarch
Pe-trar'-chan†
Pe'-trarch-ist
pet'-rel*†
pe-tres'-cent
Pe'-tri
pet-ri-fac'-tion
pet'-ri-fac'-tive
pet-ri-fi-ca'-tion

pet'-ri-fied
pet'-ri-fy
Pe'-trine
pe'-tro-chem'-i-cal*†
pe-trog'-e-ny
Pet'-ro-grad
pe-trog'-ra-pher
pet-ro-graph'-ic
pet-ro-graph'-i-cal
pe-trog'-ra-phy
pet'-rol†
pet'-ro-lage
pet-ro-la'-tum
pet'-ro-lene
pe-tro'-le:um
pe-trol'-ic
pet'-ro-lif'-er-ous
pet'-ro-lize
pet-ro-log'-ic
pet-ro-log'-i-cal
pet-ro-log'-i-cal-ly
pe-trol'-o-gist
pe-trol'-o-gy
pe-tro'-sal
pet'-rous
pe-trox'-o-lin
pet'-ti-coat
pet'-ti-fog
pet'-ti-fog-ger
pet'-ti-fog-ger:y
pet'-ti-ly
pet'-ti-ness
pet'-tish
pet'-tish-ness
pet'-ty
pet'-u-lance
pet'-u-lan-cy
pet'-u-lant
pe-tu'-nia
pe'-wit
pew'-ter
pew'-ter-er
pe-yo'-te
pe-yo'-tism
pfef'-fer-nuss
pfen'-nig
pha-com'-e-ter
pha'-e-ton
phag-e-de'-na
phag'o-cyte
phag:o-cyt'-ic
phag:o-cy-to'-sis
pha'-lange*
pha-lan'-ge-al
pha-lan'-ger
pha-lan'-ges
phal'-an-ster:y
pha'-lanx

290

phal'-a-rope
phal'-lic
phal-loi'-dine
phal'-lus
phan'-er-ite
phan'-er-o-gam
phan-er-os'-co-py
phan-er-o'-sis
phan'-o-tron
phan'-tasm
phan-tas-ma-go'-ri:a
phan-tas-ma-gor'-ic
phan-tas'-ma-gor'-i-cal
phan-tas'-mal
phan'-tom
phan'-to-scope
phar'-aoh†
Phar'-i-sa'-ic
Phar'-i-sa'-i-cal
Phar'-i-sa-ism
Phar'-i-see
phar'-ma-ceu'-ti-cal
phar'-ma-ceu'-tics
phar'-ma-ceu'-tist
phar'-ma-cist
phar-ma-cog'-no-sy
phar-mac'-o-lite
phar'-ma-co-log'-i-cal
phar-ma-col'-o-gist
phar-ma-col'-o-gy
phar-ma-co-pe'-ia
phar-ma-co-poe'-ia
phar'-ma-cy
Pha'-ros
pha-ryn'-ge-al
phar-yn-gi'-tis
pha-ryn'-go-log'-i-cal
phar-yn-gol'-o-gy
pha-ryn'-go-scope
pha-ryn-gos'-co-py
phar-yn-got'-o-my
phar'-ynx
phase
phase'-me-ter
pha-se'-o-lin
phas'-er
pha'-sic*
pha'-si-tron
pha'-sor
pheas'-ant
phel-lan'-drene
phel'-lo-gen
phen-ac'-e-tin*†
phen'-a-cite
phen'-a-cyl
phen-an'-threne*†
phen-an'-thri-dine*†
phe-nan-thri-din'-i-um

phe-nan'-thro-line
phe-nan'-thryl
phen-ar'-sa-zine
phen'-az:ine†
phe-net'-i-dine
phen'-e-tole†
phe'-nic
phen-mi-az'-ine
phe'-no-bar'-bi-tal
phe'-no-cop'-ic
phe'-no-cop'y
phe'-no-crys'-tic
phe'-nol
phe'-no-lase
phe'-no-late
phe-no'-lic*
phe-nol'-o-gist
phe-nol'-o-gy
phe'-nol-phthal'e:in
phe-nom'-e-na
phe-nom'-e-nal
phe-nom'-e-nal-ism
phe-nom'-e-no-log'-i-cal
phe-nom-e-nol'-o-gy
phe-nom'-e-non
phe'-no-plast
phe'-no-type
phen-ox'-ide*
phe-nox'y-a:ce'-tic
phen'yl†
phen'yl-ac-et-al'-de-
    hyde†
phen'yl-ate†
phen'yl-ene
phen'yl-eph'-rine
phen:yl-eth'-yl-ene
phe-nyl'-ic
phen:yl-ke-to-nu'-ric
phe-nyt'-o-in
phe:o-chro-mo-cy-to'-ma
phe:o-phor'-bide
phe:o-phy'-tin
phi'-al
Phi Be'-ta Kap'-pa
Phid'-i-as
Phil-a-del'-phia
Phil-a-del'-phian
phi-lan'-der
phi-lan'-der-er
phil'-an-throp'-ic
phi-lan'-thro-pist
phi-lan'-thro-py
phil'-a-tel'-ic
phi-lat'-e-list
phi-lat'-e-ly
Phi-le'-mon
phil'-har-mon'-ic
phil'-hel-len'-ic

phil'-i-a-ter†
Phil'-ip
Phi-lip'-pi-ans
phi-lip'-pic
Phil'-ip-pine
Phil'-is-tine†
Phi'-lo
phil-o-den'-dron
phil'-o-graph
phi-log'-y-ny
phil'-o-log'-i-cal
phi-lol'-o-gist
phi-lol'-o-gy
phil'-o-mel
phil-o-pe'-na
phil'o-pro-gen'-i-tive
phi-los'-o-pher
phil'-o-soph'-ic
phil'-o-soph'-i-cal
phil'-o-soph'-i-cal-ly
phi-los'-o-phism
phi-los'-o-phize
phi-los'-o-phiz-er
phi-los'-o-phy
phil'-ter
phle-bit'-ic
phle-bi'-tis
phleb-o-graph'-ic
phle-bog'-ra-phy
phle-bot'-o-my
phlegm
phleg-mat'-ic
phlob'-a-phene
phlo'-em
phlo-gis'-tic
phlo-gis'-ton
phlog'-o-pite
phlog-o-pi-ti-za'-tion
phlo-go'-sis
phlo-got'-ic
phlo'-i-on'-ic
phlor'-e-tin
phlor'-i-zin
phlor'-i-zin-ize*
phlor'-o-glu'-cin-ol†
phlo'-rol
phlox
phlox'-ine
pho'-bi:a
pho'-bic
pho-bo-tax'-is
pho-co-me'-li:a
phoe'-be
Phoe'-bus
Phoe-ni'-cia
Phoe-ni'-cian
Phoe'-nix
phon-as-the'-ni:a

phon-au'-to-graph†
pho'-ne-mat'-ic
pho'-neme
pho-ne'-mic
pho-ne-mic'-i-ty
pho-ne'-mics
pho-nen'-do-scope
pho-net'-ic
pho-net'-i-cal-ly
pho-ne-ti'-cian
pho-net'-i-cize
pho'-ne-tism
pho'-ne-tist†
Phone'-vi-sion
pho'-ni-at'-ric
phon'-ic
pho'-no-deik
pho'-no-gen'-ic
pho'-no-gram
pho'-no-graph
pho-no-graph'-ic
pho'-no-lite
pho'-no-log'-i-cal
pho-nol'-o-gist
pho-nol'-o-gize
pho-nol'-o-gy
pho-nom'-e-ter
pho-nom'-e-try
pho'-no-phore
pho-noph'-o-rous
pho'-no-typ:y†
pho'-ny
phor'-bin
pho-re'-sis
phor'-e-sy
pho-ret'-ic
pho-rom'-e-ter
pho-rom'-e-try
pho'-rone
Pho-rop'-tor
phos'-gene
phos'-gen-ite*
phos-pham'-ic
phos'-pha-tase
phos'-phate
phos-pha-te'-mi:a
phos'-phat'-ic
phos'-pha-tize
phos'-phide
phos'-phi-nate
phos'-phine
phos'-phin'-ic
phos'-phite
phos'-pho-a:mi-no-lip'-ide
phos-pho-di-es'-ter-ase
phos'-pho-nate

phos-phon'-ic
phos-pho'-ni-um
phos'-phor
phos'-pho-rate†
phos-pho're-al
phos'-pho-resce'†
phos-pho-res'-cence†
phos-pho-res'-cent†
phos'-phor-ic
phos'-pho-rism†
phos-phor'-o-gen
phos-pho-ro-gen'-ic†
phos-pho-rol'-y-sis
phos'-pho-rous† (adj.)
phos'-pho-rus* (n.)
phos'-pho-ryl-ase*
phos'-sy
phos'-vi-tin
pho'-tics
pho'-to
pho-to-chem'-is-try
pho'-to-chro-my
pho'-to-e:lec'-tric
pho'-to-en-grav'-ing
pho'-to-flash
pho'-to-gene
pho'-to-gen'-ic
pho'-to-gram'-me-try
pho'-to-graph
pho-tog'-ra-pher
pho'-to-graph'-ic
pho-tog'-ra-phy
pho'-to-gra-vure'
pho'-to-ki-ne'-sis
pho'-to-lith'-o-graph
pho'-to-li-thog'-ra-phy
pho-tol'-y-sis
pho'-to-lyt'-ic
pho-tom'-e-ter
pho'-to-met'-ric
pho-tom'-e-try
pho'-ton
pho'-to-nas'-tic
pho-top'-a-thy
pho'-to-phil'-ic
pho-toph'-i-lous
pho-to-pho-re'-sis
pho'-to-play
phot-op-tom'-e-ter*†
pho'-to-re-cep'-tor
pho'-to-sen'-si-tive
pho'-to-stat
pho'-to-stat-ed
pho-to-syn'-the-sis
pho-tot'-o-nus
pho'-to-tran-sis'-tor
pho-to-troph'-ic
pho-to-trop'-ic

pho-tot'-ro-pism
pho'-to-typ:y†
Pho-tron'-ic
phras'-a:ble
phras'-al†
phrase
phra'-se-o-gram
phra-se-og'-ra-phy
phra-se-ol'-o-gy
phras'-er
phras'-ing
phra'-try
phre-net'-ic
phren'ic
phren-i-cot'-o-my
phre-ni'-tis
phren-o-log'-i-cal
phre-nol'-o-gist
phre-nol'-o-gy
phren'-o-sin
Phryg'-i-an
phtha-lam'-ic†
phthal'-ate
phthal'e:in
phthal'ic
phthal'-im'-ide†
phthal'-in
phthal'-o-ni'-trile
phthal'-o-yl
phthi'-o-col
phthi-ri'-a-sis
phthis'ic
phthis'-ick:y
phthis-i-ol'-o-gy
phthi'-sis
phy-col'-o-gy
phy'-co-my-ce'-tous
phy-lac'-ter:y
Phyl'-lis
phyl'-lo-por'-phy-rin
phyl-lox'-e'ra
phy'-lo-ge-net'-ic
phy-log'-e-ny
phy'-lum
phy-ma-to'-sis
phys-i-at'-rics
phys'-ic
phys'-i-cal
phys'-i-cal-ly
phy-si'-cian
phys'-i-cist
phys'-icked
phys'-ick-ing
phys'-ics
phys'-i-o-crat
phys-i-og'-no-my
phys-i-og'-ra-pher
phys'-i:o-graph'-ic

phys-i-og'-ra-phy
phys-i-ol'-a-ter
phys'-i-o-log'-i-cal
phys-i-ol'-o-gist
phys-i-ol'-o-gy
phys-i-om'-e-try
phys-i-os'-o-phy
phys'-i:o-ther'-a-py
phy-sique'
phy'-so-car'-pous
phy-so-stig'-mine
phy-sos'-to-mous
phy'-tase
Phy'-tin
phy-to-flu'-ene
phy-tog'-a-my
phy'-to-gen'-e-sis
phy-to-gen'-ic
phy-tog'-e-ny
phy-tol'-o-gy
phy-tom'-e-ter
phy-to-met'-ric
phy-toph'-a-gous
phy-to'-sis
phy-tos'-te-rol*†
phy'-tyl
pi-ac'-u-lar
piaffe
pi'-a-nis'-si-mo
pi-an'-ist
pi-a-niste'
pi'-a-nis'-tic†
pi-a'-no (softly)
pi-an'o (instrument)
pi-an'o-forte*†
pi-an'-os
pi-as-sa'-va
pi-as'-ter
pi-az'-za
pi'-broch
pi'-ca
pic'-a-dor
Pic'-ar-dy
pic'-a-resque'
pic'-a-roon'
Pi-cas'-so
pic-a-yune'
Pic'-ca-dil'-ly
pic'-ca-lil'-li
pic'-co-lo
pic'-co-lo-ist
pic'-e-in†
pi'-cene
pic'-e-ous
pick'-a-back
pick'-a-nin-ny
pick'-ax
pick'-er

pick'-er-el
pick'-et
pick'-et-er
pick'-et-ing
Pick'-ett
pick'-ing
pick'-le
pick'-led
pick'-ling
pick'-lock
pick-pock-et
pick'-up (n.)
Pick'-wick
pic'-nic
pic'-nicked
pic'-nick-er
pic'-nick-ing
pic'-o-line
pic'-o-lin'-ic
pi'-co-pi'-co-gram
pi'-cot
pic-ram'-ic
pic-ram'-ide
pic'-rate
pic'-ric
pic-ro-cro'-cin
pic'-ro-lon'-ic
pic-rom'-er-ite
pic'-ryl
Pict'-ish
pic'-to-graph
pic'-to-graph'-ic
pic-to-graph'-i-cal-ly
pic-tog'-ra-phy
pic-to-ri-al
pic'-tur-a:ble
pic'-ture
pic-tur-esque'
pic'-tur-esque'-ness
pic'-tur-ing
pic'-ul
pid'-dle
pid'-dler
pid'-dling
pid'-gin*†
pie'-bald
pieced
pièce de ré'-sis-tance'
piece goods
piece'-meal
piec'-er
piece rate
piece'-work
pie chart
piec'-ing
pie'-crust
Pied'-mont
Pied'-mon-tese'†

294

pie'-man
pie'-plant
pierced
pierc'-er
pierc'-ing
pier'-head
Pi-e'-ri-an
Pier'-rot*
pi'-e:tism
pi-e:tis'-tic
pi'-e-ty
pi-e:zom'-e-ter
pi-e'zo-met'-ric
pi-e:zom'-e-try
pif'-fle
pi'-geon†
pi'-geon-eer'
pi'-geon-hole†
pi'-geon=toed†
pi'-geon-wing†
pig'-fish
pig'-ger:y
pig'-gish
pig'-head-ed
pig i:ron
pig'-ment
pig'-men-tar:y†
pig-men-ta'-tion
pi'-gnon*
pig'-nut
pig'-pen
pig'-skin
pig'-stick-ing
pig'-sty
pig'-tail
pig'-weed
pike'-man
pike perch
pike'-staff
pik'-er
pi-laf'
pi-las'-ter
Pi'-late
pil'-chard
pi'-le-ate
pi'-le-at-ed
pi-le'-o-lus
pi'-le-ous
pil'-er
pil'-fer
pil'-fer-age
pil'-grim
pil'-grim-age
pi-lif'-er-ous
pil'-ing
pil'-lage
pil'-lag-er

pil'-lar
pil'-lared
pill'-box
pil'-lion
pil-lo-ried
pil'-lor-ize*†
pil'-lo-ry
pil'-low
pil'-low-case
pil'-low-slip
pil'-low:y
pi-lo-car'-pi-dine
pi'-lose
pi'-lo-sine
pi-los'-i-ty
pi'-lot
pi'-lot-age
pi'-lot-house
Pil'-sner
pil'-u-lar
pim-an'-threne
pi-mar'-ic
pim'-e-late
pi-men'-ta
pi-men'-to
pi-mien'-to
pim'-per-nel
pim'-ple
pim'-pled
pim'-ply
pi'-na
pi-na'-ceous
pin'-a-coid
pin'-a-coi'-dal
pin'-a-col
pi-nac'-o-late
pi-nac'-o-lone
Pin-a-cy'-a-nol
pin'-a-fore
pi'-nane
pi-nas'-ter
pin'-ball
pince'=nez'
pin'-cers
pinch'-beck
pinch'-er
pinch'=hit
pin'-cush-ion
Pin'-dar
Pin-dar'-ic
pine'-al
pine'-ap-ple
pi'-nene
Pi-ne'-ro†
pin'-er:y
pi-ne'-tum
pi'-ney*†
pin'-feath-er

295

pin'-fold
Ping'=Pong
pin'-head
pin'-hole
pi'-nic
pin'-ion
pi'-nite*†
pi'-ni-tol
pink'-er
pink'-eye
pink'-ish
pink'-root
pin'-ky*† (finger)
pink'y (color)
pin mon-ey
pin'-na
pin'-nace
pin'-na-cle
pin'-nate
pin'-ning
pi-no-cam'-phe-ol
pi'-noch-le
pi-no'-lin*†
pi-ñon'
pi-non'-ic
pi-no-syl'-vin
pin'-point
pin'-tle
pin'-to
pin'-up (n.)
pin'-weed
pin'-wheel
pin'-worm
pinx'-ter
pin'y
pi'-nyl
pi'-o-neer'
pi'-o-neered'
pi-os'-i-ty
pi'-ous
pi'-ous-ly
pip'-age
pi-pec'-o-line
pipe dream
pipe'-ful
pipe'-line
pipe or-gan
pip'-er
pi:per'-a-zine
pi-per'-ic
pi-per'-i-dine
pip'-er-ine
pi:per'-o-nyl'-ic
pip'-er-ox'-an
pi:per'-y-lene
pipe'-stem
pipe'-stone
pi-pette'

pip'-ing
pip'-kin
pip'-pin
pi'-quan-cy
pi'-quant
pi-qué'
pique
piqued
pi-quet'
piqu'-ing*
pi'-ra-cy
Pi-rae'-us
pi-ra'-nha
pi'-rate
pi-rat'-i-cal
pi'-rogue
pir'-ou-ette'
pir'-ou-ett'-ed*†
pir'-ou-ett'-ing*†
Pi'-sa
pis'-ca-ry
pis-ca'-tion
pis-ca-tol'-o-gy
pis'-ca-to'-ri-al
pis'-ca-to-ry
Pis'-ces
pis'-ci-cul-ture
pis-ci'-na
pis'-cine
pi'-si-form
pis'-mire
pis-tach'-i:o†
pis'-til
pis'-til-late
pis'-tol
pis'-ton
pitch'-blende
pitch'-er
pitch'-fork
pitch'-ing
pitch'-stone
pitch'y
pit'-e-ous
pit'-e-ous-ly
pit'-fall
pith'-e-can'-thro-poid
Pith-e-can'-thro-pus
pith-e-col'-o-gy
pith'-i-ly
pith'-i-ness
pith'y
pit'i-a:ble
pit'-ied
pit'i-er
pit'-ies
pit'i-ful
pit'i-ful-ly
pit'i-less

pit'-man
pi-tom'-e-ter
pi'-ton
pit saw
pit'-tance
pit'-ted
pit'-ter=pat'-ter
pit'-ting
Pitts'-burg (Kans., Calif.)
Pitts'-burgh (Penn.)
pi-tu'-i-itar:y†
pi-tu'-i-tous
Pi-tu'-i-trin
pit'y
pit'y-ing
pit-y-ri'-a-sis
Pi'-us
pi-val'-ic
piv'-ot
piv'-ot-al
piv'-ot-er
pix'-ie
pix'-i-lat-ed
pix'y
Pi-zar'-ro
piz-ze-ri'a
piz'-zi-ca'-to
plac:a-bil'-i-ty
plac'a-ble
plac'-ard†
pla'-cate
pla'-cat-er
pla'-cat-ing
pla-ca'-tion
pla-ca'-tive
pla'-ca-to-ry
place'-a:ble
pla-ce'-bo
place'=kick
place'-ment
pla-cen'-ta
plac'-en-tar:y†
pla-cen'-tate
plac-en-ta'-tion
plac-en-ti'-tis
plac'-er
pla'-cet
plac'-id
pla-cid'-i-ty
plac'-id-ly
plac'-ing
plack'-et
plac'-oid
pla'-gia-rism
pla'-gia-rist
pla'-gia-ris'-tic
pla'-gia-rize
pla'-gia-riz-ing

pla'-gia-ry
pla'-gi-o-clase
pla'-gi-o-nite
pla-gi-ot'-ro-pism
plague
plagu'-ed
pla'-guey
pla-gui-ly†
plagu'-ing*
pla'-guy†
plaid
plain'=laid'
plain'-ly
plain'-ness
plains'-man
plain'-tiff
plain'-tive
plain'-tive-ly
plait
plait'-er
pla'-nar
pla-nar-i:a*†
pla-nar'-i-an†
pla-nar'-i-ty
pla-na'-tion
plan'-chet*†
plan-chette'
plan'-er (one who runs a
  plane)
pla'-ner (tree)
plan'-et
plan-e-tar'-i-um†
plan-e-tar:y†
plan-e-tes'-i-mal
plan'-et-oid†
plan'-et-oi'-dal†
plan-et-o-log'-ic†
plan-et-ol'-o-gy†
plan'-gen-cy
plan'-gent
pla-nig'-ra-phy
pla-nim'-e-ter
pla'-ni-met'-ric†
plan'-i-sphere
plank'=sheer
plank-tiv'-o-rous
plank'-ton
planned
plan'-ner
plan'-ning
pla'-no-con'-cave
plan'-o-graph*†
pla-nog'-ra-phy*
pla-nom'-e-ter
plan'-o-sol†
Plan-tag'-e-net
plan'-tain

297

plan'-tar
plan-ta'-tion
plant'-er
plan'-ti-grade
plant'-ing
plant louse
pla'-num
plaque
pla-quette'
plash'y
plas'-ma
plas-ma-pher'-e-sis
plas'-mic
plas-min'-o-gen
plas-mo-di'-a-sis
plas-mo'-di-um
plas-mol'-y-sis
plas'-mo-lyt'-ic
plas'-te-line
plas'-ter
plas'-tered
plas'-ter-er
plas'-ter-ing
plas'-ter-work
plas'-tic
plas-ti-ca-tor
plas-ti-cim'-e-ter
plas-tic'-i-ty
plas'-ti-cize
plas'-ti-ciz-er
plas'-tid
plas'-ti-noid†
plas'-ti-sol
plas-to-mer
plas-tom'-e-ter
plas'-tron
pla-teau'
plat'-ed
plate'-ful
plate glass
plat'-en
plat'-er
plat'-form
pla-ti'-na*†
plat'-ing
pla-tin'-ic
plat'-i-nize
plat'-i-no-type
plat'-i-num
plat'-i-tude
plat'-i-tu-di-nar'-i-an†
plat-i-tu'-di-nize
plat'-i-tu'-di-nous
Pla'-to
pla-ton'-ic
Pla'-ton-ism
Pla'-ton-ist
pla-toon'

Platte
plat'-ter
plat:y-kur'-tic
plat:y-kur-to'-sis
plat'-y-nite
plat'y-pus
plau'-dit
plau-si-bil'-i-ty
plau'-si-ble
plau'-sive
Plau'-tus
play'-a:ble
play'-back (n.)
play'-bill
play'-boy
play'-er
play'-fel-low
play'-ful
play'-ful-ly
play'-ful-ness
play'-go-er
play'-ground
play'-house
play'-ing card
play'-mate
play'=off (n.)
play'-room
play'-script
play'-thing
play'-time
play'-wright
plaza'*†
plea
plead'-a:ble
plead'-er
plead'-ing
plead'-ing-ly
pleas'-ance
pleas'-ant
pleas'-ant-ly
pleas'-ant-ness
pleas'-ant-ry
pleas'-ing
plea'-sur-a:ble*
plea'-sure*
pleat
pleat'-ed
pleat'-er
plebe
ple-be'-ian
ple-bis'-ci-tar:y†
pleb'-i-scite
plec'-trum
pledged
pledg-ee'
pledg'-er
pled'-get*†
pledg'-ing

pled'-gor*†
ple'-iad†
Ple'-ia-des†
plei'-o-bar
plei-ot'-ro-py
Pleis'-to-cene
ple'-nar-ty
ple'-na-ry
plen'-i-po-ten'-tia-ry*†
plen'-i-tude
plen'-i-tu'-di-nous
plen'-te-ous
plen'-ti-ful
plen'-ti-ful-ly
plen'-ty
plen'um*†
ple'-o-nasm
ple'-o-nas'-tic
ple-ro'-ma
ple-rot'-ic
ple'-si-o-saur
pleth'-o-ra
pleth'-o-ric*†
pleu'-ra
pleu'-ral
pleu'-ri-sy
pleu-rit'-ic
pleu'-ro-dont
pleu-rot'-o-my
Plex'-i-glas
plex-im'-e-ter
plex'-us
pli-a-bil'-i-ty
pli'-a-ble
pli'-an-cy
pli'-ant
pli'-cate
pli-ca'-tion
plied
pli'-ers
plight
plinth
Plin'y
Pli'-o-cene
plod'-ded
plod'-der
plod'-ding
ploi'-dy
plom'-bage'
Plo-ti'-nus
plot'-less
plot'-ter
plot'-ting
plov'er
plow
plow'-boy
plow'-er
plow'=hand

plow'-ing
plow'-man
plow'-share
pluck'-er
pluck'-i-er
pluck'y
plug'-board
plug'-ging
plug'=ug-ly
plum
plu-ma'-ceous
plu'-mage*
plu'-mate
plumb
plum-ba'-gin
plum-ba'-go
plum'-bate
plumb bob
plumb'-er
plum-bif'-er-ous
plumb'-ing
plum'-bite
plumb line
plum'-bous
plum'-ing
plum'-met
plu'-mose
plump'-er
plump'-ness
plu'-mule
plum'y
plun'-der
plun'-der-er
plun'-der-ous
plung'-er
plung'-ing
plu-per'-fect
plu'-ral
plu'-ral-ism
plu-ral'-i-ty
plu'-ral-ize
plu'-ral-ly
plu-ri-va'-lent
plush'y
Plu'-tarch
plu'-tar-chy
Plu'-to
plu-toc'-ra-cy
plu'-to-crat
plu'-to-crat'-ic
plu-to'-ni-an
plu-ton'-ic
plu'-to-nism
plu-to'-ni-um
plu'-vi-al
plu-vi-og'-ra-phy
plu-vi-om'-e-ter
plu-vi-o-met'-ric

299

plu'-vi-ous
ply'-ing
Plym'-outh
ply'-wood
pneu-drau'-lic
pneu-mat'-ic
pneu-mat'-i-cal-ly
pneu-ma-tic'-i-ty
pneu-ma-tol'-o-gy
pneu-ma-tol'-y-sis
pneu-ma-tom'-e-ter
pneu-ma-to'-sis
pneu-mec'-to-my
pneu-mo-coc'-cus
pneu-mol'-o-gy
pneu-mo'-nia
pneu-mon'-ic
pneu-mo-ni'-tis
poach'-er
Po-ca-hon'-tas
po-choir'
pock'-et
pock'-et-book
pock'-et-ful
pock'-et-knife
pock'-mark
po-co-cu-ran'-tism
po-dal'-ic
pod'-ding
po'-de-sta'*†
podg'-i-ness
podg'y
po-di'-a-trist
po-di'-a-try
po'-di-um
po'-do-lite
pod'-zol-ize
po'-em
po'-e-sy
po'-et
po'-et-as-ter
po'-et-ess
po-et'-ic
po-et'-i-cal
po-et'-i-cal-ly
po-et'-ics
po'-et-ize
po'-et-ry
po-go-nol'-o-gy
po-go-not'-ro-phy
po-grom'
poi-e'-sis
poi-et'-ic
poi'-gnan-cy*†
poi'-gnant*†
poi'-ki-lit'-ic
poi-kil'o-cy-to'-sis†

poi-lu'
Poin-ca-ré'
poin-ci-an'a'†
poin-set'-tia
point'=blank'
point'=de-vice'
point'-ed
point'-ed-ly
point'-er
poin'-til-lism
point'-less
Poi-ret'
poised
pois'-er
pois'-ing
poi'-son
poi'-son-er
poi'-son i'vy
poi'-son-ous
Poi-tiers'
pok'-er*
pok'-ing
pok'y
Po'-land
po'-lar
po-lar-im'-e-ter
po-lar'-i-met'-ric
Po-lar'-is†
po-lar'-i-scope
po-lar'-i-stro-bom'-e-ter
po-lar'-i-ty
po-lar-i:za'-tion
po'-lar-ize
po'-lar-iz-er
po'-lar-iz-ing
po-lar'-o-graph'-ic
po-lar-og'-ra-phy
Po'-lar-oid
po'-lar-on
pol'-der
pole'-ax
pole'-cat
po-lem'-i-cal
po-lem'-i-cal-ly
po-lem'-i-cist
pol'-e-mize
po-len'-ta
pol'-er
pole'-star
pole'=vault (v.)
po'-li-a-nite
po-lice'
po-lice'-man
pol'-i-cies
po-lic'-ing
pol'-i-clin'-ic
pol'-i-cy

300

pol'-i-cy-hold-er
po'-li:o†
po'-li:o-my-e-li:'-tis†
po-li-o'-sis†
pol'-ish
Pol'-ish†
pol'-ish-er
pol'-it-bu-ro*
po-lite'
po-lite'-ly
po-lite'-ness
pol'-i-tic
po-lit'-i-cal
po-lit'-i-cal-ly
pol-i-ti'-cian
po-lit'-i-cize
pol'-i-tic-ly
pol'-i-tics
pol'-i-ty
Po-litz'-er†
pol'-ka
pol'-ka=dot (v.)
pol'-kaed
pol'-lack
pol'-lard
pol'-len
pol'-len-ize
pol'-len-iz-er
poll'-er
pol'-li-nate
pol'-li-nat-ing
pol-li-na'-tion
pol'-li-nif'-er-ous
pol-lin'-i-um
pol-li-no'-sis
pol'-li-wog
poll'-ster
poll tax
pol-lu'-cite
pol-lu'-tant*
pol-lute'
pol-lut'-er
pol-lut'-ing
pol-lu'-tion
Pol'-lux
po'-lo
po'-lo-ist
pol'-o-naise'†
po-lo'-ni-um
pol-troon'
pol'y-a:cryl'-ic
pol'y-am'-ide†
pol'y-an'-drous
pol'y-an-dry
pol'y-an'-thus
pol:y-ar'-gy-rite
pol:y-ba'-sic*

pol:y-ba'-site*
Po-lyb'-i-us
pol'y-chro-ism
pol:y-chro-mat'-ic
pol'y-chrome
pol'y-chro-my
pol'y-clin'-ic
pol'y-crase
pol:y-cy-the'-mi:a
po-lyd'-y-mite*
pol'y-ene
pol'y-es-ter
pol:y-eth'-yl-ene
po-lyg'-a-la
pol'y-gam'-ic
po-lyg'-a-mist
po-lyg'-a-mous
po-lyg'-a-my
po-lyg'-e-ny
pol'y-glot
pol'y-gon
po-lyg'-o-nal
pol'y-graph
pol:y-graph'-ic
po-lyg'-ra-phy
po-lyg'-y-ny
pol'y-he'-dral
pol'y-he'-dron
pol'y-hi-dro'-sis
pol'y-i:so-bu'-tyl-ene†
pol'y-i:so-top'-ic
pol'y-kar'-y-on
pol'y-math
po-lym'-a-thy
pol'y-mer
pol'y-mer'-ic
po-lym'-er-ism
po-lym-er-i-za'-tion
po-lym'-er-ize*
po-lym'-er-iz-er
po-lym'-er-ous
pol'y-me-ter*†
pol'-ym-nite
pol'y-mor'-phic
pol'y-mor'-phism
pol'y-mor'-phous
Pol'y-ne'-sia
Pol'y-ne'-sian
pol'y-no'-mi-al
po:ly-nu-cle-o'-sis
pol'-yp
pol-yp-ec'-to-my
pol:y-pep'-tide
pol:y-pha'-gia
po-lyph'-a-gous
pol'y-phase
Pol'-y-phe'-mus

301

pol'y-phon'ic
po-lyph'o-ny†
pol'y-ploid
pol'y-ploi-dy
pol'-yp-ous*†
pol'-yp-tych
pol:y-sac'-cha-ride
pol:y-se'-mant
pol'y-se'-mous
pol'y-se-my
pol:y-so'-ma-ty
pol:y-sty'-rene
pol'y-syl-lab'-ic
pol'y-syl'-la-ble
pol'y-tech'-nic
pol'y-tech'-ni-cal
pol'y-the-ism
pol'y-the-ist
pol'y-the-is'-tic
pol:y-ton'-al-ism
pol'y-to-nal'-i-ty
pol'y-trop'-ic
pol:y-u're-thane†
pol:y-va'-lent
pol:y-vi'-nyl
pom'-ace
po-ma'-ceous
po-made'
po-ma'-tum
pome'-gran-ate
Pom-er-a'-ni:a†
Pom-er-a'-ni:an†
pom'-mel
pom'-meled
po'-mo-log'-i-cal
po-mol'-o-gy
pom'-pa-dour
pom'-pa-no
Pom-pe'-ian
Pom-peii'
Pom'-pey
pom'-pi-on
pom'=pom
pom'-pon
pom-pos'-i-ty
pomp'-ous†
Po'na-pe'-an
Pon'-ce
Pon'-ce de Le-ón'
pon'-cho
pon'-chos
pond'-age
pon'-der
pon-der-a:bil'-i-ty
pon'-der-a:ble
pon-der-o'-sa
pon-der-os'-i-ty
pon'-der-ous

pon-gee'
pon'-iard
po'-nies
pon'-tage
Pon'-ti-ac
pon'-tiff
pon-tif'-i-cal
pon-tif'-i-cate
pon-tif'-i-ca-tor
pon'-tine
Pon'-tius
pon-toon'
Pon'-tus
po'-ny
poo'-dle
pool'-room
poor farm
poor'-house
poor'-ly
poor'-ness
pop'-corn
pope'-dom
pop'-e-line
pop'-er:y†
pop'-gun
pop'-in-jay
pop'-ish
pop'-lar
pop'-lin
pop-lit'-e-al†
Po-po-ca-te'-petl
pop'-o:ver
pop'-per
pop'-pies
pop'-ping
pop'-py
pop'-py-cock
pop'-u-lace
pop'-u-lar
pop-u-lar'-i-ty
pop-u-lar-i:za'-tion
pop'-u-lar-ize
pop'-u-lar-ly
pop'-u-late
pop-u-la'-tion
pop'-u-list
pop'-u-lous
pop'-u-lous-ness
por'-ce-lain†
por-ce-la'-ne:ous
por'-cine
por'-cu-pine
pore
po'-ri-ci'-dal*
po-rif'-er-ous
po-ri'-na
po'-rism

pork'-er
por'-ky (porcupine)
pork'y (of pork)
por-nog'-ra-pher†
por-no-graph'-ic
por-nog'-ra-phy
po-rom'-e-ter
po'-ro-scope
po-ros'-co-py
po'-rose
po-ro-sim'-e-ter*
po-ros'-i-ty
po-rot'-ic
po'-rous
por'-phin
por'-phy-rin
por'-phy-rit'-ic
por'-phyr-ox'-ine†
por'-phy-ry
por'-poise
por'-ridge
por'-rin-ger
por-ta-bil'-i-ty*†
por'-ta-ble*†
por'-tage†
por'-tal
por-ta-men'-to
por'-ta-tive
Port=au=Prince
port-cul'-lis
porte co-chere'
por-tend'
por'-tent
por-ten'-tous
por'-ter
por'-ter-age
por'-ter-house
port-fo'-li:o
port'-hole
Por'-tia
por'-ti-co
por'-ti-coes
por-tiere'
por'-tion
Port'-land
port'-li-er
port'-li-ness
port'-ly
port-man'-teau
por-to-la'-no
por'-trait
por'-trai-ture
por-tray'
por-tray'-al
por'-tress
Ports'-mouth
Por'-tu-gal
Por'-tu-guese'

por-tu-lac'a*†
por'-tu-la-ca'-ceous
posed
Po-sei'-don
pos'-er
po-seur'
pos'-ing
pos'-it
po-si'-tion
po-si'-tion-er
pos'-i-ti'-val
pos'-i-tive
pos'-i-tive-ly
pos'-i-tiv-ism
pos'-i-tiv-is'-tic
pos-i-tri'-no
pos'-i-tron
pos-i-tro'-ni-um
po-sol'-o-gy
pos'-se
pos-sess'
pos-sessed'
pos-sess'-es
pos-ses'-sion
pos-ses'-sive
pos-ses'-sive-ly
pos-ses'-sive-ness
pos-ses'-sor
pos-ses'-so-ry
pos'-set
pos-si-bil'-i-ty
pos'-si-ble
pos'-si-bly
pos'-sum
post'-age
post'-al
post-ax'-i-al
post'-boy
post'-card
post'-date'
post'-di-lu'-vi:an
post'-er
pos-te'-ri-or
pos-ter'-i-ty
pos'-tern
pos'-ter:o-dor'-sal
post-ex-il'-ic
post-gla'-cial
post-grad'-u-ate
post'-haste'
post'-hu-mous†
post'-hu-mous-ly†
post'-hyp-not'-ic
pos-til'-ion
post-li-min'-i-um
post'-man
post'-mark
post'-mas-ter

303

post-me-rid'-i-an
post-mil-len'-ni-al
post'-mis-tress
post'=mor'-tem
post=o'bit
post of fire
post-or'-bit-al†
post'-paid'
post-pone'
post-pone'-ment
post-pran'-di-al
post'-script
pos'-tu-lant
pos'-tu-late
pos'-tu-lat-ing
pos-tu-la'-tion
pos'-tu-la-tor
pos'-tur-al
pos'-ture
pos'-tur-ing
post'-war'
pos'y*‡
po-ta-bil'-i-ty
po'-ta-ble
po-tage'†
po-tam'-ic
pot-a-mog'-ra-phy
pot-a-mom'-e-ter
pot'-ash
pot-as-sam'-ide*†
po-tas'-sic
po-tas'-si-um
po-ta'-tion
po-ta'-to
po-ta'-toes
po'-ta-to-ry
Pot-a-wat'-o-mi
pot'-bel-lied
pot'-bel-ly
pot'-boil-er
pot'-boy
Po-tem'-kin
po'-ten-cy
po'-tent
po'-ten-tate
po-ten'-tial
po-ten-ti-al'-i-ty
po-ten'-tial-ly
po-ten-ti-om'-e-ter
po'-tent-ly
poth'-er
pot'-herb
pot'-hole
pot'-hook
pot'-house
po'-tion
pot'-luck'
Po-to'-mac

po-tom'-e-ter
pot'-pie
pot'-pour-ri'
Pots'-dam
pot'-sherd
pot'-shot
pot'-tage
pot'-ted
pot'-ter
pot'-ter-ies
pot'-ter:y
pot'-tle
Pough-keep'-sie
poul'-ter-er
poul'-tice
poul'-try
pounc'-er
pounc'-ing
pound'-age
pound'-al
pound cake
pound'-er
pound'=fool'-ish
pour
poured
pour'-er
pour'-ing
pour'-par-ler'
pousse=ca-fé'
pout'-er
pout'-ing
pout'-ing-ly
pout'y
pov'-er-ty
pov'-er-ty=strick'-en
pow'-der
pow'-dered
pow'-der:y
pow'-er
pow'-ered
pow'-er-ful
pow'-er-ful-ly
pow'-er-house
pow'-er-less
Pow'-ha-tan'
pow'-wow
Pow'ys
poz-zo-la'-na
prac-ti-ca-bil'-i-ty
prac'-ti-ca-ble
prac'-ti-cal
prac-ti-cal'-i-ty
prac'-ti-cal-ly
prac'-ti-cal-ness
prac'-tice
prac'-ticed
prac'-tic-er
prac'-tic-ing

prac-ti'-tion-er
prae'-ci-pe*
prae'-di-al
prae-mu-ni'-re
prae'-tor
prae-to'-ri-an
prae'-tor-ship
prag-mat'-ic
prag-mat'-i-cal-ly
prag'-ma-tism
prag'-ma-tist
Prague
Pra'-ha
prai'-rie
prais'-er
praise'-wor-thy
prais'-ing
pra'-line
pranced
pranc'-er
pranc'-ing
prank'-ish
pran'-di-al
prank'-ster
prase
pra'-se:o-dym'-i-um
pras'-oid*†
prat'-er
prat'-ing
pra-tique'†
prat'-tle
prat'-tler
prax-e-ol'-o-gy
Prax-it'-e-les
prayed
prayer (act of devotion)
pray'-er (one who prays)
prayer book
prayer'-ful
preached
preach'-er
preach'-ing
preach'-ment
preach'y
pre'-am-ble
pre'-ar-range'
pre-ar-range'-ment
pre-ax'-i-al
preb'-end
pre:ben'-dal
preb'-en-dar:y†
pre-car'-i-ous
pre-car'-i-ous-ness†
prec'-a-to-ry
pre-cau'-tion
pre-cau'-tion-ar:y†
pre-cau'-tious
pre-ced'-a:ble

pre-cede'
prec'e-dence*
prec'e-den-cy*
prec'-e-dent (example)
pre:ce'-dent (foregoing)*
pre-ce-den'-tial
pre-ced'-ing
pre-cen'-tor
pre'-cept
pre-cep'-tive
pre-cep'-tor
pre-cep-to'-ri-al
pre-cep'-to-ry
pre-cep'-tress
pre-ces'-sion
pre-ces'-sion-al
pre'-cinct
pre-ci-os'-i-ty
pre'-cious
prec'-i-pice
pre-cip'-i-tance
pre-cip'-i-tan-cy
pre-cip'-i-tant
pre-cip'-i-tate
pre-cip'-i-tate-ly
pre-cip'-i-tate-ness
pre-cip-i-ta'-tion
pre-cip'-i-ta-tive
pre-cip'-i-ta-tor
pre-cip'-i-tin
pre-cip-i-tin'-o-gen
pre-cip'-i-tous
pre-cip'-i-tous-ly
Pre-cip'-i-tron
pré-cis'
pre-cise'
pre-cise'-ly
pre-cise'-ness
pre-ci'-sian
pre-ci'-sion
pre-ci'-sive
pre-clin'-i-cal
pre-clude'
pre-clud'-ing
pre-clu'-sion
pre-clu'-sive
pre-co'-cial
pre-co'-cious
pre-coc'-i-ty
pre'-con-ceive'
pre'-con-ceiv'-ing
pre-con-cep'-tion
pre-con-cert'
pre-con-cert'-ed
prec'-o-nize
pre-cor'-di-um
pre-cur'-sive
pre-cur'-sor

pre-cur'-so-ry
pre-da'-cious
pre-dac'-i-ty
pre-da'-tion
pred'-a-tism
pred'-a-tor
pred'-a-to'-ri-ly
pred'-a-to-ry
pre-de-cease'
pred'e-ces-sor
pre-den'-ta-ry
pre'-des-ti-nar'-i-an†
pres-des'-ti-nate
pre-des-ti-na'-tion
pre-des'-tine
pre-de-ter'-mi-nate
pre-de-ter-mi-na'-tion
pre-de-ter'-mine
pre-de-ter'-min-ing
pred-i-ca-bil'-i-ty
pred'-i-ca-ble
pre-dic'-a-ment
pred'-i-cant
pred'-i-cate
pred'-i-cat-ing
pred-i-ca'-tion
pred'-i-ca-tive
pred'-i-ca-to-ry
pre-dict'
pre-dict'-a:ble
pre-dic'-tion
pre-dic'-tive
pre-dic'-tor
pre'-di-gest'
pred'i-lec'-tion
pre'-dis-pose'
pre-dis-pos'-ing
pre-dis-po-si'-tion
pred-nis'-o-lone
pred'-ni-sone
pre-dom'-i-nance
pre-dom'-i-nant
pre-dom'-i-nate
pre-dom-i-na'-tion
pre-em'-i-nence
pre-em'-i-nent
pre-em'-i-nent-ly
pre-empt'
pre-emp'-tion
pre-emp'-tive
pre-emp'-tor
pre-emp'-to-ry
preened
pre'-ex-ist'
pre-ex-is'-tent*
pre-fab'-ri-cate
pre-fab'-ri-ca-tor
pref'-ace

pref'-ac-ing
pref'-a-to'-ri-ly
pref'-a-to-ry
pre'-fect
pre-fec-to'-ri-al
pre'-fec-ture
pre-fer'
pref'-er-a-bil'-i-ty
pref'-er-a-ble
pref'-er-a-bly
pref'-er-ence
pref'-er-en'-tial
pre-fer'-ment
preferred'
pre-fer'-ring
pre-fig-u-ra'-tion†
pre-fig'-u-ra-tive*†
pre-fig'-ure
pre'-fix
pre-for-ma'-tion
pre-fron'-tal
pre-ful'-gent
preg-na-bil'-i-ty
preg'-na-ble
preg'-nan-cy
preg'-nant
preg-nen-in'-o-lone
preg-nen'-o-lone
pre-hen'-si-ble
pre-hen'-sile
pre-hen-sil'-i-ty
pre-hen'-sion
pre-his-tor'-ic
pre'-his-tor'-i-cal-ly
prehn'-ite
prehn'-i-tene
prehn-it'-ic
pre'-judge'
pre-judg'-ment
prej'-u-dice
prej'-u-di'-cial
pre'=ju-di'-cial
prel'-a-cy
prel'-ate
pre-lim'-i-nar:y†
prel'-ude
pre-lu'-di-al
pre'-ma-ture'
pre'-ma-ture'-ly
pre-ma-tur'-i-ty*†
pre-med'-i-cal
pre-med'-i-tate
pre-med-i-ta'-tion
pre-med'-i-ta-tive
pre-med'-i-ta-tor
pre-mier'*†
pre-miere'
pre-mier'-ship*†

pre'-mil-le-nar'-i-an†
pre-mil-len'-i-al-ism
prem'-ise
pre'-mi-um
pre'-mo'-lar
pre-mon'-ish
pre-mo-ni'-tion
pre-mon'-i-to-ry
pre-na'-tal
pren'-tice
pre-oc'-cu-pan-cy
pre-oc-cu-pa'-tion
pre-oc'-cu-pied
pre-oc'-cu-py
pre-o'ral
pre-or-dain'
pre-or-di-na'-tion
pre-paid'
prep-a-ra'-tion
pre-par'-a-tive
pre-par'-a-to-ry
pre-pare'
pre-pared'
pre-par'ed-ness
pre-par'-er
pre-pay'
pre-pay'-ment
pre-pon'-der-ance
pre-pon'-der-ant
pre-pon'-der-ate
pre-pon'-der-at-ing
pre-pose'
prep-o-si'-tion
prep-o-si'-tion-al
pre-pos-sess'
pre-pos-sess'-ing
pre-pos-ses'-sion
pre-pos'-ter-ous
pre-pos'-ter-ous-ly
pre-po'-ten-cy
pre-po'-tent
pre'-puce
pre-req'-ui-site
pre-rog'-a-tive
pres'-age*†
pres'-age-ful*†
pres-by-o-phre'-ni:a
pres-by-o'-pi:a
pres'-by-ter
pres-byt'-er-ate
pres-by-te'-ri-al
Pres-by-te'-ri-an
Pres-by-te'-ri-an-ism
pres'-by-ter:y
pre'-school'
pre'-science*†
pre'-scient*†
pre-scind'

pre-scis'-sion
Pres'-cott
pre-scribe'
pre-scrib'-er
pre-scrib'-ing
pre'-script
pre-scrip'-ti-ble
pre-scrip'-tion
pre-scrip'-tive
pres'-ence
pres'-ent (n., adj.)
pre-sent' (v.)
pre-sent'-a:ble
pre-sen-ta'-tion*†
pre-sen'-ta-tive*
pres'-ent=day'
pres'-en-tee'
pre-sent'-er
pre-sen'-ti-ment
pres'-en-tist*†
pres'-ent-ly
pre-sent'-ment
pre-serv'-a:ble
pres-er-va'-tion
pre-serv'-a-tive†
pre-serve'
pre-serv'-er
pre-side'
pres'-i-den-cy
pres'-i-dent
pres'-i-dent=e:lect'
pres'-i-den'-tial
pre-sid'-er
pre-sid'-i-al
pre-sid'-ing
pre-sid'i:o
pre-sid'-i-um
press a:gent
press'-board
press'-er
press'=gang
press'-ing
press'-man
press'-mark
pres'-sor†
press'-room
pres'-sure
pres-sur-ize'
press'-work
pres-ti-dig-i-ta'-tion
pres-ti-dig'-i-ta-tor
pres-tige'
pres-tig'-i-ous
pres-tis'-si-mo
pres'-to
Pres'-ton
Pres'-tone
pre-sum'-a:ble

pre-sum'-a:bly
pre-sume'
pre-sumed'
pre-sum'-er
pre-sump'-tion
pre-sump'-tive
pre-sump'-tu-ous
pre-sup-pose'
pre-sup-po-si'-tion
pre-tend'
pre-tend'-ed
pre-tend'-er
pre-tense'
pre-ten'-sion
pre-ten'-tious
pre-ten'-tious-ness
pret'-er-ist
pret'-er-it
pre-ter'-i-tal
pret-er-i'-tion
pre-ter'-i-tive
pre-ter-mit'
pre'-ter-nat'-u-ral
pre'-text
Pre-to'-ri:a
pret'-ti-fied
pret'-ti-fy
pret'-ti-ly
pret'-ti-ness
pret'-ty
pre-typ'-i-fy
pret'-zel
pre-vail'
pre-vail'-ing
prev'-a-lence
prev'-a-lent
pre-var'-i-cate
pre-var-i-ca'-tion
pre-var'-i-ca-tor
pré-ve-nance'†
pre-ven'-ience†
pre-ven'-ient†
pre-vent'
pre-vent'-a:ble
pre-vent'-a:tive
pre-vent'-er
pre-ven'-tion
pre-ven'-tive
pre'-view
pre'-vi-ous
pre'-vi-ous-ly
pre-vi'-sion
pre-war'
prey
Pri'-am
Pri-a-pe'-an
pri-ap'-ic
pri'-a-pism

Pri-a'-pus
Prib'-i-lov†
price'-less
pric'-er
pric'-ing
prick'-er
prick'-ing
prick'-le
prick'-ling
prick'-ly
pride'-ful
prid'-ing
priest'-craft
priest'-ess
priest'-hood
Priest'-ley
priest'-ly
prig'-gish
pri'-ma-cy
pri'-ma don'-na
pri'-ma fa'-ci:e
pri'-mage
pri'-mal
pri'-ma-quine
pri-mar'-i-ly*†
pri-mar:y*†
pri'-mate
pri-ma'-tial
pri-ma-tol'-o-gy
pri'-ma-ve'-ral
prime'-ly
prime'-ness
prim'-er
pri-me'-val
prim'-ing
pri-mip'-a-ra
prim'-i-tive
prim'-i-tiv-ism
prim'-ness
pri'-mo-cane
pri'-mo-ge'-nial†
pri'-mo-gen'-i-tar:y†
pri'-mo-gen'-i-tor
pri'-mo-gen'-i-ture
pri-mor'-di-al
prim'-rose
prim'-u-la
prim'-u-la'-ceous
prim-u-lav'-er-in
prim'-u-line
pri'-mus
prince'-dom
prince'-li-ness
prince'-ly
prin'-ceps
prin'-cess
Prince'-ton
prin'-ci-pal

308

prin'-ci-pal'-i-ty
prin'-ci-pal-ly
prin'-ci-pal-ship
prin'-ci-pate
prin'-ci-ple
print'-a:ble
print'-er
print'-er:y
print'-ing
print'-less
pri'-on
pri'-or
pri'-or-ate
pri'-or-ess
pri-or'-i-ty
pri'-or-ship
pri'-o-ry†
Pris-cil'-la
prism
pris-mat'-ic
pris'-ma-tize
pris'-ma-toid
pris'-moid
pri-som'-e-ter
pris'-on
pris'-on-er
pris'-sy
pris'-tine
pri'-va-cy
pri'-vate
pri'-va-teer'
pri'-va-teers'-man
pri'-vate-ly
pri'-vate-ness
pri-va'-tion
priv'-a-tive
priv'-a-tize
priv'-et
priv'-i-lege
priv'-i-leged
priv'-i-ly
priv'-i-ty
priv'y
priz'-a:ble
prize'-fight
prize ring
priz'-ing
prob'-a-bi-lism†
prob-a-bil'-i-ty
prob'-a-ble
prob'-a-bly
pro'-bate
pro'-bat-ing
pro-ba'-tion
pro-ba'-tion-al
pro-ba'-tion-ar:y
pro-ba'-tion-er
pro'ba-tive

pro'-ba-to-ry
prob'-ing
pro'bi-ty
prob'-lem
prob'-lem-at'-ic
prob'-lem-at'-i-cal
prob'-lem-at'-i-cal-ly
prob'-o-la
pro-bos'-cis
pro-bos'-cis-es
pro-ca'-cious
pro'-caine
pro'-ca-the'-dral
pro-ce'-dur-al†
pro-ce'-dure
pro-ceed'
pro-ceed'-ing
pro-ce-leus-mat'-ic*†
pro-ce-phal'-ic
proc'ess
proc'ess-ing
pro-ces'-sion
pro-ces'-sion-al
pro-ces'-sion-ar:y†
proc'es-sor
pro-claim'
proc-la-ma'-tion
pro-clam'-a-to-ry
pro-clit'-ic
pro-cliv'-i-ty
pro-cli'-vous
pro-cne'-mi-al*†
pro-con'-sul
pro-con'-sul-ate*†
pro-cras'-ti-nate
pro-cras-ti-na'-tion
pro-cras'-ti-na-tor
pro'-cre-ant
pro'-cre-ate
pro-cre-a'-tion
pro'-cre-at:ive
pro'-cre-a-tor
pro-crus'-te-an
Pro-crus'-tes
proc-ti'-tis
proc-to-log'-i-cal
proc-tol'-o-gy
proc'-tor
proc-to'-ri-al
proc'-tor-ship
proc'-to-scop'-ic
proc-tos'-co-py
pro-cum'-bent
pro-cur'-a:ble
proc'-u-ra-cy
proc-u-ra'-tion
proc'-u-ra-tor
proc'-u-ra-to-ry

pro-cure'
pro-cured'
pro-cure'-ment
pro-cur'-er
pro-cur'-ess
pro-cur'-ing
prod'-ding
prod'-i-gal
prod-i-gal'-i-ty
pro-dig-i-o'-sin
pro-di'-gious†
prod'-i-gy
prod'-ro-mal
pro'-drome
pro-duce' (v.)
prod'-uce (n.)
pro-duc'-er
pro-duc'-i:ble
pro-duc'-ing
prod'-uct (n.)
pro-duct' (v.)
pro-duct-i:bil'-i-ty
pro-duc'-tion
pro-duc'-tive
pro-duc'-tive-ness
pro-duc-tiv'-i-ty
pro'-em
prof-a-na'-tion
pro-fan'-a-to-ry
pro-fane'
pro-fane'-ly
pro-fan'-er
pro-fan'-ing
pro-fan'-i-ty
pro'-fert
pro-fess'
pro-fess'-ant
pro-fessed'
pro-fess'-ed-ly
pro-fes'-sion
pro-fes'-sion-al
pro-fes'-sion-al-ism
pro-fes'-sion-al-ly
pro-fes'-sor
pro'-fes-so'-ri-al
pro-fes-so'-ri-at
pro-fes'-sor-ship
prof'-fer
prof'-fered
pro-fi'-cien-cy
pro-fi'-cient
pro'-file
pro'-fil-er
pro-fil'-o-graph
pro-fi-lom'-e-ter
prof'-it
prof'-it-a:ble
prof'-it-a:bly

prof'-i-teer'*
prof'-it-er
prof'-it-less
prof'-li-ga-cy
prof'-li-gate
prof'-lu-ence
prof'-lu-ent
pro-found'
pro-found'-ly
pro-fun'-di-ty
pro-fuse'
pro-fuse'-ly
pro-fu'-sion
pro-fu'-sive
pro-gen'-i-tor
pro-gen'-i-to'-ri-al
pro-gen'-i-ture
prog'-e-ny
pro-ges'-ter-one
prog'-na-thous
prog-no'-sis
prog-nos'-tic
prog-nos'-ti-cate
prog-nos-ti-ca'-tion
prog-nos'-ti-ca-tor
pro'-gram
pro'-gramed
pro-gram-mat'-ic
pro'-gram-mer
pro'-gram-ming
prog'-ress (n.)
pro-gress' (v.)
pro-gres'-sion
pro-gres'-sion-al
pro-gres'-sion-ist
prog'-ress-ist
pro-gres'-sive
pro-gres'-sive-ly
pro-gres'-siv-ism
pro-hib'-it
pro-hib'-it-er
pro-hi-bi'-tion
pro-hi-bi'-tion-ist
pro-hib'-i-tive
pro-hib'-i-to-ry
proj'-ect (n.)
pro-ject' (v.)
pro-ject'-ed
pro-jec'-tile
pro-jec'-tion
pro-jec'-tive
pro-jec'-tor
pro-ji'-cience
pro-ji'-cient
pro-lam'-in
pro-lapse'
pro-late'
pro-la'-tive

pro-le-gom'-e-non
pro-lep'-sis
pro'-le-tar'-i-an†
pro-le-tar'-i-an-ism†
pro-le-tar'-i-at†
pro-lif'-er-ate
pro-lif'-er-a-tive
pro-lif'-er-ous
pro-lif'-ic
pro-lif'-i-ca-cy
pro-lif'-i-cal-ly
pro-lif-i-ca'-tion
pro-li-fic'-i-ty
pro-lig'-er-ous
pro'-line
pro-lix'
pro-lix'-i-ty
pro-loc'-u-tor
pro'-log
pro'-log-ize
pro'-logue
pro-long'
pro-lon'-gate
pro-lon-ga'-tion
pro-longed'
pro-lu'-sion
pro-lu'-so-ry
pro'-ma-zine
prom'-e-nade'
prom'-e-nad'-er
Pro-me'-the:an
Pro-me'-theus
pro-me'-thi-um
prom'-i-nence
prom'-i-nent
prom'-i-nent-ly
prom-is-cu'-i-ty†
pro-mis'-cu-ous
prom'-ise
prom'-is-ee'
prom'-is-er
prom'-is-ing
prom'-i-sor†
prom'-is-so-ry
Prom'i-zole
prom'-on-to-ried
prom'-on-to-ry
pro-mote'
pro-mot'-er
pro-mot'-ing
pro-mo'-tion
pro-mo'-tion-al
pro-mo'-tive
prompt
prompt'-er
promp'-ti-tude
prompt'-ly
prompt'-ness

prom'ul-gate
prom:ul-ga'-tion
prom'ul-ga-tor
pro'-nate
pro'-na-tor
prone'-ness
pro-neph'-ros
prong'-horn
pro-nom'-i-nal
pro-no'-tus
pro'-noun
pro-nounce'
pro-nounce'-a:ble
pro-nounced'
pro-nounce'-ment
pro-nounc'-ing
pro-nun-cia-men'-to
pro-nun-ci-a'-tion
proof'-er
proof'-read
proof'-read-er
pro'-pa-di'-ene
pro-pae-deu'-tic
prop-a-ga-bil'-i-ty
prop'-a-ga-ble
prop-a-gan'-da
prop-a-gan'-dist
prop-a-gan'-dize
prop'-a-gate
prop-a-ga'-tion
prop'-a-ga-tive
prop'-a-ga-tor
pro-pam'-i-dine
pro'-pane
pro-pa-no'-ic
pro'-pa-nol
pro-par'-gyl
pro'-par-ox'-y-tone
pro-pel'
pro-pel'-lant (*n., adj.*)
pro-pelled'
pro-pel'-lent (*adj.*)
pro-pel'-ler
pro-pel'-ling
pro'-pe-no'-ic
pro-pense'
pro-pen'-si-ty
pro'-pe-nyl
prop'-er
pro'-per-din
prop'-er-ly
prop'-er-tied
prop'-er-ties
prop'-er-ty
proph'-e-cies
proph'-e-cy (*n.*)
proph'-e-sied
proph'-e-si-er

proph'-e-sy (v.)
proph'-et
proph'-et-ess
pro-phet'-ic
pro-phet'-i-cal
pro'-phy-lac'-tic
pro-phy-lax'-is
pro-pin'-qui-ty
pro'-pi-o-late
pro-pi-ol'-ic
pro'-pi-o-nate
pro-pi-on'-ic
pro'-pi:o-ni'-trile
pro'-pi-o-nyl
pro-pi-on'-y-late
pro-pi-ti-ate
pro-pi-ti-a'-tion
pro-pi-ti-a-tor
pro-pi-ti-a-to-ry
pro-pi'-tious
pro-po'-de-um
pro-po'-nent
pro-por'-tion
pro-por'-tion-a:ble
pro-por'-tion-al
pro-por'-tion-ate
pro-por'-tion-ate-ly
pro-por'-tioned
pro-pos'-al†
pro-pose'
pro-pos'-er
pro-pos'-ing
prop-o-si'-tion
prop-o-si'-tion-al
pro-pound'
pro-pound'-er
prop-ox:y-ac-et-an'-i-
  lide*
pro-pri'-e-tar:y†
pro-pri'-e-tor
pro-pri'-e-tor-ship
pro-pri'-e-to-ry
pro-pri'-e-tress
pro-pri'-e-ty
prop-to'-sis
pro-pul'-sion
pro-pul'-sive
pro-pul'-so-ry
prop-y-lae'-um
pro'-pyl-a:mine'†
pro'-pyl-ene†
pro-pyl'-ic
prop'-y-lite
pro-ra'-ta
pro-rat'-a:ble
pro-rate'
pro-rat'-er

pro-ra'-tion
pro-ro-ga'-tion
pro-rogue'
pro-sa'-ic
pro-sa'-i-cal-ly
pro-sce'-ni-um
pro-sciut'-to
pro-scribe'
pro-scrip'-tion
pro-scrip'-tive
pro-scrip'-tive-ly
prose
pros'-e-cute
pros-e-cu'-tion
pros'-e-cu-tor
pros'-e-cu-to-ry
pros-e-cu'-trix
pros'-e-lyte
pros'-e-lyt-ism†
pros'-e-lyt-ize†
pros'-e-lyt-iz-er†
pros-en-ceph'-a-lon
pros-en'-chy-ma
pros'-er
Pro-ser'-pi-na
pros'-i-er
pro'-sit
pro-slav'-er:y†
pros'-o-di'-a-cal
pro-sod'-ic
pro-sod'-i-cal
pros'-o-dist
pros'-o-dy
pros'-o-pite
pros-o-pla'-sia
pros'-pect
pro-spec'-tive
pro-spec'-tive-ly
pros'-pec-tor
pro-spec'-tus
pros'-per
pros-per'-i-ty
pros'-per-ous
pros'-per-ous-ly
pro-spi'-cience
pros'-tate
pros-ta-tec'-to-my
pros-tat'-ic
pros-ta-ti'-tis
pros-ter-na'-tion
pros-then'-ic
pros'-the-sis
pros-thet'-ic
pros'-the-tist
pros-tho-don'-tics
Pro-stig'-min
pros'-ti-tute

pros-ti-tu′-tion
pros′-trate
pros′-trat-ing
pros-tra′-tion
pros′-tra-tor
pros′y
prot-ac-tin′-i-um
pro′-ta-gon
pro-tag′-o-nist
prot′-a:mine′*†
pro-ta-no′-pi:a*
prot′-a-sis
pro′-te-an
pro′-te-ase
pro-tect′
pro-tect′-ant
pro-tect′-ing
pro-tect′-ing-ly
pro-tec′-tion
pro-tec′-tion-ism
pro-tec′-tion-ist
pro-tec′-tive
pro-tec′-tive-ly
pro-tec′-tor
pro-tec′-tor-ate
pro-tec′-to-ry
pro-tec′-tress
pro′-té-gé′
pro′-té-gée′
pro′-te-ide
pro′-tein*†
pro-tein-a′-ceous*†
pro′-tein-ase*
pro-tem′-po-re
pro-te-ol′-y-sin
pro-te-ol′-y-sis
pro′-te:o-lyt′-ic
Prot′e:ro-zo′-ic
pro′-test (n.)
pro-test′ (v.)
pro-tes′-tant (one who protests)
Prot′-es-tant (non-Catholic Christian)
Prot′-es-tant-ism
prot′es-ta′-tion
pro-test′-er
pro-test′-ing
Pro′-teus
prot-e:van-gel′-i-um*†
pro-tha-la′-mi-on
pro-thal′-li-um
proth′-e-sis
pro-thon′o-tar:y†
pro-tho′-rax
pro-throm′-bin
pro′-tide

pro′-ti-um
pro′-to-blast
pro′-to-cat′-e-chu-al′-de-hyde
pro′-to-clas′-tic
pro′-toc-neme
pro′-to-col
pro′-to-gen
pro-tog′-y-ny
pro′-ton
pro′-ton-ate
pro-to-ne′-ma
pro′-to-pine
pro′-to-plasm
pro′-to-plas′-mal
pro′-to-plas′-mic
pro′-to-plast
pro′-to-stele†
pro′-to-trop′-ic
pro-tot′-ro-py
pro′-to-typ′-al†
pro′-to-type
pro′-to-typ′-i-cal
pro′-to-ver′-a-trine†
prot-ox′-ide*†
pro-to-zo′a
pro′-to-zo′-al
pro′-to-zo′-an
pro-to-zo-i′-a-sis
pro-tract′
pro-tract′-ed
pro-tract′-i:ble
pro-trac′-tile
pro-trac′-tion
pro-trac′-tive
pro-trac′-tor
pro-trude′
pro-tru′-si-ble
pro-tru′-sion
pro-tru′-sive
pro-tru′-sive-ly
pro-tu′-ber-ance
pro-tu′-ber-ant
pro-tu′-ber-ate
proud′-ly
proust′-ite
prov′-a:ble
proved
prov′-en
prov′-e-nance†
Pro-ven-cal′
Prov′-ence†
prov′-en-der
pro-ve′-nience*†
prov′-er
prov′-erb
pro-ver′-bi-al

313

pro-vide'
pro-vid'-ed
prov'-i-dence
prov'-i-dent
prov'-i-den'-tial
pro-vid'-er
pro-vid'-ing
prov'-ince
Prov'-ince-town
pro-vin'-cial
pro-vin'-cial-ism
pro-vin-ci-al'-i-ty
pro-vin'-cial-ly
prov'-ing
pro-vi'-sion
pro-vi'-sion-al
pro-vi'-sion-al-ly
pro-vi'-sion-ar-y†
pro-vi'-sion-er
pro-vi'-so
pro-vi-so-ri-ly
pro-vi'-so-ry
pro-vi'-sos
prov-o-ca'-tion
pro-voc'-a-tive
pro-voc'-a-to-ry
pro-voke'
pro-vok'-ing
pro-vo-lo'-ne
pro'-vost*†
prov'-ost-al
pro'-vost mar'-shal†
prow'-ess
prow'-ies
prowl'-er
prox'-ies
prox'-i-mal
prox'-i-mate
prox'-i-mate-ly
prox-im'-i-ty
prox'-i-mo
prox'y
prude
pru'-dence
pru'-dent
pru-den'-tial
prud'-er-y
prud'-ish
pru-i-nes'-cence
pru'-i-nose
pru'-na-sin
pru-nel'-la
prun'-er
prun'-ing
pru'-ne-tin
pru'-ni-trin
pru'-ri-ence
pru'-ri-ent
pru-rig'-i-nous

pru-rit'-ic
pru-ri'-tus
Prus'-sia
Prus'-sian
prus'-si-ate
prus'-sic
pried
pry'-ing
pryt-a-ne'-um
pryt'-a-ny
psalm
psalm'-ist
psal:mod'-ic
psalm'o-dy
psal'-ter
psal-te'ri-um
psal'-ter-y
pseud-an-dry
pseud-ar-thro'-sis*
Pseud-e:pig'-ra-pha*
pseu'-do
pseu'-do-a:quat'-ic
pseu'-do-carp
pseu'-do-cu'-mi-dine
pseu'-do-i'o-none
pseu'-do-ni'-trole
pseu'-do-nym
pseu-don'-y-mous
pseu'-do-pod
pseu'-do-po'-di-um
pseu-dos'-co-py
pseu-dos'-to-ma
psil-an'-thro-py*†
psi-lo-mel'-ane*†
psi-lo'-sis
psi-lot'-ic
psit'-ta-cine
psit-ta-co'-sis
psit'-ta-cot'-ic
pso'-as
pso-phom'-e-ter
pso-ri'-a-sis
pso'-ri-at'-ic
pso-ro'-sis
psy'-cha-gog'-ic
psy'-cha-gog:y*
psych'-as-the'-nia*†
psy'-che
psy-che-om'-e-try
psy-chi-at'-ric
psy-chi'-a-trist
psy-chi'-a-try
psy'-chic
psy'-chi-cal
psy'-chi-cal-ly
psy-cho-a:nal'-y-sis
psy'-cho-an'-a-lyst
psy'-cho-an-a-lyt'-ic

psy-cho-an-a-lyt'-i-cal
psy-cho-an'-a-lyze
psy'-cho-gen'-ic
psy-cho-ge-nic'-i-ty
psy-chog-no'-sis
psy'-cho-graph'-ic
psy'-cho-lep-sy
psy-cho-lep'-tic
psy'-cho-log'-i-cal
psy-cho-log'-i-cal-ly
psy-chol'-o-gist
psy-chol'-o-gize
psy-chol'-o-gy
psy-chom'-a-chy
psy-chom'-e-ter
psy'-cho-met'-ric
psy-chom-e-tri'-cian
psy-chom'-e-try
psy-cho-neu-ro'-sis
psy-cho-neu-rot'-ic
psy-cho-nom'-ics
psy'-cho-path
psy'-cho-path'-ic
psy-chop'-a-thist
psy-chop'-a-thy
psy-cho'-sis
psy-cho-so-mat'-ic
psy-cho-ther'-a-py
psy-chot'-ic
psy'-cho-trine
psy-chrom'-e-ter
psy-chrom'-e-try
psyl'-li-um
psyl'-lyl
ptar'-mi-gan
pter-i-dine
pter'-i-dol'-o-gy
pter'o-dac'-tyl
pte-ro'-ic
pter'o-pod
pter'-o-yl
pte-ryg'-i-um
pter'-y-goid
pti-san'*†
Ptol'-e-ma'-ic
Ptol'-e-my
pto-maine'†
pto'-sis
pty'-a-lin
pty'-a-lism
pu-ber-ty
pu-ber'-u-lent
pu-ber'-u-lon'-ic
pu-bes'-cence
pu-bes'-cent
pu'-bic
pu-bi-ot'-o-my

pu'-bis
pub'-lic
pub'-li-can
pub-li-ca'-tion
pub'-lic house
pub'-li-cist
pub-lic'-i-ty
pub'-li-cize
pub'-lic-ly
pub'-lic=spir'-it-ed
pub'-lish
pub'-lish-a:ble
pub'-lish-er
Pub'-li-us
Puc-ci'-ni
puck'-er
puck'-ered
puck'-er:y
puck'-ish
pud'-ding
pud'-dle
pud'-dler
pud'-dling
pu'-den-cy
pu-den'-dal
pudg'-i-ness
pudg'y
pueb'-lo
pueb'-los
pu'-er-ile
pu-er-il'-i-ty
pu-er-per-al
pu-er-pe'-ri-um
Puer'-to Ri'-can
Puer'-to Ri'-co
puff'-er
puf'-fin
puff'-i-ness
puff'y
Pu'-get
pu'-gi-lism*
pu'-gi-list*
pu'-gi-lis'-tic*
pug-na'-cious
pug-na'-cious-ly
pug-nac'-i-ty
pug nose
pug'=nosed
pu'-is-sance
pu'-is-sant
Pu-las'-ki
pul'-chri-tude
pul-chri-tu'-di-nous
pu'-le-gone
pu'-li-cide
pul'-ing
Pul'-itz-er†
pull'-er

315

pul'-let
pul'-ley
pull'-ing
Pull'-man
pul-lo'-rum
pull'-o:ver (n., adj.)
pul'-lu-late
pul-lu-la'-tion
pul-mom'-e-ter
pul'-mo-nar:y†
pul-mon'-ic
Pul'-mo-tor
pulp'-er
pulp'-i-ness
pul'-pit
pul'-pi-teer'*†
pulp-ot'-o-my
pulp'-ous
pulp'-wood
pulp'y
pul'-que
pul'-sa-tance
pul'-sate
pul'-sa-tile
pul-sa'-tion
pul-sa'-tive
pul-sa'-tor
pul'-sa-to-ry
pulsed
puls'-er
pul-sim'-e-ter
puls'-ing
pul-som'-e-ter
pul'-ver-iz-a:ble
pul-ver-i-za'-tion
pul'-ver-ize
pul'-ver-iz-er
pul-ver'-u-lent
pul-vin'-ic
pu'-ma
pu'-mi-cate
pum'-ice
pu-mi'-ceous
pum'-mel
pump'-age
pump'-er
pum'-per-nick-el
pump'-kin
pun'-cheon
punch'-er
pun-chi-nel'-lo
punc'-tate
punc'-tat-ed
punc-ta'-tion
punc'-ti-form
punc-til'-i:o
punc-til'-i-ous
punc'-tu-al

punc-tu-al'-i-ty
punc'-tu-al-ly
punc'-tu-ate
punc-tu-a'-tion
punc'-tu-a-tor
punc'-tur-a:ble
punc'-ture
punc'-tured
punc'-tur-ing
pun'-dit
pun'-gen-cy
pun'-gent
Pu'-nic
pu-nic'-ic
pu'-ni-ness
pun'-ish
pun'-ish-a:ble
pun'-ish-er
pun'-ish-ment
pu'-ni-tive
pu'-ni-to-ry
Pun'-jab
Pun-ja'-bi
punned
pun'-ning
pun'-ster
punt'-er
pun'-ty
pu'-ny
pu'-pa
pu'-pal
pu-pa'-tion
pu-pif'-er-ous
pu'-pil
pu-pil-lar'-i-ty
pu'-pil-lar:y†
pu'-pil-late
pu-pil-lom'-e-ter
Pu-pin'
pu-pip'-a-rous
pup'-pet
pup'-pe-teer*
pup'-pet-ry
pup'-py
pur'-blind
Pur'-cell
pur'-chas-a:ble
pur'-chase
pur'-chased
pur'-chas-er
pur'-chas-ing
Pur-due'
pu-ree'
pure'-ly
pure'-ness
pur-ga'-tion
pur'-ga-tive
pur-ga-to'-ri-al

pur-ga-to'-ri-an
pur'-ga-to-ry
purge
purg'-er
purg'-ing
pu-ri-fi-ca'-tion
pu-rif'i-ca-to-ry
pu'-ri-fi-er
pu'-ri-fy
Pu'-rim
pu'-rine
pur'-ism
pur'-ist
pu-ris'-tic
pu'-ri-tan
pu-ri-tan'-i-cal
pu'-ri-tan-ism
pu'-ri-ty
Pur-kin'-je
Pur'-lieu
pur'-lin
pur-loin'
pu-ro-my'-cin
pur'-ple
pur-ples'-cent*
pur'-pling
pur'-plish
pur'-port
pur'-pose
pur'-pose-ful
pur'-pose-ful-ly
pur'-pose-less
pur'-pose-ly
pur'-pos-ive†
pur'-pu-ra
pur'-pu-rin
pur'-pu-rite
pur-pu-ro-gal'-lin
pur'-pu-rog'-e-nous
purr'-ing
purse=proud
purs'-er
purs'-ing
purs'-lane
pur-su'-al
pur-su'-ance
pur-su'-ant
pur-su'-ant-ly
pur-sue'
pur-sued'
pur-su'-er
pur-su'-ing
pur-suit'
pur-suit'-me-ter
pur'-sui-vant
pur'-sy†
pur'-te-nance
pu'-ru-lence

pu'-ru-lent
pur-vey'
pur-vey'-ance
pur-vey'-or
pur'-view
push'-ball
push but'-ton
push'-cart
push'-er
push'-ing
push'-o:ver
push'-pin
push'=pull'
pu-sil-la-nim'-i-ty
pu'-sil-lan'-i-mous
puss'y (cat)†
pus'-sy (with pus)
puss'y-foot†
puss'y wil'-low†
pus'-tu-lant
pus'-tu-lar
pus'-tu-late
pus-tu-la'-tion
pus'-tule
pus'-tu-lous
pu-ta'-men
pu'-ta-tive
pu'-tre-fa'-cient
pu-tre-fac'-tion
pu'-tre-fac'-tive
pu'-tre-fied
pu'-tre-fy
pu'-tre-fy-ing
pu-tres'-cence
pu-tres'-cent
pu-tres'-ci-ble
pu-tres'-cine
pu'-trid
pu-trid'-i-ty
put-tee'
putt'-er (golf club)†
put'-ter (to move
  aimlessly)
put'-ty
Puy-al'-lup†
puz'-zle
puz'-zle-ment
puz'-zler
puz'-zling
pyc-nid'-i-um
pyc-nom'-e-ter
pyc-no'-sis
pyc-not'-ic
py'-e:lit'-ic
py-e:li'-tis
py-el'o-graph'-ic
py-e'mi:a
py-gid'-i-um

317

Pyg-ma'-lion
pyg'-my
py-ja'-ma
pyk'-rete
py'-lon
py-lo-rec'-to-my†
py-lor'-ic
py-lo'-ro-plas-ty†
py-lo'-rus
py:o-cy'-a-nase
py:o-cy'-a-nin
py'-o-gen'-ic
py-or-rhe'a
pyr'a-cene
Pyr'-a-lin
Pyr'-a-mid
py-ram'-i-dal
pyr'-a-mid-er
pyr'-a-mid'-i-cal
Pyr'-a-mus
py'-ran
pyr:a-nom'-e-ter
py-ran'-o-side
pyr-ar'-gy-rite*†
pyr-a-zin'-a:mide
pyr'-a:zine†
pyr'-a:zole
py-raz'-o-lone
py-raz'-o-lyl
pyre
py'-rene
Pyr'-e-ne'-an
Pyr'-e-nees
py'-ren-em'-a-tous*
py-re'-thrin*†
py-re'-thrum*†
py-ret'-ic
pyr:e-tol'-o-gy
Py'-rex
py-rex'-i:a
py-rex'-in
pyr-ge-om'-e-ter
pyr'-he-li-om'-e-ter
pyr'-i-bole*
py-rid'-a:zine
py-rid'-ic
pyr'-i-dine
pyr-i-din'-i-um
pyr'-i-done
pyr-i-dox'-ine
pyr'-i-dyl
pyr'-i-form
py-rim'-i-dine†
py'-rite
py-rit'es
py-rit'-ic
py'-rit-if'-er-ous*†
py-ri'-to-he'-dral*†

pyr:i-tol'-o-gy
py'-ro-cat'-e-chu'-ic
py-ro-gal'-lol
py-ro-ge-na'-tion
py'-ro-graph'-ic
py-rog'-ra-phy
py'-ro-lig'-ne-ous
py-rol'-o-gy
py-ro-lu'-site
py-rol'-y-sis
py'-ro-lyze
py-ro-ma'-ni:a
py-ro-ma'-ni-ac
py-rom'-e-ter
py'-rone
py-ro'-sis
py'-ro-sphere
py'-ro-tech'-nic
py-ro-tech'-ni-cal
py-rox'-ene
py-rox'-e-nite
py-rox'-y-lin
pyr'-rhic
Pyr'-rho-nism
Pyr'-rhus
pyr-rol'-i:dine
pyr'-ro-line
pyr'-ro-lo-pyr'-i-dine
pyr'-ryl
pyr'-uv-al'-de-hyde*
pyr-u'-vic*†
py-ryl'-i-um
Py-thag'-o-ras
Py-thag-o-re'-an
Pyth'-i-an
Pyth'-i-as
py'tho-gen'-ic
py'-thon
py-thon'-ic
pyx-id'-i-um

Q

quack'-er:y
quad'-ded
Quad-ra-ges'-i-ma
quad'-ra-ges'-i-mal
quad'-ran-gle
quad-ran'-gu-lar
quad'-rant
qua-dran'-tal*†
quad'-rate
qua-drat'-ic*†
quad'-ra-ture
qua-dra'-tus*
qua-dren'-ni-al*†
qua-dren'-ni-al-ly*†
qua-dren'-ni-um*†

quad'-ric
quad'-ri-lat'-er-al
quad'-ri-lin'-gual
qua-drille'
qua-dril'-lion*†
quad-ri-ple'-gic
quad'-ri-va'-lent
qua-driv'-i-um*†
qua-droon'*†
qua-dru'-ma-nous*†
qua-drum'-vi-rate*
quad'-ru-ped
quad'-ru-pe-dal
quad-ru'-ple
quad-rup-let*†
quad'-ru-plex
qua-dru'-pli-cate*†
quad-ru'-pling
quae'-re
quaes'-tor
quaff
quaffed
quag'-ga
quag'-mire
qua'-hog
quaint'-ly
quaked
Quak'-er
quak'-ing
qual-i-fi-ca'-tion
qual'-i-fied
qual'-i-fy
qual'-i-fy-ing
qua-lim'-e-ter
qual'-i-ta-tive
qual'-i-ta-tive-ly
qual'-i-ty
qualm
qualm'-ish
quan'-da-ry
quan'-tic
quan'-tile
quan-tim'-e-ter
quan'-ti-ta-tive
quan'-ti-ta-tive-ly
quan'-ti-ty
quan-ti-za'-tion
quan'-tize
quan'-tum
quar'-an-tine
quar'-an-tin-er
quar'-rel
quar'-reled
quar'-rel-ing
quar'-rel-some
quar'-ry
quar'-tan
quar'-ter

quar'-ter-back
quar'-ter-deck
quar'-tered
quar'-ter-ing
quar'-ter-ly
quar'-ter-mas-ter
quar'-tern
quar-tet'
quar'-tile
quar'-to
quar'-tos
quarts
quartz
quartz-if'-er-ous
quartz'-ite
quartz-it'-ic
quartz'-ose
qua'-si
quas'-sia
quat'-er-nar:y†
qua-ter'-ni-on
qua-ter'-ni-ty
quat'er-ni-za'-tion
qua'-ter-phen'yl
qua-torze'
qua'-train*†
qua'-tre
qua'-ver
qua'-vered
qua'-ver-ing
qua'-ver:y
quay
quea'-si-ly
quea'-si-ness
quea'-sy
Que-bec'
que-brach'-i-tol
que-bra'-cho
queen'-li-ness
queen'-ly
Queens'-ber-ry
Queens'-land
queer'-ly
quelled
quell'-er
Que-moy'
quenched
quench'-er
quench'-less
que-nelle'
quen'-stedt-ite
Quen'-tin
quer'-ce-tin
quer-ci-mer'-i-trin
que'-ried
que'-rist
quer-u-lous
que'-ry

que'-ry-ing
ques'-tion
ques'-tion-a:ble
ques'-tion-er
ques'-tion-ing
ques'-tion-ing-ly
ques'-tion mark
ques'-tion-naire'
quet-zal'
queue
queu'-er
queu'-ing
quib'-ble
quib'-bled
quib'-bler
quib'-bling
quick'-en
quick'-en-ing
quick'=fire' *(adj.)*
quick'-lime
quick'-ly
quick'-ness
quick'-sand
quick'-set (kind of plant)
quick'=set'-ting (of cement)
quick'-sil-ver
quick'-step
quick'=tem'-pered
quick'=wit'-ted
quid'-di-ty
quid'-nunc
qui-es'-cence
qui-es'-cent
qui-et'
qui'-et-ism
qui'-et-ly
qui'-et-ness
qui-e-tude
qui-e'-tus
quilt'-ed
quilt'-ing
quin'-a-crine
quin-al-din'-i-um
quin'-a-mine†
qui-naph'-thol
qui'na-ry
quin-az'-o-line
quin-cun'-cial
Quin'-cy
qui-nel'-la
quin'-i-dine
qui-nie'-la
qui'-nine†
qui-nin'-ic
qui-niz'-a-rin
quin'-oid
qui-noi'-dine

quin'-o-line
quin'-o-lin-yl
qui-nol'-o-gy
quin'-o-lyl
qui-none'†
qui-non'-ize
qui-no'-nyl*
qui-no'-va-tan'-nic
qui-no'-vose
Quin-qua-ges'-i-ma
quin-quen'-ni-al
quin'-sy
quin'-tal
quin'-tant
quin-ter'-ni-on
quin-tes'-sence*
quin'-tes-sen'-tial
quin-tet'
quin'-tic
quin'-tile
Quin-til'-ian
quin-til'-lion
quin-tu'-ple
quin-tu'-pling
qui-nu'-cli-dine
quipped
quip'-ping
quip'-ster
qui'-pu
quire
Quir'-i-nal
quir'-i-tar'-i-an†
Quis'-ling
quit'-claim
quit'-rent
quit'-tance
quit'-ted
quit'-ter
quit'-ting
quit'-tor
quiv'-er
quiv'-ered
quiv'-er-ing
qui vive
quix-ot'-ic
quix-ot'-i-cal-ly
quix'-o-tism*†
quiz
quizzed
quiz'-zi-cal
quiz'-zing
quoin
quoit
quon'-dam
Quon'-set
quo'-rum
quo'-ta

quot'-a:bil'-i-ty
quot'-a:ble
quo-ta'-tion
quote
quot'-ed
quot'-er
quo-tid'-i-an
quo'-tient
quo'-ting

R

rab'-at (a polish)
ra'-bat (clerical dress)
Ra-bat'
ra-ba'-to
rab'-bet
rab'-bet-ed
rab'-bi
rab'-bin-ate
rab-bin'-ic
rab-bin'-i-cal
rab'-bit
rab'-bit-ry
rab'-ble
rab'-bler
Rab-e-lais'†
Rab-e-lai'-si-an
rab'-id
ra-bid'-i-ty
ra'-bies
rac-coon'
race'-course
race'-horse
rac'-e-mate
ra-ceme'
ra-ce'-mic
rac-e-mif'-er-ous
rac:e-mi-za'-tion
rac'-e-mose
rac'-er
race'-track
race'-way
Ra'-chel (feminine name)
ra-chel' (type of powder)
ra-chi-om'-e-ter
ra'-chis
ra-chit'-ic†
ra-chi'-tis
Rach-man'-i-noff†
ra'-cial
ra'-cial-ism
ra'-cial-ly
ra-ci-a'-tion
rac'-i-ly
Ra-cine'
rac'-ing
rac'-ism†

rac'-ist†
rack'-er
rack'-et
rack'-e-teer'*†
rack'-et:y
rack rail
ra'-con
rac'-on-teur†
rac'y
ra'-dar
ra'-dar-scope
Rad'-cliffe
ra'-di-ac
ra'-di-al
ra'-di-an
ra'-di-ance
ra'-di-an-cy
ra'-di-ant
ra'-di-ant-ly
ra'-di-ate
ra-di-a'-tion
ra'-di-a-tive
ra'-di-a-tor
rad'-i-cal
rad'-i-cal-ism
rad'-i-cal-ly
rad'-i-cand
rad'-i-cate
rad-i-ca'-tion
rad'-i-cle
ra'-di:i
ra'-di:o
ra'-di:o-ac'-tive
ra'-di:o-ac-tiv'-i-ty
ra'-di:o=fre'-quen-cy (adj.)
ra'-di:o fre'-quen-cy (n.)
ra'-di:o-gram
ra'-di:o-graph
ra-di-og'-ra-pher
ra'-di:o-graph'-ic
ra-di-og'-ra-phy
ra'-di:o-i'so-tope
ra'-di:o-lar'-i-an†
ra-di-o-log'-i-cal
ra-di-ol'-o-gist
ra-di-ol'-o-gy
ra-di-ol'-y-sis
ra-di-om'-e-ter
ra'-di:o-met'-ric
ra'-di-on'-ic
ra'-di:o-nu-clide
ra'-di:o-phone
ra'-di-os
ra-di-os'-co-py
ra'-di:o-sonde
ra'-di:o-tel'-e-gram
ra'-di:o-tel'-e-graph

321

ra-di:o-tel′-e-phone
ra′-di:o-te-leph′-o-ny
ra′-di:o-ther′-a-py
ra′-di:o-tho′-ri-um
rad′-ish
ra′-di-um
ra′-di-us
ra′-dix
ra′-dome
ra′-don
rad′-u-la
raf′-fi:a
raf′-fi-nase
raf′-fi-nate*
raf′-fi-nose
raff′-ish
raff′-ish-ly
raf′-fle
raf′-fled
Raf-fle′-sia
raf-fle′-si-a′-ceous
raf′-fling
raf′-ter (beam)*†
raft′-er (man on raft)
rafts′-man
rag′-a-muf-fin
rag′-ged
rag′-ged-ness
rag′-ing
rag′-lan
rag′-man
ra-gout′
rag′-pick-er
rag′-time
rag′-weed
raid′-er
rail′-er
rail′-head
rail′-ing
rail′-ler:y
rail′-road
rail′-road-ing
rail′-way
rai′-ment
rain′-band
rain′-bow
rain cloud
rain′-coat
rain′-drop
rain′-fall
rain gage
rain′-i-er
Rai-nier′
rain′-less
rain′-mak-er
rain pipe
rain′-proof
rain′-storm

rain′-tight
rain′-wa′-ter
rain′y
rais′-er
rai′-sin
rais′-ing
rai-son′
ra′-ja (ra′-jah)
Raj′-put
Raj-pu-ta′-na
raked
rake′-hell
rake′=off (n.)
rak′-er
rak′-ing
rak′-ish
Ra′-leigh
ral′-lied
ral′-ly
ral′-ston-ite
Ram′-a-dan
Ra′-man
ram′-ble
ram′-bler
ram′-bling
Ram′-bouil-let′
ram-bunc′-tious
ram′-e-kin
Ram′-e-ses
ram′-ie
ram-i-fi-ca′-tion
ram′-i-fied
ram′-i-fy
ram′-i-fy-ing
ram′-jet
rammed
ram′-ming
Ra-mo′-na
ra′-mose
ra′-mous
ram′-page
ram-pa′-geous
ram′-pag-er
ram′-pag-ing
ram′-pant*
ram′-part
ram′-pi-on
ram′-rod
ram′-shack-le
ram′-u-lose
ra-na′-li-an
ranch′-er
ran-che′-ro
ranch′-man
ran′-cho
ran′-cid
ran-cid′-i-ty
ran′-cor

ran'-cor-ous
Ran'-dolph
ran'-dom
ran'-dom-ize
ra-nee'
ranged
rang'-er
rang-ette'
rang'-ing
Ran-goon'
rang'y
ra-ni'
ra'-nine
rank'-er
ran'-kle
ran'-kled
ran'-kling
rank'-ness
ran'-sack
ran'-som
ran'-som-er
rant'-er
rant'-ing
ra-nun'-cu-la-'ce-ous
ra-pa'-cious
ra-pa'-cious-ness
ra-pac'-i-ty
ra'-pa-ki-'vi
Raph'-a-el
ra'-phe
rap'-id
rap'-id=fire
ra-pid'-i-ty
rap'-id-ly
ra'-pier
rap'-ine
rap'-ist
Rap'-pa-han'-nock
rap-pa-ree'
rapped
rap'-ping
rap-port'
rap-proche-ment'
rap-scal'-lion
rapt'-ly
rap-to'-ri-al
rap'-ture
rap'-tur-ous
rare'-bit
rar'-e-fac'-tion
rar'-e-fied
rar'-e-fy
rare'-ly
rare'-ness
rar'-i-ty
ras'-cal
ras-cal'-i-ty
ras'-cal-ly

rash'-er
rash'-ly
rash'-ness
ra-so'-ri-al
rasp'-ber-ry
rasp'-er
rasp'-ing
Ras-pu'-tin
Ras'-se-las
ras'-ter
ra'-sure
rat:i-a:bil'-i-ty
rat'-a:ble
rat-a-fee'
rat-a-fi'a
ratch'-et
ra'-tel
rate'-pay-er
rat'-er
rath'-er
raths'-kel-ler
rat-i-fi-ca'-tion
rat'-i-fied
rat'-i-fy
rat'-i-fy-ing
rat'-ing
ra'-tion
rat:i-o'ci-nate
rat:i-o:ci-na'-tion
ra-ti-om'-e-ter
ra'-tion
ra'-tio-nal*†
ra'-tio-nale'*†
ra'-tio-nal-ism*†
ra'-tio-nal-ist*†
ra-tio-nal-is'-tic*†
ra'-tio-nal'-i-ty*†
ra-tio-nal-i:za'-tion*†
ra'-tio-nal-ize*†
ra'-tio-nal-ly*†
rat'-ite
rat'-line
ra-toon'
rat'-proof
rat-tan'
rat'-tle
rat'-tler
rat'-tle-snake
rat'-tle-trap
rau'-cous
rau'-vite
rau-wol'-fi:a
rav'-age
rav'-ag-er
rav'-ag-ing
rav'-el
Ra-vel'
rav'-eled

323

rave'-lin
rav'-el-ing
ra'-ven (type of bird)
rav'-en (to devour)
rav'-en-ing
Ra-ven'-na
rav'-en-ous
rav'-in
ra-vine'
rav'-ing
rav-i-o'-li†
rav'-ish
rav'-ish-er
rav'-ish-ing
rav'-ish-ment
raw'-boned'
raw'-hide
ra'-win-sonde
Ray'-mond
ray'-on
ra'-zon
ra'-zor
ra'-zor-back
raz'-zle=daz-zle
re-act'
re-ac'-tance*
re-ac'-tion
re-ac'-tion-ar:y†
re-ac'-tive
re-ac'-tor
read-a:bil'-i-ty
read'-a:ble
re-ad-dress'
read'-er
read'-i-ly
read'-i-ness
read'-ing
Read'-ing
read'-ing room
re-ad-just'
re-ad-just'-ment
read'y
read'y=made
re-af-firm'
re-a'-gent
re-a'gin
re'-al (true)
re-al' (type of coin)
re-al'-gar
re'-al-ism
re'-al-ist
re-al-is'-tic
re-al-is'-ti-cal-ly
re-al'-i-ty
re-al-i:za'-tion
re'-al-ize
re'-al-ly
re=al-ly'

realm
re'-al-tor
re'-al-ty
ream'-er
re-an'-i-mate
reap'-er
re-ap-pear'
re-ap-pear'-ance
re-ap-point'
rear ad'-mi-ral
rear guard (n.)
rear'-guard (adj.)
re-arm'
re-ar'-ma-ment
re-ar-range'
re-ar-range'-ment
re-ar-rang'-ing
rear'-ward
re-as-cend'
rea'-son
rea'-son-a:ble
rea'-son-a:ble-ness
rea'-son-a:bly
rea'-son-er
rea'-son-ing
re-as-sem'-ble
re-as-sert'
re-as-sume'
re-as-sur'-ance
re'-as-sure'
re'-as-sur'-ing
Re'-au-mur'
reav'-er
re-a:wak'-en
re'-bate
re'-bat-er
re'-bec
Re-bec'-ca
reb'-el (n., adj.)
re-bel' (v.)
re-belled'
re-bel'-ling
re-bel'-lion
re-bel'-lious
re-bel'-lious-ly
re'-birth'
reb'-o-ant
re'-born'
re-bound'
re-buff'
re-build'
re-built'
re-buke'
re-buk'-ing
re'-bus
re-but'
re-but'-ta-ble
re-but'-tal

re-but'-ted
re-but'-ting
re-cal'-ci-trance
re-cal'-ci-trant
re-ca-les'-cence
re'-ca-les'-cent
re-call' (v., n.)
re'-call (n.)
re-cant'
re-can-ta'-tion
re'-cap
re-ca-pit'-u-late
re-ca-pit'-u-la'-tion
re-ca-pit'-u-la-to-ry
re'-capped'
re'-cap'-ping
re-cap'-ture
re-cast'
re-cede'
re-ced'-ed
re-ced'-ence†
re-ced'-er
re-ced'-ing
re-ceipt'
re-ceipt'-or
re-ceiv'-a:ble
re-ceive'
re-ceiv'-er
re-ceiv'-er-ship
re-ceiv'-ing
re'-cen-cy
re-cen'-sion
re'-cent
re'-cent-ly
re-cep'-ta-cle
re-cep'-ti-ble
re-cep'-tion
re-cep'-tion-ist
re-cep'-tive
re-cep-tiv'-i-ty
re-cep'-tor
re'-cess
re'-cess'-er
re-ces'-sion
re-ces'-sion-al
re-ces'-sive
re-charge'
ré-chauf-fé'
re-cher'-ché'
re-cid'-i-vism
re-cid'-i-vist
Re-ci'-fe
rec'-i-pe
re-cip'-i-ence
re-cip'-i-ent
re-cip'-ro-ca-ble
re-cip'-ro-cal
re-cip'-ro-cal-ly

re-cip'-ro-cate
re-cip-ro-ca'-tion
rec-i-proc'-i-ty
re-ci'-sion
re-cit'-al†
rec-i-ta'-tion
rec'-i-ta-tive'
re-cite'
re-cit'-er
re-cit'-ing
reck'-less
reck'-less-ly
reck'-less-ness
reck'-on
reck'-on-ing
re-claim'
re-claim'-a:ble
rec-la-ma'-tion
re-clin'-a:ble
rec-li-na'-tion
re-cline'
re-clin'-er
re-clin'-ing
rec'-luse*†
re-clu'-sive
rec-og-ni'-tion
rec'-og-niz-a:ble
re-cog'-ni-zance
rec'-og-nize (to
  acknowledge)
re=cog'-nize (to cognize
  again)†
re-cog'-ni-zee'
rec'-og-niz-er
re-cog'-ni-zor'†
re-coil' (to draw back)
re=coil' (to coil again)
rec-ol-lect' (to
  remember)†
re=col-lect' (to collect
  again)
rec-ol-lec'-tion
re-com-bi-na'-tion
re'-com-bine'
re-com-mence'
rec-om-mend'
rec-om-men-da'-tion
rec-om-mend'-a-to-ry
re-com-mit'
re-com-mit'-tal
re-com-mit'-ment
rec'-om-pense
rec'-om-pens-er
rec'-om-pens-ing
re-con'-cen-trate
rec-on-cil-a:ble
rec'-on-cile
rec'-on-cile-ment

325

rec'-on-cil-er
rec-on-cil-i-a'-tion
rec'-on-cil'-i:a-to-ry
rec'-on-dite
re-con-di'-tion
re-con'-nais-sance
re:con-noi'-ter
re-con'-quer
re-con'-se-crate
re-con-sid'-er
re-con-sid'-er-a'-tion
re-con'-sti-tute
re-con-struct'
re-con-struc'-tion
re-cord' (v.)
rec'-ord (n., adj.)
re-cord'-a:ble
rec-or-da'-tion
re-cord'-er
re-count'
re-coup'
re'-course
re-cov'-er
re-cov'-er-a:ble
re-cov'-er:y
rec'-re-ant
rec'-re-ate (to refresh)
re=cre-ate' (to create
    anew)
rec-re-a'-tion
re=cre-a'-tive
rec'-re-a-tive
rec'-re-ment
rec-re-men'-tal
rec'-re-men-ti'-tious
re-crim'-i-nate
re-crim'-i-nat-ing
re-crim-i-na'-tion
re-crim'-i-na-to-ry
re-cru-des'-cence
re-cru-des'-cent
re-cruit'
re-cruit'-er
re-cruit'-ment
rec'-tal
rec'-tan-gle
rec-tan'-gu-lar
rec-tan'-gu-lom'-e-ter
rec'-ti-fi-a:ble
rec'-ti-fi-ca'-tion
rec'-ti-fied
rec'-ti-fi-er
rec'-ti-fy
rec'-ti-lin'-e:ar
rec'-ti-tude
rec'-tor
rec'-tor-ate
rec'-tor-ship

rec'-to-ry
rec'-tum
rec'-tus
re-cum'-ben-cy
re-cum'-bent
re-cu'-per-ate
re-cu-per-a'-tion
re-cu'-per-a-tive
re-cur'
re-curred'
re-cur'-rence
re-cur'-rent
re-cur'-ring
re-cur'-sive
re-cur'-vate
rec'u-san-cy
rec'u-sant
re-dact'
re-dac'-tion
re-dac'-tor
re-dan'
red'-bird
red'=blood'-ed
red'-breast
red'-bud
red'-cap
red'-coat
red'-den
red'-dish
re-dec'-o-rate
re-deem'
re-deem'-a:ble
re-deem'-er
re-demp'-ti-ble
re-demp'-tion
re-demp'-tive
re-demp'-tor
re-demp'-to-ry
re-de-ploy'
re-de-ploy'-ment
red'=faced'
red'=hand'-ed
red'-head
red'-head-ed
red her'-ring
red'=hot'
red'-in-gote
re-din'-te-grate*
re-di-rect'
re-dis'-count
re-dis-cov'-er
re-dis-cov'-er:y
re-dis-trib'-ute
re-dis-tri-bu'-tion
re-dis'-trict
red lead (n.)
red'=lead' (v.)
red'=let'-ter (adj.)

red'-ness
red'-o-lence
red'-o-lent
re-dou'-ble†
re-dou'-bling†
re-doubt'
re-doubt'-a:ble
re-dound'
red'-o-wa
re-dox*
re-draw'
re-dress'
re-dress'-a:ble
re-dress'-er
red'-skin
red tape
re-duce'
re-duc'-er
re-duc'-i:ble
re-duc'-ing
re-duc'-tase
re-duc'-tion
re-duc'-tive
re-duc'-tone
re-duc'-tor
re-dun'-dan-cy
re-dun'-dant
re-du'-pli-cate
re-du-pli-ca'-tion
red'-wing
red'-wood
re-ech'o
reed'y
reef'-er
re-e:lect'
re-e:lec'-tion
reel'-er
re-em-bark'
re-en-act'
re-en-force'
re-en-force'-ment
re-en-gage'
re'-en-list'
re-en'-ter
re-en'-trant
re-en'-try
re-es-tab'-lish
re-es-tab'-lish-ment
re-ex-am-i-na'-tion
re-ex-am'-ine
re-fas'-ten†
re-fec'-tion
re-fec'-to-ry
re-fer'
ref'-er-a:ble
ref'-er-ee'†
ref'-er-ence
ref-er-en'-dum

re:fer'-ent
ref'-er-en'-tial
re-ferred'
re-fer'-ring
re-fill'
re-fill'-a:ble
re-fine'
re-fined'
re-fine'-ment
re-fin'-er
re-fin'-er:y
re-fin'-ing
re-fit'
re-flect'
re-flec'-tance*
re-flect'-i:ble
re-flec'-tion
re-flec'-tive
re-flec-tom'-e-ter
re-flec-tom'-e-try
re-flec'-tor
re-flec'-tor-ize
re'-flex
re-flex'-ive
re-flex-iv'-i-ty
ref'-lu-ent
re'-flux
re-for'-est
re-for-est-a'-tion†
re-form' (to amend)
re-form'-a:ble
ref-or-ma'-tion (reform)
re=for-ma'-tion (a
   forming again)
re-for'-ma-tive*†
re-for'-ma-to-ry*†
re-form'-er
re-fract'
re-frac'-tion
re-frac'-tive
re-frac-tom'-e-ter
re-frac'-to-met'-ric
re-frac-tom'-e-try
re-frac'-tor
re-frac'-to-ri-ness
re-frac'-to-ry
re-frain'
re-fran'-gi-ble
ref-re-na'-tion
re-fresh'
re-fresh'-ing
re-fresh'-ment
re-frig'-er-ant
re-frig'-er-ate
re-frig'-er-at-ing
re-frig-er-a'-tion
re-frig'-er-a-tor

327

re-frin'-gent
re-fu'-el
ref'-uge
ref'-u-gee
re-ful'-gence
re-ful'-gent
re'-fund (n.)
re-fund' (v.)
re-fur'-bish
re-fur'-nish
re-fus'-al
re-fuse' (to deny)
ref'-use (waste)
re=fuse' (to fuse again)
re-fus'-ing
re-fut'-a:ble*
re-fut'-a:bly*
re-fut'-al
ref-u-ta'-tion
re-fute'
re-fut'-er
re-fut'-ing
re-gain'
re'-gal
re-gale'
re-ga'-lia
re-gal'-ing
re-gal'-i-ty
re'-gal-ly
re-gard'
re-gard'-ing
re-gard'-less
re-gat'-ta
re'-ge-late
re'-ge-la'-tion
re'-gen-cy
re-gen'-er-a-cy
re-gen'-er-ate
re-gen-er-a'-tion
re-gen'-er-a-tive
re-gen'-er-a-tor
re'-gent
reg'-i-cide
re-gime'
reg'-i-men
reg'-i-ment
reg'-i-men'-tal
reg-i-men'-ta-ry
reg-i-men-ta'-tion
Re-gi'-na
Reg'-i-nald
re'-gion
re'-gion-al
reg'-is-ter
reg'-is-tered
reg'-is-tra-ble
reg'-is-trar
reg'-is-trate

reg-is-tra'-tion
reg'-is-try
reg'-let
reg'-nant
Re-gnault'
reg'-o-sol
re-gress'
re-gres'-sion
re-gres'-sive
re-gres'-sor
re-gret'
re-gret'-ful
re-gret'-ful-ly
re-gret'-ta-ble
re-gret'-ta-bly
re-gret'-ted
re-gret'-ting
reg'-u-lar
reg-u-lar'-i-ty
reg'-u-lar-ize
reg'-u-lar-ly
reg'-u-lat-a:ble
reg'-u-late
reg-u-la'-tion
reg'-u-la-tive
reg'-u-la-tor
reg'-u-la-to-ry
reg'-u-lus
re-gur'-gi-tate
re-gur-gi-ta'-tion
re-ha-bil'-i-tate
re-ha-bil-i-ta'-tion
re-ha-bil'-i-ta-tive
re'-hash'
re-hears'-al
re-hearse'
re-hears'-er
re-hears'-ing
re-heat'
Re-ho-bo'-am
Re'-ho-both
Reichs'-tag
re'-i:fy
reign
re-im-burs'-a:ble
re-im-burse'
re-im-burse'-ment
re-im-port'
re-im-por-ta'-tion
rein
re-in-car'-nate
re-in-car-na'-tion
rein'-deer
Rei'-neck:e
re-in-force'
re-in-forced'
re-in-force'-ment
re-in-sert'

re-in-stall'
re-in-stal-la'-tion
re-in-state'
re-in-state'-ment
re-in-sure'
re-in-te-gra'-tion
re-in-vest'
re-in-vig'-o-rate*†
reis
re-is'-sue
re-it'-er-ate
re-it-er-a'-tion
re-it'-er-a-tive
re-ject' (v.)
re'-ject (n.)
re-ject'-a-ble
re-ject'-er
re-jec'-tion
re-jec'-tor
re-joice'
re-joic'-ing
re-join'
re-join'-der
re-ju-ve-na'-tion
re-ju'-ve-na-tor
re-ju-ve-nes'-cence
re-kin'-dle
re-lapse'
re-lapsed'
re-laps'-er
re-laps'-ing
re-late'
re-lat'-ed
re-lat'-er
re-lat'-ing
re-la'-tion
re-la'-tion-ship
rel'-a-tive
rel'-a-tive-ly
rel'-a-tiv-ism
rel'-a-tiv'-i-ty
re-la'-tor
re-lax'
re-lax-a'-tion
re-lax'-ed-ly
re-lax-om'-e-ter
re'-lay (n.; to forward)
re-lay' (to lay again)
re'-layed
re-lease' (to let go)
re=lease' (to lease anew)
re-leased'
re-leas'-er
re-leas'-ing
rel'-e-ga-ble
rel'-e-gate
rel'-e-gat-ed

rel-e-ga'-tion
re-lent'
re-lent'-ing
re-lent'-ing-ly
re-lent'-less
rel'-e-vance
rel'-e-van-cy
rel'-e-vant
re-li-a-bil'-i-ty
re-li'-a-ble
re-li'-a-bly
re-li'-ance
re-li'-ant
rel'-ic
rel'-ict (n.)
re-lict' (adj.)†
re-lied'
re-lief'
re-lief'-er
re-liev'-a-ble
re-lieve'
re-lieved'
re-liev'-er
re-liev'-ing
re-li'-gion†
re-li-gi-os'-i-ty*†
re-li'-gious†
re-li'-gious-ly†
re-lin'-quish
rel'-i-quar:y†
rel'-ish
rel'-ish-a-ble
rel'-ish-ing
re-load'
re'-lo-cate'
re-lu-cence
re-luc'-tance
re-luc'-tant
re-luc'-tant-ly
re-luc-tiv'-i-ty
re-lume'
re-lu'-mine
re-ly'
re-ly'-ing
re-made'
re-main'
re-main'-der
re-main'-ing
re-mand'
re-mand'-ment
rem'-a-nence
rem'-a-nent
re-mark'
re-mark'-a-ble
re-mark'-a-bly
Re-marque'
re-marque'
re-mar'-riage

re-mar'-ry
Rem'-brandt
re-me'-di-a:ble
re-me'-di-al
rem'-e-died
rem'-e-dies
rem'-e-di-less
rem'-e-dy
re-mem'-ber
re-mem'-brance
re-mem'-branc-er
re-mig'-i-al
re-mind'
re-mind'-er
Rem'-ing-ton
rem-i-nisce'
rem-i-nis'-cence
rem-i-nis'-cent
rem-i-nis'-cent-ly
rem-i-nis'-cer
rem-i-nis'-cing
re-miss'
re-miss-i:bil'-i-ty*†
re-miss'-i:ble*†
re-mis'-sion
re-mis'-sive
re-miss'-ness
re-mit'
re-mit'-tance
re-mit'-ted
re-mit-tee'
re-mit'-tent
re-mit'-ter
re-mit'-ting
rem'-nant
re-mod'-el
re-mod'-eled
re-mon-e-ti-za'-tion
re-mon'-e-tize
re-mon'-strance
re-mon'-strant
re-mon'-strate
re-mon-stra'-tion
re-mon'-stra-tive
re-mon'-stra-tor
rem'-on-toir'†
rem'-o-ra
re-morse'
re-morse'-ful
re-morse'-less
re-mote'
re-mote'-ly
re-mote'-ness
re-mot'-est
re-mount
re-mov-a:bil'-i-ty
re-mov'-a:ble
re-mov'-al

re-move'
re-moved'
re-mov'-er
re-mov'-ing
re-mu'-da
re-mu'-ner-a-ble
re-mu'-ner-ate
re-mu-ner-a'-tion
re-mu'-ner-a-tive
Re'-mus
ren'-ais-sance'†
Ren'-ais-sant'
re'-nal
re-name'
Re-nan'
re-nas'-cence
re-nas'-cent
ren-coun'-ter
ren'-der (v.)
rend'-er (n.)
ren'-der-a:ble
ren'-dez-vous
rend'-i:ble*
rend'-ing
ren-di'-tion
ren-dzi'-na
Re-né'
ren'-e-gade
re-nege'
re-neg'-er
re-neg'-ing
re-new'
re-new'-a:ble
re-new'-al
re-newed'
re-new'ed-ly
ren'-gue
re'-nin†
ren'-i-tent*†
ren'-net
ren'-nin
Re'-no
Re-noir'
re-nom'-i-nate
re-nom-i-na'-tion
re-nounce'
re-nounce'-ment
re-nounc'-ing
ren'-o-vate
ren'-o-vat-ing
ren-o-va'-tion
ren'-o-va-tor
re-nown'
re-nowned'
rent'-a:ble
rent'-al
rent'-er (tenant)
ren'-ter (to repair clothing)

rent'-ing
re-nun-ci-a'-tion
re-nun'-ci-a-to-ry
re-oc'-cu-py
re-o'pen
re-or-ga-ni-za'-tion*†
re-or'-ga-nize*†
re-paid'
re-paint'
re-pair'
re-pair'-a:ble
re-pair'-er
re-pair'-man
rep'-a-ra-ble
rep-a-ra'-tion
re-par'-a-tive
re-par'-a-to-ry
rep'-ar-tee'
re-par-ti'-tion
re-past'
re-pa'tri-ate
re-pa'tri-a'-tion
re-pay'
re-pay'-ing
re-pay'-ment
re-peal'
re-peal'-a:ble
re-peal'-er
re-peat'
re-peat'-a:ble
re-peat'-ed
re-peat'-ed-ly
re-peat'-er
re-pel'
re-pelled'
re-pel'-len-cy
re-pel'-lent
re-pel'-ling
re-pent'
re-pent'-ance†
re-pent'-ant†
re:per-cus'-sion
re:per-cus'-sive
rep'-er-toire'
rep'-er-to-ry
rep'-e-tend
rep-e-ti'-tion
rep'-e-ti'-tious
rep-e-ti'-tious-ly
re-pet'-i-tive
re-pine'
re-place'
re-place'-a:ble
re-place'-ment
re-plac'-ing
re-plant'
re-plen'-ish

re-plen'-ish-er
re-plen'-ish-ment
re-plete'
re-ple'-tion
re-ple'-tive
re-plev'-in
re-plev'-i-sor
rep'-li-ca
rep'-li-cate
rep-li-ca'-tion
re-plied'
re-ply'
re-ply'-ing
re-port'
re-port'-er
rep:or-to'-ri-al
re-pose'
re-pose'-ful
re-pos'-ing
re'-po-si'-tion
re-pos'-i-to-ry
re'-pos-sess'
re'-pos-ses'-sion
re-pous-sé'
Rep'-plier
rep-re-hend'
rep-re-hen-si-bil'-i-ty
rep-re-hen'-si-ble
rep-re-hen'-sion
rep-re-hen'-sive
rep-re-sent'
rep-re-sent'-a:ble
rep-re-sen-ta'-tion
rep-re-sent'-a-tive†
rep-re-sent'-er
re-press'
re-press'-er
re-press'-i:ble
re-pres'-sion
re-pres'-sive
re-pres'-sor
re-prieve'
rep'-ri-mand
re-print' (v.)
re'-print (n.)
re-pri'-sal*
re-prise'
re-proach'
re-proach'-ful
re-proach'-ful-ly
re-proach'-ing
rep'-ro-ba-cy
rep'-ro-bate
rep-ro-ba'-tion
re'-pro-duce'
re'-pro-duc'-er
re'-pro-duc'-i:ble
re'-pro-duc'-ing

re-pro-duc'-tion
re-pro-duc'-tive
re-pro-duc-tiv'-i-ty
re-proof'
re-prove'
re-prov'-ing
re-prov'-ing-ly
rep'-tile
rep-til'-i-an
re-pub'-lic
re-pub'-li-can
re-pub'-li-can-ism
re-pub-li-ca'-tion
re-pub'-lish
re-pu'-di-ate
re-pu-di-a'-tion
re-pu'-di-a-tor
re-pug'-nance
re-pug'-nan-cy
re-pug'-nant
re-pulse'
re-puls'-ing
re-pul'-sion
re-pul'-sive
re-pur'-chase
rep'-u-ta-ble
rep'-u-ta-bly
rep-u-ta'-tion
re-pute'
re-put'-ed
re-put'-ing
re-quest'
re-quest'-er
req'ui-em†
re-qui-es'-cat†
re-quire'
re-quire'-ment
re-quir'-er
re-quir'-ing
req'-ui-site
req-ui-si'-tion
re-quit'-al†
re-quite'
re-quit'-ed
re-quit'-ing
re-read'
rer're-dos*†
re-sal'-a:ble
re'-sale
res-az'ur:in
re-scind'
re-scind'-a:ble
re-scind'-ment
re-scis'-si-ble
re-scis'-sion
re'-script
re-scrip'-tive
res'-cu-a:ble

res'-cue
res'-cued
res'-cu-er
res'-cu-ing
re'-search'
re-search'-er
re-seat'
re-seau'
re-sect'-a:ble
re-sec'-tion
re-se'-da
res'-e-da'-ceous
re-sell'
re-sem'-blance
re-sem'-ble
re-sem'-bler
re-sem'-bling
res'-ene
re-sent'
re-sent'-ful
re-sent'-ful-ly
re-sent'-ment
re-ser'-pic
re:ser'-pine
res-er-va'-tion
re-serve'
re-served'
re-serv'-ed-ly
re-serv'-ist
res'-er-voir
re-set'
re-set'-ting
re-set'-tle-ment
re-ship'
re-side'
res'-i-dence
res'-i-den-cy
res'-i-dent
res-i-den'-tial
res-i-den-ti-ar:y†
re-sid'-ing
re-sid'-u-al
re-sid'-u-ar:y†
res'-i-due
re-sid'-u-um
re-sign'
res-ig-na'-tion
re-signed'
re-sign'-ed-ly
re-sil'-ience
re-sil'-ien-cy
re-sil'-ient
re-sil'-ient-ly
re-sil-i-om'-e-ter
res'-in
res'-in-a'-ceous*†
res'-in-ate†
res-in'-ic*†

res'-in-if'-er-ous
re-sin-i-fi-ca'-tion†
res-in-og'-ra-phy
res'-in-oïd*
res'-in-ol†
res'-in-ous†
re-sist'
re-sist'-ance†
re-sist'-ant†
re-sist'-er
re-sist-i:bil'-i-ty
re-sist'-i:ble
re-sis-tiv'-i-ty
re-sist'-less
re-sis'-tor
res'-ite
res'-i-tol
res' ju-di-ca'-ta
res'-ol
re-sold'
re-sol'-u-ble†
res'-o-lute
res'-o-lute-ly
res-o-lu'-tion
res-o-lu'-tion-er
re-sol'-u-tive*†
re-solv'-a:ble
re-solve'
re-solved'
re-solv'-ed-ly
re-solv'-ent*†
re-solv'-er
re-solv'-ing
res'-o-nance
res'-o-nant
res'-o-na-tor
res-or'-cin-ol†
res'-or-cyl'-ic
re-sorp'-tive
re-sort'
res-o-ru'-fin†
re-sound'
re-sound'-ed
re-sound'-ing
re-sound'-ing-ly
re'-source
re-source'-ful
re-source'-ful-ly
re-source'-ful-ness
re-spect'
re-spect-a:bil'-i-ty
re-spect'-a:ble
re-spect'-a:bly
re-spect'-er
re-spect'-ful
re-spect'-ful-ly

re-spect'-ing
re-spec'-tive
re-spec'-tive-ly
res'-pi-ra-ble*†
res-pi-ra'-tion
res'-pi-ra-tor
res'-pi-ra-to-ry*†
re-spire'
re-spir'-ing
res-pi-rom'-e-ter
res'-pite
re-splen'-dence*
re-splen'-den-cy*
re-splen'-dent*
re-spond'
re-spon'-dence*
re-spon'-den-cy*
re-spon'-dent*
re-spond'-er
re-sponse'
re-spons'-er*
re-spon-si-bil'-i-ty
re-spon'-si-ble
re-spon'-si-bly
re-spon'-sive
re-spon'-sive-ly
re-spon'-sive-ness
re-spon'-sor
re-spon'-so-ry
re'-state'
res'-tau-rant
res'-tau-ra-teur'
rest'-ful
res'-ti-form
res-ti-tu'-tion
res'-tive
rest'-less
rest'-less-ly
rest'-less-ness
re'-stock'
res-to-ra'-tion
re-stor'-a:tive
re-store'
re-stor'-er
re-stor'-ing
re-strain'
re-strained'
re-straint'
re-strict'
re-strict'-ed
re-stric'-tion
re-stric'-tive
re-sult'
re-sult'-ant†
re-sume'
ré'-su-mé'
re-sum'-ing
re-sump'-tion

re-sump'-tive
re-su'-pi-nate
re-su-pi-na'-tion
re-sur'-gence
re-sur'-gent
res'-ur-rect'
res'-ur-rec'-tion
res'-ur-rec'-tor
re-sus-ci-ta-ble
re-sus'-ci-tate
re-sus-ci-ta'-tion
re-sus'-ci-ta-tor
re'-tail
re'-tail-er
re-tain'
re-tain'-er
re-tain'-ing
re-take'
re-tal'-i-ate
re-tal-i-a'-tion
re-tal'-i-a-tive
re-tal'-i:a-to-ry
re-tard'
re-tard'-ant†
re-tar-da'-tion
re-tard'-a-to-ry
re-tard'-ed
retch
re-tell'
re'-tene
re-tent'
re-ten'-tion
re-ten'-tive
re-ten-tiv'-i-ty
re-ten'-tor
ret'-ger-site
re'-ti-ar:y†
ret'-i-cence
ret'-i-cent
ret'-i-cle
re-tic'-u-lar
re-tic'-u-late
re-tic-u-la'-tion
ret'-i-cule
re-tic'-u-lin
re-tic-u-li'-tis
re-tic-u-lo-cy-to'-sis
re-tic'-u-lose
ret'-i-form*†
ret'-i-na
ret'-i-nal
re-tin'-a-lite
ret'-i-nene
ret-i-ni'-tis
ret-i-no-cho-roid-i'-tis
ret'-i-nol
ret-i-nop'-a-thy
ret-i-nos'-co-py

ret'-i-nue
re-tir'-al
re-tire'
re-tired'
re-tir'-ee
re-tire'-ment
re-tir'-ing
re-told'
ret-o-na'-tion*
re-tort'
re-tort'-er
re-tor'-tion
re-touch'
re-trace'
re-trace'-a:ble
re-trac'-ing
re-tract'
re-tract-a:bil'-i-ty
re-tract'-a:ble
re-trac'-tile
re-trac-til'-i-ty
re-trac'-tion
re-trac'-tive
re-trac'-tor
re'-tral
re'-tread'
re-treat'
re-trench'
re-trench'-ment
ret-ri-bu'-tion
re-trib'-u-tive
re-trib'-u-to-ry
re-triev'-a:ble
re-triev'-al
re-trieve'
re-triev'-er
re-triev'-ing
ret'-ro-ac'-tion†
ret'-ro-ac'-tive†
ret'-ro-cede'†
ret-ro-ced'-ence†
ret-ro-ces'-sion†
ret'-ro-gra'-da-to-ry
ret'-ro-grade
ret'-ro-gress†
ret-ro-gres'-sion†
ret'-ro-gres'-sive†
ret'-ro-min'-gent*†
ret-ro-ne'-cine
re-tror'-sine
ret'-ro-spect
ret-ro-spec'-tion
ret'-ro-spec'-tive
ret-ro-stal'-sis*†
ret'-rous-sé'†
ret'-ro-vert'-ed†
ret'-ting
re-turn'

re-turn'-a:ble
re-turn'-ee'
Reu'-ben
re-un'-ion†
re-u:nite'
re-u:nit'-ing
Re'-val
re-val'-u-ate
re-val-u-a'-tion
re-vamp'
re-vanche'
re-veal'
re-veal'-a:ble
rev'-eil-le
rev'-el
rev-e-la'-tion
rev'-e-la-tor
re-vel'-a-to-ry*†
rev'-eled
rev'-el-er
rev'-el-ing
rev'-el-ry
rev'-e-nant
re-venge'
re-venge'-ful
re-venge'-ful-ness
re-veng'-er
re-veng'-ing
rev'-e-nue
re-ver'-a:ble
re-ver'-ber-ant
re-ver'-ber-ate
re-ver'-ber-a'-tion
re-ver'-ber-a-tor
re-ver'-ber-a-to-ry
re-vere'
rev'-er-ence
rev'-er-end
rev'-er-ent
rev'-er-en'-tial
rev'-er-ent-ly
rev'-er-ie
re-ver'-ing
re-vers'
re-ver'-sal
re-verse'
re-vers'-er
re-vers-i:bil'-i-ty
re-vers'-i:ble
re-vers'-ing
re-ver'-sion
re-ver'-sion-ar:y†
re-vert'
re-vert'-er
re-vert'-i:ble
re-vet'-ment
re-vict'-ual
re-vict'-ual-ment

re-view'
re-view'-a:ble
re-view'-er
re-vile'
re-vile'-ment
re-vil'-er
re-vil'-ing
re-vin'-di-cate
rev'-i-res'-cence
rev'-i-res'-cent
re-vise'
re-vised'
re-vis'-er
re-vi'-sion
re-vis'-it
re-vis-i-ta'-tion*
re-vi'-so-ry
re-vi'-tal-ize
re-viv'-al†
re-viv'-al-ist†
re-vive'
re-viv'-i-fy
re-viv'-ing
rev-i-vis'-cence
rev-i-vis'-cent
re-vi'-vor
rev-o-ca-bil'-i-ty
rev'-o-ca-ble
rev-o-ca'-tion
rev'-o-ca-to-ry
re-vok'-a:ble
re-voke'
re-vok'-er
re-vok'-ing
re-volt'
re-volt'-er
re-volt'-ing
re-volt'-ing-ly
rev'-o-lu-ble
rev-o-lu'-tion
rev'-o-lu'-tion-ar:y†
rev-o-lu'-tion-ist
rev-o-lu'-tion-ize
re-volv'-a:ble
re-volve'
re-volv'-er
re-volv'-ing
re-vue'
re-vul'-sion
re-vul'-sive
re-ward'
re-ward'-a:ble
re'-write' (v.)
re'-write (n.)
Rey'-kja-vik
Rey'-nard*
Reyn'-olds
rhab'-do-man-cer

rhab'-do-man-cy
Rhad'-a-man'-thine
Rhad'-a-man'-thus
rham-na'-ceous
rham'-na-zin
rham'-ni-nose
rham'-nose
rham'-no-side
rha-pon-ti-gen'-in
rhap-sod'-ic
rhap-sod'-i-cal
rhap'-so-dist
rhap'-so-dize
rhap'-so-diz-ing
rhap'-so-dy
rhat'-a-ny
rhe'a
rhe'-a-dine
rhe-mat'-ic
Rhen'ish
rhe'-ni-um
rhe-ol'-o-gy
rhe-om'-e-ter
rhe'-o-stat
rhe'-o-stat'-ic
rhe'o-tax'-is
rhe-ot'-ro-pism
rhe'-sus
rhe'-tor
rhet'-o-ric
rhe-tor'-i-cal
rhet-o-ri'-cian
rheum
rheu-mat'-ic
rheu'-ma-tism
rheu'-ma-toid
rhig'-o-lene
rhi'-nal
rhin'-en-ceph'-a-lon*
rhine'-stone
rhi-ni'-tis
rhi-noc'-er-ost†
rhi-nol'-o-gy
rhi'-no-plas-ty
rhi-nos'-co-py
rhi-zo'-bi-um
rhi'-zo-car'-pous
rhi'-zo-ceph'-a-lous
rhi'-zoid
rhi-zom'-a-tous
rhi'-zome
rhi-zop'-ter-in
rhi-zot'-o-my
rho'-da:mine
rho'-da:nate
Rhode Is'-land
Rhode Is'-land-er
Rho-de'-sia

Rho-de'-sian
Rho'-di-an
rho'-dic
rho'-di-nol
rho'-dite
rho'-di-um
rho'-di-zon'-ic
rho-do-chro'-site
rho-do-den'-dron
rho-do'-ra
rhomb'-en-ceph'-a-lon*†
rhom'-bic
rhom'-bo-clase
rhom'-bo-he'-dral
rhom'-bo-he'-dron
rhom'-bold
rhom-boi'-dal
rhom'-bus
Rhon'-dda†
rhu'-barb
rhum'-ba-tron
rhyme
rhyme'-ster
rhym'-ing
rhy'-o-lite
rhythm
rhyth'-mic
rhyth'-mi-cal
rhyth'-mi-cal-ly
Ri-al'-to
rib'-ald
rib'-al-dry*†
rib'-and
rib'-band
ribbed
rib'-bing
rib'-bon
rib'-boned
ri'-bi-tyl
ri-bo-fla'-vin†
ri-bo-nu'-cle-ase
ri'-bo-nu-cle'-ic
ri'-bo-side
ri'-bo-some
ri'-bu-lose
Ri-car'-do
rice field
ric'-er
Rich'-ard
Riche'-lieu'
ri-chell'-ite*†
rich'-es
rich'-ly
Rich'-mond
rich'-ness
Rich'-ter
ri'cin
ri'cin-o:le'-ic

rick'-ets
rick-ett'-si-al
rick'-et:y
rick'-sha
ric'-o-chet
ric'-o-cheted
ric'-tus
rid'-a:ble
rid'-dance
rid'-den
rid'-der
rid'-ding
rid'-dle
rid'-dled
ride'-a:ble
ri'-dent
rid'-er
rid'-er-less
ridge
ridge'-pole
ridg'-ing
ridg'y
rid'-i-cule
ri-dic'-u-lous
ri-dic'-u-lous-ly
rid'-ing (form of travel)
ri'-ding (county)*†
rife'-ness
Riff'-i:an†
rif'-fle
rif'-fling
riff'-raff
ri'-fle
ri'-fle-man
ri'-fle pit
ri'-fling
Ri'-ga
rig-a-to'-ni
rigged
rig'-ger
rig'-ging
right
right'=an'-gled
righ'-teous*†
righ'-teous-ness*†
right'-er
right'-ful
right'-ful-ly
right'=hand-ed
right'-ist
right'=mind-ed
right'-ly
right'-ness
right'=of=way
rig'-id
ri-gid'-i-ty
rig'-id-ly

rig'-or mor'-tis
rig'-ma-role
rig'-or
rig'-or-ous
rig'-or-ous-ly
Ri'-ley
rime
rim'-less
rimmed
rim'-ming
ri'-mose'
ri'-mous*
rin'-der-pest
ring'-bolt
ring'-bone
ring'-dove
ringed
rin'-gent
ring'-er
ring'-ing
ring'-lead-er
ring'-let
ring'-mas-ter
ring'-side
ring'-ster
ring'-worm
rins-a:ble*
rinsed
rins'-er
rins'-ing
Ri'o de Ja-nei'-ro
Ri'o Grande*†
ri'-ot
ri'-ot-er
ri'-ot-ous
ri'-ot-ous-ly
ri-par'-i-an†
rip'-en
ripe'-ness
ri-pid'-o-lite
rip'-ping
rip'-ple
rip'-pled
rip'-pling
rip'-rap
rip'-saw
ris'-en
ris'-er
ris-i-bil'-i-ty
ris'-i-ble
ris'-ing
risk'-i-ness
risk'y
ris-qué'
ris-sole'
rite
rit'-u-al
rit'-u-al-is'-tic

ri'-val
ri'-valed
ri'-val-ing
ri'-val-ry
riv'-en
riv'-er
Ri-ve'-ra
riv'-er-ain
riv'-er-bank
riv'-er-side
riv'-et
riv'-et-er
riv'-et-ing
Riv-i-er'a†
riv'-u-let
Ri-yadh'
ri-yal'
road'-bed
road'-house
road'-side
road'-stead
road'-ster
road'-way
roam'-er
Ro'-a-noke
roast'-ed
roast'-er
robbed
rob'-ber
rob'-ber:y
rob'-bing
Rob'-ert
Robes'-pierre†
rob'-in
rob'-ing
ro'bi-nose
Rob'-in-son Cru"-soe
ro'-ble
rob'o-rant
ro'-bot
ro'-bur-ite
ro-bust'
ro-bus'-tious
ro-bust'-ness
Ro-cham-beau'
Ro-chelle'
Roch'-es-ter
rock'-bound
Rock'-e-fel-ler
rock'-er
rock'-et
rock'-e-teer*
rock'-et-er
rock'-et-ry
Rock'-ford
Rock'-ies
rock'-ing
rock'-ing chair

rock-oon'
rock'=ribbed'
rock salt
rock'-work
rock'y
ro-co'-co
ro'-dent
ro-den'-ti-ci'-dal*
ro-den'-ti-cide
ro'-de:o
Rod'-er-ick
Ro-din'
rod'o-mon-tade'
roe'-bling-ite*†
roe'-buck
roent'-gen
roent'-gen-o-graph
roent-gen-og'-ra-phy
roent-gen-ol'-o-gy
roent-gen-om'-e-ter
roent-gen-om'-e-try
roent'-gen-o-scope
roent-gen-os'-co-py
ro-ga'-tion
rog'-a-to-ry†
Rog'-er
ro-gnon'
rogue
rogu'-er:y*
rogu'-ish*
rogu'-ish-ness*
roil'y
rois'-ter*†
rois'-ter-er*†
rois'-ter-ous*†
Ro'-land
roll'-back (n.)
roll call (n.)
roll'=call' (v.)
rolled
roll'-er
roll'-er skate (n.)
roll'-er=skate (v.)
roll'-er tow-el
rol'-lick-ing
rol'-lick-some
roll'-ing
roll'-ing mill
roll'-ing pin
roll top (n.)
roll'-top (adj.)
Röl'-vaag
ro'-ly=po'-ly
Ro-ma'-gna
Ro-ma'ic
ro-maine'
Ro'-man (of Rome)
ro-man' (romance)

338

ro-mance'
ro-manc'-er
ro-manc'-ing
Ro'-man-esque'
Ro-ma'-ni:a
Ro-man'-ic
Ro'-man-ism
Ro'-man-ist
ro-ma'-ni-um
Ro'-man-ize
Ro'-ma-nov
ro-man'-tic
ro-man'-ti-cal-ly
ro-man'-ti-cism
ro-man'-ti-cist
Rom'-a-ny
ro'-me-ite
Ro'-me:o
Rom'-ish
romp'-er
romp'-ish
Rom'-u-lus
ron-deau'
ron'-del
ron'-de-let'
ron'-do
ro'-ne:o-graph
ron-geur'
Ron-sard'
roof'-er
roof gar'-den
roof'-ing
roof'-less
roof'-tree
rook'-er:y
rook'-ie
room'-er
room-ette'
room'-ful
room'-mate
room'y
Roo'-se-velt
roost'-er
root'-ed
root'-er
root'-less
root'-let
root'-stock
roped
rope'-danc-er
rop'-er
rop'er:y
rope'-walk-er
rop'-ing
Roque'-fort
roque'-laure'
ro-rif'-er-ous
Ror'-schach

ro-sa'-ceous
ro-sa'-lia†
Ros'-a-lind
Ros'-a-mond
ros-an'-i-line†
Ro-sa'-ri:o
ro'-sa-ry
rosch'er-ite
Ros'-coe
ro'-se-ate
rose'-bud
rose'-bush
rose cold
rose'=col-ored
rose fe-ver
rose'-mar:y†
ro-se'-o-la
Ro-set'-ta
ro-sette'
rose wa'-ter (n.)
rose'-wa-ter (adj.)
rose'-wood
Rosh Ha-sha'-nah
Ros:i-cru'-cian
ro'-sier (n.)
ros'-i-er (adj.)
ros'-i-ly
ros'-in
ros'-in-ate
ros'-i-ness
ro-sol'ic
Ros-set'-ti
Ros-si'-ni
Ros-tand'†
ros'-ter
ros'-trum
ros'y
ro'-tal
ro'-ta:me-ter
Ro-tar'-i-an†
ro'-ta-ry
ro'-tat-a:ble
ro'-tate
ro-ta'-tion
ro'-ta-tive
ro'-ta-tor
ro'-ta-to-ry
rote
ro'-te-noid
ro'-te-none
Roth'-schild
ro'-ti-fer
Ro-tif'-er:a
ro-tif'-er-ous
ro-tis'-ser-ie*†
ro'-to-graph
ro'-to-gra-vure'
ro'-tor

339

rot'-ten
rot'-ten-ness
rot'-ten-stone
Rot'-ter-dam
rot'-ting
ro-tund'
ro-tun'-da
ro-tun'-di-ty
ro-tund'-ly
rou:é'
Rou'-en'
rouged
rough'-age
rough=and=read:y
rough'-cast
rough'-dry
rough'-en
rough'-er
rough'-hew
rough'-house
rough'-ish
rough'-ly
rough'-neck
rough'-ness
rough-om'-e-ter
rough'-rid-er
rough'-shod
roug'-ing
rou-lade'
rou-leau'
rou-lette'
Rou-ma'-ni-an
round'-a:bout (n., adj.)
roun'-del
roun'-de-lay
round'-er
Round'-head
round'-house
round'-ish
round'-ly
round'-ness
round=shoul-dered
rounds'-man
round'-up (n.)
round'-worm
roused
rous'-ing
rous'-ing-ly
Rous-seau'
roust'-a:bout
route
rout'-ed
rout'-er†
rout'-ing
rou-ti-neer'†
ro'-ver (pirate)*†

rov'-er (wanderer)
rov'-ing
row'-an
row'-boat
row'-dies
row'-di-ness
row'-dy
row'-dy-ish
row'-dy-ism
row'-el
row'-eled
Row-e'-na
row'-er
row'-lock
roy'-al
roy'-al-ist
roy'-al-ly
roy'-al-ty
Ru-bai-yat'
ru-basse'
ru-ba'-to
rubbed
rub'-ber
rub'-ber-ize
rub'-bing
rub'-bish
rub'-ble
rub'-down
ru'-be-an'-ic
ru'-be-fa'-cient
ru-bel'-lite
Ru'-bens
ru-be'-o-la
rub-e:ryth'-ric*†
ru-bes'-cent
ru-bi-a'-ceous
Ru'-bi-con
ru'-bi-cund
ru-bi-cun'-di-ty
ru-bid'-i-um
ru-big'-i-nous
Ru'-bin-stein
ru'-ble
ru'-brene
ru'-bric
ru'-bri-cal
ru'-bri-ca-tor
ru'-by
ruche
ruch'-ing
ruck'-us
ruc'-tion
rud'-der
rud'-di-ness
rud'-dy
rude'-ly
rude'-ness

rud'-est
ru'-di-ment
ru'-di-men'-ta-ry
Ru'-dolf
Ru'-dolph
rue'-ful
rue'-ful-ly
ru-fes'-cence
ru-fes'-cent
ruffed
ruf'-fi-an
ruf'-fle
ruf'-fled
ruf'-fier
ruf'-fling
ru-fos'-i-ty
Ru'-fous (reddish)
Ru'-fus (name)
Rug'-by
rug'-ged
ru'-gose
ru-gos'-i-ty
ru'-gu-lose
Ruhr
ru'-in
ru'-in-ate
ru-in-a'-tion
ru'-ined
ru'-in-ing
ru'-in-ous
rul'-a:ble
ruled
rul'-er
rul'-ing
Ru-ma'-ni:a
Ru-ma'-ni-an
rum'-ba
rum'-ble
rum'-bler
rum'-bling
ru'-mi-nant
ru'-mi-nate
ru-mi-na'-tion
rum'-mage
rum'-mag-er
rum'-mag-ing
rum'-my
ru'-mor
rump'-er
rum'-ple
rum'-pled
rum'-pling
rum'-pus
run'-a:bout
run'-a-gate
run'-a:round
run'-a:way

run'-ci-ble
run'-ci-nate
run'-down (n.)
run=down (adj.)
ru'-nic
run'-let
run'-nel
run'-ner
run'-ner=up'
run'-ning
runt'y
run'-way
ru-pee'
Ru'-pert
ru-pic'-o-lous
rup'-tur-a:ble
rup'-ture
rup'-tured
rup'-tur-ing
ru'-ral
ru'-ral-ly
ru-rig'-e-nous
rush'-ing
rush'-light
rush'y
Rus'-kin
Rus'-sell
rus'-set
Rus'-sia
Rus'-sian
rus'-si-fy
rus'-tic
rus'-ti-cate
rus-ti-ca'-tion
rus-ti-ca'-tor
rus-tic'-i-ty
rust'-i-ly
rust'-i-ness
rus'-tle
rus'-tler
rus'-tling
rust'-proof
rust'y
ru'-ta-ba'-ga
ru-ta'-ceous
ru-tae-car'-pine
Ru-the'-ni-an
ru-then'-ic
ru-the'-nl-ous
ru-the'-ni-um
Ruth'-er-ford
ruth'-er-ford-ine
ruth'-less
ruth'-less-ly
ruth'-less-ness
ru'-tile
ru'-tin

341

ru′-tin-ose*
Rut′-land
rut′-ted
rut′-ty
ru′-ty-lene
Rwan′-da
ry-an′-o-dine
Ry:u′-kyu
Ry:u′-kyu-an

S

sab′-a-dine
Sa-bae′-an
Sa′-ba-ism
Sab′-a-oth
Sab′-a-ti′-ni
Sab-ba-tar′-i-an†
Sab′-bath
sab-bat′-i-cal
sa′-ber
Sa′bine
sab′-i-nene
sa-bi′-no
sa′-ble
sa:bot′
sab′-o-tage†
sab′-o-teur′
sa′-bra
sab-u-los′-i-ty
sab′-u-lous
sa′-bu-tan′
sac
sac′-cha-rate
sac-char′-ic
sac′-cha-ride
sac-cha-rif′-er-ous
sac-char′i-fy†
sac-cha-rim′-e-ter
sac′-cha-rin
sac′-cha-rin-ate
sac′-cha-rine
sac-cha-rin′-ic
sac-cha-rom′-e-ter
sac′-cha-rose
sac′-cu-lat-ed
sac′-er-do′-tal
sa′-chem
sa-chet′
sack
sack′-but
sack′-cloth
sack′-ful
sack′-ing
sacque
sac′ral*†
sac′-ra-ment
sac′-ra-men′-tal

sac-ra-men′-ta-ry
Sac′-ra-men′-to
sa-crar′-i-um†
sa′-cred
sac′-ri-fice
sac′-ri-fi′-cial
sac′-ri-fic-ing
sac′-ri-lege
sac′-ri-le′-gious
sa′-cring
sac′-ris-tan
sac′-ris-ty
sac-ro-il′-i-ac*†
sac′-ro-sanct
sac′-ro-sanc′-ti-ty
sac′ro-sci-at′-ic*†
sac′rum*†
sad′-den
sad′-der
sad′-dle
sad′-dle-bag
sad′-dle-bow
sad′-dler
sad′-dler:y
Sad′-du-ce′-an
Sad′-du-cee
sad′-i:ron
sa′dism*
sa′dist*
sa-dis′-tic
sa-dis′-ti-cal-ly
sad′-ly
sad′-ness
Saeng′-er-fest
sa-fa′-ri
safe=con′-duct
safe′-guard
safe′-keep-ing
safe′-ly
saf′-est
safe′-ty
safe′-ty match
safe′-ty pin
safe′-ty valve
saf′-flor-ite
saf′-fron
saf′-ra-nine
sa′-ga
sa-ga′-cious
sa-gac′-i-ty
sag′-a-more
sag-a-pe′-num
sage′-brush
sage′-ly
sag′-e-nite
sagged
sag′-ging
Sag′-i-naw

sag'-it-tal
Sag-it-tar'-i-us*†
sag'-it-tate
sa'-go
sa-gua'-ro
Sag-ue-nay'
Sa-ha'-ra
sa'-hib
Sai-gon'
sail'-boat
sail'-cloth
sailed
sail'-fish
sail'-or
saint'-ed
saint'-hood
saint'-li-ness
saint'-ly
Sai-pan'
sake
sa'-ke (drink)
Sa-kha-lin'
sa-laam'
sal-a:bil'-i-ty
sal'-a:ble
sa-la'-cious
sa-la'-cious-ly
sa-lac'-i-ty
sal'-ad
Sal'-a-din
Sal-a-man'-ca
sal'-a-man-der
sa-la'-mi
Sal'-a-mis
sal'-a-ried
sal'-a-ry
Sa'-lem
sal-e-ra'-tus
Sa-ler'-no
sales'-girl
sales'-man
sales'-man-ship
sales'-per-son
sales'-room
sales'-wom-an†
sal-i-ca'-ceous
sal'-i-cin
sal-i-cyl'-a:mide*†
sa-lic'-y-late*†
sal'-i-cyl'-ic
sa-lic'-y-lide*†
sal'-i-cyl-ize
sal'-i-cyl'-o-yl
sal'-i-cyl-u'ric*
sa'-lience†
sa'-lient†
sa-li-en'-tian
sa-lif'-er-ous

sal'-i-fy
sal-i-gen'-in*†
sa-lim'-e-ter*
sa-li'-na
sal-i-na'-tion
sa'-line
sa-lin'-i-ty
sa'-lin-o-gen'-ic*
sal-i-nom'-e-ter
Salis-bur:y
sa-li'-va
sal'-i-var:y†
sal'-i-vate
sal-i-va'-tion
sa-li'-vous
sal'-lied
sal'-low
Sal'-lust
sal'-ly
sal'-ly-ing
sal'-ly port
sal-ma-gun'-di
sal'-mi
salm'-on
Sal-mo-nel'-la
sal-mo-nel-lo'-sis
salm'-ons-ite*
Sal'-ol
Sa-lo'-me
sa-lon'
Sa-lon'-i-ka†
sa-loon'
sa-loon'-keep-er
sal-pin-gec'-to-my
sal-pin-gi'-tis
sal'-si-fy
sal-ta'-tion
sal'-ta-to'-ri-al
sal'-ta-to-ry
salt'-cel-lar
salt'-ed
salt'-er:y
salt'-i-er
sal'-tire
salt marsh
salt'-ness
salt-pe'-ter
salt'y
sa-lu'-bri-ous
sa-lu'-bri-ty
Sa-lu'-ki
sal-u-tar'-i-ly†
sal'-u-ta'r:y†
sal'-u-ta'-tion
sa-lu-ta-to'-ri-an
sa-lu'-ta-to-ry
sa-lute'
sa-lut'-ing

343

sal'-va-ble
Sal'-va-dor
Sal'-va-dor'-an*
sal'-vage
sal'-vage-a:ble
sal'-vag-er
Sal'-var-san
sal-va'-tion
salved
sal'-ver
sal'-vi:a
sal'-vi:a-nin
salv'-ing
sal'-vo
sal vo-la'-ti-le†
sal'-vor
Salz'-burg
sam'-a-ra†
Sa-mar'i:a*†
Sa-mar'-i-tan
sa-mar'-i-um*†
Sam'ar-kand†
sam'-ba
sam-bu-ni'grin
same'-ness
sam'-i-sen
sam'ite†
Sa-mo'a
Sa-mo'-an
Sa'-mos
Sam'-o-thrace
sam'-o-var
Sam'-o-yed
sam'-pan
sam'-phire
sam'-ple
sam'-pler
sam'-pling
Sam'-son
Sam'-u-el
sa'-mu-rai*
San An-to'-ni:o
san'-a-tive
san-a-to'-ri-um
san'-a-to-ry
San'-cho
sanc-ti-fi-ca'-tion
sanc'-ti-fied
sanc'-ti-fy
sanc'-ti-fy-ing
sanc-ti-mo'-ni-ous
sanc'-ti-mo-ny
sanc'-tion
sanc'-tion-er
sanc'-ti-ty
sanc'-tu-ar:y†
sanc'-tum
sanc'-tus

san'-dal
san'-daled
san'-dal-wood
sand'-bag
sand'-bank
sand'-blast
sand'-box
sand'-er
sand'-glass
san'-dhi
sand'-hog
San Di-e'-go
sand'-i-er
sand'-i-ness
sand'-man
San Do-min'-go
sand'-pa-per
sand'-pip-er
sand'-stone
sand'-storm
sand trap
San-dus'-ky
san'-dust
sand'-wich
sand'y
san'-er
sane'-ly
san'-for-ize
San Fran-cis'-co
san-ga-ree'
Sang'-er
sang-froid'
san'-gui-nar'-i-ly†
san-guin'-a-rine
san'-gui-nar:y†
san'-guine
san-guin'-e-ous
san-guin'-o-lent
San-he'-drin
san'-i-dine
sa'-ni-ous
san-i-tar'-i-an†
san'-i-tar'-i-ly†
san-i-tar'-i:um†
san'-i-tar:y†
san-i-ta'-tion
san'-i-tiz-er
san'-i-ty
San Joa-quin'
San Sal'-va-dor
sans-cu-lotte'
San Se-bas'-tian†
San'-skrit
San'-ta Bar'-ba-ra
San'-ta Claus
San'-ta Fe
san'-ta-la'-ceous
san'-ta-lene

344

san'-ta-lol
San'-ta Ma-ri'a
San-ta-ya'-na
san'-te-none
San'-ti-a'-go
San'-to Do-min'-go
san-ton'-i-ca
san'-to-nin
sa-phe'-nous
sap'-id
sa-pid'-i-ty
sap'i-ence*†
sap'i-ent*†
sap'i-en'-tial*†
sap'-in-da'-ceous
sap'-less
sap'-ling
sap-o-dil'-la
sap-o-gen'-in*†
sap'-o-na'-ceous
sa-pon-i-fi-ca'-tion
sa-pon'-i-fy
sap'-o-nin
sap'-o-rif'-ic
sap'-o-ta'-ceous
sap'-per
sap'-phic
sap'-phire
sap'-phir-ine
Sap'-pho
sap'-ping
sap'-py
sa-pre'-mi:a
sap'-ro-gen'-ic
sap-ro-ge-nic'-i-ty
sa-prog'-e-nous
sap'-ro-pel'-ic
sap'-ro-phyte
sap'-ro-phyt'-ic
sap'-suck-er
sap'-wood
sar'-a-band
Sar'-a-cen
Sar-a-cen'-ic
Sar-a-gos'-sa
Sar'-ah
Sa'-ra-je'vo
Sa-ran'
Sar-a-to'-ga
Sa-ra'-tov
Sa-ra'-wak
sar'-casm
sar-cas'-tic
sar-cas'-ti-cal-ly
sar'-coid
sar-coid-o'-sis
sar-col'-y-sis
sar-co'-ma

sar-co'-ma-toid
sar-co-ma-to'-sis
sar-com'a-tous*
sar-coph'-a-gi
sar-coph'-a-gus
sar-cop'-side
sar'-co-sine
sar'-cous
sar-dine'
Sar-din'-i:a
Sar'-dis
sar-don'-ic
sar-don'-i-cal-ly
sar-don'-yx*†
sar-gas'-so
Sar'-gent
Sar'-gon
sa'-ri
sar'-ki-nite
sar-men-to-gen'-in
sa-rong'
sar-sa-pa-ril'-la
sar'-sen
sar-to'-ri-al
sar-to'-ri-us
Sar'-tri-an
sa-shay'
Sas-katch'-e-wan
sas'-sa-fras
sas'-so-lite
Sa'-tan
sa-tan'-ic
sa-tan'-i-cal
sa-tan'-i-cal-ly
satch'-el
sat'-ed
sa-teen'
sat'-el-lite
sat'-el-lit-ed
sat'-el-lit-oid
sat-el-lit-o'-sis
sat'-el-loid
sa'-tem
sa-tia-bil'-i-ty*†
sa'-tia-ble*†
sa'-ti-ate
sa-ti-a'-tion
sa-ti'-e-ty
sat'-in
sat'-in-et'†
sat'-in-ize
sat'-in-wood
sat'in:y
sat'-ire
sa-tir'-ic
sa-tir'-i-cal
sat'-i-rist
sat'-i-rize

sat'-i-riz-ing
sat-is-fac'-tion
sat'-is-fac'-to-ri-ly
sat'-is-fac'-to-ry
sat'-is-fied
sat'-is-fy
sa'trap
sa'tra-py*†
sat-su'-ma
sat-u-ra-bil'-i-ty
sat'-u-ra-ble
sat'-u-rate
sat'-u-rat-ed
sat'-u-rat-er
sat'-u-rat-ing
sat-u-ra'-tion
sat'-u-ra-tor
Sat'-ur-day
Sat'-urn
sat-ur-na'-lia†
Sat-ur-na'-lian†
Sa-tur'-ni-an
sat'-ur-nine
sat-ur-nin'-i-ty
sa'tyr†
sa-tyr'-ic
sauce'-pan
sau'-cer
sau'-ci-ly
sau'-ci-ness
sau'-cy
Sau'-di
sau'-er-bra-ten
sau'-er-kraut*†
Sault Sainte Ma-rie'
sau'-na
saun'-ter
saun'-ter-ing
sau'-rel
sau'-ri-an
sau'-sage
saus'-sur-ite
sau-té'
sau-téd'
sau-téed'
sau-té'-ing
sau-terne'
sav'-a:ble
sav'-age
sav'-age-ly
sav'-age-ry
sa-van'-na
Sa-van'-nah
sa-vant'
sa-vate'
saved
sav'-er
sav'-in

sav'-ing
sav'-ior
sa'-voir faire'
Sav:o:na-ro'-la†
sa'-vor
sa'-vor-ous
sa'-vor:y
Sa-voy'
Sa-voy'-ard
sav'-vy
saw'-buck
saw'-dust
saw'-horse
saw'-mill
saw'-yer
sax'-i-frage
Sax'-on
Sax-o-ny
sax'-o-phone
sax'-o-phon-ist
sa'-yid†
say'-ing
scab
scab'-bard
scabbed
scab'-bing
scab'-bler
scab'-by
sca'-bies⁸†
sca-bi-o'-sa
sca-bres'-cent
scab'-rous*†
scaf'-fold
scaf'-fold-ing
sca'-lar
scal'-a-wag
scald'-ed
scald'-er
scaled
sca-lene'
sca-le'-no-he'-dral
scal'-i-ger
scal'-ing
scal'-lion
scal'-lop
scal'-loped
scal'-pel
scalp'-er
scal'y
scam'-mo-ny
scam'-per
scamp'-ish
scan'-dal
scan'-dal-i:za'-tion
scan'-dal-ize
scan'-dal-mon:ger
scan'-dal-ous

scan'-di:a
Scan-di-na'-vi:a
Scan-di-na'-vi-an
scan'-di-um
scanned
scan'-ner
scan'-ning
scan'-sion
scan-so'-ri-al
scant'-i-ly
scant'-i-ness
scant'-ling
scant'-ly
scant'y
scape'-goat
scape'-grace
sca-pig'-er-ous
scap'-o-lite
scap'-u-la
scap'-u-lar
scar'-ab
scar-a-bae'-id
scar'-a-boid*
scarce
scarce'-ly
scar'-ci-ty
scare'-crow
scared
scarf'-er
scar-i-fi-ca'-tion
scar'-i-fi-ca-tor
scar'-i-fied
scar'-i-fy
scar'-i-ly
scar'-ing
scar'-i-ous†
scar-la-ti'-na
scar'-let
scarred
scar'-ring
scar:y
scathe
scathed
scathe'-less
scath'-ing
scat-o-log'-ic
scat-o-log'-i-cal
sca-tol'-o-gy
scat'-ter
scat'-ter-brain
scat'-tered
scav'-eng-er*†
scav'-eng-ing
sce-nar'-i:o*†
sce-nar'-ist*†
sce'-ner:y*†
sce'-nic

sce'-ni-cal†
sce'-ni-cal-ly†
sce'-no-graph†
sce'-no-graph'-ic†
sce-nog'-ra-phy
scent
scent'-ed
scent'-er
scent'-less
scep'-ter
scep'-tic
scep'-ti-cal
scep'-ti-cism
sche'di-asm
sched'-ule
sched'-uled
sched'-ul-ing
schee'-lite
Sche-her-a-zade'†
Schel'-de
Scheldt
sche'-ma
sche-mat'-ic
sche'-ma-tism
sche'-ma-tist
sche-mat'o-graph
scheme
schem'-er
schem'-ing
Sche-nec'-ta-dy
Sche'-ring
scher'-zo
Sche-ven-ing-en
Schia-pa-rel'-li
schiff'-li
Schil'-ler
schil'-ling
schism
schis-mat'-ic
schist
schist'-oid
schist'-ose†
schis'-to-some
schis-to-so-mi'-a-sis
schiz'-oid
schiz'-oid-ism
schiz-o-phre'-ni:a
schiz'-o-phren'-ic
Schle'-gel
schle-miel'
Schles'-wig=Hol'-stein
Schlie'-mann
schlie'-ren
schnap'-per
Schnau'-zer
Schnei'-der
Schnitz'-ler
scho'-la can-to'-rum

schol'-ar
schol'-ar-ly
schol'-ar-ship
scho-las'-tic
scho-las'-ti-cal
scho-las'-ti-cal-ly
scho-las'-ti-cism
scho'-li-ast
school bell
school board
school'-book
school'-boy
school bus
school'-child
school'-girl
school'-house
school'-ing
school'-man
school'-mas-ter
school'-mate
school'-mis-tress
school'-room
school'-teach-er
school'-work
school'-yard
schoo'-ner*†
Scho'-pen-hauer*†
schor-la'-ceous
schot'-tische
schra'-dan
schrei'-ner-ize
Schrö'-din-ger*
schroec'-king-er-ite
Schu'-bert
Schu'-mann
Schuy'-ler
Schuyl'-kill
Schweit'-zer
Schwei'-zer
sci-ae'-noid
sci-am'-a-chy
sci-at'-ic
sci-at'-i-ca
sci'-ence
sci-en'-tial
sci-en-tif'-ic
sci-en-tif'-i-cal-ly
sci'-en-tist
scil'i-cet
scil'-li-ro-side
scim'-i-tar
scin-tig'-ra-phy
scin-til'-la
scin'-til-late
scin'-til-lat-ing
scin-til-la'-tion
scin'-til-la-tor
scin-til-lom'-e-ter

sci-o-graph'-ic
sci-om'-a-chy
sci'-on
sci-oph'-i-lous
Scip'-i:o
sci'-re fa'-ci-as
scir'-rhus
scis'-sion
scis'-sors
sci'u:roid
sclar'-e-ol
scle-rec'-to-my
scle-ren'-chy-ma
scle-ri'-a-sis
scle-ri'-tis
scle-ro-der'-ma
scle-ro'-ma
scle-rom'-e-ter
scle-ro'-sal
scle-ro'-sis
scle-ro'-tal
scle-rot'-ic
scle-ro-ti'-tis†
scle-rot'-o-my
scle'-rous
scob'-i-nate
scoff'-er
scold'-er
scold'-ing
scold'-ing-ly
scol'-e-cite
sco-li-o'-sis
sconce
sconc'-i-ble
scone
scoop'-er
scoop'-ful
scoot'-er
sco'-pa-rin
scope
scoph'-o-ny
sco'-pine
sco-pol'-a-mine†
sco-po-le'-tin
scop'-u-late
scop'-u-lite
scor-bu'-tic
scorch'-ing
scored
sco'-ri:a
sco-ri-a'-ceous
sco-ri-fi-ca'-tion
scor'-ing
scorn'-er
scorn'-ful
scorn'-ful-ly
scor'-o-dite
scor'-per*

Scor'-pi:o
scor'-pi-on
scor'-za-lite
Scotch'=I'rish
Scotch'-man
sco'-ter
scot=free'
sco'-tia†
Scot'-land
sco-to'-ma
sco-tom'-a-tous
Scots'-man
Scot'-tish
scoun'-drel
scourge
scourg'-er
scourg'-ing
scout'-ing
scout'-mas-ter
scowl'-er
scowl'-ing-ly
scrab'-ble
scrab'-bler
scrab-bling
scrag'-gly
scrag'-gy
scram'-ble
scram'-bling
Scran'-ton
scrap'-book
scraped
scrap'-er
scrap'-ing
scrapped
scrap'-ping
scrap'-ple
scrap'-py
scratch
scratch'-er
scratch'-i-ness
scratch'-proof
scratch'y
scrawl'-er
scrawl'y
scrawn'-i-ness*†
scrawn'y*†
scream'-er
scream'-ing
screech
screech'y
screed
screen
screen'-er
screw'-driv-er
scrib'-ble
scrib'-bler
scrib'-bling
scribe

scrib'-er
scrim'-mage
scrim'-mag-er
scrimp'-i-ly
scrimp'y
scrip
script
scrip-to'-ri-um
scrip'-tur-al
scrip'-ture
scriv'-en-er*
scrof'-u-la
scrof-u-lo'-sis
scrof'-u-lous
scroll
scroll'-work
scro'-tum
scrounge
scroung'-ing
scrub
scrub'-bing
scrub'-by
scrump'-tious
scru'-ple
scru-pu-los'-i-ty
scru'-pu-lous
scru'-pu-lous-ly
scru'-ti-nize
scru'-ti-ny
scud'-ded
scuf'-fle
scuf'-fling
scull
scul'-ler:y
scul'-lion
sculp'-tor
sculp'-tur-al
sculp'-ture
scum'-bled
scum'-my
scup'-per
Scup'-per-nong
scurf
scurf'y
scur-ril'-i-ty
scur'-ri-lous*
scur'-ried
scur'-ry
scur'-ry-ing
scur'-vi-ly
scur'-vy
scu'-tage
scutch'-eon
scu-tel-la'-tion
scu'-ti-form
scut'-ter
scut'-tle
scut'-tle-butt

349

scut'-tling
scu'-tum
Scyl'-la
scythe
Scyth'-i:a
Scyth'-i-an
scyth'-ing
Sea'-bee
sea'-board
sea'-coast
sea'-drome
sea'-far-er
sea'-far-ing
sea fight
sea'-food
sea'-fowl
sea'-girt
sea'-go-ing
sea'=green (*adj.*)
sea gull
sea horse
seal'-a:ble
seal'-ant
sea legs
seal'-er
seal'-er:y
sea lev'-el
seal-ine'
seal'-ing wax
sea li'-on
sea lord
seal ring
seal'-skin
Sea'-ly-ham
sea'-man
sea'-man-ship
sea'-men
sea mew
seam'-i-ness
seam'-less
seam'-stress
seam'y
sé'-ance
sea'-plane
sea'-port
search'-a:ble
search'-er
search'-ing
search'-light
search war'-rant
sea rov'-er
sea ser'-pent
sea'-shore
sea'-sick
sea'-sick-ness
sea'-side
sea'-son
sea'-son-a:ble

sea'-son-al
sea'-son-ing
seat'-ed
seat'-er
seat'-ing
Se-at'-tle
sea ur'-chin
sea'-wall
sea'-ward
sea'-way
sea'-weed
sea'-wor-thy
seb'-a-cate
se-ba'-ceous
se-bac'-ic
Se-bas'-tian
seb-or-rhe'a
sec'-a-lose
se'-cant
se-cede'
se-ced'-ed
se-ced'-er
se-ced'-ing
se-ces'-sion
se-ces'-sion-ist
se-clude'
se-clud'-ed
se-clud'-ed-ly
se-clud'-ing
se-clu'-sion
se-clu'-sive
Sec'-o-nal
sec'-ond
sec'-ond-ar'-i-ly†
sec'-ond-ar'y†
sec'-ond=class (*adj.*)
sec'-ond-er
sec'-ond-hand' (not new)
sec'-ond hand (hand on
  clock)
sec'-ond-ly
sec'-ond=rate'
se'-cre-cy
se'-cret
se-cre'-ta-gogue
sec'-re-tar'-i-al†
sec-re-tar'-i-at†
sec'-re-tar:y†
se-crete'
se-cret'-ed
se-cre'-tin
se-cre'-tion
se-cre'-tive
se'-cret-ly
se-cre'-to-ry
sect
sec-tar'-i-an†
sec-tar'-i-an-ism†

350

sec'-ta-ry
sec-til'-ity
sec'-tion
sec'-tion-al
sec'-tion-al-ism
sec'-tion-al-ly
sec'-tion-al-ize
sec'-tor
sec'-tor-al
sec-to'-ri-al
se'-cu-lar
sec'-u-lar-ism
sec'-u-lar-ist
sec-u-lar'-i-ty
sec-u-lar-i:za'-tion
sec'-u-lar-ize
se'-cund†
se-eun'-date
sec'un-dines
se-cure'
se-cure'-ly
se-cur'-i-ty*†
se'-dan
se-date'
se-date'-ly
se-date'-ness
sed'-a-tive
sed'-en-tar'-i-ly†
sed'-en-tar:y†
sedge
sedg'y
se-di'-le
se-dil'-i:a
sed'-i-ment
sed'-i-men-tar'-i-ly*†
sed'-i-men-ta:ry
sed-i-men-ta'-tion
se-di'-tion
se-di'-tion-ar:y†
se-di'-tious
se-duce'
se-duce'-ment
se-duc'-er
se-duc'-i-ble
se-duc'-ing
se-duc'-tion
se-duc'-tive
se-du'-li-ty
sed'-u-lous
se'-dum
seed'-er
seed'-ing
seed'-less
seed'-ling
seeds'-man
seed'-time
seedy
see'-ing

seek'-er
seem'-ing
seem'-ing-ly
seem'-ly
seep'-age
seer'-suck-er
see'-saw
seethe
seethed
seeth'-ing
seg'-ment
seg-men'-tal
seg-men'-tal-ly
seg-men-tar:y†
seg-men-ta'-tion
se'-gno
seg'-re-ga-ble
seg'-re-gate
seg-re-ga'-tion
seg-re-ga'-tion-ist
seg'-re-ga-tive
Seid'-litz
sei'-gneur'
sei'-gnior*
sei'-gnior-age*
sei-gno'-ri-al
seine
sei'-sin
seis'-mic
seis-mic'-i-ty
seis'-mism
seis'-mo-graph
seis-mo-graph'-er*
seis-mo-graph'-ic
seis-mog'-ra-phy
seis-mo-log'-ic
seis-mo-log'-i-cal
seis-mol'-o-gist
seis-mol'-o-gy
seis-mom'-e-ter
seis-mo-met'-ric
seiz'-a:ble
seize
seiz'-er
sei'-zin
seiz'-ing
sei'-zor
sei'-zure
se-la'-chi-an
se-lag-i-nel'-la*†
se'-lah
sel'-dom
se-lect'
se-lect'-ance
se-lect'-ee†
se-lec'-tion
se-lec'-tive
se-lec-tiv'-i-ty

se-lect'-man
se-lec'-tor
sel'-e-nate
Se-le'-ne
se-len'ic*
sel'-e-nide
se-le'-ni-ous
sel'-e-nite
se-le'-ni-um
sel'-e-no-bis'-muth-ite*
sel-e-nog'-ra-pher
se-le'-no-graph'-ic
se-le'-nog'-ra-phy
se-le'-no-lite
se-le'-no-log'-i-cal
sel-e-nol'-o-gy
sel-e-no'-ni-um
sel-e-no'-sis
Se-leu'-cid
Se-leu'-cus
self=as-sur'-ance
self=cen'-tered
self=com-mand'
self=con'-fi-dence
self=con'-fi-dent
self=con'-scious
self=con'-scious-ness
self=con-tained'
self=con-tra-dic'-tion
self=con'-trol
self=de-fense'
self=de-ni'-al
self=de-ter-mi-na'-tion
self=dis'-ci-pline
self=es-teem'
self=ev'-i-dent
self=gov'-ern-ment
self=help'
self=im-por'-tance
self=im-por'-tant
self=im-posed'
self'-ish
self'-ish-ly
self'-ish-ness
self'-less
self=made'
self=pit'y
self=pos-sessed'
self=pos-ses'-sion
self=pres-er-va'-tion
self=pro-tec'-tion
self=re-gard'
self=re-li'-ance
self=re-li'-ant
self=re-spect'
self=re-spect'-ing
self=sac'-ri-fice
self'-same

self=sat'-is-fied
self=seek'-ing
self'=start-er
self=suf-fi'-cien-cy
self=suf-fi'-cient
self=sup-port'-ing
self=willed'
Sel'-juk
Sel'-kirk
sell'-er
sell'-ing
sel'-syn
selt'-zer
sel'-vage
selves
se-man'-tic
se-man'-ti-cist
se-man'-tics
sem'-a-phore
sem'-a-phor'-ic
sem'-a-phor-ist
se-ma:si-ol'-o-gy
sem'-blance
se-mei-ol'-o-gy
se'mei-ot'-ic
Sem'-e-le
sem'-eme
se'-men
se-mes'-ter
se-mes'-tral
sem'i-an'-nu-al
sem'i-ar'-id
sem'i-cir-cle
sem'i-cir-cu-lar
sem'i-co-lon
sem'i-con-scious
sem'i-de-tached'
sem'i-dine
sem'i-fi-nal
sem'i-lu'-nar
sem'i-month'-ly
sem'i-nal
sem'-i-nar
sem'-i-nar:y†
sem'-i-na'-tion
sem'-i-nif'-er-ous
sem'-i-niv'-o-rous
Sem'-i-nole
sem'i-pre'-cious
Se-mir'-a-mis
Sem'-ite
Se-mit'-ic
Sem'-i-tism
sem'i-tone
sem-o-li'-na
sem-pi-ter'-nal
sem-pi-ter'-ni-ty
se'na-ry*†

sen'-ate
sen'-a-tor
sen-a-to'-ri-al
sen'-dal
send'-er
send'-ing
send'=off (n.)
Sen'-e-ca
se-ne'-cic
se-ne'-ci-o-nine
se-ne-ci-o'-sis
sen'-e-ga
Sen'-e-gal
Sen'-e-gal-ese'†
se-nes'-cence
se-nes'-cent
sen'-e-schal*
se-nhor'
se'nile
se-nil'-i-ty
sen'-ior†
se-nior'-i-ty*†
sen'-na
Sen-nach'-er-ib†
se-nor'
se-no'-ra
se-no-ri'-ta
sen-sa'-tion
sen-sa'-tion-al
sen-sa'-tion-al-ism
sensed
sense'-less
sen-si-bil'-i-ty
sen'-si-ble
sen'-si-bly
sen'-sile
sens'-ing
sen'-si-tive
sen'-si-tive-ness
sen-si-tiv'-i-ty
sen-si-ti:za'-tion
sen'-si-tize
sen'-si-tiz-er
sen-si-tom'-e-ter
sen-so'-ri-al
sen-so'-ri-um
sen'-so-ry
sen'-su-al
sen'-su-al-ist
sen-su-al-is'-tic
sen-su-al'-i-ty
sen'-su-ous
sen'-su-ous-ly
sen'-tence
sen-ten'-tial
sen-ten'-tious
sen'-tience*†
sen'-tient†

sen'-ti-ment
sen-ti-men'-tal
sen-ti-men'-tal-ism
sen-ti-men'-tal-ist
sen-ti-men-tal'-i-ty
sen-ti-men'-tal-ize
sen-ti-men'-tal-ly
sen'-ti-nel
sen'-ti-neled
sen'-try
Se-nus'-si
se'pal†
se'paled†
se'pal-oid*†
sep-a-ra-bil'-i-ty
sep'-a-ra-ble
sep'-a-rate
sep-a-ra-tee'
sep'-a-rate-ly
sep-a-ra'-tion
sep-a-rat-ist*†
sep'-a-ra-tor
Se-phar'-dic
Se-phar'-dim
se'-pi:a
se'-poy
sep'-sis
sep-tar'-i-um†
sep-tec'-to-my
Sep-tem'-ber
sep-ten'ar:y*†
sep-ten'-ni-al
sep-tet'
sep'-tic
sep-ti-ce'-mi:a
sep-tic'-i-ty
sep-tif'-ra-gal
sep-til'-lion
sep'-ti-mal
sep'-tu'-a:ge-nar'-i-an†
sep-tu-a-gen'ar:y*†
sep-tu-a-ges'-i-ma
Sep-tu'-a-gint
sep'-tum
sep-tu-ple
sep-tup'-let*†
sep-tu'-pli-cate
sep'-ul-cher
se-pul'-chral
sep'-ul-ture
se-qua'-cious
se-quac'-i-ty
se'-quel
se-que'-la
se'-quence
se'-quent
se-quen'-tial
se-quen'-tial-ly

353

se-ques'-ter
se-ques'-tered
se:ques'-trate
se:ques-tra'-tion†
se'-quin
se'-quined
se-quoi'a
se-ra'-glio
ser'-al
se-ra'-pe
ser'-aph
se-raph'-ic
ser'-a-phim
Ser'-bi:a
Ser'-bi-an
Ser-bo'-ni-an
ser'-e-nade'
ser'-e-nad'-er
ser'-e-nad'-ing
ser-en-dip'-i-ty
se-rene'
se-rene'-ly
se-ren'-i-ty
serf'-dom
serge
ser'-geant
ser'-geant at arms
se'-ri-al
se'-ri-al-ly
se-ri-a'tim
se-ri'-ceous
ser'-i-cin
ser'-i-cite
ser'-i-cul-ture
se'-ries
ser'-if
ser'i-graph†
se-rig'-ra-pher
se-rig'-ra-phy
ser'-ine
se-rin'-ga
ser'-in-gal*
se'-ri:o-com'-ic
se'-ri-ous
se'-ri-ous-ly
se'-ri-ous-ness
ser'-mon
ser-mon'-ic
ser'-mon-ize
se'-ro-log'-ic
se'-ro-log'-i-cal
se-rol'-o-gist
se-rol'-o-gy
se-ro-si'-tis
se-ros'-i-ty

ser'-o-tine
se-ro-to'-nin
se'-rous
ser'-pent
ser'-pen-tine
ser'-pen-tin-ite
ser-pig'-i-nous
ser-pi'-go
ser-ra'noid
ser'-rate
ser'-rat-ed
ser-ra'-tion
ser'-ried
ser'-ru-late
ser'-ry
Ser-to'-ri-us
se'-rum
ser'-vant*
served
serv'-er
Ser-ve'-tus
serv'-ice† (1)
serv'-ice-a:ble† (1)
ser'-vi-ent
ser-vi-ette'
ser'-vile
ser-vil'-i-ty
serv'-ing
ser'-vi-tor
ser'-vi-tude
ser'-vo-mech'-a-nism
ser'-vo-mo'-tor
ses'-a-me
ses'-a-min
ses'-a-moid
ses-a-moid-i'-tis
ses-a-mo-lin
ses'-qui-cen-ten'-ni-al
ses-qui-pe-da'-lian*†
ses'-sile
ses'-sion
ses-ti'-na
se'-ta
se-ta'-ceous
se'-tae
set'-back (n.)
se'-ti-ger
se-tig'-er-ous
se'-ton
set-tee'
set'-ter
set'-ting
set'-tle
set'-tle-ment
set'-tler

(1) preferred to ser'-vice, given by Webster's 3rd New
    International Dictionary

set'-tling
set'=to (n.)
set'-up
sev'-en
sev'-en-fold
sev'-en-teen'
sev'-en-teenth'
sev'-enth
sev'-en-ti-eth
sev'-en-ty
sev'-en-ty=six'
sev'-er
sev'-er-a:ble
sev'-er-al
sev'-er-al-ly
sev'-er-ance
se-vere'
sev'-ered
se-vere'-ly
se-ver'-i-ty
Sev'-ern
Se-ve'-rus
Sé-vi-gné
Se-ville'*†
Sè'-vres
sew
sew'-age
Sew'-ard
sew'-er
sew'-er-age
sew'-ing
sex-a-ge-nar'-i-an†
sex-ag'-e-nar:y†
Sex-a-ges'-i-ma
sex-en'-ni-al
sex'-tant
sex-tet'
sex-tette'
sex-til'-lion
sex'-ton
sex-tu'-ple
sex-tup'-let*†
sex-tu'-pli-cate
sex'-u-al
sex-u-al'-i-ty
Sey'-mour
sfer'-ics
shab'-bi-ness
shab'-by
shack'-le
shack'-led
shack'-ling
shade
shad'-ed
shad'-er
shad'-i-er
shad'-ing
shad'-ow

shad'-ow-graph
shad'-ow-i-ness
shad'-ow:y
Shad'-rach†
shad'y
shag'-bark
shagged
shag'-ging
shag'-gy
sha-green'
shah
Sha-hap'-ti-an
shake
shake'-down (n., adj.)
shak'-en
shak'-er
Shake'-speare
Shake-spear'-e:an
shak'-i-ly
shak'-ing
shak'o
shak'y
shale
shal'-lop
shal-lot'
shal'-low
sham
sha'-man
sha'-man-ism
sham'-ble
sham'-bles
shame
shamed
shame'-faced
shame'-ful
shame'-ful-ly
shame'-less
shame'-less-ly
sham'-ing
shammed
sham'-mer
sham'-ming
sham-poo'
sham-pooed'
sham'-rock
Shang-hai'
Shan'gri=La'
shank'-er
Shan'-non
shan-tung'
shan'-ty
shaped
shape'-less
shape'-li-ness
shape'-ly
shap'-er
shap'-ing
shap-om'-e-ter

355

shar'-a:ble
share'-crop-per
share'-hold-er
shar'-er
sha-rif'
shar'-ing
shark'-skin
Shar'-on
sharp'-en
sharp'-en-er
sharp'-en-ing
sharp'-er
sharp'-ly
sharp'-ness
sharp'-shoot-er
sharp'=sight-ed
Shas'-ta
shat'-ter
shat'-tered
shaved
shave'-ling
shave'-tail
shav'-en
shav'-er
Sha-vi-an
shav'-ing
shawl
Shaw-nee'
sheaf
shear
shear'-er
shear'-ing
sheath
sheathe
sheathed
sheath'-er
sheath'-ing
sheath knife
sheaves
She'-ba
shed'-ding
sheen
sheep
sheep'-cote
sheep dog
sheep'-fold
sheep'-herd-er
sheep'-ish
sheep'-skin
sheep'-walk
sheer
sheer'-ness
sheet'-age
sheet an'-chor
sheet'-ing
sheet i:ron
Shef'-field
sheik

shek'-el
shel'-drake
shelf
shel-lac'
shel-lacked'
shel-lack'-ing
shell'-er
Shel'-ley
shell'-fish
shell'-proof
shell shock (n.)
shell'=shocked
shell'y
shel'-ter
shel'-tered
shel'-ter-ing
shelve
shelves
shelv'-ing
Shen-an-do'-ah
she-nan'-i-gan
shep'-herd
shep'-herd-ess
Sher'-a-ton
sher'-bet
Sher'-i-dan
sher'-iff
Sher'-lock
Sher'-man
sher'-ry
Sher'-wood
Shet'-land
shib'-bo-leth
shield
shield'-er
shift'-er
shift'-i-er
shift'-i-ly
shift'-ing
shift'-less
shift'-less-ness
shift'y
shi-kim'-ic
shil-le'-lagh
shil'-ling
Shi'-loh
shim'-mer
shim'-mer:y
shim'-ming
shim'-my
shin'-bone
shin'-dig
shine
shin'-er
shin'-gle
shin'-gled
shin'-i-er
shin'-ing

shin'-ny
shin'-plas-ter
Shin'-to
shin'y
ship'-board
ship'-build-er
ship'-build-ing
ship'-load
ship'-mas-ter
ship'-mate
ship'-ment
ship'-own-er
shipped
ship'-per
ship'-ping
ship'-ping room
ship'-shape
ship'-worm
ship'-wreck
ship'-wright
ship'-yard
Shi-raz'
shire
shirk
shirk'-er
Shir'-ley
shirr
shirred
shirr'-ing
shirt'-ing
shirt'-sleeve
shirt'-waist
shiv'-er
shiv'-ered
shiv'-er:y
shoal
shoat
shock'-er
shock'-ing
shock'-proof
shod'-di-ness
shod'-dy
shoe
shoe box
shoe brush
shoe'-horn
shoe'-ing
shoe'-lace
shoe'-mak-er
shoe pol'-ish
shoe store
shoe'-string
sho'-far
sho'-gun
shoot'-er
shoot'-ing
shoot'-ing star
shop'-keep-er

shop'-lift
shop'-lift-er
shopped
shop'-per
shop'-ping
shop'-talk
shop'-walk-er
shop'-worn
sho'-ran
shore'-line
shore'-ward
shor'-ing
shorn
short'-age
short'-cake
short cir'-cuit (n.)
short=cir'-cuit (v.)
short'-com-ing
short'-en
short'-en-ing
short'-hand
short'-hand'-ed
short'-horn
short'=lived'
short'-ly
short'-ness
short-om'-e-ter
short'-sight-ed
short'-stop
short=term' (adj.)
short'-wave'
short'=wind'-ed
Sho-sho'-ne
shot'-gun
should
shoul'-der
shoul'-der blade
shoul'-dered
shout'-ed
shoved
shov'-el
shov'-eled
shov'-el-er
shov'-el-ful
shov'-el-ing
shov'-er
shov'-ing
show'-boat
show'-case
show'-down
showed
show'-er
show'-er bath
show'-er:y
show'-i-ly
show'-ing
show'-man
show'-man-ship

shown
show'-room
show'y
shrap'-nel
shred'-ded
shred'-ding
Shreve'-port
shrewd
shrewd'-ly
shrewd'-ness
shrew'-ish
Shrews'-bur:y
shriek
shrieked
shriek'-ing
shriev'-al-ty
shrill'-ness
shril'-ly†
shrimp
shrined
shrin'-er
shrink'-a:ble
shrink'-age
shrink'-er
shriv'-el
shriv'-eled
shriv'-el-ing
shriv'-en
shriv'-ing
Shrop'-shire
shroud'-ed
Shrove'-tide
shrub'-ber:y
shrub'-bi-ness
shrub'-by
shrugged
shrug'-ging
shrunk'-en
shuck'-ing
shud'-der
shuf'-fle
shuf'-fle-board
shuf'-fled
shuf'-fling
shunned
shun'-ning
shunt'-ing
shut'-down (n.)
shut'=in (n.)
shut'-off (n.)
shut'-out (n.)
shut'-ter
shut'-ting
shut'-tle
shut'-tle-cock
Shy'-lock
shy'-ly
shy'-ness

shy'-ster
si-al'-a-gog'-ic*†
si-al'-a-gogue
si-a-log'-ra-phy
si-al'-o-li-thi'-a-sis*†
Si-am'
Si'-a-mese'
Si-be'-lius
Si-be'-ri:a
Si-be'-ri-an
sib'-i-lance
sib'-i-lant
sib'-i-la-to-ry
sib'-ling
sib'-yl
si-byl'-lic
sib'-yl-line
Si-cil'-ian*†
Sic'-i-ly
sick'-en
sick'-en-ing
sick'-en-ing-ly
sick'-ish
sick'-le
sick'-led
sick'-li-er
sick'-li-ness
sick'-ly
sick'-ness
sick'-room
side arm (n.)
side'-arm (adj.)
side'-board
side'-burns
sid'-ed
side'-long
sid'-er-al
si-de'-re-al
sid'-er-ite
sid-er-og'-ra-pher
sid'-er-o-graph'-ic
sid-er-o-na'-trite
sid-er-o'-sis
side'-sad-dle
side step (n.)
side'-step (v.)
side'-swipe
side'-track
side'-walk
side'-ways
sid'-ing
si'-dle
si'-dled
si'-dling
Si'-don
Si-do'-ni-an
siè-cle
siege

Sieg'-fried
sieg'-ing
Si-en'a
si-en'-na
si-er'-o-zem
si-er'-ra
Si-er'-ra Le-one'*†
Si-er'-ra Ma'-dre'
si-es'-ta
sieve
siev'-er
sift'-er
sigh'-ing
sight'-ed
sight'-er
sight'-less
sight'-ly
sight'-see-ing
sight'-seer*†
sig'-il
sig'-il-lar:y†
sig'-il-late
sig'-lo-ite
sig'-ma
sig'-ma-tism
sig'-moid
sig-moid-ec'-to-my
sig-moid-os'-to-my†
sig'-nal
sig'-naled
sig'-nal-ing
sig'-nal-ize
sig'-nal-ly
sig'-na-ry
sig'-na-to-ry
sig'-na-ture
sign'-board
sig'-net
sig-nif'-i-cance
sig-nif'-i-cant
sig-nif'-i-cant-ly
sig-nif-i-ca'-tion
sig-nif'-i-ca-tive
sig'-ni-fied
sig'-ni-fy
sig'-ni-fy-ing
si'-gnor'
si-gno'-ra
si-gno'-re
si-gno-ri'-na
si'-gno-ry
sign'-post
Sikh
si'-lage
sil'-ane
si'-lence
si'-lenc-er
si'-lenc-ing

si'-lent
si'-lent-ly
Si-le'-nus
Si-le'-sia†
Si-le'-sian†
si'-lex
sil-hou-ette'
sil-hou-et'-ted
sil'-i-ca
sil'-i-cate
sil-i-ca-ti-za'-tion
sil'-i-ca-tor
si-li'-ceous
si-lic'-ic
sil'-i-cide
si-lic'-i-dize
si-lic'-i-cif'-er-ous
sil-lic'-i-fy
sil'-i-co-mag-ne'-si:o-
   flu'-o-rite
sil'-i-con
sil'-i-cone
sil-i-co'-sis
sil-i-cot'-ic
silk'-en
silk'-i-er
silk'-i-ness
silk=stock'-ing (adj.)
silk'-weed
silk'-worm
silk'y
sil'-li-man-ite
sil'-li-ness
sil'-ly
si'-lo
si'-los
si-lox'-ane
sil-ta'-tion
si-lun'-dum
Si-lu'-ri-an
si-lu'-rid
sil'-va
sil'-van
sil'-ver
sil'-ver gray (n.)
sil'-ver=gray (adj.)
sil'-ver=plat'-ed
sil'-ver-smith
sil'-ver-ware
sil'-ver-work
sil'-ver:y
sil'-vi-cul'-tur-al
sil'-vi-cul-ture
Sim'-e-on
sim'-i-an
sim'-i-lar
sim-i-lar'-i-ty
sim'-i-lar-ly

sim'-i-le (*n.*, figure of
  speech)
si'-mi-le (*adj.*, like)†
si-mil'-i-tude
sim'-mer
Sim'-mons
si-mo'-le:on
Si'-mon
si-mo'-ni-ac
sim'o-ni'-a-cal
si'-mo-nize
si'-mon=pure'
si'mo-ny†
si-moom'
sim-pat'i-co*
sim'-per
sim'-pered
sim'-per-er
sim'-per-ing
sim'-ple
sim'-ple-heart-ed
sim'-pler
sim'-plest
sim'-ple-ton
sim'-plex
sim-plic'-i-ty
sim-pli-fi-ca'-tion
sim'-pli-fied
sim'-pli-fy
sim'-pli-fy-ing
Sim-plon'
sim'-ply
sim-u-la'-crum
sim'-u-lant
sim'-u-late
sim'-u-lat-ing
sim-u-la'-tion
sim'-u-la-tive
sim'-u-la-tor
si'-mul-cast
si'mul-ta'-ne:ous
si'mul-ta'-ne:ous-ly
Si'-nai
Si'-na-it'-ic
si-nap'-ic†
si'-na-pine
sin'-ar-quism
Sin'-bad
sin-cere'
sin-cere'-ly
sin-cer'-est
sin-cer'-i-ty
sin'-ci-put
sine
sin'e-cure*†
sin'e-cur-ist*†
si'-ne di'e
sin'-ew

sin'-ew:y
sin'-ful
Sing'a-pore†
singe
singed
singe'-ing
sing'-er
sing'-ing
sin'-gle
sin'-gle=hand'-ed
sin'-gle=mind'-ed
sin'-gle-ness
sin'-gle-stick
sin'-glet
sin'-gle-ton
sin'-gle-tree
sin'-gling
sin'-gly
sing'-song
sin'-gu-lar
sin-gu-lar'-i-ty
sin'-gu-lar-ly
Sin'-ha-lese'
sin'-is-ter
sin'is-tral
sin'is-trorse'
Si-nit'-ic
sink'-age
sink'-er
sink'-hole
sink'-ing
sink'-ing fund
sin'-less
sinned
sin'-ner
sin'-ning
Si-nol'-o-gy
si-nom'-e-nine
sin'-ter
sin-u-os'-i-ty
sin'-u-ous
si'-nus
si-nus-i'-tis†
si'-nus-oi'-dal
Siou'-an
Sioux
Sioux Cit'y
si'-phon
si'-phon-age
si-pid'-i-ty
sipped
sip'-ping
sir'-dar
sired
si'-ren
si-re'-ni-an
si-ri'-a-sis
sir'-ing

Sir'-i-us
sir'-loin
si-roc'-co
si-roc'-cos
sir'-up
sir-vente'
si'-sal†
sis'-sy
sis'-ter
sis'-ter-hood
sis'-ter=in=law
sis'-ter-ly
Sis'-tine
Sis'-y-phe'-an
Sis'-y-phus
site
Sit'-ka
si-tol'-o-gy
si'-to-ster'ol*†
sit'-ter
sit'-ting
sit'-ting room
sit-u-ate
sit-u-at-ed
sit-u-a'-tion
si'-tus
Si'-va
six'-fold
six=foot'
six'-pence
six=shoot-er
six'-teen'
six'-teenth'
sixth
six'-ti-eth
six'-ty
siz'-a:ble
siz'-a:ble-ness
siz'-ar
sized
siz'-ing
siz'-zle
siz'-zled
siz'-zling
siz'-zling-ly
skald
skat'-ed
skat'-er
skat'-ing
skat'-ole
skeet'-er
skein
skel'-e-tal
skel'-e-ton
skel'-e-ton-ize
skep'-tic
skep'-ti-cal
skep'-ti-cism

sketch
sketch'-book
sketched
sketch'-i-est
sketch'-i-ly
sketch'y
skew'-er
ski
ski-am'-e-try
ski-as'-co-py
skid'-ded
skid'-ding
skied
skies
ski'-ing
skilled
skil'-let
skill'-ful
skill'-ful-ly
skill'-ful-ness
skimmed
skim'-mer
skim'-ming
skimp'-i-est
skimp'-i-ly
skimp'-ing
skimp'y
skin=deep'
skin'-flint
skinned
skin'-ner
skin'-ni-est
skin'-ni-ness
skin'-ning
skin'-ny
skin-tight'
skip'-per
skip'-ping
skir'-mish
skir'-mish-er
skirt'-er
skirt'-ing
skit'-ter
skit'-tish
skit'-tles
skiv'-er
skul-dug'-ger:y
skulk'-er
skulk'-ing
skull
skull'-cap
skunk
sky'=blue'
sky'-ey
sky'-lark
sky'-light
sky'-line

sky'-rock-et
sky'-scrap-er
sky'-ward
sky'-writ-ing
slack'-en
slack'-ened
slack'-er
slack'-ness
slag'-gy
slain
slake
slaked
slak'-er
slak'-ing
slam'=bang'
slammed
slam'-ming
slan'-der
slan'-der-er
slan'-der-ous
slang'-i-ly
slang'y
slant'-ing
slant'-wise
slapped
slap'-ping
slap'-stick
slash'-ing
slate
slat'-ed
slath'-er
slat'-ing
slat'-ted
slat'-tern
slat'-ting
slat'y
slaugh'-ter
slaugh'-ter-house
slave'-hold-er
slav'-er (n., v.)
slav'-er-y
Slav'-ic
Slav'-i-cist
slav'-ish
Slav'-ism
slav-oc'-ra-cy
Sla-vo'-ni:an
Sla-von'-ic
Slav'-o-phile†
slay'-er
slay'-ing
slea-zi-er
slea'-zy
sled'-ding
sledge
sledge'-ham-mer
sleek'-ly
sleep'-er

sleep'-i-ly
sleep'-i-ness
sleep'-ing
sleep'-ing car
sleep'-less
sleep'-walk-er
sleep'-walk-ing
sleep'y
sleet'-i-ness
sleet'y
sleeve'-less
sleigh
sleigh'-ing
sleight
slen'-der
slen'-der-ize
slen'-der-ness
slept
sleuth
slew
sliced
slic'-er
slic'-ing
slick'-en-side
slick'-er
slick'-ness
slid'-a:ble
slide
slide rule
slid'-ing
slid-om'-e-ter†
sli'-er
slight
slight'-ing
slight'-ly
slime
slim'-i-er
slim'-i-ness
slim'-ness
slim'y
sling'-er
sling'-shot
slink'-ing
slipped
slip'-per
slip'-pered
slip'-per-i-ness
slip'-per-y
slip'-ping
slip'-shod
slith'-er
slith'-er-y
slit'-ting
sliv'-er (splinter)
sli'-ver*† (textile fiber)
slob'-ber
slob'-ber-ing
sloe

sloe'-ber-ry
sloe gin
slo'-gan
slog'-ging
sloop
slope
sloped
slop'-ing
slopped
slop'-pi-ly
slop'-ping
slop'-py
slosh'y
sloth'-ful
slot'-ted
slouch
slouch'-i-ly
slouch'-ing
slouch'y
slough
Slo'-vak
Slo-vak'-i:a
Slo-vak'-i:an
slov'-en
Slo'-vene
Slo-ve'-ni:an
slov'-en-li-ness
slov'-en-ly
slow'-ly
slow'-ness
slow'-worm
sludge
sludg'-er
sludg'y
slug'-gard
slug'-gish
sluice
sluice'-way
sluic'-ing
slum'-ber
slum'-ber-ous
slum'-ming
slurred
slur'-ring
slush
slush'-i-ness
slush'y
slut'-tish
sly'-ly
sly'-ness
smack'-ing
small'-ish
small'-ness
small'-pox
small'=time' (adj.)
sma-rag'-dine
smart'-en
smart'-ly

smart'-ness
smart'-weed
smashed
smash'-up (n.)
smat'-ter
smat'-ter-ing
smeared
smell'-er
smell'-ing
smell'y
smelt
smelt'-er
smi'-la-ca'-ceous
smi-la-gen'-in
smi'-lax
smiled
smil'-ing
smil'-ing-ly
smirch
smirk'-ing
smite
smith-er-eens'
Smith-so'-ni-an
smith'y
smit'-ten
smock'-ing
smok'-a:ble
smoke'-house
smoke'-jack
smoke'-less
smok'-er
smoke'-stack
smok'-i-er
smok'-ing
smok'y
smol'-der
smol'-dered
smol'-der-ing
smooth
smooth'-bore
smooth'-en
smooth'-ly
smooth'-ness
smor'-gas-bord
smoth'-er
smoth'-ered
smudge
smudg'-er
smudg'-i-ly
smudg'-ing
smudg'y
smug'-gle
smug'-gler
smug'-ly
smut'-ti-ness
smut'-ty
Smyr'-na
snaf'-fle

sna'-fu'
snagged
snag'-ging
snake'-root
snak'-i-ly
snak'y
snap'-drag-on
snap'-per
snap'-pi-ly
snap'-pish
snap'-py
snap'-shot
snared
snare drum
snar'-ing
snarled
snarl'-ing
snarl'-ing-ly
snarl'-ish
snatch'-er
snatch'y
sneaked
sneak'-er
sneak'-i-ly
sneak'-i-ness
sneak'-ing
sneak'y
sneer'-ing
sneeze
sneezed
sneez'-er
sneez'-ing
snick'-er
snick'-er-ing
sniff'-er
sniff'-ing
snif'-fle
snif'-ter (drink)
snift'-er valve†
snig'-ger
snip'-er
snip'-ing
snipped
snip'-pet
snip'-pi-er
snip'-ping
snip'-py
sniv'-el
sniv'-el-er
sniv'-el-ing
snob'-ber:y
snob'-bish
Sno-ho'-mish
snook'-er
snoop'-er
snoop'-er:y
snored
snor'-er

snor'-ing
snor'-kel
snort'-er
snort'-ing
snout
snow'-ball
snow'-bank
snow'-bird
snow=blind
snow'-bound
snow'-drift
snow'-drop
snow'-fall
snow'-flake
snow'-i-er
snow line
snow'-plow
snow'-shed
snow'-shoe
snow'-storm
snow=white
snow'y
snubbed
snub'-ber
snub'-bing
snub'-by
snub=nosed
snuff'-box
snuff'-er
snuf'-fle
snuf'-fled
snug'-gle
snug'-gled
snug'-gling
snug'-gly (adj.)
snug'-ly (adv.)
snug'-ness
soak'-age
soak'-ing
soap'-box
soap'-er
soap'-i-er
soap'-i-ness
soap op'-er:a
soap'-stone
soap'-suds
soap'y
soar
soar'-ing
sob'-bing
so'-ber
so'-ber-ly
so'-ber=mind-ed
so-bri'-e-ty
so'-bri-quet
soc'-age
so=called
soc'-cer

so-cia-bil'-i-ty
so'-cia-ble
so'-cial
so'-cial-ism
so'-cial-ist
so-cial-is'-tic
so'-cial-ite
so-ci-al'-i-ty
so-cial-i:za'-tion
so'-cial-ize
so'-cial-ly
so-ci'-a-try
so-ci'-e-tal
so-ci'-e-ty
so-ci-oc'-ra-cy
so'-ci-o-log'-ic
so'-ci-o-log'-i-cal
so'-ci-o-log'-i-cal-ly
so-ci-ol'-o-gist
so-ci-ol'-o-gy
so-ci-om'-e-try
so-ci-op'-a-thy
sock-dol'-a-ger
sock'-et
soc'-le*†
Soc'-ra-tes
So-crat'-ic
so'-da
so'-da-lite
so-dal'-i-ty
so'-da-mide*†
so'-dar
so'-da wa'-ter
sod'-den
sod'-ding
so'-di-um
Sod'-om
sod'-om-ite
sod'-om:y
so'-fa
so'-far
sof'-fit
So-fi'a
soft=boiled
soft'-en*†
soft'-en-er*†
soft'-en-ing*†
soft'-heart-ed
soft'-ly
soft'-ness
soft'=shell
soft'=soap (v.)
soft'y
sog'-gi-ly
sog'-gi-ness
sog'-gy
soi'=di-sant'
soi-gné'

soil'-age
soiled
soi-rée'
Sois-sons'
so'-journ
so'-journ-er
So'-kol
sol'-ace
sol'-aced
sol'-ac-er
sol'-ac-ing
so'-la-na'-ceous†
so-lan'-der
so-lan'-i-dine
so'-la-nine*†
so-la'-no
so'-lar
so'-lar-ism
so-lar'-i-um†
so-lar-i:za'-tion
so-las'-o-nine
so-la'-ti-um
sol'-der
sol'-dered
sol'-dier
sol'-dier-ly
sol'-dier:y
sol'e-cism
sol'e-cist
sol'e-cis'-tic
sole'-ly
sol'-emn
so-lem'-ni-ty
sol-em-ni-za'-tion
sol'-em-nize
sol'-emn-ly
so'-le-noid
so-le-noi'-dal†
sol-feg'-gio
sol-fe-ri'-no
so-lic'-it
so-lic-i-ta'-tion
so-lic'-i-tor
so-lic'-i-tous*
so-lic'-i-tude
so-lic-i-tu'-di-nous
sol'-id
sol'-i-dar'-ic
sol'-i-da-ris'-tic
sol-i-dar'-i-ty
so-lid-i-fi-ca'-tion
so-lid'-i-fied
so-lid'-i-fy
so-lid'-i-ty
sol'-id-ly
sol'-id-ness
sol'-i-dus
so-lig'-e-nous

365

so-lil'-o-quist
so-lil'-o-quize
so-lil'-o-quy
so'-li-lu'-nar
sol'-ing
sol'-ip-sism
sol'-i-taire
sol'-i-tar-i-ly†
sol'-i-tar:y†
sol'-i-tude
sol'-lar
sol-mi-za'-tion
so'-lo
so'-lod-ize†
so'-lo-ist
Sol'-o-mon
So'-lon
sol'-o-netz'
so-lo'-ni-an
so'-los
sol'-stice
sol-sti'-tial
sol-u-bil'-i-ty
sol'-u-bi-liz-er*
sol'-u-ble
so'-lum
sol'-ute†
so-lu'-tion
sol'-u-tizer
solv-a:bil'-i-ty
solv'-a:ble
solved
sol'-ven-cy
sol'-vent
solv'-ing
sol-vol'-y-sis
Sol'-way
so'-ma
So-ma'-li
So-ma'-li-land
so-mat'-ic
so-mat'-i-cal-ly
so-ma-ti-za'-tion
so'-ma-to-gen'-ic
so-ma-tol'-o-gy
som'-ber
som'-ber-ly
som'-ber-ness
som-bre'-ro
som-bre'-ros
som'-brous
some'-bod:y
some'-day
some'-how
some'-one
som'-er-sault
Som'-er-set
Som'-er-ville

some'-thing
some'-time
some'-times
some'-what
some'-where
som-nam'-bu-late
som-nam'-bu-la-tor
som-nam'-bu-lism
som-nam'-bu-list
som-nam'-bu-lis'-tic
som-nif'-er-ous
som-nif'-ic
som-nil'-o-quist
som-nil'-o-quy
som-niv'-o-len-cy
som'-no-lence
som'-no-lent
som'-no-lent-ly
so'-na-ble
so'-nance
so'-nant
so-nan'-tal
so'-nar
so-na'-ta
son-a-ti'-na*†
song'-bird
song'-ster
song'-stress
son'-ic
so-nif'-er-ous
son=in=law
son'-net
son'-ne-teer'*†
son'-ny
son'-o-buoy
so-nom'-e-ter
So-no'-ra
so-no'-rant
son-o-res'-cent†
son'-o-rif'-er-ous
so-nor'-i-ty
so:no'-rous
so:no'-rous-ly
soon'-er
soon'-est
sooth
soothe
soothed
sooth'-er
sooth'-ing
sooth'-ing-ly
sooth'-say-er
soot'-i-ness
soot'y
So-phi'a
soph'-ism
soph'-ist
soph'-is-ter*†

so-phis'-tic
so-phis'-ti-cate
so-phis'-ti-cat-ed
so-phis-ti-ca'-tion
soph'-is-try*
Soph'-o-cles
soph'-o-more
soph'-o-mor'-ic
so'-por
sop'o-rif'-er-ous*
sop'o-rif'-ic*†
sop'-ping
sop'-py
so-pra'no†
sor'-be-fa'-cient
sor'-bent
sor'-bi-tan
sor'-bite
sor'-bi-tol
Sor-bon'-ist
Sor-bonne'
sor'-bose*
sor'-bo-side*
sor'-cer-er
sor'-cer-ess
sor'-cer:y
sor'-did
sor'-did-ly
sore'-ly
sore'-ness
sor'-ghum
so-ri'-tes
so-rit'-i-cal
So-rop'-ti-mist
so-ror'-i-cide
so-ror'-i-ty
so-ro'-sis
sor'-rel
sor'-ri-ness
sor'-row
sor'-row-ful
sor'-row-ful-ly
sor'-ry
sort'-a:ble
sort'-er
sor'-tie
sor'-ti-lege
so'-rus
so-ste-nu'-to*†
so-te-ri-ol'-o-gy
So'-thic
sot'-tish
sot'-to vo'-ce
sou-brette'
sou-chong'
souf-flé'
sough'-ing

sought
soul'-ful
soul'-ful-ly
soul'-less
soun'-der (swine)
sound'-er
sound'-ing
sound'-less
sound'-ly
sound'-ness
sound'-proof
soup-çon'
soup'-i-er
soup'y
source
sour'-ly
sour'-ness
Sou'-sa
sou-tache'
South-amp'-ton
South Car-o-li'-na
South Car-o-lin'-i-an
South Da-ko'-ta
South Da-ko'-tan
south-east'
south-east'-er-ly
south-east'-ern
south'-er-ly
south'-ern
south'-ern-er
south'-ern-most
south'-land
south'-ward
South'-wark
south-west'
south-west'-er-ly
south-west'-ern
sou-ve-nir'
sov'-er-eign
sov'-er-eign-ty
so'-vi-et†
so'-vi-et-ism†
sov-khoz'
Soxh'-let
soy
soy'a*†
soy'-bean
so-zol'-ic
spaced
spac'-ing
spa'-cious
spa'-cis-tor
spad'-ed
spad'-er
spa-di'-ceous
spad'-ing
spa-ghet'-ti
spa:gyr'ic

spall'-er
spal-peen'
span'-drel
spa-ne'-mi:a
span'-gle
span'-gled
span'-gly
Span'-iard
span'-iel
Span'-ish
spank'-er
spank'-ing
spanned
span'-ner
span'-ning
spared
spare'-ness
spare'-rib
sparg'-er
spar'-ing
spar'-ing-ly
spar'-kle
spar'-kler
spark'-let
spar'-kling
spar'-kling-ly
sparred
spar'-ring
spar'-row
spar'-row hawk
sparse'-ly
spar'-si-ty
Spar'-ta
Spar'-tan
Spar'-tan-burg
spar'-te-ine
spasm
spas-mod'-ic
spas-mod'-i-cal-ly
spas-mol'-y-sis
spas-mo-lyt'-ic
spas'-tic
spas'-ti-cal-ly
spas-tic'-i-ty
spate
spa-tha'-ceous
spath'-ic
spa'-tial
spa-ti-al'-i-ty
spa'-tial-ly
spa-ti-og'-ra-phy
spat'-ter
spat'-ting
spat'-u-la
spav'-in
spav'-ined
spawned
spawn'-er

speak'-a:ble
speak'-eas:y
speak'-er
speak'-ing
spear'-fish
spear'-head
spear'-man
spear'-mint
spe'-cial
spe'-cial-ism
spe'-cial-ist
spe-ci-al'-i-ty
spe-cial-i:za'-tion
spe'-cial-ize
spe'-cial-ly
spe'-cial-ty
spe'-cie (coin)
spe'-cies (category)
spec'-i-fi-a:ble
spe-cif'-ic
spe-cif'-i-cal-ly
spec-i-fi-ca'-tion
spec-i-fic'-i-ty
spec'-i-fied
spec'-i-fi-er
spec'-i-fy
spec'-i-fy-ing
spec'-i-men
spe-ci-os'-i-ty
spe'-cious
speck'-le
speck'-led
speck'-ling
spec'-ta-cle
spec'-ta-cled
spec-tac'-u-lar
spec-tac-u-lar'-i-ty
spec-tac'-u-lar-ly
spec'-ta-tor
spec'-ta-to'-ri-al
spec'-ter
spec'-tral
spec-trog'-ra-phy
spec-tro-he'-li:o-gram
spec-trom'-e-ter
spec-trom'-e-try
spec'-tro-scope
spec'-tro-scop'-ic
spec'-tro-scop'-i-cal
spec-tros'-co-pist
spec-tros'-co-py
spec'-trum
spec'-u-lar
spec'-u-late
spec'-u-lat-ing
spec-u-la'-tion
spec-u-la'-tive

spec'-u-la-tor
spec'-u-lum
sped
speech
speech'-i-fy
speech'-less
speed'-boat
speed'-er
speed'-i-ly
speed'-ing
speed lim'-it
speed-om'-e-ter
speed'-ster
speed'-way
speed'-well
speed'y
spe-lae'-an
spe'-le-ol'-o-gist
spe'-le-ol'-o-gy
spell'-bind-er
spell'-bound
spell'-er
spell'-ing
spelt
spel'-ter
spe-lunk'-er†
Spen'-cer
Spen-ce'-ri-an
spend'-er
spend'-ing
spend'-thrift
Spen-gle'-ri-an
Spen'-ser
Spen-se'-ri-an
spent
sper-ma-ce'ti
sper-mat'-ic
sper-ma-tif'-er-ous
sper'-ma-tin
sper-ma-ti-za'-tion
sper-mat'o-cele*†
sper-mat'o-ci'-dal†
sper-mat'o-cyte*†
sper'-ma-to-gen'-e-sis
sper-mat'o-phyte*†
sper-mat'o-phyt'-ic*†
sper-ma-tor-rhe'a
sper'-ma-to-zo'-ic
sper'-ma-to-zo'-id
sper-ma-to-zo'-on
sperm'-ine†
sperm'-ism
sphac'-e-late
sphal'-er-ite
sphe-nog'-ra-phy
sphe'-noid
sphe-noi'-dal

spher'-al
sphere
spher'i-cal
spher:i-cal'-i-ty
sphe-ric'-i-ty
sphe'roid
sphe-roi'-dal
sphe-roi'-dal-ly
sphe:roid-ic'-i-ty*†
sphe-rom'-e-ter
spher'ule
spher'u-lite
sphinc'-ter
sphinc-ter-ot'-o-my
sphin-gom'-e-ter
sphin'-go-sine
sphinx
sphra-gis'-tic
sphyg'-mic
sphyg'-mo-graph
sphyg'-mo-ma-nom'-e-ter
sphyg-mom'-e-ter
spice'-bush
spiced
spic'-i-ly
spic'-i-ness
spic'-ing
spic'-u-la
spic'-u-lar
spic'-ule
spic'y
spi'-der
spi'-der web
spi'-der:y
spie'-gel-ei-sen
spiel'-er
spig'-ot
spiked
spike'-let
spike'-nard
spik'-i-ness
spik'-ing
spik'y
spi'-lite
spill'-age
spilled
spill'-er (one who spills)
spil'-ler (type of fish)
spill'-ing
spill'-way
spi-lo'-ma
spi'-lo-site†
spi-na'-ceous
spi'-nach
spi'-nal
spi'-na-ster'ol
spi'-nate
spin'-dle

369

spin'-dler
spin'-dling
spin'-dly
spin'-drift
spi-nel'†
spine'-less
spi-nes'-cence
spin'-et
spi-nif'-er-ous
spin'-na-ker
spin'-ner
spin-ner-et'
spin'-ning
spin'-ning wheel
spin'-or
spi'-nose
spi-nos'-i-ty
spi'-nous
Spi-no'-za
Spi-no'-zism
spin'-ster
spin'-ster-hood
spin-thar'-i-scope
spi'-nule†
spi'-nu-les'-cent*†
spi'-nu-lose*†
spin'y
spir'a-cle
spi-rac'-u-lar
spi-rae'a
spi'-ral
spi-ral'e*
spi'-raled
spi'-ral-ing
spi'-ral-ly
spi'-rant
spi-re'a
spi'-reme
spi-rif'-er-ous
spi-ril'-lum
spir'-it
spir'-it-ed
spir'-it-ism
spir'-it-is'-tic
spir'-it-less
spir'-i-tu-al*
spir'-i-tu-al-ism*
spir'-i-tu-al-ist*
spir'-i-tu-al-is'-tic*
spir-i-tu-al'-i-ty*
spir'-i-tu-al-ize*
spir'-i-tu-al-ly*
spir'-i-tu-el'*
spir-i-tu-os'-i-ty*
spir'-i-tu-ous*
spi'-ro-chete
spi-ro-chet-o'-sis*†

spi'-ro-graph
spi'-roid
spi-rom'-e-ter
spi'-ro-met'-ric
spi'-ro-pen'-tane
spir'y
spite
spit'-ed
spite'-ful
spit'-fire
spit'-ing
Spits'-ber-gen
spit'-ting
spit'-tle
spit-toon'
splanch'-nic
splanch-ni-cec'-to-my
splash'-ing
splash'y
splat'-ter
spleen'-ish
splen'-dent
splen'-did
splen'-did-ly
splen-dif'-er-ous
splen'-dor
splen'-dor-ous
sple-net'-ic
sple'nic*†
sple-ni'-tis
sple'-ni-um
sple-not'-o-my
spliced
splic'-er
splic'-ing
splin'-ter
splin'-tered
split=lev'-el
split'-ting
splotch'y
splurge
splurged
splut'-ter
spo'-di-um
spod'-u-mene
spoil'-age
spoiled
spoil'-er
spoil'-ing
spoils'-man
Spo-kane'
spo'-ken
spoke'-shave
spokes'-man
spo-li-a'-tion
spo'-li-a-tive
spon-da'-ic
spon'-dee

spon-dy-li′-tis
sponge
sponged
spong′-er
spong′-i-ness*
spong′-ing
spon-gi-ol′-o-gy
spong′y*
spon′-si-ble
spon′-son
spon′-sor
spon-so′-ri-al
spon′-sor-ship
spon-ta-ne′-i-ty
spon-ta′-ne-ous
spook′-ish
spook′y
spoon′-er-ism
spoon′-ful
spoor
spo-rad′-ic
spo-rad′-i-cal-ly
spo-ran′-gi:a
spo-ran′-gi-um
spore
spo′-ri-ci′-dal
spo-rif′-er-ous
spo′-ro-cyst
spo′-ro-gen′-e-sis
spo-ro-gen′-ic
spo-ro-go′-ni-um
spo′-ro-phyll
spo′-ro-phyte
spo-ro-zo′-an
spo-ro-zo′-ite
spor′-ran
sport′-ing
spor′-tive
sports′-cast-er
sports′-man
sports′-man-ship
sport′y
spor-u-la′-tion
spor′-ule
spot′-less
spot′-less-ness
spot′-light
spot′-ted
spot′-ter
spot′-ti-er
spot′-ting
spot′-ty
spous′-al†
spouse
spout′-er
sprained
sprawl′-er
sprawl′-ing

sprayed
spray′-er
spread′-er
spread′-ing
sprig′-gy
spright′-li-ness
spright′-ly
spring′-board
spring′-bok
spring′-er
Spring′-field
spring′-i-ness
spring′-ing
spring′-time
spring′y
sprin′-kle
sprin′-kler
sprin′-kling
sprint′-er
sprite
sprit′-sail
sprock′-et
sprout
spruce
spruce′-ly
spruc′-ing
spry′-ly
spume
spu-mes′-cent
spu-mo′-ni
spu′-mous
spum′y
spunk′-i-ness
spunk′y
spurge
spu′-ri-ous
spu′-ri-ous-ly
spurn′-ing
spurred
spur′-ring
spurt′-ed
spur′-tive
sput′-nik
sput′-ter
sput′-ter-ing
spu′-tum
spy′-glass
spy′-ing
squab′-ble
squab′-bled
squab′-bling
squad
squad′-ron
squa′-lene*
squal′-id
squa-lid′-i-ty
squall

371

squall'-er
squall'y
squal'-or
squa-mo'-sal
squa'-mous
squam'u-lose
squan'-der
squan'-dered
squan'-der-ing
square
squared
square dance
square knot
square'-ly
squar'-er
square root
squar'-ing
squash
squash'-i-ness
squash'-ing
squash'y
squat'-ted
squat'-ter
squat'-ting
squat'-ty
squaw
squawk
squawked
squawk'-er
squeak
squeak'-i-ly
squeak'-ing
squeak'y
squeal'-er
squeal'-ing
squea'-mish*†
squee'-gee
squeezed
squeez'-er
squeez'-ing
squelched
squid
squil'-la
squint'-ed
squint'-er
squint'-ing
squire
squir'-ing
squirm'y
squir'-rel
squirt
squirt'-ed
squirt'-ing
stabbed
stab'-bing
sta'-bile
stab-i-lim'-e-ter
sta-bil'-i-ty

Sta'-lin
Sta'-lin-grad
sta-bi-li-za'-tion†
sta'-bil-i-za'-tor*†
sta'-bi-lize†
sta'-bi-liz-er†
sta'-ble
sta'-bled
sta'-ble-mate
sta'-bling
stac-ca'-to
stach'-y-drine
stacked
stack'-er
stac'-te
stac-tom'-e-ter
sta-dim'-e-ter
sta'-di-um
stadt'-hold-er
staffed
staff'-er
Staf'-ford
stage'-coach
stage'-craft
staged
stage'-hand
stag'-er
stag'-ger
stag'-ger-ing
stag'-hound
stag'-ing
stag-mom'-e-ter
stag'-nan-cy
stag'-nant
stag'-nate
stag'-nat-ing
stag-na'-tion
stag'y
staid
stain'-er
stain'-ing
stain'-less
stair'-case
stair'-way
staked
Sta-kha'nov-ite*†
stak'-ing
sta:lac'-tite
stal'-ac-tit'-ic
stal'-ac-tit'-i-cal-ly
sta'-lag
sta:lag'-mite
stal'-ag-mit'-ic
stal'-ag-mit'-i-cal-ly
stal-ag-mom'-e-ter
stale'-mate
stale'-ness
stal'-er

372

stalk'-er
stalk'-ing
stal'-lion
stal'-wart
sta'-men
Stam'-ford
stam'-i-na
stam'-i-nal
stam'-i-nate
sta-min'-e-al†
stam'-i-no-dy
stam'-mer
stam'-mer-er
stam'-mer-ing
stamped
stam-pede'
stamp'-er
stance
stanch
stan'-chion
stan'-dard*†
stan'-dard=bear-er*†
stan'-dard-i:za'-tion*†
stan'-dard-ize*†
stand'-by (n., adj.)
stand'-ee'
stand'-ing
Stan'-dish*
stand'-ish
stand'-off (n.)
stand'-pipe
stand'-point
stand'-still
Stan'-ford
Stan'-hope
sta'-nine
Stan-i-slav'-ski
Stan'-ley
stan'-na-ries
stan'-nic
stan'-nite
stan'-nous
stan'-num
Stan'-ton
stan'-za
sta'-pes
staph-y-lo-coc'-cus
staph-y-lot'-o-my
sta'-ple
sta'-pled
sta'-pler
sta'-pling
star'-board
star-cham'-ber (adj.)
starch'-er
starch'-i-ness
starch'y
stared

sta'-re de-ci'-sis
star'-er
sta'-rets
star'-fish
star-gaz-er
star'-ing
stark'-ly
star'-less
star'-let
star'-light
star'-like
star'-ling
star'-lit
star'-lite
starred
star'-ring
star'-ry
star'-ry=eyed
star=shaped
star shell
star=span'-gled
start'-er
star'-tle
star'-tling
star-va'-tion
starve
starved
starve'-ling
starv'-er
starv'-ing
sta'sis
state'-craft
stat'-ed
state'-hood
state'-house
state'-li-ness
state'-ly
state'-ment
Stat'-en Is'-land
stat'-er (one who states)
sta'-ter (coin)
state'-room
states'-man
states'-man-ship
state'-wide
stat'-ic
stat'-i-cal-ly
stat'-i-ce
sta'-tion
sta-tion-ar:y†
sta'-tio-ner*†
sta'-tio-ner:y*†
sta'-tion-mas-ter
stat'-ism
stat'-ist
sta-tis'-tic
sta-tis'-ti-cal
sta-tis'-ti-cal-ly

373

stat-is-ti′-cian
sta-tis′-tics
stat′-i-tron
sta-tom′-e-ter
sta′tor†
stat′o-scope
stat′-u-ar:y†
stat′-ue
stat′-u-esque′
stat′-u-ette′
stat′-ure
sta′tus
stat′-ut-a:ble*
stat′-ute
stat′-u-to-ry
staunch
staunch′-ly
stau′-ro-lite
stau′-ro-scop′-ic
stay′-ing
stay′-sail
stead′-fast
stead′-i-ly
stead′-i-ness
stead′y
steal
steal′-age
stealth
stealth′-i-ly
stealth′-i-ness
stealth′y
steam′-boat
steam boil′-er
steam en′-gine
steam′-er
steam′-fit-ter
steam′-roll-er
steam′-ship
steam shov′-el
steam ta′-ble
steam′-tight
steam′y
ste-ap′-sin
ste′a-rate
ste-ar′-ic
ste′a:rin
ste′a-rone
ste:ar′-o-yl
ste′a-ryl
ste′-a-tite
ste′-a-tit′-ic
ste-a-tol′-y-sis
ste′-a-to-py′-gous†
ste-a-to′-sis
steel
steel′-works
steel′y
steel′-yard

steen′-bok
steep′-en
steep′-er
stee′-ple
stee′-ple-chase
stee′-ple-jack
steep′-ly
steep′-ness
steer′-age
steer′-age-way
steers′-man
Ste′-fan
Ste′-fans-son
steg:o-my′-ia
steg′o-saur
steg:o-sau′-rus
Stein′-metz
stele*†
stel′-lar
stel′-late
stel-lif′-er-ous
Stel′-lite
stel′-lu-lar
stem′-less
stemmed
stem′-ming
sten′-cil
sten′-ciled
sten′-cil-ing
Sten′-dhal
ste-nog′-ra-pher
sten′o-graph′-ic
sten′o-graph′-i-cal-ly
ste-nog′-ra-phy
sten′o-ha′-line*
ste-nom′-e-ter
sten′o-sis
sten′o-type
sten′o-typ-ist
sten′o-typ:y
sten-to′-ri-an
step′-child
step′-daugh-ter
step′-fa-ther
Steph′-a-nie
Ste′-phen
Ste′-phens
step=in (n.)
step′-lad-der
step′-moth-er
steppe
step′-per
step′-ping
step′-ping=stone
step′-son
ste-ra′-di-an
ster-co-bi-lin′-o-gen
ster′-co-ra′-ceous

374

ster'-co-ric'-o-lous
ster'-co-rite
ster-cu'-li-a'-ceous
ster-cu'-lic
ste:re-og-no'-sis*†
ste're:o-graph*†
ste:re-og'-ra-pher*†
ste're:o-graph'-ic*†
ste-re-om'-e-ter*†
ste're:o-met'-ric*†
ste're:o-phon'-ic*†
ste're:o-phon'-ic*†
ste:re-oph'-o-ny*†
ste:re-op'-sis*
ste're-op'-ti-con*†
ste're-op'-tics
ste're:o-scope*†
ste're:o-scop'-ic*†
ste:re-os'-co-pist*†
ste:re-os'-co-py*†
ste:re-ot'-o-my*†
ste're-ot'-ro-pism*†
ste're:o-type*†
ste're:o-typ-er*†
ste're:o-typ-ing*†
ste're:o-typ:y*†
ster'ic
ster'i-cal-ly
ster'-ile
ste-ril'-i-ty
ster-i-li:za'-tion†
ster'-i-lize†
ster'-i-liz-er†
ster'-let
ster'-ling
stern'-ly
stern'-ness
ster'-num
ster-nu-ta'-tion
ster-nu'-ta-to-ry
ster'oid
ste-roi'-dal
ster'ol
ster'-to-rous†
ste-thom'-e-ter†
steth'o-scope
steth'o-scop'-ic
ste-thos'-co-py†
Stet'-son
stet'-ted
Stet-tin'
Steu'-ben
Steu'-ben-ville
ste've-dore
Ste'-vens
Ste'-ven-son
ste'-vi-o-side
stew'-ard

ster'-co-ric'-o-lous
ster'-co-rite
ster-cu'-li-a'-ceous
ster-cu'-lic
stew'-ard-ess
stew'-ard-ship
Stew'-art
stew'-pan
sthene
sthe'-ni:a
sthen'-ic
stib'-a:mine
stib'-ine
sti-bin'-ic
stib'-i-o-pal'-la-di-nite
stib'-i-um
sti-bon'-ic
sti-bo'-ni-um
stib'-o-phen
sti-chom'-e-try
stick'-er
stick'-ful
stick'-i-er
stick'-i-ness
stick'-ing
stick'-le
stick'-le-back
stick'y
stiff'-en
stiff'-en-er
stiff'-en-ing
stiff'-ly
stiff=necked
stiff'-ness
sti'-fle
sti'-fling
stig'-ma
stig-mas'-ter-ol
stig-mat'-ic
stig-mat'-i-cal
stig'-ma-tism
stig'-ma-tist
stig-ma-ti-za'-tion
stig'-ma-tize
stil'-bene
stil-bes'-trol
sti-let'-to
still'-born
still'=hunt (v.)
still'-ness
stil'-ly (adv.)†
still'y (adj.)
stilp-no-mel'-ane*†
stilt'-ed
stim'-u-lant
stim'-u-late
stim-u-la'-tion
stim'-u-la-tive
stim'-u-la-tor
stim'-u-li
stim'-u-lus
sting'-er

stin'-gi-er
stin'-gi-ness
sting'-ing
sting'y (stinging)
stin'-gy (mean)
stink'-er
stink'-ing
stink'-weed
stint'-ing
sti'-pend
sti-pen'-di-ar:y†
sti'-pes
sti'-pi-form
stip'-i-tat'-ic
stip'-ple
stip'-pled
stip'-pling
stip'-u-late
stip'-u-lat-ing
stip-u-la'-tion
stip'-u-la-tor
stip'-u-la-to-ry
stip'-ule
stir
Stir'-ling
stirred
stir'-ring
stir'-rup
stitch'-er
stitch'-ing
sti'-ver
sto'a
stoc-ca'-do
sto-chas'-tic
sto-chas'-ti-cal-ly
stock-ade'
stock'-bro-ker
stock dove
stock'-hold-er
Stock'-holm
stock'-i-nette'
stock'-ing
stock'-job-ber
stock'-man
stock mar'-ket
stock'-pile
stock'=still'
Stock'-ton
stock'y
stock'-yard
stodg'-i-ness
stodg'y
sto'-gie
sto'-ic
sto'-i-cal
stoi-chi-ol'-o-gy
stoi'-chi-o-met'-ric
stoi-chi-om'-e-try

sto'-i-cism
stoked
stoke'-hold
stok'-er
stok'-ing
sto'-len
stol'-id
sto-lid'-i-ty
stol'-id-ly
sto'-lon
sto'-ma
stom'-ach
stom'-ach-ache
stom'-ach-er
sto-mach'-ic
stom'a-ta*†
stom'a-tal†
stom:a-ti'-tis*†
sto-ma-tol'-o-gy
sto-mat'-o-my
stone'-bass
stone'-boat
stone crush'-er
stone'-cut-ter
stoned
Stone'-henge
stone'-ma-son
stone proof
stone'-wall (v.)
stone'-ware
stone'-work
ston'-i-ly
ston'-i-ness
ston'-ing
ston'y
stop'-cock
stop'-gap
stop'-page
stopped
stop'-per
stop'-ping
stop'-pled
stop'-watch
stor'-age
sto'-rax
stored
store'-house
store'-keep-er
store'-room
sto'-ried
sto'-ri-ette'
stor'-ing
stork
storm'-i-ly
storm'-i-ness
storm'-proof
storm'y
sto'-ry

sto'-ry-tell-er
stout'-ness
sto'-ver (cattle feed)
stov'-er (stove worker)
stow'-age
stow'-a:way (n.)
stra-bis'-mal
stra-bis-mom'-e-ter
stra-bis'-mus
Stra'-bo
stra-bot'-o-my
Stra'-chey
strad'-dle
strad'-dler
strad'-dling
Strad:i-var'i-us†
strafed
straf'-ing
strag'-gle
strag'-gler
strag'-gling
strag'-gly
straight
straight'-a:way
straight'-edge
straight'-en
straight'-en-er
straight'-for'-ward
strained
strain'-er
strait
strait'-en
strait'-ened
strait'-jack-et
strait'-laced
stra-min'-e:ous
stra-mo'-ni-um
strand'-er
strange'-ly
strange'-ness
stran'-ger (n.)
strang'-er (adj.)
stran'-gle
stran'-gler
stran'-gling
stran-gu-late
stran-gu-la'-tion
strapped
strap'-ping
stra'ta
strat'-a-gem
stra-te'-gic†
stra-te'-gi-cal†
strat'-e-gist
strat'-e-gy
Strat'-ford
stra-tic'-u-late

strat-i-fi-ca'-tion
strat'-i-fied
strat'-i-fy
strat'-i-fy-ing
strat-i-graph'-ic
stra-tig'-ra-phy
strat'o-cu'-mu-lus*†
strat'o-sphere†
strat'o-spher'-ic
stra'tum
stra'tus
straw'-ber-ry
straw'-board
stray'-er
stray'-ing
streak'-i-ness
streak'y
stream
stream'-er
stream'-let
stream'-line
stream'-lined
street
street'-car
strength
strength'-en
strength'-en-ing
strength'-less
stren'-u-ous
strep'-i-tous
strep:o-gen'-in
strep'-ta-mine
strep-to-coc'-cic
strep-to-coc-co'-sis
strep-to-coc'-cus
strep-to-my'-cin
strep-to-thri'-cin
stressed
stretch'-er
strewed
strewn
stri'-at-ed
stri-a'-tion
strick'-en
strick'-le
strict'-ly
strict'-ness
stric'-ture
stri'-den-cy
stri'-dent
strid'-er
strid'-ing
stri'-dor
strid'-u-late
strid-u-la'-tion
strid'-u-la-to-ry
strid'-u-lous
strife

strig'-il
strig'-i-late
stri'-gose
strik'-er
strik'-ing
stringed
strin'-gen-cy
strin'-gent
string'-er
string'-i-ness
string'-ing
string'-piece
string'y
striped
strip'-er
strip'-ing
strip'-ling
stripped
strip'-ping
strive
striv'-en
striv'-ing
strob'-ic
strob'-i-la'-ceous
strob'-ile
stro'-bo-scop'-ic*†
stro'-bo-tron*†
stro'-ga-noff
stroked
strok'-er
strok'-ing
stroll'-er
stro'-ma
stro-mat'-ic
stro'-ma-tin
strong'=arm (*adj., v.*)
strong'-box
strong'-hold
strong'-ly
strong'-point
strong room
stron'-gyle
stron-gy-lo'-sis
stron'-tia†
stron'-ti-an-if'-er-ous
stron'-ti-an-ite
stron'-ti-um
stro-phan'-thi-din
stro'-phe
stroph'-ic
stroph'-u-lus
strop'-ping
struc'-tur-al
struc'-tur-al-ly
struc'-ture
stru'-del
strug'-gle
strug'-gled

strug'-gling
strum'-ming
stru'-mose
stru'-mous
strum'-pet
strut'-ted
strut'-ting
strych'-nine
strych'-nin-ism
Stu'-art
stubbed
stub'-ber
stub'-bi-ness
stub'-bing
stub'-ble
stub'-bly
stub'-born
stub'-born-ness
stub'-by
stuc'-co
stuc'-co-er
stuc'-co-work
stuck'=up
stud'-book
stud'-ded
stud'-ding
Stu'-de-bak-er
stu'-dent
stud'-ied
stud'-ied-ly
stu'-di:o
stu'-di:ous
stud'y
stud'y-ing
stuff
stuffed
stuff'-i-ly
stuff'-i-ness
stuff'-ing
stuff'y
stul-ti-fi-ca'-tion
stul'-ti-fied
stul'-ti-fy
stul'-ti-fy-ing†
stum'-ble
stum'-bling
stum'-bling block
stump'-age
stump'y
stunned
stun'-ning
stunt'-ed
stu'-pe-fa'-cient
stu-pe-fac'-tion
stu'-pe-fied
stu'-pe-fi-er
stu'-pe-fy
stu'-pe-fy-ing

stu-pen'-dous	sub'-di-vide
stu'-pid	sub'-di-vid-ing
stu-pid'-i-ty	sub'-di-vi-sion
stu'-pid-ly	sub-due'
stu'-por	sub-du'-ing
stu'-por-ous	sub-ed'-i-tor
stur'-died	su'-ber-ate
stur'-di-ly	su-be're-re-ous
stur'-di-ness	su-ber'-ic
stur'-dy	su'-ber-in
stur'-geon	su'-ber-ize
stut'-ter	su'-ber-ose
stut'-tered	su'-ber-yl-ar'-gi-nine
stut'-ter-ing	sub'-head'
Stutt'-gart	sub-ja'-cen-cy
Stuy'-ve-sant	sub-ja'-cent
Styg'-ian*†	sub'-ject (n., adj.)
styled	sub-ject' (v.)
sty'-let	sub-jec'-tion
styl'-ing	sub-jec'-tive
styl'-ish	sub-jec'-tiv-ism
styl'-ist	sub-jec-tiv'-i-ty
sty-lis'-tic	sub'-join'
sty'-lite	sub'-ju-gate
styl-i-za'-tion	sub'-ju-gat-ing
sty'-lize	sub-ju-ga'-tion
sty'-lo-graph'-ic	sub'-ju-ga-tor
sty-lom'-e-try	sub-junc'-tive
sty'-lus	sub-lease'
sty'-mie	sub'-les'-see'
sty'-mied	sub'-les'-sor
sty'-mie-ing	sub'-let'
styp'-sis	sub-let'-ting
styp'-tic	sub-lim'-a:ble†
sty'ra-ca'-ceous	sub'-li-mate
sty-rac'-i-tol	sub'-li-mat-ing
sty're-nate	sub-li-ma'-tion
sty're-nate	sub-lime'
sty'rene	sub-lime'-ly
Styr'-i-an	sub-lim'-in-al*†
sty'ryl	sub-lim'-i-ty
Styx	sub'-li-mize
Sua'-kin	sub-lu'-nar
sua'-si-ble	sub'-lu-nar:y†
sua'-sion	sub-ma-rine
sua'-sive-ness	sub-max'-il-lar:y†
suave	sub-me'-di-al
suave'-ly	sub-merge'
suav'-i-ty	sub-merged'
sub-al'-tern	sub-mer'-gence
sub-a:tom'-ic	sub-mer'-gi:ble†
sub-ce-les'-tial	sub-mer'-sal
sub'-cel-lar	sub-merse'
sub'-cla'-vi-an	sub-mersed'
sub'-com-mit-tee	sub-mers'-i:ble
sub-con'-scious	sub-mers'-ing
sub'-con-trac-tor	sub-mer'-sion
sub'-cu-ta'-ne-ous	sub-mis'-sion
sub-dea'-con	

sub-mis'-sive
sub-mit'
sub-mit'-ted
sub-mit'-ting
sub-nor'-mal
sub-nor-mal'-i-ty
sub-or'-di-nate
sub-or'-di-nate-ly
sub-or-di-na'-tion
sub-or'-di-na-tive
sub-orn'
sub-or-na'-tion
sub-pe'-naed
sub-poe'-na
sub-poe'-naed
sub-poe'-na-ing
sub'-ro-gate
sub-ro-ga'-tion
sub ro'-sa
sub-scribe'
sub-scrib'-er
sub-scrib'-ing
sub-scrip'-tion
sub-scrip'-tive
sub'-sec'-tion
sub'-se-quence
sub'-se-quent
sub'-se-quen'-tial
sub-serve'
sub-ser'-vi-ence
sub-ser'-vi-ent
sub-serv'-ing
sub-side'
sub-sid'-ence†
sub-sid'-i-ar:y†
sub-sid'-ing
sub-si-di-za'-tion
sub'-si-dize
sub'-si-dy
sub-sist'
sub-sist'-ence†
sub-sist'-ent†
sub'-soil
sub-son'-ic
sub'-stance
sub-stan'-tial
sub-stan-ti-al'-i-ty
sub-stan'-tial-ly
sub-stan'-ti-ate
sub-stan-ti-a'-tion
sub'-stan-tive
sub-sta'-tion
sub-stit'-u-ent
sub'-sti-tute-a:ble
sub'-sti-tute
sub'-sti-tut-ed
sub'-sti-tut-ing
sub-sti-tu'-tion

sub'-sti-tu-tive
sub'-stra:tum
sub'-struc'-ture
sub-sump'-tive
sub-tend'
sub'-ter-fuge
sub-ter-ra'-ne:an
sub-ter-ra'-ne-ous
sub'-tile
sub'-ti-lin
sub-til'-i-ty
sub'-ti-tle
sub'-tle
sub'-tle-ty
sub'-tly
sub-tract'
sub-tract'-er
sub-trac'-tion
sub-trac'-tive
sub-tra-hend
sub'-trea'-sur:y*
sub-trop'-i-cal
sub'u-late
sub'-urb
sub-ur'-ban
sub-ur'-ban-ite
sub-ven'-tion
sub-ver'-sion
sub-ver'-sion-ar:y†
sub-ver'-sive
sub-vert'
sub-vert'-er
sub-vert'-i:ble
sub'-way
suc'-ce-da'-ne-ous
suc-ce-da'-ne-um
suc-ce'-dent
suc-ceed'
suc-cen'-tor
suc-cess'
suc-cess'-ful
suc-cess'-ful-ly
suc-ces'-sion
suc-ces'-sive
suc-ces'-sor
suc-cin'-a-mate*†
suc'-ci-nam'-ic*†
suc'-ci-na-mide*†
suc'-ci-nate
suc-cinct'
suc-cinct'-ly
suc-cin'-ic
suc'-ci-nyl*†
suc'-cor
suc'-co-ry
suc'-co-tash
suc-cu-bus
suc'-cu-lence

suc'-cu-lent
suc-cumb'
suck'-er
suck'-le
suck'-ler
suck'-ling
Su'-cre
su'-crose
suc'-tion
suc-to'-ri-al
su-da'-men
Su-dan'
Su'-da-nese'
su-da-ry
su-da-to'-ri-um
su'-da-to-ry
sud'-den
sud'-den-ly
Su'-der-mann
su'-do-rif'-er-ous*†
su-do-rif'-ic*†
suds'y
sue
sued
suede
su'-et
Sue-to'-ni-us
su'-et:y
Su'-ez'
suf'-fer
suf'-fer-a:ble
suf'-fer-ance
suf'-fer-er
suf'-fer-ing
suf-fice'
suf-ficed'
suf-fic'-er
suf-fi'-cien-cy
suf-fi'-cient
suf-fic'-ing
suf'-fix
suf'-fo-cate
suf'-fo-cat-ing
suf-fo-ca'-tion
suf'-fo-ca-tive
Suf'-folk
suf'-fra-gan
suf'-frage
suf-fra-gette'*†
suf-frag-ett'-ism*†
suf'-frag-ist*†
suf-fus'-a:ble
suf-fuse'
suf-fus'-ing
suf-fu'-sion
suf-fu'-sive
Su'-fism
sug'-ar

sug'-ar beet
sug'-ar-boat
sug'-ar bush
sug'-ar cane
sug'-ared
sug'-ar-i-ness
sug'-ar-loaf (n.)
sug'-ar=loaf (adj.)
sug'-ar ma'-ple
sug'-ar-plum
sug'-ar:y
sug-gest'
sug-gest-i:bil'-i-ty
sug-gest'-i:ble
sug-ges'-tion
sug-ges'-tive
su'-i-ci'-dal*†
su'-i-ci'-dal-ly*†
su'-i-cide
su'i ge'-ner-is†
su'-ing
suit-a:bil'-i-ty
suit'-a:ble
suit'-a:bly
suit'-case
suite
suit'-ing
suit'-or
su-ki-ya'-ki
sul'-fa
sul-fa-cet'-a-mide
sul-fa-di'-a-zine†
sul-fa-gua'-ni-dine*†
sul-fa-mer'-a-zine
sul'-fa-meth'-yl-thi'-a-
  zole
sul'-fam'-ic*†
sulf-am'-ide
sul-fam'-o-yl
sul-fa-nil'-a-mide†
sul'-fa-nil'-ic*†
sul-fan'-i-lyl
sul'-fa-pyr'-i-dine†
sulf-ar'-se-nide
sulf-ars-phen'-a-mine
sul'-fat-ase
sul'-fate
sul-fa-thi'-a-zole†
sul'-fa-tize*
sul-fen'-ic
sulf'-hy'-dryl
sul'-fide
sul-fin'-ic
sul-fi-nyl
sul'-fite
Sul'-fo-nal
sul-fon'-a-mide*†
sul-fo-nat-ed

381

sul'-fo-na-tor	sun'-bon-net
sul'-fon-eth'-yl-meth'-ane	sun'-burn
sul-fon'-ic	sun'-burned
sul-fo'-ni-um	sun'-burst
sulf-ox'-ide	sun'-dae
sul'-fur	Sun'-day
sul'-fu-rate	Sun'-day school
sul-fu'-re-ous	sun'-der
sul'-fu-ret-ed	sun'-der-ance
sul-fu'-ric	sun'-dew
sul'-fu-rize†	sun'-di-al
sul-fu'-rous†	sun'-down
sul'-fur-yl	sun'-down-er
sulk'-i-ly	sun'-dries
sulk'-i-ness	sun'-dry
sulk'y	sun'-fast
sul'-len	sun'-fish
Sul'-la	sun'-flow-er
sul'-len-ly	sun'-glass-es
sul'-len-ness	sunk'-en
sul'-lied	sun'-lamp
Sul'-li-van	sun'-less
sul'-ly	sun'-light
sulph- (*see* sulf-)	sun'-lit
sul'-tan	sun'-ni-er
sul-tan'a†	sun'-ning
sul'-tan-ate	sun'-ny
sul-tan'-ic	sun'-rise
sul'-tri-er	sun'=room
sul'-tri-ness	sun'-set
sul'-try	sun'-shade
su'-mac	sun'-shine
Su-ma'-tra	sun'-shin:y
Su-ma'-tran	sun'-spot
Su-mer'i-an*†	sun'-stroke
sum'-ma cum lau'-de	sun'-struck
sum-mar'-i-ly*†	sun'-up
sum-ma-ri-za'-tion	su'-per
sum'-ma-rize	su-per-a-bil'-i-ty
sum'-ma-ry	su'-per-a-ble
sum-ma'-tion	su-per-a:bun'-dance
sum'-mer	su-per-a:bun'-dant
sum'-mer-house	su-per-an'-nu-ate
sum'-mer-time	su-per-an'-nu-at-ed
sum'-mer:y	su-per-an-nu-a'-tion
sum'-ming	su-perb'
sum'-mit	su-perb'-ly
sum'-mit-ry	su'-per-car-go
sum'-mon	su-per-cil'-i-ar:y†
sum'-moned	su-per-cil'-i-ous
sum'-mon-er	su-per-co-lum'-nar
sum'-mon-ing	su-per-er'-o-gate
sum'-monsed	su-per-er-o-ga'-tion
sump'-ter	su'-per-e:rog'-a-to-ry
sump'-tu-ar:y†	su'-per-fe-ta'-tion
sump-tu-os'-i-ty	su-per-fi'-cial
sump'-tu-ous	su-per-fi-ci-al'-i-ty
sun'-beam	su-per-fi'-cial-ly

su-per-fi'-cies*†
su'-per-fine
su-per-flu'-i-ty
su-per'-flu-ous
su'-per-heat'-ed
su-per-het'-er:o-dyne
su'-per-hu'-man
su-per-im-pose'
su'-per-im-po-si'-tion
su-per-in-duce'
su'-per-in-tend'
su'-per-in-tend'-en-cy†
su-per-in-tend'-ent†
su-pe'-ri-or
su-pe-ri-or'-i-ty
su'-per-la-tive
su'-per-man
su-per'-nal
su'-per-na'-tant
su-per-nat'-u-ral
su'-per-nat'-u-ral-is'-tic
su'-per-nu'-mer-ar:y†
su'-per-pose
su-per-po-si'-tion
su'-per-pow-er
su-per-scrip'-tion
su-per-sede'
su-per-se'-de-as
su-per-sed'-ence†
su'-per-sed'-ing
su-per-se'-dure
su-per-sen'-si-ble
su-per-sen'-si-tive
su-per-sen'-so-ry
su-per-son'-ic
su-per-sti'-tion
su-per-sti'-tious
su'-per-struc'-ture
su'-per-vene'
su-per-ve'-nience*
su'-per-ven'-ing
su-per-ven'-tion
su'-per-vise
su-per-vis-ee'
su'-per-vis-ing
su'-per-vi'-sion
su'-per-vi-sor
su'-per-vi'-so-ry
su'-pi-nate
su'-pi-na-tor
su-pine' (face up)
su'-pine (grammar)
su-pine'-ly
sup'-per
sup'-per-time
sup-plant'
sup-plan-ta'-tion
sup-plant'-er

sup'-ple
sup'-ple-ment
sup'-ple-men'-tal
sup'-ple-men-tar'-i-ly*†
sup'-ple-men-tar:y*†
sup-ple-men-ta'-tion
sup-ple-ness
sup-ple'-tive
sup'-pli-ance
sup'-pli-ant
sup'-pli-cant
sup'-pli-cate
sup'-pli-cat-ing
sup-pli-ca'-tion
sup'-pli-ca-to-ry
sup-plied'
sup-pli'-er
sup-ply'
sup-ply'-ing
sup-port'
sup-port-a:bil'-i-ty
sup-port'-a:ble
sup-port'-er
sup-port'-ing
sup-port'-ive*†
sup-pos'-a:ble
sup-pos'-al
sup-pose'
sup-posed'
sup-pos'-ing
sup-po-si'-tion
sup'-po-si'-tion-al-ly
sup-pos'-i-ti'-tious
sup-pos'-i-to-ry
sup-press'
sup-press'-i:ble
sup-pres'-sion
sup-pres'-sive
sup-pres'-sor
sup'-pu-rate
sup'-pu-rat-ing
sup-pu-ra'-tion
sup'-pu-ra-tive
sup-pu-ta'-tion
su'-pra
su'-pra-re'-nal
su-prem'a-cy
su-preme'
su-preme'-ly
su'-ra
su'-rah
su'-ral
sur'-a-min
sur'-base
sur-cease'
sur'-charge
sur'-cin-gle
sur'-coat

sure'-fire'	sur'-tax
sure'-foot-ed	sur'-tout
sure'-ly	sur-veil'-lance
sure'-ness	sur-veil'-lant
sur'-er	sur-vey' (v.)
sur'-est	sur'-vey (n.)
sure'-ty	sur-vey'-ing
sur'-face	sur-vey'-or
sur'-faced	sur-viv'-al
sur'-fac-er	sur-vive'
sur'-fac-ing	sur-vi'-vor
sur-fac'-tant	sur-vi'-vor-ship
sur'-feit	Su'-san
surf'y	sus-cep-ti-bil'-i-ty
surge	sus-cep'-ti-ble
sur'-geon	sus'-pect (n.)
sur'-ger:y	sus-pect' (v.)
sur'-gi-cal	sus-pend'
surg'-ing	sus-pend'-ed
su'-ri-cate	sus-pend'-er
Su'-ri-nam	sus-pend'-i:ble
Su'-ri-nam-ese'	sus-pense'
sur'-li-ly	sus-pen'-si-ble
sur'-li-ness	sus-pen'-sion
sur'-ly	sus-pen'-so-ry
sur-mis'-a:ble	sus-pi'-cion
sur-mise'	sus-pi'-cious
sur-mis'-ing	sus-pi-ra'-tion
sur-mount'	Sus'-que-han'-na
sur-mount'-a:ble	Sus'-sex
sur-mount'-ed	sus-tain'
sur'-name	sus-tained'
sur-pass'	sus-tain'-ing
sur-pass'-ing	sus-tain'-ment
sur'-plice	sus'-te-nance
sur'-plus	sus-ten-tac'-u-lar
sur'-plus-age	sus'-ten-ta'-tion
sur-pris'-a:ble	sus'-ten-ta-tive
sur-pris'-al	su-sur-ra'-tion
sur-prise'	su-sur'-rus
sur-prised'	sut'-ler
sur-pris'-ed-ly	su'-tra
sur-pris'-ing	sut-tee'
sur-re'-al-ism	su'-tur-al
sur-re'-al-ist	su'-ture
sur-re'-al-is'-tic†	su'-tur-ing
sur-re-but'-ter	su'-ze-rain
sur'-re-join'-der	su'-ze-rain-ty
sur-ren'-der	svelte
sur-rep-ti'-tious	swabbed
sur'-rey	swab'-bing
sur'-ro-gate	swab'-ble
sur'-ro-gat-ed	Swa'-bi:a
sur'-ro-gat-ing	Swa'-bi-an
sur-round'	swad'-dle
sur-round'-ed	swad'-dled
sur-round'-ing	swad'-dling

swag'-ger
swal'-low
swal'-low-tail
swal'-low=tailed
swal'-low-wort
swa'-mi
swamp
swamp'-er
swamp'-land
swamp'y
swank'-i-ness
swank'y
swan'-like
swan'-ner:y
swans'-down
swarmed
swarm'-er
swarm'-ing
swarth'-i-ly
swarth'-i-ness
swarth'y
swash'-buck-ler
swas'-ti-ka
swatch
swath
swathe
sway'-backed
sway'-ing
swear'-ing
sweat'-er
sweat'-i-ly
sweat'-i-ness
sweat'-shop
sweat'y
Swe'-den
Swe'-den-borg'
Swe'-den-bor'-gi:an
Swed'-ish
swee'-ny
sweep'-er
sweep'-ing
sweep'-stakes
sweet'-bread
sweet'-bri-er
sweet corn
sweet'-en
sweet'-ened
sweet'-en-ing
sweet fern
sweet flag
sweet'-heart
sweet'-ish
sweet'-ly
sweet'-meats
sweet'-ness
sweet pea
sweet'-shop

sweet Wil'-liam
swelled
swell'-ing
swel'-ter
swel'-ter-ing
swerve
swerved
swerv'-ing
swift'-er
swift'-ly
swift'-ness
swim'-mer
swim'-mer-et'
swim'-ming
swim'-ming-ly
Swin'-burne
swin'-dle
swin'-dler
swin'-dling
swine'-herd
swing'-ing
swin'-ish
Swin'-ner-ton
swiped
swip'-ing
swirl'-ing
switch
switch'-back
switch'-board
switch'-er
switch'-man
Switz'-er-land†
swiv'-el
swiv'-eled
swiv'-el-ing
swol'-len
swoon
swoon'-ing
swoop
sword
sword'-fish
sword grass
sword knot
sword'-play
swords'-man
swords'-man-ship
sworn
syb'-a-rite
syb'-a-rit'-ic
syc'-a-more
sych'-no-car'-pous
sy-co'-ni-um
syc'o-phan-cy
syc'o-phant
sy-co'-sis
Syd'-en-ham
Syd'-ney

385

sy'-e-nite
syl'-la-bar:y†
syl-lab'-ic
syl-lab'-i-cate
syl-lab'-i-cat-ing
syl-lab-i-ca'-tion
syl-lab-i-fi-ca'-tion
syl-lab'-i-fied
syl-lab'-i-fy
syl-lab'-i-fy-ing
syl'-la-bize
syl'-la-ble
syl'-la-bus
syl-lep'-sis
syl'-lo-gism
syl-lo-gis'-ti-cal
sylph
sylph'-id
sylph'-like
Syl'-phon
syl'-van
syl'-van-ite
Syl'-ves-ter
syl-ves'-trene
Syl'-vi:a
syl'-vite
sym-bi'-o-sis
sym'-bi-ot'-ic
sym'-bol
sym-bol'-ic
sym-bol'-i-cal
sym'-bol-ism
sym'-bol-is'-tic
sym-bol-i:za'-tion
sym'-bol-ize
sym-bol'-o-gy
sym-met'-ri-cal
sym'-me-trize
sym'-me-try
Sym'-onds
sym-pa-thec'-to-my
sym-pa-thet'-ic
sym-path'-i-co-trop'-ic
sym'-pa-thin
sym'-pa-thize
sym'-pa-thiz-er
sym'-pa-thiz-ing
sym-pa-tho-lyt'-ic
sym'-pa-thy
sym-phon'-ic
sym-pho'-ni-ous
sym'-pho-nize
sym'-pho-ny
sym'-phy-sis
sym-phyt'-ic
sym-po'-di-um
sym-po'-si-ac

sym-po'-si-um
symp'-tom
symp-to-mat'-ic†
symp-to-mat'-i-cal-ly†
symp'-tom-a-tize
symp-tom-a-tol'-o-gy
syn'-a-gogue
syn'-apse
syn-ap'-sis
syn-ar-thro'-sis
syn-chon-drot'-o-my
syn'-chro-nism
syn'-chro-nis'-tic
syn-chro-ni-za'-tion
syn'-chro-nize
syn'-chro-niz-er
syn'-chro-niz-ing
syn-chron'-o-graph
syn'-chro-nous
syn'-chro-ny
syn'-chro-scope
syn'-chro-tron
syn-clas'-tic
syn-cli'-nal
syn'-cline
syn'-co-pate
syn'-co-pat-ed
syn'-co-pat-ing
syn-co-pa'-tion
syn'-co-pa-tor
syn'-co-pe
syn-cop'-ic
syn-cret'-ic
syn'-cre-tism
syn'-cre-tize
syn-cri'-sis
syn-des-mo'-sis
syn-det'-ic
syn'-dic
syn-di-cal-ism
syn'-di-cate
syn'-di-cat-ing
syn-di-ca'-tion
syn'-di-ca-tor
syn'-drome*†
syn-ec'-do-che†
syn'-ec-doch'-i-cal
syn-ec'-do-chism
syn-e:col'-o-gy
syn-er'-e-sis
syn-er'-gic
syn'-er-gism
syn-er-gis'-ti-cal
syn-e:sis
syn-es-the'-sia*†
syn'-ga-my
syn-ge-nite

386

syn-i-ze′-sis
syn′-od
syn-od-al
syn-od′-i-cal†
syn-od′-i-cal-ly†
syn-oe′-cious†
syn′-o-nym
syn′-o-nym′-ic
syn-o-nym′-i-ty
syn-on′-y-mous†
syn-on′-y-my†
syn-op′-sis†
syn-op′-tic†
syn-o′vi:a†
syn-o:vi′-is
syn-tac′-ti-cal
syn′-tax
syn-tec′-tic
syn′-the-sis
syn′-the-sist
syn′-the-size
syn′-the-siz-er
syn′-the-siz-ing
syn′-the-tase
syn-thet′-ic
syn-thet′-i-cal
syn-thet′-i-cal-ly
syn′-the-tize
syn′-thol
syn-to-ni-za′-tion
syph′-i-lis
syph′-i-lit′-ic
syph-i-lol′-o-gy
sy′-phon
Syr′-a-cuse
Syr′-i:a
Syr′-i-ac
Syr′-i-an
sy-rin′-ga
sy-ringe′
sy-rin′-ge-al
sy-rin′-gic
sy-rin′-gin
syr-in-gi′-tis
sy-rin-go-my-e′-lia*†
syr-in-got′-o-my
syr′-inx
syr′-up
sys-tal′-tic
sys′-tem
sys′-tem-at′-ic
sys′-tem-at′-i-cal-ly
sys′-tem-a-ti-za′-tion
sys′-tem-a-tize
sys-tem′-ic
sys-tem-i:za′-tion
sys′-tem-ize

sys′-to-le
sys-stol′-ic
sy-zyg′-i-al
syz′-y-gy

T

tab′-ard
Ta-bas′-co
tabbed
tab′-bing
tab′-by
tab′-er-na-cle*
tab′-er-nac′-u-lar
tab-er-nan′-thine
ta′-bes
ta-bes′-cent
ta′-bes dor-sa′-lis
ta-bet′-ic
tab′-id
tab′-i-net
Tab′-i-tha
tab′-la-ture
ta′-ble
tab′-leau
tab′-leaux
ta′-ble-cloth
ta′-ble d'hôte′
ta′-ble-land
ta′-ble-spoon
ta′-ble-spoon-ful
tab′-let
ta′-ble-ware
ta′-bling
tab′-loid
ta-boo′
ta′-bor
tab′-o-ret′
tab′-u-lar
tab′-u-late
tab′-u-lat-ing
tab-u-la′-tion
tab′-u-la-tor
tach′-i-na†
ta-chis′-to-scope
tach′-o-graph
ta-chom′-e-ter
tach′-o-met′-ric
ta-chom′-e-try
tach′y-car′-di:a
tach′y-gen′-ic
ta-chyg′-ra-pher
tach′y-graph′-ic
tach:y-graph-om′-e-ter
ta-chyg′-ra-phy
tach′y-lyte
tach′y-lyt′-ic

387

ta-chym'-e-ter
tach'y-met'-ric
ta-chys'-ter-ol
tac'-it
tac'-it-ly
tac'-it-turn
tac-i-tur'-ni-ty
Tac'-i-tus
tack'-le
tack'-ler
tack'-ling
tack'y
Ta-co'-ma
tac'-o-nite
tact'-ful
tact'-ful-ly
tac'-ti-cal
tac'-ti-cal-ly
tac-ti'-cian
tac-tic'-i-ty
tac'-tics
tac'-tile
tac-til'-i-ty
tact'-less
tac-tom'-e-ter
tac'-to-sol
tac'-tu-al
tad'-pole
tae-ni'a
tae-ni'a-cide
tae-ni'-a-sis
taf'-fe-ta
taff'-rail
taf'-fy
Ta-ga'-log
tag'-a-tose
tag'-e-tone
tagged
tag'-ging
Ta-gore'
Ta'-gus
Ta-hi'-ti
Ta-hi'-tian*†
Ta'-hoe
tail'-board
tail'-er
tail'-less
tail'-light
tai'-lor
tai'-lored
tai'-lor-ing
tai'-lor=made'
tail'-piece
tail'-race
tail'-spin
tail'-stock
tail wind
taint

Tai-wan'-ese'
take'-down (n., adj.)
tak'-en
take'-off (n.)
tak'-er
tak'-ing
ta-lar'-i:a*†
Tal'-bot
talc
talc'-ose
tal'-cum
tale'-bear-er
tal'-ent
tal'-ent-ed
ta'-les (law)
tales'-man
tal'-i-on
tal'-is-man
tal'-ites
tal'-i-tol
talk'-a-thon
talk'-a-tive
talk'-er
tal'-lage
Tal'-la-has'-see
tall'-ate
Tal'-ley-rand
tal'-lied
tal'-lith
tal'-low
tal'-ly
Tal'-mud
Tal-mud'-ic
Tal'-mud-ist
tal'-on
ta-lon'-ic
Ta'-los
tal'-ose
tal-pa-ta'-te
ta'-lus
tam'-a:ble
ta-ma'-le
tam'-a-rack
tam'-a-rind
tam'-a-risk
ta-ma-sha'
tam'-bour
tam'-bou-rine'
tame'-a:ble
tamed
tame'-ness
tam'-er
tam'-ing
Tam'-ma-ny
tam'=o'=shan-ter
Tam'-pa
tamp'-er (n.)
tam'-per (v.)

Tam-pi'-co
tam'-pon
tam'-pon-ade'
tan-a-ce'-tin
tan'-a-ger
Tan'-a-gra
Ta-nan'-a-rive†
tan'-bark
Tan'-cred
tan'-dem
Tan'-gan-yi'-ka†
Tan'-gan-yi'-kan†
tan-ge-lo
tan'-ge-los
tan'-gent
tan-gen'-tial
tan-gen'-tial-ly
tan-ger-e'-tin
tan'-ger-ine*
tan-gi-bil'-i-ty
tan'-gi-ble
Tan-gier'
tan'-gle
tan'-gled
tan'-gling
tan'-go
tan'-goed
tang'y
tan'-ist-ry
tank'-age
tan'-kard*†
tank'-er
tan'-nate
tanned
tan'-ner
tan'-ner:y
Tann'-hau-ser
tan'-nic
tan'-nin
tan'-ning
tan-nom'-e-ter
tan-tal'-ic
tan'-ta-lite
tan'-ta-lize
tan'-ta-liz-er
tan'-ta-lum
Tan'-ta-lus
tant'-a:mount*†
tan'-trum
Tao'-ism
taped
tape'-line
ta'-per (candle, cone; v.)
tap'-er (one who tapes)
ta'-per-ing
tap'-es-try
ta-pe'-tum

tape'-worm
tap-i-o'-ca
ta'-pir
tap-is'†
tapped
tap'-ping
tap'-room
tap'-root
tap'-ster
tar-an-tel'-la
tar'-an-tism*†
ta-ran'-tu-la
ta-rax'-e-in
tar'-di-ly
tar'-di-ness
tar'-dy
tar'-get
tar'-ge-teer*†
tar'-iff
Tar'-king-ton
tar'-la-tan
tar'-nish
tar'-nish-a:ble
ta'-ro
tar-pau'-lin
Tar-pe'-ian
tar'-pon
tar'-ra-gon
tarred
tar'-ried
tar'-ring
tar'-ry
tar'-ry-ing
tar'-sal
tar-sec'-to-my*†
tar'-si-er
tar'-so-met'a-tar-sal
tar'-so-met'a-tar-sus
tar-sor'-rha-phy
tar'-sus
tar'-tan
tar'-tar
Tar-tar'-e:an†
tar-tar'-e-ous†
Tar-tar'-i:an†
tar-tar'-ic
tar'-tar-ous
Tar'-ta-rus
Tar'-ta-ry
tar-tram'-ic
tar'-trate
tar'-trat-ed
Tash'-kent
ta-sim'-e-ter
tas-i-met'-ric
task'-mas-ter
Tas-ma'-ni:a

Tas-ma'-ni-an
tas'-ma-nite†
tas'-sel
tas'-seled
tas'-sel-ing
Tas'-so
taste'-ful
taste'-less
tast'-er
tast'-i-ness
tast'-ing
tast'y
Ta'-tar
tat'-ter
tat-ter-de-ma'-lion*
tat'-tered
tat'-tle
tat'-tler
tat'-tle-tale
tat-too'
tat-too'-er
taught
taunt
taunt'-er
taunt'-ing
taunt'-ing-ly
Taun'-ton
taupe
tau-rine
tau-ro-cho'-late
tau'-ro-cho'-lic†
tau-rom'-a-chy
Tau'-rus
tau'-ryl
tau-to-log'-i-cal
tau-tol'-o-gism
tau-tol'-o-gy
tau'-to-mer'-ic
tau-tom'-er-ism
tau'-to-met'-ric
tau-toph'-o-ny
tav'-ern
taw'-dri-ness
taw'-dry
tawn'-i-er*†
tawn'y*†
tax-a:bil'-i-ty
tax'-a:ble
tax-a'-tion
tax'=ex-empt'
tax'i-cab
tax'-i-der'-mic
tax'-i-der-mist
tax'-i-der-my
tax'-ied
tax-i-fo'-lin
tax'-i-me-ter†
tax'-ing

tax'-o-nom'-ic
tax-on'-o-my
tax'-pay-er
Tay'-lor
Tchai-kov'-sky
Tche-by-cheff'†
teach'-a:ble
teach'-er
teach'-ing
tea'-cup
tea'-house
tea'-ket-tle
teal
team'-mate
team'-ster
team'-work
tea par'-ty
tea'-pot
tear'-ful
tear gas
tear'-ing
tear'-less
tea'-room
tear sheet
teased
tea'-sel
teas'-er
teas'-ing
tea'-spoon
tea'-spoon-ful
tea'-time
tea wag'-on
Te-bet'
tech-ne'-ti-um
tech'-ni-cal
tech-ni-cal'-i-ty
tech-ni'-cian
Tech'-ni-col-or
tech'-nics
tech-nique'
tech-noc'-ra-cy
tech'-no-crat
tech-nog'-ra-phy
tech-no-log'-i-cal
tech-nol'-o-gy
tec-ton'-ics
tec'-ton-ite
Te-cum'-seh
te'-di-ous
te'-di-um
teen'=ag'-er
tee'-ter
teethed
teeth'-ing
tee'-to-tal-er
Tef'-lon
teg-men'-tal
teg'-mi-nal

390

teg'-u-men
teg'-u-ment
teg'-u-men'-tar:y
Te-he-ran'
Teh-ran'
Te-huan'-te-pec
Te-huan'-te-pec-er
Tel-Au'-to-graph
Tel' A:viv'
tel'e-cast'
tel-e-gon'-ic
te-leg'-o-ny
tel'-e-gram
tel'-e-graph
te-leg'-ra-pher
tel'-e-graph'-ic
te-leg'-ra-phy
tel:e-ki-ne'-sis
Te-lem'-a-chus
tel'e-me-ter*†
tel'e-met'-ric
te-lem'-e-try
tel'e-mo-tor
tel'-en-ceph'-a-lon
tel'-e-o-log'-i-cal
tel-e-ol'-o-gy
tel'-e-ost
tel'-e-path'-ic
te-lep'-a-thy
tel'-e-phone
tel'-e-phon'-ic
te-leph'-o-ny
tel'e-pho'-to
tel'e-pho-tog'-ra-phy
Tel'e-Promp'-Ter
tel'-e-ran
tel'-e-scope
tel'-e-scop'-ic
tel'-e-scop'-i-cal-ly
tel-les'-co-py
tel'-e-sis
tel'-es-the'-sia*
Tel'e-type
tel'-e-typ-ist
tel'-e-vise
tel'e-vi-sion
tel'-e-vi-sor
te'-li:o-spore†
te'-li:o-stage†
tell'-er
tell'-tale
tel-lu'-ri-an
tel-lu'-ric
tel-lu'-ride
tel-lu'-ri-um
tel-lu-rom'-e-ter
tel-lu-ro'-ni-um

tel'-lu-rous
te'-lome
tel-o-mer-i:za'-tion
tel'-pher
tel'-pher-age
tem'-blor
te-mer'-i-ty
tem'-per
tem'-per:a†
tem'-per-a-ment
tem'-per-a-men'-tal
tem'-per-ance
tem'-per-ate
tem'-per-a-ture
tem'-pered
tem'-per-er
tem'-pest
tem-pes'-tu-ous
tem'-plar
tem'-plate
tem'-ple
tem'-plet
tem'-po
tem'-po-ral
tem-po-ral'-i-ty
tem'-po-rar'-i-ly†
tem'-po-rar:y†
tem'-po-rize
tem'-po-riz-er
tempt
tempt'-a:ble
temp-ta'-tion
tempt'-er
tempt'-ing
tempt'-ress
tem'-pus fu'-git
ten-a-bil'-i-ty
ten'-a-ble
te-na'-cious
te-nac'-i-ty
te-nac'-u-lum
ten'-an-cy
ten'-ant
ten'-ant-a:ble
ten'-ant-ry
tend'-ance†
tend'-en-cy†
tend'-er (boat, an attendant)
ten'-der (to offer; *adj.*, soft)
ten'-der-foot
ten'-der-heart-ed
ten'-der:iz-er
ten'-der-loin
ten'-der-ness
ten-der-om'-e-ter
ten-di-ni'-tis
ten'-di-nous

ten'-don
ten'-dril
Ten'-e-brae
ten-e-bres'-cence
ten'-e-brous
ten'-e-ment
Ten'-er-iffe
ten'-et
ten'-fold
te-nien'-te
Ten'-ite
Ten-nes-se'-an
Ten'-nes-see'
ten'-nis
Ten'-ny-son
ten-o-de'-sis
ten'-on
ten-o-ni'-tis
ten'-or
te-not'-o-my
ten'-pen-ny
ten'-pins
ten'-si-ble
ten'-sile
ten-sil'-i-ty
ten-sim'-e-ter
Ten-si-om'-e-ter
ten'-sion
ten'-son
ten'-sor
ten-so'-ri-al
ten=strike
ten'-ta-cle
ten-tac'-u-lar
ten-tac'-u-lo-cyst
tent'-age
tent'-ta-tive
tent'-ed
tent'-er (one in a tent)
tent'-ter (frame)
ten'-ter-hook
ten'-u-is
te-nu'-i-ty*
ten'-u-lin
ten'-u-ous
ten'-ure
te-nu'-to
te-o-cal'-li
te-o-sin'-te
te-pa'-che
te'-pee
tep'-e-fy
teph'-rite
teph'-ro-ite
teph'-ro-sin†
tep'-id
tep-i-dar'-i-um†
te-pid'-i-ty

te-qui'-la
ter'-a-con'-ic
ter'-a-cryl'-ic
ter'-aph
ter'-a-phim
ter-a-to-log'-i-cal
ter-a-tol'-o-gy
ter-a-to'-ma
ter'-bi:a
ter'-bi-um
cer-cen-ten'-a-ry*†
ter-e-ben'-thene
te-reb'-ic
ter'-e-binth
ter-e-bin'-thi-nate
ter'e-bin'-thine
te-re'-do
Ter'-ence
ter-eph-thal'-ate*†
ter'-eph-thal'-ic
ter'-gite
ter'-gi:ver-sate
ter-gi-ver-sa'-tion
ter'-gi-ver-sa-tor
ter'-gum
term'-er
ter'-mi-na-ble
ter'-mi-nal
ter'-mi-nate
ter-mi-na'-tion
ter'-mi-na-tor
ter'-mi-ni
ter-mi-nol'-o-gy
ter'-mi-nus
ter'-mite
ter'-mit'-ic
ter'-mor*†
ter'-na-ry
ter'-ni-on
ter'-pene
ter'-pe-nyl'-ic
ter'-pi-nene*
ter-pin'-e-ol
ter-pin'-o-lene
ter'-pi-nyl
Terp-sich'-o-re
terp'-si-cho-re'-an
ter'-race
ter'-ra=cot'-ta
ter'-ra fir'-ma
ter-rain'
Ter-ra-my'-cin
ter'-ra-pin
terr-a'que-ous*†
ter-rar'-i-um†
ter-raz'-zo
Ter'-re Haute

ter-rene'
ter'-re-plein
ter-res'-tri-al
ter'-ri-ble
ter'-ri-bly
ter-ric'-o-lous
ter'-ri-er
ter-rif'-ic
ter-rif'-i-cal-ly
ter-ri-fied
ter'-ri-fy
ter-rig'-e-nous
ter-ri-to'-ri-al
ter'-ri-to-ry
ter'-ror
ter'-ror-ism
ter'-ror-ist
ter'-ror-ize
ter'-ry-cloth
terse
terse'-ly
terse'-ness
ter'-tial
ter-tian
ter'-ti:ar:y†
Ter-tul'-lian*†
ter'-va'-lent
tes'-sel-late
tes'-sel-lat-ed
tes-sel-la'-tion
tes'-ser:a
tes'-ta
test'-a:ble
tes-ta'-cean†
tes-ta'-ceous
tes'-ta-cy
tes'-ta-ment
tes'-ta-men'-ta-ry
tes'-tate
tes'-ta-tor
tes-ta'-trix
test'-er (one who tests)
tes'-ter (canopy)
tes'-ti-cle
tes-tic'-u-lar
tes-ti-fi-ca'-tion
tes'-ti-fy
tes-ti-mo'-ni-al
tes'-ti-mo-ny†
tes'-ti-ness
tes'-tis
tes-tos'-ter-one
test tube
tes-tu'-di-nal
tes-tu-di-nar'-i-ous†
tes'-ty
tet'-a-nal
te-tan'-ic

tet'-a-nize
tet'-a-no-gen'-ic
tet'-a-nus
tet'-a-ny
te-tar'-to-he'-dral
te'-tar-toi'-dal
tête=à=tête
teth'-er
teth'-ered
tet'-ra-ba'-sic*
tet'-ra-bro'-mo
tet'-ra-cene
tet'-ra-chlo'-ride
tet-ra-chlo'-ro
te-trac'-id
tet'-ra-co'-sa-no'-ic
tet-ra-cy'-cline
tet'-rad
te-trad'-ic
tet'-ra-eth'-yl
tet'-ra-gon
te-trag'-o-nal
tet'-ra-he'-dral
tet-ra-he'-drite
tet'-ra-he'-dron
tet'-ra-hy'-dro-fu'-ran
tet'-ra-kis-az'o
te-tral'-o-gy
te-tram'-er-ous
te-tram'-e-ter
tet'-ra-mine†
tet'-ra-ni'-tro-meth'-ane
tet-ra-ple'-gia*†
tet'-ra-ploi-dy
tet'-ra-pod
te-trap'-o-dy
te-trap'-ter-an
te'trarch†
te-trar'-chic†
te'trar-chy*†
tet-ra-som'-a-ty
tet'-ra-stich
te-tras'-ti-chous
tet-ra-thi'-o-nate†
tet'-ra-tom'-ic
tet-ra-va'-lent
tet'-ra-zine†
tet-ra-zo'-li-um
te-traz'-o-lyl
tet'-ra-zone
tet'-ri-tol
te-tron'-ic
tet'-rose
te-trox'-ide
tet'-ryl
Teu'-ton
Teu-ton'-ic
Tex'-an

Tex-ar-kan'a
Tex'-as
text'-book
tex'-tile
tex'-tu-al
tex'-tu-ar:y†
tex'-tur-al
tex'-ture
Thack'-er-ay
Thai'-land
Tha'-is
tha-lam'-ic
thal-a-mot'-o-my
thal'-a-mus
tha-las'-sic
thal-as-som'e-ter
Tha'-les
Tha'-li:a
tha-lid'-o-mide
thal-lif'-er-ous
thal'-line
thal'-li-um
thal'-lo-phyte
thal'-lus
Thames
than-a-top'-sis
than-a-to'-sis
thank'-ful
thank'-ful-ness
thank'-less
thanks'-giv'-ing
thatch'-er
thau-ma-site
thau-ma-tol'-o-gy
thau'-ma-tur'-gic
thau-ma-tur-gy
the-a'-ceous
the'-an-throp'-ic
the-an'-thro-pism
the'-ar-chy
the'-a-ter
the-at'-ri-cal
the'-ba-ine
The'-ban
Thebes
thegn
the'-ine
the'-ism
the'-ist
the-is'-tic
the-mat'-ic
the-mat'-i-cal-ly
The-mis'-to-cles
them-selves'
the'-nar
thence'-forth
thence'-for'-ward
then'-o-yl

the-oc'-ra-cy
the'-o-crat'-ic
The-oc'-ri-tus
the-od'-i-cy
the-od'-o-lite
the-od'-o-lit'-ic
The'-o-dore
The-od'-o-ric
The'-o-do'-sia*
the'-o-gon'-ic
the-og'-o-ny
the-o-lo'-gian*†
the'-o-log'-i-cal
the-ol'-o-gize
the-ol'-o-gy
the-om'-a-chy
the'-o-mor'-phic
the'-o-pa-thet'-ic
the'-o-path'-ic
the-op'-a-thy
the-oph'-a-ny
the-o-phyl'-line
the-or'-bo
the'-o-rem
the'-o-re-mat'-ic†
the-o-ret'-i-cal
the-o-re-ti'-cian
the'-o-rist
the-o-ri-za'-tion
the'-o-rize
the'-o-ry
the'-o-soph'-ic
the-os'-o-phist
the-os'-o-phy
ther'-a-peu'-tic
ther'-a-peu'-ti-cal-ly
ther'-a-pist
ther'-a-py
there'-a:bouts
there'-af'-ter*
there'-by'
there'-fore'
there-in'
there-of'
there-on'
The-re'-sa
there'-up:on'
there'-with'
the'-ri-ac
the'-ri-an-throp'-ic
the-ri-an'-thro-pism
the-ri-at'-rics
ther'-mal
ther'-mi-cal-ly
Ther'-mi-dor
therm'-i'on
therm'-i:on'-ic
therm'-is'-tor*

ther'-mite
ther'-mo-chro-mism
ther'-mo-cou-ple†
ther'-mo-du'-ric†
ther'-mo-dy-nam'-ic
ther'-mo-e:lec'-tric
ther-mog'-ra-pher
ther'-mo-graph'-ic
ther'-mo-lyt'-ic
ther-mom'-e-ter
ther'-mo-met'-ric
ther-mo-met'-ri-cal-ly
ther-mom'-e-try
ther'-mo-nu'-cle-ar
ther-moph'-i-ly
ther'-mo-pile
Ther-mop'-y-lae
Ther'-mos
ther'-mo-scop'-ic
ther'-mo-stat
ther'-mo-stat'-ic
ther'-mo-ther'-a-py
ther-mot'-ro-pism
Ther'-si-tes
ther-sit'-i-cal
the-sau'-rus
the'-ses
the'-sis
The'-seus
Thes'-pi-an
Thes'-pis
Thes'-sa-lo'-ni-an
Thes'-sa-ly
the'-ta
the'-tin
The'-tis
the-ur'-gic
the'-ur-gy
the-ve'-tin*
thi-am'-ide
thi-am'i-nase
thi-am'ine
thi:a-naph'-thene
thi-an'-threne
thi'-a-zole
thi-az'-o-line
thi'-a-zol-sul'-fone
thick'-en
thick'-en-ing
thick'-et
thick'-ness
thick'-set'
thick'=skinned'
thief
thiev'-er:y
thieves
thiev'-ing

thiev'-ish
thigh'-bone
thim'-ble
thim'-ble-ful
thi-mer'o-sal
think'-er
think'-ing
thin'-ner
thin'-ness
thin'=skinned'
thi'o-fla'-vine
thi:o-naph'-thene
thi-on'-ic
thi'-o-nine
thi-o'-ni-um
thi-oph'-e-nine
thi'o-u'ra-cil
thi'o-u:re'a
third
third'-ly
thirl'-age
thirst
thirst'-i-ly
thirst'-i-ness
thirst'y
thir'-teen'
thir'-ti-eth
thir'-ty
this'-tle
this'-tle-down
thith'-er
thi-u-ro'-ni-um
thix-ot'-ro-py
Thom'-as
Tho'-mism
thong
thon-zyl'-a-mine
tho-ra-cen-te'-sis
tho-rac'-ic
tho-rac'-i-co-lum'-bar
tho-ra'-co-scope
tho-ra-cos'-to-my
tho'-rax
Tho-reau'
tho'-ri:a
tho'-ri-a-nite
tho'-ri-ate
thor'-ic†
tho-rif'-er-ous
tho'-rite
tho'-ri-um
thorn'y
tho'-ron†
thor'-ough
thor'-ough-bred
thor'-ough-fare
thor'-ough-go-ing
thor'-ough-ly

thor'-ough-ness
though
thought'-ful
thought'-ful-ly
thought'-ful-ness
thought'-less
thought'-less-ness
thou'-sand
thou'-sand-fold
thou'-sandth
Thra'-cian
thrall'-dom
thrash'-er
thra-son'-i-cal
thread'-bare
thread'-er
thread'-worm
thread'y
threat'-en
threat'-en-ing
three'-fold
three'-pence
three'-score
three'-some
thre'-i-tol
threm-ma-tol'-o-gy
thre'-node†
thre-nod'-ic
thren'-o-dist
thren'-o-dy
thre'-o-nine
thresh'-er
thresh'-old
threw
thrift'-i-er
thrift'-i-ly
thrift'-i-ness
thrift'-less
thrift'y
thrill'-er
thrill'-ing
thrips
thrive
thriv'-ing
throat
throat'-i-ness
throat'y
throb'-bing
throe
throm'-bin
throm-bo-an'-gi-i'-tis
throm-bo-cy-to'-sis
throm-bo-plas'-tin
throm-bo-bo'-sis
throm-bot'-ic
throm'-bus
throng
thros'-tle

throt'-tle
throt'-tled
through
through-out'
throw
thrush
thrust'-er
thrust'-ing
Thrus'-tor
thu'-cho-lite
Thu-cyd'-i-des
thud'-ding
thu-ja-pli'-cin
thu'-jyl
thu'-le
thu'-li-um
thumb'-nail
thumb'-screw
thump'-er
thun'-der
thun'-der-bird
thun'-der-bolt
thun'-der-cloud
thun'-der-er
thun'-der-head
thun'-der-ous
thun'-der-ous-ly
thun'-der-show-er
thun'-der-storm
thun'-der-struck
thun'-der:y
thu'-ri-ble
thu'-ri-fer
thu-rif'-er-ous
Thu-rin'-gi:a
Thurs'-day
thwart
thy'-la-cine
thyme
thy'-mic*†
thy'-mi-dine
thy'-mi-dyl'-ic
thy'-mine
thy'-mol†
thy-mol-phthal'e:in
thy'-mo-nu-cle'-ic
thy'-mus
Thy'-ra-tron
Thy'-rite
thy'-roid
thy-roi'-dal
thy-roid-ec'-to-my
thy-roid-i'-tis
thy'-ro-nine
thy-rot'-ro-phin
thy-rox'-ine
thyr'-soid
thyr'-sus

thy′sa-nu′-ran
thy′sa-nu′-rous
ti-ar′a†
Ti′-ber
Ti-be′-ri-as
Ti-bet′
Ti-bet′-an
tib-i:a
tib′-i-al
tick′-er
tick′-et
tick′-et-er
tick′-i-ci′-dal
tick′-i-cide
tick′-ing
tick′-le
tick′-ler
tick′-lish
Ti-con-der-o′-ga
tid′-al†
tid′-bit
tid′-dly-winks
tide′-wa-ter
ti′-di-ly
ti′-di-ness
ti′-ding (news)
tid′-ing (tide)
ti′-dy
tie′=in (n., adj.)
tie′-mann-ite†
Tien′-tsin′†
tier (layer)
ti′-er (one who ties)
Ti:er′-ra del Fue′-go†
tie′=up (n.)
tif′-fa-ny
tif′-fin
ti′-ger
ti′-ger-ish
ti′-ger lil:y (plant)
ti′-ger-lil:y (color)
tight′-en
tight′-en-er
tight′-en-ing
tight′-rope
tight′-wad
tig-lal′-de-hyde
Tig′-lath-pi-le′-ser
tig′-lic
ti-gnon′
ti-go′-nin
ti′-gress
ti′-grine
Ti′-gris
ti-grol′-y-sis
til′-bur:y*
til′-de

Til′-den
tiled
til′-i-a′-ceous
til′-ing
till′-a:ble
till′-age
till′-er
tilt′-er
tim′-bal
tim′-bale
tim′-ber
tim′-bered
tim′-ber-man
tim′-ber wolf
tim′-ber-work
tim′-bre
tim′-brel
tim′-brelled
Tim′-buk-tu′
time′=hon′-ored
time′-keep-er
time′-li-er
time′-li-ness
time′-ly
time′-piece
tim′-er
time′-ta-ble
tim′-id
ti-mid′-i-ty
tim′-ing
ti-moc′-ra-cy
tim′-o-rous*†
tim′-o-thy
tim′-pa-ni
tim′-pa-nist
tin-cal′-co-nite
tinc-to′-ri-al
tinc′-ture
tin′-der
tin′-e:a
tin′-foil
tinge′-ing
tin′-gle
tin′-gled
tin′-gling
ti′-ni-er
tin′-ker*†
tin′-kle
tin′-kling
tin′-ner
tin′-ni-er
tin-ni′-tus
tin′-ny
tin′-sel
tin′-seled
tin′-smith
tint′-er
tin-tin-nab-u-la′-tion

tin-tin-nab'-u-lous
tint-om'-e-ter†
Tin-to-ret'-to
tin'-type
tin'-ware
ti'-ny
tip'-off (n.)
Tip-pe-ca-noe'
tip'-per
Tip-pe-rar'y†
tip'-pet
tip'-ping
tip'-ple
tip'-si-ly
tip'-staff
tip'-ster
tip'-sy
tip'-toe
tip'=top
ti-queur'
ti-rade'
ti-rail-leur'
tired'-ly
tire'-less
tire'-some
tir'-ing
Tish-chen'-ko
tis'-sue
ti'-tan
ti'-ta-nate*†
ti-ta'-ni:a
ti-tan'-ic
ti-ta-nif'-er-ous*†
ti'-ta-nite*†
ti-ta'-ni-um
ti-tan'-ous
ti'-ter
tith'-a:ble
tithe
tith'-er
tith'-ing
Ti'-tian
ti'-tian-esque'
Ti'-ti-ca'-ca†
tit'-il-late
tit'-i-vate
ti'-tle
ti'-tled
tit'-mouse
Ti'-to-ism
ti'-trat-a:ble
ti'-trate
ti-tra'-tion
Ti-trim'-e-ter
ti'-tri-met'-ri-cal-ly†
tit'-ter
tit-u-ba'-tion
tit'-u-lar

tit-u-lar'-i-ty
tit'-u-lar:y†
Ti'-tus
Tiv'-o-li†
tme'-sis
toad'-stool
toad'y
toast'-er
toast'-mas-ter
to-bac'-co
to-bac'-co-nist
to-bac'-cos
to-bog'-gan
to-bog'-gan-er
To'-by
toc-ca'-ta
to-col'-o-gy
to-coph'-er-ol
toc'-sin
to-day'
tod'-dle
tod'-dler
tod'-dy
tof'-fee
to'-ga
to'-gaed
to'-gat-ed
to-geth'-er
to-geth'-er-ness
tog'-ging
tog'-gle
tog'-gler
toil'-er
toi'-let
toi'-let-ry
toi-lette'
toil'-some
toil'-worn
To'-kay'
to'-ken
To'-ky:o
tol-bu'-ta-mide
To-le'-do
tol'-er-a-ble
tol'-er-a-bly
tol'-er-ance
tol'-er-ant
tol'-er-ate
tol-er-a'-tion
tol'-i-dine
toll'-booth
toll'-gate
Tol'-stoy
Tol'-tec
to'-lu
tol'-u-ate†
tol'-u-ene†
to:lu'-ic

to-lu'-i-dine
tol'-u-ol†
to-lu'-ric
tol'-u-yl-ene†
tol'-yl-ene†
tom'-a-hawk
to-mat'-i-dine
tom'-a-tine
to-ma'-to
to-ma'-toes
tom'-boy
tomb'-stone
tom'-cat
to-men'-tose
tom-fool'-er:y
to-mog'-ra-phy
to-mor'-row
tom'=tom
to-nal'-i-ty
tone'-less
to'-neme
ton'-er
to-net'-ics
tongue
tongue'-less
tongu'-er
tongue'=tied
tongu'-ing
ton'-ic
to-nic'-i-ty
to-night
to'-nite*†
ton-neau'
ton'-nage
ton'-o-log'-i-cal
to-nom'-e-ter
ton'-o-met'-ric
to-nom'-e-try
ton'-sil
ton-sil-lec'-to-my
ton-sil-li'-tis
ton-sil-lot'-o-my
ton-so'-ri-al
ton'-sure
ton'-tine
to'-nus
tool bit
tool'-box
tool crib
tool'-er
tool'-hold-er
tool'-ing
tool kit
tool'-room
tooth'-ache
tooth'-brush
tooth'-less

tooth'-paste
tooth'-pick
tooth pow-der
tooth'-some
to'-paz
to'-paz-ine
top'-coat
to-pec'-to-my
to-pee'
To-pe'-ka
top'-er
top'-flight'
top-gal'-lant
top hat (n.)
top'=heav:y
to'-pi-ar:y†
top'ic
top'-i-cal
top'-knot
top'-mast
top'-most
top'=notch'
top'o-deme
to-pog'-ra-pher
top:o-graph'-i-cal
top:o-graph'-i-cal-ly
to-pog'-ra-phy
top'o-log'-i-cal
to-pol'-o-gy
top'-o:nym'-ic
to-pon'-y-my
top'-per
top'-ping
top'-ple
top'-pling
top'-sail
top'-side
top'-soil
top'-sy=tur'-vy
toque
To'-rah
torch'-bear-er
torch'-light
tor'-chon
torch'-wood
to'-re-a:dor*
to-reu'-tic
to'-ric*
to-ri:i
to-rin'-gin
tor-ment' (v.)
tor'-ment (n.)
tor-men'-tor
tor-na'-do
tor-na'-does
to'-roid
to-roi'-dal
To-ron'-to

399

tor-pe'-do
tor-pe'-do boat
tor-pe'-does
tor'-pid
tor-pid'-i-ty
tor'-por
tor'-por-if'-ic†
torque
Tor-que-ma'-da
torque'-me-ter
tor'-re-fac'-tion
Tor'-rens
tor'-rent
tor-ren'-tial
tor'-rid
tor-si-bil'-i-ty
tor-si-om'-e-ter
tor'-sion
tor'-sion-al
tor'-so
tor-som'-e-ter
tort
tor'-te
tor-ti'-lla*†
tor'-tious
tor'-toise
tor'-toise-shell
tor-tu-os'-i-ty
tor'-tu-ous
tor'-tu-ous-ly
tor'-ture
tor'-tur-er
tor'-tur-ing-ly
tor'-tur-ous
to'-rus
To'-ry
To'-ry-ism
Tos-ca-ni'-ni
toss'-ing
toss'=up (n.)
tos'-yl-ate
tot'-a:ble
to'-tal
to'-taled
to'-tal-ing
to-tal'-i-tar'-i-an
to-tal-i-tar'-i-an-ism
to-tal'-i-ty
to'-tal-i-za'-tor
to'-tal-ize
to'-tal-iz-er
to'-tal-ly
to'-ta-quine
to'-tem
to'-tem-ism
tot'-ing
tot'-ter
tou'-can

touch'-down
tou-ché'
touch-i-ly
touch'-i-ness
touch'-ing
touch'-stone
touch'y
tough
tough'-en
tough'-ness
Tou-lon'
Tou-louse'
tou-pee'
tou'-ra-co'
tour'-ism
tour'-ist
tour'-ma-line
tour'-na-ment
tour'-ney
tour'-ni-quet
tou'-sle
tou'-sled
tout'-er
to-va'-rish
tow'-age
to'ward
tow'-boat
tow'el
tow'el-ed
tow'el-ing
tow'-er
tow'-ered
tow'-er-ing
tow'-head
tow'-line
town' house
towns'-folk
town'-ship
towns'-man
towns'-peo-ple
tow'-path
tow'-rope
tox-e'-mi:a
tox-e'-mic
tox'-ic
tox-ic'-i-ty
tox'-i-co-log'-i-cal
tox-i-col'-o-gist
tox-i-col'-o-gy
tox-i-co'-sis
tox-if'-er-ous
tox'i-ge-nic'-i-ty
tox'-in
tox'i-pho'-bi:a
tox-oph'-i-lite
toy'-on*
tra'-be-at-ed
tra-bec'-u-la

trace'-a:ble
trac'-er
trac'-er:y
tra'-che:a
tra'-che-al
tra-che'-i:dal
tra-che-i'-tis
tra-che-ot'-o-my
tra-cho'-ma
tra-chom'a-tous
tra-chyt'-ic
trac'-ing
track'-age
track'-er
track'-less
track'-man
track'-walk-er
trac-ta-bil'-i-ty†
trac'-ta-ble†
Trac-tar'-i-an-ism†
trac'-tate
trac'-tile
trac-til'-i-ty
trac'-tion
trac'-tive
trac'-tor
trade'=in (n.)
trade'=last (n.)
trade'-mark
trade name
trad'-er
trade school
trades'-man
trade un'-ion†
tra-dev'-man
trade wind
trad'-ing
tra-di'-tion
tra-di'-tion-al
tra-di'-tion-ar:y†
trad'-i-tive
trad'-i-tor
tra-duce'
tra-duc'-er
tra-du'-cian-ism
tra-duc'-i:ble
Tra-fal'-gar
traf'-fic
traf'-fic-a:ble
traf'-ficked
traf'-fick-er
traf'-fick-ing
rag'-a-canth
trag-a-can'-thin
tra-ge'-di-an
tra-ge'-di-enne'
rag'-e-dy

trag'-ic
trag'-i-cal
trag'-i-cal-ly
trag'-i-com'-e-dy
trag'-o-pan
tra'-gus
trail'-er
train-ee'
train'-er
train'-ing
train'-load
train'-man
trait
trai'-tor
trai'-tor-ous
trai'-tress
Tra'-jan
traj'-ect (n.)
tra-ject' (v.)
tra-jec'-tile
tra-jec'-to-ry
tram'-mel
tram'-meled
tram'-mel-ing
tra:mon'-tane
tramp'-er
tram'-ple
tram'-pling
tram'-po-line'
tram'-way
tran'-quil
tran'-quil-ize
tran'-quil-iz-er
tran-quil'-li-ty
trans-act'
trans-ac'-tion
trans-am'-i-nase
trans'-at-lan'-tic
Trans-cau-ca'-sian
trans-ceiv'-er
tran-scend'
tran-scen'-den-cy*
tran-scen'-dent*
tran'-scen-den'-tal
tran'-scen-den'-tal-ism
trans-con-ti-nen'-tal
tran-scribe'
tran-scrib'-er
tran'-script
tran-scrip'-tion
trans-duc'-er
trans-duc'-tor
tran-sect'
tran'-sept
trans-e-unt
trans'-fer (n., v.)
trans-fer' (v.)
trans-fer'-a:ble

401

trans'-fer-ase
trans'-fer-ee'
trans'-fer-ence
trans'-fer-en'-tial
trans-ferred'
trans-fer'-rer
trans-fer'-ring
trans-fig-u-ra'-tion†
trans-fig'-ure
trans-fix'
trans-fix'-ion
trans-form' (v.)
trans'-form (n.)
trans-for-ma'-tion
trans-form'-a-tive
trans-form'-er
trans-fus'-a-ble
trans-fuse'
trans-fu'-sion
trans-gress'
trans-gres'-sion
trans-gres'-sor
trans-hu'-mance
tran'-sien-cy
tran'-sient
tran'-sient-ly
tran-sil'-ience*†
tran-sil'-ient*†
tran'-sis-tor
tran'-sit*
tran'-sit-er
tran-si'-tion†
tran'-si-tion-al†
tran'-si-tive
tran'-si-to-ry
tran'-si-tron
trans-late'
trans-la'-tion
trans-la'-tive
trans-la'-tor
trans-lit'-er-ate
trans-lit'-er-a-tor
trans-lu'-cence
trans-lu'-cen-cy
trans-lu'-cent
trans-mi'-grate
trans-mi-gra'-tion
trans-mi'-gra-to-ry
trans-mis'-si-ble
trans-mis'-sion
trans-mis-som'-e-ter
trans-mit'
trans-mit'-ta-ble
trans-mit'-tal
trans-mit'-ter
trans-mog'-ri-fy
trans-mut-a-bil'-i-ty
trans-mut'-a-ble

trans-mu-ta'-tion
trans-mute'
trans-o:ce-an'-ic
tran'-som
tran-son'-ic
trans-pa-cif'-ic
trans-par'-en-cy
trans-par'-ent
tran-spir'-a:ble
tran-spi-ra'-tion
tran-spir'-a-to-ry
tran-spire'
tran-spi-rom'-e-ter†
trans-plant'
trans-plan-ta'-tion
tran-spon'-der
trans-po'-ni-ble
trans-pon'-tine
trans-port' (v.)
trans'-port (n.)
trans-por-ta'-tion
trans-pose'
trans-po-si'-tion
trans-ship'
trans-ship'-ping
trans=son'-ic
tran-sub-stan'-ti-ate
tran-sub-stan-ti-a'-tion
tran-su-da'-tion
tran-su'-da-to-ry
tran-sude'
trans'-u:ra'-ni-um
Trans-vaal'
trans-ver'-sal
trans-verse'
trans-vers'-er
trans-vert'-er
trans-vert'-i:ble
Tran'-syl-va'-nia*†
trap'-door
tra-peze'
tra-pe'-zi-form
tra-pe'-zi-um
tra:pe'-zo-he'-dron*†
trap'-e-zoid
trap'-e-zoi'-dal
trap'-per
trap'-pings
Trap'-pist
trap'-shoot-ing
trash'y
trau'-ma
trau-mat'-ic
trau'-ma-tism
tra:vail'†
trav'-el
trav'-eled
trav'-el-er

trav'-el-ing
trav'-el-og*
trav'-el-ogue*†
tra-vers'-a:ble*†
tra-vers'-al*†
trav'-erse (n.)
tra-verse'† (v., n.)
trav'-er-tine
travois*†
trawl'-er
treach'-er-ous
treach'-er:y
trea'-cle
tread'-ing
trea'-dle†
tread'-mill
trea'-son
trea'-son-a:ble
trea'-son-ous
trea'-sure*
trea'-sur-er*
trea'-sure trove*
trea'-sur:y*
treat
treat'-er
trea'-ties
trea'-tise
treat'-ment
trea'-ty
tre'-ble†
tre'-bled†
treb'-u-chet
tree fern
tree frog
tree'-ing
tree'-less
tree'-nail
tree toad
tree'-top
tre'-foil
tre'-ha-lose
trek'-king
trel'-lis
trel'-lised
trel'-lis-work
Trem-a-to'-da*
trem'-a-tode
trem'-ble
trem'-bling
trem'-bling-ly
tre-men'-dous
tre-men'-dous-ly
trem'-e-tol
trem'-o-lant
trem'-o-lo
trem'-or
trem'-u-lous
trench

tren'-chan-cy*†
tren'-chant*†
tren'-cher (board, cap)*†
trench'-er (digger)
Tren'-ton
tre-pan'
trep-a-na'-tion
tre-pan'-ning
tre-phine'
treph'-o-cyte
treph'-one
trep-i-da'-tion
tre-pid'-i-ty
trep-o-ne'-ma
trep-o-ne-ma-to'-sis
trep'-o-ne'-mi-ci'-dal*
tres'-pass
tres'-pass-er
tres'-tle
tres'-tle-man
Tre-vel'-yan
tri'-a:ble
tri'-ad
tri'-al
tri'-an-gle
tri-an'-gu-lar
tri-an'-gu-late
tri-an-gu-la'-tion
tri-ap'-sal
tri-ap'-si-dal
tri-ar'-yl-meth'-ane
Tri-as'-sic
tri'-a:tom'-ic
tri'-a-zine†
tri-az'-i-nyl
tri'-a-zole†
tri-az'-o-lyl
trib'-al†
tribe
tribes'-man
tri-bom'-e-ter
tri-bro'-mo-eth'-a-nol
tri-bro'-mo-eth'-yl
trib-u-la'-tion
tri:bu'-nal
trib'-u-nate
trib'une
trib'-u-ni'-cial
trib'-u-tar:y†
trib'-ute
tri'-ceps
tri-chi'-a-sis
tri-chi'-na
trich'-i-nize
trich-i-no'-sis
tri-chit'-ic
tri-chlo'-ride
tri-chlo'-ro-meth'-ane

trich-o-mo-ni'-a-sis
tri-cho'-sis
tri-chot'-o-my
trick'-er:y
trick'-i-ly
trick'-i-ness
trick'-le
trick'-ster
trick'y
tri'-cli'-no-he-he'-dric*†
tri'-col-or
tri'-cot
tric'-o-tine'
tri-crot'-ic
tri'-cro-tism
tri-cus'-pid
tri'-cy-cle
tri-cy'-clic
tri-dec'-yl-ene†
tri'-dent
tri-en'-ni:al
tri'-er
Trier
tri'-er-ar-chy*
Tri-este'
tri-eth-a-nol'-a:mine'†
tri-far'-i-ous†
tri'-fle
tri'-fler
tri'-fling
tri-fo'-cal
tri-fo'-li-ate
tri-fo'-li-o-late
tri-fo'-ri-um
tri-gem'-i-nal
trig'-ger
tri'-gon
trig'-o-nal
tri-go-ni'-tist†
trig-o-nom'-e-ter
trig-o-no-met'-ric
trig-o-nom'-e-try
trig'-o-nous
tri-hal'ide
tri-he'-dral
tri-he'-dron
tri-hy'-dric
tri-ke'-tone
tri-lat'-er-al
tril'-lion
tril'-li-um
tri'-lo-bite
tri-log'-ic
tril'-o-gy
tri'-mer-ide
trim'-er-ous
tri-mes'-ic
trim'-e-ter

tri-meth'-yl-ene-tri-ni'-
    tra-mine
tri-met'-ro-gon
trim'-mer
trim'-ming
tri'-na-ry
Trin'-i-dad
Trin'-i-tar'-i-an†
tri-ni'-tro-tol'-u-ene
Trin'-i-ty
trin'-ket
tri-no'-mi-al
tri'o
tri'-o-let'
Tri'-o-nal
tri-ox'-ide
tri-par'-ti-ble*†
tri-par'-tite
tri-par-ti'-tion
tri'-pe-dal†
trip'=ham-mer
tri-phen'yl-ene
tri-phib'-i-ous
triph'-thong
triph'-y-lite
tri'-ple†
tri-ple'-gi:a
trip'-let*
trip'lex*†
trip'-li-cate
trip-li-ca'-tion
trip-lic'-i-ty
trip'-loi-dy
tri'-pod
trip'-o-dal
tri-pod'-ic
Trip'-o-li
Tri-pol'-i-tan
tri'-pos
trip'-ping-ly
trip'-tych
trip-tyque'
tri-que'tra†
tri-quet'-ric
tri'-reme
tri-sect'
tri-sec'-tion
tri-se'-mic†
tri-skel'-i-on*†
tri-so'-mic
tris'-ti-chous*
Tris'-tram
tri-syl-lab'-ic*
tri-syl'-la-ble
trite'-ness
tri-thi'-o-nate
trit'i-um
tri'-ton

trit'-u-rate
trit-u-ra'-tion
trit'-u-ra-tor
tri'-tyl†
tri'-umph
tri-um'-phal
tri-um'-phant
tri'-umph-ing
tri-um'-vir
tri-um'-vir-al*†
tri-um'-vi-rate
tri'-une
tri-va'-lence
tri-va'-lent
triv'-et
triv'-ia*†
triv'-i-al
triv-i-al'-i-ty
triv'-i-um
tro'-car
tro-cha'-ic
tro-chan'-ter
tro'-che
troch-e-am'-e-ter
tro'-chee
troch'-i-lus
troch'-le-ar
tro-choi'-dal
tro-chom'-e-ter
trod'-den
trog'-lo-dyte
Troi'-lus
Tro'-jan
troll'-er
trol'-ley
trol'-lop
Trol'-lope
trom-bi-di'-a-sis
trom-bone'
trom-bon'-ist
tro-mom'-e-ter
tro-nom'-e-ter
troop
troop'-er
troop'-ship
tro-pae'-o-lin
tro'-pane
trope
tro'-pe-ine
troph'-ic
tro'-phied
tro'-phy
trop'-ic
trop'-i-cal
trop'-ic acid†
tro-pism†
tro-pol'-o-gy
trop'-o·lone

tro-pom'-e-ter
tro-poph'-i-lous
trop'-o-phyte
tro'-po-sphere*†
trop-tom'-e-ter
tro'-pyl
Trot'-sky
trot'-ter
trot'-ting
trou'-ba-dour
trou'-ble†
trou'-bled†
trou'-bler†
trou'-ble-some†
trou'-blous†
trough
trounce
troupe
troup'-er
troup'-i-al
trou'-sers
trous'-seau
trou-vère'
tro'-ver
trow'-el
trow'-eled
tru'-an-cy
tru'-ant
Truck'-ee
truck'-er
truck'-le
truck'-ling
truck'-man
truc'u-lence†
truc'u-lent†
trudge
trud'-gen*†
trudg'-ing
tru'-est
truf'-fle
tru'-ism
tru-is'-tic
tru'-ly
trum'-per:y*†
trum'-pet
trum'-pet-er
trun'-cate
trun'-cat-ed
trun-ca'-tion
trun'-cheon
trun'-dle
trunk'-ful
trunk line
trun'-nion
truss'-ing
trust'-ee'*†
trust-ee'-ship*†
trust'-ful

405

trust'-i-ly
trust'-ing
trust'-wor-thi-ness
trust'-wor-thy
trust'y
truth'-ful
truth'-ful-ness
tru-xil'-lic*†
try'-ing
try'-out (n.)
try:pan'o-ci'-dal*
try:pan'o-some*†
tryp:ar'-sa-mide*†
tryp'-o-graph
tryp'-o-sin
tryp-sin'-o-gen
tryp'-to-phan
try'-sail
try square
tryst
tryst'-er
tsar
tset'-se
tsu-nam'i*†
tsu-tsu-ga-mu'-shi
tu'-ba
tub'-al†
tub'-ba-ble
tu-bec'-to-my
tu'-ber
tu'-ber-cle
tu-ber'-cu-lar
tu-ber'-cu-lin
tu-ber-cu-lo'-sis
tu-ber'-cu-lous
tube'-rose (flower)
tu'-ber-ose (with tubers)
tu-ber-os'-i-ty
tu'-ber-ous
tu'-bi-fa'-cient
tub'-ing
tu-bo-cu-ra'-rine
tu'-bu-lar
tu-bu-la'-tion
tu'-bule
tuck'-er
Tuc-son'
Tu'-dor
Tues'-day
tu'-fa
tu-fa'-ceous
tuff-a'-ceous
tuft'-ed
tuft'-er
tug'-boat
tug'=of=war'
Tui'-ler-ies†
tu-i'-tion

tu-la-re'-mi:a
tu'-lip
tu'-lip-wood
tulle
Tul'-sa
tum'-ble
tum'-ble-down
tum'-bler
tum'-ble-weed
tum'-bling
tum'-brel
tu'-me-fa'-cient
tu-me-fac'-tion
tu'-me-fy
tu-mes'-cent
tu'-mid
tu'-mor
tu'-mu-lar
tu'-mu-lose
tu-mu-los'-i-ty
tu'-mult
tu-mul'-tu-ar:y†
tu-mul'-tu-ous
tu'-mu-lus
tu'-na
tun'-a:ble
tun'-dra
tune'-ful
tune'-less
tung'-sten
tung'-stic
tung'-stite
tu'-nic
tu'-nicked
tun'-ing
tun'-ing fork
Tu'-nis
Tu-ni'-sia†
Tu-ni'-sian†
tun'-nel
tun'-neled
tun'-nel-er
tun'-ny
tu'-pe-lo
tu'-ran-ose
tur'-ban
tur'-baned
tur'-bid
tur-bi-dim'-e-ter
tur-bi-di-met'-ric
tur-bid'-i-ty
tur'-bi-nal
tur'-bi-nate
tur'-bine
tur-bi-nec'-to-my
tur'-bo-charg-er
tur'-bo-jet
tur'-bo-prop

tur'-bot
tur'-bu-la-tor
tur'-bu-lence
tur'-bu-lent
tu-reen'
turf'-man
tur'-gen-cy
Tur-ge'-nev
tur'-gent-ly
tur-ges'-cence
tur-ges'-cent
tur'-gid
tur-gid'-i-ty
tur'-gor
Tu'-rin
Tur'-ke-stan'
tur'-key
tur'-keys
Turk'-ish
tur'-mer-ic
tur'-moil
turn'-buck-le
Turn'-bull
turn'-coat
turn'-down (n.)
Tur'-ner
turn'-er
turn'-nip
turn'-key
turn'-out (n.)
turn'-o:ver (n., adj.)
turn'-pike
turn'-spit
turn'-stile
turn'-ta-ble
tur'-pen-tine
tur'-pi-tude
tur'-quoise
tur'-ret
tur'-ri-lite
tur'-tle
tur'-tle-dove
Tus'-ca-loo'-sa
Tus'-can
Tus'-ca-ny
Tus-ke'-gee
tusk'-er
tus'-sah
tus'-sle
tus'-sock
tu'-te-lage
tu'-te-lar
tu'-te-lar:y†
tu'-tor
tu'-tored
tu-to'-ri-al
tu-to'-ri-al-ly

tut'-ti=frut'-ti
Tu-tu-i'-lan
tux-e'-do
tu-yere'
twad'-dle
twan'-gle
twang'y
tweet'-er
tweez'-ers
twelfth
twen'-ti-eth
twen'-ty
twid'-dle
twi'-light
twing'-ing
twi'=light
twin'-ing
twin'-kle
twin'-kling
twin'-ning
twist'-er
twitch
twitch'-er
Twitch'-ell
twit'-ter
twit'-ting
two'-fold
two'-pence
two'-some
two'=step
ty'-chism
Ty-chon'-ic
ty-coon'
ty'-ee
ty'-ing
Ty'-ler
tym-pan'-ic
tym'-pa-nist†
tym-pa-ni'-tes
tym-pa-nit'-ic
tym'-pa-num
tym'-pa-ny
Tyn-dall
tyn-dall-om'-e-ter
typ'-a:ble
type'-cast
type'-found-er
type met'-al
type'-script
type'-set-ter
type wash
type'-write
type'-writ-er
type'-writ-ing
type'-writ-ten
typh-li'-tis
typh-lol'-o-gy
typh-lo'-sis

407

ty'-phoid
ty-phoi'-dal
ty-phoi'-din
ty-phon'-ic
ty-phoon'
ty'-phous
ty'-phus
typ'-i-cal
typ-i-fi-ca'-tion
typ'-i-fy
typ'-ist
ty-pog'-ra-pher
ty-po-graph'-ic
ty-po-graph'-i-cal
ty-pog'-ra-phy
ty'-po-nym
ty-poth'-e-tae
ty'-ra-mine
ty-ran'-ni-cal
ty-ran'-ni-cide
tyr'-an-nize
tyr'-an-nous
tyr'-an-nous-ly
tyr'-an-ny
ty'-rant
Tyr'-i-an
ty'-ro
ty-ro-ci'-dine
Ty'-rode
Ty:rol'*†
Ty:ro'-le-an
Tyr'o-lese'
Ty-rone'
ty'ro-sin-ase
ty'ro-sine
ty-ro-sin-o'-sis
Tyr-rhe'-ni-an

U

U:ban'-gi
u:bi'-e-ty
u:biq'-ui-tar'-i-an†
u.biq'-ui-tar:y†
u:biq'-ui-tous
u:bi'-qui-ty*†
ud'-der
u:dom'-e-ter
u'do-me'-tric*†
U:gan'-da
U:gan'-dan
ug'-li-fy
ug'-li-ness
ug'-ly
uh-lan'
u:in'-ta-ite
u:kase'
U:kraine'

U:krain'-i-an
u:ku-le'-le
u'la-ma'
ul'-cer
ul'-cer-ate
ul-cer-a'-tion
ul'-cer-a-tive
ul'-cer-ous
u:le-ma'
ul-ma'-ceous
ul'-na
ul'-nar
ul-nar'e*†
ul'-no-con'-dy-lar
ul'-ster
ul-te'-ri-or
ul'-ti-ma
ul'-ti-ma-cy
ul'-ti-mate
ul-ti-ma'-tum
ul'-ti-mo
ul'-ti-mo-gen'-i-ture
ul'-tra
ul'-tra-cen'-tri-fuge
ul'-tra-ism
ul'-tra-ma-rine'
ul-tra-mon'-tan-ism
ul-tra-mun'-dane'
ul-tra-son'-ic
ul-tra-vi'-o-let
ul'-tra vi'-res
ul'-tra-vi'-rus
ul'u-lant
ul'u-late
ul'u-la'-tion
U:lys'-ses
um-bel-lif'-er-one
um-bel-lif'-er-ous
um'-ber
um-bil'-i-cal
um-bil'-i-cus†
um'-bo-nal
um'-bo-nate
um'-bra
um'-brage
um-bra'-geous
um-brel'-la
Um'-bri-an
um-brif'-er-ous
um'-laut
u'mo-ho-ite
um'-pir-age
um'-pire
un-a:bat'-ed
un-a:ble
un-a:bridged'
un-ac-cept'-a:ble
un-ac-com'-pa-nied

un-ac-count'-a:ble
un-ac-cus'-tomed
un-ac-quaint'-ed
un-a:dorned'
un-a:dul'-ter-at-ed
un-af-fect'-ed
un-a:fraid'
un-aid'-ed
un-al'-loyed
un-al'-ter-a:ble
un-al'-tered
un-am-bi'-tious
un=A:mer'-i-can
un-a'mi-a:ble
u:na-nim'-i-ty
u:nan'-i-mous
un-an-nounced'
un-an'-swer-a:ble
un-ap-proach'-a:ble
un-ar'-gued
un-armed'
u'na-ry
un-a:shamed'
un-asked'
un-as-sail'-a:ble
un-as-sist'-ed
un-as-sum'-ing
un-at-tached'
un-at-tain'-a:ble
un-at-tend'-ed
un-at-trac'-tive
un-au'-tho-rized*†
un-a:vail'-ing
un-a:void'-a:ble
un-a:ware'
un-bal'-anced
un-bear'-a:ble
un-beat'-en
un-be-com'-ing
un-be-lief'
un-be-liev'-a:ble
un-be-liev'-er
un-be-liev'-ing
un-bend'
un-bend'-ing
un-ben'-e-ficed
un-bent'
un-bi'-ased
un-bid'-den
un-bind'
un-blam'-a:ble
un-bleached'
un-blem'-ished
un-blink'-ing
un-blush'-ing
un-bolt'-ed
un-born'

un-bos'-om†
un-bound'
un-bound'-ed
un-break'-a:ble
un-bri'-dled
un-bro'-ken
un-buck'-le
un-bur'-den
un-but'-ton
un-called=for
un-can'-ny
un-ceas'-ing
un-cer-e-mo'-ni-ous
un-cer'-tain
un-cer'-tain-ty
un-chained'
un-chal'-lenged
un-change'-a:ble
un-changed'
un-char'-i-ta-ble
un-chart'-ed
un-chaste'
un-checked'
un-chris'-tian
un'-cial*
un-ci-na-ri'-a-sis
un'-ci-nate
un-cir'-cum-cised
un-civ'-il
un-civ'-il-ized
un-clad'
un-clasped'
un'-cle
un-clean'
un-cloud'-ed
un-com'-fort-a:ble
un-com'-mon
un-com-mu'-ni-ca-tive
un-com-plain'-ing
un-com'-pro-mis-ing
un-con-cern'
un-con-cerned'
un-con-di'-tion-al
un-con'-quer-a:ble
un-con'-quered
un-con-scio-na-ble*†
un-con'-scious
un-con'-scious-ness
un-con-sti-tu'-tion-al
un-con-trol'-la-ble
un-con-trolled'
un-con-ven'-tion-al
un-cor-rupt'-ed
un-count'-ed
un-cou'-ple†
un-couth'
un-cov'-er
un-cov'-ered

409

un-crowned'
unc'-tion
unc'-tu-ous
un-cul'-ti-vat-ed
un-cul'-tured
un-cured'
un-daunt'-ed
un-de-cid'-ed
un-dec'-yl-ene†
un'-dec'-y-len'-ic
un-de-feat'-ed
un-de-filed'
un-de-fined'
un-dem-o-crat'-ic
un-de-mon'-stra-ble
un-de-mon'-stra-tive
un-de-ni'-a-ble
un'-der
un'-der-brush
un'-der-clothes
un'-der-cloth'-ing
un'-der-cov'-er
un'-der-cur-rent
un'-der-cut
un'-der-dog
un-der-es'-ti-mate
un'-der-foot'
un'-der-glaze
un'-der-go'
un'-der-gone'
un-der-grad'-u-ate
un'-der-ground
un'-der-growth
un'-der-hand-ed
un'-der-line
un'-der-ling
un'-der-ly-ing
un'-der-mine'
un'-der-neath'
un-der-nour'-ished
un'-der-paid'
un'-der-pass
un-der-priv'-i-leged
un'-der-rate'
un'-der-score
un'-der-sec'-re-ta-ry†
un'-der-sell'
un'-der-shirt
un'-der-side
un'-der-signed'
un'-der-sized
un'-der-slung
un'-der-stand'
un-der-stand'-a:ble
un-der-stand'-ing
un'-der-state-ment
un'-der-stood'
un'-der-stud:y

un'-der-take
un'-der-tak-er
un'-der-tak'-ing
un'-der-tone
un'-der-took'
un'-der-tow
un-der-val-u-a'-tion
un'-der-wa'-ter
un'-der-wear
un'-der-weight
un'-der-went'
un'-der-world
un'-der-write
un'-der-writ-er
un'-der-writ'-ten
un-de-served'
un-de-sir'-a:ble
un-de-vel'-oped
un-dis'-ci-plined
un-dis-cov'-ered
un-dis-mayed'
un-dis-put'-ed
un-dis-turbed'
un-di-ver'-si-fied
un-di-vid'-ed
un-do'
un-do'-ing
un-done'
un-doubt'-ed-ly
un-dreamed'
un-dress'
un-due'
un'-du-lant
un'-du-late
un'-du-lat-ed
un-du-la'-tion
un'-du-la-to-ry
un-du'-ly
un-dy'-ing
un-earned'
un-earth'
un-earth'-ly
un-eas'-i-ly
un-eas'-i-ness
un-eas'y
un-ed'-u-cat-ed
un-em-ployed'
un'-em-ploy'-ment
un-end'-ing
un-e'qual
un-e'qualed
un-e:quiv'-o-cal
un-err'-ing
un-e'ven
un-e'ven-ness
un-e:vent'-ful
un-ex-am'-pled

un-ex-cep'-tion-al
un-ex-pect'-ed
un-ex-plained'
un-ex-plored'
un-ex'-pur-gat-ed
un-fail'-ing
un-fair'
un-faith'-ful
un-fa-mil'-iar
un-fas'-ten†
un-fath'-om-a:ble
un-fa'-vor-a:ble
un-feel'-ing
un-feigned'
un-feign'-ed-ly
un-fet'-tered
un-fil'-i:al†
un-fin'-ished
un-fit'
un-fit'-ted
un-fit'-ting
un-fledged'
un-flag'-ging
un-flinch'-ing
un-fold'
un-fore-seen'
un-for-get'-ta-ble
un-for-giv'-a:ble
un-for'-tu-nate
un-found'-ed
un-fre'-quent-ed
un-friend'-ly
un'-ful-filled'
un-furl'
un-fur'-nished
un-gain'-ly
un-gen'-er-ous
un-god'-ly
un-gov'-ern-a:ble
un-gra'-cious
un-grate'-ful
un-ground'-ed
un'-gual
un-guard'-ed
un'-guent
un'-guen-tar:y†
un-guen'-tous
un-guic'-u-late
un'-gui-nous
un'-gu-la
un'-gu-lar
un'-gu-late
un-hal'-lowed
un-ham'-pered
un-hap'-pi-ly
un-hap'-pi-ness
un-hap'-py
un-harmed'

un-har'-ness
un-health'-y
un-heard'
un-heed'-ed
un-heed'-ing
un-hes'-i-tat-ing-ly
un-hinge'
un-ho'-ly
un-hon'-ored
un-horse'
un-hur'-ried
un-hurt'
u'ni-bi'-va'-lent
u'ni-cam'-er-al
u'ni-cel'-lu-lar
u:nic'-i-ty
u'ni-corn
un-i:de'aed
un-i:den'-ti-fied
un-id'-i-o-mat'-ic†
u'ni-fi-a:ble
u:ni-fi-ca'-tion
u:nif'-ic
u'ni-fied
u'ni-fi'-lar
u:ni-fo'-li-o-late
u'ni-form
u'ni-form-i-tar'-i-an†
u:ni-form'-i-ty
u'ni-fy
u'ni-fy-ing
u:ni-ju'-gate*†
u:ni-lat'-er-al
un-im:ag'-i-na-tive
un-im-paired'
un-im-peach'-a:ble
un-im-por'-tance
un-im-por'-tant
un-im-proved'
un-in-cor'-po-rat-ed
un-in-flam'-ma-ble
un-in-formed'
un-in-hab'-it-ed
un-in-i'-ti-at-ed
un-in'-jured
un-in-tel'-li-gi-ble
un-in-ten'-tion-al
un-in'-ter-est-ed
un-in-ter-rupt'-ed
un-in-vit'-ed
un'-ion†
un'-ion-ism†
un'-ion-ist†
un'-ion-ize†
u:nip'-a-rous
u:ni-pla'-nar
u:nip'-o-tent
u:nique'

411

u·nique′-ly
u′ni-son
u·nis′-o-nance
u·nis′-o-nous
u′nit
u·nit′-a·ble
U:ni-tar′-i-an†
u′ni-tar:y†
u·nite′
u·nit′-ed
u·nit′-ing
u′ni-tive
u′nit-ize
u′ni-ty
u′ni-va′-lence
u′ni-va′-lent
u′ni-valve
u′ni-ver′-sal
U:ni-ver-sal′-ist
u:ni-ver-sal′-i-ty
u′ni-verse
u:ni-ver′-si-ty
u:niv′-o-cal
un-just′
un-jus′-ti-fi-a:ble
un-kempt′
un-kind′
un-kind′-li-ness
un-kind′-ness
un-known′
un-lace′
un-law′-ful
un-learned′
un-leash′
un-leav′-ened
un-less′
un-let′-tered
un-like′
un-like′-li-hood
un-like′-ly
un-lim′-ber
un-lim′-it-ed
un-liq′-ui-dat-ed
un-list′-ed
un-load′
un-lock′
un-loose′
un-luck′y
un-man′-age-a:ble
un-man′-ly
un-man′-ner-ly
un-mar′-ried
un-masked′
un-mea′-sur-a:ble*
un-mel′-lowed
un-mend′-a:ble
un-men′-tion-a:ble
un-mer′-chant-a:ble

un-mer′-ci-ful
un-mis-tak′-a:ble
un-mit′-i-gat-ed
un-mixed′
un-mor′-al
un-mort′-gaged
un-moved′
un-nat′-u-ral
un-nec-es-sar′-i-ly†
un-nec′-es-sar:y†
un-nerve′
un-no′-ticed
un-ob-served′
un-ob-tru′-sive
un-oc′-cu-pied
un-of-fi′-cial
un-o′pened
un-or′-ga-nized*†
un-o:rig′-i-nal
un-or′-tho-dox
un-os′-ten-ta′-tious
un-pack′
un-paid′
un-pal′-at-a:ble
un-par′-al-leled
un-par′-don-a:ble
un-par-lia-men′-ta-ry
un-per′-fo-rat-ed
un-per-turbed′
un-pleas′-ant
un-pleas′-ant-ness
un-pol′-ished
un-pop′-u-lar
un-pop-u-lar′-i-ty
un-prac′-ti-cal
un-prec′-e-dent-ed
un-pre-dict′-a:ble
un-prej-u-diced
un-pre-med′-i-tat-ed
un-pre-pared′
un-pre-ten′-tious
un-prin′-ci-pled
un-print′-a:ble
un-proc′essed
un-pro-duc′-tive
un-pro-fes′-sion-al
un-prof′-it-a:ble
un-pro-pi′-tious
un-pro-tect′-ed
un-pro-voked′
un-pub′-lished
un-pun′-ished
un-qual′-i-fied
un-quench′-a:ble
un-ques′-tion-a:ble
un-ques′-tioned
un-qui′-et
un-quote′

un-rav'-el
un-read'y
un'-re'-al
un-re-al'-i-ty
un-rea'-son-a-ble
un-rec'-og-niz-a:ble
un-re-con-struct'-ed
un-reel'
un-re-flec'-tive
un-re-gen'-er-ate
un-re-lent'-ing
un-re-li'-a:ble
un-re-li'-gious†
un-re-mit'-ting
un-re-mu'-ner-at-ed
un-re-mu'-ner-a-tive
un-rep-re-sent'-a-tive†
un-re-quit'-a:ble
un-re-quit'-ed
un-re-served'
un-rest'
un-re-strained'
un-re-strict'-ed
un-rid'-dle
un-righ'-teous*†
un-ripe'
un-ri'-valed
un-roll'
un-ruf'-fled
un-ru'-ly*
un-safe'
un-sal'-a:ble
un-san'-i-tar:y†
un-sat-is-fac'-to-ry
un-sat'-is-fied
un-sat'-u-rat-ed
un-sa'-vor:y
un-scathed'
un-schol'-ar-ly
un-sci-en-tif'-ic
un-scram'-ble
un-scru'-pu-lous
un-search'-a:ble
un-sea'-son-a-ble
un-seat'
un-seem'-ly
un-seen'
un-self'-ish
un-self'-ish-ness
un-set'-tled
un-shak'-a:ble
un-shak'-en
un-shav'-en
un-sheathe'
un-shod'
un-sight'-ly
un-signed'
un-skilled'

un-skill'-ful
un-snarl'
un-so'-cia-ble
un-sol'-der†
un-so-lic'-it-ed
un-so-lic'-i-tous*
un-so-phis'-ti-cat-ed
un'-sound'
un-spar'-ing
un-speak'-a:ble
un-spe'-cial-ized
un-spec'-u-la-tive
un-spoiled'
un-spot'-ted
un-sta'-ble
un-stained'
un-stead'-i-ly
un-stead'y
un-strung'
un-stud'-ied
un-sub-stan'-tial
un-suc-cess'-ful
un-suit'-a:ble
un-suit'-ed
un-sul'-lied
un-sup-port'-ed
un-sur-passed'
un-sus-pect'-ed
un-sym-pa-thet'-ic
un-taint'-ed
un-tam'-a:ble
un-tamed'
un-tan'-gle
un-tar'-nished
un-taught'
un-ten'-a:ble
Un'-ter-mey-er
un-think'-a:ble
un-think'-ing
un-ti'-dy
un-tie'
un-til'
un-time'-ly
un-tir'-ing
un-ti'-tled
un-told'
un-touch'-a:ble
un-touched'
un-to'ward
un-trained'
un-tram'-meled
un'-trans-lat'-a:ble
un-tra-vers'-a:ble*†
un-tried'
un-trou'-bled†
un-true'
un-truth'
un-truth'-ful

413

UNTUTORED

un-tu'-tored	up'-right
un-used'	up'-right-ness
un-u'su-al	up'-ris-ing
un-u'su-al-ness	up'-roar
un-ut'-ter-a:ble	up'-roar'-i-ous
un-var'-nished	up-roar'-i-ous-ly
un-var'y-ing†	up'-root
un-veil'	up'-set (n.)
un-ven'-ti-lat-ed	up-set' (v., adj.)
un-ver'-i-fied	up'-shot
un-vir'-tu-ous-ly	up'-si-lon
un-vit'-ri-fied	up'-stage
un-want'-ed	up-stairs'
un-war'-i-ly†	up-stand'-ing
un-war'-rant-a:ble	up'-start
un-war'-rant-ed	up'-state'
un-war'y†	up'-stat-er
un-washed'	up'-stream'
un-wa'-ver-ing	up'-stroke
un-wea'-ried	up'-thrust
un-wel'-come	up'=to=date'
un-whole'-some	up'-turn
un-wield'y	up'-ward
un-will'-ing	u'ra-chus
un-will'-ing-ness	u'ra-cil
un-wise'	U'ral
un-wit'-ting	u'ral-ite
un-wont'-ed	u:ral'-i-tize
un-work'-a:ble	u'ra-nate
un-world'-ly	U:ra'-ni:a
un-wor'-thi-ness	U:ra'-ni:an
un-wor'-thy	u:ran'-ic
un-wo'-ven†	u'ra-nif'-er-ous
un-wrap'	u'ra-nin
un-writ'-ten	u'ra-nin-ite*†
un-yield'-ing	u:ra'-ni-um
u'pas	u'ra-no-graph'-ic
up'-braid'	u:ra-nog'-ra-phy
up'-bring-ing	u'ra-no-log'-i-cal
up'=coun'-try	u:ra-nol'-o-gy
up'-date'	u:ra-nom'-e-try
up'-end'	u:ra-nos'-co-py
up'-grade'	u'ra-nous
up-heav'-al	U'ra-nus
up-held'	u'ra-nyl
up-hill'	u'ra-zine
up-hold'	ur'-ban
up-hol'-ster	ur'-bane'
up-hol'-ster-er	ur-ban'-i-ty
up-hol'-ster:y	ur-bi-cul'-ture
up'-keep	ur-ce-o-late
up'-land	ur'-chin
up'-lift (n.)	u:re'a
up-lift' (v.)	u:re-am'-e-ter
up:on'	u:re-mi:a
up'-per	u:re'-mic
up'-per-cut	u:re-om'-e-ter
up'-per-most	u:re'-ter

414

u:re′-ter-al
u:re-ter-i′-tis
u′re-thane†
u:re′-thra
u:re-thri′-tis
u:ret′-ic
u:re′-yl-ene
ur′-gen-cy
ur′-gent
ur′-gent-ly
urg′-ing
U:ri′-ah
u′ric
u:ri-col′-y-sis
u′ri-co-lyt′-ic
u′ri-nal
u:ri-nal′-y-sis
u′ri-nar:y†
u′ri-nate
u:ri-na′-tion
u′rine
u:ri-nif′-er-ous
u′ri-no-cry-os′-co-py
u′ri-nol′-o-gy
u:ri-nom′-e-ter
u′ro-fla′-vin
u′ro-gen′-i-tal
u:rog′-ra-phy
u′ro-leu′-cic
u:ro-li-thi′-a-sis†
u:ro-li-thol′-o-gy†
u′ro-log′-ic
u:rol′-o-gist
u:rol′-o-gy
u:ro-poi-e′-sis
u′ro-poi′-et′-ic
u′ro-por′-phy-rin
u:ro-pyg′-i-um
u:ros′-co-py
u:rot′-ro-pine
ur′-si-gram
ur′-sine
Ur′-su-la
Ur′-su-line
ur-ti-ca′-ceous
ur-ti-car′-i:a*†
ur-ti-ca′-tion
U′ru-guay
U′ru-guay′-an
us-a:bil′-i-ty
us-a:ble
us′-age
us′-ance
use′-ful
use′-ful-ness
use′-less
use′-less-ness

us′-er
ush′-er
us′-que-baugh
us′-ti-lag′-i-na′-ceous
us-tu-la′-tion
u′su-al
u′su-al-ly
u′su-fruct
u:su-fruc′-tu-ar:y
u′su-rer
u:su′-ri-ous
u:surp′
u:sur-pa′-tion
u:surp′-er
u′su-ry
U′tah
U′tah-an
u:ten′-sil
u′ter-ine
u:ter-og′-ra-phy
u′ter-us
U′ti-ca
u:til-i-tar′-i-an†
u:til-i-tar′-i-an-ism†
u:til′-i-ty
u′ti-li-za′-tion†
u′ti-lize†
u′ti-liz-er†
ut′-most
U:to′-pi:a
u:to′-pi-an
u′tri-cle
u:tric′-u-lar
u:tric′-u-li-form
ut′-ter
ut′-ter-ance
ut′-ter-most
u:va′-rov-ite†
u′ve:a
u:ve-i′-tis
u:vi-ton′-ic
u′vu-la
u′vu-lar
u:vu-li′-tis
ux-o′-ri-al
ux-or′-i-cide
ux-o′-ri-ous
u:zar-i-gen′-in
u:za′-rin

V

va′-can-cy
va′-cant
va′-cate
va′-cat-ing
va-ca′-tion
va-ca′-tion-ist

vac'-ci-nal
vac'-ci-nate
vac-ci-na'-tion
vac'-ci-na-tor
vac-cine'
vac-cin'-i-a'-ceous
vac-cin'-i-form
vac'-il-late
vac'-il-lat-ing
vac-il-la'-tion
vac'-il-la-to-ry
vac'-u-ist
va-cu'-i-ty
vac-u-o-la'-tion
vac'-u-ole
vac-u-om'-e-ter
vac'-u-ous
vac'-u-ous-ly
vac'-u-um
va'-de me'-cum
va'-dose
vag'-a-bond
vag'-a-bond-age
va-gar'-i-ous†
va-gar:y†
va-gil'-i-ty
va-gi'-na
va:gi'-nal*†
vag'-i-nate
vag-i-nec'-to-my
vag-i-ni'-tis
va-got'-o-my
va'-gran-cy
va'-grant
vague
vague'-ly
va'-guish
va'-gus
vain-glo'-ri-ous
vain'-glo-ry
vain'-ness
val'-ance
val-e-dic'-tion
val-e-dic-to'-ri-an
val'-e-dic'-to-ry
va'-lence
Va-len'-cia*†
Va-len'-ci-ennes'*†
va'-lent
val'-en-tine
Va-le'-ra
va-le'-ri-an
va-le'-ri-a-na'-ceous
va-ler'ic
va-le'-ryl*†
val'-et
val-e-tu-di-nar'-i-an†
Val-hal'-la

val'-ian-cy
val'-iant
val'-id
val'-i-date
val-i-da'-tion
va-lid'-i-ty
val'ine
va-lise'
Val-kyr'ie
val-lec'-u-la
val-lec'-u-lar
val'-ley
val'-leys
Val-ois'
va-lo'-ni:a
val'-or
val-o-ri-za'-tion*†
val'-o-rize*†
val'-or-ous
val'-or-ous-ly
Val'-pa-rai'-so
val'-u-a:ble
val'-u-a:bly
val-u-a'-tion
val'-ue
val'-ued
val'-ue-less
val'-u-ing
val'-val*
val'-vate
valve
val'-vu-lar
val'-vu-late
val-vu-li'-tis
val-vu-lot'-o-my
vam'-pire
vam'-pir-ism
va-na'dic*†
van'-a-dif'-er-ous
va-na'-di-nite*†
va-na'-di-um
va-na'-dous*
Van Bu'-ren
Van-cou'-ver
van'-dal
van'-dal-ism
van-dyke'
Va-nes'-sa (insect)
Van-es'-sa (Swift's love)†
van'-guard
va-nil'-la
va-nil'-lic
va:nil'-lin*
van'-ish
van'-i-ty
van'-quish
van'-quish-er
van'-tage

vap'-id
va-pid'-i-ty
vap'-id-ly
va-pog'-ra-phy
va'-por
va-por-es'-cence
va'-por-if'-ic
va-por-im'-e-ter
va'-por-iz-a:ble
va-por-i:za'-tion
va'-por-ize
va'-por-iz-er
va'-por-ous
va-que'-ro
var'-i-a-bil'-i-ty†
var'-i-a-ble†
Var'-i-ac
var'-i-ance†
var'-i-ant†
var'-i-at-ed†
var-i-a'-tion†
var-i-cel'-la
var'-i-ces
var'-i-co-cele
var'i-col-ored†
var'-i-cose
var-i-co'-sis
var-i-cos'-i-ty
var-i-cot'-o-my
var'-ied†
var'-i:e-gate†
var'-i:e-gat-ed†
var-i:e-ga'-tion†
va-ri'-e-tal
va-ri'-e-ty
var'-i-form†
var'-i-o-late†
var-i-o-la'-tion†
var'-i-o-lite†
var'-i-o-lit'-ic†
var'-i-o-loid†
va-ri'-o-lous
var-i-om'-e-ter†
var-i-o'-rum†
var'-i-ous†
var'-i-ous-ly†
var-is'-tor
var'-i-type
var'-ix†
var'-let
var'-nish
var'-nish-er
var'-si-ty
var'-us†
var'y†
vas-cu-lar
vas-cu-lar'-i-ty

vas-ec'-to-my†
Vas'-e-line
vas'o-dil'-a-tin*
vas'o-di-la'-tor
vas'o-mo'-tor
vas'-sal
vas'-sal-age
Vas'-sar
vas'-ti-tude
vast'-ly
vast'-ness
vat'-ic
Vat'-i-can
va-tic'-i-nal
va-tic'-i-na'-tion*
va-tic'-i-na-tor
vaude'-ville
vault'-ing
vaunt'-ing
vav'-a-sor
vec'-tion
vec'-tor
vec-to'-ri-al
Ve'-da
Ve-dan'-tic
ve-dette'
veer'-ing-ly
vee'-ry*†
veg'-e-ta-ble
veg'-e-tal
veg-e-tar'-i-an†
veg-e-tar'-i-an-ism†
veg'-e-tate
veg-e-ta'-tion
veg-e-ta'-tion-al
veg'-e-ta-tive
veg'-e-tism
veg'-e-tive
ve'-he-mence
ve'-he-ment
ve'-he-ment-ly
ve'-hi-cle
ve-hic'-u-lar
veil'-ing
veined
vein'-ing
ve-la'-men
ve'-lar
ve-lar'-i-um†
Ve-las'-quez
ve'-late
veldt
vel-i-ta'-tion
vel-le'-i-ty
vel'-li-cate
vel-li-ca'-tion
vel'-lum
vel-o-cim'-e-ter†

417

ve-loc'-i-pede
ve-loc'-i-ty
ve-lom'-e-ter
ve-lour'
ve'-lum
ve-lu'-men
ve-lu'-ti-nous
vel'-vet
vel'-vet-een'
vel'-vet:y
ve'-nal
ve-nal'-i-ty
ve-nat'-ic
ve-na'-tion
ven'-dace
ven'-dage
vend-ee'†
vend'-er
ven-det'-ta
ven-det'-tist
vend'-i:ble
ven-di'-tion
ven'-dor
ve-neer'
ve-neer'-er
ven'-e-nif'-er-ous
ven'-er-a:ble
ven'-er-ate
ven-er-a'-tion
ven'-er-a-tor
ve-ne'-re-al
ve-ne-re-ol'-o-gy
ven'-er:y
ven'-e-sect
ven-e-sec'-tion
Ve-ne'-tian
Ven-e-zu-e'-la*†
ven'-geance*
venge'-ful
ve'-ni:al
Ven'-ice
ven'i-punc-ture†
ve-ni're
ve-ni're fa'-ci-as
ve-ni're-man
ven'-i-son
ven'-om
ven'-om-ous
ve-nos'-i-ty
ve'-nous
ve'-nous-ly
ven'-ter (belly)
vent'-er (utterer)
ven'-ti-duct
ven'-ti-late
ven-ti-la'-tion
ven'-ti-la-tor
ven-tom'-e-ter

ven'-tral
ven'-tri-cle
ven-tric'-u-lar
ven'-tri-lo'-qui-al
ven-tril'-o-quism
ven-tril'-o-quist
ven-tril'-o-quis'-tic
ven-tril'-o-quy
ven'-ture
ven'-tur-er
ven'-ture-some
ven-tu'-ri
ven'-tur-ing
ven'-tur-ous
ven'-ue
ven'-ule
ven'-u-lose
Ve'-nus
Ve-nu'-sian*
ve-ra'-cious
ve-ra'-cious-ly
ve-rac'-i-ty
Ve'-ra-cruz
ve-ran'-da
ver'-a-scope
ver-a-tral'-de-hyde
ver-a-tram'-ine
ver'a-trate
ve-rat'-ric†
ver'-a-trine†
ve-rat'-ro-yl
ve-ra'-trum
ver-a-tryl'-i-dene
ver'-bal (adj.)
verb'-al*† (n.)
ver-bal'-i-ty
ver-bal-i:za'-tion
ver'-bal-ize
ver'-bal-iz-er
ver'-bal-ly
ver-ba'-tim
ver-be'-na
ver'-be-na'-ceous
ver-be'-na-lin
ver'-bi-age
verb'-i:fy
ver-big'-er-ate
ver'-bile
ver-bose'
ver-bos'-i-ty
ver-bo'-ten
ver'-dan-cy
ver'-dant
ver'-der-er
Ver'-di
ver'-dict
ver'-di-gris
ver'-din

ver'-di-ter
Ver-dun'
ver'-dure
ver'-dur-ous
ver'-dur-ous-ness
ver'-e-cund
verge
verg'-er*†
Ver'-gil
Ver-gil'-i:an
verg'-ing
ve-rid'-i-cal
ve-rid'-i-cal-ly
ver'-i-fi-a:ble
ver'-i-fi-ca'-tion
ver'-i-fied
ver'-i-fy
ver'-i-ly
ver:i-sim'-i-lar
ver:i-si-mil'-i-tude
ve'-rism*
ve'-rist*
ver'-i-ta-ble
ver'-i-tas
ver'-i-ty
ver'-juice
ver'-meil
ver-mi-cel'-li
ver'-mi-ci'-dal*†
ver'-mi-cide
ver-mic'-u-lar
ver-mic-u-la'-tion
ver-mic'-u-lite
ver'-mi-form
ver'-mif'-u-gal
ver'-mi-fuge
ver-mil'-ion
ver'-min
ver-mi-na'-tion
ver-mi-no'-sis
ver'-min-ous†
ver'-min-ous-ly†
Ver-mont'
Ver-mont'-er
Ver-mont'-ese'
ver-mouth'
ver-nac'-u-lar
ver-nac'-u-lar-ism
ver'-nal
ver-nal-i-za'-tion
ver'-nal-ize
ver'-nal-ly
ver-na'-tion
Ver'-ner
ver'-ni-er
Ver'-non
Ve-ro'-na
Ver'-o-nal

Ver'-o-nese' (of Verona)
Ve'-ro-ne'-se (painter)
ve-ron'-i-ca
ver-ru'-ca
ver-ru-co'-sis
ver-ru'-cous
Ver-sailles'
ver'-sa-tile
ver'-sa-tile-ly
ver-sa-til'-i-ty
versed
ver'-si-cle
ver'-si-col'-or
ver-sic'-u-lar
ver-si-fi-ca'-tion
ver'-si-fied
ver'-si-fi-er
ver'-si-fy
ver'-sion
ver'-sus
ver'-te-bra
ver'-te-brae
ver'-te-bral
ver'-te-brate
ver'-te-bro-chon'-dral
ver'-tex
ver'-ti-cal
ver'-ti-cal-ly
ver'-ti-ces
ver'-ti:cil'-late*†
ver-tic'-i-ty
ver-tig'-i-nous
ver'-ti-go
verve
ver'y
ves'-i-cal
ves'-i-cant
ves'-i-cate
ves'-i-ca-to-ry
ves'-i-cle
ve-sic'-u-lar
Ves-pa'-si:an
ves'-per
ves'-per-al
ves'-pi-ar:y†
Ves-puc'-ci
ves'-sel
Ves'-ta
ves'-tal
vest'-ed
vest-ee'
ves'-ti-ar:y†
ves-tib'-u-lar
ves'-ti-bule
ves-ti-bu-li'-tis
ves'-tige
ves-tig'-ial*†
ves-tig'-ial-ly*†

419

ves'-ti-ture
vest'-ment
ves'-try
ves'-try-man
ves'-tur-al
ves'-ture
Ve-su'-vi:an
Ve-su'-vi-us
vetch
vet'-er-an
vet-er-i-nar'-i-an†
vet'-er-i-nar:y†
ve'-to
ve'-toed
ve'-to-er
ve'-toes
ve'-to-ing
vex-a'-tion
vex-a'-tious
vex'-ed-ly
vex'-il-lar:y†
vi'a
vi-a-bil'-i-ty
vi'-a-ble
vi'a do-lo-ro'-sa*
vi'-a-duct
vi'-al
vi'-and
vi-at'-i-cum
vi-a'-tor
vi'-brac'-u-lum
vi'-bran-cy
vi'-brant
vi'-brate
vi'-bra-tile
vi'-brat-ing
vi-bra'-tion
vi-bra'-tion-al
vi-bra'-to
vi'-bra-tor
vi'-bra-to-ry
vib'-ri:o
vib'-ri-on'-ic
vib-ri-o'-sis
vi-bris'-sa
vi-brom'-e-ter
vi-bur'-num
vic'-ar
vic'-ar-age
vic'-ar=gen'-er-al
vi-car'-i-al†
vi-car'-i-ate†
vi-car'-i-ous†
vi-car'-i-ous-ly†
vice ad'-mi-ral
vice=chan'-cel-lor
vice=con'-sul

vice-ge'-rent
vic'-e-nar:y†
vi-cen'-ni-al
vice=pres'-i-den-cy
vice=pres'-i-dent
vice-re'-gal
vice'-roy
vice'-roy-al-ty
vi'ce ver'-sa
Vi'-chy
Vi'-chy-ite
vi-chys-soise'
Vi'-ci
vi'-ci-a-nin
vi'-ci-a-nose
vic'-i-nage
vic'-i-nal
vi-cin'-i-ty
vi'-cious
vi'-cious-ness
vi-cis'-si-tude
vi-cis'-si-tu'-di-nous
vi-con'-ti-el
vic'-tim
vic'-tim-ize
vic'-tor
Vic-to'-ri:a
Vic-to'-ri-an
vic-to'-ri-ous
vic'-to-ry
Vic-tro'-la
vict'-ual
vict'-ualed
vict'-ual-er
vi-cu'-na
vi-de-li-cet†
vid'-e:o
Vi-en'-na
Vi'-en-nese'
Vi-et' Nam'*
Vi-et'-nam-ese'*
view'-point
vi-ges'-i-mal
vig'-il
vig'-i-lance
vig'-i-lant
vig-i-lan'-te
vig-i-lan'-tism
vi-gnette'
vi-gnet'-ter†
vig'-or
vig'-or-ous
vi'-king
vi-la-'yet
vile'-ly
vile'-ness
vil-i-fi-ca'-tion

vil'-i-fi-er
vil'-i-fy
vil'-i-fy-ing
vil'-i-pend
vil'-la
vil'-lage
vil'-lag-er
vil'-lain
vil'-lain-ous
vil'-lain:y
vil-la-nel'-la
vil-la-nelle'
vil-lat'-ic
vil'-lein
vil'-li
vil'-li-form
vil-los'-i-ty
vil'-lus
Vil'-na
vi-min'-e-ous
vi'-na
vi-na'-ceous
vin-ai-grette'
vi-nasse'
Vin-cennes'
Vin'-cent
vin-ci-bil'-i-ty
vin'-ci-ble
vin'-cu-lum
vin'-di-ca-ble
vin-di-ca'-tion
vin'-di-ca-tive*
vin'-di-ca-tor
vin'-di-ca-to-ry
vin-dic'-tive
vin-dic'-tive-ly
vin'-e-gar
vin'-e-gar:y
vin'-er:y
vine'-yard
vi'-nic
vin'i-cul'-tur-al
vi-nif'-er:a
vin-i-fi-ca'-tion
vin-ol'-o-gy
vin-om'-e-ter†
vi-nos'-i-ty
vi'-nous
vin'-tage
vin'-tag-er
vint'-ner
vin'y
vi'-nyl
vi'-nyl-a'-tion
vi'-nyl-ene
vi-nyl'-i-dene

Vi'-nyl-ite
vi-nyl'-o-gous
Vin'-yon
vi'-ol
vi-o'-la
vi'-ol-a:ble†
vi'-o-la'-ceous
vi-o-lan'-throne
vi'-o-late
vi-o-la'-tion
vi'-o-la-tive
vi'-o-la-tor
vi'-o-lence
vi'-o-lent
vi'-o-les'-cent
vi'-o-let
vi-o-lin'
vi-o-lin'-ist
vi-o-lon-cel'-list
vi-o-lon-cel'-lo
vi-o-lo'-ne*
vi'-o-lu'-ric
vi-os'-ter-ol
vi'-per
vi'-per-ous
vi-ra'-go
vi'-ral
vi-re'-mi:a
vir'-e:o
vi-res'-cence
vi-res'-cent
Vir'-gil
vir'-gin
vir'-gin-al†
Vir-gin'-ia†
Vir-gin'-ian*†
vir-gin'-i-ty
vir-gin'-i-um
vir'-gule
vir'-i-al
vi'-ri-ci'-dal
vir'-i-des'-cent
vi-rid'-i-ty
vir'-ile
vir'-il-ism*†
vi-ril'-i-ty
vi-rol'-o-gy
vi-ro'-sis
vir-tu'
vir'-tu-al
vir-tu-al'-i-ty
vir'-tue
vir-tu-os'-i-ty
vir-tu-o'-so
vir'-tu-ous
vir'-u-lence
vir'-u-lent

vi'-rus
vi'-sa
vis'-age
vis'-aged
vis'=a=vis'
vis'-cer:a
vis'-cer-al
vis'-cid
vis-cid'-i-ty
vis'-cin
Vis'-co-liz-er
vis-com'-e-ter
vis'-co-scope
vis'-cose
vis-co-sim'-e-ter
vis-cos'-i-ty
vis'-count
vis'-count-ess
vis'-cous
vi'-sé
Vish'-nu
vis-i-bil'-i-ty
vis'-i-ble
Vis'-i-goth
vi'-sion
vi'-sion-ar:y†
vi'-sioned
vis'-it
vis'-i-tant*
vis-i-ta'-tion*
vis'-i-tor
vi'-sor†
vis'-ta
Vis'-tu-la
vi'-su-al*†
vis-u-al'-i-ty
vi-su-al-i:za'-tion*†
vi'-su-al-ize*†
vi'-su-al-iz-er*†
vi'-su-al-ly*†
vi-ta'-ceous
vi'-tal
vi-tal'-i-ty
vi-tal-i:za'-tion
vi'-tal-ize
vi'-ta-min
vi-ta-min-ol'-o-gy
vi'-ta-scope
vi-tel'-lin
vi'-ti-ate
vi'-ti-at-ed
vi-ti-a'-tion
vi'-ti-a-tor
vit'i-cul-ture
vit'i-cul'-tur-ist
vit-i-li'-go
vit'-rain
vit-re-os'-i-ty

vit'-re-ous
vi-tres'-cence
vi-tres'-cent
vi-tres'-ci-ble
vit'-ri-fi-a:ble
vit-ri-fi-ca'-tion
vit'-ri-form
vit'-ri-fy
vit'-ri-ol
vit'-ri-o-lat-ed
vit-ri-ol'-ic
vit-ri-os'-i-ty
vit'-u-line
vi-tu'-per-ate
vi-tu'-per-a'-tion
vi-tu'-per-a-tive
vi'-va
vi-va'-cious
vi-va'-cious-ly
vi-vac'-i-ty
vi'-van-dier'
vi-vant'
vi-var'-i-um†
vi'-va vo'-ce
Viv'-i-an
viv'-id
vi-vid'-i-ty
viv'-id-ly
viv'-id-ness
viv-i-fi-ca'-tion
viv'-i-fied
viv'-i-fy
viv:i-par'-i-ty
vi-vip'-a-rous
vi-vip'-a-rous-ly
viv'-i-sect
viv'-i-sec'-tion
vix'-en
vix'-en-ish
viz'-ard
vi-zier'
vizs'-la
Vlad'-i-vos-tok'†
vo'-ca-ble
vo-cab'-u-lar:y†
vo'-cal
vo'-cal-ist
vo-cal-i:za'-tion
vo'-cal-ize
vo'-cal-iz-er
vo-ca'-tion
vo-ca'-tion-al
voc'-a-tive
voc'-a-tive-ly
vo-cif'-er-ant
vo-cif'-er-ate
vo-cif-er-a'-tion
vo-cif'-er-ous

vo-cif'-er-ous-ly
vo-cod'-er
vod'-ka
vogue
voice'-less
voic'-ing
void'-a:ble
voile
vo'-lant
vo'-lar
vol'-a-tile
vol-a-til'-i-ty
vol-a-til-i:za'-tion
vol'-a-til-ize
vol-can'-ic
vol-ca'-no
vol-ca'-noes
vol'-ca-nol'-o-gy*†
vo-lem'-i-tol
Vol'-ga
Vol'-go-grad
vol-i-ta'-tion
vo-li'-tion
vol'-i-tive
vol'-ley
vol'-ley-ball
vol'-plane
vol'-plan-ist
Vol'-stead-ism
Vol'-ta
volt'-age
vol-ta'-ic
vol-tam'-e-ter†
vol'-ta-met'-ric†
volt'=am'-me-ter
volt'-me-ter
vol-u-bil'-i-ty
vol'-u-ble
vol'-ume
vol-u-me-nom'-e-ter
vo-lu'-me-ter
vol'-u-met'-ric
vo-lu-mi-nos'-i-ty
vo-lu'-mi-nous
vol'-un-tar'-i-ly†
vol'-un-ta-rism
vol'-un-tar:y†
vol'-un-tar:y-ism†
vol'-un-teer'
vol'-un-teered
vo-lup'-tu-ar:y†
vo-lup'-tu-ous
vo-lup'-tu-ous-ly
vo-lup'-tu-ous-ness
vo-lute'
vol'-u-tin
vo-lu'-tion

vol'-vu-lus
vo'-mer
vo'mer-ine
vom'-i-ca
vom'-i-cine
vom'-it
vom'-it-er
vom'-i-to-ry
vom'-i-tus
voo'-doo
voo'-doo-ism
vo-ra'-cious
vo-rac'-i-ty
vo-ra'-go
vor'-tex
vor'-ti-cal-ly
vor-ti-cel'-la
vor'-ti-ces
vor-tic'-i-ty
vor-tig'-i-nous
Vosges
vot'-a:ble
vo'-ta-ress
vo'-ta-rist
vo'-ta-ry
vot'-er
vot'-ing
vo'-tive
vouch'-er
vouch-safe'
vow'-el
vox po'-pu-li
voy'-age
voy'-ag-er
voy'-a-geur'*
v=shaped
Vul'-can
Vul-ca'-ni-an
Vul'-can-ite
vul-can-i:za'-tion
vul'-can-ize
vul'-can-iz-er
vul'-gar
vul-gar'-i-an†
vul'-gar-ism
vul-gar'-i-ty
vul-gar-i:za'-tion
vul'-gar-ize
vul'-gar-ly
Vul'-gate
vul-ner-a-bil'-i-ty
vul'-ner-a-ble
vul'-ner-ar:y†
vul'-pine
vul-pin'-ic
vul'-pi-nite
vul'-ture
vul'-tur-ous

423

vul'-va
vul'-var
vul-vi'-tis
vy'-ing

W

Wa'-bash
wab'-ble
wa-be'-no
wack'y
wad'-ding
wad'-dle
wad'-dled
wad'-dling
wad'-er
wad'-ing
wa'-fer
waf'-fle
waft'-age
waft'-er
wage earn'-er
wag'-er (one who wages)
wa'-ger (a bet)
wag'-est†
wage'-work-er
wag'-gish
wag'-gle
wag'-gling
wag'-ing
Wag'-ner
Wag-ne'-ri-an
Wag'-ner-ism
wag'-on
wag'-on-er
wag'-on-ette'
wag'-on-load
wag'-tail
waif
Wai-ki-ki'
wail'-ing
wain'-scot
wain'-scot-ing
wain'-wright
waist'-band
waist'-coat
waist'-line
wait'-er
wait'-ing room
wait'-ress
waive
waiv'-er
wake'-ful
wake'-ful-ness
wak'-en
wak'-en-er
wak'-en-ing
Wa-la'-chi-an

Wal'-den
Wal'-den'-si-an
Wal'-do
Wal'-dorf
walk-a:way
walk'-er
walk'-ie=talk'-le
walk'-ing
walk'-out (n.)
walk'=up (n., adj.)
wal'-la-by
Wal'-lace
Wal-la'-chi:a
wall'-board
Wal'-len-stein
Wal'-ler
wal'-let
wall'-eyed
wall'-flow-er
Wal-loon'
wal'-lop
wal'-lop-er
wal'-lop-ing
wal'-low
wall'-pa-per
wal'-nut
Wal'-pole
wal'-rus
Wal'-ter
Wal'-tham
Wal'-ton
waltz
waltz'-er
wam'-pum
wan'-der
wan'-der-er
wan'-der-ing
wan'-der-lust
wan'-gle
wan'-gled
wan'-gling
wan'-ing
wan'-ly
wan'-ness
want'-ing
wan'-ton
wan'-ton-ly
wan'-ton-ness
wap'-en-take
wap'-i-ti
war'-ble
war'-bler
war'-bling
war cry
war'-den*
war'-den-ship*
ward'-er
war'-der-ship*

ward'-robe
ward'-room
ward'-ship
ware'-house
ware'-room
war'-fare
war'-fa-rin
war'-i-ly†
war'-i-ness†
war'-like
war'-lock
warm'-er
warm'-heart-ed
war'-mon:ger
warmth
warn'-er
warn'-ing
warp
warp'-age
war'-path
warp'-ing
war'-ra-gal
war'-rant
war'-rant-ee'†
war'-rant-er
war'-ran-tor'
war'-ran-ty
war'-ren
war'-rior*
War'-saw
war'-ship
war'-time
wart'y
War'-wick
war'y†
wash'-a:ble
wash'-ba-sin
wash'-board
wash'-bowl
wash'-cloth
washed=out
wash'-er
wash'-er-wom-an†
wash'-ing
Wash'-ing-ton
Wash'-ing-to'-ni-an
wash'-out (n.)
wash'-room
wash'-stand
wash'-tub
wasp'-ish
was'-sail
was'-sail-er
Was'-ser-mann
wast'-age
waste'-bas-ket
waste'-ful
waste'-land

waste'-pa-per
wast'-er
wast'-ing
was'-trel*†
watch'-case
watch'-dog
watch'-er
watch'-ful
watch'-ful-ness
watch'-mak-er
watch'-man
watch'-tow-er
watch'-word
wa'-ter
wa'-ter bug
Wa'-ter-bur:y
wa'-ter clock
wa'-ter-col-or
wa'-ter-course
wa'-ter-cress
wa'-ter-fall
wa'-ter-fowl
wa'-ter-front
wa'-ter gap
wa'-ter gas
wa'-ter-glass
wa'-ter lev-el
wa'-ter lil:y
wa'-ter-line
wa'-ter-log
wa'-ter-logged
Wa'-ter-loo'
wa'-ter main
wa'-ter-man
wa'-ter-mark
wa'-ter-mel-on
wa'-ter me-ter
wa'-ter mill
wa'-ter pipe
wa'-ter po-lo
wa'-ter-pow-er
wa'-ter-proof
wa'-ter rat
wa'-ter-shed
wa'-ter-side
wa'-ter snake
wa'-ter-spout
wa'-ter ta-ble
wa'-ter-tight
wa'-ter tow-er
wa'-ter wag-on
wa'-ter-way
wa'-ter-wheel
wa'-ter-works
wa'-ter:y
watt'-age†
Wat-teau'
wat'-tle

425

watt'-me-ter
Wau-ke'-gan
Wau'-sau
wave'-length
wave'-let
wave'-me-ter
wav'-er (one who waves)
wa'-ver (to vacillate)
wa'-ver-er
wa'-ver-ing
wa'-ver-ing-ly
Wa'-ver-ley
wav'-i-est
wav'-ing
wav'y
wax'-en
wax'-i-est
wax'-i-ness
wax'-ing
wax pa-per
wax'-works
wax'y
way'-bill
way'-far-er
way'-far-ing
way'-laid
way'-lay
way'-side
way'-ward
way'-worn
wayz'-goose
wa-zir'
weak
weak'-en
weak'-ened
weak'-fish
weak'-ling
weak'=mind-ed
weak'-ness
wealth
wealth'-i-er
wealth'y
wean'-er
weap'-on
weap'-on-eer'
wear-a:ble
wear'-er
wea'-ri-ful
wea'-ri-less
wea'-ri-ly
wea'-ri-ness
wear'-ing
wea'-ri-some
wea'-ri-some-ly
wea'-ry
wea'-sand
wea'-sel
wea'-seled

weath'-er
weath'-er=beat-en
weath'-er-board
weath'-er-cock
weath'-ered
weath'-er-ing
weath'-er-man
Weath'-er-Om'-e-ter
weath'-er-proof
weath'-er=strip (v.)
weath'-er vane
weave
weav'-er
weav'-er-bird
weav'-ing
webbed
web'-bing
We'-ber
web'=foot-ed
Web'-ster
Web-ste'-ri-an
Wechs'-ler
wed'-ded
wed'-ding
wedge=shaped
Wedg'-ies
wedg'-ing
Wedg'-wood
wed'-lock
Wednes'-day
weed'-er
weed'y
week
week'-day
week'-end
week'-ly
weep'-er
weep'-ing
wee'-vil
wee'-viled
wei-ge'-la
weigh
weight
weight'-i-ness
Weight-om'-e-ter
weight'y
Wei'-mar
Wei'-mar-an-er
weir
weird
weird'-ly
weird'-ness
wel'-come
weld'-er
wel'-fare
wel'-kin
well=bal'-anced
well=be-haved'

well'=be'-ing
well'-born
well'-bred'
Wel'-ling-ton
well'=known'
well'=nigh'
wells'-ite
well'-spring
well'=to=do'
well'=trained'
welsh'-er
Welsh'-man
wel'-ter (wallow)
welt'-er (makes welts)
wel'-ter-weight
Wen'-ces-laus
wend'-ing
were'-wolf
Wes'-ley
Wes'-ley-an
Wes'-sex
West Ches'-ter
West'-ches-ter
west'-er
west'-er-ly
west'-ern
west'-ern-er
West In'-dies
West'-ing-house
West'-min-ster
West'-more-land (U.S.)
West'-mor-land (Can., Brit.)
West-pha'-lia*†
West-pha'-lian*†
West Vir-gin'-ia†
west'-ward
wet'-back
weth'-er
wet'-ness
wet'-ting
Wey'-mouth
whack'-ing
whale'-back
whale'-boat
whale'-bone
whal'-er
whal'-er:y
whal'-ing
wharf
wharf'-age
wharf'-in-ger
Whar'-ton
wharves
what-ev'-er
what'-not
what-so-ev-er
wheal

wheat'-en
whee'-dle
whee'-dled
wheel'-bar-row
wheel'-base
wheeled
wheel'-er
wheel'-horse
wheel'-house
Wheel'-ing
wheel'-wright
wheeze
wheez'-i-ly
wheez'-i-ness
wheez'-ing-ly
wheez'y
whelp
when'-as'
whence
when-ev'-er
when-so-ev'-er
where'-a:bouts
where'-as'
where'-at'
where'-by'
where'-fore'
where'-in'
where'-of'
where-so-ev'-er
where-up:on'
wher-ev'-er
where'-with'
where'-with-al
wher'-ry
wher'-ry-man
weth'-er
whet'-stone
whet'-ting
whey
whey'=faced
which-ev'-er
which'-so-ev'-er
whif'-fen-poof
whif'-fet
whif'-fle
whif'-fle-tree
while
whi'-lom
whim'-per
whim'-pered
whim'-per-ing
whim'-si-cal
whim-si-cal'-i-ty
whim'-sy
whin'-chat
whined
whin'-ing
whin'-ing-ly

whin'-nied
whin'-ny
whip'-cord
whip hand
whip'-lash
whip'-per-snap-per
whip'-pet
whip'-ping
whip'-poor-will
whip'-saw
whip'-stitch
whirl'-er
whirl'-i-gig
whirl'-pool
whirl'-wind
whirl'y-bird
whir'-ring
whisk'-er
whisk'-ered
whis'-key
whis'-kies
whis'-ky
whis'-per
whis'-pered
whis'-per-ing
whist
whis'-tle
whis'-tler
Whis-tle'-ri-an
whis'-tling
white'-bait
white'-cap
white'=col'-lar (adj.)
white'-fish
White'-hall
white=hot
white lead
white'-ly
whit'-en
white'-ness
whit'-en-ing
white'-wall
white'-wash
white wa'-ter
white'-wood
whith'-er
whit'-ing
whit'-ish
whit'-low
Whit'-man
Whit'-sun-day
Whit'-ti-er
whit'-tle
whit'-tled
whit'-tling
whiz'-zer
who-dun'-it
who-ev'-er

whole'-heart-ed
whole'-sale
whole'-sal-er
whole'-some
whole wheat
whol'-ly
whom-so-ev'-er
whoop
whoop'-ee
whoop'-ing
whoop'-ing cough
whop'-per
whop'-ping
whore
whorl
whor'-tle-ber-ry
who-so-ev'-er
Wich'-i-ta
wick'-ed
wick'-ed-ly
wick'-ed-ness
wick'-er
wick'-ered
wick'-er-work
wick'-et
wick'-i-up
wide'=eyed
wid'-en
wide'-spread
wid'-geon*†
wid'-get
wid'-ow
wid'-ow-er
wid'-ow-hood
width
wield
wield'-er
wield'y
wie'-ner
wie'-ner schnit'-zel
wie'-ner-wurst
Wies'-ba-den
wie'-sen-bo-den
wife
wife'-hood
wife'-ly
wigged
wig'-gle
wig'-gling
wig'-gly
wig'-wag
wig'-wam
Wil'-ber-force
wild'-cat
Wilde
wil'-de-beest†
Wil'-der (writer)
wild'-er (adj.)

428

wil'-der-ness
wild'=eyed
wild'-fire
wild'-fowl
wild'-ness
wild'-wood
Wil'-fred
wil'-ful
W:l'-helm
Wil'-helms-ha-ven
Wil'-helm-stras'-se
wil'-i-ly†
wil'-i-ness†
Wilkes=Bar'-re
Wil-lam-ette†
wil-lem-ite†
will'-ful
will'-ful-ly
will'-ful-ness
Wil'-liam
Wil'-liams-burg
will'-ing
will'-ing-ness
will'=o'=the=wisp
wil'-low
wil'-low:y
wil'-ly=nil'-ly
Wil'-ming-ton
Wil'-son
Wil'-ton
wil'y†
wim'-ble
wim'-ple
wince
Win'-ches-ter
winc'-ing
wind'-age
wind'-bag
wind'-blown
wind'-break
wind'-break-er
wind'-ed
wind'-er
Win'-der-mere
wind'-fall
wind'-flow-er
wind'-i-er
wind'-i-ness
wind'-ing
wind'-ing=sheet
wind'-jam-mer
wind'-lass
win'-dle
wind'-less
win'-dle-straw
wind'-mill
win'-dow
win'-dow-pane

win'-dow=shop-ping
win'-dow-sill
wind'-pipe
wind'-row
wind'-shield
Wind'-sor
wind'-storm
wind'-up (n.)
wind up (v.)
wind'-ward
wind'y
wine cel'-lar
wine'-glass
wine'-grow-er
wine'-press
win'-er:y
Wine'-sap
wine'-skin
winged
wing'-ed (poetic)
wing'-ed-ly
wing'-less
wing'-spread
wink'-ing
win'-kle
Win-ne-ba'-go
win'-ner
win'-ning
Win'-ni-peg
win'-now
win'-now-er
win'-now-ing=fan
Wins'-low
win'-some
win'-some-ness
Win'-ston=Sa'-lem
win'-ter
win'-ter-green
win'-ter-ize
win'-ter-time
Win'-throp
win'-try
win'y
wip'-er
wip'-ing
wire'-less
wire'-pho-to
wire'=pull-ing
wir'-er
wire'-weed
wir'-i-ness
wir'-ing
wir'y
Wis-con'-sin
Wis-con'-sin-ite
wis'-dom
wise'-a:cre
wise'-crack

wise'-ly
wis'-est
wish'-bone
wish'-ful
wish'y=wash:y
wisp'y
wis-tar'-i:a*†
Wis-te'-ri:a
wist'-ful
wist'-ful-ly
wi'-tan*†
witch'-craft
witch'-er:y
witch ha-zel
witch'-ing
wi'-te-na-ge-mot'*†
with-al'
with-draw'
with-draw'-al
with-drawn'
with-drew'
with'-er
with'-ered
with'-er-ing
with-held'
with-hold'
with-hold'-ing
with-in'
with-out'
with-stand'
with-stand'-ing
with'y
wit'-less
wit'-ness
wit'-ti-cism
wit'-ti-ly
wit'-ting-ly
wit'-ty
wiz'-ard
wiz'-ard-ry
wiz'-ened
woad
wob'-ble
wob'-bly
wob'-bu-la-tor
Wo'-den
woe'-be-gone
woe'-ful
woe'-ful-ness
wolf
Wolfe
Wolff'-i:an
wolf'-hound
wolf'-ish
wolf'-ish-ly
wolf'-ram
wolf-ra-min'-i-um
wolf'-ram-ite

wol'-las-ton-ite
Wol'-sey
wol'-ver-ine'
wolves
wom'-an†
wom'-an-hood†
wom'-an-ish†
wom'-an-kind†
wom'-an-like†
wom'-an-ly†
womb
wom'-bat
wom'-en†
wom'-en-folk†
won'-der
won'-dered
won'-der-ful
won'-der-land
won'-der-ment
won'-der=work-er
won'-drous
won'-drous-ly
wont (custom)
won't (will not)
wont'-ed
wood'-bine
wood'-chuck
wood'-cock
wood'-craft
wood'-cut
wood'-cut-ter
wood'-ed
wood'-en
wood'-en-ware
wood'-i-er
wood'-land
wood'-lot
wood'-man
wood'-peck-er
wood'-pile
wood pulp
wood'-ruff
wood'-shed
woods'-man
Wood'-stock
woods'y
wood'-work
wood'y
woo'-er
woof
woof'-er
wool'-en
wool'-gath-er-ing (n.)
wool'-li-ness
wool'-ly
wool'-sack
Wool'-worth
Woos'-ter

Worces'-ter
word'-age
word'-i-est
word'-i-ly
word'-ing
word'-less
word'-ster
Words'-worth
word'y
work-a:bil'-i-ty
work-a:ble
work'-a-day
work'-bas-ket
work'-bench
work'-book
work'-box
work'-day
work'-er
work'-horse
work'-house
work'-ing
work'-ing-man
work'-man
work'-man-like
work'-man-ship
work'-men
work'-out (n., adj.)
work'-room
work'-shop
work'-ta-ble
work'-week
world'-li-ness
world'-ling
world'-ly
world'-ly=wise
world'-wide'
worm'=eat-en
worm'-hole
worm'-wood
worm'y
worn=out
wor'-ried
wor'-ri-ment
wor'-ri-some
wor'-ry
wor'-ry-ing
wors'-en
wor'-ship
wor'-shiped
wor'-ship-er
wor'-ship-ful
wor'-ship-ing
worst'-ed (v.)
wor'-sted† (yarn)
wor'-thi-ly
wor'-thi-ness
worth'-less
worth'-while'

wor'-thy
would
wound
wound'-ed
wo'-ven†
wrack
wraith
Wran-gell'
wran'-gle
wran'-gler
wran'-gling
wrap'-per
wrap'-ping
wrath'-ful
wrath'-i-ly
wreak
wreath
wreathe
wreath'-ing
wreck
wreck'-age
wreck'-er
wrench
wrest
wres'-tle
wres'-tler
wres'-tling
wretch
wretch'-ed
wretch'-ed-ness
wrig'-gle
wrig'-gler
wrig'-gly
wright
wring'-er
wring'-ing
wrin'-kle
wrin'-kled
wrin'-kling
wrin'-kly
wrist
wrist'-band
wrist'-let
wrist'-lock
wrist pin
wrist'-watch
write'=off (n.)
writ'-er
write'=up (n.)
writhe
writhed
writh'-er
writh'-ing
writ'-ing
writ'-ten
wrong
wrong'-do-er
wrong'-do-ing

431

wrong'-ful
wrong'-ly
wroth
wrought
wrought i:ron
wry'-ly
Wurt'-tem-berg
Wy'-an-dotte
Wyc'-liffe
Wyc'-liff-ite*
Wy'-lie
Wy-o'-ming
Wy-o'-ming-ite

X

xan'-tha-mide*†
xan'-thate
xan'-thene
xan'-the-nyl
xan'-thine
Xan-thip'-pe
xan'-tho-chroid†
xan'-tho-gen-ate
xan-tho'-ma
xan'-thom'a-tous
xan-thom'-e-ter
xan'-tho-phyll
xan-thop'-ter-in
xan'-thous
xan-thox-y-le'-tin
xan-thy'-drol
Xa-ve'-ri-an
Xav'-i-er
xe'-bec
xe'-ni:a
xe'-ni:al
xe-nog'-a-my
xen'o-gen'-e-sis
xen'o-ge-net'-ic
xen'o-lith
xen'o-lith'-ic
xen'o-mor'-phic
xe'non
xen:o-pho'-bi:a
xen:o-pho'-bic
Xen'-o-phon
xen'yl
xe'-ric†
xe-ro-der'-ma
xe'-ro-gel
xer'o-graph'-ic
xe-rog'-ra-phy
xe-roph'-i-lous
xe-roph-thal'-mi:a
xe'-ro-phyte
xe-ro-phyt'-ic

xe'-ro-sere
xe-ro'-sis
Xer'-xes†
xiph'-oid
xi-phop'-a-gus†
xiph'-os-u'ran*†
x ray (n.)
x=ray (v.)
xy'-lem
xy'-lene
xy'-le-nol
xy'-le-nyl
xy'-lic
xyl'i-dine*†
xy-lin'-de-in
xy'-lo-graph'-ic
xy-log'-ra-phy
xy'-loid
xy-lol'-o-gy
xy-lom'-e-ter
xy-loph'-a-gous
xy'lo-phone
xy'lo-phon-ist*
xy'-lo-side
xy-lot'-o-my
xy'-lo-yl
xy'-lu-lose
xy'-lyl-ene†
Xy'-ris
xys'-tus

Y

yacht'
yacht'-ing
yachts'-man
Yah'-weh
Yah-wis'-tic
yak
Yak'-i-ma
Yak'-u-tat*†
yam
ya'-men
Yang'-tze'
Yan'-kee
yap'-ping
Ya'-qui
yard'-age
yard'-arm
yard'-stick
yar'-row
yat'-a-ghan
yau'-pon
yaw'-ing
yawl
yaw'-me-ter
yawn
yawn'-ing-ly

Yaz'oo
year'-book
year'-ling
year'-long
year'-ly
yearn
yearn'-ing
yeast
yeast'-i-ness
yeast'y
Yed'-do
yel'-low
yel'-low-fin
yel'-low-bird
yel'-low fe'-ver
yel'-low-ish
yel'-low jack-et
Yel'-low-stone
yelp'-er
Yem'-en
Yem'-en-ite
yeo'-man
yeo'-man-ry
yes'-ter-day
yes'-ter-morn
yes'-ter-year
yet'i
yew
Ygg-dra-sil
Yid'-dish
yield
yield'-a:ble
yield'-ing
yipped
yip'-ping
yo'-del
yo'-del-er
yo'-del-ing
yo'-ga
yo'-gi
yo-him'-bine
yoke
yoke'-fel-low
yo'-kel
Yo'-ko-ha'-ma
yolk
Yom Kip'-pur
yon'-der
Yon'-kers
yore
York'-ist
York'-shire
Yo-sem'-i-te
young
young'-ber-ry
young'-ish
young'-ling

young'-ster
Youngs'-town
youn'-ker
your-self'
youth'-ful
youth'-ful-ly
Yo'=Yo
y'per-ite
yp-sil'-i-form†
yt-ter'-bi-um
yt-ter'-bous
yt-trif'-er-ous
yt'-tri-um
yt'-tro-tan'-ta-lite
Yu'-ca-tan'
yuc'-ca
Yu'-go-slav'
Yu-go-slav'-i:a†
Yu'-kon
Yule
Yule'-tide
Yun'-nan
Y:vonne'

Z

Zach-a-ri'-ah
zai-ba'-tsu
Zam-be'-si
Zam-be'-zi
za:min'-dar
za'-ni-ness
za'-ny
Zan'-zi-bar'
za-pa-te-a'-do
zar'a-tite*†
za-re'-ba
Zea'-land
zeal'-ot
zea-lot'-i-cal
zeal'-ot-ry
zeal'-ous
ze-a-xan'-thin
Zeb'-e-dee
ze'-bra
ze'-bu
Zech-a-ri'-ah
ze-na'-na
ze'-nith
Ze'-no
ze-nog'-ra-phy
ze'-o-lite
ze-ol'-i-tize
zeph'-yr
zeph'-yr-e'-an
Zep'-pe-lin
ze'-ro

433

ze′-roes
ze′-ro-ize
ze′-ros
zest
zest′-ful
zest′-ful-ly
ze′-ta
Zeus
zib′-el-ine†
zig′-gu-rat
zig′-zag
zig′-zag-ging
zinc
zinc′-ate
zinc′-ic
zinc-if′-er-ous
zinc′-i-fy
zincked
zinck′y
zin′-co-graph
zin-cog′-ra-phy
zinc′-oid
zinc′-ous
Zin′-fan-del
zin′-ger-one
zin′-gi-ber-ene
zin′-ni:a
Zi′-on
Zi′-on-ism
Zi′-on-ist
zip′-per
zip′-py
zirc′-ite
zir′-con
zir′-con-ate
zir-co′-ni-um
zir′-co-nyl
zith′-er
Ziz′-i-phus
zlo′-ty
zo-an′-thro-py
zo′-di-ac
zo-di′-a-cal
Zo-is′-i:a
zois-it-i:za′-tion†
Zo′-la
Zoll′-ver-ein
zom′-bi
zon′-al†
zo′-na-ry*
zon′-ate†
zo-na′-tion
zoned
zo-nif′-er-ous
zon′-ing
zo-og′-a-my
zo′-o-gen′-ic

zo′-o-ge′-o-graph′-ic
zo′-o-ge-og′-ra-phy
zo-o-gle′a
zo-og′-ra-pher
zo-og′-ra-phy
zo-ol′-a-ter
zo-o-log′-i-cal
zo-ol′-o-gist
zo-ol′-o-gy
zo-om′-e-ter
zo′-o-mor′-phic
zo-on′-o-sis
zo-o-phil′-i:a
zo-oph′-o-rus
zo′-o-phyte
zo-os′-co-py
zo′-o-sperm
zo′-o-sper-mat′-ic
zo′o-spo-ran′-gi-um
zo′-o-spore
zo-os′-ter-ol
zo-ot′-o-my
Zo′-ro-as-ter
Zo′-ro-as′-tri-an
Zou-ave′
Zo-ys′-i:a
zuc-chet′-to
zuc-chi′-ni
Zu′-lu
zu-mat′-ic
Zu′-ñi
zun′-yite
Zu′-rich
zwie-back
Zwing′-li
Zwing′-li-an-ism
zwit′-ter-i′on
zyg-a-de′-nine
zy′-gal
zy′-go-dac′-tyl
zy′-go-mat′-ic
zy′-gote
zy-got′-ic
zy′-mase
zy′-min
zy′-mo-gen
zy′-mo-gen′-ic
zy-mog′-e-nous
zy-mo-hy-drol′-y-sis
zy-mol′-o-gy
zy-mom′-e-ter
zy′-mo-plas′-tic
zy-mo′-sis
zy-mos′-ter-ol
zy′-mos-then′-ic
zy-mot′-ic
zy′-mur-gy

Appendix of Variants

*indicates alternate word division according to *Webster's New International Dictionary, Second Edition*

†indicates alternate word division according to Funk & Wagnalls *New Standard Dictionary of the English Language*

*†Aar′-on
*ab′a
*a:ba-ca′
†a:bat-toir′
†a:bi′-dance
*†ab-i-o-gen′-e-sis
*†ab-i-o-ge-net′-ic
*†ab-i-og′-e-nist
*ab-ju′-ra-to-ry
*ab-lu′-tion-a-ry
*†a:bor′-tive
*†ab-ra′-dant
*†ab-rad′-ed
*†ab-rad′-ing
*ab-ra-si-om′-e-ter
*†ab-ra′-sion
*†ab-ra′-sive
*ab-sor′-bent
†a:bys′-sal
*†a:cad-e-mi′-cian
*ac-au-les′-cent
†ac-ce′-dence
*ac-cel-er-an′-do
†ac-cep′-tance
*ac-cli′-ma-ta-ble
*ac-cu′-sa-to-ry
*†ac′-e-rate
*†ac′-e-rose
*†ac′-e-rous
*†ac′-er-vate
*†ac-et-am′-ide
*†a:cet′-i-fy
*†ac′-e-tous
*†ac′-e-tyl
*†ac′-e-tyl-ac′-e-tone
*ac-e-tyl-a′-tion
†A:cha′-ia
†Ach′-e-ron
*†ach-la-myd′-e-ous
*†ac-i-di-met′-ric
†ac-quain′-tance
†ac-quain′-tance-ship
*ac′-ryl-yl
*†ac′-tin-ism
*ac-tu-a′-ri-al
†ac′-tu-a-ries
†ac′-tu-a-ry
†a:cyc′-lic
*†ac′-y-late
*a:dap′-tive
†Ad′-dis A′ba-ba
†ad-du′-ci-ble
†ad-i-a-ther′-man-cy
*†ad in′-te-rim
†a:di-os′
†ad-ju′-ra-to-ry
†ad-jur′-or

*†A:do′-nis
*Ad-ren′-al-in
†Ad-re′-nal-in
*A:dri-an-o′-ple
†Ad-ri-a-no′-ple
†ad-u-la′-ri:a
*ad-ven′-ience
*†ad-ver′-bi-al
†ad′-ver-sa-ries
†ad′-ver-sa-ry
*†ad-ver′-tence
*ad-ver′-tent
*†ad-ver′-tent-ly
*†ad-vi′-so-ry
†ad′-vo-ca-to-ry
*†ad-y-na′-mi:a
*ad-y-nam′-ic
*†a:e′-ri-al
*†a:e′-ri-al-ist
*†a′er-ie
†a:fe′-brile
*†af-flic′-tive
*†af-for-est-a′-tion
*†af-fron′-tive
*aft′-er-
*aft′-er-birth
*aft′-er-burn-er
*aft′-er-care
*aft′-er-deck
*aft′-er-ef-fect
*aft′-er-glow
*aft′-er-life
*aft′-er-math
*aft-er-noon′
*aft′-er-taste
*aft′-er-thought
*aft′-er-ward
*aft′-er-wards
*ag′-a-ma
*†ag-a-mo-gen′-e-sis
*ag′-a-pe
*†a:gar′-ic
†ag′-a-tize
*†a:ger′-a-tum
†A:gin-court′
*†ag′-i-o-tage
†a:gra′-ri-an
†ag-ron′-o-mist
†ag-ron′-o-my
*ai′-ler-on
*†Al-a-ba′-ma
†A′la-mo
*al-bu′-men-ize
*al-bu′-min-ize
*†al-bu-mi-nu′-ri:a
*†al-bu-mi-nu′-ric
*al-caz′-ar
†al′-de-hy-dase

437

*†a:leu'-rone
*†Al'-e-ut
†Al-e-u'-tian
*†a:li-un'-de
†al-i-vin'-cu-lar
†al-ka-loi'-dal
†al'-ky-lene
†al'-ky-lize
†Al-le-ghen'-i-an
†Al'-le-ghen-ies
†Al'-le-ghen:y
†al'-lyl-am-ine
*†al'-mon-er
†al-ti-tu-di-na'-ri-an
*a:mal'-gam-ate
*a:mal-gam-a'-tion
*a:mal'-gam-a-tor
†am-bro'-sial
†am-bro'-sian
*†am-bu-la'-crum
†am-bur'-bi-al
*A:mel'-ia
*a:mel'-io-ra-ble
*a:mel'-io-rate
*a:mel'-io-ra'-tion
*a:mel'-io-ra-tive
*a:mel'-io-ra-tor
*†A:mer-i-ca'-na
†a:mid'-o-gen
†am'-ine
†am'-i-no
†am'-i-no ac'-id
†am'-i-no-ben-zo'-ic
†am'-i-to'-sis
*†am-i-tot'-ic
†am'-mon-ite
†am-ne'-si:a
*†a:mor-ti-za'-tion
*†a:mor'-tize
*†a:mor'-tiz-ing
*Am-oy-ese'
†am'-pli-fi-ca-to-ry
*†a:mu'-sive
†am'-y-lene
*am'-yl-ose
†an-a-er-ob'-ic
*†an'-arch-ism
*†an'-arch-ist
†an-arch-is'-tic
*an'-arch:y
†an-a-stig'-mat
*†an-as-tig-mat'-ic
†an'-cil-la-ry
*†an-cy-los-to-mi'-a-sis
*an'-des-ite
*†an-ec-do-tal
†an'-e-roid

*†an-es'-the-tist
*†an-es'-the-tize
*†An'-na-mese'
*a'no-rak
*An-ta'-res
†an-te-ce'-dence
†an-te-ce'-den-cy
†an-te-ce'-dent
*an-thel-min'-tic
*†an-thro-po-mor'-phic
†an'-ti-do-tal
†an'-tim'-e-rism
*an-ti-mo'-nic
†an-tiph'-o-na-ry
†an-ti-qua'-ri-an
†an'-ti-qua-ry
*†an-tit'-ra-gus
†a:nu'-rous
*†a:pé-ri-tif'
†a:pet'-a-lous
†a:phe'-li-on
*†a:phe-li-ot'-ro-pism
†aph'-id
†aph-lo-gis'-tic
†a:pi-a'-ri-an
†a'pi-a-ry
*A:pol-li-na'-ris
*†a:poph'-yl-lite
†a:poth'-e-ca-ries
†a:poth'-e-ca-ry
†ap-o-the'-o-sis
*a:poth'-e-o-size
*†Ap'-pa-lach'-i-an
†ap-pa-ra'-tus
†ap-pen'-dage
†ap-pen'-daged
†ap-pen'-dant
*†ap'-pe-ti-tive
†ap-plau'-sive
*ap-point-ee'
*ap-poin'-tive
*†ap-pre'-ci-a-ble
*†ap-pre'-ci-a-tive
*†ap-pre'-ci-a-tive-ly
*†ap-pre'-ci-a-to-ry
†ap-y-ret'-ic
†a'qua
†a:qua-ma-rine'
†a'qua-plane
†a:qua'-ri-um
†A:qua'-ri-us
†a'qua-tint
†Ar'-a-bist
†ar'-bi-tra-ri-ly
†ar'-bi-tra-ry
*†ar'-bor-ize
†ar'-che-ty-pal
*†a're:a

*†a're-al
*†a're-a-way
*†ar'-e-ca
*†A:re-op'-a-gus
†A:ri-ad'-ne
†A'ri-an
†A'ri-el
*†ar'-i-ose
†ar-is-to-crat'-ic
†ar-is-to-crat'-i-cal-ly
†ar'-mil-la-ry
*ar'-mor:y
†ar-ri'-val
†ar-ro'-yo
†ars-phen-am'-ine
*†art'-ist-ry
†As'-bur:y
†as-cen'-dan-cy
†as-cen'-dant
*†as-cos'-po-rous
†a:scribe'
†a:scrib'-ing
†a:scrip'-tion
†Ash'-ur
†asp'-en
*†as-pir'-ant
†as-sert'-or
†as-sis'-tance
†as-sis'-tant
†a:ston'-ish
†a:ston'-ished
†a:ston'-ish-ing
†a:ston'-ish-ing-ly
†a:ston'-ish-ment
†a:stound'
†a:stound'-ed
†a:stound'-ing
†a:stound'-ing-ly
†as'-ym-ptote
*†a:tav'-ic
†at'-el-ier
†ath'-el-ing
*†at'-mos-phere
*†at-mos-pher'-ic
*†at-mos-pher'-i-cal
*†at-mos-pher'-i-cal-ly
†a:toll'
†at-om-ic'-i-ty
†at'-om:y
†at-ten'-dance
†at-ten'-dant
†at-tes'-tant
†at-trac'-tant
*†at-trac'-tive
*†at-trac'-tive-ly
†at-trac'-tive-ness
†at-trib'-u-ta-ble
*aug-ment'-a-tive

*†au-ro'-ra bo-re-a'-lis
*†Aus-tral-a'-sia
*†Aus-tral-a'-sian
*Aus-tral'-ia
*Aus-tral'-ian
*au'-tarch:y
†au-thor-i-ta'-ri-an
*†au-thor-i-za'-**tion**
*†au'-thor-ize
*†au'-thor-ized
*†au'-thor-iz-ing
†au-tot'-y-py
*a'vi-ar-ist
†a'vi-a-ry
*†awn'-ing
†ax'-il-la-ry
†Az-o-to-bac'-ter
*†az'-u-rite

†bab-oon'
†bac'-il-la-ry
*bac'-ter-oid
*†ba-cu'-li-form
†ba-di-nage'
†baf'-fy
*†bagn'-io
*Bah-i'a
*bail'-iff
*bail'-i-wick
*Bak'-e-lite
*†bal'-a-ta
*†bal-is-tra'-ri:a
†ba'-nal
*†band'-age
*†band'-ag-ing
†bar-ba'-ri-an
†bar-ba'-ri-an-ism
†bar-bit'-u-rate
†ba'-rite
†ba'-ri-um
*bark'-en-tine
*†bar'-o-ny
*bas'-al
*bas'-al-ly
*bas'-al me-tab'-o-lism
*†ba-salt'-ic
*†ba-salt'-i-form
*bas'-ic
*bas'-i-cal-ly
*bas'-tar-dy
†bau'-chle
†Ba-va'-ri:a
†Ba-va'-ri-an
†bech'-a-mel
*Bech-u-a'-na-land
*†be-diz'-en
†be-ha'-vior
†be-ha'-vior-ism

†be-ha′-vior-is′-tic
*†ben-e-dic′-i-te
*ben-e-fi′-ci-ar-ies
*ben-e-fi′-ci-ar:y
*†Ben-ga-lese′
†ben-zal′-de-hyde
*Ben-zed′-rine
*ben-zi-mid′-a-zole
*benz-ox′-y-a-cet′-ic
*†Ber-e-ni′-ce
†ber′-et
*†Be′-ring
†Ber′-nar-dine
*†Ber-nese′
†bes′-ti-a-ry
†Bet′-el-geuse
†Bi-ar-ritz′
†bibe′-lot
†bi-car′-bo-nate
†bi-cen′-te-nar:y
†bi-cen′-te-na-ry
†bi-cyc′-lic
†bi-fa′-ri-ous-ly
†bil′-i-a-ry
*bi-oc′-el-late
†biv′-ou-ac
†biv′-ou-acked
†biv′-ou-ack-ing
†Blé-ri-ot′
*Bod-le′-ian
*†bo′-lus
*bom-bard-ier′
*bond′-serv-ant
†bond′-wo-man
†boom′-er-ang
†boom′-e-rang
†boot-ee′
†bo′-rak
†bo′-som
*bra-chi-al
*bra′-chi-ate
*bra′-chi-o-pod
*brass′-age
*Brem′-en
*†Bres′-cia
*bre-vi-ar:y
†bri′-dal
*†Bridg′-et
*bro-mel′-lite
†bru′-cine
†Bru′-ges
†budg′-et-a-ry
†buf′-fer
*bulb′-ar
†bulb′-ous
†Bul-ga′-ri:a
*Bul-ga′-ri-an

*bull′-ock
*bunk′-er
†bu-reau′-cra-cy
*burg′-age
*†burgh′-er
*bur-gla′-ri-ous
†bur′-nish
*bur-sa′-ri-al
*bu′-ty-lene
*bu-ty-ra′-ceous
*bu′-ty-rate
*†By-zan′-tine
*†ca-ba′-na
*†ca-bo-chon′
*†ca-bril′-la
†ca-da′-ver
*†ca′-dre
*Caes-a-re′a
*Cae-sa′-re-an
†caf′-fe-ine
†Ca-gay-an′
†cage′y
†cag′-i-er
†cag′-i-ly
*cal′-a-ma-ry
*cal-a-ve′-rite
†cal-ca′-re-ous
*cal-ce-o-la′-ri:a
*cal′-i-ces
*cal′-iph-ate
*cal′-i-phate
*†cal′-ma-tive
*cal′-o-yer
*cal′-y-coid
*Ca-mem-bert′
†ca-mou-flage′
*Camp′-bel-lite
†ca-na′-ries
†ca-na′-ry
*can-de-lil′-la
†can′-ti-lev-er
†caout′-chouc
†cap′-il-la-ry
*cap′-re-o-line
*†cap′-ryl-ate
*cap′-ut
*†cap-y-ba′-ra
†ca-ra-ba′o
†car′-a-bin-eer′
*†ca-ra-ca′-ra
*Ca-rac′-as
*†car-ban′-i-lide
†car′-bin-ol
*car-bon-a′-ceous
*ca-res′-sive
*ca-res′-sive-ly
*†Car′-ib-an

*car´-i-es
†ca´-ri-es
†ca-ril-lon-neur´
†ca´-ri-ous
†Carl´-ist
†car´-nal-lite
†Car-neg´-ie
*car-nel´-ian
†ca-rou´-sal
†car´-ven
*Ca´-ry
*car-y-at´-i-dal
*Ca-sa-no´-va
†cas´-ca-ra
†ca´-se-in
*ca´-se-in-ate
†ca-shew´
†cas-sit´-e-rite
†cas-so-wa´-ry
*cas´-u-al
*cas´-u-al-ly
*cas´-u-al-ness
*cas´-u-al-ty
*cas´-u-ist
†cas-u-is´-tic
*cas-u-is´-ti-cal-ly
*cas´-u-ist-ry
†ca-taph-o-re´-sis
†cat-e-chu´-me-nal
†cat´-e-na-ry
†Cath´-e-rine
†cause-rie´
†cau´-tion-a-ry
*ca-va-ti´-na
*Cec´-il
*ced´-u-la
*cel-lu-lo´-sic
†cem-en-ta´-tion
†cem-en-ti´-tious
†cen-o-ge-net´-ic
†cen-te-na´-ri-an
*cen´-te-nar:y
†cen´-te-na-ry
†Ceph´-e-id
*†cer´-a-mist
†Cer´-be-rus
*†cer-ca´-ri:a
*ce-rot´-ic
†Ce-sa´-re-an
†cet´-yl
*Cey-lo-nese´
*†chaf´-er
†chaf´-fer
*†cha-me´-le-on
†chant´-ey
†chant´-ry
*†cha-pa-ra´-jos
*†char-i-ot-eer´

*†Cha´-ron
*†Chart´-ism
*†Chart´-ist
†char-tu-la-ry
†char´-wo-man
†chas´-my
†chast´-en
†chat´-e-lain
*†chat´-e-laine
†che-lic´-e-ra
†chel´-i-form
†Che´-ops
†cheq´-uer
†chi-a-ro-scu´-ro
†chi-can´-er:y
*†chic´-le
†Chi´-le
†Chin-ki-ang´
†chi´-ti-nous
*†chiv´-al-ric
*†chla´-mys
*chlo-ra-mine´
*chlo´-rid-ize
†chlo-rin-ate
†cho-lan´-threne
†chor-e-og´-ra-pher
†chor-e-og´-ra-phy
*chor´-is-ter
†Chris-ti-a´-ni:a
*chro´-ma-to-gram
*chro´-ma-to-scope
*†chrys-an´-the-mum
*†chrys´-ene
†chuf´-fy
†church´ war-den
†ci-ce-ro´-ne (n.)
†ci-ce-rone (v.)
†cil´-i-a-ry
*ci-mar-ron´
†cim´-i-coid
†Cin-cin-na´-ti
†Cin-cin-na´-tus
*†cin-e-ra´-ri:a
†cin´-er-a-ry
*cit´-ri-nin
*†cit-ron-el´-la
†civ´-il ser´-vice
†clam´-ant
†clan´-gor
†clan´-gor-ous
*cla´-vi-er
†Cle-o-pa´-tra
†cli´-ent-al
†clique´y
†cliqu´-ish
*†cli´-to-ris
*clon´-ic
†club´-wo-man

441

†co′-balt-ous
†cob′-le
†co′-ca-ine
†co′-ca-in-ism
*†cock′-chaf-er
*co-de-fen′-dant
†co′-de-ine
†coen-es-the′:si:a
*co-er′-ci-ble
*co-ex-ist′-ence
*co-ex-ist′-ent
†cog′-nac
†co-hab′-it-ant
*co-le-op′-ter-ous
†col-e-op′-ter-ous
†col-le′-gi-an
†col-le′-gi-ate
*†colo′-nel
*colo′-nel-cy
*†Col-o-ra′-dan
*†Col-o-ra′-do
*col-o-ra-tu′-ra
*†Co-los′-sian
†col′-um-ba-ry
†col′-umn-ist
*com′-a-tose
*com′-a-tose-ly
*†com-ba′-tive
†com-ba-tive-ness
*com-bin-a-to′-ri-al
*com-meas′-ure
*†com-mend′-a-to-ry
†com-men-ta-ry
†com-mis-sa′-ri-at
†com-mis-sa-ry
*†com-mis′-su-ral
*com-mun′-ion
*†com′-pa-ra-tor
†com-pu′-tist
*†Com′-ti-an
†Com′-tism
*con′-a-tive
†con-ces′-sion-a-ry
*†con-chif′-er-ous
*con′-ci-erge
*†con-cil′-i-a-to-ry
*con-cord′-ance
*con-cord′-ant
†con-cre′-tion-a-ry
*con-cu′-bi-na-ry
*con-den′-sa-ble
†con-de-scen′-dence
†con-do′-nance
†con-duc′-tance
†con-fec′-tion-a-ry
†con-fig-ur-a′-tion
*†con-firm′-a-to-ry

*con-fut′-a-tive
*con-gen′-ial
*†con-ge′-ri-es
*†con-gres′-sion-al
†Con′-gress-wo-man
*co′-ni-fer
*†con-jur′-or
†con′-ning
†con′-ning=tow-er
†con-ni′-vent
*con-not′-a-tive
*con-not′-a-tive-ly
*con-ser′-van-cy
†con-ser′-va-tism
*con-ser′-va-tive
*con-ser′-va-to-ry
†con-sis′-tence
†con-sis′-ten-cy
†con-sis′-tent
†con-sis′-tent-ly
†con-stab′-u-la-ry
†con-sue-tu′-di-na-ry
*con′-su-lar
*†con′-su-late
*con-sult′-ant
*†con-sult′-a-tive
*†con-tan′-go
†con-tem′-ner
†con-tem′-po-ra-ry
*con-test′-ant
*†con-trac-tile
*†con-tra′-ri-ness
*†con-tra′-ri-wise
*†con′-tra-ry
*con-tri′-vance
*con-ven′-ience
*con-ven′-ient
*con-ven′-ient-ly
*con-vert′-or
*con-vul′-sion-a-ry
*Cool′-idge
†coo′-per
†coo′-per-age
*coop′-ra
*†cop-roph′-a-gous
†co-quet′-tish
*Cor-del′-ia
*co-re-spond′-ent
*Cor-i-o′-lis
*Cor-nel′-ia
*cor-nel′-ian
*Cor-nel′-ius
†cor′-ol-la-ry
*co-ro′-nal
†cor′-o-na-ry
*cor-rect′-ant
*cor-rect′-i-tude
*cor-re-spond′-ence

*cor-re-spond'-ent
†corse'-let
*†co-rym'-bose
*co-ry-phée'
*†cos'-ter-mon-ger
†cos'-tu-mier'
*coun'-se-lor
†coun'-try-wo-man
*coup'-le
†coup'-ler
†coup'-let
†coup'-ling
*cour'-i-er
*cour'-ti-er
†court'-ier
†co-va'-ri-ance
†co-va'-ri-ant
*†cov'-e-nant-er
*†cov'-et-ous
*†cov'-et-ous-ness
†co-yo'-te
†cres-cen'-do
†cre'-syl
*†Cro'-at
*†cro'-co-ite
†Cro═Ma-gnon'
†cryp-ta-nal'-y-sis
*cte'-noid
*†cudg'-el
*†cudg'-el-er
*cu'-li-nar:y
†cu'-li-na-ry
*†cul'-ver-in
*†cur'-a-tive
*curl'-i-cue
*†cur-mudg'-eon
*curv-om'-e-ter
†cus'-tom-a'-ri-ly
†cus'-tom-a-ry
†cus'-tum-al
*cy-an-am'-ide
†cy-an-u'-ric
*†cyc-a-da'-ceous
*cyc'-la-men
†cyc'-lic
†cyc'-li-cal
*†cy-per-a'-ceous
*†Cy-re-na'-ic
*cyst'-ic
†Cyth-e-re'a
*Czech :o-Slo-vak'-i-an

*†dac'-ty-lo-gram
†Da-ghes-tan'
†dah'-lia
†dai'-ries
†dai'-ry

†dai'-ry-ing
†dai'-ry-man
*Dak'-ar
*†Da-le-car'-li-an
†dam-as-cene'
†dam'-ning
†dam'-ning-ly
†Da'-na:e
†Da-ri-en'
*†dav'-it
†de-bac'-le
†deb-au-chee'
†dé-bu-tante'
†de-ca'-dence
*†de-ca'-dent
†dec'-a-me-ter
†dec'-a-nal
†dec-ath'-lon
†de'-cene
†de-cli'-na-to-ry
†dec'-li-vous
†de-co'-rous
*†de-cus'-sate
†dec'-y-lene
†def-al-ca'-tion
†de-fen'-dant
†def-er-ves'-cence
†de-for-es-ta'-tion
†def-or-ma'-tion
*†de-form'-a-tive
†de-form'-i-ty
†de-fraud-a'-tion
*de-lo-cal-i-za'-tion
*dem'-a-gog-uer:y
†de-man'-dant
†de-mo-bil-i-za'-tion
†de-mo'-bil-ize
*†de-my'
†de-na'-ri-us
*†den'-a-ry
*†de-na'-tion-al-ize
†de-na'-tu-rant
*†den'-tist-ry
†den'-u-date
*†den-u-da'-tion
*de-pend'-ence
*de-pend'-en-cy
*de-pend'-ent
*de-plo-ra'-tion
†de-por-tee'
†de-pos'-i-ta-ry
†de-pres'-si-ble
†de-scen'-dant
*†de-scry'
*de-scry'-ing
*de-sist'-ance
*†des'-pi-ca-ble
*†des-pit'-e-ous-ly

443

DESPONDENCE

*de-spond'-ence
*de-spond'-en-cy
*de-spond'-ent
*†des'-pot-ism
*de-spu'-mate
*de-struct'-i-ble
†de-sul'-fur-ize
*†de-ter'-mi-na-ble
*†de-ter'-min-ism
*†de-ter'-min-ist
*deu'-ced
*de-vi'-sor
*di-ac'-e-tyl
†di-am'-ine
†di-a-stas'-ic
*†di-as-tol'-ic
*†di-az'o (prefix)
†di-az'-ole
†di-cet'-yl
†di-cot-y-le'-do-nous
†dic'-tion-ar-ies
†dic'-tion-a-ries
†dic'-tion-ar:y
†dic'-tion-a-ry
*†Di-eppe'
†di'-et-a-ry
†dig'-it-al
†dig-i-ta-lin
†dig-i-ta'-lis
*dig'-i-tal-ize
†dig'-ni-ta-ries
*dig'-ni-ta-ry
*di-lat'-ant
*dil-et-tan'-te
*†din'-ghy
*Di-o-ny'-sian
†Di-o-nys'-i-us
*di-o-ra'-ma
†di-phe'-nyl
*diph-thon'-gal
†dip-lod'-o-cus
*di-rec'-to-rate
*†dis-as'-ter
*†dis-as'-trous
*†dis-as'-trous-ly
*dis-ci-pli'-nal
*dis-ci-pli-na'-ri-an
†dis'-ci-pli-na-ry
*dis'-cord-ance
*dis-cord'-ant
†dis-cre'-tion-a-ry
*dis-in-fect'-ant
*dis-miss'-al
*†dis-or-gan-i-za'-tion
*dis-or'-gan-ize
*dis'-pa-rate
*†dis-pen-sa-bil'-i-ty
*dis-pers'-ant

*dis-pers'-oid
*†dis-pir'-it
*†dis-pir'-it-ed
*dis-pleas'-ure
*†dis-port'
*dis-po'-sal
*†dis-pu-ta-bil'-i-ty
*†dis'-pu-ta-ble
*dis-sei-see'
*dis-ser'-vice
†dis-so-lu-bil'-i-ty
†dis'-so-lu-ble
*dis'-tich-ous
†dis-til'-la-ble
*dis-til'-ler
*dis-til'-ler:y
*dis-til'-ling
†di-sto'-ma-tous
*dis-trib'-u-ta-ry
*dis-turb'-ance
*dis-u'-nion
*†diz'-en
*do'-dec-yl
*doll'y
*†dol'-o-mite
†dol'-or-ous
†dol'-o-rous
†do'-mi-cal
†dom-i-cil'-i-a-ry
*dom'-i-cine
*†don'-a-tive
*†Don Quix'-ote
*dope'y
*do'-pey
†Do'-ris
*dos'-si-er
†do'-tage
*†do'-tard
†do'-tish
†do'-ty
*doub'-le
*doub'-le=bar'-reled
†doub'-le cross
†doub'-le=cross (v.)
†doub'-le=head-er
†doub'-le=quick (adj., v.)
†doub'-let
*doub'-ling
†doub-loon'
*doub'-ly
*†dow'-di-ness
*dow'-dy
*†dram'-a-tis per-so'-nae
*dra'-per:y
*drom'-e-da-ry
†dro'-mond
*†drow'-si-ly

*†drow'-si-ness
*†drow'-sy
*†dudg'-eon
*duff'-er
*†Dul-cin'-e:a
*†dull'-ard
†dun'-ite
*Dunk'-ard
*Dunk'-er
*†du-o-den'-a-ry
†du-ra-lu'-min
*†dur'-ance

*†East'-er
*†East'-er-tide
*Eb-en-e'-zer
†eb'-o-nite
*eb'-on:y
*e:bur-na'-tion
*†ech'-i-nate
†ech'-o-ic
*e'co-nom'-ic
*e'co-nom'-i-cal
*e'co-nom'-i-cal-ly
†é'cru
*ec-tos-to'-sis
†ec-to-sto'-sis
*†ec'-ty-pal
*Ec-ua-do'-ran
*†Ec-ua-do'-ri-an
*ec-u-men-ic'-i-ty
*†ec-zem'-a-tous
*†ed'-u-ca-tive
*ef-fer-ves'-ci-ble
*ef-front'-er:y
*e:gal-i-ta'-ri-an
†eg'o
†eg-o-cen'-tric
†eg-o-cen-tric'-i-ty
†eg'-o-ism
†eg'-o-ist
†eg-o-is'-tic
†eg-o-is'-ti-cal
†eg'-o-tism
†eg'-o-tist
†eg-o-tis'-tic
†eg-o-tis'-ti-cal
†eg-o-tis'-ti-cal-ly
*E:gypt-ol'-o-gist
*E:gypt-ol'-o-gy
*†eight-een'
*†eight-eenth'
*†ei-se-ge'-sis
*†eld'-er (older)
*†eld'-er-ly
*†eld'-est
†El-e-a-no'-ra
†e:lec'-to-ral

†e:lec'-to-rate
†e:lec'-tu-a-ry
†el-e-e-mos'-y-na-ry
†e:le'-gi-ac
*†el-e-men'-ta-ri-ly
†E:liz'-a-beth-an
*el-lips'-oid
†el-o-cu'-tion-a-ry
†El Pa'-so
*†elv'-ish
†E:lyr'-i:a
†E:lys'-i-an
†E:lys'-i-um
†em-bo'-som
†em'-en-da-tor
†e:mend'-a-to-ry
†em'-er-ald-ine
†em'-is-sa-ries
†em'-is-sa-ry
*†em-is-siv'-i-ty
*†em-pyr'-e-al
*en-cy'-clic
*en-cy'-cli-cal
*†En-da-moe'-ba
*†en-dar-te-ri'-tis
†en-do-cri'-nous
*en-dor-see'
*†en-dos-mo'-sis
*†en-dos'-po-rous
*†en-dos'-te-um
*en-dos-to'-sis
*en-do-sto'-sis
*en-doth'-e-loid
*en-for'-ced-ly
†Eng'-els
*Eng'-land
*Eng'-land-er
*Eng'-lish
*Eng'-lish-ism
*Eng'-lish-man
*Eng'-lish-wom'-an
†En'-glish-wo-man
†en-li'-ven
†en-thro-ni-za'-tion
†ep'-act
†ep-ei-ro-gen'-ic
†eph'-e-drine
*†ep-i-phys'-e-al
†ep-i-ste-mo-log'-i-cal
†ep-i-ste-mol'-o-gy
*†e:pis'-to-la-ry
†e:qua-bil'-i-ty
†e'qua-ble
†e:qual-i-ta'-ri-an
†e:qual-i-ta'-ri-an
†e:qui-len'-in
†e:qui-li'-brant
*†e:qui-li'-brate
*†e:qui-li-bra'-tion

445

*†e:quil'-i-brist
*†e'qui-poise
†er'-go-ster-ol
†E'rin
*er'-i-nite
*e:ri-o-dic'-ty-ol
*e-ri-om'-e-ter
*er-is'-tic
*†E:ri-tre'a
*er-ra-bil'-i-ty
*†e:ryth'-rism
†e:ryth'-rite
*†es-ca-pee'
*es-cap'-ism
*†e:so-phag'e-al
†es-pou'-sal
†es'-tu-a-ry
*†et'-a-mine
†eth'-yl-am-ine
†eth'-yl-i-dene
†eth'-y-nyl
*eu'-ge-nist
*e:va'-cu-ée
†ev-an-gel'-ic
†ev-an-gel'-i-cal
†e:van'-gel-ism
†e:van'-gel-ist
†e:van'-gel-is'-tic
†e:van'-gel-ize
*†ev-o-ca'-tion
*e:vo'-ca-tive
*†ev'-o-ca-tor
†ev-o-lu'-tion-a-ry
*†ex-act'-i-tude
†ex-am'-i-na-ble
*†ex-cheq'-uer
†ex-ci'-ta-tive
†ex-ci'-ta-to-ry
*ex-ha'-lant
*ex-hor'-ta-to-ry
*ex-ist'-ence
*ex-ist'-ent
†ex of-fic'-i:o
†ex-pec'-tan-cy
†ex-pec'-tant
†ex-pec'-tant-ly
*ex-pec'-ta-tive
†ex-pe-di'-tion-a-ry
†ex-pen'-di-ture
*†ex'-pli-ca-ble
*†ex'-pli-ca-tive
*†ex'-pli-ca-to-ry
*†ex'-qui-site
*†ex'-qui-site-ly
†ex-tem'-po-ra-ry
*†ex-tor'-tive
†ex-traor-di-na'-ri-ly
†ex-traor'-di-na-ry

†ex'-tra-po-late
†ex'-tra-po-lat'-ed
†ex'-tra-po-la'-tion
*†ex-trem'-ism
*†ex'-tri-ca-ble
†ex-ul'-tance
†ex-ul'-tant
*†eye'-let-eer'

*faer'y
†Fah'-ren-heit
†fal'-co-net
*†fan-fa-ron-ade'
†fa-ran'-dole
†fast'-en
†fast'-en-er
†fast'-en-ing
*fa-ti'-guing
*fa-ti'-guing-ly
*†fay'-al-ite
*fe'-brile
†Feb'-ru-a-ry
†fec'-und
*fe'-cun-date
*fe-cun-da'-tion
†fenc'-i-ble
*†fe-nes'-trat-ed
†feoff'-or
†fer-men'-ta-tive
*fer-ti-liz-a-ble
*fer-ti-li-za'-tion
*fer'-ti-lize
*fer'-ti-liz-er
*†fet-e-ri'-ta
*fe'-ti-cid'-al
†fet'-i-ci'-dal
†fet'-i-cide
*fe'-tish
*fe'-tish-ism
†feu-ille-ton'
*fi'-bril-la-ry
†fi-bril-la'-tion
†fi-brin-og'-e-nous
*fi'-bri-nous
fi-bro'-ma-tous
*†fidg'-et
*†fidg'-et:y
†fi-du'-ci-a-ry
*fier'-i-ness
†fier'y
*fies'-ta
†Fi'-ga-ro'
†fig-u-ral
*†fig'-ur-ate
*fig'-ur-ate-ly
†fig-ur-a'-tion
*†fig'-ur-a-tive
*†fig'-ur-a-tive-ly

446

*†fi-la′-ri:a
†fi-la′-ri-al
fi-la-ri′-a-sis
*fil-i-cid′-al
*†fi-na′-le
*†fi′-nis
  †Fi-u′-me
*fla-con′
  †flaut′-ist
  †flex′-u-ral
*†flunk′y
*flu-or-an′-thene
  †flu′-or-ene
  †flu′-or-ite
*flu-or-og′-ra-phy
  †flu′-or-o-scope
*†flu-or-os′-co-py
  †flux′-ion-a-ry
*†fog-ram
*folk′-sy
  †foot′-le
  †fo-ra-min′-i-fer
*for′-ci-ble
*for′-ci-bly
  †fore′-wo-man
  †for-mal′-de-hyde
*form′-ant
  †for′-mi-ca-ry
*for′-mu-la-ry
  †For-set′i
  †for-sy′-thi:a
  †fort′-a-lice
  †foun′-dries
  †foun′-dry
*Fowl′-er
  †frag′-men-ta-ry
*†frank′-in-cense
  †frat′-ri-cid′-al
  †Freu′-di-an
*Frig′-id-aire
  †Fris′-ian
  †frit′-il-la-ry
  †frizz′-ly
  †Frob′-ish-er
*†fron-tol′y-sis
*frowz′-i-er
*frowz′-i-ness
*frowz′y
*full′-er
  †full′y
*†ful-mi-nu′-ric
  †func′-tion-a-ry
  †fu′-ner-a-ry
  †fun′-gi-cid′-al
*†fu′-ran-ose
*fur′-fur-al

*fur-fur-yl′-i-dene
*†fu-sa′-ri-um
*fu-sil-ier′
*†fust′-i-er
*†fust′-i-ly
*fust′y
  †fu-til-i-ta′-ri-an
*fu′-tur-al

*†gadg′-et
  †gad′-id
  †gain′-er
  †ga-len′-ic
  †gal′-va-no-scope
*gam′-et:e
*†gam-e-to-gen′-e-sis
  †gam′-e-to-phore
  †gam′-e-to-phyte
  †gam′-o-pet′-al-ous
  †gam′-o-sep′-al-ous
  †gang′-ling
  †gang′-ly
*†Gar′-and
  †Ga′-ry
  †ge-lat′-i-nase
  †gel-a-tin′-o-chlo′-ride
  †gel-id′-i-ty
  †ge′-lose
  †gel-sem′-ic
*†gen-dar-me-rie′
*gen-darm′-er:y
*†gen-er-al-is′-si-mo
  †ge-net′
  †ge-neth-li′-a-cal
*gen′-ial
*gen′-ial-ly
  †gen-i-to-u′ri-na-ry
*gen′-ius
*gen′-o-cid′-al
*†gen′-ome
*gen′-o-type
*gen′-o-typ′-ic
  †gen′-thite
  †gen-tian-a′-ceous
*†gen-tian-el′-la
  †gen′-tle-wo-man
*gen′-tly
*ger-man′-ite
*ger′-mi-cid′-al
  †ge-run′-div-al
  †ges-ta′-po
  †gi-go-lo′
  †gild′-er (coin)
  †gil′-der (one who gilds)
  †gi′t-a-lin
  †gi′t-al-in
*gi-tox-i-ge′-nin
*glad-i-o′-lus

447

*†glam′-or-ous
*†gle′-noid
†glo′-bal
†glo′-bal-ly
*Glo-big-er-i′-na
†Glo-bi-ger-i′-na
†glos-sa′-ri-al
*gloss′-i-ly
*gloss′-i-ness
*glu-cos-a:mine′
†glu-co-sam′-ine
†glue′y
*†glu-ta-con′-ic
†glu-tam′-ine
†glu′-te-nous
†glyc′-er-ic
†glyc′-ine
†gly-co-cy-am′-ine
†gly-co-pro′-te-in
*†gly-co-su′-ri:a
†gnath-on′-ic
*goat-ee′
*Goid′-el-ic
†go′-li-ard
†go′-li-ard-ic
*†gon′-ad
†gon′-ad-al
†gon-a-do-tro′-phin
*goos-an′-der
†Go′-tham
†Go′-tham-ite
†gov′-ern-ess
*go′-ya-zite
*grain′-ing
†gra′-ma
†gram-ma′-ri-an
*†gran′-a-ry
*grang′-er-ize
*gran-tee′
*graph-ol′-o-gy
*†gra-tin′
†gra′-zer
*green′-ock-ite
*†gre-ga′-ri-ous
*gre-ga′-ri-ous-ness
*†gri-mace′
*†grop′-er
†gro-tes′-quer-ie
†gro-tesque′-rie
*†group′-er
*grous′-er
*†gryph′-on
†Gua-dal-quiv′-ir
†gua-nam′-ine
†guan′-i-dine
*gudg′-eon
*†Gui-a′-na
†gui′-dance

†gul-li-bil′-i-ty
†gul′-li-ble
†gym-no-sto′-ma-tous
*†gyn-ae-ce′-um
*†gy-nan′-drous
*†gy-nan′-dry
†gyn-ar-chy
*†gyn-e-coc′-ra-cy
*†gyn-e-co-log′-i-cal
†gyn-e-col′-o-gist
*†gyn-e-col′-o-gy
*†gyn-e-co-mor′-phous
†gyn-e-ol′-a-try
*†gyn′-o-phore

†Ha-bak′-kuk
*hab′-it-ant
†hach′-ure
†ha-cien′-da
†ha-gi-oc′-ra-cy
*Ha-gi-og′-ra-pha
†ha-gi-og′-ra-pher
†ha-gi-ol′-a-ter
†ha-gi-o-log′-ic
†ha-gi-ol′-o-gy
*hal′-ber-dier′
*†ha-lis-ter-e′-sis
*hall′-ing
†ham′-al
†ham-a-me-li-da′-ceous
†Ha-mit′-ic
*hang′-ar
†ha′-ra=ki′-ri
*†har′-ass
*†har′-assed
*†har′-ass-ing
*†har′-ass-ment
†hast′-en
†Ha′-thor
*†Ha-van′a
†haz′-i-ly
†haz′-i-ness
†haz′y
*†he′-don-ism
*he′-don-ist
†hed′-on-ist
†hed-on-is′-tic
†hed-on-is′-ti-cal
†he-ge-mon′-ic
†he′-ge-mo-ny
*Heg′-i-ra
*Hel′-len-ism
*Hel-len-is′-tic
†hem-a-cy-tom′-e-ter
*†hem-a-fi′-brite
†hem-ag-glu′-ti-nin
†hem-al′-bu-men
†hem-a-poi-e′-sis

†hem-ar-thro′-sis
†hem-a-te′-in
†hem-a-ti-nom′-e-ter
†hem′-a-toid
*†hem-a-tol′o-gy
†hem-a-to′-ma
†hem-a-tom′-e-ter
†hem-a-to′-sis
†hem-a-tox′-y-lin
†hem-i-cyc′-lic
*he-mis′-ti-chal
†hem-o-chro′-mo-gen
†hem-o-chro-mom′-e-ter
†hem-o-co-ni-o′-sis
†hem-o-cy′-a-nin
†hem′-o-cyte
†hem-o-cy-tol′-y-sis
†hem-o-glo′-bin
†hem-o-glo-bi-nom′-e-ter
†hem′-o-lymph
*he-mol-y′-sin
†hem-o-ly′-sin
†hem-o-lyt′-ic
†hem-o-phil′-i:a
†hem-o-phil′-i-ac
†hem-op′-ty-sis
†hem-o-sid′-er-in
†hem-o-sid-e-ro′-sis
†hem-o-stat′-ic
*hep′-tarch:y
†her-ba′-ri-um
*here-aft′-er
†he-red-i-ta′-ri-ly
†he-red′-i-ta-ry
*here′-in-aft′-er
†her′-e-si-arch
†her-it-a-bil′-i-ty
*†her′-it-a-ble
*her′-it-age
†her′-it-ance
†her-ni-a′-rin
†he-ro′-in
†Her′-on
†het-e-ro-chro-mat′-ic
†het-er-o-cyc′-lic
†het′-er-o-gam-ete
†hex′-y-lene
*hi′-er-arch:y
†hi-la′-ri-ous
†hill′-bil-ly
*†Hi-ma′-la-ya
*†Hi-ma′-la-yan
*†Hin-du-sta′-ni
*†Hi′-ro-shi′-ma
†His-pa-nio′-la
*†home′y
*hom-i-cid′-al

†ho-mog′-e-ni-zer
†ho′-mo-graph
*†hom′o-log
†hom-o-log′-i-cal
*†hom′-o-logue
†ho-mo-nym′-ic
*Ho′mo sa′-pi-ens
*†ho-mos′-po-rous
†ho-mo-zyg′-ote
†hon′-ky≡tonk
†hon-o-ra′-ri-um
†hon′-or-a-ry
*hook′-ah
†horse′-wo-man
*horse′y
*†hos′-pi-ta-ble
*†hos′-pi-ta-bly
*house′-wif-er:y
*how′-itz-er
†hu-man-i-ta′-ri-an
†hu-man-i-ta′-ri-an-ism
†Hun-ga′-ri-an
*†Hunt′-ing-don
†Hunt′-ing-ton
*hurl′y≡burl′y
*hurt′-er
*hus′-ky
†hust′-ing
*hy-dra-cryl′-ate
*hy-dram′-ine
*hy-dro-quin′-one
*hy-drox′-yl-am′-ine
*hy′-gi-en-ist
*†Hy-men-o-cal′-lis
†Hy-men-op′-ter:a
†hy-men-op′-ter-ous
†hyp-ae′-thral
*hy-perp-ne′a
*†hy-per-troph′-ic
*†hyp′-o-caust
*†hyp-o-ge′-um
*hy-po-phys′-e-al
*hy-po-phys′-i-al
*†hyp′-o-style
*hy-poth′-e-ca-ry

†i:a-tro-chem′-is-tr**y**
*i:bi′-dem
*†I:ca′-ri-an
*i′ci-ly
*i′ci-ness
*i′cy
*id′-e-o-gram
*id′-e-o-graph
*id-e-og′-ra-phy
*id-e-o-log′-i-cal
*id-e-ol′-o-gist
*id-e-ol′-o-gy

449

IDIOMATIC

†id-i-om-at′-ic
†i′dyl-list
*†ig′-no-min:y
*†I:go-rot′
*I:guan′-o-don
*†im′-age-ry
*†im-ag′-i-na-ble
*†im-ag′-i-nal
†im-ag′-i-na-ry
*i:mi′-do
*i:min′-a-zole
*i:mine′
*i:mi′-no
†im-mar′-gi-nate
†im-ma-tu′-ri-ty
†im-meas′-ur-a-ble
†im-meas′-ur-a-bly
†im-men′-sur-a-ble
†im-mo′-bil-ize
†im-mun-i-za′-tion
†im-mun′-ize
†im-pe′-dance
†im-pen′-dent
*†im-pre-sa′-ri:o
†im-prob′-i-ty
†im-put′-a-tive
*†in-ad-vert′-ence
*in-ad-vert′-ent
*in-ad-vert′-ent-ly
*†in-apt′-i-tude
†in-cen′-di-a-ry
†in-ci′-tant
*†in′-ci-vism
*in-co-er′-ci-ble
*in-con-den′-sa-ble
*in-con-sis′-ten-cy
*in-con-sis′-tent
*†in-con-ven′-ience
*in-con-ven′-ien-cy
*in-con-ven′-ient
*in-con-vinc′-i-ble
†in-dam′-ine
*in-dec′-o-rous
*in-de-co′-rous
*in-de-pend′-ence
*in-de-pend′-en-cy
*in-de-pend′-ent
*in-de-pend′-ent-ly
*in-de-struct-i-bil′-i-ty
*in-de-struct′-i-ble
*in-de-ter′-mi-na-ble
*†in-di-ca-to-ry
*†in′-di-go-lite
†in′-di-go-tin
*†in-dis-pen′-sa-ble
*†in-dis′-pu-ta-ble
*†in-dis′-so-lu-ble
†in-dor-see′
*†in-duct′-ance
450

†in-duc-tee′
*in-ept′-i-tude
*†in-er′-ra-ble
*†in-ex-act′-i-tude
*in-ex-ist′′-ence
*in-ex-ist′-ent
†in′-fan-til-ism
†in-fec′-tant
*†in-for′-mal-ize
*†in-form′-ant
†in-fus′-i-ble
*in-gen′-ious
*in-gen′-ious-ly
*in-hab′-it-ant
*in-ha′-lant
*in-her′-it-ance
*†ink′-ling
†in-san′-i-ta-ry
*†in-sa′-ti-ate
*in-sec-ti-cid′-al
*insect-ol′-o-gy
*†in-se-cu′-ri-ty
*in-sist′-ence
*in-sist′-ent
*in-sist′-ent-ly
*†in-tagl′-io
*in-tel-li-gent′-si:a
†in-tell-i-gent′-si:a
*†in-ten′-dance
†in-ten′-dan-cy
†in-ten′-dant
†in-ter′-ca-la-ry
†in-ter-fe-rom′-e-ter
*†in-ter-ne′-cine
†in-tern′-ist
†in-ter-plan′-e-ta-ry
*†in-tra-va-sa′-tion
*in-tri′-guer
*in-tri′-guing
*in-tri′-guing-ly
†in-va′-ri-a-ble
†in-va′-ri-a-bly
†in-va′-ri-ant
†in-ver′-tase
*†in-vig′-or-ate
*†in-vig′-or-at-ing
*†in-vig-or-a′-tion
*†in-vol′-un-ta-ri-ly
*†in-vol′-un-ta-ry
*in′-wov-en
*†i′o-din-ate
*i:ri-sa′-tion
*ir-ra′-tion-al
*†ir-ref′-ra-ga-ble
*ir-ref′-u-ta-ble
†ir-re-lig′-ion
†ir-re-lig′-ious
*†ir-rem′-e-a-ble
*ir-re-pres′-si-ble

†ir-re-sis′-ti-ble
†ir-re-sis′-ti-bly
*†ir-res′-o-lu-ble
*i:so-glos′-sal
†is′-o-late
†is-o-la′-ble
†is-o-la′-tion
†is-o-la′-tion-ist
†i:soph-thal′-ic
*†i:soth′-er-al
*i:sot′-o-py
†i:tin′-er-a-ry

†jac′-a-na
†Jacque-rie′
†ja-lou-sie′
†Ja-net′
†jan′-is-sa-ry
†Jan′-u-a-ry
†jar′-o-site
†jaunt′-i-ly
†jaunt′y
*†jeal-ous′y
*†Je′-kyll
*†jeop′-ard-ize
*†jeop′-ard-iz-ing
*†jeop′-ard:y
*†jerk′y
†Jo′-seph-ine′
†ju-di′-ci-a-ry
†ju′-gu-lar
†ju′-gu-late
†Jul′-ia
*Jul′-ian
*Jul′-ius
*jun-ior′-i-ty
*jun-i-or′-i-ty
*jus′-ti-fi-ca-to-ry

†kai′-no-site
†kak-e-mo′-no
†ka-ra-kul′
†kar-y-om′-i-tome
†Kash-mi′-ri-an
*kef′-ir
†Ker′-en-sky
†ker′-me-site
†kil′o
*†kil′-o-me-ter
†kin′-ase
†ki-net′-o-graph
†ki-net′-o-graph′-ic
†ki-net′-o-phone
†ki-net′-o-scope
*†King′-ston
†kins′-wo-man
†Kla′-math

†kohl-ra′-bi
*ko′-ni-me-ter
*†Kshat′-ri-ya
†ky′-an-ize

†lab′-ile
†lab′-il-ize
†lab′-roid
*†la-cer′-tine
*lac-tal-bu′-min
†lac′-u-na-ry
*La-fa-yette′
†la′-gan
†lam′-el-lar
†lam′-el-lose
*†lam-i-na′-ri-a′-ceous
†la′-ni-a-ry
†lap′-i-da-ry
†la-pin′
*lap′-is laz′-u-li
*la′-pis laz′-u-li
†lard′-er
*†lar-vi-ci-dal
*lar-viv′-or-ous
†la-ta-ki′a
*lat-i-tu-di-na′-ri-an
*laud′-a-to-ry
*lav′-age
†law′-ren-cite
†la-yette′
*†la′-zar
*lea′-guer
†leg′-en-da-ry
†le′-gion-a-ry
*†leish-man-i′-a-sis
†le′-man
*Le′-nin
†Le′-nin-grad
†Le′-nin-ism
†le′-on-ite
†lep-i-doc′-ro-cite
†lep′-i-do-lite
†lep-ro-sa′-ri-um
*lep-ro′-sis
*†Let′-tish
*†leu-co′-ma-ine
*Le-van′-tine
*Le-vant′-ine
*†lev′-ee
*le′-ver
*le′-ver-age
†li-an′a
†lib-er-ta′-ri-an
†lib′-er-ti-cide
†li-bra′-ri-an
†li′-bra-ry
*†li-cen-see′
†lig-nal′-oe
*lim′-ber

451

*†lim′-i-nal
†lim′-i-ta-ry
†li-mou-sine′
*†lin-a-ma′-rin
†li-no′-le-ic
*Lin′-o-type
lip′-ase
*†lip-o-pro′-te-in
*liq′-uor
†lit′-er-a-ry
†lith-e′-mi:a
†lith-i′-a-sis
*lith-o-chol′-ic
†lith-og′-ra-pher
†lith-og′-ra-phy
†lith-ol′-o-gy
†lith-ot′-o-my
†lith-ot′-ri-ty
†lith-u′-ri-a
*li-tig′-ious
†li-tig′-ious-ly
†lit′-o-tes
*lit-té-ra-teur′
*lo-che′-tic
*log′-a-nin
*†log-i′a
*†log′-i-on
*†Log′-os
*Lom′-bard:y
†long′-er
*†loon′y
†loph′-ine
*†lo′-pho-phore
†loq′-ui-tur
†Lo-tha′-ri:o
†Lo-yo′-la
*lu′-ci-fer-ase
*†Lud′-dism
*†Lud′-dite
†lu′-mi-na-ry
†lu-na′-ri-an
†lu-ni-ti′-dal
†lyd′-dite
*lym-phad-e-ni′-tis
*lym-phad-e-nop′-a-thy
†lymph-an′-gi-al
†lymph′-o-cyte
†lymph-o-sar′-co-ma
†lyr′-i-form

*mac-é-doine′
*†ma-che′-te
*Ma-chi-a-vel′-li
†mach-i-co-la′-tion
*†ma-chin′-al
*mac′-le
†mac-ro-cyc′-lic
*†ma-crog′-ra-phy

†*ma-crop′-si:a
*mad′-ame
†ma-es′-tro
*Ma′-fe-king
†mag-net-om′-e-ter
†mag′-net-o-met′-ric
†mag-net-om′-e-try
†mag-net-o-mo′-tive
†mag-net-o-stric′-tion
*mag′-uey
*maid′-serv-ant
*†ma-jus′-cule
*ma-laise′
†ma-la′-ri:a
†ma-la′-ri-al
*ma′-lic
†ma-lon′-ic
†mam′-mil-la-ry
†man′-da-ta-ry
*†ma′-nic
*†ma′-nic=de-pres′-sive
*man′-serv-ant
*†mar′-chion-ess
†mar′-gi-nal
†Ma′-ri-an
†Ma-ri-et′-ta
†ma-ri-ol′-a-try
†Ma′-ri-us
†mar′-quet-ry
*Ma′-ry
*Ma′-ry-land
*Ma′-ry-land-er
*mas-o-chis′-tic
*mas′-quer
†mass′-ive
†mas-toi-di′-tis
†mat′-i-nal
†ma-tri-ar′-chate
*ma′-tri-arch:y
†ma-tri-cid′-al
*†mat-ro-cli′-nous
*ma-tur′-a-tive
*ma-tu′-ri-ty
*matz′-oth
*maun′-der
*†mauv′-ine
*max′-il-la-ry
†Maz-a-rin′
*ma′-zi-ly
*meas-ur-a-bil′-i-ty
*meas′-ur-a-ble
*meas′-ure
*meas′-ured
*meas′-ure-less
*meas′-ure-ment
*meas′-ur-er
†med′-i-ca-ment
*†med′-i-ta-tor

†med′-ul-la-ry
†meg-a-gam′-ete
*†meis′-ter
*†Meis′-ter-sing-er
*me-lam′-ine
*me-lang′-er
*me-lib′-i-ose
*mel′-io-rate
*mel′-io-ra′-tion
*mel′-io-ra-tive
*mel′-io-rism
*mel′-io-rist
*mel-ior′-i-ty
*me-nar′-che
*Men′-non-ite
*men′-o-paus-al
†men-sur-a-bil′-i-ty
*men′-sur-a-ble
†mer′-ce-na-ry
*mé-sal-liance′
†mé-sal-li-ance′
†mes-ar-ter-i′-tis
*mes-cal′-ine
*†mes-en′-chy-ma
†mes′-i-al
*me′-sic
*†mesn′-al-ty
†mes-og′-na-thous
†met′-a-mer-ism
†met′-a-mer-ized
*me-temp-sy-cho′-sis
*†me-te-or-og′-ra-phy
*†me-te-or-ol′-o-gist
*†me-te-or-ol′-o-gy
†meth-an-ol
†meth-ox′-y-car′-bon-yl
†meth-yl-am′-ine
†meth′-y-late
†meth′-y-lene
*met′-o-pe
*me-to′-pon
*†mi-cro-or′-gan-ism
*mid-aft-er-noon′
†Mil-an-ese′
†mil-i-a-ry
†mil-i-ta′-ri-ly
†mil′-i-ta-ry
†mil-le-na′-ri-an
†mil′-le-na-ry
†mil′-li-a-ry
*mi-ne-stro′-ne
*†Mis-e-re′-re
*mis′-er-i-cord′
†mis-gui′-dance
†mis-og′-a-mist
†mis-og′-a-my

*†mis-og′-y-nist
†mis-og′-y-ny
*mis-ol′-o-gy
†mis-sha′-pen
†mis′-sion-a-ries
†mis′-sion-a-ry
†mis-u′-sage
†mith′-ri-dat-ism
†mi-trai-lleuse′
†mo-bil-i-za′-tion
†mo′-bil-ize
†mo′-dal
†mo′-dal-ism
*†mod-e-ra′-to
*mois′-ten
*mois′-ten-er
†Mo′-lin-ism
†mo-men-ta′-ri-ly
†mo′-men-ta-ry
*†mon′-ad
†mon-ad′-ic
†mon′-a-dis′-tic
*†mon′-arch-ism
*†mon′-arch-ist
*mon′-arch:y
†mon-e-ta′-ri-ly
†mon′-e-ta-ry
†Mon′-go-loid
*mon-o-bas′-ic
*mon-o-dac′-ty-lism
*mon-o-spo′-rous
*mo-nos′-tro-phe
†Mon-ta′-na
†Mon-te-vid′-e:o
*†mont-mo-ril′-lo-nite
†mon-troyd′-ite
†mor′-a-to-ry
†mor′-tu-a-ry
*mu′-cin-ous
*mul-ti-fa′-ri-ous
*mul-ti-for′-mi-ty
*mul′-ti-pli-ca-ble
*mus′-ket-eer′
*mus′-ti-ness
*mus′-ty
*myr′-i-a-me-ter
†myr′-rhic

*nai′-ad
†naph-tho-quin′-one
*naph-thyl-am′-ine
*naph′-thyl-ene
*nap-rap′-a-thy
†na′-res
†na′-ri-al
†nar-in-ge′-nin
†na′-ris

†nat'-ro-lite
†na'-var
†nec-es-sa'-ri-ly
†nec'-es-sa-ry
†ne-ces-si-ta'-ri-an
†ne-ces-si-ta'-ri-an-ism
*†nec'-rop-sy
†nec-ta'-re-ous
†nee'-dle-wo-man
†ne-fa'-ri-ous
†neg-lect'
*†neg-lect'-er
*†neg-lect'-ful
*†ne-mer'-tine
†ne-o-ars-phen-am'-ine
*†nerv'-ate
*†nerv'-ine
*†nerv'-ous
*†nerv'-ous-ly
*†nerv'-ous-ness
†nes'-ci-ence
†nes'-cience
†nes'-ci-ent
†nes'-cient
†nes'-tling
†neu-ras-the'-ni:a
†neu-ras-then'-ic
†neu-ro-ly'-sis
*†Ne-va'-da
†Ne-va'-dan
†Nietzsch'e
*Nie'-tzsche-ism
*†ni'-hil-ism
*†ni'-hil-ist
†*ni-hil-is'-tic
*†Nis'-sl
†Niss'l
†ni-tram'-ine
*†ni-trol'-ic
†ni-tro-sam'-ine
†no-bil'-i-a-ry
†no'-ble-wo-man
†no'-dal
†nom'-ad
†nom'-ad-ism
*nom'-arch:y
†no'-mo-gram
†no'-mo-graph'-ic
†non-ac-cep'-tance
†non-a-ge-na'-ri-an
†non'-ane
†non=com'-ba-tant
†non=ex-ist'-ence
†non=ex-ist'-ent
†non pro-seq'-ui-tur
†non=sec-ta'-ri-an
†non seq'-ui-tur
†non=u'nion

†non-yl'-ic
†no-ta'-ri-al
†no'-vo-ca-in
†nu'-dism
†nu'-dist
†nu'-mer-a-ry
†Nu'-rem-berg
*†nurs'-er:y
*†nurs'-er-y-man
*†nym-pha-lid

†oak'-um
*†o:bes'-i-ty
*†ob'-i-ter dic'-tum
†o:bit'-u-a-ries
†o:bit'-u-a-ry
†o'blast
†ob'-li-ga-tory
*†ob-scur'-ant
*†ob-scur'-ant-ism
†ob-se'-qui-ty
†ob-ser'-vance
†ob-ser'-vant
†ob-ser'-va-tive
†ob-ser'-va-to-ry
†ob-tun'-dent
†oc-clu'-dent
*†o:ce-a-nog'-ra-pher
*†o:ce-a-nog'-ra-phy
*†oc'-el-late
*†o:chron'-o-sis
*†o:co-til'-lo
†o:co-til'-lo
†oc'-tant-al
†oc-to-ge-na'-ri-an
†oc-tog'-e-na-ry
†oc'-to-na-ry
*†oc'-tu-plet
†o'dic
†of-fi'-ci-a-ry
†oft'-en
†oft'-en-times
†o'ko-nite
†o:le-cra'-non
*†ol'-i-garch:y
†ol'-i-gon-ite
†ol'-i-va-ry
†ol'-i-ven-ite
*†o:me'-ga
†om-ni-fa'-ri-ous
*†om-nis'-cience
*†om-nis'-cient
*†On-ta'-ri-an
†On-ta'-ri:o
†oo'-zy
†o-pa'-quing
†op-e-ret'-ta
*†O:phel'-ia

†op-por-tu'-nism
†op-por-tu'-nist
†op-por-tu-nis'-tic
†or'-bi-tal
†or'-ci-nol
†or'-de-al
†or-di-na'-ri-ly
†or'-di-na-ry
*†o:ré'-ga-no
*†or'-gan-ism
*†or-gan-iz-a-ble
*†or-gan-i-za'-tion
*†or'-gan-ize
*†or'-gan-iz-er
*†or'-gan-iz-ing
*o:ris-mol'-o-gy
†or'-ne-ry
*or-ni-thu'-ric
*†or-o-ban-cha'-ceous
†or'-re-ry
*†or-yc-tog'-no-sy
*†or-yc-tol'-o-gy
†os'-a-zone
†os-si-fi-ca-to-ry
†os'-su-a-ry
†Os-tend'
†os-te-o-cla'-sis
†os'-ti-a-ry
†o:va'-ri-an
†o:va-ri-ec'-to-my
†o:va'-ri-ole
†o:va-ri-ot'-o-my
†o'-ver-se'-er
*o'vi-cid'-al
†O'wen

*†ox'-a-lis
*†ox-a-lu'-ric
*†ox-az'-ine
†ox-y-hem'-o-glo-bin
†ox-y-toc'-ic
*†o'yer
*†o'yez
*†o'-zo-nide
*†o'-zo-nif'-er-ous
*†o'zo-niz-er
*†o'zo-nous

*pa-cif'-i-ca-tor
†Pa-de-rew'-ski
†Pa-ki-stan'
*pal-ma'-ri-an
*pal-mi-to-le'-ic
*†pam'-phlet
*†pam-phlet-eer'
*†pan-o-ra'-ma
*†Pan-tag'-ru-el
*pan'-tarch:y

†pan-ti-soc'-ra-cy
*pa'-parch:y
†pa-pa'-ya
†pa-pe-teries'
†pap'-il-la'-ry
†Pa'-pu:a
†par-a=am'-i-no-ben-zo'-ic
*par-a-bas'-ic
*†par-a-chor'-dal
*†par-ach'-ro-nism
†par-am'-ide
*par-a-pleg'-ic
*par-a-sit-i-cid'-al
*†par'-a-sit-ize
†par'-ce-na-ry
†par'-e-sis
†Pa'-ri-an
†pa-ri mu-tu-el'
*†pa-rish'-ion-er
†par-lia-men-ta'-ri-an
†Pa'-ros
†pa-rot'-ic
*†par'-quet-ry
*par-ri-cid'-al
†part'-age
†part-i-bil'-i-ty
†pas'-tor-al
*†pas-to-ra'-le
†pas'-tor-al-ism
†pas'-tor-al-ist
†pas'-tor-al-ize
†past'-ries
†past'-ry
†past'-ry=cook
*†past'y
†pa-tchou'-li
*pa'-ten-cy
*pat-ent-ee'
†pa-tib'-u-la-ry
*†pa'-ti:o
†pa-tisse-rie'
*pat'-ois
*†pa'-tri-arch:y
*pat'-ri-ci-dal
*†Pa-tri-pas'-si-an
†pat'-ron-age
†pa-tro'-nite
†pat'-ron-ize
*pat'-ron-iz-ing
†pawn'-brok-er
*pawn'-bro-king
*pe-cul'-iar
*pe-cul'-iar-ly
*pe-cu'-ni-a'-ri-ly
*pe-cu'-ni-a-ry
*†ped'-a-go-gy
†ped-al'-fer

†pei-gnoir′
*†pe′-jo-ra-tive
†pe-lo′-ric
*†pelt′-ry
*†pen′-chant′
*pend′-ant
*pend′-en-cy
*pend′-ent
*pen-in′-su-la
*pen-in′-su-lar
*pen-tac′-id
*pen′-tarch:y
†pen-tox′-id
*†pep-to-ni-za′-tion
*†per-cen′-tile
*†per′-emp′-to-ri-ly
*†per′-emp′-to-ri-ness
*†per′-emp′-to-ry
*†per-en′-ni-al
*†per′-i-do′-tite
*†per′-i-lous
†per′-i-lous-ly
†per-im′-e-ter
†per-im′-e-try
†per-i-pe-te′-ia
*†per-i-so′-mal
*per-me-am′-e-ter
*†per-nick′-et:y
*†per-plex′-ed-ness
†per-sis′-tence
†per-sis′-ten-cy
†per-sis′-tent
†per-sis′-tent-ly
*†per-snick′-et:y
†pe-ru′-sal
*†Pe-shaw′-ar
*†pes-ti-cid′-al
†pet-a-lif′-er-ous
†pet′-a-line
†pet′-a-lite
†pet′-a-lous
†pe-tech′-i-al
*pet′-i-ol-ar
†pe-ti′-tion-a-ry
*†Pe′-trarch-an
*†pet′-rel
*†pet-ro-chem′-i-cal
†pe-trol′
†phal′-ange
†pha′-raoh
†phas′-oid
*†phe-nac′-e-tin
*†phe-nan′-threne
*†phe-nan′-thri-dine
†phe′-na-zine
†phe′-ne-tole
*phe-nol′-ic (n., plastic)

*phe-nox′-ide
†phe′-nyl
†phe-nyl-ac-et-al′-de-
hyde
†phe′-nyl-ate
†phi-li′-a-ter
*Phi-lis′-tine
†phlo′-ri-zin-ize
†phlo-ro-glu′-ci-nol
†pho-nau′-to-graph
†pho′-net-ism
†pho′-net-ist
†pho′-no-ty-py
*phos′-ge-nite
†phos′-phor-ate
†phos-phor-esce′
†phos-phor-es′-cence
†phos-phor-es′-cent
†phos′-phor-ism
†phos-phor-o-gen′-ic
†phos′-phor-ous
†phos′-phor-us
*phos-phor′-yl-ase
*†pho-top-tom′-e-ter
*†pho′-to-ty-py
†phra′-sal
†phthal-am′-ic
†phthal′-i-mide
*†phy-tos′-ter-ol
†pi-an-is′-tic
*†pi-an′-o-for′-te
†pi′-ce-in
*†pidg′-in
†Pied-mont-ese′
*Pi′-er-rot
†pig′-eon
†pig′-eon-hole
†pig′-eon=toed
†pig′-eon-wing
†pig′-men-ta-ry
*pign′-on
*†pil′-lo-rize
†Pi-ner′o
*pin′-ey
†pine′y
*†pin′-ite
*pink′y
*†pi′-nol-in
†pi′-quing
*†pir-ou-et′-ted
*†pir-ou-et′-ting
†pis-ta′-chi:o
†pit′-u-i-ta-ry
†pla-card′(v.)
†pla-cen′-ta-ry
†plagu′-i-ly
*pla′-guing
†plagu′y

*†pla-na'-ri:a
†pla-na'-ri-an
*†planch'-et
†plan-e-ta'-ri-um
†plan'-e-ta-ry
†plan'-e-toid
†plan-e-toi'-dal
†plan-e-to-log'-ic
†plan-e-tol'-o-gy
†plan-i-met'-ric
*pla'-no-graph
*plan-og'-ra-phy
†pla'-no-sol
†plas'-tin-oid
*†plat'-i-na
†plat-i-tu-di-na'-ri-an
*pla'-za
*pleas'-ur-a-ble
*pleas'-ure
*†ple-bis'-ci-ta-ry
*†pledg'-et
*†pledg'-or
†plei'-ad
*Plei'-a-des
†plen-i-po-ten'-ti-ar:y
†plen-i-po-ten'-ti-a-ry
*†ple'-num
*†ple-thor'-ic
*plum'-age
*†po-des-ta'
*†poign'-an-cy
*†poign'-ant
†Poin-ci-a'-na
*po'-ker (game)
*†Po-la'-ris
†pol'-i:o
†pol-i-o-my-e-li'-tis
†pol-i-o'-sis
†Po'-lish
*Po-lit'-bu-ro
†Po'-lit-zer
*pol'-lut-ant
†po-lo-naise'
†pol-y-a'-mid
†pol-y-bas'-ic
†pol-y-bas'-ite
†pol-y-dym'-ite
†pol-y-i-so-bu'-ty-lene
†pol'-y-mer-ize
*†po-lym'-e-ter
†pol'-y-pho-ny
*†pol'-y-pous
†pol-y-u-reth'-ane
†Pom-e-ra'-ni:a
†Pom-e-ra'-ni-an
†pom'-pous
†po'-per:y

†pop-li-te'-al
†porce'-lain
*po-ri-cid'-al
†por-nog'-raph-er
†po-ros-im'-e-ter
†por-phy-rox'-ine
*†port-a-bil'-i-ty
*†port'-a-ble
†port'-age
*†por-tu-la'-ca
†pos'-thu-mous
†pos'-thu-mous-ly
†post-or'-bi-tal
*†po'-sy
†pot'-age
*†pot-ass-am'-ide
*praec'-i-pe
*†pra'-soid
†prat'-ique
†preb'-en-da-ry
*pre-ca'-ri-ous-ness
*pre-cau'-tion-a-ry
*pre-ced'-ence
*pre-ced'-en-cy
*pre-ced'-ent
*pre-des-ti-na'-ri-an
*pre=ex-ist'-ent
*pre-fig-ur-a'-tion
*†pre-fig-ur-a'-tive
†pre-lim'-i-na-ry
*†pre-ma-tu'-ri-ty
*†pre'-mi-er
*pre'-mi-er-ship
*pre-mil-le-na'-ri-an
*pre-sage' (v.)
*pre-sage'-ful
*†pre'-sci-ence
*pre'-sci-ent
*pres-en-ta'-tion
*pre-sent'-a-tive
*pres'-ent-ist
†pre-ser'-va-tive
†press'-or
†prev'-e-nance
†pre-ve'-nience
†pre-ve'-nient
*Pri'-bi-lov
*†pri'-ma-ri-ly
*†pri'-ma-ry
†pri-mo-ge'-ni-al
†pri-mo-gen'-i-ta-ry
†pri'-or:y
†prob'-a-bil-ism
†pro-ce'-du-ral
*†proc-e-leus-mat'-ic
†pro-ces'-sion-a-ry
*proc-ne'-mi-al
*†pro-con'-su-late

†pro-dig'-ious
*prof-it-eer'
*pro-le-ta'-ri-an-ism
†pro-le-ta'-ri-an-ism
†pro-le-ta'-ri-at
*pro-mis-cu'-i-ty
†prom'-is-or
*pro-po'-sal
*pro-pox'y-ac-et-an-i'-lide
†pro-pri'-e-ta-ry
†pro-pyl-am'-ine
*pro'-py-lene
*pros'-e-ly-tism
*pros'-e-ly-tize
*pros'-e-ly-tiz-er
*pro-sla'-ver:y
*pro'-ta-mine
*pro-tam'-ine
*pro-tan-o'-pi:a
*†pro'-te-in
*†pro-te-i-na'-ceous
*pro'-te-in-ase
*†pro-te-van-gel'-i-um
*pro-thon'-o-ta-ry
*pro'-to-ste'-le
*pro'-to-ty-pal
*pro-to-ve-ra'-trine
*†pro-tox'-ide
*pro-ve-nance'
†Pro-vence'
*†pro-ve'-ni-ence
*pro-vi'-sion-a-ry
*†prov'-ost
†prov'-ost mar-shal
*pseu-dar-thro'-sis
*pseu-de-pig'-ra-pha
*†psi-lan'-thro-py
*†psi-lom'-e-lane
*psy'-cha-go-gy
*†psy-chas-the'-ni:a
*ptis'-an
†pto'-ma-ine
*pu'-gil-ism
*pu'-gil-ist
*pu-gil-is'-tic
†Pu'-lit-zer
*pul'-mo-na-ry
*†pul-pit-eer'
*pu'-pil-la-ry
*pup-pet-eer'
*pur-pl-es'-cent
*pur'-po-sive
†purs'y
*pus'-sy
†pus'-sy=foot
†pus'-sy=wil'-low
†put'-ter

†Pu-yal'-lup
†pyl-o-rec'-to-my
*py-lor'-o-plas-ty
*†pyr'-ar'-gy-rite
*py'-ra-zine
*pyr-e-nem'-a-tous
*py-reth'-rin
*pyr'-eth-rin
*py-reth'-rum
*pyr'-eth-rum
*pyr'-i-bole
*pyr'-i-mi-dine
*pyr-i-tif'-er-ous
*pyr-i-to-he'-dral
*py-ru-val'-de-hyde
*†py-ru'-vic

*†quad-ran'-tal
*†quad-rat'-ic
*†quad-ra'-tus
*†quad-ren'-ni-al
*†quad-ren'-ni-al-ly
*†quad-ren'-ni-um
*†quad-ril'-lion
*†quad-riv'-i-um
*†quad-roon'
*†quad-ru'-ma-nous
*quad-rum'-vi-rate
*quad'-ru-plet
*†quad-ru'-pli-cate
†qua'-ter-na'-ry
*†quat'-rain
†quin-am'-ine
†quin'-ine
†quin'-one
*quin'-o-nyl
*quint-es'-sence
*quin'-tu-plet
*†quir-i-ta'-ri-an
*†quix'-ot-ism

†Ra-be-lais'
†Ra-chi'-tic
†Rach-ma'-ni-nof
†ra'-cism
†ra'-cist
*†rack-et-eer'
†ra-con-teur'
†ra-di-o-la'-ri-an
*raf'-fin-ate
†raft'-er
*ramp'-ant
*†ra'-tion-al
*†ra-tion-ale'
*ra-tio-na'-le
*†ra'-tion-al-ism
*†ra'-tion-al-ist
*†ra-tion-al-is'-tic

*†ra-tion-al′-i-ty
*†ra-tion-al-i-za′-tion
*†ra′-tion-al-ize
*†ra′-tion-al-ly
†ra-vi-o′-li
*re-act′-ance
†re-ac′-tion-a-ry
†re-ce′-dence
†re-ci′-tal
*†re-cluse′
†rec′-og-nize
†rec′-og-niz-or
†re-col-lect′
†red-in′-te-grate
†re-doub′-le
†re-doub′-ling
*red′-ox
†re-fast′-en
†ref-e-ree′
†re-flect′-ance
†re-for-es-ta′-tion
*†re-form′-a-tive
*†re-form′-a-to-ry
*ref′-u-ta-ble
*ref′-u-ta-bly
*†re-in-vig′-or-ate
†rel′-ict
†re-lig′-ion
*†re-lig-i-os′-i-ty
†re-lig′-ious
†re-lig′-ious-ly
†rel′-i-qua-ry
*†re-mis-si-bil′-i-ty
*†re-mis′-si-ble
†re-mon-toir′
†re-nais-sance′
*ren′-di-ble
†ren′-in
*†re-ni′-tent
*†re-or-gan-i-za′-tion
*†re-or′-gan-ize
†re-pen′-tance
†re-pen′-tant
†rep-re-sen′-ta-tive
†re-pris′-al
†re′-qui-em
†req-ui-es′-cat
†re-qui′-tal
*†rere′-dos
†res-i-den′-ti-a-ry
†re-sid′-u-a-ry
*†res-i-na′-ceous
†res′-i-nate
*†re-sin′-ic
†res′-in-i-fi-ca′-tion
†res′-i-noid
†res′-i-nol
†res′-i-nous

†re-sis′-tance
†re-sis′-tant
†res′-o-lu-ble
*†res′-o-lu-tive
*†re-sol′-vent
†re-sor′-ci-nol
†re-so-ru′-fin
*†re-spir′-a-ble
*†re-spir′-a-to-ry
†re-splend′-ence
†re-splend′-en-cy
†re-splend′-ent
†re-spond′-ence
†re-spond′-en-cy
†re-spond′-ent
*re-spon′-ser
†re-sul′-tant
†re-tar′-dant
†re′-ti-a-ry
*†re′-ti-form
†re-to-na′-tion
†re′-tro-ac′-tion
†re′-tro-ac′-tive
†re-tro-ce-dence′
†re-tro-ces′-sion
†re-tro-gress′
†re-tro-gres′-sion
†re-tro-gres′-sive
*†re-tro-min′-gent
*†re-tro-stal′-sis
†re-trous-sé′
†re-tro-vert′-ed
†re-u′-nion
*†rev′-e-la-to-ry
†re-ver′-sion-a-ry
*†re-vis-it-a′-tion
†re-vi′-val
†re-vi′-val-ist
†rev-o-lu′-tion-a-ry
*Reyn′-ard
*rhi-nen-ceph′-a-lon
†rhi-noc′-e-ros
*†rhom′-ben-ceph′-a-lon
†Rhond′-da
*†rib′-ald-ry
†rib-o-flav′-in
*†ri-chel′-ite
*†rid′-ing
†Rif′-fi-an
*†right′-eous
*†right′-eous-ness
†rim′-ous
*rin′-sa-ble
*Ri:o Gran′-de
†ri-pa′-ri-an
†Ri-vi-e′-ra
†Ro′-bes-pierre

*rock-et-eer′
*ro-den′-ti-cid′-al
*†roeb′-ling-ite
*ro′-ga-to-ry
*ro′-guer:y
*ro′-guish
*ro′-guish-ness
*†roist′-er
*†roist′-er-er
*†roist′-er-ous
*ro-sal′-ia
*ro-san′-i-line
rose′-ma-ry
Ro-stand′
*Ro-ta′-ri-an
*ro-tis-se-rie′
*trou′-ter
*rou′-tin-eer′
*†rov′-er
*†ru-be-ryth′-ric
*ru′-ti-nose

†Sab-ba-ta′-ri-an
†sa-bo-tage′
†sac′-cha-ri-fy
*sa′-cral
†sa-cra′-ri-um
*†sa′-cro-il′-i-ac
*†sa′-cro-sci-at′-ic
*†sa′-crum
sad′-ism
*sad′-ist
*†Sag-it-ta′-ri-us
†sales′-wo-man
*†sal-i-cyl-am′-ide
*†sal′-i-cyl′-ate
*†sal-i-cyl′-ide
*sal-i-cyl′-u-ric
†sa′-li-ence
†sa′-li-ent
*†sa-lig′-e-nin
†sal-im′-e-ter
*sa-li′-no-gen′-ic
†sal′-i-va-ry
*†sal-mons-ite
†Sa-lo-ni′-ci
†sal′-u-ta-ri-ly
†sal′-u-ta-ry
*Sal-va-do′-ran
*sal vol′-a-tile
†sa-ma′-ra
*†Sa-ma′-ri:a
*†sa-ma′-ri-um
†Sa-mar-kand′
†sa′-mite
*sam′-u-rai
†sanc′-tu-a-ry
†san′-gui-na-ri-ly

†san′-gui-na-ry
†san-i-ta′-ri-an
†san′-i-ta-ri-ly
†san-i-ta′-ri-um
†san′-i-ta-ry
†San Se-bas-ti-án′
*†sa′-pi-ence
*†sa′-pi-ent
*†sa-pi-en′-tial
*†sa-pog′-e-nin
*sar-co′-ma-tous
*†sar′-do-nyx
*†sa-ti-a-bil′-i-ty
*†sa′-ti-a-ble
†sat-i-net′
*†sa′-trap:y
†Sat-ur-na′-li:a
†Sat-ur-na′-li-an
†sat′-yr
*sauer′-kraut
†Sa-vo-na-ro′-la
†say′-id
*†sca′-bi-es
*†sca′-brous
*scar′-ab-oid
†sca′-ri-ous
†scav′-en-ger
*†sce-na′-ri:o
*†sce-na′-rist
*scen′-er:y
†scen′-i-cal
†scen′-i-cal-ly
†scen-o-graph
†scen-o-graph′-ic
†Sche-he-ra-za′-de
†schis′-tose
*†schoon′-er
*†Scho′-pen-hau-er
*Schrö′-ding-er
†scler-o-ti′-tis
†sco-po-lam′-in
†scorp′-er
†sco′-ti:a
*†scraw′-ni-ness
*†scraw′-ny
*scrive′-ner
*scur′-ril-ous
†sec′-on-da-ri-ly
†sec′-on-da-ry
†sec-re-ta′-ri-al
†sec-re-ta′-ri-at
†sec′-re-ta-ry
†sec-ta′-ri-an
†sec-ta′-ri-an-ism
†sec′-und
*†se-cu′-ri-ty
†sed′-en-ta-ri-ly
†sed′-en-ta-ry

*†sed-i-men'-ta-ri-ly
†se-di'-tion-a-ry
†seg'-men-ta-ry
†seign'-ior
*seign'-ior-age
*seis-mog'-raph-er
*†sel-a-gi-nel'-la
†se'-lec-tee'
†se-le'-nic
*se-le'-no-bis'-muth-ite
†sem'-i-na-ry
*†sen'-a-ry
†Sen-e-ga-lese'
†sen'-es-chal
†se'-nior
*sen-ior'-i-ty
†se-ni-or'-i-ty
†Sen-nach'-e-rib
*†sen'-ti-ence
†sen'-ti-ent
†sep'-al
†sep'-aled
†sep'-al-oid
†sep'-a-loid
*†sep'-a-ra-tist
†sep-ta'-ri-um
*sep'-te-nar:y
†sep'-te-na-ry
†sep-tu-a-ge-na'-ri-an
*sep-tu-ag'-e-nar:y
†sep-tu-ag'-e-na-ry
*†sep'-tu-plet
†seq-ues-tra'-tion
†se'-ri-graph
*se-rin'-gal
*serv'-ant
†ser'-vice
†ser'-vice-a-ble
*†Sev'-ille
†sex-a-ge-na'-ri-an
†sex-ag'-e-na-ry
*†sex'-tu-plet
†Sha'-drach
†shrill'y
*†si-a-la-gog'-ic
*†si'-a-lo-li-thi'-a-sis
*†Si-er'-ra Le-o'-ne
*†sight'-se-er
†sig'-il-la-ry
†sig-moi-dos'-to-my
*†Si-le'-si:a
*†Si-le'-si-an
†sim'-i-le
†sim'-o-ny
*sim-pa'-ti-co
†sin'-a-pic

*†si'-ne-cure
*†si'-ne-cur-ist
†Sin-ga-pore'
†si-nu-si'-tis
†sis'-al
*†si-tos'-ter-ol
†Sla'-vo-phile
†sli-dom'-e-ter
*†sliv'-er
†snif'-ter=valve
*so'-cle
*sod-am'-ide
*†sof'-ten
†sof'-ten-er
†sof'-ten-ing
†sol-a-na'-ceous
†sol'-a-nine
†so-la'-ri-um
†sol-e-noi'-dal
*so-lic'-it-ous
†sol'-i-ta-ri-ly
†sol'-i-ta-ry
†so'-lo-dize
*sol'-u-bil-iz-er
†so-lute'
*†so-na-ti'-na
†son-net-eer'
†so-no-res'-cent
*†soph'-is-ter
†soph'-ist-ry
*so-po-rif'-er-ous
*†so-po-rif'-ic
†so-pra'-no
†sor'-bic
*sorb'-ose
*sorb'-o-side
*†sos-te-nu'-to
†so'-viet
†so'-viet-ism
*†so'-ya
†spe-lun'-ker
*†sper'-ma-to-cele
*†sper'-ma-to-ci-dal
†sper'-ma-to-cyte
*sper'-ma-to-phyte
*†sper-ma-to-phyt'-ic
*sper'-mine
*†sphe-roi-dic'-i-ty
*spil'-o-site
†spin'-el
†spin'-ule
*†spin-u-les'-cent
*†spin'-u-lose
*spi-ra'-le
*spir'-it-u-al
*spir'-it-u-al-ism
*spir'-it-u-al-ist
*spir'-it-u-al-is'-tic

*spir-it-u-al′-i-ty
*spir′-it-u-al-ize
*spir′-it-u-al-ly
*spi-ri-tu-el′
*spir′-it-u-os′-i-ty
*spir′-it-u-ous
*†spi-ro-che-to′-sis
*†splen′-ic
*spon′-gi-ness
*spon′-gy
†spou′-sal
*squal′-ene
*†squeam′-ish
†stab-i-li-za′-tion
*sta′-bi-li-za-tor
†stab′-i-li-sa-tor
†stab′-i-lize
†stab′-i-liz-er
*†Sta-kha′-no-vite
†stam′-i-ne′-al
*†stand′-ard
*†stand′-ard=bear′-er
*†stand-ard-i-za′-tion
*†stand′-ard-ize
  Stand′-ish
*†sta′-tion-a-ry
*†sta′-tion-er
*†sta′-tion-er:y
†stat′-or
†stat′-u-a-ry
  stat′-u-ta-ble
†ste-a-top′-y-gous
*†ste′-le
  sten-o-hal′-ine
*†ster-e-og-no′-sis
*†ster′-e-o-graph
*†ster-e-og′-ra-pher
*†ster-e-o-graph′-ic
*†ster-e-om′-e-ter
*†ster-e-o-met′-ric
*†ster-e-om′-e-try
*†ster-e-o-phon′-ic
*†ster-e-o-oph′-o-ny
  *ster-e-op′-sis
*†ster-e-op′-ti-con
*†ster-e-o-scope
*†ster-e-o-scop′-ic
*†ster-e-os′-co-pist
*†ster-e-os′-co-py
*†ster-e-ot′-o-my
*†ster-e-o-ro′-ro-pism
*†ster′-e-o-type
*†ster′-e-o-typ-er
*†ster′-e-o-typ-ing
*ster′-e-o-typ:y
  †ster-il-i-za′-tion
  †ster′-il-ize
  †ster′-il-iz-er

†ster′-tor-ous
†steth-om′-e-ter
†steth-os′-co-py
†still′y
*†stilp-nom′-e-lane
†sti-pen′-di-a-ry
*†sto′-ma-ta
†sto′-ma-tal
*†sto-ma-ti′-tis
†Strad-i-va′-ri-us
†stra-teg′-ic
†stra-teg′-i-cal
*†stra-to=cu′-mu-lus
†stra′-to-sphere
*†strob-o-scop′-ic
*†strob′-o-tron
†stron′-ti:a
*†sub-li′-ma-ble
*†sub-lim′-i-nal
†sub′-lu-na-ry
*†sub-max′-il-la-ry
†sub-merg′-i-ble
†sub-si′-dence
†sub-sid′-i-a-ry
†sub-sis′-tence
†sub-sis′-tent
*sub-treas′-ur:y
†sub-ver′-sion-a-ry
*†suc-cin-am′-ate
*†suc-cin-am′-ic
*†suc-cin-am′-ide
*†suc′-cin-yl
*†su-dor-if′-er-ous
*†su-dor-if′-ic
†suf-fra-gette′
*†suf-fra-get′-tism
*suf′-fra-gist
*†su-i-cid′-al
*†su-i-cid′-al-ly
†su′i gen′-er-is
*sulf-a-di′-a-zine
*sul-fa-guan′-i-dine
†sul-fa-guan′-i-dine
*†sulf-am′-ic
†sulf-a-nil′-a-mide
*sulf-a-nil′-ic
†sulf-a-pyr′-i-dine
†sulf-a-thi′-a-zole
*sul′-fat-ize
*†sul-fon-am′-ide
†sul′-fur-ize
†sul′-fur-ous
†sul-ta′-na
*†Su-me′-ri-an
*†sum′-ma-ri-ly
†sump′-tu-a-ry
†su-per-cil′-i-a-ry

*†su-per-fi′-ci-es
†su-per-in-ten′-den-cy
†su-per-in-ten′-dent
†su-per-nu′-mer-a-ry
†su-per-se′-dence
*su-per-ven′-ience
*†sup-ple-men′-ta-ri-ly
*†sup-ple-men′-ta-ry
*†sup-por′-tive
†sur-re-al-ist′-ic
†syl-la-ba′-ry
*Swit′-zer-land
†symp-tom-at′-ic
†symp-tom-at′-i-cal-ly
*†syn′-dro-me
†sy-nec′-do-che
*†syn-es-the′-si:a
†sy-nod′-i-cal
†sy-nod′-i-cal-ly
†sy-noe′-cious
†sy-non′-y-mous
†sy-non′-y-my
†sy-nop′-sis
†sy-nop′-tic
†sy-no′-vi:a
†sy-rin′-go-my-e′-li:a
*tab′-er-nac-le
*†Ta-hi′-ti-an
†ta-chi′-na
†Ta-na-na-rive′
†Tan-ga-nyi′-ka
†Tan-ga-nyi′-kan
†ta′-pis
*†tank′-ard
*†tan′-ta-mount
†tape meas′-ure
†ta′-pis
†tar′-ant-ism
†tar′-get-eer′
*†tars-ec′-to-my
†Tar-ta′-re-an
†tar-ta′-re-ous
†Tar-ta′-ri-an
*†tar-tram′-ide
†tas′-man-ite
†tat-ter-de-mal′-ion
†tau-ro-chol′-ic
*†taw′-ni-er
†taw′-ny
†tax-im′-e-ter
†Tcheb′-y-sheff
*†te-lem′-e-ter
*tel-es-the′-si:a
†tel′-i-o-spore
†tel′-i-o-stage
†tem′-pe-ra
†tem′-po-ra-ri-ly

†tem′-po-ra-ry
†ten′-dance
†ten′-den-cy
†ten-u′-i-ty
†te-phro′-sin
†tep-i-da′-ri-um
*ter-cen′-te-nar′y
†ter-cen′-te-na-ry
†ter-eph′-tha-late
†te-reph′-tha-late
**†term′-or
*ter′-pin-ene
*†ter-ra′-que-ous
†ter-ra′-ri-um
†ter′-ti-a-ry
*†Ter-tul′-li-an
†tes-ta′-ce-an
†tes′-ti-mon:y
†tes-tu-di-na′-ri-ous
†tet-ra-bas′-ic
†te-tram′-ine
*†tet-ra-ple′-gi:a
†tet′-rarch
†tet-rar′-chic
†te′-trarch:y
†tet′-rarch:y
†tet-ra-thi′-on-ate
†te-traz′-ine
*tex′-tu-a-ry
*The-o-do′-si:a
*†the-o-lo′-gi-an
†the-o-rem-at′-ic
†there-aft′-er
*ther-mis′-tor
†ther′-mo-coup-le
†ther-mo-dur′-ic
*thev′-e-tin
†tho′-ric
†thor′-on
†thren′-ode
*†thym′-ic
†thym′-ol
†ti-a′-ra
†ti′-dal
†tie′-man-ite
†Ti-en-tsin′
†Ti-er′-ra del Fu-e′-go
*til′-bu-ry
*†tim′-or-ous
*†tink′-er
†tin-tom′-e-ter
†Tip-pe-ra′-ry
*†ti′-tan-ate
*†ti-tan-if′-er-ous
*†ti′-tan-ite
†Tit-i-ca′-ca
†tit-ri-met′-ri-cal-ly
†tit′-u-la-ry

463

†Ti′-vo-li
†to′-lu-ate
†to′-lu-ene
†to′-lu-ol
†tol′-u-y-lene
†tol′-y-lene
*†ton′-ite
†to′-pi-a-ry
†tor′-e-a-dor
†tor′-ic
†tor-po-rif′-ic
*†tor-til′-la
†to′-yon
†tract-a-bil′-i-ty
†tract′-a-ble
†Trac-ta′-ri-an-ism
*†trad-es-can′-ti:a
†trade u:nion
†tra-di′-tion-a-ry
*†tran-scend′-en-cy
*†tran-scend′-ent
†trans-fig-ur-a′-tion
*†tran-sil′-i-ence
*†tran-sil′-i-ent
†trans′-it
†trans-i′-tion
†trans-i′-tion-al
†trans-pi-rom′-e-ter
*†Tran-syl-va′-ni:a
*†trap-e-zo-he′-dron
*†trav′-ail
*†trav′-e-log
*†trav′-e-logue
*†trav′-ers-a-ble
*†trav′-ers-al
†trav′-er-sal
†trav′-erse (v.)
*†tra-vois′
†tread′-le
*†treas′-ure
*†treas′-ur-er
*†treas′-ure=trove
*†treas′-ur:y
†treb′-le
†treb′-led
*Tre-ma-to′-da
*†trench′-an-cy
*†trench′-ant
*†trench′-er
*trep-o-ne-mi-cid′-al
†tri-az′-ine
†tri-az′-ole
†tri′-bal
†trib′-u-ta-ry
*†tri-cli-no-hed′-ric
†tri-dec′-y-lene
*tri′-er-arch′y
†tri-eth-an-ol-a-mine′

†tri-fa′-ri-ous
†trig-o-ni′-tis
*Trin-i-ta′-ri-an
*†tri-part′-i-ble
†trip′-e-dal
†trip′-le
*†tri′-plet
*†tri′-plex
†tri-quet′-ra
†tri-sem′-ic
*†tris-kel′-i-on
†tris′-tich-ous
*†tris-yl-lab′-ic
†trit′-yl
*†tri-um′-vi-ral
*†triv′-i:a
†tro′-pic (acid)
†trop′-ism
*†trop′-o-sphere
†troub′-le
†troub′-led
†troub′-ler
†troub′-le-some
†troub′-le-lous
†tru′-cu-lence
†tru′-cu-lent
*†trudg′-en
*†trump′-er:y
*†trus-tee′
*†trus-tee′-ship
*†trux-il′-lic
*tryp-a-no-cid′-al
*†tryp′-a-no-some
*†tryp-ars-am′-ide
*†tsu-na′-mi
†tu′-bal
†Tuile-ries′
†tu-mul′-tu-a-ry
†Tu-nis′-i:a
†Tu-nis′-i-an
†tu′-te-la-ry
†tym′-pan-ist
*†Tyr′-ol

†u:biq-ui-ta′-ri-an
†u:biq-ui-ta-ry
†u:biq-ui-ty
*†u:do-met′-ric
*†ul-na′-re
†um-bi-li′-cus
*†un-au′-thor-ized
†un-bo′-som
†un′-ci-al
*†un-con′-scion-a-ble
†un-coup′-le
†un-dec′-y-lene
†un-der-sec′-re-ta-ry
†un-fast′-en

464

†un-fil'-ial
†un'-guen-ta-ry
†un-id-i-om-at'-ic
†u:ni-form-i-ta'-ri-an
*†u:nij'-u-gate
*u'nion
*u'nion-ism
*u'nion-ist
*u'nion-ize
†U:ni-ta'-ri-an
†u'ni-ta-ry
†un-meas'-ur-a-ble
†un-nec'-es-sa-ri-ly
†un-nec'-es-sa-ry
*†un-or'-gan-ized
†un-re-lig'-ious
†un-rep-re-sen'-ta-tive
†un-right'-eous
†un-rul'y
†un-san'-i-ta-ry
†un-sold'-er
*un-so-lic'-it-ous
*†un-trav'-ers-a-ble
†un-troub'-led
†un-va'-ry-ing
†un-wa'-ri-ly
†un-wa'-ry
†un-wov'-en
*u:ran'-i-nite
*u:reth'-ane
†u'ri-na-ry
†u:ro-lith-i'-a-sis
†u:ro-lith-ol'-o-gy
*ur-ti-ca'-ri:a
†u:til-i-ta'-ri-an
†u:til-i-ta'-ri-an-ism
†u:til-i-za'-tion
†u'til-ize
†u'til-iz-er
†u:var'-o-vite

†va-ga'-ri-ous
†va-ga'-ry
*†Va-len'-ci:a
*†Va-len-ciennes'
*val'-er-yl
†val-e-tu-di-na'-ri-an
*val-or-i-za'-tion
*val'-or-ize
*valv'-al
*†va-nad'-ic
*†va-nad'-i-nite
*van'-a-dous
*Va-nes'-sa
*van'-il-lin
†va-ri-a-bil'-i-ty
†va'-ri-a-ble

†va'-ri-ance
†va'-ri-ant
†va'-ri-at-ed
†va'-ri-a'-tion
†va'-ri-col'-ored
†va'-ried
†va'-ri-e-gate
†va'-ri-e-gat-ed
†va-ri-e-ga'-tion
†va'-ri-form
†va'-ri-o-late
†va'-ri-o-la'-tion
†va'-ri-o-lite
†va-ri-o-lit'-ic
†va'-ri-o-loid
†va-ri-om'-e-ter
†va-ri-o'-rum
†va'-ri-ous
†va'-ri-ous-ly
†va'-rix
†va'-rus
†va'-ry
†va-sec'-to-my
*vas-o-di-la'-tin
*vat-i-ci-na'-tion
*†veer'y
†veg-e-ta'-ri-an
†veg-e-ta'-ri-an-ism
†ve-la'-ri-um
†ve-loc'-i-me-ter
†ven-dee'
*†Ven-e-zue'-la
†venge'-ance
†ve'-ni-punc-ture
*Ve-nu'-si-an
†ve-ra'-tric
†ve-ra'-trine
*†ver'-bal
*†ver'-ger
*ver'-ism
*ver'-ist
*†ver'-mi-cid'-al
†ver'-mi-nous
†ver'-mi-nous-ly
*†ver-tic'-il-late
†ves'-pi-a-ry
†ves'-ti-a-ry
*†ves-tig'-i-al
*†ves-tig'-i-al-ly
†vet-er-i-na'-ri-an
†vet'-er-i-na-ry
†vex'-il-la-ry
*vi'a dol'-o-ro'-sa
†vi-ca'-ri-al
†vi-ca'-ri-ate
†vi-ca'-ri-ous
†vi-ca'-ri-ous-ly
†vic'-e-na-ry

465

†vi-del′-i-cet
*Viet′-nam′
*Viet′-nam-ese′
†vi-gnett′-er
*vin-dic′-a-tive
†vi-nom′-e-ter
†vi′-o-la-ble
*vio-lo′-ne
†vir′-gi-nal
†Vir-gin′-i:a
*†Vir-gin′-i-an
*†vir′-i-lism
†vi′-sion-a-ry
*vis′-it-ant
*vis-it-a′-tion
†vis′-or
*†vis′-u-al
*†vis-u-al-i-za′-tion
*†vis′-u-al-ize
*†vis′-u-al-iz-er
*†vis′-u-al-ly
†vi-va′-ri-um
†Vla-di-vos-tok′
†vo-cab′-u-la-ry
*†vol-can-ol′-o-gy
†volt-am′-e-ter
†volt-a-met′-ric
†vol′-un-ta-ri-ly
†vol′-un-ta-ry
†vol′-un-ta-ry-ism
†vo-lup′-tu-a-ry
*vo-ya-geur′
†vul-ga′-ri-an
†vul′-ner-a-ry

†wa′-ges
*ward′-en
*ward′-en-ship
*ward′-er-ship
†wa′-ri-ly
†wa′-ri-ness
†war-ran-tee′
*war′-ri-or
†wa′-ry
†wash′-er-wo-man
*†wast′-rel

†wat′-tage
*†West-pha′-li:a
*†West-pha′-li-an
†West Vir-gin′-i:a
*†widg′-eon
†wilde′-beest
†wi′-li-ly
†wi′-li-ness
†Wil-la′-mette
†will′-em-ite
†wi′-ly
*†wis-ta′-ri:a
*†wit′-an
*†wit′-e-na-ge-mot
†wo′-man
†wo′-man-hood
†wo′-man-ish
†wo′-man-kind
†wo′-man-like
†wo′-man-ly
†wo′-men
†wo′-men-folk
†wors′-ted
†wov′-en
*Wyc′-lif-fite

*†xanth-am′-ide
†xan-thoch′-ro-id
†xer′-ic
†Xerx′-es
†xiph-op′-a-gus
*†xiph-o-su′-ran
*†xy′-li-dine
*xy-loph′-o-nist
†xy′-ly-lene

*†Ya-ku-tat′
†yp′-si-li-form
†Yu-go=Sla′-vi:a

*†za′-ra-tite
†zib′-e-line
†zois-i-ti-za′-tion
†zo′-nal
*zon′-a-ry
†zo′-nate

466